THE MINOR AGREEMENTS OF MATTHEW AND LUKE AGAINST MARK
with
A CUMULATIVE LIST

BIBLIOTHECA EPHEMERIDUM THEOLOGICARUM
LOVANIENSIUM

XXXVII

The Minor Agreements of Matthew and Luke against Mark

with a Cumulative List

EDITED BY

Frans NEIRYNCK

IN COLLABORATION WITH

THEO HANSEN AND FRANS VAN SEGBROECK

LEUVEN UNIVERSITY PRESS

© 1974 by Leuven University Press, Krakenstraat 3, B-3000 Leuven/Louvain
(Belgium)

D 1974/1869/10
ISBN 90 6186 021 0

Distribution : Éditions Duculot, B-5800 Gembloux (Belgium)

TABLE OF CONTENTS

APPENDIX

THE ARGUMENT FROM ORDER AND ST. LUKE'S TRANSPOSITIONS

FOREWORD

" Nevertheless it must be of use to all students of the
Synoptic Gospels to have before them a table of the
corrections of Mark adopted by Matthew and Luke ".
Edwin A. Abbott (Diatessarica II, p. 55).

The first draft of this list was set up by Dr Theo Hansen as part of his
doctoral dissertation which was accepted by the Theological Faculty in
1969. It was submitted to the Seminar on the Synoptic Problem at the
Claremont Meeting of the Society for New Testament Studies in 1972 and
the members of the Seminar Group expressed the wish that the list be
made available in a printed form. The material is now presented in a
revised arrangement. New entries are inserted and it has been comple-
mented by the collation of recent studies and a classification of the
stylistic agreements, with comparative material from the Triple Tradition. Our first purpose is to give a neutral description of the evidence in
a comprehensive tool, with a complete list of the Minor Agreements,
and to inform the reader about the significance of the phenomenon for
Synoptic studies. The related problem of the agreements in order is
treated in the Appendix [1].

Thanks are due to Dr Frans Van Segbroeck who assisted in preparing
the text for publication.

Leuven, January 1974.   F. NEIRYNCK

---

1. First published in *Eph. Theol. Lov.* 49 (1973) 784-815.

THE STUDY OF THE MINOR AGREEMENTS

1

The study of the minor agreements of Matthew and Luke against Mark originated with the Marcan hypothesis. On the traditional assumption of a common source, original gospel or oral tradition, no special attention was given to smaller coincidences between Matthew and Luke, and as long as the Augustinian and Griesbachian hypotheses were predominant the supposed dependence of Luke upon Matthew precluded any query about such agreements. Nevertheless, on the Griesbach hypothesis Mark is the latest gospel, a combination of Matthew and Luke, and the commentator is able to describe Mark's editorial activity by noticing the peculiar elements, not found in Matthew and Luke [1]. Those ' negative ' agreements became a problem with Wilke's exposition of the priority of Mark [2].

---

1. Cf. W. M. L. DE WETTE, *Kurze Erklärung der Evangelien des Lukas und Markus* (Kurzgefasstes exegetisches Handbuch zum Neuen Testament I,2), Leipzig, 1836 ; [3]1846. The ' negative ' agreements Matthew/Luke are signaled here as ' additions '. Characteristically Marcan are " eine Menge theils abweichender theils hinzugefügter Nebenumstände, welche alle von einer eigenthümlichen Liebe zur Umständlichkeit und Ausmalerei zeugen " (p. 3). For instance, Mk 1,20 : " kleine Nebenzüge, welche Mark. hinzuzufügen liebt " (p. 173) ; 1,33, cf. 1,45 ; 2,2 : " Schilderungen " ; 2,3 : " Vorliebe für Umständlichkeit " (p. 176) ; 2,6 : " malerisch nach Mark. Gewohnheit " (*ib.*) ; 2,32 : " malender und erklärender Zusatz des Mark. " (p. 184) ; 5,13, cf. 6,37 : " Mark. liebt genaue Zahlen anzugeben " (p. 190) ; 10,21, cf. 3,5 ; 8,12 : " Mark. malt gern und giebt die Gemüthsbewegungen an " (p. 221) ; 11,17 (quotation) : " Mark. führt sorgfältiger an " (p. 228) ; 12,23 : " Mark. schreibt bisweilen so weitschweifig " (p. 232) ; 14,30, cf. 14,68.72 : " Mark. hat Vorhersagung Jesu bestimmter gefasst " (p. 242) ; 14,36, cf. 5,41 : " Mark. liebt Aramäisches einzumischen " (p. 243) ; 15,43 : " ein Zusatz im Geiste des Mark. " (p. 251). — The ' positive ' agreements Matthew/Luke against Mark are scarcely considered, although De Wette observed : " er liebt die kleineren Abweichungen " (p. 250).
2. C. G. WILKE, *Der Urevangelist, oder exegetisch-kritische Untersuchung über das Verwantschaftsverhältnis der drei ersten Evangelien*, Dresden, 1838.

Wilke   Christian Gottlob WILKE attributed some peculiar elements in Mark [3]
             to later copyists, sometimes on the basis of external evidence but also on
(t)   mere internal grounds [4]. Other traits, such as repetitions, pleonastic
             expressions, correspondences between saying and narrative, are character-
(r)   istically Marcan and the absence in both Matthew and Luke is an acci-
             dental coincidence in their independent editing of the Gospel of Mark [5].
             A number of positive agreements [6] can likewise be accidental. According
             to Wilke, however, Matthew's acquaintance with Luke provides an
             explanation for some similarities in Mt 3,1-12 ; 10,1-14 ; 12,9-14 ; 12,22-
             32 and 13,1-35 [7], and it is not impossible that there are Lukan reminis-
             cences (*Anklänge*) in common narrative sections [8].

             Wilke has been criticized by Heinrich Julius HOLTZMANN in *Die
             synoptischen Evangelien* (1863) [9], especially for his immoderate admission
             of textual glosses in Mark [10] and his recourse to Matthew's dependence

---

3. Lists of *Zusätze* in saying material : p. 323. " Die kleinern " are in Mk 1,7 ;
2,9.25.26 ; 4,7.11.19 ; 6,9.37.39 ; 8,35 ; 10,29 ; 11,30 ; 12,14.27 ; (13,32) ; 14,20.30.
(42).(44).72 ; 16,7 ; " die grössern " are Mk 2,19 ; 2,27 ; 10,30. There is a much
longer list of additions in narrative material : in Mk 1,29.33.40.41.42.43 ; 2,(1-2).3.13.
14.15 ; 3,5.22.30 ; 4,10.(35-36).38.39 ; 5,4(cf. 3).13.41 ; 6,13.(30-33).34.40.41.43 ;
9,3.6.14-16.21-24.26 ; 10,13.14.16.17.21.22.23.24.32.46.49.50 ; 11,4.16 ; 12,27.38 ;
13,3 ; 14,68.72 ; 15,21.25.39.41.44.46 (pp. 552-554). See also n. 17.

4. *Ibid.*, pp. 463-466 (saying) and 471-674 (narrative) : " Wie viele Interpola-
tionen mögen nun aber noch ausserdem in dem Markus sein ! " (p. 674) ; " Ein
entscheidender Beweis gegen die Annahme, dass Matthäus und Lukas aus Markus
geschöpft, sind also ... die betrachteten Zusätze auch nicht " (p. 466).

5. *Ibid.*, pp. 674-677. " Nun ist aber das Zusammentreffen der beiden andern
Texte im Ausschluss dessen, was Markus den Worten hinzusetzt, oft nur zufällig
(eine Folge gemachter Abänderungen) ". E.g., in Mk 1,29.33.43 ; 3,32 ; 4,38.39 ;
5,23 ; 6,34 ; 10,21 ; 11,16 ... (cf. p. 677 : " die in Markus Text hervortretenden
scheinbaren Zusätze "). — On the characteristics of Marcan style comp. also C. G.
WILKE, *Die neutestamentliche Rhetorik. Ein Seitenstück zur Grammatik des Sprach-
idioms*, Dresden-Leipzig, 1843, pp. 436-438.

6. *Ibid.*, pp. 295-296 : " (die Stellen) wo das Uebereinstimmige der beiden
Andern, an dem Markus nicht Theil hat, nur in einem oder in einem Paar Worten
oder in einer Phrase besteht " (par. Mk 2,21.22 ; 3,32 ; 4,11 ; 6,8.9.10.11 ; 8,33.36 ;
9,19.31 ; 11,2 ; 12,22.37 ; 13,2) ; p. 554 : " die Stellen, wo Matthäus und Lukas
in Ausdrücken übereinstimmen, welche Markus Text nicht hat " (par. Mk 2,3bis.
5.12.22.23 ; 3,18.33 ; 4,38.41 ; 5,27 ; 6,34 ; 9,19 ; 10,22.47 ; 14,11.72 ; 15,39).

7. *Ibid.*, pp. 460-462.

8. *Ibid.*, p. 465 : " Gehört aber der Zusatz (Mk 10,30) wirklich dem Markus an,
so ist es auch nichts Unmögliches, dass die Andern, schöpfend aus Markus, ihn
weggelassen haben (zumal da der Matthäische Kopist sich auch anderwärts nach
Lukas gerichtet hat, und Markus kann sonach immer der Schriftsteller sein, von
dem die Relation ihren Ursprung hat) ".

9. H. J. HOLTZMANN, *Die synoptischen Evangelien. Ihr Ursprung und geschichtlicher
Charakter*, Leipzig, 1863.

10. *Ibid.*, p. 111 : " Vorschnell ... erklärt Wilke eine Reihe solcher, zu seiner
Theologie freilich nicht passender, Partien für Glossen ". — It should be noted,

on Luke. In the passages of Mt 10, 12 and 13, quoted above, both Matthew and Luke depend on a second non-Marcan source ($\Lambda = Logia$-$Quelle$),   (q) and in Mt 3 there is a pre-Marcan common gospel source ($A = Aposto$-$lische\ Quelle$) [11]. This assumption of an Ur-Marcus is Holtzmann's own answer to the problem of the minor agreements. Some of them are the result of independent editing, but in many instances of positive and   (r) negative agreement Matthew and Luke preserved the original text of the   Holtzmann common source [12].

Thus Holtzmann, in spite of his critique of the Griesbachian theory, comes close to it by assigning to Mark's edition of A an important number of smaller changes, omissions and additions. The criticism he addressed to F. C. Baur [13] will be repeated against his own solution by Bernhard WEISS in almost identical words [14]. The purpose of such a

---

however, that Wilke is not the only one who expresses some doubt about the original text of Mark. De Wette (1846) may be quoted : " Merkwürdig und noch nicht genug aufgeklärt ist der schwankende kritische Zustand des Textes des Mark., wovon eine Ursache in dessen combinirten Beschaffenheit liegen mag " (p. 4). Comp. also Holtzmann on the text of Mark " welcher gemäss seinem höheren Alter auch anerkanntermassen viel verdorbener ist, als der Text der andern Synoptiker " ($op.\ cit.$, p. 62). According to the principles adopted in textual criticism a number of agreements against Mark can be removed (Wilke) but they could increase as well : " Diese Stellen ($positive\ agreements$) könnten noch vermehrt werden, wenn wir ... nach den textkritischen Grundsätzen Derer verfahren würden, die zum Theil die auffällendsten, von allen Parallelen abweichenden, Lesarten für die ächten halten " (p. 62, with reference to F. Hitzig). More recently, a similar observation against Streeter's method has been made by F. M. Keech and W. R. Farmer (cf. $infra$, n. 131).

11. The double tradition texts of the first part of the gospel (before Lk 7, 18) belong to the Apostolic Source and were omitted by Mark : Lk 3,7-9.16-17 (Mt 3,7-12) ; 4,1-13 (Mt 4,1-11) ; 6,20-49 (Mt 5-7) ; 7,1-10 (Mt 8,1.5-10.13).

12. The list of positive minor agreements " in der Wahl einzelner Wörter und Ausdrücke " : par. Mk 1,10 ; 2,3bis.5.12.21.22.23 ; 3,16-17.32.33 ; 4,11.38.41 ; 5,27bis ; 6,9.10.11.34 ; 8,31.36 ; 9,19.31 ; 10,22.47 ; 11,3 ; 12,15.22.37 ; 13,2 ; 14,11.72 ; 15,39.46 ; 16,6 (pp. 61-62 ; see also p. 60 : Mk 14,65). Negative minor agreements, " eine Anzahl von ganz kurzen, erläuternden Zusätze und Einfügungen ". Mk 1,7.13.20.33 ; 2,14.16.18.25.26.27 ; 3,17.26 ; 4,3.7.8.11.19 ; 5,13.19.23.34 ; 6,3.13.37.(48.50.52) ; 8,32.35.38 ; 9,(12).49-50 ; 10,19.29.32.46 ; 11,10.13.16 ; 12, 14.27 ; (13,32) ; 14,20.(44).68 ; 15,21.40.43 ; 16,1 (pp. 110-111) ; in addition : 14,30.68.72 (p. 60) ; 9,21-24 ; 10,23.49 (p. 63). " Allerdings müssen in manchen reine Zuthaten des Marcus anerkannt werden ... Zum mindesten ebenso oft aber haben Matthäus und Lukas ausgelassen " (p. 111 ; instances of common omission are underlined).

13. Cf. p. 112 : " Er (Marcus) bringt es höchstens zu Zusätzen, Motivirungen, Modificationen, frappanten Detaillirungen und Pointen, zu neuen Namen und Situationen " (with reference to F. C. Baur's interpretation of Mark).

14. B. WEISS, ' Die Redestücke des apostolischen Matthäus. Mit besonderer Berücksichtigung von " Dr. H. J. Holtzmann, die synoptischen Evangelien, ihr Ursprung und geschichtlicher Charakter Leipzig 1863 " ', in $Jahrbücher\ für\ Deutsche$

Marcan redaction is unthinkable : it would be a recension of the text
rather than a redaction [15]. On the other hand, B. Weiss concedes that
the Ur-Marcus hypothesis has some attractiveness because it explains
so well the Matthew-Luke contacts [16], especially in the passion story [17].
In this last section (and in some other portions of the gospel) B. Weiss
readily admits the influence of the oral tradition [18] but the fundamental
solution he defends is that of the Apostolic Matthew. It is the fixation of
the oral tradition in a primitive gospel, without the passion story but
including the discourse material found in Matthew and Luke ; i.e., the
Redenquelle enlarged with narrative material and overlapping with the
gospel of Mark. The Matthew/Luke agreements, if they are not merely
insignificant coincidences of independent redaction [19], are attributed to

(or)
Weiss

(r)

Theologie 9 (1864) 49-140 ; ' Die Erzählungsstücke des apostolischen Matthäus ',
ibid. 10 (1865) 319-376.

15. ' Redestücke ', p. 138 ; ' Erzählungsstücke ', pp. 362-363 : " Eine Bear-
beitung desselben, die sich auf solche Aenderungen verlegte, wäre ja keine Redaction
mehr, sondern lediglich eine Text-recension, und dann müssten wir in unseren
Textquellen die Spuren davon aufsuchen und alle diese Differenzen durch Confor-
mation fortschaffen ". (See also pp. 366-367, on Mk 14,68.72, for the possibility
of " eine vor der Zeit unserer Textquellen gemachte Textnachbesserung " ; comp.
Wilke).

16. ' Redestücke ', p. 51. He even declares, at least in the beginning of his study,
that those contacts (*Berührungen*) between Matthew and Luke " sich auf dem
von Dr. Holtzmann gewiesenen Wege leichter erklären, als durch Zuhülfenahme
des apostolischen Matthäus " (*ibid.*).

17. Since the Apostolic Matthew did not contain a passion story, the agreements
Matthew-Luke in this section constitute a special difficulty for B. Weiss. See already
in ' Zur Entstehungsgeschichte der synoptischen Evangelien ', *Theologische Studien
und Kritiken* 34 (1861) 29-110.644-713, espec. p. 84. The possibility of a special
Lukan source, formulated there (*ibid.*, and p. 702), is abandoned in ' Erzählungsstücke ', pp. 364-367.

18. On the agreements in the passion story, see ' Erzählungsstücke ', pp. 364-376 ;
p. 365 : " Mir will es das Natürlichste scheinen, dass in diesen Fällen der von
Marcus verlassene mündliche Erzählungstypus, wie er sich auch für gewisse Ereig-
nisse der Leidenstage gebildet hatte, für die Abweichung der beiden Evangelisten
von ihrer Quelle massgebend gewesen ist ".

19. Cf. ' Erzählungsstücke ', pp. 361-364 (on Holtzmann's " Uebereinstimmun-
gen zwischen dem ersten und dritten Evangelium ", i.e. the list of positive agreements in *Die synoptischen Evangelien*, pp. 61-62 ; cf. *supra*, n. 12). Insignificant
(" nichts bedeutend ") are the coincidences in the use of $\delta\acute{\epsilon}$ instead of $\kappa\alpha\acute{\iota}$, of $\epsilon\hat{\iota}\pi\epsilon\nu$
instead of $\lambda\acute{\epsilon}\gamma\epsilon\iota$, etc. : " wenn das nicht ein Spiel des Zufalls ist ... " (p. 362). It is
more important that two observations are made by Weiss which are essential in a
discussion of the redactional character : some instances of Luke's agreement with
Matthew become less significant (1) because they correspond to Luke's general
literary usage (e.g. Lk 5,37, par. Mk 2,22 : " so ist zu erwägen, dass er überhaupt
dies angehängte $\gamma\epsilon$ liebt " ; 19,31, par. Mk 11,3 : " so ist zu erinnern, dass er diess
Wort [$\dot{\epsilon}\rho\epsilon\hat{\iota}\nu$] überhaupt am häufigsten gebraucht " ; *ibid.*, p. 363) ; or (2) because
Luke's agreement with Matthew is only partial, merely verbal or apparent (e.g.

the influence of the Apostolic Matthew, which is the common source of Matthew/Luke (and Mark) [20]. Weiss's hypothesis is exposed with more details in Das Marcusevangelium (1872), in which the exposition of every pericope is followed by a brief comment of the synoptic parallels and the Matthew/Luke agreements [21].

The first specific study of the minor agreements is that of Eduard SIMONS (1880) [22]. He is a defender of the Marcan hypothesis without the proto-gospel compromises of Holtzmann and Weiss [23]. He clearly maintains the distinction between the extra-Marcan common material of Matthew and Luke (Logia source) and the coincidences against Mark in the Marcan material [24]. Luke's use of Matthew as a *Nebenquelle* is the best explanation for the great number and the variety of these agreements [25]. Simons enumerates the Matthew/Luke contacts pericope after

---

par. Mk 12,22 : " nicht ganz gleich " ; 2,23 : " der Ausdruck (ist) keineswegs gleich " ; 12,15 ; 8,36 ; 10,47 ; 16,6 ; 6,8 : " Jede Uebereinstimmung fehlt ... " ; *ibid.*, pp. 363-364).

20. In our list " Weiss " (without any specification) indicates that solution. The letter q is added only when the author considered also another possibility (r/q or q/or). Farmer's historical survey should be corrected when he notes that Weiss's solution has " an integrity of method " (!) because he explains *all* the agreements by the Ur-gospel (*The Synoptic Problem*, p. 105 and 107). The author clearly ignores Weiss's insistance on oral tradition (p. 103).

(q)

21. *Das Marcusevangelium und seine synoptischen Parallelen*, Berlin, 1872. For a summary of his critique of the Ur-Marcus hypothesis of Holtzmann and K. Weizsäcker (*Untersuchungen über die evangelische Geschichte*, Gotha, 1864), see pp. 17-21. He maintains his position in *Die Evangelien des Markus und Lukas* (Meyer's *Kritisch-exegetischer Kommentar über das Neue Testament* I, 2), Göttingen, [9]1901, espec. pp. 256-258, against Johannes Weiss's adherence to Ur-Marcus ([8]1892, p. 278) and rejects Luke's subsidiary dependence on Matthew (cf. *infra*, n. 22 ; already in the 6th ed., 1878, p. 238, against the view of H. A. W. Meyer). Compare also his later work on Luke : *Die Quellen des Lukasevangeliums*, Stuttgart-Berlin, 1907 ; *Die Quellen der synoptischen Überlieferung* (TU 32, 3), Berlin, 1908.

22. E. SIMONS, *Hat der dritte Evangelist den kanonischen Matthäus benutzt ?*, Bonn, 1880.

23. Cf. J. SCHMID, *Matthäus und Lukas*, p. 10 : " Dieser Mittelweg, der sicher zwischen der Szulla der Urmarkushypothese und der Charybdis der Urmatthäus-hypothese eines B. Weiss hindurchführen sollte ... ".

24. See his conclusion : " Dabei ist die Stellung der Λ als 2. Hauptquelle wie ihre Eigenschaft als *Spruch*sammlung vollauf gewahrt geblieben. ... Wir gewinnen einen Standort, von welchem aus ein im weitesten Umfang primärer Charakter des Mr.-Textes sich mit Erfolg vertheidigen lässt " (p. 112).

25. There is deliberate use of Matthew but there are also unconscious reminiscences : " Stellt man sich aber vor, dass Lc. Vieles aus dem Mt.-Evangelium im Kopf hatte (*he calls it* " *eine gedächtnissmässige Aneignung* ") und erwägt man gleichzeitig, dass dasselbe für ihn eine Schrift von höchstens sekundärem Rang sein musste, so begreift man vollauf, dass er es bald sorgfältig zu Rathe zieht, bald blosse Einzelheiten von grösserer oder geringerer Bedeutung von ihm entlehnt, bald nur durch unwillkürliche Anklänge beweist, dass er es überhaupt gelesen " (p. 108).

Simons
pericope and openly declares the ineptness of other solutions (common source, oral tradition, accidental editorial coincidence) [26].

Rushbrooke's *Synopticon* was published in the same year as Simons's book. But before we come to the synoptic studies in England, we should mention two German works published at the end of the nineteenth

Veit
century: the horizontal-line synopsis of Karl VEIT [27] and the well-balanced exposition of the two-document hypothesis in Paul WERNLE's *Die synoptische Frage* (1899) [28]. Wernle gives a description of the evidence in a list of the common (*a*) omissions, (*b*) additions, (*c*) inversions and alterations, and (*d*) linguistic contacts: coincidences in the use of the same words, in grammatical changes, in the avoidance of Mark's constructions [29]. In the author's opinion most of the agreements result from an independent but similar reflection of Matthew and Luke upon

Wernle
(t)
Mark [30]. The text of Mark, however, shows secondary glosses and alterations and in some instances Matthew and Luke could have used either a slightly revised gospel text, concurrently attested by the ' Western '

---

26. Simons admits also a subsidiary dependence on Matthew for the Logia texts, especially regarding their combination with Mark (Mt 3,7-12 ; 4,1-12 and 12,22ff. ; the insertion of the Sermon on the Mount, etc.). " Ja Lc. eignet sich von Mt. frei geschaffenen Stoff an (s. Lc. 11,30 ; 16,17 ; 20,18 ; vgl. auch 6,22.23) " (p. 107). For Lk 16,17 = Mt 5,18 the possibility of Luke's dependence on Matthew was already envisaged by Holtzmann in *Jahrbücher für protestantische Theologie* 4 (1878) 553-554 ; *TLZ* 3 (1878) 553, and subsequently Holtzmann espoused his student's thesis : cf. *TLZ* 6 (1881) 180-183 ; *Lehrbuch der historisch-kritischen Einleitung in das Neue Testament*, Leipzig, 1885 ; ³1892, pp. 350 and 356-358.

27. K. VEIT, *Die synoptischen Parallelen und ein alter Versuch ihrer Enträtselung mit neuer Begründung*, Gütersloh, 1897. In the second part of the book (*Enträtselung der synoptischen Parallelen*) the author defends Gieseler's tradition hypothesis. The first part, *Die synoptischen Parallelen*, is a horizontal-line synopsis of the text of Mark and the synoptic parallels (including the following Matthew-Luke parallels : Mt 3,7-10 ; 5 - 7 ; 8,5-13 ; 8,19-22 ; 9,32-34 ; 10,5 - 11,1 ; 11,2-27 ; 12,38-45 ; 13,33 ; 18,12-14 ; 23,1-39). Two classes of agreements Matthew/Luke against Mark are clearly marked : (1) strictly identical words : replaced by an asterisk in the text of Luke, third line ; (2) inversions of order : the text of Mark, second line, is printed in the order of Matthew (and Luke) and the inverted elements are enclosed in round brackets and numbered : 2( ) 1( ).

28. P. WERNLE, *Die synoptische Frage*, Freiburg i.B., 1899. Espec. pp. 45-61 : " Der Marcustext bei Matthäus und Lucas ".

29. *Ibid.*, pp. 45-49. " Bei dem nun folgenden kompliziertesten Teil der synoptischen Frage ist vor allem nötig ein vollständiger Überblick über den Thatbestand " (p. 45).

30. Wernle rejects the hypothesis of a common source (rather a text recension of Mark ?) and also the interdependence theory : " kein einziger Zug, der für Mt oder für Lc charakteristisch wäre... Thatsächlich steht es so, dass Lc gerade alle sicheren Änderungen des Mt am Mrtext nicht befolgt... und umgekehrt folgt Mt keiner einzigen sichern Korrektur des Lc " (p. 51).

witnesses D sy^c ^s [31], or a text form which is more original than the text of our Mark [32].

2

Edwin A. ABBOTT is at the origin of the special interest of British scholars in the problem of the minor agreements. It starts with his article on the ' Gospels ' in the *Encyclopaedia Britannica* (1879) [33]. There he examines Mk 12,1-11 as a specimen of Triple Tradition and notices that Matthew and Luke agree in adding three words to the common texts, " trifling words ", " that any early editor of Mark might naturally insert " [34]. Nevertheless, he did not infer that Matthew and Luke borrowed " from the complete Mark as we have it " : " For though each of the three additions οὖν, ἰδόντες, οἱ γεωργοί, is in itself natural enough, yet the hypothesis that Matthew and Luke independently adopted precisely these and no other additions is most improbable " [35]. He uses expressions

---

31. " Allerdings scheint dieser ' occidentalische ' Text seine Entstehung einer uralten Redaktion zu verdanken, die darauf ausgieng, die Differenzen der synoptischen Texte möglichst auszugleichen. Dabei ist es jedoch nicht unwahrscheinlich, dass in dieser Redaktion vielfach gerade der ursprüngliche Mrtext sich erhielt " (p. 54). Examples are : Mk 1,7-8 (" Konformation ist hier wahrscheinlich ") ; 2,19.26.27 ; 4,10.11.15.19 ; 5,15 (" Vielleicht ist es wirklich Glosse " ; cf. p. 220) ; 9,35 ; 10,24.29 (pp. 54-56).

32. *Ibid.*, pp. 56-57 : Mk 1,20.29 ; 2,9.15-16(dubious).2̲1̲ ; 3,9.14-15.16*a* ; 4,36 ; 5,27 ; 6,3 ; 9,19 ; 11,1.17 ; 14,3̲0̲.6̲8̲.7̲2̲. See also pp. 220-22̲1̲ : " ein paar annähernd sichere Glossen und Textverderbnisse " ; in addition to the underlined instances : Mk 6,8-9 ; 9,49 ; 10,46 ; 15,21. — The position is well formulated in the following passage : " Die 3. und 4. Hypothese treffen darin zusammen, dass sie den gemeinsamen Abweichungen des Mt und Lc von Mr *kein so grosses Gewicht* beilegen. Zu ihrer Erklärung genügt entweder die Annahme *eines freien fliessenden* Mrtextes oder *des frei reflectierenden* Verhältnisses beider Evangelisten zu Mr. Dabei erwächst uns hier der Vorteil, dass diese letzten Hypothesen *sich* keinerwegs ausschliessen, sondern *ergänzen*, dass die eine das erklären kann, was sich der andern entzieht " (p. 54 ; the underlining is ours). See also p. 61 : " Jede andere Hypothese ist darum falsch, weil sie überflüssig ist ", and : " die Unabhängigkeit des Lc von Mt (ist) ein sicheres Ergebnis ".

33. E. A. ABBOTT, ' Gospels ', in *Encyclopaedia Britannica*, 9th ed., Vol. X, Edinburgh, 1879, pp. 789-843. Espec. in the first part on ' Synoptical Gospels : Internal Evidence ' (pp. 789-813) : ' The Triple Tradition ', pp. 789-792 ; ' The Additions and Peculiarities of Mark ', pp. 801-803.

34. *Ibid.*, p. 791.

35. The quotation is taken from the 1879 article (*ibid.*). It is not quite correct when Farmer observes that " by 1901... Abbott *reversed his position* on the grounds that these agreements were of such a nature as to lead him to the conclusion that

as " some form of Mark " and " a slightly modified edition of Mark ".
In 1880 the theory of an early edition or correction of Mark is formulated
by W. G. RUSHBROOKE in the introduction to his *Synopticon* [36] and shortly
after by Abbott in *The Common Tradition of the Synoptic Gospels* [37].
Finally, in 1901 the full evidence is published by Abbott in *The Corrections of Mark Adopted by Matthew and Luke* [38]. He distinguishes amendments of style from amendments of fact. " The comparatively unimportant class referring to Greek style or grammatical improvement " [39]
are " *Minor* Agreements of Matthew and Luke ", modifications " as
might be expected from a Corrector desirous of improving style and

---

they could not be due to the coincidental modifications made by two independent
editors (Matthew and Luke), but must be due to the conscious effort of a single
mind " (*The Synoptic Problem*, p. 95 ; see also pp. 136-137). The " conscious effort
of a single mind " is another inaccuracy. Comp. *Corrections* (see n. 38), p. 55, n. 1 :
" ' The Corrector ' will sometimes be used to denote the origin of any reading in
which Matthew and Luke agree (in the Triple Tradition) against Mark. But the term
is not to commit us to any definite view as to *one* Corrector or Editor. There may
have been a score of editions of Mark, all trying to make the Gospel less obscure
and ungrammatical, and some of them trying to make it more edifying. About
such details we can know nothing " ; and p. 54, n. 1 : " It does not follow that
Matthew and Luke used the *same* edition of Mark ". Farmer unduly assimilates
Abbott's position with that of Sanday (cf. the quotation on p. 96).

36. W. G. RUSHBROOKE, *Synopticon. An Exposition of the Common Matter of
the Synoptic Gospels*, London, 1880. The work is dedicated to Abbott, " the first
suggester of this work, ... by his former pupil " and a large extract from Abbott's
article (pp. 789-791) is quoted in the introduction (pp. V-IX). It is one of the facilities
the *Synopticon* should afford that " the additional matter common to St. Matthew
and St. Luke [*indicated by spaced type in Matthew and by capitals in Luke*] (scanty
though it is in most passages) will enable the reader, with altogether new advantages,
to consider the supposition that both St. Matthew and St. Luke may have had
before them, as a basis of part of their Gospels, some identical edition of the tradition contained in St. Mark's Gospel, in which edition an attempt had been made to
correct some of the roughnesses in style and language which still characterize our
present edition of that Gospel " (p. XI).

37. E. A. ABBOTT - W. G. RUSHBROOKE, *The Common Tradition of the Synoptic
Gospels* (in the Text of the Revised Version), London, 1884. On p. VII, n. 2 : " Where
Matthew and Luke agree in slight deviations from Mark, they probably used some
' similar edition ' of the original tradition, from which there had been removed
some of the abruptnesses perceptible in Mark's form of the tradition " (the Introduction, pp. V-XXXIX, is written by Abbott). *The Common Tradition of the Synoptic Gospels* is a ' translation ' of the first part of *Synopticon* (pp. 1-133), with the
complete text of Mark and the parallel passages in Matthew and Luke. The Common
Tradition, exhibited in red in *Synopticon*, is printed in thick type. A special column
is added with the matter peculiar to Mark (Portions not found in Matthew or
Luke), which is printed in ordinary type in *Synopticon*.

38. E. A. ABBOTT, *The Corrections of Mark Adopted by Matthew and Luke* (Diatessarica-Part II), London, 1901.

39. *Ibid.*, p. 61.

Rushbrooke

removing obscurities " [40]. Other corrections assume a different character, partly " due to a Hebrew original, which Mark appeared to the Corrector to have mistranslated ", and " amounting to an edition, or editions, of Mark, later than our Mark [41] but earlier than Matthew and Luke, edited at a time when the Hebrew original of the gospel still exercised influence " [42]. Those are " the *principal* corrections of Mark ", the proper object of Abbott's study. However, the best known part of his book is the appendix, in which he exhibits an exhaustive list of " the Greek textual agreements of Matthew and Luke against Mark, in the Triple Tradition " [43]. It is based on Rushbrooke's *Synopticon* and forms a most convenient supplement for the study of the positive agreements (" Corrections "), comparable with *The Common Tradition* for the negative agreements (" Portions not found in Matthew or Luke ") [44]. Less atten-

---

40. *Ibid.*, p. 300. He distinguishes eight classes of *minor* agreements (pp. 300-304) :
Abbott
  I. Corrections defining subject or object (about twelve instances) ;   (I)
  II. Corrections of the abrupt construction caused by the absence of a connecting word (about fifteen instances ; see also VII) ;   (II)
  III. Corrections of Mark's historic present (about thirteen instances ; see also V) ;   (III)
  IV. Substitutions of the participle for the indicative with " and ", or for the relative and the subjunctive (about twelve instances) ;   (IV)
  V. Substitutions of the word " said (εἶπεν) " for Mark's " says (λέγει) ", or corrections of Mark's imperfect " used to say " or " began to say " (ἔλεγεν, more rarely ἤρξατο λέγειν) (about twenty-three instances) ;   (V)
  VI. Substitutions of δέ for καί (at least thirty instances) ;   (VI)
  VII. Improvement of Greek construction or style, by softening abruptness (of a different kind from that mentioned under II), changing interrogatives into statements, introducing μέν ... δέ, ἀλλά, or other particles, and altering Hebraic or vernacular words or phrases ;   (VII)
  VIII. Less important instances of agreement in returning to a Hebrew Original, e.g. in the use of " behold (ἰδού) ".   (VIII)

41. *Ibid.*, p. 54, n. 1 : " Later than our Mark (at all events in parts)... Our Mark may combine *late interpolations* — not known to Matthew (and perhaps not to Luke) — with a *text earlier* than that which was used by Matthew and Luke ".

42. *Ibid.*, pp. 53-54.

43. *Ibid.*, pp. 307-324 : " Appendix I : A Complete Table of the Corrections of Mark ". The most important are explained in pp. 59-304 (Book II : The Principal Corrections of Mark), and marked (†). Of the rest, a few are explained by footnotes, but most belong to the eight classes of stylistic improvement (cf. n. 40). In our list the important instances which he explains as translation variants of a Hebrew original are indicated by (H). The corrections due to Greek corruption or   (H) editorial improvement are indicated by the name of Abbott without additament. Additions belonging to the Double Tradition are not inserted, although the author admits that there may be doubt whether an expression should be treated as a *correction* of the Triple Tradition, or an *addition* belonging to the Double Tradition ; e.g. par. Mk 1,7 : καὶ πυρί (p. 61).

44. Cf. n. 37.

tion is paid by Rushbrooke and Abbott to the inversions of order. For this class of agreements the *Synopsis* of Arthur WRIGHT may be helpful [45].

The position of William SANDAY, although he abandons the supposition of corrections of Mark under the influence of the Hebrew original, is in many respects related to that of Abbott. He had already suggested in 1891 that textual corruption and the freedom of early copyists could explain the facts [46]. " Here we have a *vera causa*, which may be introduced if we want it. I hope some day to test more exactly how far it will carry us " [47]. In *Oxford Studies* (1911) [48] he no longer maintains his clear distinction between editorial and textual and formulates the hypothesis that Matthew and Luke used a *recension* of the text of Mark [49].

---

45. A. WRIGHT, *A Synopsis of the Gospels in Greek*, London, 1896 ; [2]1903 ; [3]1906. Where Matthew and Luke agree in order against Mark the text of Mark is marked Wright by an obelus (†). (In Rushbrooke's *Synopticon* the same sign calls attention to variation in order but as it is printed in the three texts the Matthew/Luke agreements are not marked.) A. Wright attempts to combine the two-document theory with the oral tradition hypothesis. " Oral tradition is flexible, ... oral tradition grows like a tree " (p. V). According to " a golden rule, that if a section is not found in an Evangelist, the presumption is that he was not acquainted with it " (p. XI), he distinguishes three stages in the expansion of the oral Mark, the proto-Mark : as it was used by Luke ; the deutero-Mark : as it was used by Matthew ; the trito-Mark : when there had been still further expansion (p. X). He gives a list of negative agreements (" the trito-Marcan additions ") on pp. LIX-LXI ; in the *Synopsis* they are enclosed in square brackets and marked in the margin by the figure (iii). For Wright's theory of the three editors of Mark as a documentary hypothesis, cf. W. W. HOLDSWORTH, ' The Markan Narrative in the Synoptic Gospels ', *Expositor* 8th Ser., 1 (1911) 449-460.

46. W. SANDAY, ' A Survey of the Synoptic Problem ', *Expositor* 4th Ser., 3 (1891) 81-91.179-194.302-316.345-361.411-426, espec. pp. 179-194 : II. ' Points Proved or Probable '. On p. 191 : " One hypothesis, which I am myself much inclined to keep in sight, ... is, that these facts were not so much editorial as textual, that they did not mark any deliberate recension of the Gospel, but were only incidental to the process of copying ".

47. *Ibid.*, p. 191.

48. W. SANDAY, ' The Conditions under which the Gospels were written, in their Bearing upon some Difficulties of the Synoptic Problem ', in *Studies in the Synoptic Problem* By Members of the University of Oxford (ed. W. SANDAY), Oxford, 1911, pp. 3-26, espec. pp. 19-24 : ' The copying and transmission of texts, in their bearing upon (a) the agreements of Mt Lk against Mk '.

49. *Ibid.*, p. 21 : " But I believe that by far the greater number of the coincidences of Mt Lk against Mk are due to the use by Mt Lk ... *of a recension of the text of Mk different from that from which all the extant MSS. of the gospel are descended.* I reject the idea of an *Ur-Marcus*, or older form of the gospel, because the great majority of the coincidences seem to me to belong to a later form of text rather than an earlier. And I call this form of text a recension, because there is so much method and system about it that it looks like the deliberate work of a particular editor, or scribe exercizing to some extent editorial functions. This appears to come out clearly from Dr. Abbott's classification of the corrections ". He enumerates the

Sanday was impressed by the large number of agreements collected by Abbott [50] and he proposed his suggestion as a general explanation for the phenomenon of the coincidences [51]. The recension theory gained momentary acceptance among the Oxford scholars [52] but was definitely abandoned in C. H. Turner's Inaugural Lecture of 1920 : " A post-Marcan ' recension ' is open to the same sort of objections as a pre-Marcan ' Ur-Marcus ' : in deference to 1 per cent of the evidence it

---

eight classes of Abbott (cf. *supra*, n. 40) and concludes : " The number and the recurrence of these phenomena is evidently due to design, and not to accident " (p. 22).

50. *Ibid.*, p. 10 : " too numerous to be entirely the result of accident " ; p. 19 : " the examples (many of them simple, but many also complex) given by Dr. Abbott number in all about 230 ".

51. *Ibid.*, p. 21 : " by far the greater number ". Other causes will account for some of the examples : obvious correction in Matthew and Luke, textual corruption and overlapping of Mark and Q (p. 20).

52. J. C. Hawkins, *Horae Synopticae* (see n. 62), [2]1909, p. 212 : " But it appears to me now that others of them, and perhaps the majority, may be best accounted for by Dr. Sanday's suggestion ".

Id., ' Probabilities as to the so-called Double Tradition of St. Matthew and St. Luke ', in *Oxford Studies* (see n. 48), pp. 95-138, espec. p. 103 (with reference to Sanday's essay in n. 2) : " they are much more reasonably explained either by subsequent harmonizations ..., or else, and I now think in very many cases, by Mt and Lk having used a copy of Mk in which small alterations and supposed corrections had been already made ". Subsequent harmonization was the only cause he mentioned in the first edition of *Horae Synopticae* (cf. p. 212 : " as I sugges-ted in my first edition as to all of them "). It should be clear from those quota-tions that Hawkins came to the recension theory under the influence of Sanday. On p. 152 (1st ed., p. 122) Hawkins suggested the possibility of " a later editor's hand " for a few cases of additional matter in Mark. This has to do with Ur-Marcus and is completely misunderstood by R. T. Simpson as the suggestion " that both St Matthew and St Luke made use of a deutero-Mark " ; cf. ' The Major Agreements of Matthew and Luke against Mark ', *NTS* 12 (1965-66) 273-284, p. 282. The same mistake appears in Schmid's *Einleitung* (cf. *infra*, n. 104), p. 288, n. 35 ; other cor-rection : Simpson's hypothesis is not Deutero-Mark (*ibid.*) but Luke's dependence on Matthew.

— B. H. Streeter, ' St. Mark's Knowledge and Use of Q ', in *Oxford Studies*, pp. 166-183, p. 178 : " These are more likely to be due to posterior scribal improve-ments on the text of Mark, *before* it was used by Matthew and Luke (cf. Dr. Sanday's essay, p. 21)... ". Id., ' The Synoptic Problem ', in *Peake's Commentary on the Bible*, London, 1920, pp. 672-680, espec. p. 675 : " But 220 instances of concurrent stylistic or grammatical improvement, however natural and obvious and however minute, are too many to be put down to mere coincidence. A far more probable explanation is that the text of Mk had undergone a slight grammatical revision before it was made use of by Matthew and Luke ". Cf. *infra*, n. 53.

— T. Stephenson, ' The Overlapping of Sources in Matthew and Luke ', *JTS* 21 (1920) 127-145, espec. pp. 127-132 : " I believe that the key to the solution of this problem is given by Dr Sanday " (p. 127) ; " Their frequency is an important factor, and affords cumulative evidence of a common original " (p. 128). Cf. *infra*, n. 68.

introduces a new factor, of the existence of which we have, otherwise, not the slightest indication " [53]. Obviously, Turner did not expect that his own method of reducing the agreements with the help of ' Western ' textual authorities [54] could prepare for a new chance for Sanday's theory. In 1943 Thomas Francis GLASSON was to collect twenty variant readings of D in Mark which differ from the original reading in the same way as Matthew and Luke differ from Mark. Thus, besides overlapping of Mark and Q and independent corrections and alterations, he adds a third factor : " the use by Matthew and Luke of copies of Mark in which the same corruptions occurred — corruptions which have been transmitted to us in the Western MS. tradition " [55]. In 1959 John

---

53. C. H. TURNER, *The Study of the New Testament 1883 and 1920*, Oxford, 1920 ; [2]1924, p. 43 : " That is a conclusion to which I should come very reluctantly " (*ibid.*). — Hawkins took notice of it ; cf. 'Hawkins's Additional Notes to His *Horae Synopticae* ' (ed. F. NEIRYNCK), *ETL* 46 (1970) 79-111, p. 110 ; and in 1924 Streeter simply adds to the passage on independent editing : " If, however, any one thinks the proportion too large to be accidental, it is open to him to accept Dr. Sanday's hypothesis " (*The Four Gospels*, pp. 304-305). — It requires to be noted that C. H. Turner in a former study (January 1909) had mentioned as one of the causes of coincidences " the opinion of one who has long presided over these studies among us " ; cf. ' Historical Introduction to the Textual Criticism of the New Testament ', *JTS* 10 (1908-09) 161-182, pp. 175-176. — Compare also W. C. ALLEN, *Matthew* (cf. *infra*, n. 89), 1907, pp. XXXIX-XL : " Some of the agreements in question are probably due to the fact that the copy of Mk. used by Mt. and Lk. had already undergone textual correction from the original form of the gospel ". The position of both Allen and Turner (a possible factor, not an over-all explanation for the majority of the cases) is different from Sanday's theory which is based on " the number and the recurrence of these phenomena ". Comp. C. S. PATTON, *Sources of the Synoptic Gospels* (University of Michigan Studies. Humanistic Series, V), New York, 1915, pp. 30-31.70-71 and 88-93 : " Ur-Marcus was at the most not a different Mark from ours, but only a different copy or text of our Mark " (p. 92).

54. Cf. *The Study*, pp. 45-47 ; ' Historical Introduction ', pp. 176-179. Cf. *infra*, n. 81 (and 80). Compare Wernle (*supra*, n. 28) who accepts some of the Western readings as original (cf. Turner), others as corruptions (cf. Glasson).

55. T. F. GLASSON, ' Did Matthew and Luke Use a ' Western ' Text of Mark ? ', *Expos. Tim.* 55 (1943-44) 180-184 ; 57 (1945-46) 53-54 ; 77 (1965-66) 120-121. Glasson

replaces Sanday's recension (or deliberate revision of the text of Mark ; cf. Abbott's corrections) by corruptions of the text. The examples are : 1,10.43[*] ; 2,9[*].16. 19b.23.26[*].27-28a ; 4,10a.10b.11.16 ; 5,14 ; 8,27 ; 9,3.35 ; 10,24.27 ; 12,7.14[*] ; 14,48 ; 15,15.24.25. The asterisk indicates four instances which he added in 1965 (p. 121). Three more instances are indicated in *JBL* 85 (1960), p. 233 (cf. *infra*, n. 57) : Mk 10,19 ; 11,17 ; 12,7a.

— Comp. C. S. C. WILLIAMS, ' Did Matthew and Luke Use a ' Western ' Text of Mark ? ', *Expos. Tim.* 56 (1944-45) 41-45 ; 58 (1946-47) 251 ; cf. Glasson's reply in *Expos. Tim.* 57 (1945-46). Although Williams disagreed with the particular instances (Tatian is the source of the Western readings), he did admit that some variant readings of the Marcan text perhaps lay before Matthew and Luke, and were later incorporated in the Western tradition. In *Expos. Tim.* 77 (1965-66)

Pairman BROWN proposed an amendment to Glasson's suggestion : there existed in the first century a revised version or versions of Mark, which accounts for many textual variants in our MSS. of Mark and for the bulk of the agreements of Matthew and Luke against Mark ; the best witness to this recension is not the Western (D) but the Caesarean (particularly fam. 13). The author brings forward 71 cases where a textual variant of Mark corresponds to an agreement of Matthew and Luke against Mark [56]. Since Brown's article [57] the suggestion of Sanday is cited again among the possible solutions of the problem of the minor agreements [58]. Joachim GNILKA holds it for the best solution [59]. For others the edited form of Mark is not a scribal revision but a complete gospel redaction, for H.

Glasson signals the support of Klijn : " Not all examples are of equal value, but his thesis cannot be denied. This shows that ' Western ' readings go back to the very beginnings of Christianity " ; cf. A. F. J. KLIJN, ' A Survey of the Researches into the Western Text of the Gospels and Acts ', NT 3 (1959) 1-27.161-173, p. 162.

56. J. P. BROWN, ' An Early Revision of the Gospel of Mark ', JBL 78 (1959) 215-227. He gives a list of 15 instances of variant reading with MS. citation from the edition of Legg : Mk 1,40a ; 1,40b, 1,41a ; 1,41b ; 1,42 ; 2,22 ; 4,11 ; 6,3 ; 6,43 ; 9,19 ; 11,29 ; 14,30.68.72 ; 14,62 ; 14,65 ; 15,25 ; and 56 further readings (without MS. evidence) in the following classification : **Brown**
— Additions : 1,14 ; 2,3.22.26 ; 3,1.14 ; 4,3.15 ; 5,22.27 ; 6,33 ; 8,29 ; 9,4.7 ; 12,9.23 ; 13,6.7.31 ; 14,20.
— Transpositions : 2,10 ; 9,1 ; 12,1.8.17 ; 15,14.
— Other changes : 1,29 ; 2,16bis ; 3,1.7 ; 4,1.9.10.41 ; 5,14.38bis ; 6,14 ; 8,31bis ; 9,18 ; 10.28.51 ; 11,2.7 ; 12,17.37 ; 13,2.30 ; 14,10.38.54.72 ; 15,1.24.
For the omissions in 2,19.26.27 ; 10,24 and 15,15 (with overwhelmingly Western   **(W)**
attestation) some different cause might be at work.

57. Comp. Glasson's reaction in Expos. Tim. 77 (1965-66) 120-121 ; ' An Early Revision of the Gospel of Mark ', JBL 85 (1966) 231-233.
— However, see O. LINTON, ' Evidences for a Second-Century Revised Edition of St. Mark's Gospel ', NTS 14 (1967-68) 321-335 : a revision which includes later harmonistic readings besides corrections independent from Matthew and Luke. Cf. F. NEIRYNCK, Duality in Mark. Contributions to the Study of the Markan Redaction (Bibl. ETL, 31), Leuven, 1972, pp. 37-39.

58. Cf. N.T.-introductions of W. G. Kümmel (Einleitung, p. 32), D. Guthrie (The Gospels and Acts, p. 129, n. 1), J. Schmid (Einleitung, p. 288 : " nicht bloss überflüssig, sondern auch durchaus unwahrscheinlich "). Nevertheless, G. Schneider (Verleugnung, 1969, cf. infra, n. 144) who enumerates all possible theories, does not even mention that possibility (pp. 48-49). — There is no reference to Glasson in the introductions of Kümmel (1963), Guthrie (1965) and Schmid (1973 ; see also the correction regarding Simpson, supra, n. 52) ; in the new edition of KÜMMEL's Einleitung in das Neue Testament (Heidelberg, 1973) the JBL article of 1966 is now mentioned (p. 36, n. 45a).

59. J. GNILKA, Die Verstockung Israels. Isaias 6,9-10 in der Theologie der Synoptiker (StANT, 3), Munich, 1961, p. 123 : " Die beste Lösung dieser ausserordentlich schwierigen Frage (minor agreements) " (in an examination of Mk 4,11) ; and more recently in Theologische Revue 69 (1973) 458-460, p. 459.

Philip WEST a Primitive Luke [60], for Albert FUCHS a Deutero-Mark which includes the Q material [61].

3

John C. HAWKINS's *Horae Synopticae* (1899) is representative for another direction in the study of the minor agreements [62]. A first contribution is his exposition on the peculiar matter of Mark [63]. He brings together and classifies the Marcan peculiarities, " so that we may see how far they are such as would be likely to be omitted or altered " [64].

---

60. H. Philip WEST Jr., ' A Primitive Version of Luke in the Composition of Matthew ', *NTS* 14 (1967-68) 75-95, p. 94 : " The agreements of Matthew and Luke against Mark strongly suggest that both knew an edited form of Mark. If Matthew used Mark and Primitive Luke, then the agreements of Matthew and Luke against Mark, both positive changes and omissions, are easily explicable. Matthew could save himself a great deal of work if he chose to abide by some of the modifications of Mark made by the editor of Primitive Luke ".

61. A. FUCHS, *Sprachliche Untersuchungen zu Matthäus und Lukas. Ein Beitrag zur Quellenkritik* (Analecta Biblica, 49), Rome, 1971. The specific object of the study is the deutero-Marcan origin of two displaced pericopes : Mt 9,27-31, par. Mk 10, 46-52 (Mt 20,29-34), and Lk 12,11-12, par. Mk 13,11 (Lk 21,14-15). With his observation that the minor agreements are part of a theological redaction and some of them (e.g. " Änderungen der Satzstruktur oder längere Ergänzungen ", p. 109) are clearly more than textual corrections, he is far from Brown's *basic observation* : " the agreements of Matthew and Luke against Mark seldom are more extensive than the variants in the text of Mk itself " (*art. cit.*, p. 220).

Fuchs — In the course of his stylistic analysis the author calls attention to the conglomeration of agreements in the following passages : par. Mk 1,40-45 (p. 156, n. 120) ; 4,35-41 (pp. 67-68) ; 5,27 (p. 146) ; 6,7-11 (pp. 61-62) ; 6,32-44 (pp. 55-56 and 69, n. 34) ; 10,23-30 (pp. 75-77) ; 11,27-33 (pp. 10-107) ; 12,18-22 (p. 108) ; 13,9-11. (p. 174) ; 14,54 (pp. 72-73) ; 15,37 (p. 90) ; 15,54 (pp. 72-73). The author announces a *Habilitationsarbeit* on Deutero-Mark ; cf. ' Die Überschneidungen von Mk und ' Q ' nach B. H. Streeter und E. P. Sanders ' (SNTS Seminar Paper, 1973), p. 25, n. 30. On the insertion of Q material, *ibid.*, pp. 21-22.

62. J. C. HAWKINS, *Horae Synopticae. Contributions to the Study of the Synoptic Problem*, Oxford, 1899 ; [2]1909 (repr. 1968). Cf. F. NEIRYNCK (ed.), ' Hawkins's Additional Notes to His *Horae Synopticae* ', *ETL* 46 (1970) 78-111 (= Analecta Lovaniensia Biblica et Orientalia, V, 2).

63. *Ibid.*, [2]1909, pp. 114-153 : " Part III. Further Statistics and Observations bearing on the Origin and Composition of each Gospel : A. On the Gospel of St. Mark ".

64. *Ibid.*, p. 115. The material is collected from Rushbrooke's *Synopticon* and *The Common Tradition* (cf. p. 114, n. 1). On the sections IV, V and VI, cf. *infra*.
Hawkins The collection of the sections I, II and III is important with regard to the negative agreements. In our list we mentioned (with the number of the section) the instances where both Matthew and Luke disagree with Mark :

That examination leads to the result that " not an ' *Ur-Marcus* ', but St Mark's Gospel almost as we have it now " is the source used by the two later Synoptists [65]. Still he adds : " Almost ; not quite ", and gives II instances where " a later editor's hand is to be seen " [66]. The positive agreements are treated in an appendix to that part of the book [67]. He distinguishes three categories : (1) Agreements in sections chiefly consisting of discourse and probably due to the influence of the Logia source [68] ; (2) About 218 slight verbal agreements in the other

---

I. Passages which may have been omitted or altered as being liable to be misunderstood, or to give offence, or to suggest difficulties :

A. Passages seeming (*a*) to limit the power of Jesus Christ, or (*b*) to be otherwise (IA) derogatory to, or unworthy of, Him (pp. 117-121).

B. Passages seeming to disparage the attainments or character of the Apostles (IB) (pp. 121-122).

C. Other passages which might cause offence or difficulty (pp. 122-125). (IC)

II. Enlargements of the narrative, which add nothing to the information con- (II) veyed by it, because they are expressed again, or are directly involved, in the context (' context-supplements ') (pp. 125-126).

III. Minor additions to the narrative (pp. 127-131). (On pp. 130-131 : 1. Aramaic (III) or Hebrew phrases ; 2. Unimportant proper names.)

IV. Rude, harsh, obscure or unusual words or expressions, which may therefore (IV) have been omitted or replaced by others :

(*a*) Various unusual words and constructions (pp. 131-135) ; (IVa)

(*b*) Instances of anacoluthon, or broken or incomplete construction (pp. 135-137). (IVb)

(*c*) Cases of ' asyndeton ', or want of connexion (pp. 137-138). (IVc)

V. Duplicate expressions in Mark, of which (one or) both of the other synoptists (V) use one part, or its equivalent (pp. 139-142).

VI. The historic present in Mark (pp. 143-149). (VI)

VII. The conjunction καί preferred to δέ in Mark (pp. 150-152). (VII)

Comp. ' Hawkins's Additional Notes ', pp. 94-111.

65. *Ibid.*, p. 152.

66. *Ibid.*, p. 152 ; *very probably* in 1,1 (" Jesus Christ ") and 9,41 (" Christ's ") ; *probably* in 8,35 ; 10,29 (" the gospel ") and 10,30 (" persecutions ") ; *perhaps* in 7,3 (" the Jews ") ; 6,37 ; 14,5 (the numerals 200 and 300) ; *possibly* in 5,13 (" 2000 ") and 15,56.59 (the disagreement of the witnesses). In his ' Additional Notes ' (pp. 100-101) he refers to further literature (Stanton, Moffatt, Menzies, Rashdall, Bacon), but mentions also C. H. Turner's Inaugural Lecture (p. 40) with regard to the numerals in 5,13 ; 6,37 ; 14,5. Cf. his letter (June 1, 1920) quoted by Turner in *JTS* 26 (1925) p. 338 : " What you say about Mark's *constant* fondness for numerals is a weighty argument for the genuineness of the 200 and 300, and 2,000 about which I was doubtful ".

67. *Ibid.*, pp. 208-212 : ' The Alterations and Small Additions in which Matthew and Luke agree against Mark '.

68. *Ibid.*, p. 208 (and notes) : Mk 1,1-8 (cf. n. 3 : possibly abbreviated by a subsequent editor) ; 1,12-13 ; 3,20-30 ; 4,30-34 ; 6,7-13 ; 9,33-50 ; 12,28-34 ; 12,38-40 ; 13,14-37. Hawkins simply indicates 10 sections of Tischendorf's *Synopsis*. Stanton, Sanday, Streeter, Schmid, will give more precise lists (with variations). Cf. also T. STEPHENSON, ' The Overlapping of Sources in Matthew and Luke ', *JTS* 21 (1920) 127-145. The overlapping of Mark and Q is the cause of *major agreements*

sections which are explicable by accidental coincidence and editorial
improvement [69]; (3) A list of 20 (or 21) instances of supplements and
modifications " which seem to be owing to some influence, direct or
indirect, of a common source " [70]. Although Hawkins observes that it
is reasonable to suspect a common source in other sections also, his
fundamental solution for the agreements is that Matthew and Luke
accidentally concurred in making them. They can be explained by one
of three causes. " Either (a) they consist of words so ordinary and
colourless and so nearly synonymous with Mark's that the use of them
may be merely accidental ; or (β) they are such obvious amplifications
or explanations as it would be natural for any writers to introduce ;
or (γ) they are changes to a more smooth and usual Hellenistic vocabulary and style from the comparative harshness and ' unusualness ' of
Mark " [71]. That explanation is insufficient only in a limited number of
agreements, the twenty instances which appear to him " least unim-

---

par. Mk 1,1-8.12-13 ; 3,20-30 (and 8,11) ; 4,21.30-32 ; 6,7-13 ; 8,12.34 ; 9,35 and
10,43-44 ; 9,42 ; 11,22-23.25 ; 12,28-34.39 ; 13,15-16. The cases of agreements in
1,1-8 and 3,20-30 are inserted in our list ; also the inversion in 1,13 (pp. 133-137).

(q)   From the *minor agreements* (explicable by Sanday's theory ; cf. *supra*, n. 52)
Stephenson   the section Mk 1,40-45 (pp. 129-130) and εὐθύς (pp. 131-132) are in the list.
        — The terms used by Stephenson : *major agreements* (for " the larger and more
complex agreements " explained by Q influence) and *minor agreements* (for " the
lesser agreements ", " a large number of quite small agreements " explained by the
recension theory), can be compared with the terminology of Abbott who distinguishes between " the *principal* corrections of Mark " and the " minor agreements of
Matthew and Luke " (less significant stylistic corrections) (cf. *supra*, n. 40 and 43).
Farmer notes about the *minor* agreements that " they were later (i.e., after Hawkins)
so termed by Burkitt " (*The Synoptic Problem*, p. 105), but the assertion is undoc-
umented and Burkitt does not use the term where he treats the list of Hawkins
(cf. *infra*, n. 81). R. L. Lindsey declares : " It is true that the use of the word ' minor '
appears to have been first applied to these Mt-Lk agreements against Mark by
Streeter, who was unquestionably anxious to deprecate the importance of these
phenomena " (*Mark*, p. 27 ; cf. *infra*, n. 141). In fact, the title given to Chapter XI
of *The Four Gospels* (cf. *infra*, n. 96) contributed to the fixation of the term, but it
was not unprepared. Compare also *Oxford Studies*, p. 178 (cf. *supra*, n. 52) for the
distinction between *substantial* and *minute* verbal agreements (Stephenson's two
classes).
        69. *Ibid.*, p. 209. About 118 of them occur in sections in which also the 21 " least
unimportant " agreements are found.
Hawkins(*)   70. *Ibid.*, pp. 210-211 : (No. *1*) par. Mk 2,22 ; (*2*) 4,11 ; (*3*) 5,27 ; (*4*) 6,14 ; (*5*) 6,33
(and 34) ; (*6*) 8,29 ; (*7*) 9,7 ; (*8*) 9,19 ; (*9*) 10,30 ; (*10*) 11,11 ; (*11*) 11,27 ; (*12*) 14,45 ;
(*13*) 14,72 ; (*14*) 14,65 ; (*15*) 15,30 ; (*16*) 15,39 ; (*17*) 15,46 ; (*18*) 16,2 ; (*19*) 16,5 ;
(*20*) 16,8. — Mk 11,1 (om. Βηθφαγή) is added within brackets (No. *21*). Cf. ' Additional Notes ', pp. 109-110 : Mk 14,25 and 62.
        71. The account (γ) is to be given to the great majority of the agreements. He
refers to the Marcan peculiarities, sections IV-VI, in particular to Mark's preference
for the historic present and the conjunction καί. *Ibid.*, p. 209.

portant " [72]. His first suggestion [73] is that they are due to subsequent harmonization (whether made intentionally or unconsciously), either by copyists or more probably in the course of oral transmission [74]. Other phenomena too, like words differently applied and transpositions of the order of words and sentences, would take place easily in the course of oral transmission [75].

Hawkins's list of twenty notable instances of agreement will become the object of thorough examination in subsequent studies. In 1904 Ernest DeWitt BURTON proceeds in his own way to a similar reduction of the significant agreements [76]. Of the 275 words of agreement distributed in about 175 instances, many changes are explicable as due to causes which affected both Matthew and Luke alike [77]. He concludes by enumerating 15 instances (37 words) of common addition " which affect the sense of the passage further than by the change of tense or an unimportant exchange of prepositions " [78]. The agreements are " an unexplained remainder. To make them determinative for the whole theory is, however, to set the pyramide on its apex " [79]. Only three (or perhaps four) agreements listed by Burton coincide with those of Hawkins's list [80]. In 1906 the 20 instances were examined by F. Crawford BURKITT who dismissed them all : some are too different as to be called agreement,

---

72. Cf. *Oxford Studies* (see n. 48), p. 103, n. 1.

73. In the second edition he adopts the theory of Sanday (cf. *supra*, n. 52). It should be observed, however, that Sanday suggested his solution not for a limited number of difficult cases but for the large number of agreements collected in Abbott's list, and without considering them in conjunction with the agreements in omission (cf. Hawkins's exposition on the peculiar matter of Mark).

74. *Horae Synopticae*, 1899, pp. 174-175. In the second edition he still maintains it as a reasonable explanation for " some of them " (p. 212 ; cf. *Oxford Studies*, p. 103).

75. *Ibid.*, pp. 67-77 and 77-80. He gives only the principal cases of transpositions (and only one instance of Matthew/Luke agreement against Mark : Mk 1,7-8) and refers to the works of Veit and Wright (cf. *supra*, n. 27 and 45) where " other and briefer instances may be conveniently examined " (p. 80).

76. E. DeWitt BURTON, *Some Principles of Literary Criticism and Their Application to the Synoptic Problem*, in *The Decennial Publications of the University of Chicago*, Ser. 1, Vol. V, Chicago, 1904, pp. 194-264 (= pp. 1-72).

77. *Ibid.*, p. 209 (= p. 17). Many are due to a common impulse to improve Mark's Greek, or to conform the statement more exactly to the facts as understood by them. Other changes affect only the merest details.

78. *Ibid.* : (No. *1*) par. Mk 1,5 ; (*2*) 1,8 ; (*3*) 2,12 ; (*4*) 3,1 ; (*5*) 3,18 ; (*6*) 4,10 ; (*7*) 4,41 ; (*8*) 5,27 ; (*9*) 6,7 ; (*10*) 6,34 ; (*11*) 9,2 ; (*12*) 13,19 ; (*13*) 14,62 ; (*14*) 14,65 ; (*15*) 14,72.

79. *Ibid.*, p. 245 (= p. 53) : " This unexplained remainder probably owes its origin to causes that belong to the border line between editorial revision and scribal corruption, or also to some slight influence of one of those gospels in its final form on the mind of the writer of the other " (*ibid.*).

80. Mk 5,27 ; (6,34) ; 14,65 and 72. (Cf. *infra*, n. 156.)

others are coincident editorial changes and in four cases the text is not certain [81]. Following the lines of Burkitt, C. H. Turner observes that more weight should be given to the Old Latin and Old Syriac evidence [82], and in his second edition Hawkins will " agree that textual criticism has diminished, and is likely to diminish further, from the force of several of the instances " [83]. Marie-Joseph LAGRANGE discusses Hawkins's list in his commentary on Luke. His analysis of the 20 instances is only slightly different from that of Burkitt. He reduces the list to nine and adds eleven other instances of his own [84]. But most of them are explicable by independent editing and only in a few cases he suggests, not without hesitation, some influence of the Lucan text on Matthew [85]. Lagrange brings a more essential contribution in his commentary on

---

81. F. C. BURKITT, *The Gospel History and Its Transmission*, Edinburgh, 1906, pp. 42-58. Text uncertain in Mk 4,11 (Mt) ; 5,27 (Lk) ; 10,30 (Mt, Lk) ; 14,72 (Lk) ; also Mk 11,1.

82. Cf. *supra*, n. 67. He examines the four instances from Burkitt's discussion and adds Mk 12,28.

83. *Horae Synopticae*, p. 210, n. 1.

84. M.-J. LAGRANGE, *Évangile selon saint Luc* (Études Bibliques), Paris, 1921 ; [4]1948, pp. LXX-LXXIII. His list includes nine of Hawkins's instances (cf. n. 70 : Nos. 1, 2, 3, 4, 5, 7 [= no. 6 in his list], 8[= 7], 13[= 8], 14[= 9]) and eleven other agreements : (No. *10*) par. Mk 1,40bis ; (*11*) 2,3bis ; (*12*) 2,12*a* ; (*13*) 2,12*b* ; (*14*) 2,21 ; (*15*) 2,23 ; (*16*) 2,26 ; (*17*) 14,30.72 ; (*18*) 6,41.43 ; (*19*) 6,8 ; (*20*) 5,22. Nos. 17 and 18 are common omissions.

85. In particular, for his Nos. 4 (par. Mk 6,14 : ὁ τετραάρχης) and 6 (par. Mk 9,7 : ἔτι αὐτοῦ λαλοῦντος) : the style is Lucan rather than Matthean. But he continues : " Il est sage cependant de réserver le concours de plusieurs causes, le même besoin d'être clair (n°s 2.14) ou complet (n°s 12.15), des habitudes courantes de parler et d'écrire, enfin même ce concours de causes non ordonnées que l'on nomme le hasard " (*ibid.*, p. LXXIII). — See also p. LXXII, for no. 18 (par. Mk 6,41.43), and p. 310 (par. Mk 12,28, νομικός and πειράζων, " un emprunt à Luc "). The influence of Luke is not mentioned in his comment on Mt 14,1 and 17,4 ; in the latter he seems to suggest a common source : " La coïncidence ..., si elle peut être une rencontre non intentionnelle, pourrait aussi suggérer un récit ancien indépendant de Mc " (*Évangile selon saint Matthieu*, Paris, 1923 ; [8]1948, p. 335), and textual harmonization for Mt 22,35 (par. Mk 12,28) : " On peut croire que les deux autres mots sont venus de Lc et dus à des copistes " (p. 431). — The subsidiary dependence of Matthew on Luke is proposed also as a solution for the minor agreements by E. von DOBSCHÜTZ, ' Matthäus als Rabbi und Katechet ', ZNW 27 (1928) 338-348, espec. p. 347 (with the example of par. Mk 6,14). More information about similar views of J. E. Carpenter ([4]1906), P. Dausch (1914) and B. Heigh (1916) can be found in J. SCHMID, *Matthäus und Lukas* (cf. *infra*, n. 103), p. 3, n. 1 and p. 6, n. 4 ; and about earlier defenders of a more radical dependence on Luke : A. F. Büsching (1766), E. Evanson (1792), Vogel (1805), C. G. Wilke (1838, cf. *supra*, n. 2), F. Hitzig (1843), G. Volkmar (1866 ; 1870), O. Pfleiderer (1887), G. Schläger (1896), W. Küppers (1902), H. Delafosse [= H. Turmel] (1924) (*ibid.*, pp. 2-3). On W. Lockton (and R. L. Lindsey), cf. *infra*, n. 141.

Mark. There he continues the work of Hawkins in a survey of the linguistic and stylistic peculiarities of the Marcan style and language [86], as it will be done in a more complete form in Cuthbert H. TURNER's articles on ' Marcan Usage ' [87].

---

86. M.-J. LAGRANGE, *Évangile selon saint Marc* (Études Bibliques), Paris, 1911 ; [8]1947, pp. LXVII-LXXXIII. He refers to Hawkins and Swete ; cf. H. B. SWETE, *The Gospel according to St. Mark*, London, 1898 ; [3]1907, pp. XLIV-L. Compare also V. TAYLOR, *The Gospel according to St. Mark*, London, 1952, pp. 44-54. From this commentary only a few instances of verbal agreements were selected for our list, for obvious reasons (e.g. Mk 1,41). See further study of Mark's style in F. NICOLARDOT, *Les procédés de rédaction des trois premiers évangélistes*, Paris, 1908 ; and the works of W. C. Allen, W. Larfeld, J. Schmid (cf. *infra*), and F. NEIRYNCK, *Duality in Mark*, pp. 20-24 (on pleonasms and repetition).

Taylor

87. C. H. TURNER, ' Marcan Usage : Notes, Critical and Exegetical, on the Second Gospel ', *JTS* 25 (1924) 377ff. :
1. The impersonal plural, *ibid.*, 378-386 ;
2. Φέρειν in St. Mark, 26 (1925) 12-14 ;
3. εἰς and ἐν in St. Mark, *ibid.*, 14-20 ;
4. Parenthetical clauses in Mark, *ibid.*, 145-156 ;
5. The movements of Jesus and his disciples and the crowd, *ibid.*, 225-228 (i. The impersonal plural, followed by the singular, 228-231 ; ii. The singular followed by mention of the disciples/or the Twelve, 231-233 ; iii. The Lord, the disciples and the multitude, 234-235 ; iv. ' His disciples ', ' the disciples ' [οἱ μαθηταὶ αὐτοῦ, οἱ μαθηταί], 235-237 ; v. ' The crowd ' or ' the multitude ', 237-238 ; vii. The word ' to follow ' [ἀκολουθεῖν], 238-240) ;
6. The use of numbers in St. Mark's Gospel, *ibid.*, 337-346 ;
7. Particles : (1) Ὅτι interrogative, 27 (1926) 58-62 ; (2) Ὅτι recitative (after λέγειν or similar verbs), 28 (1927) 9-15 ; (3) Asyndeta or absence of particles in Mark, *ibid.*, 15-19 ; (4) Particles absent from Mark : i. ναί ; ii. οὖν ; iii. ἰδού in narrative, *ibid.*, 19-22 ;
8. ' The disciples ' *and* ' the Twelve ', *ibid.*, 22-30 ;
8(!). Auxiliary and quasi-auxiliary verbs, *ibid.*, 349-362 (i. The past tense of the substantive verb ἦν ἦσαν with present active, present or perfect passive, participle, 349-351 ; ii. The verb ἄρχομαι (ἤρξατο ἤρξαντο) with present infinitive, 352-353 ; iii. The verb δύναμαι, 354-355 ; iv. The verb θέλω, 355-357 ; v. The verb ἔχω, 357-360 ; Appendix : εἰδέναι, γινώσκειν, ἐπιγινώσκειν, substantially identical in sense in Mark, 360-362 ;
9. Lexical notes on (1) some ἅπαξ λεγόμενα : words used once in Mark, and nowhere else in the Gospels ; (2) some words or phrases of common occurrence in Mark but rare in Matthew and Luke, 29 (1928) 275-289 : (1) ἀποστερεῖν, 275-276 ; κεφαλιόω, 276-277 ; προδοῦναι, 277-278 ; πυγμῇ, 278-279 ; (2) ἀλλά 279-280 ; (πρὸς) ἑαυτούς, 280-281 ; ἐκ, ἀπό, 281-282 ; πάλιν, 283-287 ; ὑπάγω and πορεύεσθαι (with its compounds), 287-289 ;
10. Usage of Mark, *ibid.*, 346-361 : (1) Titles used in addressing Christ : Ῥαββεί (Ῥαββουνεί), Διδάσκαλε, Κύριε, Ἰησοῦ, 347-349 ; (2) Diminutives in Mark : θυγάτριον, ἰχθύδιον, κοράσιον, κυνάριον, σανδάλιον, ψιχίον, ὠτάριον, 349-352 ; (3) The verb at the end of the sentence, after noun or personal pronoun : (a) with the verb ἅπτεσθαι, (b) other instances, 352-356 ; (4) ἵνα, 356-359 ; (5) Absence of λέγων (λέγοντες) after verbs introducing a statement or a question, 359-361.

Turner's studies were " intended to be a contribution ... also to the better understanding of that department of the Synoptic problem which is concerned with the agreements of Matthew and Luke against Mark "[88]. The series started in 1924, the year of the publication of Streeter's *The Four Gospels*. But before leaving the pre-Streeter period two earlier studies should be mentioned here.

In the introduction of his commentary on Matthew, Willoughby C. ALLEN (1907) printed some suggestive examples of Matthew/Luke agreements [89]. " Many of the more important agreements " may be due to independent revision of Mark by Matthew and Luke. Sometimes they may be explained by the use of a second tradition (the Logia) and three other factors must probably be taken into account : the use of a corrected copy of Mark, textual assimilation and Luke's acquaintance with Matthew [90]. That last cause is rejected as unsatisfactory by Vincent Henry STANTON [91], though this author is a decided defender of a variety of causes. He has printed a valuable table of agreements, indicating for each instance the explanation which seems to him most probable [92].

---

88. *Ibid.*, *JTS* 25 (1924), p. 377 (introduction) : " So long as it is supposed that there is a residuum of agreements between Matthew and Luke against Mark in matter taken from Mark — apart, that is, from passages found also in Q — which cannot be explained without assuming literary contact either of Matthew and Luke with one another or of both with some other document than our extant Mark, so long will research into the Synoptic question be hampered and final solution delayed ".

Allen   89. W. C. ALLEN, *A Critical and Exegetical Commentary on the Gospel according to S. Matthew* (ICC), Edinburgh, 1907, pp. XXXVI-XXXVIII. — J. C. Hawkins (" whose *Horae Synopticae* is the invaluable companion of every student of the Gospels ") read the proof of the Introduction, " and it owes much to his correction and additions " (Preface, p. XII).

90. *Ibid.*, pp. XXXVIII-XL. Cf. *infra*, n. 117.

91. V. H. STANTON, ' Some Points in the Synoptic Problem ', *Expositor* 4th Ser., 7 (1893) 81-97.179-196.256-266,336-353 ; pp. 256-266 : 2. Some Secondary Features, espec. 263-266 ; *The Gospels as Historical Documents. Part II. The Synoptic Gospels*, Cambridge, 1909, espec. pp. 140-141. The absence in Luke of more considerable Matthean additions, Luke's redactional freedom in revising Mark and the agreements in omission should show the inappropriateness of the supposition of reminiscences (E. Simons). See also p. 207, n. 1 : " Wernle ( ) and ( ) Hawkins explain ... as I do, in a way as to render the assumption that Luke was acquainted with St. Matthew unnecessary ".

92. *Ibid.*, pp. 207-219 : " Additional Note II to chapter III : The coincident
Stanton   differences from St. Mark in the First and the Third Gospels, due to :
(1)   (1) Revision of the original Marcan document.
(2)   (2) Undesigned agreements between the first and the third evangelists in the revision of their Marcan document.
(3a)   (3) *a.* The influence of the Logian document.
(3b)   *b.* The influence of some document distinct from both the Marcan and the Logian, or of oral tradition, or habits of oral teaching.
(4)   (4) Textual assimilation between the first and the third Gospels by copyists ". For some remarks in regard to those different causes, see pp. 142-150. Concerning

He takes a position which is at the opposite of Sanday's simple recension theory [93]. He calls attention not only to slight verbal agreements, attributable to a revised form of Mark, but also to the coincident omissions which are more easily explicable on the hypothesis that Matthew and Luke used the original proto-Marcan document. In fact, he is a late defender of the Ur-Marcus hypothesis : the larger passages omitted by Luke [94] as well as a number of common omissions and other small differences in which Matthew and Luke agree may be later insertions in Mark [95].

The strongest opposition to that view will come from Burnett Hillmann STREETER. He concludes his chapter on the minor agreements in this way : " The investigation summarized in this chapter has shown, I claim, that the only valid objection to the theory that the document used by Matthew and Luke was our Mark — that, namely, based on the existence of the minor agreements of those gospels against Mark — is completely baseless " [96]. According to Streeter textual corruption (i.e., accidental omission or alteration of the text of Mark and assimilation between the parallel texts of Matthew and Luke) is to be seen as the most probable explanation of the agreements which are not explained

---

the second class (2) see also pp. 51-53 : " Indications that our first and third evangelists have revised Mark, or a source closely resembling St Mark " (agreements indicated in brackets). — The table itself is far from identical with Abbott's list of corrections : not only (positive) verbal agreements but also the common omissions and inversions of order are included. On the other hand, oft-recurring coincidences such as $\delta\acute{\epsilon}$ and $\epsilon\hat{\imath}\pi\epsilon\nu$ (or the frequent omission of $\pi\hat{a}s$, $\pi o\lambda\lambda\acute{a}$, $\mu\acute{\epsilon}\gamma as$, $\dot{o}\lambda\acute{\imath}\gamma os$, $\pi\acute{a}\lambda\iota\nu$, $\epsilon\dot{v}\vartheta\acute{v}s$) are not included.

93. " There is a charm — an appearance of simplicity and completeness — in any theory which assigns a single cause for a large group of phenomena. But we ought not to attach much weight to a consideration of that kind " (p. 141). Compare with Sanday's remark : " The suggestions made in this essay are all very simple. It is just their simplicity which has had the chief attraction for me " (Oxford Studies, p. 26).

94. Ibid., p. 167, n. 1 : Mk 3,22-30 ; 4,13b.24b.26-34 ; 6,45 - 7,23 ; 8,1-10.14.16-21 ; 9,41-50 ; 10,2-12 ; 11,11b-14.19-25 ; 13,10.34-37 ; 14,3-9. Comp. pp. 204-206 : " Style as a means of distinguishing the passages added to Proto-Mark " (Additional Note I to chapter III).

95. Ibid., pp. 142-145. Insertions are in Mk 2,26.27 ; 6,13 ; 8,35 ; 9,14.30-31a.35 ; 10,29 ; 11,17 ; 14,30.72 ; 15,25 and other changes in 4,35-36 ; 6,3 ; 9,35 ; 11,12-14. In our list : Stanton (1) ; cf. supra, n. 92. (" Revision of the original Marcan document ", that means : not the revision but the original Mark is the text used by Matthew and Luke !). — For a more recent Ur-Marcus theory, cf. n. 151 ; compare in our list : Stanton (1) and Boismard (McR).

96. B. H. STREETER, The Four Gospels. A Study of Origins, London, 1924, Chapter XI : " The Minor Agreements of Matthew and Luke against Mark ", pp. 299-331. (The quotation is from p. 331.) In his former studies Streeter defended Sanday's recension theory (cf. supra, n. 52), which he proposed as " the very opposite to an Ur-Marcus hypothesis " (Peake's Commentary, p. 675 ; The Four Gospels, p. 305).

by editorial improvement or by the influence of Q [97]. Thus he adopts
Sanday's opinion that the problem of the minor agreements " belongs
to the sphere, not of documentary, but of textual criticism " [98] and the
essential part of his study is to describe, with due attention to the
grouping of the MSS. in local texts, the MS. evidence for a number of
significant agreements [99]. In one case he follows a suggestion made by
Turner and admits that the words τίς ἐστιν ὁ παίσας σε ; (par. Mk 14,65)
which occur in all extant MSS. of the text, are an interpolation into
Matthew from Luke [100]. And after discussing his selection of minor
agreements he concludes : " The residue are agreements still more
minute. Of these textual assimilation is the probable explanation.
Indeed, it would perhaps be a better explanation of some of those which
in the earlier part of this chapter I have attributed to the coincident
activity of Matthew and Luke " [101].

4

Shortly after Streeter's book Burton Scott EASTON printed " a fairly
full list " of the minor agreements in his commentary on Luke. The

---

97. Cf. *infra*, n. 99.

98. Cf. *supra*, n. 46 and 48.

99. *The Four Gospels*, pp. 309-329. Streeter's list of *significant* agreements
include Hawkins's Nos. 1,2,3,5,7,8,9,11,13,14,16,17,18,19,21 and Burton's Nos. 8,
10,11,13,14,15 (cf. *supra*, n. 70 and 78) ; " also all those in Abbott's exhaustive list
which are in the slightest degree remarkable " (cf. Mk 1,40-42 ; 2,21.22.23.24.26 ;
6,32.36.43.44 ; 9,19 ; 10,25 ; 11,29 ; 12,(11).12.22.28 ; 14,70.72 ; 15,43.46), " along
with certain others I have myself noticed " (only a few instances, noticed already
by other authors : diff. Mk 1,42 εὐθέως ; 2,24 ποιεῖν ; 14,62 σὺ εἶπας/ὑμεῖς λέγετε ;
15,46 ἔθηκεν). — All instances discussed by Streeter are mentioned in our list
and his explanation is indicated :

Streeter   *Irrelevant* agreements (which " have no significance whatever ") : coincident
omissions and corrections of style and grammar ; they " constitute considerably
more than half the total number " (pp. 295-298) ;

(d)   *Deceptive* agreements (which " at first sight appear significant ") : corrections
of a word which is linguistically inadmissible and other " alterations which would
naturally occur to independent editors " (Hawkins's Nos. 4,6,10,12,15,20 and
Burton's Nos. 3,4,5,6,12 are in this class) (pp. 298-305) ;

(q)   *Influence of Q* : " in passages where, *on other grounds*, we have reason to believe
that Mark and Q overlapped " (pp. 305-306) ;

(t)   *Textual corruption* : agreements due to later scribes, by accidental omission (in the
text of Mark) or by assimilation (of Matthew and Luke) (cf. first part of this note).

100. *Ibid.*, pp. 325-328. Cf. C. H. TURNER, *The Study of the New Testament*,
p. 47 : " an undetected insertion by scribes ". *Ibid.* : " I want to claim a legitimate,
if modest, place for conjectural emendation in the text of the New Testament ".
It was suggested already in 1909 by V. H. STANTON (*op. cit.*, p. 149).

101. *Ibid.*, p. 328.

" Lk-Mt contacts " and the " common omissions " are indicated in the critical discussion of each Marcan section. Most of them are attributed to independent editing [102]. The same explanation will be defended more vigorously by Josef SCHMID in his *Matthäus und Lukas* [103]. In Schmid's opinion the (source-critical) problem of the minor agreements is reducible to a small number of residual cases of coincidence which are not easily explicable by independent editing [104] and in some instances like Mk 14,65 Streeter's hypothesis of textual corruption remains a possibility [105]. But Streeter is blamed for neglecting the redactional characteristics of each gospel in his evaluation of the verbal agreements [106]. Schmid particularly stresses the importance of those small alterations, omissions or additions for the study of the gospels : " Aus ihnen lernen wir nämlich das schriftstellerische Verfahren des Mt und Lk und die sprachlichen Eigentümlichkeiten der drei Synoptiker kennen " [107]. His survey of the characteristics of Mark's style and of its corrections in Matthew and Luke is an exhaustive collection of those phenomena. The agreements are not merely shown to be " alterations which naturally occur to inde-

---

102. B. S. EASTON, *The Gospel according to S. Luke. A Critical and Exegetical Commentary*, Edinburgh, 1926. *Ibid.*, p. XXII : " Most of them are of no importance, as they involve only such modifications of Mk as would naturally suggest themselves to editors. Of the other cases, some may be due to ' primitive ' textual influence of Lk on Mt (or *vice versa*), but such influence must be predicated with caution. A few agreements may indicate that the text of Mark has changed since it was used by Lk and Mt, and this explanation has been adopted in one or two instances. In a residuum of cases a genuine Q influence may be attested ". He admits Q influence in par. Mk 1,2-4.7-8 ; 4,21-25 ; 6,7-13 (comp. Streeter and others), but also in par. Mk 6,32-44, cf. p. 137 : " distinct traces of a (brief) pre-Markan source underlying Lk and Mt, a source that Mk seems to have expanded (cf. Weiss) " ; and " with less probability " in par. Mk 1,40-45 and 2,1-12, cf. p. 67 : " the cumulative effect is certainly impressive... And Weiss's assumption of a Q version is even more attractive than in the last section ".

Easton

(t)

(q)

103. J. SCHMID, *Matthäus und Lukas. Eine Untersuchung des Verhältnisses ihrer Evangelien* (Biblische Studien, 23), Freiburg i.B., 1930 ; espec. pp. 31-182 : " Die gemeinsamen Abweichungen des Mt und Lk vom Mk-Text ".

104. *Ibid.*, p. 179 : " nur einige Übereinstimmungen ... deren Erklärung durch zufälliges Zusammentreffen nicht so überzeugend wirkt wie in der grossen Masse der übrigen Fälle " ; cf. n. 1 : " Mk 2,21-22 ; 5,27 ; 6,33.43 ; 9,2-3.19 ; 10,30 ; 11,27-29 ; 12,28 ; 14,62 ; 15,46 ; 16,1.5.8. Die überwiegende Zahl hat sich aber als harmloser Natur erwiesen ". Comp. J. SCHMID, *Einleitung in das Neue Testament* (6th ed. of A. Wikenhauser's *Einleitung*), Freiburg i.B., 1973, p. 289 ; " Ihre Zahl ist allerdings sehr gering. Die wichtigsten... : Mk 4,11 ; 14,72 ; 8,35 ; 10,29 ; 14,65 ".

105. *Matthäus und Lukas*, pp. 157-159 ; p. 159, n. 2 : " Diese von mir nicht ohne Bedenken — als die im ganzen plausibelste betrachtete Lösung des Problems ", with reference to Stanton, Turner, Streeter, Taylor and Burkitt. Comp. p. 182 : " Die grundsätzliche mögliche Annahme von Textangleichungen (aber) beseitigt auch den letzten ungeklärten Rest des Problems ". See also *Einleitung*, p. 289.

106. *Matthäus und Lukas*, p. 181, n. 1.

107. *Ibid.*, p. 32.

pendent editors " (Streeter) but to correspond to what happens in other passages of Matthew's and Luke's editing of Mark [108]. In a subsequent

---

108. *Ibid.*, pp. 33-81 : " Die wichtigsten darstellerischen Eigentümlichkeiten
Schmid der drei synoptischen Evangelien ". The author classifies the alterations in Matthew and Luke in improvements of Mark's style (Nos. 1-28), changes of content (Nos. 29-32) and stylistic additions (No. 33) (cf. p. 59).

(1)   1. Aramaic words (p. 35).

(2)   2. Latinisms (p. 36).

(3)   3. Cases of asyndeton (pp. 36-37).

(4)   4. Frequent use of καί instead of δέ and rarity of οὖν, ἄρα, μέν - δέ (p. 37).

(5)   5. The historic present (p. 38).

(6)   6. The imperfect (especially ἔλεγεν) (pp. 38-39).

(7)   7. The paratactic construction and the concatenation of participles (pp. 39-40).

(8)   8. The verb ἄρχεσθαι with infinitive (p. 40).

(9)   9. The *constructio periphrastica* (pp. 40-41).

(10)   10. Εὐθύς (pp. 41-42).

(11)   11. Πάλιν (p. 42).

(12)   12. The impersonal plural (p. 43).

(13)   13. Instances of (*a*) parenthesis (pp. 43-45) and (*b*) anacoluthon (pp. 45-46).

(14)   14. The verb placed after its object (pp. 46-47).

(15)   15. Ἀλλά (p. 47).

(16)   16. Πολλά (p. 48).

(17)   17. The use of tenses : present, perfect, imperfect, aorist are interchanged (p. 48).

(18)   18. The active voice in Mark and the passive in Matthew and Luke (pp. 48-49).

(19)   19. Simple verbs and compound verbs (pp. 49-50).

(20)   20. Interchange of prepositions : (*a*) ἐν and εἰς (pp. 50-51) ; (*b*) ἐκ and ἀπό (p. 51) ; (*c*) other prepositions (pp. 51-52).

(21)   21. Ὅτι recitativum (p. 53).

(22)   22. Ὅτι interrogativum (p. 53).

(23)   23. Ἵνα without its proper sense of purpose (pp. 53-54).

(24)   24. (Πρὸς) ἑαυτούς (p. 54).

(25)   25. The genitive absolute (pp. 25-26).

(26)   26. Diminutives (p. 55).

(27)   27. Other vulgarisms in Mark (pp. 55-58).

(28)   28. Other changes of Mark, not classified (pp. 58-59).

(29)   29. The use of numbers (pp. 59-62).

(30)   30. The position of Jesus and his disciples (pp. 62-64).

(31)   31. Pleonasms and duplicate expressions (pp. 64-69).

(32)   32. Unimportant additional details (pp. 69-75).

(33)   33. Stylistic augmentations in Matthew and Luke : (*a*) subject or object ; (*b*) verb ; (*c*) particles ; (*d*) λέγων ; (*e*) ἀποκριθείς (εἶπεν) ; (*f*) (καὶ) ἰδού ; (*g*) κύριε ; (*h*) προσελθών ; (*i*) participles ; (*k*) clarifications (pp. 75-80).

Comp. also pp. 27-30 : " Kürzungen an Mk-Perikopen ".

— The author acknowledges his indebtedness to Hawkins's *Horae Synopticae* and Turner's ' Marcan Usage ' (cf. p. 32, note, and the frequent references). He refers also to the commentaries of Swete, Allen and Lagrange (see n. 86, 89 and 84), to H. J. CADBURY, *The Style and Literary Method of Luke* (Harvard Theological Studies, 6), Cambridge (Mass.), 1920 (*passim*) ; J. H. SCHOLTEN, *Das paulinische Evangelium*, Elberfeld, 1881, pp. 80-103.122-131 ; and W. LARFELD, *Die neutestamentlichen Evangelien nach ihrer Eigenart und Abhängigkeit*, Gütersloh, 1925.

part he examines the agreements in their context and their conglomeration (*Häufung*) in certain sections [109]. " The author's thorough and
systematic study of the phenomenon of the minor agreements, with
the aid of the linguistic characteristics of each evangelist, has not as
such been superseded in later research " [110].

A more recent study can be mentioned in connexion with the work
of J. Schmid : Bruno DE SOLAGES's Greek Synopsis and his new book
on the composition of Matthew and Luke [111]. He attributes most of
the agreements to independent correction of Mark. The majority of them
(between 2/3 and 3/4 of 393 words) are grammatical and stylistic variants
and a thoroughgoing description and classification of all differences
between Mark and Luke and between Mark and Matthew should
prove that the ' convergent ' corrections are due to editorial tendencies
shown in the transformation of Mark's vocabulary, grammar, style and
content [112]. De Solages has collected the positive agreements in a table
of 323 instances (or 393 words). He distinguishes different classes (and
subdivisions) and considers separately the most characteristic cases
(δέ, εἶπεν) and in a last class a few instances which are probably due
to the influence of a second source [113]. The list can be helpful for counting the words in which Matthew and Luke agree, but the absence of
any reference to the context of the agreements, their isolation from the

---

— In Larfeld's opinion the agreements in omission and stylistic corrections of   Larfeld
Mark (cf. pp. 28-35) are unimportant (accidental coincidence) but a number of
agreements (some of which are attributed by others to the influence of Q) point
to Luke's subsidiary dependence on Matthew, strongly contradicted by Schmid.

109. *Ibid.*, pp. 81-167. Some passages of overlapping Mark and Q are treated in
the second part, e.g. Mk 3,22-30 (pp. 289-297), 4,30-32 (pp. 299-301).

110. F. NEIRYNCK, ' Minor Agreements Matthew-Luke in the Transfiguration
Story ' (cf. *infra*, n. 160), p. 253.

111. B. DE SOLAGES, *Synopse grecque des évangiles. Méthode nouvelle pour résoudre le problème synoptique* ; = *A Greek Synopsis of the Gospels. A New Way
of Solving the Synoptic Problem*, Leiden-Toulouse, 1959 ; *La composition des évangiles de Luc et de Matthieu et leurs sources*, Leiden, 1973.

— Bibliographical references, other than to his *Synopse*, are inexistent. The
date he gives is 1958, but my copy has 1959 (and 1958 for the preface of Cardinal
Tisserant). In the introduction (date : 1950) the author tells that his method originated in 1929 (thus about contemporaneously with the work of Schmid).

112. *La composition*, pp. 102-152 : ' Les transformations du texte de Marc dans
les paraphrases de Luc et de Matthieu '. (Comp. p. 305 : " un phénomène synoptique
de convergence ").

— The negative agreements are listed only here ; cf. 130-140 : " D. Cas plus
littéraires ou touchant davantage au fond des choses. II. Mt/Lc supprime εὐθύς
(Nº 102), πάλιν (Nº 103), ἤρξατο (Nº 104), des noms propres (Nº 106), des préci-
sions locales (Nº 107), des répétitions (Nº 110), ce qu'il juge choquant (Nº 111),
sémitismes (Nº 112) ".

113. *Synopse*, pp. 1055-1065 ; *La composition*, pp. 306-318. He divides the

negative agreements and some overclassification are obvious defects of this table [114]. De Solages seems to have collected the agreements independently of Abbott's table and " the two most complete published lists of these agreements " are complementary in their form of presentation and in the number of instances they have listed [115].

De Solages

agreements over the following seven classes (the main subdivisions are indicated and the numbers refer to Chapter IV of *La composition*, cf. n. 111) :

(a)   a. *The most characteristic cases* : the substitution of δέ for καί (No. 23), of εἶπεν for λέγει, ἔλεγεν or ἤρξατο λέγειν (No. 81), etc. Total : 64 words.

(b)   b. *Words of the same root* : (α) nouns and pronouns : change of number (No. 74), of gender, of case (simplification, grammatical corrections, change of preposition) ; (β) verbs : changes of tense (No. 81²), substitution of participle for καί with finite verb (No. 87), other changes of mood or voice ; (γ) substitutions of words. Total : 79.

(c)   c. *Synonyms* : nouns, pronouns, prepositions, adverbs, verbs (more common verb, compound verb, etc.). Total : 52.

(d)   d. *Analogous expressions* : additions of conjunctions (No. 93), the subject (No. 84), the object (No. 90), the article (No. 82), ἰδού (No. 94), εἰμί (No. 86), λέγων or other participle (No. 118), explicative (No. 122). Total : 69.

(e)   e. *Other analogous expressions* : substitution of a noun (e.g., ὁ ὄχλος) for a pronoun, or *vice versa* (No. 83) ; more simple locutions ; accidentally coincident modifications. Total : 51.

(f)   f. *Additions* : related to style, content, or theology ; various and accidental additions. Total : 56.

(g)   g. *Probable influence of a second common source* : par. Mk 1,38b-39a ; 3,7b-8a.10 ; 9,2b.7a ; 14,61b.62b^bis.65. Total : 22.

In *La composition*, p. 318, he attributes Mk 14,61b.62b^bis to " convergence d'ajouts assez naturels ", and " convergence de hasard " ; on p. 305 he enumerates possible causes of ' convergence ' : particular reasons, a second common source, textual corruption, recension of Mark, accidental convergence.

114. The table is reprinted in *La composition* (1973), "avec quelques corrections" (*ibid.*, p. 305). He gives no list of those corrections. It may be helpful for owners of the *Synopse* : p. 1055 col. A, 6th instance : 15,2 (instead of 14,2) ; p. 1057 B, 3th : λέγει (εἶπεν) ; p. 1060 A, 6th : 9,18β(9,16β) ; p. 1064 A, 9th : 14,70β(13,70β) ; p. 1065 B, 1st : 16,8 (16) ; 8th : 14,65 (14,63) ; ἐνείλησεν Mk 15,46 is transferred from (b) (p. 1057 B) to (c), substitution of the verbs, with the new total of 9 (8) (p. 1059 B). The figure for the total of (b) is corrected : 80 (72) (p. 1055 B), but after that transference the figures should be changed in 79 for (b) (*ibid.*), in 8 for " tempora " (p. 1057 A) and 52 for (c) (p. 1058 B).

— A few other misprints remain uncorrected : p. 1055, δέ: 12,35 (12,33) ; p. 1057 A, 7th : ἀφίενται (ἀφίεται) ; last line : 14,69 (14,6) ; p. 1058 B, 1st : ἀρχισυναγώ-γων (-ουν), p. 1060 B, καί: 12,24 δέ/καί (12,2) ; p. 1062 A, 6th: 14,10 (4,10) ; p. 1063 B, 1st : συνακολουθοῦσαι (συνηκ.) ; p. 1065 B, 2nd : 5,27 (5,25).

The author gives no explanation about his Greek text. Some instances are taken from the *Textus Receptus*, e.g. par. Mk 2,5.9 ; 14,24 (Matthew).

115. The two tables include only positive agreements, excluding the agreements in omission, the inversions of order and other variations different from Mark in both Matthew and Luke but without (at least partially) identical words. As can be seen in our list B. de Solages gives about 80 additional instances (= 90 words). On the other hand about 45 instances from Abbott's list are not included : cf. Mk 2,11.18 ; 3,1.10 ; 4,1.38 ; 5,2.12.13.14.22 ; 6,36 ; 8,14 ; 9,30 ; 10,25.30.42^bis.47 ;

5

The main stream of synoptic studies goes in the line of J. Schmid : the influence of Q in a limited number of passages and the coincidences of the independent editing of Matthew and Luke for the bulk of the instances can explain the minor agreements ; only in a few exceptional cases the textual factor is a last expedient. By way of simplification, however, Streeter's *The Four Gospels*, and his overemphasis of textual corruption, is frequently cited as the classical treatment of the " unexplained remainder " in the two-document hypothesis. Particularly in England the problem of the minor agreements has become a topic of the anti-Streeter reaction [116]. With John CHAPMAN and Basil Christopher BUTLER who defend the Augustinian hypothesis the discussion concentrates upon the ' major agreements ' [117]. In 1955 Austin M. FARRER

11,1.7.9.11(= 19).18 ; 12,9,17.18.19.36.38 ; 13,31 ; 14,1.29.69.70 ; 15,1.5.9^{bis}.12bis. 14.24.26.39 ; 16,2.6.7. Moreover, De Solages did not consider in this list the sections with overlapping sources (Q or special source) : Abbott's instances par. Mk 1,5.7.8. (Q) 10.12.13.16 ; 3,20-21.22.23-26.27.28-29 ; 4,21.22.23.30-32 ; 6,2.4.6.7-13 ; 8,12 ; 9,35.50 ; 10,1.11-12 ; 11,22 ; 12,28.29.30 ; 13,21.

The view of McLoughlin is far too optimistic when he writes : " Deux listes indépendantes et (presque) complètes de ces accords... Les mots cités par les deux coïncident presque parfaitement " (' Les accords mineurs ', [cf. *infra*, n. 154], p. 19, n. 16).

— De Solages has counted 393 words of agreement. In Abbott's list about 446 words (+ Mt 12,30 ; 21,44) are distributed over 229 instances (or 228 : cf. p. 316 for 9,29) ; with exclusion of the portions not considered by De Solages : about 326 words. — Compare similar calculations (of instances of agreement, not of words, and excluding the so-called Q passages) : Hawkins : about 240 (cf. *supra*, n. 69 and 70) ; Burton : 175 phrases (275 words) (cf. *supra*, n. 77) ; Streeter : " some 220 cases " (*Peake's Commentary*, p. 675 ; cf. *The Four Gospels*, p. 328 : Hawkins and Burton) ; Schmid : about 250 (*Matthäus und Lukas*, p. 169) ; McLoughlin : about 342 (cf. *infra*, n. 154 ; p. 19, n. 6 : " en comptant comme un seul accord les mots [ou parties de mots] solidaires "). The figure which is more commonly cited is " about 230 " with reference to Abbott's ' Complete Table ' (cf. Sanday in *Oxford Studies*, p. 10 and 19-20 : " many of them simple, but many also complex ").

116. See Farmer's book on *The Synoptic Problem* (cf. *infra*, n. 125). Not mentioned there : W. Lockton and F. Torm (cf. *infra*, n. 141 and 142).

117. J. CHAPMAN, *Matthew, Mark and Luke. A Study in the Order and Interrelation of the Synoptic Gospels* (ed. J. M. T. BARTON), London, 1937. The so-called Q passages in Luke are taken from Matthew (pp. 110-127), but minor agreements are less significant : " The most that can be said is that there is some probability that in Marcan parallels Lk. has a few, but very few, words borrowed from Mt. But the resemblances are quite possibly due to accidental coincidence, or (in a few cases) to textual harmonization at an early date. Even as accumulated above they are not impressive. I should not venture to urge them as proofs that Lk. revised his MS. according to Mt. On the contrary, their extreme fewness and unimportance suggests that Lk. regarded Mk. as the best possible authority, never to be controlled or to be collated with any other " (p. 129 ; cf. his list of ' The remaining   Chapman Agreements ', pp. 127-129).

who dispenses with Q but maintains the Marcan priority, proceeds to a radical critique of Streeter's treatment of the minor agreements. He explains them by Luke's subsidiary dependence on
Matthew [118]. He will be followed by Nigel TURNER [119], A. W.

— B. C. BUTLER, 'St. Luke's Debt to St. Matthew', *HTR* 32 (1939) 237-308 ;
The Originality of St Matthew. A Critique of the Two-Document Hypothesis, Cambridge, 1951.

Butler too renounces the minor agreements as an argument : " the similarities
between Matthew and Luke in the ' triple tradition ' are not, as a rule [*Note* : The
qualifying clause is intended to allow for possible occasional agreements between
Matthew and Luke against Mark, in case they cannot be explained away.], due to
immediate dependence of Matthew on Luke or *vice versa* " (p. 65).

— The Augustinian hypothesis (and Luke's acquaintance with Matthew) was
a very common view among Catholic exegetes in the 19th and in the beginning
of the 20th century. Cf. J. SCHMID, *Matthäus und Lukas*, pp. 4-6. In particular, we
should mention Cladder who calls attention to the agreements of order (sequences

Cladder   of pericopes) : H. J. CLADDER, *Unsere Evangelien. I. Zur Literaturgeschichte der
Evangelien*, Freiburg i.B., 1919, pp. 141-145. In England the hypothesis was supported against the current theory by E. W. LUMMIS, *How Luke was Written*, Cambridge,
1915, and H. J. JAMESON, *The Origin of the Synoptic Gospels. A Revision of the
Synoptic Problem*, Oxford, 1922. On the minor agreements : chap. VII, §§ 72-77
(pp. 54-57). Although he admits that " Luke takes the substance of his narrative
from Mark wherever he can " (p. 57), Jameson maintains that the coincidences in
the triple tradition " would imply that at least Luke was acquainted with, and to
some extent influenced by, the First Gospel. More than this is not claimed here,
as to *these* parts of Luke " (p. 54). In answer to Stanton's objection he suggests
that the omissions may be due to discrepancies between Mark and Matthew or to
the fact that Luke recognized that they were additions made by Mark to Matthew's
original account (p. 57). A similar subsidiary dependence on Matthew will be defended on the Marcan hypothesis, dispensing with Q (Farrer) or not (Morgenthaler) ;
cf. *infra*, n. 118-124 and *supra*, n. 22 (Simons) and 108 (Larfeld).

118. Cf. A. FARRER, ' On Dispensing with Q ', in D. E. NINEHAM (ed.), *Studies
in the Gospels. Essays in Memory of R. H. Lightfoot*, Oxford, 1955, pp. 55-86, espec.
pp. 61-62. " Now this is just what one would expect, on the supposition that St.
Luke had read St. Matthew, but decided to work direct upon the more ancient
narrative of St. Mark for himself. He does his own work of adaptation, but small
Matthaean echoes keep appearing, because St. Luke is after all acquainted with
St. Matthew " (p. 61). And on Streeter's treatment : " He divides the evidence into
several groups and finds a distinct hypothesis for each... Thus the forces of evidence
are divided by the advocate, and defeated in detail " (p. 62). Comp. R. McL. WIL-
SON, ' Farrer and Streeter on the Minor Agreements of Matthew and Luke against
Mark ', in *Studia Evangelica* I (TU, 73), Berlin, 1959, pp. 254-257, espec. p. 255 :
" an example of the demolition of one's opponent by means of the gentle art of
ridicule " ; E. L. BRADBY, ' In Defence of Q ', *Expos. Times* 68 (1956-57) 315-318.
(The author examines Mk 2,23 - 3,6 ; 4,1-20 ; 6,7-11 and 8,27 - 9,1 : Luke seems to
ignore Matthew.)

119. N. TURNER, ' The Minor Verbal Agreements of Mt. and Lk. against Mark ',
in *Studia Evangelica* I (TU, 73), Berlin, 1959, pp. 223-234. Turner (in Oxford Con-
gress, 1957) discusses in answer to Bradby's article (cf. n. 118) some examples within

Turner   the same four passages : Mk 2,26[bis] ; 4,4.9.19.20 ; 6,7 ; 8,31[bis].34[bis].35.36 (cf. our

ARGYLE [120] and R. T. SIMPSON [121], and by two continental authors, Wilhelm WILKENS [122] and more recently Robert MORGENTHALER [123] who restates the hypothesis of Simons [124].

---

list). " The effect is cumulative, not confined to the weight of any single example in itself " (p. 233). " There cannot be any other reason than *literary* dependence to explain these apparently irrelevant agreements of style and grammar... Because these agreements are so often inconsistent with St. Luke's style elsewhere, it is more likely that Lk. depends on Mt. than vice-versa " (p. 234).

120. A. W. ARGYLE, ' The Agreements between Matthew and Luke ', *Expos. Times* 73 (1961-62) 19-22 ; comp. R. S. CHERRY, ' Agreements between Matthew and Luke ', *Expos. Times* 74 (1962-63) 63 ; A. W. ARGYLE, ' Evidence for the View that St. Luke Used St. Matthew's Gospel ', *JBL* 83 (1964) 390-396 (with emphasis on the common omissions).

121. R. T. SIMPSON, ' The Major Agreements of Matthew and Luke against Mark ', *NTS* 12 (1965-66) 273-284. Mk 1,1-13 ; 12,28-31 ; 3,22-27 = ' Major agreements ' : " the inclusion of Q material alongside certain of the minor agreements gives them an importance which distinguishes them from the other agreements against Mark " (p. 275, n. 1 ; compare *supra*, n. 68). " St Luke must have known a version of Mark which incorporated the same editorial improvements as those which are found in Matthew " (p. 275) ; " it is simpler to suppose that Matthew itself is the second edition of Mark on which St Luke relied " (p. 282).   Simpson

122. W. WILKENS, ' Zur Frage der literarischen Beziehung zwischen Matthäus und Lukas ', *NT* 8 (1966) 48-57. In Lk 3,7-9.16-17 ; 6,41-42 ; 10,2 ; 12,22-31 ; 13,28-30 ; 7,1-10 ; 12,39-46 the similarity of the vocabulary points to Luke's dependence on Matthew. " Zur Bestimmung des Q-Textes fällt jedenfalls in diesen Punkten Lukas aus " (p. 57). The minor agreements (list on p. 56) : " Lukas reproduziert den Markus-Stoff und hat dabei die Version des Matthäus mit im Ohr " (p. 56).

123. R. MORGENTHALER, *Statistische Synopse*, Zürich-Stuttgart, 1971. Cf. pp. 301-303 : " Indizien für eine Bekanntschaft Mt → Lk : 1. Die kleineren Wortlautübereinstimmungen Mt → Lk ", espec. p. 303 : " Es gibt etliche Texte der reinen Mk-Tradition, in denen wir eine Häufung dieser kleineren Übereinstimmungen antreffen. Es handelt sich um die folgenden Perikopen : Mk 2,1-12 ; 4,35-41 ; 6,30-44 ; 9,2-8 ; 9,14-29 ; 10,17-31 ; 11,1-10 ; 11,27-33 ; 14,66-72 ; 15,42-47 und ihre jeweiligen Parallelen. Anderseits existiert praktisch kein einziger dreifacher Mk-Text, in dem nicht 2, 3 vereinzelte Koinzidenzen erscheinen, und die naheliegendste Erklärung für dieses Phänomen bleibt die Annahme, dass entweder Mt den Lk oder Lk den Mt kannte. Nur muss diese Annahme nicht sofort in eine Alternativlösung zur Q-Hypothese verwandelt werden ! Wir stehen tatsächlich kleineren Übereinstimmungen gegenüber ". On the second and third category of *minor* agreements " in den Satzfolgen, — in den Perikopenfolgen " (pp. 303-305), comp. F. NEIRYNCK, ' The Argument from Order and St. Luke's Transpositions ', *ETL* 49 (1973) 784-815, espec. pp. 785-790 (E. P. Sanders) and 799-804 (R. Morgenthaler) ; in this volume, pp. 292-297 and 306-311.

124. Rudolf PESCH seems to be tempted by the hypothesis of some acquaintance of Luke with Matthew : " eine Möglichkeit, die ernsthaft überlegt werden kann " (with reference to the ' eleven ' disciples), cf. ' Levi-Matthäus (Mc 2 14/Mt 9 9/10 3). Ein Beitrag zur Lösung eines alten Problems ', *ZNW* 59 (1968) 40-56, p. 52, n. 46.

The criticism of Streeter's treatment of the minor agreements was the focal point of William R. FARMER's book on *The Synoptic Problem* [125]. This author defends the view that the minor agreements constitute " a category of literary phenomena which is more readily explicable on a hypothesis where Mark is regarded as third with Matthew and Luke before him than on any alternative hypothesis " [126]. The agreements between Matthew and Luke against Mark " tend to be minor in extent, inconsequential in substance, and sporadic in occurrence " [127] : that means that Mark departed from the text of his predecessors " only when to do so would not affect the sense or the intention of the text to which his sources bore concurrent testimony " [128]. In response to Streeter's arguments he made three more general methodological observations : the concatenation of agreements within a particular passage should not be dissipated by dividing them into different categories [129] ; agreements in omission may be significant if they occur in conjunction with positive agreements [130] ; the method used to decrease the agreements by citing textual variants can also be used to increase the number of agreements against Mark [131]. In his opinion the grammatical and stylistic agreements could emanate from the usage and preference of Mark

---

125. W. R. FARMER, *The Synoptic Problem. A Critical Analysis*, New York-London, 1964, espec. pp. 118-152 : " Streeter's Treatment of the Minor Agreements ". See also pp. 94-117 : " A Survey of the Pre-Streeter Treatment of the Minor Agreements of Matthew and Luke against Mark ". He refers to Abbott, Sanday, Stanton, Hawkins, Burton, Burkitt, Turner, Lummis, Jameson, and indirectly to Holtzmann, Weiss and Simons. The survey is written in a polemic tone (cf. ' A Skeleton in the Closet of Gospel Research ') and somewhat inaccurate (cf. *supra*, n. 20, 35 and 52). For the period after Streeter the author is extremely brief : " his (Streeter's) proposed solution in terms of textual assimilation satisfied the majority of critics for thirty years until the subject was reopened by N. Turner at Oxford in 1957 " (p. 50). Authors like Easton, Schmid, Vaganay, Glasson (and for the pre-Streeter period : Wernle, Stephenson, Lagrange) are not even mentioned.

126. *Ibid.*, pp. 215-217.

127. *Ibid.*, p. 216.

128. *Ibid.*, p. 217. See also *infra*, n. 132.

129. *Ibid.*, p. 119. Compare Farrer's criticism (cf. *supra*, n. 118). For a similar observation he refers to F. M. KEECH, *The Agreements of Matthew and Luke Against Mark in the Triple Tradition*, Madison (New Jersey), 1962 (unpublished thesis, Drew University Library), pp. 38-41. (Cf. *infra*, n. 136.)

130. *Ibid.*, p. 120. With reference to Stanton (1893), (cf. *supra*, n. 91). See also the remark of L. Vaganay (cf. *infra*, n. 145).

131. *Ibid.*, pp. 146-147 (again with an unspecified reference to Keech, cf. *supra*, n. 129). See also R. Morgenthaler : " Wir müssen unbedingt damit rechnen, dass anstelle einer jeden einzelnen kleineren Übereinstimmung Mt-Lk gegen Mk, die durch Textverderbnis aus der Welt zu schaffen ist, bei umfassender Überprüfung der Lesarten eine andere tritt, die jetzt wegen Textverderbnis nicht sichtbar wird ! " (*Statistische Synopse*, p. 302). See *supra*, n. 10.

conflating the texts of Matthews and Luke [132] and the argument for
Marcan primitivity has no probative value [133]. In that connexion he is
the inspiration behind Ed Parish SANDERS's work on *The Tendencies
of the Synoptic Tradition* [134]. It should be mentioned also that he is the
promoter of ' objective ' tools of study : his *Synopticon* [135] and the table

---

132. *Ibid.*, pp. 120-141 (on ' irrelevant ' and ' deceptive ' agreements).

— " This extent of exact verbatim agreement, extending to the smallest points of
grammar, such as case, number, person, tense, voice, mood, gender, etc., constitutes
prima-facie evidence for direct literary dependence between Matthew and Luke "
(p. 139). In the Griesbachian hypothesis the minor agreements reflect Matthaean
usage and Mark created " an agreement between Matthew and Luke against his
Gospel, whenever he permitted the style and grammar of his own Greek to deviate
from the text to which Matthew and Luke bore concurrent testimony " (p. 137).

133. *Ibid.*, pp. 159-169 (discussion of Mk 1,32.34 ; 3,15.20-21 ; 6,5,8,24 ; 10,18.35 ;
11,21 ; 15,44 ; 16,4 ; cf. Abbott) and pp. 121-124. On the agreements in Mk 2,1-12,
see pp. 131-139.

— For further discussion of the criticism on Streeter see J. A. FITZMYER, ' The
Priority of Mark and the " Q " Source in Luke ', in *Jesus and Man's Hope (Per-
spective*, XI, 1-2), vol. I, Pittsburgh, 1970, pp. 131-170, espec. pp. 142-146.

134. E. P. SANDERS, *The Tendencies of the Synoptic Tradition* (SNTS Monogr.
Ser., 9), Cambridge, 1969. The author investigates the categories of length, detail,
semitism, direct discourse and conflation ; compare Farmer's and Burton's " canons
of criticism " in *The Synoptic Problem*, pp. 227-229. Comp. C. H. TALBERT and
E. V. McKNIGHT, ' Can the Griesbach Hypothesis Be Falsified ? ', *JBL* 91 (1972)
338-368. Three pericopes are examined by C. H. Talbert, with due attention to
the minor agreements : Mk 16,1-8 ; 8,27-33 ; 2,23-28 (pp. 339-357 : no evidence for
Luke's dependence upon Matthew). See also, on conflation and direct discourse,
F. NEIRYNCK, *Duality in Mark*, pp. 40-41.64-71.

— Other studies of Sanders : ' The Argument from Order and the Relationship
between Matthew and Luke ', *NTS* 15 (1968-69) 249-261, with a list of supposed
agreements of order pointing to Luke's use of Matthew   Sanders
(comp. F. NEIRYNCK, ' The Argument from Order ', pp. 784-790 ; cf. *supra*, n. 123) ;
' Priorités et dépendances dans la tradition synoptique ', *RSR* 60 (1972) 519-540,
with lists of agreements par. Mk 10,17-31 (pp. 520-522) ; 2,23-28 (pp. 530-531) ;
1,29-31 (p. 535) ; ' The Overlaps of Mark and Q and the Synoptic Problem ', *NTS*
19 (1972-73) 453-465 (on Mt 1,1-8.9-11.12-13 ; 3,22-30 ; 4,30-32 : evidence for *both*
interdependence *and* overlapping traditions).

135. W. R. FARMER, *Synopticon. The Verbal Agreement Between the Greek Texts
of Matthew, Mark and Luke Contextually Exhibited*, Cambridge, 1969. Comp. R.
MORGENTHALER, *Statistische Synopse*, pp. 25-27, and W. R. FARMER, ' A Response
to Robert Morgenthaler's Statistische Synopse ', *Biblica* 54 (1973) 417-433.

— The verbal agreement is marked by the use of colors in the text of Matthew,
Mark and Luke (Nestle-Aland, 25th ed., large size) : red for Matthew-Luke, green
for Luke-Mark, yellow for Mark-Matthew, blue for Matthew-Mark-Luke. Complete
verbal agreement (the same word in the same form) is marked by the ground color,
incomplete agreement by underlining, agreement in word sequence by a colored
line between the words. That method can be used for the detection of the Matthew/
Luke agreements (and for some agreements not already noted elsewhere the name
Farmer is inserted in our list), but it has obvious limitations : the procedure is   Farmer

of the minor agreements compiled under his direction by Finley Morris
KEECH [136].

6

In the two-document hypothesis it is a common assumption that in
particular sections some of the minor agreements can be assigned to
Q [137]. But the Logia source is not the only non-Marcan source which has
been suggested. A minimal form is to explain a few residual instances of
agreement by the influence of oral tradition [138]. For some authors the

---

purely mechanical and many coincidences in content (not in wording) cannot be
considered ; it is not useful for inversions of groups of words and the line between
the words is ambiguous (inversion or omission) ; the real extent of the agreements
becomes visible only after consulting the parallel gospel text (e.g., a complete
agreement can be an addition, a substitution, or a small grammatical change).
Moreover, I noted a considerable number of inaccuracies or misprints in the use
of the colored lines. — Farmer's defence of the ' objectivity ' (in *Biblica*, p. 421)
will make the reader only more cautious. E.g., for " the presence of red in almost
all the passages common to Matthew, Mark and Luke ", it should be observed
that the blue line (for an incomplete agreement Matthew/Mark/Luke) is entirely
unemployed and it may be clear from an example how the image of the synoptic
data can be distorted : ἄνθρωπος par. Mk 8,36 is in full red in Matthew (underlined
in yellow) and Luke (underlined in green) and ἄνθρωπον in Mark is underlined in
yellow and green. (That means, no triple tradition color, only the combination of
the parallels !).

136. F. M. KEECH, *The Agreements of Matthew and Luke against Mark in the
Triple Tradition*, Compiled and Edited by F. M. Keech (For Private Circulation
Only), Madison (New Jersey), 1959 (cf. *supra*, n. 129), in 4°, pp. I-XII (introduction) and pp. 1-31 : " A Complete Table of the Agreements of Matthew and
Luke against Mark in the Triple Tradition ". The text of the agreements is printed
in a synopsis (in Luke's order). The positive agreements are underlined with solid
underlining for complete verbal identity, dotted underlining for less than complete
but still significant verbal identity, the underlining is interrupted where the sequence of identical words is broken. For agreements in ' substitution ' and agreements in word order Mark's equivalent is also shown ; agreements in ' omission '
are in Mark's column only (circumscribed with a special line). After each pericope a
small comment is added with some observations on the instances listed by Abbott,
Burton, Hawkins, Streeter and Easton. Keech's table is a valuable tool and is in
some respects comparable with the list compiled by T. Hansen (cf. *infra*, n. 158).
The booklet was put at my disposal by Prof. W. R. Farmer (November, 1970).

137. The following passages are commonly accepted as overlapping with Q :
Mk 1,7-8.12-13 ; 3,22-30 ; 4,30-32 ; 6,7-11.(12-13). Are also taken in consideration :
4,21-25 ; 8,11-12.15 ; and, less convincingly, 1,2-6.9-11 ; 12,38-40 and some individual verses : 8,34.35.38 ; 9,35.37.40.42.50 ; 10,11-12 ; 11,23 ; 13,11.15-16.21-22.31.33.35.

138. W. G. KÜMMEL, *Einleitung in das Neue Testament* (12th ed. of P. FEINE-
J. BEHM's *Einleitung*), Heidelberg, 1963, p. 32 : " Diese wenigen Fälle lassen sich
durch den Einfluss der mündlichen Tradition erklären ". The text on the minor
agreements (pp. 31-32) remained unchanged in the new edition (1973, pp. 35-36).
In n. 45 he refers to McLoughlin " in seiner vorzüglichen Untersuchung " (cf. *infra*,

Keech

minor agreements are more important and show clearly that the so-called
rigid Marcan hypothesis requires to be mitigated by the acceptance of
the oral tradition factor. It is emphasized by Nils Alstrup DAHL for
the passion story [139]. Tim SCHRAMM attributes the minor agreements
in a series of pericopes to the influence of *Traditionsvarianten* [140]. Others
defend the more specific literary theory of a primitive gospel source [141].

---

n. 154) and concludes : " aber wenn das (*the conjecture in Mt 26,68*) auch problema-
tisch bleibt, ergibt sich auf alle Fälle, dass die Zahl der wirklich erklärungsbedürfti-
gen Übereinstimmungen des Mt und Lk gegen Mk sehr gering ist. "

— For a late representative of the (radical) oral tradition theory (cf. *supra*,
n. 27 and 45) see Aloisius Gonzaga DA FONSECA, *Quaestio Synoptica*, Rome, ³1952.
He gives a list of 37 positive agreements (pp. 82-83) and refers to Abbott's table : Da Fonseca
" Hic enumerat 230 exempla ; sed in multis convenientia est mere fortuita " (p. 82).

139. N. A. DAHL, ' Die Passionsgeschichte bei Matthäus ', *NTS* 2 (1955-56)
17-32, p. 21 : " eine neben Markus weiterbestehende oder auf Grund von Markus
entstandene mündliche Überlieferung " ; see also p. 31 (a list of minor agreements).
— Comp. *supra*, n. 18.

140. T. SCHRAMM, *Der Markus-Stoff bei Lukas. Eine literarkritische und redak-
tionsgeschichtliche Untersuchung* (SNTS Monogr. Ser., 14), Cambridge, 1971. On
the evidence of the minor agreements (besides Luke's peculiar matter and semi-
tisms), see pp. 72-77, and passim. The pericopes with significant agreements are
par. Mk 1,40-45 ; 2,1-12.18-22 ; 3,13-19 ; 4,1-9.10-12.21-25.35-41 ; 6,7-13.30-44 ;
8,27-31 ; 8,34 - 9,1 ; 9,2-10.14-29.30-32 ; 10,32-34 ; 11,1-10 ; 12,1-12. — The influence
of B. Weiss is undeniable ; cf. p. 57 : " Mit B. Weiss festzuhalten sind dagegen
M. E. auch heute noch die Einsicht in das quellenkombinatorische Arbeitsver-
fahren der Grossevangelien und die aufgrund dieser Einsicht gewonnene differen-
zierte Beurteilung des Mk-Stoffes bei Mt und Lk ".

141. " The Minor Agreements, if used as indications of the knowledge by Matthew
and Luke of a parallel source to Mark, may be said to provide a corrective to the
Markan hypothesis ". Cf. Robert Lisle LINDSEY, *A Hebrew Translation of the
Gospel of Mark. Greek-Hebrew Diglot with English Introduction*, Jerusalem, *s.d.*
(1971), p. 22. The author insists particularly on the importance of the minor agreements (cf. pp. 14-19). For his own synoptic theory see the ' Introduction ' of his
book on Mark (pp. 9-84) and the article : ' A Modified Two-Document Theory
of the Synoptic Dependence and Interdependence ', *NT* 6 (1963) 239-263 (on the
minor agreements, p. 244). He holds Luke as the most primitive gospel, based on
two principal sources Q and PN (Proto-narrative) which is the common source of
Luke, Mark (who used Luke) and Matthew (who used Mark and Q). For the suggestion that Luke is the earliest gospel he refers to W. LOCKTON, ' The Origin of
the Gospels ', *Church Quarterly Review* 94 (1922) 216-239 ; *The Three Traditions
in the Gospels*, London, 1926 : three lines of traditions, the Petrine, the Jacobean
and the Johannine, are at the origin of the Synoptic Gospels ; Matthew is dependent
upon the earlier two gospels ; *Certain Alleged Gospel Sources*, London, 1927 : he
maintained that the agreements amount to about 750 (cf. J. SCHMID, *Matthäus
und Lukas*, p. 181, n. 2).

— A common source, non-Marcan but parallel with Mark, is the solution of Ema-
nuel HIRSCH for the minor agreements against Mark in 14,45.62.65.75 ; 15,46 and
Mt 28,19/Lk 24,47 : the passion narrative in Q ; cf. *Frühgeschichte des Evangeliums.
II. Die Vorlagen des Lukas und das Sondergut des Matthäus*, Tübingen, 1941, pp. 243-
246 and 400-401.

The multiple-document hypothesis holds an intermediate position. It was suggested by Frederik TORM in reaction against Streeter's treatment of the negative agreements [142] and more recently it is strongly supported by Xavier LÉON-DUFOUR [143], in particular with reference to the minor agreements in the passion story, as an alternative for Vaganay's primitive gospel hypothesis [144]. The negative minor agree-

---

142. Cf. F. TORM, ' A Note on the Synoptic Problem. Have the First and Third Gospel made use of Mark ? ', *Church Quarterly Review* 104 (1927) 354-364 ; comp. *Indledning til det Ny Testamente*, Kopenhagen, [4]1951, pp. 69ff. For his solution he refers to the *Diegesen* of Schleiermacher and the *corpuscula historiae evangelicae* of Lachmann. See his critique of Streeter : " The agreement of Matthew and Luke in ' omissions ' is what is striking, and not so much their agreement in individual words and sentences against Mark " (p. 354 ; cf. the list on pp. 356-357).

143. X. LÉON-DUFOUR, ' Les évangiles synoptiques ', in *Introduction à la Bible. II. Nouveau Testament* (ed. A. ROBERT and A. FEUILLET), Tournai, 1959, pp. 143-334, espec. pp. 291-295. Cf. p. 292 : " C'est sous cette appellation de ' *documentation multiple* ' qu'il convient de ranger les récents essais de L. Cerfaux " (cf. *infra*, n. 148) ; p. 295 : " Des *contacts littéraires* ont eu lieu, non pas nécessairement entre les évangiles, mais dans la documentation présynoptique plus ou moins systématisée " ; see also p. 283. For the minor agreements the author refers to the study of L. Vaganay (cf. *infra*, n. 145), but his solution is found unsatisfactory (pp. 280-282). — The view of Léon-Dufour gained a wide divulgation by the several editions of the *Introduction*, translated in English, German, Spanish and Portuguese. Comp. *Les évangiles et l'histoire de Jésus*, Paris, 1963, p. 235.

144. X. LÉON-DUFOUR, art. ' Passion (Récits de la) ', *DBS* 6 (fasc. 35), Paris, 1960, col. 1419-1492, espec. col. 1444-1447 ; = ' Mt et Mc dans le récit de la Passion ', *Biblica* 40 (1959) 684-696, pp. 690-694 ; reprinted in *Studia Biblica et Orientalia. II. Novum Testamentum* (Analecta Biblica, 11), Rome, 1959, pp. 116-128, espec. pp. 122-126. The minor agreements require " des contacts littéraires au stade présynoptique " (col. 1447), " un stade présynoptique de la tradition, au cours duquel les traditions se contaminèrent " (col. 1444). He classifies them in the following categories (" selon leur importance et leur nature ") :

Léon-Dufour
(1)   *a.* common omissions ;
(2)   *b.* agreements affecting the sense and the form ;
(3)   *c.* agreements affecting principally the sense ;
(4)   *d.* agreements affecting principally the form ;
(5)   *e.* agreements only affecting the form.

X. Léon-Dufour is largely dependent on the article of N. A. Dahl (cf. *supra*, n. 139) ; he proposes his theory as a complement to the explanation by interaction of oral tradition and written gospel, and as an alternative for Vaganay's Proto-Matthew (' Les évangiles synoptiques ', p. 288 ; ' Passion ', col. 1447).

— More recently the minor agreements in the passion story (at least in one section, Mk 14,53-72) are studied more carefully by Gerhard SCHNEIDER, *Verleugnung, Verspottung und Verhör Jesu nach Lukas 22,54-71. Studien zur lukanischen Darstellung der Passion* (STANT, 22), Munich, 1969, pp. 47-60. He gives a list of 41 agreements which he assigns to one of the following causes (he excludes Luke's dependence on Matthew, p. 48, n. 136, and does not mention the recension theory, cf. *supra*, n. 49) :

Schneider
(I)   I. Literary contact in the pre-synoptic stage of the tradition (cf. Léon-Dufour) :
       Mk 14,61(two).62(five).

ments are essential in the argument of Léon VAGANAY [145]. He refuses to explain them by accidental coincidence for three reasons : (1) the negative agreements are too numerous ; (2) they are related to similar phenomena : other anecdotic details omitted either by Matthew or by Luke and positive agreements of Matthew and Luke against Mark ; (3) the negative agreements are distributed throughout the pericopes in an alternation with triple tradition elements (Matthew /Mark /Luke) [146]. The negative agreements require a second source besides Mark and their special character (*éléments accessoires, détails anodins*) reveals the ' schematic ' style of the primitive gospel [147].

II. Textual harmonization (cf. Streeter) : Mk 14,72.   (II)
III. Oral tradition (cf. Dahl) : Mk 14,65(?).   (III)
IV. Small special source : Mk 14,65(?).   (IV)
 V. Independent editing.   (V)
VI. Common theological intention.   (VI)
    Most of the agreements are explicable by the editorial factor (V and VI).

145. L. VAGANAY, *Le problème synoptique. Une hypothèse de travail* (Bibliothèque de Théologie, III, 1), Tournai, 1954, pp. 69-74, 293, 319 and 423-425. Cf. p. 425 : "Bien loin d'être sans portée, la plupart des accords négatifs de Mt.-Lc. contre Mc., envisagés non pas isolément, mais en groupe dans une péricope, intéressent au plus haut point la solution du problème synoptique ". On the number of negative agreements : " Sauf erreur, on ne les a jamais comptés. Et pour cause : il serait trop difficile de les expliquer... A coup sûr, dans l'ensemble des récits évangéliques, ces accords négatifs de Mt.-Lc. contre Mc. doivent dépasser plusieurs centaines " (pp. 69-70).

146. The principal illustrations are Mk 6,31-44 (pp. 69 and 71-72) ; 4,35-41 (p. 73) and 9,14-29 in ' Excursus V. Les accords négatifs de Matthieu-Luc contre Marc : L'épisode de l'enfant épileptique (Mt. 17,14-21 ; Mc. 9,14-29 ; Lc. 9,37-43a) ' (pp. 405-425). The agreements noted by Vaganay are in our list ; in addition those   Vaganay of Mk 1,1-6 ; 9,33-50 and 3,13-19, cf. ' Excursus III : Les traits rédactionnels de Mc. dans la première péricope synoptique (Mt. 3,1-6 ; Mc. 1,1-6 ; Lc. 3,1-6) ' (pp. 345-360) ; ' Excursus IV. Le schématisme du discours communautaire (Mt. 18,1-35 ; Mc. 9,33-50 ; Lc. 9,46-50) ' (pp. 361-404) ; and his article ' L'absence du sermon sur la montagne chez Marc ', *RB* 58 (1951) 5-56. On the positive agreements, see *Le problème synoptique*, pp. 319-321 (with the distinction : " éléments en plus, — mis à une place différente, — conservés sous une forme différente ").

147. *Ibid.*, p. 67 : " Le schématisme de M. Nous entendons par schématisme dans les synoptiques non pas seulement une certaine indigence de vocabulaire, caractérisée par la répétition fréquente des mêmes termes, mais plutôt l'allure stylisée du développement, c'est-à-dire, une rédaction réduite à ses éléments essentiels ".

— For criticism of Vaganay's use of the minor agreements see J. LEVIE, ' L'évangile araméen de S. Matthieu est-il la source de l'évangile de S. Marc ? ', *NRT* 76 (1954) 689-715.812-843, espec. pp. 710-714 and 816-818, with a discussion of Mk 1, 1-6 (pp. 819-820) ; 6,30-44 (pp. 820-826) ; 9,14-29 (pp. 826-833) ; 9,33-50 (pp. 833-835) ; see p. 818 : " C'est sur ces *accords* négatifs que M. Vaganay, me semble-t-il, fonde l'essentiel de sa démonstration " ; J. SCHMID, ' Markus und der aramäische Matthäus ', in *Synoptische Studien Alfred Wikenhauser*, Munich, 1953, pp. 148-183, espec. pp. 159-165. Cf. *infra*, n. 155.

The Proto-Matthew theory of L. Vaganay is in many respects related
to the synoptic studies of Lucien CERFAUX [148], but the special emphasis
on the negative agreements, which reminds us of the Proto-Mark hypothesis [149], is undoubtedly Vaganay's personal contribution. The more
recent synoptic theory of Marie-Émile BOISMARD now unambiguously
returns to the Proto-Mark [150]. The Gospel of Mark known to Matthew
and Luke is not our Mark but the *Marc-intermédiaire*, and the inter-
ventions of a final redactor gave rise to agreements between Matthew
and Luke against Mark : the numerous agreements in omission are
redactional additions in Mark and some positive agreements are due
to omissions or changes in Mark by the same redactor [151]. The bulk of
the positive agreements he assigns to Luke's dependence on Matthew,
not in the final stage of the gospel redaction but on the level of the
' intermediate ' gospels : Proto-Luke borrowed them from *Matthieu-
intermédiaire* [152]. Boismard admits that some agreements can be explained

---

148. L. CERFAUX, ' A propos des sources du troisième Évangile : proto-Luc
ou proto-Matthieu ? ', *ETL* 12 (1935) 5-27 ; = *Recueil Lucien Cerfaux* I (Bibl.
ETL, 6), Gembloux, 1954, pp. 389-414 ; ' Encore la question synoptique ', *ETL* 15
(1938) 330-337 ; = *Recueil* I, pp. 415-424 (cf. p. 424 : *Note*) ; ' La mission de Galilée
dans la tradition synoptique ', *ETL* 27 (1951) 369-389 ; 28 (1952) 629-647 ; = *Recueil* I, pp. 425-469. See L. VAGANAY, *Le problème synoptique*, pp. 30-31. Compare
the *Préface* written by Cerfaux, and the presentation of the book in ' Le problème
synoptique. A propos d'un livre récent ', *NRT* 76 (1954) 494-505 ; on the minor
agreements : pp. 497-498 ; = *Recueil* III (Bibl. ETL, 18), Gembloux, 1962, pp. 87-88.

149. The argument of the minor agreements is not the only rapprochement
with the Proto-Mark theory. Vaganay's primitive gospel (*Matthieu grec*) is much
less ' Matthean ' than Cerfaux's *proto-Matthieu*. In fact, the gospel source of Vaganay could be called an Ur-Marcus : his argument for the inclusion of the Sermon
on the Mount in Mk 3,19/20 is that of Ewald and Holtzmann ; he admits besides
Mg a second source for double tradition texts (*Sg*, comp. the Logia source) ; the
order of the pericopes in *Mg* was that of Mark (diff. Mt 4 - 13) and many archaic
elements of *Mg* are preserved in Mark. (The origin of Mark's peculiar matter, i.e.
the negative agreements of Matthew and Luke, is the Roman preaching of Peter
which combined with the primitive tradition.)

150. M.-É. BOISMARD, *Commentaire*, in P. BENOIT and M.-É. BOISMARD, *Synopse
des quatre évangiles en français*, vol. II, Paris, 1972.

151. *Ibid.*, pp. 23-29 (*Introduction* II B). For a description of the redactional
intervention see pp. 28-29 : repetitions of words, composition of summaries, insertion of O. T. quotations, explicatory glosses, ' pittoresque ' details, proper names,
theological or apologetical additions and explanations for a gentile audience.
Moreover, the Marcan redactor knew *Matthieu-intermédiaire* and Proto-Luke and
both Matthean and Lucan influences can be shown in Mark. For criticism see F. NEI-
RYNCK, ' Urmarcus redivivus ? Examen critique de l'hypothèse des insertions
matthéennes dans Marc ', in M. SABBE (ed.), *L'Évangile de Marc* (Bibl. ETL, 34),
Leuven-Gembloux, 1974, pp. 103-145.

152. *Ibid.*, pp. 30-32 (*Introduction IIC,1c* : ' Les accords Mt/Lc contre Mc ')
and pp. 41-42 (*E,1d* : ' Les accords Mt/Lc contre Mc '). Boismard repeatedly refers
to the Proto-Luke hypothesis of many other authors (p.16 : " à la suite de beaucoup

Cerfaux

Boismard
(McR)

(Mt)

by textual harmonisation and by accidental coincidence of independent editing but he refuses to follow the defenders of the two-document hypothesis " dans les excès de leurs méthodes critiques " [153].

7

In a concluding section I would mention three dissertations of Louvain students. In a critical evaluation of X. Léon-Dufour's synoptic studies Swithun MCLOUGHLIN examined more particularly the minor agreements in the theories of L. Vaganay and X. Léon-Dufour [154]. He denied the probative value of the objection against the two-document hypothesis which is based on the number of the minor agreements and their disposition within the pericopes [155] and studied the four partially overlapping lists of significant agreements compiled by J. C. Hawkins, E. D. Burton, M.-J. Lagrange and B. de Solages [156]. The synthesis of the four lists contains only 42 agreements, to which McLoughlin added

---

d'auteurs " ; p. 40 : " beaucoup d'auteurs admettent aujourd'hui "), but it should be clear that in that Proto-Luke hypothesis the two stages in the composition of Luke are understood quite differently. They consider the Marcan material as later insertions in Proto-Luke (Q + L) : the (relatively pure) Marcan blocks. The Proto-Luke of Boismard includes already a gospel narrative concurrent with the Marcan stories but dependent on Matthew (Mt-intermédiaire). The explanation of the agreements by the influence of a common source is not absolutely excluded, although the Lucan dependence on the Document A cannot be proven (p. 32).

153. Ibid., p. 30. Boismard has listed a great number of agreements in his commentary ; they are noted in our list with the author's explanation where clearly indicated : Marcan redaction (McR), dependence of Proto-Luke on Intermediate Matthew (Mt), common dependence on Q (q), textual corruption (t), coincidence (q) (t) in the redaction of Matthew and Luke (r). A few instances are marked by (Mc) (r) indicating that Mc-intermédiaire has made an addition (or omission) in the common (Mc) source.
— For a recent short study in defence of Ur-Marcus, see T. BAARDA, ' Markus 14,11 : ΕΠΗΓΓΕΙΛΑΝΤΟ ' Bron ' of ' Redaktie ' ? ', Gereformeerd Theologisch Tijdschrift 73 (1973) 65-75.
154. S. McLOUGHLIN, The Synoptic Theory of Xavier Léon-Dufour. An Analysis and Evaluation (Doctoral Dissertation), Leuven, 1965. (Cf. ' The Gospels and the Jesus of History ', The Downside Review 87 (1969) 183-200 ; 90 (1972) 201-206.) On the minor agreements : pp. 236-291 ; see also 59-69.90-91.119-126.135-137.140-145.319-320.389-390.507-510. — S. McLOUGHLIN, ' Les accords mineurs Mt-Lc contre Mc et le problème synoptique. Vers la théorie des deux sources ', ETL 43 (1967) 17-40 ; = I. DE LA POTTERIE (ed.), De Jésus aux Évangiles (Bibl. ETL, 25), Gembloux-Paris, 1967 (same pagination).
155. Vaganay's argument of the alternation (cf. the criticism of Levie, art. cit., pp. 823-824) is now employed by Boismard : " l'alternance chez Lc d'accords Mt/Lc contre Mc et Mc/Lc contre Mt prouve la dépendance de Lc par rapport à deux textes différents, l'un matthéen et l'autre marcien " (op. cit., p. 41).
156. Cf. supra, n. 70, 78, 84 and 113(g).

48 HANSEN

a further four cases which in his view also merit consideration. He applied
to them nine criteria which could lessen the value of an agreement
against Mark [157]. He retained six instances, in order of decreasing
importance: Mk 14,65; 14,72; 9,2; 2,12; 9,19 and 5,27 which he explained along the lines of Schmid and Streeter with a special consideration
for Streeter's case of textual conjecture (Mk 14,65). In a more contextual
approach Theo HANSEN examined the agreements of Matthew and Luke,
positive and negative, in a particular section of the gospel (first chapter
of Mark) on the hypothesis of independent editing of Mark by the later
synoptists [158] and Donald SENIOR's analysis of the passion narrative
in Matthew called attention to the Matthean redaction [159]. In the same
line of redactional interpretation the minor agreements in the transfiguration story were studied in a contribution to the *Festschrift* for
J. Schmid [160].

---

157. The 46 instances are mentioned in our list with the criteria applied by
McLoughlin :

McLoughlin

(P) *Position* : the different place in Matthew and Luke.
(D) *Différence* : differences in the words used by Matthew and Luke.
(M) *Matthéen* : Matthean vocabulary or style.
(L) *Lucanien :* Lucan vocabulary or style.
(R) *Raisonnement à partir de Mc* : editorial reflexion based on the text of Mark.
(I) *Instigateur de corrections* : corrections provoked by Mark.
(Q) *Q* : a minor agreement in close contact with a major one.
(T) *Texte incertain* : textual uncertainty.
(C) *Connaissance* : either Matthew or Luke is acquainted with our text of Mark.

158. T. HANSEN, *De overeenkomsten Mattheus-Lucas tegen Marcus in de drie-
voudige traditie. I. Historisch overzicht van de problematiek met cumulatieve lijst
van overeenkomsten ; II. Onderzoek van Mc I en paralleltiteksten* (Doctoral Dissertation), Leuven, 1969. The first part contains the first draft of our cumulative list of

Hansen agreements. Hansen's name is given for some new entries not mentioned by earlier
authors.

159. D. SENIOR, *The Passion Narrative according to Matthew. A Redactional
Study of Mt 26,1 - 27,56* (Doctoral Dissertation), Leuven, 1972. Cf. ' The Fate of
the Betrayer. A Redactional Study of Matthew XXVII, 3-10 ', *ETL* 48 (1972)
372-426.

160. F. NEIRYNCK, ' Minor Agreements Matthew-Luke in the Transfiguration
Story ', in *Orientierung an Jesus. Zur Theologie der Synoptiker. Für Josef Schmid*
(ed. P. HOFFMANN), Freiburg i.B., 1972, pp. 253-266 (with a special examination
of Mk 9,2 and 7).

A CUMULATIVE LIST
OF THE MINOR AGREEMENTS
OF MATTHEW AND LUKE AGAINST MARK

INTRODUCTION

The following table attempts to give an exhaustive description of the minor agreements. It includes the instances mentioned in the exegetical discussion and in former compilations and indicates for each case authors who refer to it (in a chronological order).

*Wilke (1838) : p. 12.
*Holtzmann (1863) : p. 13.
*Weiss (1865, 1872) : p. 14-15.
Simons (1880) : p. 15-16.
Rushbrooke (1880, 1884) : p. 18, n. 36.37.
Wright (1896) : p. 20, n. 45.
Veit (1897) : p. 16.
*Wernle (1899) : p. 16.
†*Hawkins (1899) : p. 24-26, n. 64.70.
†*Abbott (1901) : p. 19, n. 40.
Burton (1904) : p. 27, n. 78.
Allen (1907) : p. 30, n. 89.
*Stanton (1909) : p. 30, n. 92.
Cladder (1919) : p. 38, n. 117.
*Stephenson (1919): p. 26, n. 68.
Lagrange (1921) : p. 28, n. 84.
*Streeter (1924) : p. 32, n. 99.
Larfeld (1925) : p. 35, n. 108.
*Easton (1926) : p. 33, n. 102.
†*Schmid (1930) : p. 34, n. 108.
Cerfaux (1935) : p. 46, n. 148.

Chapman (1937) : p. 37, n. 117.
Glasson (1943) : p. 22, n. 55.
Taylor (1952) : p. 29, n. 86.
Da Fonseca (1952) : p. 43, n. 138.
Vaganay (1954) : p. 45, n. 146.
†*De Solages (1959) : p. 35-37, n. 113.115.
Keech (1959) : p. 42, n. 136.
Brown (1959) : p. 23, n. 56.
Turner (1959) : p. 38, n. 119.
†*Léon-Dufour (1960) : p. 44, n. 144.
*McLoughlin (1965, 1967) : p. 48, n. 157.
Simpson (1966) : p. 39, n. 121.
Farmer (1969) : p. 41, n. 135.
Sanders (1969) : p. 41, n. 134.
Hansen (1969) : p. 48, n. 158.
*Schneider (1969) : p. 44, n. 144.
Fuchs (1971) : p. 24, n. 61.
*Boismard (1972) : p. 46-47, n. 151-153.

The page references in the list above are from ' The Study of the Minor Agreements ' (pp. 11-48). The asterisk (*) indicates that the list contains some information about the causal factor by which the author explains the agreement (e.g., q for Q influence, t for textual corruption, r for redactional, i.e., independent editing of Mark). For some names (e.g., Glasson and Brown for the revision theory) no further sign is needed and for others (Hawkins, Stanton, Streeter, McLoughlin,

Schneider) the author's own signs or numbers are adopted. The obelus
(†) indicates that the author distinguishes specific categories of agreement ; e.g., the historic present in Mark : Hawkins (VI), Abbott (III),
Schmid (5) ; the conjunction καί in Mark : Hawkins (VII), Abbott (VI),
1 2   Schmid (4). The numbers printed in heavy type at the end of the line
refer to our classification of stylistic agreements (pp. 197ff.).

* * *

The table contains, in a horizontal line synopsis, a contextual presentation of the agreements between Matthew and Luke against Mark,
following the order of the gospel of Mark. The words in agreement are
underlined. For agreements in addition or substitution (positive agreements) a full line is used in the text of Matthew and Luke, with a
complete underlining for additional matter and the specific underlining
of the agreement where a word is used in a form different from Mark.
For agreements in omission (negative agreements) the text of Mark
is underlined with a dotted line ; occasionally the two elements of
a b   duplicate expressions are numbered by **a b**. Agreements in inverted
/   order are indicated in Matthew and Luke by the sign / between the two
//   inverted words and by // for more complex transpositions.

* * *

In each set the individual agreements are numbered in the order of
the text of Matthew (first line) and Mark (second line). Complex agreements (i.e., more than one word) are covered by one number, unless
differentiation is needed by the apparatus of authors. Where the agreement is indicated by continuous underlining, the number at the beginning
refers to the whole phrase and can be followed by another number
2 ٦   referring to a part of the same phrase (compare, e.g., Mk 4,2-3).

* * *

The gospel text printed in the table is that of Aland's *Synopsis*
(Stuttgart, 1964) with exception only for agreements based on a deviating
textual variant (marked by the use of parentheses). With a view to the
study of the minor agreements a small apparatus informs about the
variant readings printed in the following editions.

TR   *Textus Receptus.*
Ti   C. TISCHENDORF, *Synopsis Evangelica*, Leipzig, [1]1851 ; [2]1864.
T   C. TISCHENDORF, *Synopsis Evangelica*, Leipzig, [3]1870 - [7]1898.
     Unless otherwise indicated the text of Ti is that of his N.T. edition of
     1859 and the text of T that of the *Octava* (1869).

B. F. Westcott - J. F. A. Hort, *The New Testament in the Original*   H h
Greek, Cambridge-London, 1881 (h = a marginal reading).

W. G. Rushbrooke, *Synopticon*, London, 1880.   Ru
The text only in a very few cases deviates from Westcott-Hort,
especially in the earlier chapters.

B. Weiss, *Das Neue Testament* I, Leipzig, 1894.   W

H. von Soden, *Die Schriften des Neuen Testaments. II. Text mit Apparat*,   S s
Göttingen, 1913 (s = a reading in his first apparatus).

A. Huck - H. Lietzmann, *Synopse der drei ersten Evangelien*, Tübingen,   L
^{9}1936 ; ^{10}1950.
The text printed in the *Synopse* of A. Huck (^{1}1892-^{8}1931) is that of
Tischendorf (T).

E. Nestle - K. Aland, *Novum Testamentum graece*, Stuttgart, ^{25}1963.   N

K. Aland - M. Black - B. M. Metzger - A. Wikgren, *The Greek New*   GNT^1 ^{2}
Testament, Stuttgart, ^{1}1966 ; ^{2}1968.

Cf. B. M. Metzger, *A Textual Commentary on the Greek New Testament*.   GNT^3
A Companion Volume to the *United Bible Societies' Greek New Testa-*
ment (third edition), London-New York, 1971.

All variant readings adopted by GNT are included in so far as they
are of influence on the agreement between Matthew and Luke. When
the ratings *A B C D* of the edition are added (in parentheses), a textual   (*A*)
apparatus of the variant readings can be found in GNT.

The siglum is put in brackets where brackets are used for the text   [ ]
in the edition.

§ 1. Mc 1,1-6 ; Mt 3,1-6 ; Lc 3,1-6

Mt   om.
Mc 1,1   <u>ἀρχὴ τοῦ εὐαγγελίου Ἰησοῦ Χριστοῦ.</u>
Lc   om.

        Rushbrooke, Stanton(1), Schmid, Vaganay.
        Mc : + υιου του θεου TR [S] ; υιου θεου Ti h W [GNT](C).

Mt 3,1   <u>ἐν</u>   δὲ ταῖς ἡμέραις ἐκείναις
Mc 1,1   om.
Lc 3,1   <u>ἐν</u> ἔτει δὲ πεντεκαιδεκάτῳ τῆς ἡγεμονίας Τιβερίου Καίσαρος,

        Rushbrooke, De Solages(Q). **2n**
        Indicatio temporis : Weiss, Simons, Stephenson(q), Vaganay.

Mt 3,1-3   παραγίνεται   Ἰωάννης...// (3) *verba prophetae*
Mc 1,2-4   *verba prophetae*   (4) ἐγένετο Ἰωάννης...
Lc 3,2-4   ἐγένετο ῥῆμα θεοῦ ἐπὶ Ἰωάννην...// (4) *verba prophetae*

        Simons, Wright, Veit, Stanton(1), Easton, Schmid(13), Vaganay, DeSolages(Q)
        Keech, Simpson, Sanders, Boismard(McR). **8A   35**

Mt 3,3   οὗτος γάρ ἐστιν ὁ ῥηθεὶς διὰ   [1]Ἡσαΐου τοῦ προφήτου λέγοντος·
Mc 1,2   [2]καθὼς γέγραπται   ἐν [3]τῷ   Ἡσαΐᾳ <u>τῷ προφήτῃ</u>·
Lc 3,4   <u>ὡς</u>   γέγραπται ἐν βίβλῳ λόγων Ἡσαΐου <u>τοῦ προφήτου</u>·

        1 : Rushbrooke, Veit, Easton, De Solages(Q), Keech, Simpson.
        2 : Rushbrooke.
        3 : Farmer. **33b**

Mt 3,3   om. (cf. 11,10)
Mc 1,2   <u>ἰδοὺ ἀποστέλλω τὸν ἄγγελόν μου πρὸ προσώπου σου, ὃς κατασκευάσει τὴν ὁδὸν</u>
              <u>σου·</u>
Lc 3,4   om. (cf. 7,27)

        Wilke, Weiss, Simons, Rushbrooke, Wright, Stanton(1), Stephenson(t),
        Streeter(q), Schmid, Vaganay, Keech, Simpson, Sanders, Boismard(McR). **35**

Mt (11,10)   τὴν ὁδόν σου <u>ἔμπροσθέν σου.</u>
Mc 1,2   τὴν ὁδόν σου·
Lc (7,27)   τὴν ὁδόν σου <u>ἔμπροσθέν σου.</u>

        Weiss, Veit, Keech, Simpson.

Mt 3,1-2   'Ιωάννης ὁ βαπτιστὴς   κηρύσσων ... (2) λέγων· μετανοεῖτε·
Mc 1,4   'Ιωάννης ὁ ᵃβαπτίζων   ... κηρύσσων ᵇβάπτισμα   μετανοίας
Lc 3,2-3   'Ιωάννην ... (3) καὶ ἦλθεν ... κηρύσσων βάπτισμα   μετανοίας

        Hawkins(II). **34**
        Mc (καὶ) κηρύσσων : Rushbrooke.
        Mc κηρυσσων : και κ. TR T Ru S GNT(C).
        Mc ο βαπτιζων : — ο TR S GNT¹²(C) [GNT³].

Mt 3,5   τότε   ἐξεπορεύετο ...   'Ιεροσόλυμα καὶ πᾶσα
Mc 1,5   ¹καὶ   ἐξεπορεύετο ... πᾶσα ... καὶ οἱ 'Ιεροσολυμῖται ²πάντες,
Lc 3,7   ἔλεγεν οὖν τοῖς ἐκπορευομένοις   ὄχλοις

        1 : Rushbrooke. **2n**
        2 : Rushbrooke.

Mt 3,5   πᾶσα ἡ 'Ιουδαία καὶ πᾶσα ἡ περίχωρος τοῦ 'Ιορδάνου,
Mc 1,5   πᾶσα ἡ 'Ιουδαία   χώρα
Lc (3,3)   πᾶσαν τὴν   περίχωρον τοῦ 'Ιορδάνου

        Weiss, Simons, Rushbrooke, Veit, Wernle, Abbott(H), Burton, Stanton(3a),
        Stephenson(q), Streeter(q), Larfeld, Easton(q), Schmid, Chapman, Vaganay,
        De Solages(Q), Keech, McLoughlin(PMLQ?).

§ 2. Mc 1,7-8; Mt 3,7-12; Lc 3,7-17

Mt 3,7-10   Ioannes paenitentiam praedicat.
Mc 1,6   om.
Lc 3,7-9   Ioannes paenitentiam praedicat.

        Wilke, Weiss, Simons, Stephenson(q), Vaganay, Keech, Simpson, Sanders.

Mt (3,7)   ἰδὼν δὲ πολλοὺς ...   εἶπεν   ¹αὐτοῖς·
Mc 1,7   ²καὶ   ³ἐκήρυσσεν λέγων·
Lc (3,7)   ἔλεγεν οὖν τοῖς ... ὄχλοις
Lc 3,15-16 προσδοκῶντος δὲ τοῦ λαοῦ ..., (16) ἀπεκρίνατο λέγων   πᾶσιν

        1 : **23**
        2 : Rushbrooke. **1**
        3 : Rushbrooke.

Mt 3,11   ἐγὼ [1]μὲν ὑμᾶς βαπτίζω ἐν ὕδατι...[2]//ὁ [3]δὲ ὀπίσω μου ἐρχόμενος ἰσχυρότερος
Mc 1,7-8   ἔρχεται ὁ ἰσχυρότερός μου ὀπίσω μου, ... (8) ἐγὼ ἐβάπτισα ὑμᾶς ὕδατι,
Lc 3,16   ἐγὼ μὲν ὕδατι βαπτίζω ὑμᾶς·   //ἔρχεται δὲ ὁ ἰσχυρότερός μου,

> 1 : Rushbrooke, Wright, Veit, Abbott(VII), Streeter(q), Schmid, De Solages(Q), Keech, Simpson. **4**
> 2 : Weiss, Simons, Wright, Veit, Wernle, Hawkins, Stanton(3a), Stephenson(q), Streeter(q), Schmid, Vaganay, Keech, Simpson, Sanders. **35**
> 3 : Rushbrooke, Veit, Abbott(VII), Streeter(q), De Solages(Q), Keech. Cf. 1.

Mt 3,11   οὗ οὐκ εἰμὶ ἱκανὸς   τὰ ὑποδήματα   βαστάσαι·
Mc 1,7   οὗ οὐκ εἰμὶ ἱκανὸς κύψας λῦσαι τὸν ἱμάντα τῶν ὑποδημάτων αὐτοῦ.
Lc 3,16   οὗ οὐκ εἰμὶ ἱκανὸς   λῦσαι τὸν ἱμάντα τῶν ὑποδημάτων αὐτοῦ·

> Wilke, Holtzmann, Weiss, Rushbrooke, Wright, Wernle, Hawkins(II), Stephenson(r), Schmid, Boismard(McR).

Mt 3,11   ἐγὼ μὲν ὑμᾶς βαπτίζω   ἐν ὕδατι εἰς μετάνοιαν· ὁ δὲ ὀπίσω μου
Mc 1,8   ἐγὼ   ἐβάπτισα ὑμᾶς ὕδατι,   αὐτὸς δὲ βαπτίσει
Lc 3,16   ἐγὼ μὲν ὕδατι βαπτίζω ὑμᾶς·   ἔρχεται δέ

> Simons, Rushbrooke, Wright, Veit, Abbott, Streeter(q), Schmid, De Solages(Q), Keech. **11n**

Mt 3,11   αὐτὸς   ὑμᾶς [1]/ βαπτίσει [2]ἐν πνεύματι ἁγίῳ [3]καὶ πυρί·
Mc 1,8   αὐτὸς [4]δὲ βαπτίσει ὑμᾶς   πνεύματι ἁγίῳ.
Lc 3,16   αὐτὸς   ὑμᾶς / βαπτίσει ἐν πνεύματι ἁγίῳ καὶ πυρί·

> 1 : Simons, Wright, Veit, Streeter(q), Keech, Simpson. **(21A)**
> 2 : Wernle, Abbott, Stephenson(q), Schmid, Keech, Simpson. **31a**
>   Mc : + ἐν TR T Ru GNT(*A*).
> 3 : Simons, Rushbrooke, Wright, Veit, Wernle, Abbott(H?), Burton, Stanton(3a), Stephenson(q), Streeter(q), Schmid, Chapman, Da Fonseca, Vaganay, De Solages(Q), Keech, McLoughlin(Q), Simpson.
> 4 : Rushbrooke, Keech. Cf. Mc 1,8*a*. **(4)**

Mt 3,12   οὗ τὸ πτύον ἐν τῇ χειρὶ αὐτοῦ, καὶ διακαθαριεῖ τὴν ἅλωνα αὐτοῦ,
           καὶ συνάξει τὸν σῖτον αὐτοῦ εἰς τὴν ἀποθήκην,
           τὸ δὲ ἄχυρον κατακαύσει πυρὶ ἀσβέστῳ.
Mc 1,8   om.
Lc 3,17   οὗ τὸ πτύον ἐν τῇ χειρὶ αὐτοῦ   διακαθᾶραι τὴν ἅλωνα αὐτοῦ
           καὶ συναγαγεῖν τὸν σῖτον   εἰς τὴν ἀποθήκην αὐτοῦ,
           τὸ δὲ ἄχυρον κατακαύσει πυρὶ ἀσβέστῳ.

> Simons, Rushbrooke, Veit, Schmid, Vaganay, De Solages(Q), Keech, Simpson.
> Mt αποθηκην : + αυτου h [GNT[12]](*C*).

§ 3. Mc 1,9-11; Mt 3,13-17; Lc 3,21-22

Mt 3,13   τότε παραγίνεται   ὁ Ἰησοῦς
Mc 1,9   [1]καὶ ἐγένετο [2]ἐν ἐκείναις ταῖς ἡμέραις [3]ἦλθεν Ἰησοῦς
Lc 3,21   ἐγένετο δὲ   ἐν τῷ βαπτισθῆναι ...   καὶ Ἰησοῦ βαπτισθέντος

     1 : Rushbrooke, Schmid(4).   **2**
       Mc και εγενετο : — και h W.
     2 : Rushbrooke.   **2n**
     3 : Rushbrooke.

Mt 3,13   ἀπὸ   τῆς Γαλιλαίας ... τοῦ [1]βαπτισθῆναι ὑπ' αὐτοῦ.
Mc 1,9   ἀπὸ [2]Ναζαρὲθ τῆς Γαλιλαίας   καὶ ἐβαπτίσθη ... ὑπὸ Ἰωάννου.
Lc 3,21   ἐν τῷ   βαπτισθῆναι ἅπαντα τὸν λαόν

     1 : Rushbrooke, Keech.
     2 : Rushbrooke, Easton.

Mt 3,16   [1]βαπτισθεὶς δὲ ὁ [2]Ἰησοῦς
Mc 1,9   καὶ   ἐβαπτίσθη   [3]εἰς τὸν Ἰορδάνην
Lc 3,21   καὶ Ἰησοῦ   βαπτισθέντος

     1 : Easton, De Solages(Q).
     2 : Easton, De Solages(Q).   **22**
     3 : Rushbrooke, Schmid(20).

Mt 3,16   καὶ ἰδοὺ   [1]ἠνεῴχθησαν οἱ   οὐρανοί,   καὶ εἶδεν
Mc 1,10   [2]εἶδεν   σχιζομένους τοὺς οὐρανοὺς   καὶ
Lc 3,21-22 ἐγένετο δὲ ... ἀνεῳχθῆναι τὸν   οὐρανὸν (22) καὶ

     1 : Holtzmann, Weiss, Rushbrooke, Veit, Wernle, Hawkins(IVa), Abbott(H),
       Allen, Stanton(3a), Streeter(q), Easton, Schmid, Chapman, Glasson,
       Da Fonseca, De Solages(Q), Keech, Simpson.   **32**
       Mt ηνεωχθησαν : + αυτω TR Ti h S [GNT](C).
     2 : Weiss, Simons, Wernle, Schmid, Keech.

Mt 3,16   καὶ εἶδεν   πνεῦμα θεοῦ
Mc 1,10   καὶ   τὸ πνεῦμα
Lc 3,22   καὶ καταβῆναι τὸ πνεῦμα τὸ ἅγιον

     Weiss(r), Schmid(33).   **23**
     Mt πνευμα : το πν. του TR Ti S [GNT].

Mt 3,16   καταβαῖνον   ¹/ὡσεὶ περιστεράν,   ἐρχόμενον ²ἐπ᾽ αὐτόν·
Mc 1,10   ὡς   περιστερὰν καταβαῖνον   εἰς αὐτόν·
Lc 3,22   καταβῆναι ... /ὡς   περιστερὰν   ἐπ᾽ αὐτόν,

    1 : Weiss, Veit. **21B**
    2 : Weiss, Simons, Rushbrooke, Veit, Wernle, Abbott(VII), Easton, Schmid(20),
        De Solages(Q), Keech, Simpson. **31c**
        Mc εις : επ TR s ; Mt ερχομενον : και ε. TR GNT¹(B) [GNT² ³](C).

§ 4. Mc 1,12-13; Mt 4,1-11; Lc 4,1-13

Mt 4,1   τότε   ὁ ¹᾽Ιησοῦς   ²ἀνήχθη ...³//ὑπὸ τοῦ πνεύματος
Mc 1,12   ⁴καὶ ⁵εὐθὺς τὸ πνεῦμα αὐτὸν   ⁶ἐκβάλλει
Lc 4,1   ᾽Ιησοῦς δὲ ..., καὶ ἤγετο   //ἐν τῷ πνεύματι

    1 : Rushbrooke, Abbott, Easton(q), De Solages(Q), Keech, Boismard(McR).
        Mt ο Ιησους : — ο Ti [H]. **22**
    2 : Weiss, Simons, Rushbrooke, Hawkins(IAb,VI), Abbott(H,III), Allen,
        Streeter(q), Easton(q), Schmid(5,18,27), Vaganay, De Solages(Q), Keech,
        Boismard(McR). **17**
    3 : Veit, Easton(q). **21B**
    4 : **2**
    5 : Rushbrooke, Wernle, Schmid(10). **26**
    6 : Cf. 2. **10**

Mt 4,1   ἀνήχθη   εἰς τὴν ἔρημον
Mc 1,12-13 ἐκβάλλει ᵃεἰς τὴν ἔρημον. (13) καὶ ᵇἦν ἐν τῇ ἐρήμῳ
Lc 4,1   καὶ ἤγετο ...   ἐν τῇ ἐρήμῳ

    Wilke (t : καὶ ἦν — σατανᾶ), Rushbrooke(b), Hawkins(a.b : II), Boismard(b :
    McR). **34**

Mt (4,2)   νηστεύσας ἡμέρας / τεσσεράκοντα καὶ τεσσεράκοντα νύκτας
Mc 1,13   τεσσεράκοντα ἡμέρας   πειραζόμενος
Lc 4,2   ἡμέρας / τεσσεράκοντα   πειραζόμενος

    Weiss(r), Simons, Veit, Stephenson(q), Keech. **21B**

Mt 4,1   πειρασθῆναι ὑπὸ τοῦ ¹διαβόλου.
Mc 1,13   ²ἦν ... πειραζόμενος ὑπὸ τοῦ σατανᾶ, ³καὶ ἦν μετὰ τῶν θηρίων,
Lc 4,2   πειραζόμενος ὑπὸ τοῦ διαβόλου.

    1 : Weiss, Simons, Rushbrooke, Veit, Wernle, Abbott(H), Stanton(3a), Stree-
        ter(q), Easton(q), Schmid(1), Da Fonseca, Vaganay, De Solages(Q), Keech,
        Simpson. **32**
    2 : **12**
    3 : Holtzmann, Simons, Rushbrooke, Wright, Wernle, Abbott(H), Allen,
        Schmid(31), Boismard(Mc).

Mt 4,2   καὶ νηστεύσας ἡμέρας τεσσεράκοντα καὶ τεσσεράκοντα νύκτας   ὕστερον
              <u>ἐπείνασεν.</u>

Mc 1,13   om.

Lc 4,2   καὶ οὐκ ἔφαγεν οὐδὲν ἐν ταῖς ἡμέραις ἐκείναις, καὶ συντελεσθεισῶν αὐτῶν
              <u>ἐπείνασεν.</u>

              Weiss, Simons, Rushbrooke, Veit, Abbott(H), Streeter(q), Da Fonseca, Keech,
              Simpson.

Mt 4,3-10   *Tentatio Jesu.*

Mc 1,13   om.

Lc 4,3-12   *Tentatio Jesu.*

              Holtzmann, Sanders.

Mt 4,11   τότε   <u>ἀφίησιν αὐτὸν ὁ διάβολος,</u>

Mc 1,13

Lc 4,13   καὶ συντελέσας πάντα πειρασμὸν <u>ὁ διάβολος ἀπέστη ἀπ' αὐτοῦ</u>

              Rushbrooke, Veit, Streeter(q), Keech.

§ 5. Mc 1,14-15; Mt 4,12-17; Lc 4,14-15

Mt 4,12-13 ἀνεχώρησεν   εἰς τὴν Γαλιλαίαν. (13) καὶ καταλιπὼν τὴν [1]<u>Ναζαρά</u>

Mc 1,14   [2]ἦλθεν ...   εἰς τὴν Γαλιλαίαν

Lc 4,14   ὑπέστρεψεν ... εἰς τὴν Γαλιλαίαν·

Lc (4,16)   καὶ ἦλθεν   εἰς   <u>Ναζαρά</u>

          1 : Weiss, Wernle, Stephenson(q), Streeter(q), Larfeld, Schmid, Keech, Bois-
             mard(Mt).
             Lc Ναζαρα : την N. S ; την Ναζαρετ TR Ti(-εθ).
             In Nazareth praedicat (cf. Lc 4,16-30) : Simons, Cladder.
          2 : Simons, Rushbrooke, Schmid.   **32**

Mt 4,17   ἀπὸ τότε ἤρξατο ὁ Ἰησοῦς κηρύσσειν καὶ λέγειν·
          μετανοεῖτε·   ἤγγικεν γὰρ ἡ βασιλεία τῶν οὐρανῶν.

Mc 1,14-15 ἦλθεν ...   κηρύσσων [1]<u>τὸ εὐαγγέλιον τοῦ θεοῦ</u> (15) καὶ λέγων, [2]<u>ὅτι</u>
          [3]<u>πεπλήρωται ὁ καιρὸς</u> καὶ ἤγγικεν ἡ βασιλεία τοῦ θεοῦ·
          μετανοεῖτε καὶ [4]<u>πιστεύετε ἐν τῷ εὐαγγελίῳ.</u>

Lc 4,15   καὶ αὐτὸς ἐδίδασκεν ἐν ταῖς συναγωγαῖς αὐτῶν,

          1 : Rushbrooke, Stanton(1).
          2 : Rushbrooke.
          3 : Rushbrooke, Hawkins(V), Stanton(1).
          4 : Rushbrooke, Hawkins(V), Stanton(1).

§ 6. Mc 1,16-20; Mt 4,18-22; (Lc 5,1-11)

Mt 4,18	περιπατῶν [1]δὲ	παρὰ τὴν θάλασσαν ...	εἶδεν [2]δύο ἀδελφούς, Σίμωνα
Mc 1,16	καὶ [3]παράγων	παρὰ τὴν θάλασσαν ...	εἶδεν Σίμωνα
Lc 5,1-2	ἐγένετο δὲ ... ἑστὼς παρὰ τὴν λίμνην ..., (2) καὶ εἶδεν δύο πλοιάρια

1 : Rushbrooke, Abbott(VI), Keech. **1**
2 : Rushbrooke, Veit, Abbott(H), Keech.
3 : Rushbrooke.

Mt 4,19	καὶ ποιήσω ὑμᾶς ἁλεεῖς ἀνθρώπων.
Mc 1,17	καὶ ποιήσω ὑμᾶς γενέσθαι ἁλεεῖς ἀνθρώπων.
Lc 5,10	ἀπὸ τοῦ νῦν ἀνθρώπους ἔσῃ ζωγρῶν.

Rushbrooke, Hawkins(II).

Mt 4,22	ἀφέντες τὸ πλοῖον καὶ τὸν πατέρα αὐτῶν
Mc 1,20	ἀφέντες τὸν πατέρα αὐτῶν [1]Ζεβεδαῖον ἐν τῷ πλοίῳ [2]μετὰ τῶν μισθωτῶν
Lc 5,11	ἀφέντες πάντα

1 : Rushbrooke.
2 : Holtzmann(r), Rushbrooke, Wright, Wernle(t), Hawkins(II,III), Stanton(2).

Mt 4,22	ἀφέντες τὸ πλοῖον ...	ἠκολούθησαν αὐτῷ.
Mc 1,20	ἀφέντες τὸν πατέρα ...	ἀπῆλθον ὀπίσω αὐτοῦ.
Lc 5,11	ἀφέντες πάντα	ἠκολούθησαν αὐτῷ.

Rushbrooke, Veit. **32**

§ 7. Mc 1,21-22; Mt 7,28-29; Lc 4,31-32

Mt (4,13.15)	καὶ ... [1]ἐλθὼν κατῴκησεν εἰς Καφαρναοὺμ ... (15) ... [2]Γαλιλαία τῶν ἐθνῶν,
Mc 1,21	καὶ [3]εἰσπορεύονται	εἰς Καφαρναούμ·
Lc 4,31	καὶ κατῆλθεν	εἰς Καφαρναοὺμ πόλιν τῆς Γαλιλαίας.

1 : Rushbrooke, De Solages(c). **20**
    Ante vocationem discipulorum : Cladder.
2 : Rushbrooke.
3 : Rushbrooke. Cf. 1. **10**

§ 8. Mc 1,23-28; (Mt 4,24); Lc 4,33-37

Mt (9,26)   καὶ ἐξῆλθεν ἡ [1]φήμη αὕτη εἰς ὅλην τὴν γῆν ἐκείνην.

Mt 4,24   καὶ ἀπῆλθεν ἡ ἀκοὴ αὐτοῦ εἰς ὅλην τὴν Συρίαν·

Mc 1,28   καὶ ἐξῆλθεν ἡ ἀκοὴ αὐτοῦ [2]εὐθὺς [3]πανταχοῦ
                 εἰς ὅλην τὴν περίχωρον [4]τῆς Γαλιλαίας.

Lc 4,37   καὶ ἐξεπορεύετο ἦχος περὶ αὐτοῦ
                 εἰς πάντα τόπον τῆς περιχώρου.

Lc (4,14)   καὶ φήμη ἐξῆλθεν   καθ' ὅλης τῆς περιχώρου περὶ αὐτοῦ.

> 1 : Farmer.
> 2 : Rushbrooke, Schmid(10). **26**
> 3 : Rushbrooke, Hawkins(V).
> 4 : Rushbrooke, Wright.
>   Mc και εξηλθεν : ε. δε TR S.

§ 9. Mc 1,29-31; Mt 8,14-15; Lc 4,38-39

Mt 8,14   καὶ   [1]ἐλθὼν ὁ Ἰησοῦς εἰς

Mc 1,29   καὶ [2]εὐθὺς ἐκ τῆς συναγωγῆς [3]ἐξελθόντες ἦλθον   εἰς

Lc 4,38   ἀναστὰς δὲ ἀπὸ τῆς συναγωγῆς   εἰσῆλθεν   εἰς

> 1 : Schmid(12,30), Brown. **(33c)**
>   Mc εξελθοντες ηλθον : -ων ηλθεν h W L.
> 2 : Rushbrooke, Wernle, Stephenson, Easton, Schmid(10).
> 3 : Rushbrooke, Stanton(2), Easton.

Mt 8,14   εἰς τὴν οἰκίαν Πέτρου

Mc 1,29   εἰς τὴν οἰκίαν Σίμωνος καὶ Ἀνδρέου μετὰ Ἰακώβου καὶ Ἰωάννου.

Lc 4,38   εἰς τὴν οἰκίαν Σίμωνος.

> Wilke(Γr), Weiss(r), Simons, Rushbrooke, Wright, Wernle, Hawkins(III), Allen, Stanton(1 vel 2), Easton, Schmid(32), Vaganay, Keech, Boismard(McR).

Mt 8,14   εἶδεν ... βεβλημένην καὶ πυρέσσουσαν·

Mc 1,30   [1]κατέκειτο πυρέσσουσα, καὶ [2]εὐθὺς [3]λέγουσιν αὐτῷ

Lc 4,38   ἦν συνεχομένη πυρετῷ μεγάλῳ καὶ ἠρώτησαν αὐτόν

> 1 : Rushbrooke. **11**
> 2 : Rushbrooke, Schmid(10).
> 3 : Rushbrooke.

Mt 8,15   καὶ   ἥψατο   τῆς χειρὸς ¹αὐτῆς,
Mc 1,31   καὶ ²προσελθὼν ἤγειρεν αὐτὴν ³κρατήσας τῆς χειρός·
Lc 4,39   καὶ ἐπιστὰς ἐπάνω αὐτῆς

    1 : Rushbrooke, Stanton(2).
    2 : Rushbrooke, Stanton(2), Schmid(7).
    3 : Rushbrooke, Schmid(7).

Mt 8,15   καὶ ἀφῆκεν αὐτὴν ...· //καὶ ¹ἠγέρθη,
Mc 1,31   καὶ ... ²ἤγειρεν αὐτὴν ...· καὶ ἀφῆκεν αὐτήν
Lc 4,39   καὶ ἀφῆκεν αὐτήν· // ... ἀναστᾶσα

    1 : Weiss(r), Wernle, Schmid, Boismard(McR). 21B
    2 : Rushbrooke. Cf. 1.

§ 10. Mc 1,32-34; Mt 8,16-17; Lc 4,40-41

Mt 8,16   ὀψίας δὲ γενομένης
Mc 1,32   ªὀψίας δὲ γενομένης, ᵇὅτε ἔδυσεν   ὁ ἥλιος,
Lc 4,40   δύνοντος δὲ τοῦ ἡλίου

    Weiss(r), Hawkins(V), Allen, Schmid(31), Boismard(McR). 34

Mt 8,16   προσήνεγκαν   αὐτῷ
Mc 1,32   ἔφερον   πρὸς αὐτόν
Lc 4,40   ἤγαγον αὐτοὺς πρὸς αὐτόν·

    Rushbrooke, Allen, Schmid(27). 11 29

Mt 8,16   (cf. v. 16b)   δαιμονιζομένους πολλούς·
Mc 1,32   ¹πάντας ²ªτοὺς κακῶς ἔχοντας ᵇκαὶ τοὺς δαιμονιζομένους·
Lc 4,40   ἀσθενοῦντας νόσοις ποικίλαις   (cf. v. 41)

    1 : Rushbrooke, Vaganay.
    2 : Rushbrooke, Stanton(2), Schmid. 34

Mt 8,16   om.
Mc 1,33   καὶ ἦν ὅλη ἡ πόλις ἐπισυνηγμένη πρὸς τὴν θύραν.
Lc 4,40   om.

    Wilke(r), Holtzmann, Weiss, Simons, Rushbrooke, Wright, Wernle, Hawkins
    (III), Allen, Stanton(2), Easton, Schmid(32), Keech.

Mt 8,16   καὶ   πάντας τοὺς κακῶς ἔχοντας ἐθεράπευσεν·
Mc 1,34   καὶ ἐθεράπευσεν πολλοὺς   κακῶς ἔχοντας
Lc 4,40   ὁ δὲ   ἑνὶ ἑκάστῳ αὐτῶν ...   ἐθεράπευεν αὐτούς.

    Hawkins(IAa), Schmid.

Mt 8,16   καὶ ἐξέβαλεν || τὰ πνεύματα λόγῳ,
Mc 1,34   καὶ δαιμόνια πολλὰ ἐξέβαλεν,
Lc 4,41   ἐξήρχετο δὲ καὶ || δαιμόνια ἀπὸ πολλῶν,

            Wright, Veit.   21A

§ 11. Mc 1,35-38; Lc 4,42-43

Mt (4,25)   καὶ ἠκολούθησαν αὐτῷ ὄχλοι πολλοί
Mc 1,36-37 καὶ κατεδίωξεν   αὐτὸν Σίμων καὶ οἱ μετ' αὐτοῦ, (37) ... λέγουσιν αὐτῷ
            ὅτι πάντες   ζητοῦσίν σε.
Lc 4,42   καὶ οἱ ὄχλοι ἐπεζήτουν   αὐτόν,

            (Schürmann).

§ 12. Mc 1,39; (Mt 4,23); Lc 4,44

Mt 4,23   καὶ   κηρύσσων τὸ εὐαγγέλιον τῆς βασιλείας
Mc 1,38-39 ἵνα ... κηρύξω· ... (39) καὶ ἦλθεν κηρύσσων
Lc (4,43)   εὐαγγελίσασθαί με δεῖ   τὴν βασιλείαν τοῦ θεοῦ,

            Rushbrooke, Abbott, Stanton(2), Larfeld, Schmid(33), De Solages(g), Keech,
            Brown(cf. 1,14), McLoughlin (PDLMRI).
            Mc 1,14 το ευαγγελιον : + της βασιλειας TR.

Mt 4,23   περιῆγεν   ἐν ὅλῃ τῇ Γαλιλαίᾳ,
            [1]διδάσκων ἐν ταῖς συναγωγαῖς αὐτῶν καὶ κηρύσσων
Mc 1,39   [2]ἦλθεν κηρύσσων εἰς τὰς συναγωγὰς αὐτῶν [3]εἰς ὅλην τὴν Γαλιλαίαν
Lc 4,44   ἦν κηρύσσων εἰς τὰς συναγωγὰς   τῆς Ἰουδαίας.
Lc (4,15)   ἐδίδασκεν ἐν ταῖς συναγωγαῖς αὐτῶν,

            1 : Farmer.
            2 : Rushbrooke.   32
               Mc ηλθεν : ην TR Ti.
            3 : Rushbrooke.

Mt 4,23   καὶ θεραπεύων πᾶσαν νόσον καὶ πᾶσαν μαλακίαν ἐν τῷ λαῷ.
Mc 1,39   καὶ τὰ δαιμόνια ἐκβάλλων.
Lc 4,44   om.

            Rushbrooke, Wright.

§ 13. Mc 1,40-45; (Mt 8,1-4); Lc 5,12-16

Mt 8,1   καταβάντος δὲ   αὐτοῦ ἀπὸ τοῦ ὄρους
Mc 1,40   om.
Lc 5,12   καὶ ἐγένετο ἐν τῷ εἶναι αὐτὸν ἐν μιᾷ τῶν πόλεων

            De Solages(e).

Mt 8,2   καὶ ¹ἰδοὺ   λεπρὸς προσελθών
Mc 1,40   καὶ ²ἔρχεται πρὸς ³αὐτὸν λεπρὸς   ⁴παρακαλῶν αὐτόν
Lc 5,12   καὶ ἰδοὺ   ἀνὴρ πλήρης λέπρας·

1 : Weiss, Simons, Rushbrooke, Wright, Veit, Wernle, Abbott(H), Stanton(3b),
    Stephenson, Lagrange, Easton, Schmid(33), Chapman, De Solages(d), Keech,
    McLoughlin(MLI), Fuchs, Boismard(Mt). **25**
2 : Weiss, Rushbrooke, Hawkins(VI), Abbott(III), Schmid(5). **10**
3 : Rushbrooke. **(23)**
4 : Rushbrooke, Fuchs.

Mt 8,2   προσεκύνει   αὐτῷ ¹/ λέγων·
Mc 1,40   ²καὶ γονυπετῶν   λέγων ³αὐτῷ
Lc 5,12   πεσὼν ἐπὶ πρόσωπον ἐδεήθη αὐτοῦ / λέγων·

1 : Veit, Stephenson. **21B**
2 : Wilke, Weiss, Rushbrooke, Brown. **32**
    Mc καὶ γονυπετων : — Ti ; [H] [GNT](D).
3 : Fuchs. **(23)**

Mt 8,2   ¹κύριε, ἐὰν θέλῃς, δύνασαί με καθαρίσαι.
Mc 1,40   ²ὅτι   ἐὰν θέλῃς, δύνασαί με καθαρίσαι.
Lc 5,12   κύριε, ἐὰν θέλῃς, δύνασαί με καθαρίσαι.

1 : Wilke, Weiss, Simons, Rushbrooke, Wright, Veit, Wernle, Abbott(H),
    Stanton(3b), Stephenson, Lagrange, Streeter(t), Easton, Schmid(33),
    Chapman, Da Fonseca, De Solages(f), Keech, Brown, McLoughlin(MLI),
    Fuchs, Boismard(Mt). **30**
    δύνασαι (Mc δύνῃ B) : Simons.
2 : Weiss, Simons, Rushbrooke, Easton, Schmid(21), Keech, Fuchs, Boismard
    (Mt). **5**

Mt 8,3   καὶ   ἐκτείνας τὴν χεῖρα
Mc 1,41   ¹(ὁ δὲ Ἰησοῦς) ²σπλαγχνισθεὶς ἐκτείνας τὴν χεῖρα
Lc 5,13   καὶ   ἐκτείνας τὴν χεῖρα

1 : Wilke.
    Mc καὶ : ο δε Ιησους TR S.
2 : Wilke, Weiss, Simons, Rushbrooke, Wernle, Hawkins(III), Allen, Stanton(2),
    Stephenson(r), Easton, Schmid(32), Keech, Brown, Fuchs.
    ὀργισθείς : Taylor, Boismard(McR).
    Mc : οργισθεις hʳ.

Mt 8,3   καὶ ἐκτείνας τὴν χεῖρα ἥψατο ¹/αὐτοῦ   ²λέγων·
Mc 1,41   καὶ ... ἐκτείνας τὴν χεῖρα αὐτοῦ ἥψατο καὶ λέγει ³αὐτῷ·
Lc 5,13   καὶ ἐκτείνας τὴν χεῖρα ἥψατο /αὐτοῦ   λέγων·

1 : Simons, Wright, Veit, Wernle, Stanton(3b), Stephenson, Streeter(t), Easton,
    Schmid(14), Vaganay, Keech, Brown, Fuchs, Boismard(Mt). **21A**
2 : Simons, Rushbrooke, Wernle, Hawkins(VI), Abbott(IV), Stanton(3b),

Stephenson, Schmid(5,7), Easton, Chapman, De Solages(b), Keech, Brown,
Fuchs, Boismard(Mt). **3   10   15**
Lc λέγων : ειπων TR Ti T S.
3 : Schmid, Keech, Fuchs, Boismard. **(23)**
Mc αυτω : — T.

Mt 8,3   καὶ   [1]εὐθέως ἐκαθαρίσθη αὐτοῦ ἡ λέπρα.
Mc 1,42   καὶ [2](εἰπόντος αὐτοῦ) εὐθὺς ἀπῆλθεν ἀπ᾽ αὐτοῦ ἡ λέπρα,
Lc 5,13   καὶ   εὐθέως ἡ λέπρα ἀπῆλθεν ἀπ᾽ αὐτοῦ.

1 : Simons, Rushbrooke, Veit, Wernle, Stephenson, Streeter(d vel t), Easton,
Schmid(10), De Solages(c), Keech, Brown, Fuchs, Boismard(Mt). **26**
2 : Wilke.
Mc : + ειποντος αυτου TR S.

Mt 8,3   ἐκαθαρίσθη αὐτοῦ ἡ λέπρα.
Mc 1,42   [a]ἀπῆλθεν ἀπ᾽ αὐτοῦ ἡ λέπρα, [b]καὶ ἐκαθαρίσθη.
Lc 5,13   ἡ λέπρα ἀπῆλθεν ἀπ᾽ αὐτοῦ.

Weiss, Hawkins(V), Allen, Schmid(31), Boismard(McR). **34**

Mt (9,30)   καὶ ἐνεβριμήθη   αὐτοῖς
Mt 8,3   om.
Mc 1,43   καὶ ἐμβριμησάμενος αὐτῷ εὐθὺς ἐξέβαλεν αὐτόν,
Lc 5,13   om.

Wilke(r)(cf. Mt 9,30), Weiss, Simons, Rushbrooke, Wright, Wernle, Hawkins
(IAb,II), Allen, Stephenson(r), Easton, Schmid(32), Glasson, Keech, Brown,
Fuchs, Boismard(McR).

Mt (9,30)   καὶ   [1]ἐνεβριμήθη αὐτοῖς [2]ὁ Ἰησοῦς λέγων· ὁρᾶτε μηδεὶς γινωσκέτω.
Mt 8,4   καὶ   λέγει   αὐτῷ ὁ Ἰησοῦς·   ὅρα μηδενὶ   εἴπῃς,
Mc 1,44   καὶ   λέγει   αὐτῷ·   ὅρα μηδενὶ [3]μηδὲν εἴπῃς,
Lc 5,14   καὶ αὐτὸς παρήγγειλεν αὐτῷ   μηδενὶ   εἰπεῖν,

1 : Boismard(Mt).
2 : Hansen. **22**
3 : Weiss, Simons, Rushbrooke, Easton, Schmid(28), Keech, Brown, Fuchs. **(23)**

Mt 8,4   τὸ δῶρον ὃ προσέταξεν Μωϋσῆς,
Mc 1,44   ἃ προσέταξεν Μωϋσῆς,
Lc 5,14   καθὼς   προσέταξεν Μωϋσῆς,

Weiss(r), Rushbrooke.

Mt (9,31)   οἱ δὲ ἐξελθόντες   διεφήμισαν αὐτὸν ἐν ὅλῃ τῇ γῇ ἐκείνῃ.
Mt 8,4   om.
Mc 1,45   ⌜ὁ δὲ ἐξελθὼν⌝ ἤρξατο κηρύσσειν πολλὰ ⌜καὶ διαφημίζειν⌝ τὸν λόγον,
Lc 5,15   διήρχετο δὲ μᾶλλον   ὁ λόγος περὶ αὐτοῦ,

          Rushbrooke, Wright, Hawkins(V), Schmid, Boismard(McR ⌜⌝)

Mt 8   om.
Mc 1,45   ὥστε μηκέτι αὐτὸν δύνασθαι φανερῶς εἰς πόλιν εἰσελθεῖν, ἀλλ' ἔξω
Lc 5,15   om.

          Rushbrooke, Wright, Hawkins(I), Allen, Schmid, Boismard(McR).

§ 14. Mc 2,1-12; Mt 9,1-8; Lc 5,17-26

Mt 9,1   καὶ   ἦλθεν   εἰς τὴν ἰδίαν πόλιν.
Mc 2,1   καὶ εἰσελθὼν ¹πάλιν εἰς Καφαρναοὺμ δι' ἡμερῶν ²ἠκούσθη ὅτι ἐν οἴκῳ ἐστίν.
Lc 5,17   καὶ ἐγένετο   ἐν μιᾷ τῶν ἡμερῶν

          1 : Rushbrooke, Easton.
          2 : Weiss, Rushbrooke, Easton, Schmid(32).
             Mc εν οικω : εις οικον TR Ti h W S.

Mt 9,1   om.
Mc 2,2   ¹καὶ συνήχθησαν πολλοί, ὥστε μηκέτι χωρεῖν μηδὲ τὰ πρὸς τὴν θύραν,
            ²καὶ ἐλάλει αὐτοῖς τὸν λόγον.
Lc 5,17   καὶ αὐτὸς ἦν διδάσκων, καὶ..., οἳ ἦσαν ἐληλυθότες ἐκ πάσης κώμης

          1 : Weiss, Wernle, Hawkins(II), Allen, Easton, Schmid.
          2 : Rushbrooke, Boismard(McR).

Mt 9,2   καὶ ¹ἰδοὺ προσέφερον   αὐτῷ   παραλυτικόν
Mc 2,3   καὶ ²ἔρχονται φέροντες πρὸς αὐτὸν   παραλυτικόν
Lc 5,18   καὶ ἰδοὺ ἄνδρες φέροντες ... ἄνθρωπον ὃς ἦν παραλελυμένος,

          1 : Wilke, Holtzmann, Weiss, Simons, Rushbrooke, Veit, Wernle, Abbott(H),
             Stanton(3b), Lagrange, Easton, Schmid(33), Chapman, Da Fonseca, De
             Solages(d), Keech, Brown, McLoughlin(ML), Boismard(Mt). 25
          2 : Rushbrooke, Hawkins(VI), Abbott(III), Schmid(5). 10

Mt 9,2   παραλυτικὸν ¹ἐπὶ κλίνης βεβλημένον.
Mc 2,3   παραλυτικὸν   ²αἰρόμενον ὑπὸ τεσσάρων.
Lc 5,18   ἐπὶ κλίνης ἄνθρωπον ὃς ἦν παραλελυμένος,

          1 : Wilke, Holtzmann, Weiss, Simons, Rushbrooke, Wright, Veit, Wernle,
             Hawkins(VIA), Abbott(H), Stanton(3b), Lagrange, Streeter(d), Easton,

Schmid(33), Chapman, Da Fonseca, De Solages(f), Keech, McLoughlin(RI), Boismard(Mt).

2 : Wilke(t), Simons, Rushbrooke, Wernle, Easton, Schmid(29), Keech, Boismard(Mt).

Mt 9,2   om.

Mc 2,4   ¹ἀπεστέγασαν τὴν στέγην ²ὅπου ἦν⌉, καὶ ³ἐξορύξαντες

Lc 5,19   διὰ τῶν κεράμων

1 : Rushbrooke, Schmid.
2 : Easton.
3 : Wright.

Mt 9,2   om.

Mc 2,4   χαλῶσι ¹τὸν κράβατον ²ὅπου ὁ παραλυτικὸς κατέκειτο.

Lc 5,19   καθῆκαν αὐτὸν σὺν τῷ κλινιδίῳ εἰς τὸ μέσον   ἔμπροσθεν τοῦ Ἰησοῦ.

1 : Rushbrooke.
2 : Easton.

Mt 9,2   καὶ ἰδὼν ὁ Ἰησοῦς τὴν πίστιν αὐτῶν εἶπεν τῷ παραλυτικῷ· θάρσει, τέκνον,

Mc 2,5   καὶ ἰδὼν ὁ Ἰησοῦς τὴν πίστιν αὐτῶν λέγει τῷ παραλυτικῷ·   τέκνον,

Lc 5,20   καὶ ἰδὼν   τὴν πίστιν αὐτῶν εἶπεν·   ἄνθρωπε,

Weiss, Simons, Rushbrooke, Veit, Hawkins(VI), Abbott(V), Easton, Schmid(5), De Solages(a). **10**
Mc (ἰδὼν δέ) : Wilke, Holtzmann(?).
Mc καὶ ἰδὼν : ἰδ. δε TR S.

Mt 9,2   (ἀφέωνταί) σου αἱ ἁμαρτίαι.

Mc 2,5   ἀφίενταί σου αἱ ἁμαρτίαι.

Lc 5,20   ἀφέωνταί σοι αἱ ἁμαρτίαι σου.

De Solages(b).
Mt αφιενται : αφεωνται TR Ti S.

Mt 9,3   ¹καὶ ἰδού τινες τῶν γραμματέων   ²εἶπαν ἐν ἑαυτοῖς·

Mc 2,6   ἦσαν δέ τινες τῶν γραμματέων ³ἐκεῖ καθήμενοι

     ⁴καὶ διαλογιζόμενοι ⁵ἐν ταῖς καρδίαις αὐτῶν·

Lc 5,21   καὶ ἤρξαντο διαλογίζεσθαι οἱ γραμματεῖς καὶ οἱ Φαρισαῖοι λέγοντες·

(5,17)   καὶ ἦσαν καθήμενοι Φαρισαῖοι καὶ νομοδιδάσκαλοι

1 : Rushbrooke, Veit, Abbott(?), Easton, De Solages(a), Keech. **(1)**
2 : De Solages(d). **32**
3 : Rushbrooke.
4 : Schmid(9). **12**
5 : Rushbrooke, Schmid(31).

Mt 9,3   οὗτος   βλασφημεῖ·
Mc 2,7   [1]τί   οὗτος [2]οὕτως λαλεῖ ; βλασφημεῖ·
Lc 5,21   τίς ἐστιν οὗτος   ὃς λαλεῖ βλασφημίας ;

    1 : Schmid. **6**
      Mc τι : Οτι h, οτι· W (λαλει·).
    2 : Rushbrooke, Schmid.

Mt 9,4   καὶ   εἰδὼς   ὁ Ἰησοῦς
Mc 2,8   καὶ [1]εὐθὺς ἐπιγνοὺς   ὁ Ἰησοῦς [2]τῷ πνεύματι αὐτοῦ
Lc 5,22   ἐπιγνοὺς δὲ ὁ Ἰησοῦς

    1 : Rushbrooke, Easton, Schmid(10). **26**
    2 : Rushbrooke,Wright, Hawkins(II), Stanton(2), Easton, Schmid(31,33), Keech.
      Mt ειδως : ιδων TR Ti T h Ru S GNT[3](C).

Mt 9,4   [1]τὰς ἐνθυμήσεις   [2]αὐτῶν
Mc 2,8   [3]ὅτι οὕτως διαλογίζονται ἐν ἑαυτοῖς,
Lc 5,22   τοὺς διαλογισμοὺς   αὐτῶν,

    1 : Easton, Schmid(27), De Solages(e), Keech. **14n**
    2 : Rushbrooke, Veit, Easton, De Solages(e), Keech.
    3 : Simons, Rushbrooke, Schmid, Keech.
      Mc ουτως : [H] ; + αυτοι TR Ti W.

Mt 9,4   [1]εἶπεν·   ἱνατί   ἐνθυμεῖσθε πονηρά
Mc 2,8   λέγει   αὐτοῖς·   τί [2]ταῦτα διαλογίζεσθε
Lc 5,22   ἀποκριθεὶς εἶπεν πρὸς αὐτούς·   τί   διαλογίζεσθε

    1 : Weiss, Simons, Rushbrooke, Veit, Wernle, Hawkins(VI), Abbott(V), Easton,
      Schmid(5), De Solages(a), Keech. **10**
    2 : Rushbrooke, Schmid.

Mt 9,5   εἰπεῖν·   [1](ἀφέωνταί) σου αἱ ἁμαρτίαι,
Mc 2,9   εἰπεῖν [2]τῷ παραλυτικῷ· ἀφίενταί σου αἱ ἁμαρτίαι,
Lc 5,23   εἰπεῖν·   ἀφέωνταί σοι αἱ ἁμαρτίαι σου,

    1 : De Solages(b).
      Mt αφιενται : αφεωνται TR Ti S.
    2 : Wilke, Weiss, Rushbrooke, Hawkins(II), Easton, Schmid(31), Keech. **(23)**

Mt 9,5   ἢ εἰπεῖν· ἔγειρε   καὶ [1]περιπάτει ;
Mc 2,9   ἢ εἰπεῖν· ἔγειρε [2]καὶ ἆρον τὸν κράβατόν σου καὶ (ὕπαγε) ;
Lc 5,23   ἢ εἰπεῖν· ἔγειρε   καὶ   περιπάτει ;

    1 : Weiss, Simons, Rushbrooke, Veit, Wernle(t), Stanton(3b), Easton(?),
      Schmid(27), Chapman.
      Mc περιπατει : υπαγε T Ru S.
    2 : Wilke(t), Weiss, Simons, Rushbrooke, Wright,Wernle(t), Easton, Schmid(31),
      Glasson, Keech.
      Mc εγειρε : εγειρου Ti H Ru ; και αρον : αρον Ti S, [και] αρον H.

Mt 9,6   ἐπὶ τῆς γῆς || ἀφιέναι ἁμαρτίας
Mc 2,10   ἀφιέναι ἁμαρτίας ἐπὶ τῆς γῆς,
Lc 5,24   ἐπὶ τῆς γῆς || ἀφιέναι ἁμαρτίας,

             Weiss, Wright, Easton, Keech, Brown.   21B
             Mc : 1 3-4-5 2 TR Ti S ; 3-4-5 1 2 T h.

Mt 9,6   ἔγειρε   ἆρόν σου τὴν κλίνην   καὶ ὕπαγε εἰς τὸν οἶκόν σου.
Mc 2,11   ἔγειρε   ἆρον   τὸν κράβατόν σου   καὶ ὕπαγε εἰς τὸν οἶκόν σου.
Lc 5,24   ἔγειρε καὶ ἄρας   τὸ κλινίδιόν σου   πορεύου εἰς τὸν οἶκόν σου.

             Simons, Rushbrooke, Hawkins(IVa), Abbott(VII), Allen, Streeter(d), Easton,
             Schmid(27), Keech.   32

Mt 9,7   καὶ   [1]ἐγερθείς
Mc 2,12   καὶ   ἠγέρθη καὶ [2]εὐθὺς ἄρας [3]τὸν κράβατον
Lc 5,25   καὶ παραχρῆμα ἀναστὰς ...,   ἄρας ἐφ' ὃ κατέκειτο,

             1 : Weiss, Schmid(7).   3
             2 : Rushbrooke, Stephenson, Schmid(10).   26
             3 : Rushbrooke, Hawkins(IVa), Schmid(27).

Mt 9,7   [1]ἀπῆλθεν   εἰς τὸν οἶκον αὐτοῦ.
Mc 2,12   ἐξῆλθεν [2]ἔμπροσθεν πάντων,
Lc 5,25   ἐνώπιον αὐτῶν, ... ἀπῆλθεν   εἰς τὸν οἶκον αὐτοῦ

             1 : Wilke, Holtzmann, Weiss, Simons, Rushbrooke, Wright, Veit, Wernle,
                 Hawkins, Abbott(H), Burton, Stanton(3b), Lagrange, Streeter(d), Easton,
                 Schmid(20), Chapman, De Solages(c,f), Keech, McLoughlin(I), Boismard(Mt).
                 31b
             2 : Rushbrooke, Wright.

Mt 9,8   ἰδόντες δὲ οἱ ὄχλοι [1]ἐφοβήθησαν καὶ ἐδόξασαν τὸν θεόν
Mc 2,12   [2]ὥστε ἐξίστασθαι   πάντας καὶ δοξάζειν τὸν θεόν
Lc 5,26   καὶ ἔκστασις ἔλαβεν ἅπαντας, καὶ ἐδόξαζον τὸν θεόν, καὶ ἐπλήσθησαν φόβου

             1 : Weiss, Simons, Rushbrooke, Wernle, Abbott(H), Lagrange, Easton,
                 Schmid, De Solages(e), Keech, McLoughlin(I), Boismard(Mt).   32
             2 : Rushbrooke, Easton, Schmid.

             § 15. Mc 2,13-17 ; Mt 9,9-13 ; Lc 5,27-32

Mt 9,9   καὶ   παράγων ὁ Ἰησοῦς ἐκεῖθεν
Mc 2,13   καὶ   ἐξῆλθεν πάλιν παρὰ τὴν θάλασσαν·
             καὶ πᾶς ὁ ὄχλος ἤρχετο πρὸς αὐτόν, καὶ ἐδίδασκεν αὐτούς. (14) καὶ παράγων
Lc 5,27   καὶ μετὰ ταῦτα ἐξῆλθεν, καί

             Wilke, Weiss(r), Simons, Rushbrooke, Wright, Wernle, Stanton(1 vel 2),
             Easton, Schmid(32), Keech.
             Mc παρα τ. θ. : εις τ. θ. T.

Mt 9,9   εἶδεν   ἄνθρωπον ..., Μαθθαῖον ¹λεγόμενον,
Mc 2,14   εἶδεν   Λευὶν   ²τὸν τοῦ Ἀλφαίου
Lc 5,27   ἐθεάσατο τελώνην ὀνόματι Λευίν

1 : Simons, Veit, Schmid. **15n**
2 : Wilke(t), Holtzmann, Simons, Rushbrooke, Wernle, Hawkins(III), Easton,
Schmid(32).

Mt 9,9   καὶ   ἀναστὰς (ἠκολούθει) αὐτῷ.
Mc 2,14   καὶ   ἀναστὰς ἠκολούθησεν αὐτῷ.
Lc 5,28   καὶ καταλιπὼν πάντα ἀναστὰς ἠκολούθει αὐτῷ.

Rushbrooke, Veit, Stanton(1,2 vel 3b), Schmid(?). **(11)**
Mt ηκολουθησεν : -θει T Ru S.

Mt 9,10   καὶ ἐγένετο αὐτοῦ ἀνακειμένου   ἐν τῇ οἰκίᾳ,
Mc 2,15   καὶ γίνεται κατακεῖσθαι αὐτὸν   ἐν τῇ οἰκίᾳ αὐτοῦ,
Lc 5,29   καὶ ἐποίησεν δοχὴν μεγάλην Λευὶς αὐτῷ ἐν τῇ οἰκίᾳ αὐτοῦ·

Hansen. **10**
Mc γινεται : εγενετο TR.

Mt 9,10   om.
Mc 2,15   ἦσαν γὰρ πολλοί, καὶ ἠκολούθουν αὐτῷ.
Lc 5,29   om.

Wilke, Rushbrooke, Wright, Wernle, Hawkins(II,III?), Allen, Easton, Schmid
(13), Keech, Boismard(McR). **8A**

Mt 9,11   καὶ ἰδόντες   οἱ Φαρισαῖοι
Mc 2,16   καὶ   οἱ γραμματεῖς τῶν Φαρισαίων ἰδόντες
Lc 5,30   καὶ ἐγόγγυζον οἱ Φαρισαῖοι καὶ οἱ γραμματεῖς αὐτῶν

Rushbrooke, Veit, Abbott, Stanton(2), Easton, Schmid, De Solages(b), Keech,
Brown.
Mc των Φαρισαιων : και οι Φαρισαιοι TR Ti ; οι γραμματεις : γραμματεις T S ;
αυτω. και οι γρ. των Φαρ. ιδοντες : αυτω και οι γρ. των Φαρ., και ιδοντες T(— οι)
GNT¹²(C).

Mt 9,11   om.
Mc 2,16   ὅτι ἐσθίει μετὰ τῶν ἁμαρτωλῶν καὶ τελωνῶν
Lc 5,30   om.

Holtzmann, Weiss(r), Simons, Rushbrooke, Wright, Wernle, Hawkins(II),
Allen, Easton, Schmid(31), Keech, Boismard(McR).
Mc οτι εσθιει : οτι ησθιεν T S ; αυτον εσθιοντα TR Ti.

Mt 9,11   ¹διὰ τί μετὰ τῶν τελωνῶν καὶ ἁμαρτωλῶν ἐσθίει   ὁ διδάσκαλος ²ὑμῶν ;
Mc 2,16   ὅτι   μετὰ τῶν τελωνῶν καὶ ἁμαρτωλῶν ἐσθίει ;
Lc 5,30   διὰ τί μετὰ τῶν τελωνῶν καὶ ἁμαρτωλῶν ἐσθίετε καὶ πίνετε ;

> 1 : Weiss(r), Simons, Rushbrooke, Veit, Wernle, Hawkins(IVa), Abbott(H),
> Stanton(2), Easton, Schmid(22), Glasson, De Solages(c), Keech, Brown,
> Boismard(r). **6**
> Mc οτι : τι οτι TR S ; εσθιει· W.
> 2 : Weiss(r), Schmid. **22**
> Mc εσθιει : ε. και πινει TR Ti T h Ru S.

Mt 9,12   ὁ δὲ ἀκούσας   ¹εἶπεν·
Mc 2,17   καὶ ἀκούσας   ὁ Ἰησοῦς λέγει   αὐτοῖς ²[ὅτι]
Lc 5,31   καὶ   ἀποκριθεὶς ὁ Ἰησοῦς εἶπεν πρὸς αὐτούς.

> 1 : Weiss(r), Simons, Rushbrooke, Veit, Wernle, Hawkins(VI), Abbott(V),
> Easton, Schmid(5), De Solages(a), Keech. **10**
> 2 : Schmid(21). **5**
> Mc οτι : — TR Ti T Ru S ; + W L ; [H][N][GNT].

§ 16. Mc 2,18-22; Mt 9,14-17; Lc 5,33-39

Mt 9,14   om.
Mc 2,18   καὶ ἦσαν οἱ μαθηταὶ Ἰωάννου καὶ οἱ Φαρισαῖοι νηστεύοντες.
Lc 5,33   om.

> Holtzmann, Simons, Rushbrooke, Wright, Wernle, Hawkins(II), Stanton(1
> vel 2), Easton, Schmid(31), Boismard(McR).
> Mc Φαρισαιοι : των Φαρισαιων TR S.

Mt 9,14   τότε ¹προσέρχονται αὐτῷ ²οἱ μαθηταὶ Ἰωάννου   λέγοντες·   διὰ τί
Mc 2,18   ³καὶ   ἔρχονται   καὶ ⁴λέγουσιν αὐτῷ· διὰ τί
Lc 5,33   οἱ δὲ   εἶπαν πρὸς αὐτόν·

> 1 : Rushbrooke, Abbott, Keech.
> 2 : Rushbrooke, Stanton(2), Schmid(12), Boismard(r). **22**
> 3 : Rushbrooke, Schmid(4,7). **2**
> 4 : Hawkins(VI).

Mt 9,14   ἡμεῖς   καὶ   οἱ   Φαρισαῖοι νηστεύομεν,
Mc 2,18   οἱ μαθηταὶ Ἰωάννου καὶ οἱ μαθηταὶ τῶν Φαρισαίων νηστεύουσιν,
Lc 5,33   οἱ μαθηταὶ Ἰωάννου νηστεύουσιν πυκνὰ ... καὶ οἱ τῶν Φαρισαίων,

> Rushbrooke, Easton, Schmid(31).
> Mt νηστευομεν : ν. πολλα TR Ti h S GNT¹²(C), [GNT³](C).

Mt 9,15   om.
Mc 2,19   ὅσον χρόνον ἔχουσιν τὸν νυμφίον μετ᾽ αὐτῶν, οὐ δύνανται νηστεύειν.
Lc 5,34   om.

> Wilke, Simons, Rushbrooke, Wright, Wernle(t), Hawkins(II), Allen, Stanton
> (1 vel 2), Easton, Schmid(31), Glasson, Keech, Brown(W), Boismard(McR).

Mt 9,16   οὐδεὶς δέ
Mc 2,21   οὐδείς
Lc 5,36   ἔλεγεν δὲ καὶ παραβολὴν πρὸς αὐτοὺς ὅτι οὐδείς

> Hawkins(IVc). **4**

Mt 9,16   οὐδεὶς δὲ ἐπιβάλλει ἐπίβλημα ῥάκους ἀγνάφου
Mc 2,21   οὐδεὶς _____ ἐπίβλημα ῥάκους ἀγνάφου   ἐπιράπτει
Lc 5,36   οὐδεὶς   ἐπίβλημα ἀπὸ ἱματίου καινοῦ σχίσας ἐπιβάλλει

> Wilke, Holtzmann, Weiss(r), Simons, Rushbrooke, Veit, Wernle, Hawkins
> (IVa), Abbott, Allen, Stanton(3b), Lagrange, Streeter(d), Easton, Schmid(27),
> Chapman, De Solages(c), Keech, McLoughlin(I), Boismard(Mt). **32**

Mt 9,17   εἰ δὲ μή γε, ῥήγνυνται   οἱ   ἀσκοί,
Mc 2,22   εἰ δὲ μή,   ῥήξει ὁ οἶνος   τοὺς ἀσκούς,
Lc 5,37   εἰ δὲ μή γε, ῥήξει ὁ οἶνος ὁ νέος τοὺς ἀσκούς,

> Wilke, Holtzmann, Weiss(r), Simons, Rushbrooke, Veit, Wernle, Abbott,
> Stanton(3b vel 4), Streeter(t), Easton, Schmid(28), De Solages(b), Keech,
> Boismard(Mt).

Mt 9,17   καὶ ὁ οἶνος [1]ἐκχεῖται   καὶ οἱ ἀσκοὶ [2]//[3]ἀπόλλυνται.
Mc 2,22   καὶ ὁ οἶνος ἀπόλλυται   καὶ οἱ ἀσκοί.
Lc 5,37   καὶ αὐτὸς   ἐκχυθήσεται καὶ οἱ ἀσκοὶ // ἀπολοῦνται.

> 1 : Weiss(r), Simons, Rushbrooke, Wright, Hawkins(*), Abbott, Stanton(2
>   vel 3b), Lagrange, Streeter(t), Easton, Schmid, Da Fonseca, De Solages(c),
>   Keech, Brown, McLoughlin(DRI), Boismard(Mt). **24**
> 2 : Weiss, Wright, Veit. **21B**
> 3 : Weiss(r), Simons, Rushbrooke, Abbott, Stanton(2 vel 3b), Lagrange,
>   Streeter(t), Easton, Schmid, McLoughlin(DRI), Boismard(Mt). Cf. 1. **24**

Mt 9,17   ἀλλὰ βάλλουσιν οἶνον νέον εἰς ἀσκοὺς καινούς,
Mc 2,22   ἀλλὰ _____ οἶνον νέον εἰς ἀσκοὺς καινούς.
Lc 5,38   ἀλλὰ   οἶνον νέον εἰς ἀσκοὺς καινοὺς βλητέον.

> Weiss(r), Simons, Rushbrooke, Wright, Veit, Abbott, Stanton(2 vel 3b),
> Schmid(13), De Solages(f), Keech, Brown, Boismard(Mt). **8A 24**
> (ἀλλὰ οἶνον νέον εἰς ἀσκοὺς καινούς om. Mc) : Wernle(t), Easton, Brown.
> Mc αλλα ... καινους : — Ti T ; [H][N] ; + βλητεον TR.

§ 17. Mc 2,23-28; Mt 12,1-8; Lc 6,1-5

Mt 12,1   ἐν ἐκείνῳ τῷ καιρῷ   ἐπορεύθη ὁ Ἰησοῦς... διὰ τῶν σπορίμων·
Mc 2,23   [1]καὶ ἐγένετο   αὐτὸν ... [2]παραπορεύεσθαι   διὰ τῶν σπορίμων,
Lc 6,1   ἐγένετο δὲ ...   διαπορεύεσθαι αὐτὸν   διὰ σπορίμων,

     1 : Rushbrooke, Schmid(4). **2**
     2 : Weiss(r), Schmid(19). **32**
     Mc παραπορευεσθαι : δια- H (h παρα-) Ru.

Mt 12,1   οἱ δὲ μαθηταὶ αὐτοῦ..., καὶ ἤρξαντο   τίλλειν
Mc 2,23   καὶ οἱ μαθηταὶ αὐτοῦ   ἤρξαντο ὁδὸν ποιεῖν τίλλοντες
Lc 6,1   καὶ   ἔτιλλον   οἱ μαθηταὶ αὐτοῦ

     Weiss(r), Simons, Rushbrooke, Wernle, Hawkins(IC), Stanton(3b vel 1),
     Streeter(d), Easton, Schmid(2), Glasson, Keech, Boismard(McR).
     Mc οδον ποιειν : οδοποιειν h.

Mt 12,1   τίλλειν   στάχυας καὶ ἐσθίειν.
Mc 2,23   τίλλοντες τοὺς στάχυας.
Lc 6,1   ἔτιλλον ...   καὶ ἤσθιον τοὺς στάχυας ψώχοντες ταῖς χερσίν.

     Wilke, Holtzmann, Weiss(r), Simons, Rushbrooke, Wright, Veit, Wernle,
     Hawkins, Abbott, Stanton(3b vel 1), Lagrange, Streeter(d), Easton, Schmid(33),
     Chapman, Da Fonseca, De Solages(f), Keech, McLoughlin(RI), Boismard(Mt).
     24

Mt 12,2   οἱ   [1]δὲ   Φαρισαῖοι ἰδόντες [2]εἶπαν αὐτῷ·
Mc 2,24   καὶ οἱ   Φαρισαῖοι   ἔλεγον αὐτῷ·
Lc 6,2   τινὲς δὲ τῶν Φαρισαίων   εἶπαν·

     1 : Weiss(r), Simons, Rushbrooke, Wernle, Abbott(VI), Easton, Schmid(4),
     De Solages(a), Keech, Boismard(Mt). **1**
     2 : Weiss(r), Simons, Rushbrooke, Wernle, Abbott(V), Easton, Schmid(6),
     De Solages(a), Keech, Boismard(Mt). **11**
     Lc ειπαν : ειπον TR Ti T S.

Mt 12,2   ἰδοὺ οἱ μαθηταί σου ποιοῦσιν ὃ οὐκ ἔξεστιν [1]ποιεῖν [2]//ἐν σαββάτῳ.
Mc 2,24   ἴδε τί   ποιοῦσιν   τοῖς σάββασιν ὃ οὐκ ἔξεστιν ;
Lc 6,2   τί   ποιεῖτε ὃ οὐκ ἔξεστιν (ποιεῖν) //τοῖς σάββασιν ;

     1 : Weiss(r), Rushbrooke, Veit, Stanton(3b vel 1), Streeter(t), Easton, Schmid
     (33), Chapman. **24**
     Lc : ποιειν TR Ti T Ru S.
     2 : Weiss(r), Simons, Wright, Veit, Stanton(3b vel 1), Easton, Schmid, Keech,
     Boismard(Mt). **21B**

Mt 12,3   ¹ὁ δὲ   ²εἶπεν   αὐτοῖς·
Mc 2,25   καὶ   λέγει   αὐτοῖς·
Lc 6,3   καὶ ἀποκριθεὶς πρὸς αὐτοὺς εἶπεν ὁ Ἰησοῦς·

> 1 : Farmer. **22**
>   Mc καὶ : + αυτος TR Ti W, [S].
> 2 : Simons, Rushbrooke, Veit, Wernle, Hawkins(VI), Abbott(V), Easton,
>   Schmid(5), De Solages(a), Keech, Boismard(Mt). **10**
>   Lc προς αυτους ειπεν ο Ιησους : 4-5 1-2-3 T Ru S ; o : [H].

Mt 12,3   οὐκ   ἀνέγνωτε τί ἐποίησεν Δαυίδ, ὅτε
Mc 2,25   οὐδέποτε   ἀνέγνωτε τί ἐποίησεν Δαυίδ, ὅτε
Lc 6,3   οὐδὲ   τοῦτο ἀνέγνωτε ὃ ἐποίησεν Δαυίδ, ὁπότε

> Schmid.
> Lc οποτε : οτε H.

Mt 12,3   ὅτε   ἐπείνασεν   καὶ οἱ μετ' αὐτοῦ ;
Mc 2,25   ὅτε   χρείαν ἔσχεν καὶ ἐπείνασεν αὐτὸς καὶ οἱ μετ' αὐτοῦ ;
Lc 6,3   ὁπότε   ἐπείνασεν αὐτὸς καὶ οἱ μετ' αὐτοῦ ὄντες ;

> Wilke, Holtzmann, Weiss(q /r), Simons, Rushbrooke, Wright, Wernle, Hawkins
> (V), Allen, Schmid(31), Keech, Boismard. **34**
> ἐπείνασεν καὶ οἱ μετ' αὐτοῦ (om. Mc : 255) : Boismard.
> Lc οντες : — H.

Mt 12,4   πῶς εἰσῆλθεν εἰς τὸν οἶκον τοῦ θεοῦ
Mc 2,26   πῶς εἰσῆλθεν εἰς τὸν οἶκον τοῦ θεοῦ ἐπὶ Ἀβιαθὰρ ἀρχιερέως
Lc 6,4   ὡς εἰσῆλθεν εἰς τὸν οἶκον τοῦ θεοῦ

> Wilke(t), Holtzmann(r), Weiss(r /q), Simons, Rushbrooke, Wright, Wernle(t),
> Hawkins(IC,III), Allen, Stanton(1 vel 2), Easton, Schmid(32), Glasson, Vaga-
> nay, Keech, Brown(W), Boismard(McR).

Mt 12,4   ὃ οὐκ ἐξὸν ἦν αὐτῷ φαγεῖν οὐδὲ τοῖς ¹μετ' αὐτοῦ, ²//εἰ μὴ τοῖς ἱερεῦσιν ³μόνοις ;
Mc 2,26   οὓς οὐκ ἔξεστιν φαγεῖν εἰ μὴ τοὺς ἱερεῖς, καὶ ἔδωκεν καὶ τοῖς σὺν αὐτῷ ⁴οὖσιν ;
Lc 6,4   καὶ ἔδωκεν τοῖς μετ' αὐτοῦ, οὓς οὐκ ἔξεστιν φαγεῖν //εἰ μὴ μόνους τοὺς ἱερεῖς ;

> 1 : Weiss(r), Simons, Wernle, Easton, Schmid(20), De Solages(c,b), Keech,
>   Turner, Boismard(McR). **31c**
> 2 : Stanton(3b vel 1), Schmid(13). **8A**
> 3 : Weiss(r /q), Simons, Rushbrooke, Veit, Wernle, Hawkins, Abbott, Stanton
>   (3b vel 1), Lagrange, Streeter(t), Easton, Schmid(33), Da Fonseca, De
>   Solages(f), Keech, Brown, McLoughlin(I), Boismard(Mt).
> 4 : Schmid, Turner, Boismard(McR). **(24)**

Mt 12,7   om.
Mc 2,27   τὸ σάββατον διὰ τὸν ἄνθρωπον ἐγένετο, καὶ οὐχ ὁ ἄνθρωπος διὰ τὸ σάββατον·
Lc 6,5   om.

        Wilke, Holtzmann, Weiss(r/q), Simons, Rushbrooke, Wright, Wernle(t),
        Hawkins(IC), Stanton(1), Easton, Schmid, Glasson, Vaganay, Keech, Brown(W)
        Boismard(McR).

Mt 12,8   κύριος γάρ ἐστιν τοῦ σαββάτου [1]// ὁ υἱὸς τοῦ ἀνθρώπου.
Mc 2,28   [2]ὥστε κύριός   ἐστιν ὁ υἱὸς τοῦ ἀνθρώπου [3]καὶ τοῦ σαββάτου.
Lc 6,5   κύριός   ἐστιν τοῦ σαββάτου // ὁ υἱὸς τοῦ ἀνθρώπου.

        1 : Weiss(r/q), Simons, Wright, Easton, Schmid, Keech, Boismard(Mt). Cf. 3. **21B**
        2 : Weiss(r/q), Rushbrooke, Wright, Easton, Schmid, Glasson, Keech.
        3 : Weiss(r/q), Simons, Easton, Keech, Boismard(Mt).
        Lc του σαββατου ο υι. τ. α. : ο υι. τ. α. και του σαββατου TR Ti T h Ru S.

§ 18a. Mc 3,1-6; Mt 12,9-14; Lc 6,6-11

Mt 12,9   καὶ μεταβὰς ἐκεῖθεν   ἦλθεν   εἰς [1]τὴν συναγωγὴν αὐτῶν.
Mc 3,1   καὶ   εἰσῆλθεν [2]πάλιν εἰς   συναγωγήν.
Lc 6,6   ἐγένετο δὲ ἐν ἑτέρῳ σαββάτῳ εἰσελθεῖν αὐτὸν εἰς τὴν συναγωγὴν καὶ διδάσκειν·

        1 : Simons, Rushbrooke, Wright, Veit, Abbott(VII), Burton, Stanton(4),
        Streeter(d), Easton, Schmid, Keech, Brown, McLoughlin(I). **(33b)**
        Mc : την TR S GNT.
        2 : Rushbrooke, Easton, Schmid(11), Brown. **27**

Mt 12,10   καὶ ἰδοὺ   ἄνθρωπος   χεῖρα   ἔχων   [1]//[2]ξηράν·
Mc 3,1   καὶ ἦν   ἐκεῖ ἄνθρωπος   ἐξηραμμένην   ἔχων τὴν χεῖρα·
Lc 6,6   καὶ ἦν   ἄνθρωπος ἐκεῖ καὶ ἡ χεὶρ αὐτοῦ ἡ δεξιὰ ἦν   // ξηρά·

        1 : Veit. **21B**
        2 : Simons, Wernle, Stanton(2), Streeter(d), Easton, Schmid, Keech, Brown. **11n**

Mt 12,10   καὶ ἐπηρώτησαν   αὐτὸν λέγοντες· (cf. v. 9 : αὐτῶν)
Mc 3,2   καὶ παρετήρουν   αὐτόν
Lc 6,7   παρετηροῦντο δὲ αὐτὸν οἱ γραμματεῖς καὶ οἱ Φαρισαῖοι

        Stanton(2). **22n**

Mt 12,10   εἰ ἔξεστιν τοῖς σάββασιν θεραπεῦσαι ;
Mc 3,2   εἰ   τοῖς σάββασιν θεραπεύσει αὐτόν,
Lc 6,7   εἰ   ἐν τῷ   σαββάτῳ θεραπεύει,

        Rushbrooke, Easton, Keech. **23**

Mt 12,11   [1]ὁ [2]δὲ [3]εἶπεν   αὐτοῖς·
Mc 3,4   καὶ λέγει   αὐτοῖς·
Lc 6,9   εἶπεν δὲ ὁ Ἰησοῦς πρὸς αὐτούς·

     1 : Keech. **22**
     2 : Weiss(r), Rushbrooke, Wernle, Hawkins(VII), Abbott(VI), Easton, Schmid
     (4), De Solages(a), Keech. **1**
     3 : Simons, Rushbrooke, Veit, Wernle, Hawkins(VI), Abbott(V), Easton,
     Schmid(5), De Solages(a), Keech. **10**

Mt (12,10)   καὶ [1]ἐπηρώτησαν   αὐτὸν λέγοντες·   [2]εἰ ἔξεστιν
Mc 3,4   καὶ λέγει   αὐτοῖς·   ἔξεστιν
Lc 6,9   εἶπεν δὲ ὁ Ἰησοῦς πρὸς αὐτούς·   ἐπερωτῶ ὑμᾶς εἰ ἔξεστιν

     1 : De Solages(c). **(19n)**
     2 : De Solages(d). Cf. Mc 3,2.

Mt 12,12   om.
Mc 3,4   οἱ δὲ ἐσιώπων.
Lc 6,9   om.

     Rushbrooke, Stanton(2), Easton, Schmid.

Mt 12,12   om.
Mc 3,5   καὶ περιβλεψάμενος   αὐτοὺς μετ᾽ ὀργῆς, συλλυπούμενος ἐπὶ τῇ πωρώσει
     τῆς καρδίας αὐτῶν,
Lc 6,10   καὶ περιβλεψάμενος πάντας αὐτούς

     Wilke, Simons, Rushbrooke, Wright, Wernle, Hawkins(IAb), Stanton(2),
     Easton, Schmid(32), Vaganay, Boismard(McR).

Mt 12,13   ἔκτεινόν σου τὴν χεῖρα.
Mc 3,5   ἔκτεινον   τὴν χεῖρα.
Lc 6,10   ἔκτεινον   τὴν χεῖρά σου.

     Simons, Veit, Wernle, Easton, Schmid(33), Keech. **23**
     Mc χειρα : χ. σου H(h χειρα) Ru s¹(s² σου τ. χ.).

Mt 12,14   ἐξελθόντες [1]δὲ οἱ Φαρισαῖοι
Mc 3,6   καὶ ἐξελθόντες οἱ Φαρισαῖοι [2]εὐθὺς [3]μετὰ τῶν Ἡρῳδιανῶν
Lc 6,11   αὐτοὶ   δὲ ἐπλήσθησαν ἀνοίας,

     1 : Rushbrooke, Easton, De Solages(a), Keech. **1**
     2 : Rushbrooke, Stephenson, Easton, Schmid(10). **26**
     3 : Wilke(t), Simons, Rushbrooke, Wright, Wernle, Stanton(1 vel 2), Easton,
     Schmid.

Mt 12,14	συμβούλιον ἔλαβον	κατ' αὐτοῦ,
Mc 3,6	συμβούλιον ἐδίδουν	κατ' αὐτοῦ,
Lc 6,11	καὶ διελάλουν πρὸς ἀλλήλους	

Rushbrooke, Schmid(2).

Mc εδιδουν : εποιησαν T h, εποιουν TR.

§ 18b. Mc 3,1-6; Mt 12,9-14; (Lc 14,1-6)

Mt 12,9	καὶ μεταβὰς ἐκεῖθεν ἦλθεν	εἰς τὴν συναγωγὴν αὐτῶν.
Mc 3,1	καὶ	εἰσῆλθεν πάλιν εἰς συναγωγήν.
Lc 14,1	καὶ ἐγένετο	ἐν τῷ ἐλθεῖν αὐτὸν εἰς οἶκόν τινος τῶν ἀρχόντων

Larfeld. **(18)**

Mt 12,10	καὶ ἰδοὺ ἄνθρωπος	χεῖρα	ἔχων ξηράν·
Mc 3,1	καὶ ἦν ἐκεῖ ἄνθρωπος	ἐξηραμμένην ἔχων τὴν χεῖρα·
Lc 14,2	καὶ ἰδοὺ ἄνθρωπός τις ἦν ὑδρωπικὸς	ἔμπροσθεν αὐτοῦ.

Weiss, Larfeld. **25**

Mt 12,10	καὶ ἐπηρώτησαν αὐτὸν	λέγοντες·
Mc 3,2	καὶ παρετήρουν αὐτόν	
Lc 14,3	καὶ ἀποκριθεὶς ὁ Ἰησοῦς εἶπεν πρὸς τοὺς ... λέγων·	

Larfeld. **15a**

Mt 12,10	εἰ ἔξεστιν τοῖς σάββασιν θεραπεῦσαι ;
Mc 3,2	εἰ τοῖς σάββασιν θεραπεύσει αὐτόν,
Lc 14,3	ἔξεστιν τῷ σαββάτῳ θεραπεῦσαι ἢ οὔ ;

Wilke, Weiss, Larfeld.

Mt (12,10)	εἰ ἔξεστιν τοῖς σάββασιν θεραπεῦσαι
Mt 12,12	ὥστε ἔξεστιν τοῖς σάββασιν καλῶς ποιεῖν.
Mc 3,4	ἔξεστιν τοῖς σάββασιν ἀγαθὸν ποιῆσαι
Lc 14,3	ἔξεστιν τῷ σαββάτῳ θεραπεῦσαι

Boismard(q).

Mt 12,11	ὁ δὲ εἶπεν αὐτοῖς· τίς ἔσται ἐξ ὑμῶν ἄνθρωπος ὃς ἕξει πρόβατον ἕν, καὶ ἐὰν ἐμπέσῃ τοῦτο τοῖς σάββασιν εἰς βόθυνον, οὐχὶ κρατήσει αὐτὸ καὶ ἐγερεῖ ;
Mc 3,4	om.
Lc 14,5	καὶ πρὸς αὐτοὺς εἶπεν· τίνος ὑμῶν υἱὸς ἢ βοῦς εἰς φρέαρ πεσεῖται, καὶ οὐκ εὐθέως ἀνασπάσει αὐτὸν ἐν ἡμέρᾳ τοῦ σαββάτου ;

Wilke, Weiss, Veit, Larfeld, Easton, Boismard(q).

§ 19. Mc 3,7-12; Mt (4,24-25); 12,15-16; Lc 6,17-19

Mt 12,15   ὁ δὲ Ἰησοῦς γνοὺς   ἀνεχώρησεν ἐκεῖθεν.
Mc 3,7   καὶ ὁ Ἰησοῦς   μετὰ τῶν μαθητῶν αὐτοῦ ἀνεχώρησεν πρὸς τὴν θάλασσαν·
Lc 6,17   καὶ καταβὰς   μετ' αὐτῶν   ἔστη ἐπὶ τόπου πεδινοῦ,

> Rushbrooke, Wright, Wernle, Stanton(3a), Easton.
> Mc προς τ. θ. : εις τ. θ. Ti T.

Mt (4,25)   καὶ ἠκολούθησαν αὐτῷ [1]ὄχλοι πολλοὶ ἀπὸ τῆς Γαλιλαίας
Mt 12,15   καὶ ἠκολούθησαν αὐτῷ   πολλοί,
Mc 3,7-8   καὶ [2a]πολὺ πλῆθος ἀπὸ τῆς Γαλιλαίας ἠκολούθησεν· καὶ …(8) … [b]πλῆθος πολύ,
          … ἦλθον πρὸς αὐτόν.
Lc 6,17-18 καὶ ὄχλος πολὺς μαθητῶν αὐτοῦ, καὶ πλῆθος πολὺ τοῦ λαοῦ … (18) οἳ ἦλθον

> 1 : Simons, Rushbrooke, Easton, Schmid, De Solages(g), Keech, Brown,
> McLoughlin(DML), Boismard(McR). **32**
> Mt 12,15 πολλοι : οχλοι π. TR Ti s [GNT³](C).
> 2 : Hawkins(IVB,II), Boismard. **34**
> Mc ηκολουθησεν : [GNT³](D) ; -σαν TR T.

Mt 4,25   ἀπὸ τῆς Γαλιλαίας   καὶ   Δεκαπόλεως   καὶ   Ἱεροσολύμων
          καὶ   Ἰουδαίας   καὶ πέραν τοῦ Ἰορδάνου.
Mc 3,7-8   ἀπὸ τῆς Γαλιλαίας … καὶ [1]ἀπὸ   τῆς Ἰουδαίας (8) καὶ ἀπὸ Ἱεροσολύμων
          [2]καὶ ἀπὸ τῆς Ἰδουμαίας [3a]καὶ πέραν τοῦ Ἰορδάνου [b]καὶ περὶ Τύρον καὶ Σ.
Lc 6,17   ἀπὸ   πάσης τῆς Ἰουδαίας   καὶ   Ἱερουσαλὴμ
                          καὶ   τῆς παραλίου Τύρου καὶ Σ.

> 1 : Rushbrooke.
> 2 : Rushbrooke, Wright, Wernle, Easton, Schmid(31), Boismard(McR).
> 3 : Schmid(31), Boismard(McR). **34**

Mt 12,15   om.
Mc 3,9   καὶ εἶπεν τοῖς μαθηταῖς αὐτοῦ ἵνα πλοιάριον προσκαρτερῇ αὐτῷ διὰ τὸν
          ὄχλον, ἵνα μὴ θλίβωσιν αὐτόν·
Lc 6,18   om.

> Rushbrooke, Wright, Wernle(t), Hawkins(III), Allen, Stanton(2), Easton,
> Schmid(30,32), Boismard(McR).

Mt 12,15   [1]καὶ   ἐθεράπευσεν αὐτοὺς [2]πάντας,
Mc 3,10   πολλοὺς [3]γὰρ ἐθεράπευσεν,   [4]ὥστε ἐπιπίπτειν αὐτῷ
Lc 6,19   καὶ   ἰᾶτο   πάντας.

> 1 : Hansen. Cf. 3. **(1)**
> 2 : Abbott(H), Hawkins(IA), Keech.
> 3 : Rushbrooke.
> 4 : Rushbrooke, Wright, Easton.

Mt (4,24)   πάντας τοὺς κακῶς ἔχοντας ποικίλαις ¹νόσοις ²καί
Mc 3,10   ὅσοι εἶχον μάστιγας.
Lc 6,18   καὶ ἰαθῆναι   ἀπὸ τῶν νόσων αὐτῶν, καί

        1 : Rushbrooke, Abbott, Keech. **32**
        2 : νόσοις καί De Solages(g), McLoughlin (Mt 4,24 = Mc 1,34).

Mt 12,15   om.
Mc 3,11   καὶ τὰ πνεύματα τὰ ἀκάθαρτα, ὅταν αὐτὸν ἐθεώρουν, προσέπιπτον αὐτῷ⌉
             καὶ ἔκραζον λέγοντα ὅτι σὺ εἶ ὁ υἱὸς τοῦ θεοῦ.
Lc 6,18   καὶ οἱ ἐνοχλούμενοι ἀπὸ πνευμάτων ἀκαθάρτων ἐθεραπεύοντο·
Lc (4,41)   κραυγάζοντα καὶ λέγοντα ὅτι σὺ εἶ ὁ υἱὸς τοῦ θεοῦ.

        Rushbrooke, Wright, Easton, Schmid, Boismard(McR : ⁊).

Mt 12,16   καὶ   ἐπετίμησεν αὐτοῖς   ἵνα μὴ φανερὸν ¹// αὐτὸν ποιήσωσιν·
Mc 3,12   καὶ ²πολλὰ ἐπετίμα   αὐτοῖς   ἵνα μὴ αὐτὸν φανερὸν   ποιήσωσιν.
Lc (4,41)   καὶ   ἐπιτιμῶν ...,   ὅτι ᾔδεισαν // τὸν χριστὸν αὐτὸν εἶναι.

        1 : Schmid(14), Vaganay. **21A**
        2 : Rushbrooke, Schmid(16). **28**

Mt 5-7   Sermo Jesu.
Mc 3,12(19) om.
Lc 6,20-49   Sermo Jesu.

        Holtzmann, Simons, Cladder, Easton, Keech, Sanders. **35**

§ 20. Mc 3,13-19; (Mt 10,1-4); (Lc 6,12-16)

Mt (5,1)   ἰδὼν ¹δὲ τοὺς ὄχλους   ἀνέβη   εἰς τὸ ὄρος·
Mc 3,13   καὶ   ²ἀναβαίνει   εἰς τὸ ὄρος,
Lc 6,12   ἐγένετο δὲ ἐν ταῖς ἡμέραις ταύταις ἐξελθεῖν αὐτὸν εἰς τὸ ὄρος προσεύξασθαι,

        1 : **1**
        2 : **10**

Mt (5,1)   καὶ ...   προσῆλθαν αὐτῷ ¹οἱ μαθηταὶ αὐτοῦ.
Mc 3,13   καὶ ²ᵃπροσκαλεῖται οὓς ἤθελεν αὐτός, καὶ ᵇἀπῆλθον πρὸς αὐτόν.
Lc 6,13   καὶ ... προσεφώνησεν τοὺς μαθητὰς αὐτοῦ,

        1 : **23**
        2 : Hawkins(II). **34**

Mt 10,1   καὶ προσκαλεσάμενος ¹τοὺς δώδεκα μαθητὰς αὐτοῦ
Mc 3,13   καὶ ²προσκαλεῖται   ³οὓς ἤθελεν αὐτός,   ⁴καὶ ἀπῆλθον πρὸς αὐτόν.
Lc 6,13   προσεφώνησεν   τοὺς   μαθητὰς αὐτοῦ, καὶ ἐκλεξάμενος ἀπ' αὐτῶν δώδεκα,

    1 : Simons, Easton, De Solages(e), Keech. Cf. Mc 6,7.
    2 : Rushbrooke, Hawkins(VI).
    3 : Rushbrooke, Easton.
    4 : Rushbrooke, Easton.

Mt 10,1   τοὺς δώδεκα μαθητὰς αὐτοῦ ἔδωκεν αὐτοῖς
           ἐξουσίαν πνευμάτων ἀκαθάρτων ὥστε ἐκβάλλειν αὐτά,
Mc 3,14-15 καὶ ἐποίησεν δώδεκα ἵνα ὦσιν μετ' αὐτοῦ, καὶ ἵνα ἀποστέλλῃ αὐτοὺς κηρύσσειν
           (15) καὶ ἔχειν ἐξουσίαν ἐκβάλλειν τὰ δαιμόνια·
Lc 6,13   καὶ ἐκλεξάμενος ἀπ' αὐτῶν δώδεκα, οὓς καὶ ἀποστόλους ὠνόμασεν,

    Wright, Veit, Wernle(t), Stanton(2), Easton.

Mt 10,2   τῶν δὲ δώδεκα ¹ἀποστόλων τὰ ὀνόματά ἐστιν ταῦτα·
Mc 3,14.16 ²ᵃκαὶ ἐποίησεν δώδεκα ... ἵνα ἀποστέλλῃ αὐτοὺς ... (16) ᵇκαὶ ἐποίησεν τοὺς
            δώδεκα,
Lc 6,13   οὓς καὶ   ἀποστόλους ὠνόμασεν,

    1 : Easton, Schmid(30), Keech, Brown. **14n**
      Mc δωδεκα : + ους και αποστολους ωνομασεν H Ru [GNT](C).
    2 : Rushbrooke, Wernle(v. 16 : t), Easton.
      Mc και εποιησεν τους δωδεκα : — TR Ti ; [GNT](C).

Mt 10,2   πρῶτος Σίμων   ¹ὁ λεγόμενος   Πέτρος
Mc 3,16   καὶ ἐποίησεν τοὺς δώδεκα, ²καὶ ἐπέθηκεν ὄνομα τῷ Σίμωνι Πέτρον·
Lc 6,14   Σίμωνα,   ὃν καὶ ὠνόμασεν   Πέτρον,

    1 : Vaganay. **16n**
    2 : Rushbrooke, Hawkins(IVb), Schmid, Boismard(McR). **8B**

Mt 10,2-4   Apostoli bini et bini recensentur.
Mc 3,16-19 Tabula duodecim.
Lc 6,14-16 Apostoli bini et bini recensentur.

    Schmid, Vaganay.

Mt 10,2   Σίμων ... καὶ 'Ανδρέας ¹ὁ ἀδελφὸς αὐτοῦ, ²// καὶ 'Ιάκωβος ... καὶ 'Ιωάννης
Mc 3,16-18 Σίμωνι ... (17) καὶ 'Ιάκωβον ...   καὶ 'Ιωάννην ... (18) καὶ 'Ανδρέαν
Lc 6,14   Σίμωνα... καὶ 'Ανδρέαν τὸν ἀδελφὸν αὐτοῦ, // καὶ 'Ιάκωβον   καὶ 'Ιωάννην,

    1 : Wilke, Holtzmann, Simons, Rushbrooke, Veit, Abbott, Burton, Stanton(3b),

Streeter(d), Easton, Schmid, Da Fonseca, De Solages(d), Keech, McLough-
lin(MI).   **23**
2 : Wilke, Holtzmann, Weiss(or), Simons, Wright, Veit, Wernle, Stanton(3b),
Streeter(d), Easton, Schmid, Chapman, Vaganay, Keech, Boismard(McR).
21B

Mt 10,2   Ἰάκωβος ὁ   τοῦ Ζεβεδαίου καὶ Ἰωάννης ὁ   ἀδελφὸς αὐτοῦ,
Mc 3,17   Ἰάκωβον τὸν τοῦ Ζεβεδαίου καὶ Ἰωάννην τὸν ἀδελφὸν ¹τοῦ Ἰακώβου,
           ²καὶ ἐπέθηκεν αὐτοῖς ὄνομα Βοανηργές, ὅ ἐστιν υἱοὶ βροντῆς·
Lc 6,14   Ἰάκωβον   καὶ Ἰωάννην,

1 : Rushbrooke, Hawkins(II), Schmid(31).
2 : Wilke(t), Holtzmann, Rushbrooke, Wright, Wernle, Hawkins(III,IVB), Allen,
Stanton(1 vel 2), Easton, Schmid(1,13,31), Vaganay, Keech, Boismard(McR).

Mt 10,3-4   καὶ (Λεββαῖος), (4) Σίμων ὁ   Καναναῖος
Mc 3,18   καὶ Θαδδαῖον   καὶ Σίμωνα τὸν Καναναῖον
Lc 6,15-16   καὶ Σίμωνα τὸν καλούμενον ζηλωτήν, (16) καὶ Ἰούδαν

Mt Θαδδαιος : Λεββαιος Ti T hʳ¹ ; Λεββαιος ο επικληθεις Θαδδαιος TR hʳ² S.

Mt 10,4   καὶ Ἰούδας ὁ Ἰσκαριώτης ὁ   καὶ   παραδοὺς   αὐτόν.
Mc 3,19   καὶ Ἰούδαν   Ἰσκαριώθ, ὃς καὶ   παρέδωκεν αὐτόν.
Lc 6,16   καὶ Ἰούδαν   Ἰσκαριώθ, ὃς   ἐγένετο προδότης.

Hansen.

§ 21. Mc 3,20-21

Mt   om.
Mc 3,20-21   καὶ ἔρχεται εἰς οἶκον· καὶ συνέρχεται πάλιν ὁ ὄχλος, ὥστε μὴ δύνασθαι αὐτοὺς
             μηδὲ ἄρτον φαγεῖν. (21) καὶ ἀκούσαντες οἱ παρ᾽ αὐτοῦ ἐξῆλθον κρατῆσαι αὐτόν·
             ἔλεγον γὰρ ὅτι ἐξέστη.
Lc   om.

Rushbrooke, Wright, Wernle, Hawkins(III), Allen, Stanton(3a vel 2), Schmid
(32), Vaganay, Keech, Boismard(Mc).

§ 22. Mc 3,22-30; Mt 12,22-32; (Lc 11,14-23)

Mt 12,22   τότε προσηνέχθη αὐτῷ ¹δαιμονιζόμενος τυφλὸς   καὶ κωφός·
Mt (9,32-33) ἰδοὺ προσήνεγκαν αὐτῷ κωφὸν δαιμονιζόμενον. (33) καὶ ²ἐκβληθέντος
Mc 3,22   om.
Lc 11,14   καὶ ἦν ἐκβάλλων δαιμόνιον, καὶ αὐτὸ ἦν κωφόν·... τοῦ δαιμονίου

1 : Simons, Veit, Abbott, Stephenson, Chapman, De Solages(Q), Keech.
2 : Simpson.

Mt 12,22   καὶ ἐθεράπευσεν αὐτόν, ὥστε τὸν κωφὸν   λαλεῖν καὶ βλέπειν.
Mt (9,33)   καὶ ἐκβληθέντος τοῦ δαιμονίου   ἐλάλησεν ὁ κωφός.
Mc 3,22   om.
Lc 11,14   ἐγένετο δὲ   τοῦ δαιμονίου ἐξελθόντος ἐλάλησεν ὁ κωφός·

        Simons, Veit, Abbott, Stephenson, Larfeld, Chapman, De Solages(Q), Keech.
        (ἐκβληθέντος) : Larfeld.
        Lc εξελθοντος : εκβληθεντος (C A φ al lat) Lachmann.

Mt 12,23   καὶ ἐξίσταντο πάντες οἱ ὄχλοι
Mt (9,33)   καὶ ἐθαύμασαν   οἱ ὄχλοι
Mc 3,22   om.
Lc 11,14   καὶ ἐθαύμασαν   οἱ ὄχλοι·

        Simons, Veit, Abbott, Stephenson, Larfeld, Chapman, De Solages(Q), Keech.

Mt 12,24   οἱ [1]δὲ Φαρισαῖοι   ἀκούσαντες   [2]εἶπον·
Mt (9,34)   οἱ δὲ Φαρισαῖοι   ἔλεγον·
Mc 3,22   καὶ οἱ   γραμματεῖς [3]οἱ ἀπὸ Ἱεροσολύμων καταβάντες ἔλεγον
Lc 11,15   τινὲς δὲ ἐξ αὐτῶν   εἶπαν·

        1 : Simons, Rushbrooke, Veit, Abbott(VI), Larfeld, Chapman, De Solages(Q),
          Keech. 1
          Mt 9,34 : [H], — NEB.
        2 : Simons, Rushbrooke, Veit, Abbott(V), Larfeld, Chapman, De Solages(Q),
          Keech. 11
          Lc ειπαν : ειπον TR Ti T S.
        3 : Wilke, Rushbrooke, Schmid(32), Keech.

Mt 12,24   εἰ μὴ [1]ἐν τῷ Βεεζεβοὺλ   ἄρχοντι τῶν δαιμονίων.
Mt (9,34)   ἐν τῷ ἄρχοντι τῶν δαιμονίων
Mc 3,22   [2]ὅτι Βεεζεβοὺλ ἔχει, καὶ ὅτι ἐν τῷ ἄρχοντι τῶν δαιμονίων
Lc 11,15   ἐν   Βεεζεβοὺλ   τῷ ἄρχοντι τῶν δαιμονίων

        1 : Veit, Stephenson, Keech.
        2 : Rushbrooke, Schmid(21), Keech. 5 34

Mt 12,25   [1]εἰδὼς δὲ τὰς ἐνθυμήσεις αὐτῶν   [2]εἶπεν αὐτοῖς·
Mc 3,23   καὶ [3]προσκαλεσάμενος αὐτοὺς ἐν παραβολαῖς ἔλεγεν αὐτοῖς·
Lc 11,17   αὐτὸς δὲ εἰδὼς αὐτῶν τὰ διανοήματα   εἶπεν αὐτοῖς·

        1 : Weiss, Simons, Rushbrooke, Wright, Veit, Abbott(H,VI), Stephenson,
          Streeter(q), Chapman, De Solages(Q), Keech, Simpson. 1
        2 : Simons, Rushbrooke, Veit, Wernle, Abbott(V), Stephenson, Streeter(q),
          Chapman, De Solages(Q), Keech, Simpson. 11
        3 : Rushbrooke, Hawkins(III), Schmid(32), Keech.

Mt(12,26)   καὶ εἰ ὁ σατανᾶς τὸν σατανᾶν ἐκβάλλει,

Mt 12,25   om.

Mc 3,23   ⌜πῶς δύναται⌝ σατανᾶς σατανᾶν ἐκβάλλειν ;

Lc 11,17   om.

     Rushbrooke (⌜⌝), Keech.

Mt 12,25   ¹πᾶσα βασιλεία μερισθεῖσα καθ᾽ ἑαυτῆς ἐρημοῦται,

Mc 3,24   ²καὶ ἐὰν βασιλεία ἐφ᾽ ἑαυτὴν μερισθῇ, ³οὐ δύναται σταθῆναι ἡ βασιλεία ἐκείνη·

Lc 11,17   πᾶσα βασιλεία ἐφ᾽ ἑαυτὴν διαμερισθεῖσα ἐρημοῦται,

     1 : Simons, Rushbrooke, Abbott(H), Stephenson, Streeter(q), Chapman, De Solages(Q), Keech, Simpson.
     Lc (διαμερισθεῖσα /ἐφ᾽ ἑαυτήν) : Veit.
     Lc εφ εαυτην διαμερισθεισα : 3 1-2 T h S.
     2 : Rushbrooke, Keech.
     3 : Rushbrooke, Keech.

Mt 12,26   καὶ εἰ ὁ σατανᾶς τὸν σατανᾶν ἐκβάλλει,   ἐφ᾽ ἑαυτὸν ἐμερίσθη·

Mc 3,26   καὶ εἰ ὁ σατανᾶς ¹ἀνέστη ἐφ᾽ ἑαυτὸν ²καὶ   ἐμερίσθη,

Lc 11,18   εἰ δὲ καὶ ὁ σατανᾶς   ἐφ᾽ ἑαυτὸν διεμερίσθη,

     1 : Holtzmann, Rushbrooke.
     2 : Rushbrooke, Keech.
     Mc εφ εαυτον και εμερισθη, ου : εφ εαυτον εμ., και ου T ; εμερισθη : μεμερισται TR Ti S.

Mt 12,26   ¹πῶς οὖν σταθήσεται ἡ βασιλεία αὐτοῦ ;

Mc 3,26   ²οὐ δύναται στῆναι   ἀλλὰ τέλος ἔχει.

Lc 11,18   πῶς σταθήσεται ἡ βασιλεία αὐτοῦ ;

     1 : Simons, Rushbrooke, Veit, Stephenson, Streeter(q), Chapman, De Solages(Q), Keech.
     2 : Rushbrooke, Hawkins(V), Keech. **9B**

Mt 12,27   καὶ εἰ ἐγὼ ἐν Βεεζεβοὺλ ἐκβάλλω τὰ δαιμόνια, οἱ υἱοὶ ὑμῶν ἐν τίνι ἐκβάλλουσιν ; διὰ τοῦτο αὐτοὶ κριταὶ ἔσονται ὑμῶν.

Mc 3,26   om.

Lc 11,19   εἰ δὲ ἐγὼ ἐν Βεεζεβοὺλ ἐκβάλλω τὰ δαιμόνια, οἱ υἱοὶ ὑμῶν ἐν τίνι ἐκβάλλουσιν ; διὰ τοῦτο αὐτοὶ ὑμῶν κριταὶ ἔσονται.

     Rushbrooke, Chapman, De Solages(Q), Keech, Sanders.

Mt 12,28   εἰ δὲ ἐν πνεύματι θεοῦ ἐγὼ ἐκβάλλω τὰ δαιμόνια, ἄρα ἔφθασεν ἐφ᾽ ὑμᾶς ἡ βασιλεία τοῦ θεοῦ.

Mc 3,26   om.

Lc 11,20   εἰ δὲ ἐν δακτύλῳ θεοῦ [ἐγὼ] ἐκβάλλω τὰ δαιμόνια, ἄρα ἔφθασεν ἐφ᾽ ὑμᾶς ἡ βασιλεία τοῦ θεοῦ.

     Rushbrooke, Chapman, De Solages(Q), Keech, Sanders.

Mt 12,29   ἢ πῶς δύναται..., ἐὰν μὴ πρῶτον δήσῃ [1]/ τὸν ἰσχυρόν ;
Mc 3,27   [2]ἀλλ' οὐ δύναται..., ἐὰν μὴ πρῶτον τὸν ἰσχυρὸν δήσῃ,
Lc 11,21-22 ὅταν...·   (22) ἐπὰν δὲ... ἐπελθὼν νικήσῃ / αὐτόν,

          1 : Veit. 21
          2 : 9A

Mt 12,30   ὁ μὴ ὢν μετ' ἐμοῦ κατ' ἐμοῦ ἐστιν, καὶ ὁ μὴ συνάγων μετ' ἐμοῦ σκορπίζει.
Mc 3,27   om.
Lc 11,23   ὁ μὴ ὢν μετ' ἐμοῦ κατ' ἐμοῦ ἐστιν, καὶ ὁ μὴ συνάγων μετ' ἐμοῦ σκορπίζει.

          Rushbrooke, Veit, Abbott, Stephenson, Chapman, Da Fonseca, De Solages(Q),
          Keech, Simpson, Sanders.

Mt 12,31   om.
Mc 3,28   ὅσα ἐὰν βλασφημήσωσιν·
Lc (12,10) om.

          Rushbrooke, Hawkins(II), Boismard(McR).

Mt 12,32   καὶ ὃς ἐὰν εἴπῃ λόγον κατὰ τοῦ υἱοῦ τοῦ ἀνθρώπου, ἀφεθήσεται αὐτῷ·
Mc 3,28   om.
Lc (12,10) καὶ πᾶς ὃς ἐρεῖ λόγον εἰς τὸν υἱὸν τοῦ ἀνθρώπου, ἀφεθήσεται αὐτῷ·

          Simons, Rushbrooke, Abbott(H), Streeter(q), Chapman, Da Fonseca, De
          Solages(Q), Keech.

Mt 12,32   οὐκ [1]ἀφεθήσεται αὐτῷ οὔτε ἐν τούτῳ τῷ αἰῶνι οὔτε ἐν τῷ μέλλοντι.
Mc 3,29   οὐκ [2]ἔχει ἄφεσιν [3]εἰς τὸν αἰῶνα, [4]ἀλλὰ ἔνοχός ἐστιν αἰωνίου ἁμαρτήματος.
Lc (12,10) οὐκ ἀφεθήσεται.

          1 : Simons, Rushbrooke, Abbott(H), Chapman, De Solages(Q), Keech, Bois-
              mard(McR).
          2 : Rushbrooke, Boismard(McR).
          3 : Rushbrooke, Boismard(McR).
          4 : Rushbrooke, Hawkins(IC,V), Wright, Boismard(McR). 9B

Mt   om.
Mc 3,30   ὅτι ἔλεγον· πνεῦμα ἀκάθαρτον ἔχει.
Lc   om.

          Wilke, Rushbrooke, Wright, Hawkins(II), Schmid(31).

§ 23. Mc 3,31-35; Mt 12,46-50; (Lc 8,19-21)

Mt 12,46   [1]ἔτι (δὲ) αὐτοῦ λαλοῦντος τοῖς ὄχλοις, ἰδοὺ   ἡ μήτηρ
Mc 3,31   [2]καὶ   [3]ἔρχονται ἡ μήτηρ [4]αὐτοῦ
Lc 8,19   παρεγένετο δὲ πρὸς αὐτὸν ἡ μήτηρ
Lc (11,27) ἐγένετο δὲ ἐν τῷ λέγειν αὐτὸν ταῦτα ...γυνὴ ἐκ τοῦ ὄχλου

1 : Weiss.
   Mt ετι : ε. δε TR S.
2 : Rushbrooke.
   Mc και ερχονται : ε. ουν TR.
3 : Rushbrooke, Hawkins(VI), Schmid(5). **10**
   Mc ερχονται : -εται T GNT ; ερχονται οι αδελφοι και η μητηρ αυτου TR Ti
   (+ αυτου) S.
4 : Weiss, Rushbrooke, Hawkins(II), Easton, Schmid, Keech. **(22n)**
   Lc μητηρ : μ. αυτου T.

Mt 12,46   ¹εἰστήκεισαν ἔξω   ζητοῦντες   ²αὐτῷ λαλῆσαι.
Mc 3,31   καὶ ἔξω στήκοντες ³ἀπέστειλαν πρὸς αὐτὸν καλοῦντες αὐτόν.
Lc 8,19-20   καὶ οὐκ ἠδύναντο   συντυχεῖν   αὐτῷ διὰ τὸν ὄχλον.(20) ... ἐστήκασιν ἔξω

   1 : Simons, Schmid.
   2 : Veit, De Solages(b).
   3 : Rushbrooke.

Mt 12,46   om.
Mc 3,32   καὶ ἐκάθητο περὶ αὐτὸν ὄχλος,
Lc 8,19   διὰ τὸν ὄχλον.

   Wilke(r), Rushbrooke, Schmid(32).

Mt [12,47]   [εἶπεν ¹δέ τις αὐτῷ· ... καὶ οἱ ἀδελφοί σου]
Mc 3,32   καὶ ²λέγουσιν αὐτῷ· ... καὶ οἱ ἀδελφοί σου ³καὶ αἱ ἀδελφαί σου
Lc 8,20   ἀπηγγέλη δὲ αὐτῷ· ... καὶ οἱ ἀδελφοί σου

   1 : Rushbrooke, Hawkins(VII), Abbott, Easton, Schmid(4), De Solages(a), Keech.
     1
   2 : Rushbrooke, Hawkins(VI), Easton. **10 22n**
   3 : Weiss, Simons, Hawkins(III), Easton, Keech.
     Mc και αι αδελφαι σου : — TR H(h+) Ru GNT¹ ²(B) ; [GNT³](C).

Mt [12,47]   [ἔξω ἑστήκασιν ζητοῦντές σοι λαλῆσαι.]
Mc 3,32   ἔξω   ζητοῦσίν σε.
Lc 8,20   ἑστήκασιν ἔξω ἰδεῖν θέλοντές σε.

   Wilke, Holtzmann, Weiss, Rushbrooke, Veit, Abbott, Stanton(4), Easton,
   Chapman, De Solages(f), Keech.

Mt 12,48   ¹ὁ δὲ ἀποκριθεὶς ²εἶπεν ³/ τῷ λέγοντι αὐτῷ·
Mc 3,33   καὶ ἀποκριθεὶς ⁴αὐτοῖς λέγει·
Lc 8,21   ὁ δὲ ἀποκριθεὶς εἶπεν / πρὸς αὐτούς·

   1 : Wilke, Holtzmann, Weiss(r), Simons, Rushbrooke, Veit, Abbott(VI),
     Easton, Schmid(4), Chapman, De Solages(d,a), Keech. **1 22**
   2 : Wilke, Holtzmann, Weiss(r), Simons, Rushbrooke, Veit, Abbott(V), Easton,
     Schmid(5), Chapman, De Solages(a), Keech. Cf. Mc 3,34.
     Wilke : Mc καὶ ἀπεκρίθη αὐτοῖς.
     Mc αποκριθεις ... λεγει : απεκριθη ... λεγων TR S.
   3 : Veit. **21A**
   4 : Simons, Keech.

Mt 12,49   καὶ ἐκτείνας τὴν χεῖρα αὐτοῦ ἐπὶ τοὺς μαθητὰς αὐτοῦ [1]εἶπεν·
Mc 3,34   καὶ [2]περιβλεψάμενος τοὺς περὶ αὐτὸν κύκλῳ καθημένους λέγει·
Lc 8,21   ὁ δὲ ἀποκριθεὶς   εἶπεν πρὸς αὐτούς·

> 1 : Hawkins(VI), Schmid(5). **10**
> 2 : Rushbrooke, Hawkins(III), Easton, Schmid(32).

§ 24. Mc 4,1-9; Mt 13,1-9; Lc 8,4-8

Mt 13,1   ἐν τῇ ἡμέρᾳ ἐκείνῃ ἐξελθὼν ὁ Ἰησοῦς τῆς οἰκίας ἐκάθητο παρὰ τὴν θάλασσαν·
Mc 4,1   καὶ πάλιν   ἤρξατο διδάσκειν παρὰ τὴν θάλασσαν·
Lc 8,4   συνιόντος δέ

> Rushbrooke, Wernle, Easton, Schmid(4 : καί; 11 : πάλιν). **2 27**

Mt 13,2   καὶ συνήχθησαν πρὸς αὐτὸν ὄχλοι [1]πολλοί,
Mc 4,1   καὶ [2]συνάγεται   πρὸς αὐτὸν ὄχλος πλεῖστος,
Lc 8,4   συνιόντος δὲ   ὄχλου πολλοῦ καὶ ... ἐπιπορευομένων πρὸς αὐτόν

> 1 : Rushbrooke, Veit, Abbott(VII), Stanton(3b), Easton, Schmid, Keech, Brown. **32**
> 2 : Rushbrooke, Hawkins(VI), Schmid(5). **10**

Mt 13,3   καὶ ἐλάλησεν αὐτοῖς πολλὰ ἐν παραβολαῖς   λέγων·
Mc 4,2   καὶ [1]ἐδίδασκεν αὐτοὺς ἐν παραβολαῖς πολλά, καὶ [2]ἔλεγεν
Lc 8,4   εἶπεν   διὰ παραβολῆς·

> 1 : Rushbrooke, Allen, Schmid(6). **11**
> 2 : Rushbrooke. Cf. 1.

Mt 13,3   λέγων·
Mc 4,2-3 καὶ ἔλεγεν [1]αὐτοῖς [2]ἐν τῇ διδαχῇ αὐτοῦ·⌉(3) [3]ἀκούετε.
Lc 8,4   εἶπεν διὰ παραβολῆς·

> 1 : Rushbrooke, Wernle, Hawkins(II,V), Easton, Keech.
> 2 : Schmid(31).
> 3 : Holtzmann.

Mt 13,3   ἰδοὺ ἐξῆλθεν ὁ σπείρων τοῦ σπείρειν.
Mc 4,3   ἰδοὺ ἐξῆλθεν ὁ σπείρων   σπεῖραι.
Lc 8,5   ἐξῆλθεν ὁ σπείρων τοῦ σπεῖραι τὸν σπόρον αὐτοῦ.

> Weiss, Simons, Rushbrooke, Wright, Veit, Wernle, Abbott(VII), Stanton(3b), Easton, Schmid, De Solages(f), Keech, Brown, Boismard(Mt). **(33b)**
> Mc : + τοῦ TR s.

Mt 13,4   καὶ   ἐν τῷ σπείρειν [1]αὐτόν
Mc 4,4   καὶ [2]ἐγένετο ἐν τῷ σπείρειν
Lc 8,5   καὶ   ἐν τῷ σπείρειν αὐτόν

1 : Weiss, Simons, Rushbrooke, Wright, Veit, Abbott(I), Stanton(3b), Easton,
    Schmid(33), De Solages(d), Keech. **22**
2 : Simons, Rushbrooke, Easton, Schmid, Keech, Turner, Boismard(McR).

Mt 13,4   καὶ ἐλθόντα τὰ πετεινὰ   κατέφαγεν αὐτά.
Mc 4,4   καὶ ἦλθεν   τὰ πετεινὰ   καὶ κατέφαγεν αὐτό.
Lc 8,5   καὶ   τὰ πετεινὰ τοῦ οὐρανοῦ   κατέφαγεν αὐτό.

Schmid(7).
Mt ελθοντα τα πετεινα : ηλθον τ. π. και h, ηλθεν τ. π. και TR T.

Mt 13,7   ἐπὶ τὰς ἀκάνθας,   καὶ ... [1]ἀπέπνιξαν αὐτά.
Mc 4,7   [8]εἰς τὰς ἀκάνθας,   καὶ ... συνέπνιξαν αὐτό, [3]καὶ καρπὸν οὐκ ἔδωκεν.
Lc 8,7   ἐν μέσῳ τῶν ἀκανθῶν, καὶ ... ἀπέπνιξαν αὐτό.

1 : Simons, Easton, Schmid(20), De Solages(c), Keech. **31c**
    Mt απεπνιξαν : επνιξαν T h Ru S GNT.
2 : Rushbrooke.
3 : Wilke(t), Holtzmann, Simons, Rushbrooke, Wernle, Hawkins(II), Easton,
    Schmid(31), Keech, Boismard(Mt).

Mt 13,8   καὶ   ἐδίδου καρπόν,
Mc 4,8   καὶ   ἐδίδου καρπὸν [1]ἀναβαίνοντα καὶ αὐξανόμενα [2]καὶ ἔφερεν
Lc 8,8   καὶ φυὲν ἐποίησεν καρπόν

1 : Holtzmann, Rushbrooke, Wernle, Hawkins(II,V), Easton, Schmid(1,31),
    Keech.
    Mc αυξανομενα : -ενον TR Ti T S.
2 : Rushbrooke, Easton, Keech. **34**

Mt 13,8   ὃ μὲν ἑκατόν, ὃ δὲ ἑξήκοντα, ὃ δὲ τριάκοντα.
Mc 4,8   εἰς τριάκοντα καὶ ἐν ἑξήκοντα καὶ ἐν ἑκατόν.
Lc 8,8   ἑκατονταπλασίονα.

Rushbrooke, Hawkins(IVb).
Mc εις ... εν ... εν : ter εις Ti T h[1], ter εἱς S, ter ἕν TR, GNT(C) εἰς ... ἕν ... ἕν ... h[2].

Mt 13,9   [1]ὃ ἔχων ὦτα   ἀκουέτω.
Mc 4,9   [2]καὶ ἔλεγεν·   ὃς ἔχει ὦτα ἀκούειν ἀκουέτω.
Lc 8,8   ταῦτα λέγων ἐφώνει· ὁ ἔχων ὦτα ἀκούειν ἀκουέτω.

1 : Weiss, Rushbrooke, Veit, Wernle, Abbott(IV), Stanton(3b), Easton,
    Schmid, Chapman, De Solages(e,b), Keech, Brown, Turner. **14n**
2 : Rushbrooke.

§ 25. Mc 4,10-12; Mt 13,10-15; Lc 8,9-10

Mt 13,10   καὶ   προσελθόντες οἱ ¹μαθηταὶ   εἶπαν αὐτῷ·
Mc 4,10   καὶ ²ὅτε ἐγένετο κατὰ μόνας, ἠρώτων αὐτὸν οἱ ³περὶ αὐτὸν ⁴σὺν τοῖς δώδεκα
Lc 8,9   ἐπηρώτων δὲ αὐτὸν οἱ μαθηταὶ αὐτοῦ

1 : Weiss(r), Simons, Rushbrooke, Veit, Wernle(t), Abbott(H), Burton, Stanton (1 vel 3b), Streeter(d), Easton, Schmid(30), Chapman, Glasson, De Solages (e), Keech, Brown, McLoughlin(MLRI), Boismard(McR).
2 : Wilke, Rushbrooke, Wright, Stanton(1 vel 3b), Easton, Schmid(32), Boismard(McR).
3 : Rushbrooke.
4 : Wilke(t), Rushbrooke.

Mt 13,10   εἶπαν   αὐτῷ·   διὰ ¹τί   ἐν παραβολαῖς λαλεῖς ... ;
Mc 4,10   ἠρώτων   αὐτὸν ...   ²τὰς παραβολάς.
Lc 8,9   ἐπηρώτων δὲ αὐτὸν ...   τίς αὕτη εἴη ἡ παραβολή.

1 : De Solages(e).
2 : Rushbrooke, Schmid.
    Mc τας παραβολας : την -λην TR S.

Mt 13,11   ¹ὁ δὲ ἀποκριθεὶς ²εἶπεν·
Mc 4,11   καὶ   ἔλεγεν ³αὐτοῖς·
Lc 8,10   ὁ δὲ   εἶπεν·

1 : Weiss(r), Simons, Rushbrooke, Veit, Hawkins(VII), Abbott(VI), Easton, Schmid(4), De Solages(d,a), Keech, Boismard(McR). **1 22**
2 : Weiss(r), Simons, Rushbrooke, Veit, Wernle, Abbott(V), Easton, Schmid(6), De Solages(a), Keech, Boismard(McR). **11**
3 : Weiss(r), Rushbrooke, Easton, Schmid, Keech, Boismard(McR).
    Mt ειπεν : ε. αυτοις TR Ti h GNT. **(23)**

Mt 13,11   ὑμῖν δέδοται ¹//²γνῶναι ³τὰ μυστήρια τῆς βασιλείας τῶν οὐρανῶν,
Mc 4,11   ὑμῖν τὸ μυστήριον δέδοται   τῆς βασιλείας τοῦ θεοῦ·
Lc 8,10   ὑμῖν δέδοται // γνῶναι   τὰ μυστήρια τῆς βασιλείας τοῦ θεοῦ,

1 : Weiss(r /or), Simons, Wright, Veit, Hawkins(*), Easton, Keech, Brown, Boismard. **21B**
2 : Weiss(r /or), Simons, Rushbrooke, Wright, Veit, Wernle(t), Hawkins(*), Abbott(VII), Stanton(3a vel 3b), Lagrange, Streeter(d), Schmid, Chapman, Glasson, Da Fonseca, De Solages(f), Keech, Brown, McLoughlin(RI). **24**
3 : Wilke, Holtzmann, Weiss(r /or), Simons, Rushbrooke, Veit, Wernle, Hawkins(*), Abbott(VII), Stanton(3a vel 3b), Lagrange, Streeter(t), Easton, Schmid, Chapman, Glasson, Da Fonseca, De Solages(b), Keech, Brown, McLoughlin(RI), Boismard(McR). **33c**

Mt 13,11.13   ἐκείνοις δὲ ...(13)... ἐν παραβολαῖς αὐτοῖς λαλῶ,
Mc 4,11   ἐκείνοις δὲ ¹τοῖς ἔξω ἐν παραβολαῖς ²τὰ πάντα γίνεται,
Lc 8,10   τοῖς δὲ λοιποῖς ἐν παραβολαῖς,

        1 : Wilke, Holtzmann, Rushbrooke, Schmid, Boismard(McR).
        2 : Rushbrooke, Easton, Schmid, Boismard(McR).

Mt 13,13   ὅτι βλέποντες   ¹οὐ βλέπουσιν
           καὶ ἀκούοντες   οὐκ ἀκούουσιν οὐδὲ συνίουσιν.
Mc 4,12   ἵνα βλέποντες ²βλέπωσιν καὶ μὴ ἴδωσιν,
           καὶ ἀκούοντες ²ἀκούωσιν καὶ μὴ συνιῶσιν,
Lc 8,10   ἵνα βλέποντες   μὴ βλέπωσιν
           καὶ ἀκούοντες   μὴ συνιῶσιν.

        1 : Veit, Easton, Keech.
        2 : Schmid(7), Boismard(McR).

Mt 13,15   μήποτε ... καὶ ἐπιστρέψωσιν, καὶ ἰάσομαι αὐτούς.
Mc 4,12   μήποτε   ἐπιστρέψωσιν καὶ ἀφεθῇ αὐτοῖς.
Lc 8,10   om.

        Boismard(McR).

§ 26. Mc 4,13-20; Mt 13,18-23; Lc 8,11-15

Mt 13,18   om.
Mc 4,13   καὶ λέγει αὐτοῖς·
Lc 8,11   om.

        Rushbrooke.

Mt 13,18   ὑμεῖς οὖν ἀκούσατε τὴν παραβολὴν τοῦ σπείραντος.
Mc 4,13   οὐκ οἴδατε   τὴν παραβολὴν ταύτην,
           καὶ πῶς πάσας τὰς παραβολὰς γνώσεσθε ;
Lc 8,11   ἔστιν δὲ αὕτη   ἡ παραβολή.

        Wilke, Rushbrooke, Wright, Wernle, Hawkins(IB), Allen, Schmid, Vaganay,
        Keech.

Mt 13,19   παντὸς ἀκούοντος τὸν λόγον ¹τῆς βασιλείας
Mc 4,14   ὁ σπείρων   τὸν λόγον   ²σπείρει.
Lc 8,11   ὁ σπόρος ἐστὶν   ὁ λόγος τοῦ θεοῦ.

        1 : De Solages(d).   **23**
        2 : Rushbrooke.

Mt 13,19   παντὸς ¹ἀκούοντος τὸν λόγον τῆς βασιλείας
Mc 4,15   ²ὅπου σπείρεται ὁ λόγος, ³καὶ ὅταν ἀκούσωσιν,
Lc 8,12   οἱ   ἀκούσαντες,

    1 : Hansen. **14n**
    2 : Weiss(r), Simons, Rushbrooke, Hawkins(II), Easton, Schmid(13), Boismard
        (McR).
    3 : Simons, Rushbrooke, Wernle.

Mt 13,19   ἔρχεται ὁ πονηρός
Mc 4,15   ¹εὐθὺς ἔρχεται ὁ ²σατανᾶς
Lc 8,12   εἶτα ἔρχεται ὁ διάβολος

    1 : Rushbrooke, Stephenson, Schmid(10). **26**
    2 : Rushbrooke, Schmid(1). **32**

Mt 13,19   καὶ ἁρπάζει   τὸ ἐσπαρμένον ἐν ¹τῇ καρδίᾳ αὐτοῦ·
Mc 4,15   καὶ αἴρει   ²ᵃτὸν λόγον ᵇτὸν ἐσπαρμένον ³εἰς αὐτούς.
Lc 8,12   καὶ αἴρει   τὸν λόγον   ἀπὸ τῆς καρδίας αὐτῶν,

    1 : Simons, Rushbrooke, Veit, Wernle(t), Abbott(H), Stanton(3b vel 2), Easton,
        Schmid(33), De Solages(e), Keech, Brown.
    2 : Rushbrooke, Schmid. **(23) 34**
    3 : Rushbrooke.
        Mc εις αυτους : εν αυτοις T S, εν ταις καρδιαις αυτων TR s.

Mt 13,20   ὁ ¹δὲ   ἐπὶ τὰ πετρώδη σπαρείς, οὗτός ἐστιν ὁ
Mc 4,16   καὶ οὗτοί εἰσιν ²ὁμοίως οἱ ἐπὶ τὰ πετρώδη σπειρόμενοι,   οἳ ὅταν
Lc 8,13   οἱ δὲ   ἐπὶ τῆς πέτρας   οἳ ὅταν

    1 : Simons, Rushbrooke, Veit, Abbott(VI), Easton, Schmid(4), De Solages(a),
        Keech. **1**
    2 : Simons, Rushbrooke, Hawkins(II), Easton, Schmid(31), Glasson.
        Mc ομοιως : — GNT(B).

Mt 13,21   γενομένης δὲ θλίψεως ἢ διωγμοῦ
Mc 4,17   εἶτα γενομένης   θλίψεως ἢ διωγμοῦ
Lc 8,13   καὶ ἐν καιρῷ πειρασμοῦ

             Rushbrooke.

Mt 13,22   ¹ὁ δὲ   εἰς τὰς ἀκάνθας σπαρείς,
Mc 4,18   ²καὶ ἄλλοι εἰσὶν οἱ εἰς τὰς ἀκάνθας σπειρόμενοι·
Lc 8,14   τὸ δὲ   εἰς τὰς ἀκάνθας πεσόν,

    1 : Simons, Rushbrooke, Veit, Hawkins(VII), Abbott(VI), Easton, Schmid(4),
        De Solages(a), Keech. **1 (23c)**
        εἰς (ἐπί in Mc) : Veit, Easton.
        Mc εις : επι T S.
    2 : Rushbrooke.

Mt 13,22   καὶ ἡ ἀπάτη τοῦ [1]πλούτου
Mc 4,19   καὶ ἡ ἀπάτη τοῦ (κόσμου) καὶ [2]αἱ περὶ τὰ λοιπὰ ἐπιθυμίαι
Lc 8,14   καὶ   πλούτου καὶ ἡδονῶν τοῦ βίου

> 1 : Turner.
> Mc πλουτου : κοσμου (D Θ pc it).
> 2 : Wilke(t), Holtzmann, Rushbrooke, Wernle(t), Schmid(31), Keech.

Mt 13,23   [1]ὁ δὲ   ἐπὶ τὴν καλὴν [2]/ γῆν σπαρείς, [3]// [4]οὗτός ἐστιν
Mc 4,20   [5]καὶ ἐκεῖνοί εἰσιν οἱ ἐπὶ τὴν γῆν τὴν καλὴν σπαρέντες,
Lc 8,15   τὸ δὲ   ἐν τῇ καλῇ   γῇ,   // οὗτοί εἰσιν

> 1 : Simons, Rushbrooke, Veit, Hawkins(VII), Abbott(VI), Easton, Schmid(4),
>   De Solages(a), Keech. 1 (23c)
> 2 : Veit, Easton, Vaganay, Turner. 21B
> 3 : Wright, Easton. 21B
> 4 : Simons, Rushbrooke, Veit, Hawkins, Abbott(VI), Easton, Schmid, De
>   Solages(c), Keech.
> 5 : Rushbrooke.

Mt 13,23   ὁ τὸν λόγον ἀκούων   καὶ συνιείς,
Mc 4,20   οἵτινες   ἀκούουσιν τὸν λόγον καὶ παραδέχονται
Lc 8,15   οἵτινες ... ἀκούσαντες τὸν λόγον   κατέχουσιν

> Schmid. 14n

§ 27. Mc 4,21-25; Lc 8,16-18

Mt (5,15)   [1]οὐδὲ   καίουσιν λύχνον
Mc 4,21   [2]καὶ ἔλεγεν αὐτοῖς ὅτι μήτι   [3]ἔρχεται ὁ λύχνος...;
Lc 8,16   οὐδεὶς δὲ   λύχνον ἅψας
Lc (11,33)   οὐδεὶς   λύχνον ἅψας

> 1 : Rushbrooke, Abbott(H), Keech.
> 2 : Rushbrooke.
> Mc οτι : — TR S GNT.
> 3 : Rushbrooke.

Mt (5,15)   καὶ [1]τιθέασιν αὐτὸν [2]/ ὑπὸ τὸν μόδιον,   [3]ἀλλ᾽ ἐπὶ τὴν λυχνίαν,
Mc 4,21   [4]ἵνα ὑπὸ τὸν μόδιον   τεθῇ ἢ ὑπὸ τὴν κλίνην ;   οὐχ ἵνα ἐπὶ τὴν λυχνίαν
Lc 8,16   καλύπτει αὐτὸν / σκεύει ἢ ὑποκάτω κλίνης τίθησιν, ἀλλ᾽ ἐπὶ   λυχνίας
Lc (11,33) εἰς κρύπτην τίθησιν / οὐδὲ ὑπὸ τὸν μόδιον,   ἀλλ᾽ ἐπὶ τὴν λυχνίαν,

> 1 : Rushbrooke, Veit, Abbott(H), Streeter(q), Keech.
> 2 : Veit.
> Lc 11,33 ουδε υπο τον μοδιον : — NEB (P[45.75] L Ξ 0124 λ 700 al sy[s] sa).
> 3 : Rushbrooke, Veit, Abbott(VII), Streeter(q), Keech.
> 4 : Rushbrooke.

Mt (5,15)   καὶ λάμπει πᾶσιν τοῖς ἐν τῇ οἰκίᾳ.
Mc 4,21   om.
Lc 8,16   ἵνα οἱ εἰσπορευόμενοι βλέπωσιν τὸ φῶς.
Lc (11,33)   ἵνα οἱ εἰσπορευόμενοι τὸ φέγγος βλέπωσιν.

        Stanton(3a).

Mt (10,26)   [1]οὐδὲν γάρ ἐστιν κεκαλυμμένον   ὃ οὐκ ἀποκαλυφθήσεται,
                καὶ   κρυπτὸν   ὃ οὐ γνωσθήσεται.
Mc 4,22   οὐ   γάρ ἐστίν [2]τι   κρυπτόν, ἐὰν μὴ ἵνα φανερωθῇ·
        οὐδὲ   ἐγένετο   ἀπόκρυφον,   ἀλλ' ἵνα ἔλθῃ εἰς φανερόν.
Lc 8,17   οὐ   γάρ ἐστιν   κρυπτὸν   ὃ οὐ   φανερὸν γενήσεται,
        οὐδὲ   ἀπόκρυφον   ὃ οὐ μὴ γνωσθῇ καὶ εἰς φανερὸν ἔλθῃ.
Lc (12,2)   οὐδὲν δὲ   συγκεκαλυμμένον ἐστὶν ὃ οὐκ ἀποκαλυφθήσεται,
                καὶ   κρυπτὸν   ὃ οὐ γνωσθήσεται.

       1 : Rushbrooke, Veit, Abbott(H), Stanton(3a), Streeter(q), Keech, Boismard.
       2 : Rushbrooke.
       Mc τι : — Ti H (h+) Ru GNT.

Mt (11,15)   [1]ὁ ἔχων   ὦτα   ἀκουέτω.
Mt 13,23   om.
Mc 4,23   [2]εἴ τις ἔχει ὦτα ἀκούειν ἀκουέτω.
Lc 8,17   om.
Lc (14,35)   ὁ ἔχων   ὦτα ἀκούειν ἀκουέτω.

       1 : Rushbrooke, Abbott(IV), Keech. **14n**
       2 : Wright, Sanders.

Mt (6,33)   καὶ [1]ταῦτα πάντα προστεθήσεται ὑμῖν.
Mt (7,2)   [2]καὶ ἐν ᾧ μέτρῳ μετρεῖτε μετρηθήσεται ὑμῖν.
Mt 13,23   om.
Mc 4,24   [3]καὶ ἔλεγεν αὐτοῖς· ... [4]ἐν ᾧ μέτρῳ μετρεῖτε μετρηθήσεται ὑμῖν,
        [5]καὶ   προστεθήσεται ὑμῖν.
Lc 8,18   om.
Lc (6,38)   ᾧ γὰρ μέτρῳ μετρεῖτε ἀντιμετρηθήσεται ὑμῖν.
Lc (12,31)   καὶ ταῦτα   προστεθήσεται ὑμῖν.

       1 : Rushbrooke.
       2 : **4**
       3 : Rushbrooke, Wright.
       4 : Wright, Stanton(1), Sanders.
       5 : Wright, Hawkins(II), Stanton(1), Streeter(q), Sanders.

§ 28. Mc 4,26-29

Mt 13,24-30   λέγων· ... ἡ βασιλεία ... ἀνθρώπῳ ... (25) καθεύδειν ... (26) ἐβλάστησεν ... (29) σῖτον... (30) τοῦ θερισμοῦ

Mc 4,26-29   καὶ ἔλεγεν· οὕτως ἐστὶν ἡ βασιλεία τοῦ θεοῦ, ὡς ἄνθρωπος βάλῃ τὸν σπόρον ἐπὶ τῆς γῆς, (27) καὶ καθεύδῃ καὶ ἐγείρηται νύκτα καὶ ἡμέραν, καὶ ὁ σπόρος βλαστᾷ καὶ μηκύνηται ὡς οὐκ οἶδεν αὐτός. (28) αὐτομάτη ἡ γῆ καρποφορεῖ, πρῶτον χόρτον, εἶτεν στάχυν, εἶτεν πλήρης σῖτος ἐν τῷ στάχυϊ. (29) ὅταν δὲ παραδοῖ ὁ καρπός, εὐθὺς ἀποστέλλει τὸ δρέπανον, ὅτι παρέστηκεν ὁ θερισμός.

Lc   om.

> Rushbrooke (cf. Mt 13,24-30), Wright, Hawkins(IC), Schmid, Vaganay, Boismard.

§ 29. Mc 4,30-32; Mt 13,31-32; (Lc 13,18-19)

Mt 13,31   ἄλλην ... λέγων·   [1]ὁμοία ἐστὶν   ἡ   βασιλεία ...   κόκκῳ

Mc 4,30-31   [2]καὶ ἔλεγεν·   πῶς ὁμοιώσωμεν τὴν βασιλείαν... ; (31) [3]ὡς   κόκκῳ

Lc 13,18-19   ἔλεγεν οὖν·   τίνι ὁμοία ἐστὶν   ἡ   βασιλεία ... ; (19) ὁμοία ἐστὶν κόκκῳ

> 1 : Wilke, Rushbrooke(Lc 13,19), Abbott(VII), Veit, Streeter(q), Da Fonseca, De Solages(Q), Keech.
> 2 : Rushbrooke. **2**
> 3 : Rushbrooke, Hawkins(IVb).

Mt 13,31-32   [1]ὃν λαβὼν ἄνθρωπος ἔσπειρεν ἐν τῷ ἀγρῷ [2]αὐτοῦ· (32) ὃ μικρότερον

Mc 4,31   ὃς [3]ὅταν   σπαρῇ [4]ἐπὶ τῆς γῆς,   μικρότερον [5]ὂν

Lc 13,19   ὃν λαβὼν ἄνθρωπος ἔβαλεν εἰς   κῆπον ἑαυτοῦ,

> 1 : Wilke, Rushbrooke, Veit, Hawkins(IV), Abbott(H), Streeter(q), Da Fonseca, De Solages(Q), Keech.
> 2 : Wilke, Rushbrooke, Abbott, Streeter(q), De Solages(Q), Keech.
> 3 : Wilke(t), Rushbrooke.
> 4 : Rushbrooke, Schmid(20). **31c**
> 5 : Hawkins(IVb). **8B**

Mt 13,32   πάντων τῶν σπερμάτων,   ὅταν δὲ   [1]αὐξηθῇ,

Mc 4,31-32   πάντων τῶν σπερμάτων [2]τῶν ἐπὶ τῆς γῆς, (32) καὶ ὅταν [3]σπαρῇ, ἀναβαίνει

Lc 13,19   καὶ   ηὔξησεν

> 1 : Wilke, Rushbrooke, Wright, Abbott, Streeter(q), De Solages(Q), Keech. **32**
> 2 : Rushbrooke, Hawkins(II).
> 3 : Rushbrooke, Hawkins(II,IVb).

Mt 13,32   *γίνεται*   ¹*δένδρον,*   *ὥστε ... κατασκηνοῦν* ²//³*ἐν τοῖς κλάδοις αὐτοῦ.*

Mc 4,32   ⁴*ποιεῖ κλάδους μεγάλους, ὥστε δύνασθαι ὑπὸ τὴν σκιὰν αὐτοῦ ... κατασκηνοῦν.*

Lc 13,19   *ἐγένετο εἰς δένδρον, καὶ ...*   *κατεσκήνωσεν //* *ἐν τοῖς κλάδοις αὐτοῦ.*

      1 : Rushbrooke, Veit, Abbott(H), Streeter(q), Da Fonseca.
      2 : Wright. **21B**
      3 : Abbott(H), Da Fonseca, De Solages(Q), Keech.
      4 : Rushbrooke.

Mt 13,33   *Parabola fermenti.*

Mc 4,32   om.

Lc 13,20-21 *Parabola fermenti.*

      Sanders.

§ 30. Mc 4,33-34; Mt 13,34-35

§ 31. Mc 4,35-41; (Mt 8,18-27); Lc 8,22-25

Mt 8,18   *ἰδὼν*   ¹*δὲ* ²*ὁ Ἰησοῦς ὄχλον περὶ αὐτὸν*   *ἐκέλευσεν ἀπελθεῖν*

Mc 4,35   *καὶ* ³*λέγει αὐτοῖς ἐν* ⁴*ἐκείνῃ τῇ ἡμέρᾳ* ⁵*ὀψίας γενομένης·*

Lc 8,22   *ἐγένετο δὲ*   *ἐν μιᾷ τῶν ἡμερῶν καὶ αὐτὸς ...,*   *καὶ εἶπεν πρὸς αὐτούς·*

      1 : Hawkins(VII), Easton, Schmid(4). **1**
      2 : **22**
      3 : Hawkins(VI), Schmid(5). **10**
      4 : Rushbrooke, Easton.
      5 : Simons, Rushbrooke, Hawkins(III), Stanton(1), Easton, Schmid(31), Boismard(McR).

Mt (13,36) *τότε ἀφεὶς τοὺς ὄχλους*

Mt 8,23   om.

Mc 4,36   ¹*καὶ ἀφέντες τὸν ὄχλον παραλαμβάνουσιν αὐτὸν ὡς ἦν ἐν τῷ πλοίῳ,* ²*καὶ ἄλλα πλοῖα ἦν μετ᾽ αὐτοῦ.*

Lc 8,22   *καὶ ἀνήχθησαν.*

      1 : Weiss, Simons, Rushbrooke, Stanton(1), Easton (*ὡς ἦν*).
      2 : Weiss, Simons, Wright, Wernle(t), Hawkins(IAa), Stanton(1), Easton, Schmid(32), Vaganay, Fuchs, Boismard(McR).

Mt 8,23   *καὶ*   ¹*ἐμβάντι αὐτῷ*   ²*εἰς τὸ πλοῖον,*

Mc 4,36   *καί ...* ³*παραλαμβάνουσιν αὐτὸν ὡς ἦν ἐν τῷ πλοίῳ,*

Lc 8,22   *καὶ*   *αὐτὸς ἐνέβη*   *εἰς*   *πλοῖον*

      1 : Simons, Rushbrooke, Wernle, Abbott(H), Easton, Stanton(1), Streeter(d), Schmid, De Solages(e), Keech, Fuchs.
      2 : Simons, Rushbrooke, Wernle, Abbott(H), Easton, Stanton(1), Streeter(d), Schmid, De Solages(c), Keech, Fuchs. **(31a)**
         Mt *το* : — Ti H, [GNT].
      3 : Abbott(III), Easton, Schmid(5). **10**

Mt 8,23   ἠκολούθησαν αὐτῷ οἱ μαθηταὶ αὐτοῦ.
Mc 4,36   καὶ ἄλλα πλοῖα   ἦν μετ᾽ αὐτοῦ.
Lc 8,22   καὶ οἱ μαθηταὶ αὐτοῦ,

Weiss, Simons, Rushbrooke, Wernle, Abbott(H), Streeter(d), Easton, Chapman, De Solages(f), Keech, Fuchs, Boismard.

Mt 8,24   καὶ ἰδοὺ   σεισμὸς μέγας   ἐγένετο [1]ἐν τῇ θαλάσσῃ,
Mc 4,37   καὶ [2]γίνεται λαῖλαψ μεγάλη ἀνέμου,
Lc 8,23   καὶ κατέβη λαῖλαψ   ἀνέμου εἰς τὴν λίμνην,

1 : Weiss, Wright, Easton, Schmid(33), De Solages(f).
2 : Hawkins(VI), Schmid(5).   **10**

Mt 8,24   ὥστε τὸ πλοῖον καλύπτεσθαι ὑπὸ τῶν κυμάτων·
Mc 4,37   καὶ τὰ κύματα ἐπέβαλλεν εἰς τὸ πλοῖον, [1]ὥστε [2]ἤδη⌉ γεμίζεσθαι τὸ πλοῖον.
Lc 8,23   καὶ συνεπληροῦντο καὶ ἐκινδύνευον.

1 : Rushbrooke, Hawkins(II).
2 : Easton.

Mt 8,24   αὐτὸς [1]δὲ   ἐκάθευδεν.
Mc 4,38   καὶ αὐτὸς ἦν [2]ἐν τῇ πρύμνῃ ἐπὶ τὸ προσκεφάλαιον [3]καθεύδων.
Lc (8,23) πλεόντων δὲ αὐτῶν   ἀφύπνωσεν.

1 : **1**
2 : Wilke(r), Simons, Rushbrooke, Wright, Hawkins(III), Allen, Stanton(1 vel
    2), Easton, Schmid(32), Fuchs, Boismard.
3 : **12**

Mt 8,25   καὶ [1]προσελθόντες [2]ἤγειραν   αὐτὸν   [3]λέγοντες·
Mc 4,38   καὶ   ἐγείρουσιν αὐτὸν καὶ λέγουσιν [4]αὐτῷ·
Lc 8,24   προσελθόντες δὲ διήγειραν   αὐτὸν   λέγοντες·

1 : Wilke, Holtzmann, Simons, Rushbrooke, Veit, Wernle, Abbott(H), Stanton
    (2 vel 1), Easton, Schmid(33), Chapman, De Solages(d), Keech, Fuchs,
    Boismard. **18**
2 : Simons, Rushbrooke, Veit, Wernle, Hawkins(VI), Abbott(III), Stanton
    (2 vel 1), Easton, Schmid(5), Chapman, Keech, Fuchs, Boismard. **10**
3 : Hawkins(VI), Abbott(IV), Schmid(7), De Solages(b), Fuchs. **3 10**
4 : Rushbrooke, Schmid, Keech, Fuchs, Boismard. **(23)**

Mt 8,25-26 κύριε,   σῶσον, ἀπολλύμεθα. (26) ... τότε ἐγερθεὶς
Mc 4,38-39 [1]διδάσκαλε,   [2]οὐ μέλει σοι ὅτι ἀπολλύμεθα ; (39) [3]καὶ [4]διεγερθεὶς
Lc 8,24   ἐπιστάτα ἐπιστάτα,   ἀπολλύμεθα.   ὁ δὲ διεγερθεὶς

1 : Weiss(r /q), Rushbrooke, Schmid. **30**
2 : Weiss(r /q), Simons, Rushbrooke, Hawkins(IB), Easton, Schmid(31),
    Vaganay, Keech, Fuchs, Boismard.
3 : Rushbrooke, Schmid(4). **2**
4 : Mc ἐγείρουσιν διεγερθείς : Mt ἤγειραν ἐγερθείς, Lc διήγειραν διεγερθείς.
    Mc εγειρουσιν : διεγ- TR S.

Mt 8,26   ἐπετίμησεν τοῖς ἀνέμοις καὶ   τῇ θαλάσσῃ,

Mc 4,39   ἐπετίμησεν τῷ ἀνέμῳ καὶ εἶπεν τῇ θαλάσσῃ·   σιώπα, πεφίμωσο.

Lc 8,24   ἐπετίμησεν τῷ ἀνέμῳ καὶ   τῷ κλύδωνι τοῦ ὕδατος·

Wilke(r), Weiss(r /q), Rushbrooke, Wernle, Hawkins(II), Stanton(2 vel 1), Easton, Schmid(31), Fuchs, Boismard.

Mt (8,26)   καὶ ἐγένετο γαλήνη μεγάλη.

Mc 4,39   καὶ ἐκόπασεν ὁ ἄνεμος, καὶ ἐγένετο γαλήνη μεγάλη.

Lc 8,24   καὶ ἐπαύσαντο.   καὶ ἐγένετο γαλήνη.

Weiss, Rushbrooke.

Mt (8,26)   καὶ λέγει αὐτοῖς· τί δειλοί ἐστε,   ὀλιγόπιστοι ;

Mc 4,40   καὶ εἶπεν αὐτοῖς· [a]τί δειλοί ἐστε οὕτως ; [b]πῶς οὐκ ἔχετε πίστιν ;

Lc 8,25   εἶπεν δὲ αὐτοῖς·   ποῦ   ἡ πίστις ὑμῶν ;

Hawkins(V). **34**

(οὔπω) : Rushbrooke.

Mc εστε ουτως ; πως : εστε ; ουπω H Ru GNT(A).

Mt 8,27   οἱ [1]δὲ ἄνθρωποι   [2]ἐθαύμασαν [3]λέγοντες·

Mc 4,41   καὶ ἐφοβήθησαν [4]φόβον μέγαν,   καὶ ἔλεγον πρὸς ἀλλήλους·

Lc 8,25   φοβηθέντες δὲ   ἐθαύμασαν, λέγοντες πρὸς ἀλλήλους·

1 : Rushbrooke, Abbott(VI), Stanton(2 vel 1), Easton, Schmid(4), De Solages (a), Keech, Fuchs. **1**

2 : Wilke, Holtzmann, Weiss, Simons, Rushbrooke, Wright, Wernle, Abbott(H), Burton, Stanton(2 vel 1), Easton, Schmid, Chapman, De Solages(e), Keech, McLoughlin(RI), Fuchs, Boismard. **32**

3 : Simons, Rushbrooke, Wernle, Abbott(IV), Burton, Stanton(2 vel 1), Easton, Schmid(7), De Solages(b), Keech, McLoughlin(RI), Fuchs, Boismard. **3 11**

4 : Rushbrooke, Schmid.

Mt 8,27   ὅτι καὶ οἱ [1]ἄνεμοι   καὶ ἡ θάλασσα αὐτῷ [2]ὑπακούουσιν ;

Mc 4,41   ὅτι καὶ ὁ   ἄνεμος   καὶ ἡ θάλασσα ὑπακούει αὐτῷ ;

Lc 8,25   ὅτι καὶ τοῖς ἀνέμοις ἐπιτάσσει καὶ τῷ ὕδατι, καὶ   ὑπακούουσιν αὐτῷ ;

1 : Weiss, Simons, Wernle, Easton, Schmid(33), Brown, Boismard. **33c**

2 : Rushbrooke, Abbott(VII), Stanton(2 vel 1), Easton, De Solages(b), Keech, Fuchs.

§ 32. Mc 5,1-20 ; (Mt 8,28-34) ; Lc 8,26-39

Mt 8,28   καὶ ἐλθόντος αὐτοῦ εἰς τὸ πέραν   εἰς τὴν χώραν τῶν Γαδαρηνῶν

Mc 5,1   καὶ [1]ἦλθον   εἰς τὸ πέραν [2]τῆς θαλάσσης εἰς τὴν χώραν τῶν Γερασηνῶν.

Lc 8,26   καὶ κατέπλευσαν   εἰς τὴν χώραν τῶν Γερασηνῶν,

1 : Rushbrooke.

2 : Rushbrooke, Hawkins(II), Easton.

Lc Γερασηνων : Γεργεσηνων T h[r1] S GNT[12](D), Γαδαρηνων TR h[r2].

Mt 8,28   καὶ   ἐλθόντος αὐτοῦ...   [1]ὑπήντησαν αὐτῷ
Mc 5,2   καὶ ἐξελθόντος αὐτοῦ [2]ἐκ τοῦ πλοίου, [3]εὐθὺς (ἀπήντησεν) αὐτῷ
Lc 8,27   ἐξελθόντι δὲ   αὐτῷ ἐπὶ τὴν γῆν   ὑπήντησεν

    1 : Simons.
        Mc υπηντησεν : απ- TR Ti S.
    2 : Rushbrooke.
    3 : Stephenson, Easton, Schmid(10).
        Mc ευθυς : — W, [H][N][GNT], ευθεως TR.

Mt 8,28   ὑπήντησαν αὐτῷ   δύο δαιμονιζόμενοι
Mc 5,2   ὑπήντησεν αὐτῷ ... ἄνθρωπος ἐν πνεύματι ἀκαθάρτῳ,
Lc 8,27   αὐτῷ... ὑπήντησεν   ἀνήρ τις ... ἔχων δαιμόνια,

    Rushbrooke, Veit, Hawkins(IVa), Abbott, Schmid(27), Keech. **32**

Mt 8,28   ἐκ τῶν μνημείων ἐξερχόμενοι,
Mc 5,2-3   [a]ἐκ τῶν μνημείων ..., (3) ὃς τὴν κατοίκησιν εἶχεν   [b]ἐν τοῖς μνήμασιν,
Lc 8,27   ἐκ τῆς πόλεως ...,   καὶ ἐν οἰκίᾳ οὐκ ἔμενεν ἀλλ' ἐν τοῖς μνήμασιν.

    1 : **34**

Mt   om.
Mc 5,3   καὶ οὐδὲ ἁλύσει οὐκέτι οὐδεὶς ἐδύνατο αὐτὸν δῆσαι,
Lc   om.

    Rushbrooke, Wright, Hawkins(III), Schmid, Keech.

Mt 8,28   χαλεποὶ λίαν, ὥστε μὴ ἰσχύειν τινὰ παρελθεῖν διὰ τῆς ὁδοῦ ἐκείνης.
Mc 5,4   καὶ διὰ τὸ αὐτὸν πολλάκις πέδαις καὶ ἁλύσεσιν δεδέσθαι,
         καὶ διεσπάσθαι ὑπ' αὐτοῦ τὰς ἁλύσεις καὶ τὰς πέδας συντετρίφθαι,
         ⌐καὶ οὐδεὶς ἴσχυεν αὐτὸν δαμάσαι⌐·
Lc 8,27   om.
Lc (8,29) πολλοῖς γὰρ χρόνοις συνηρπάκει αὐτόν, καὶ ἐδεσμεύετο ἁλύσεσιν καὶ πέδαις
         φυλασσόμενος, καὶ διαρήσσων τὰ δεσμά

    Wilke(⌐ t), Rushbrooke, Wright, Keech, Boismard(McR).

Mt   om.
Mc 5,5   καὶ διὰ παντὸς νυκτὸς καὶ ἡμέρας ἐν τοῖς μνήμασιν καὶ ἐν τοῖς ὄρεσιν ἦν
        κράζων καὶ κατακόπτων ἑαυτὸν λίθοις.
Lc 8,27   om.
Lc (8,29) καὶ ... ἠλαύνετο ἀπὸ τοῦ δαιμονίου εἰς τὰς ἐρήμους.

    Rushbrooke, Wright, Wernle, Hawkins(V), Easton, Schmid, Keech, Boismard
    (McR).

Mt 8,29   καὶ ἰδοὺ   ἔκραξαν   λέγοντες·
Mc 5,6-7   καὶ ἰδὼν τὸν Ἰησοῦν ¹ἀπὸ μακρόθεν ἔδραμεν καὶ προσεκύνησεν αὐτόν,
                             (7) καὶ κράξας   φωνῇ μεγάλῃ ²λέγει·
Lc 8,28   ἰδὼν δὲ   τὸν Ἰησοῦν ἀνακράξας προσέπεσεν αὐτῷ καὶ φωνῇ μεγάλῃ εἶπεν·

         1 : Rushbrooke, Hawkins(III), Easton.
         2 : Hawkins(VI), Schmid(5). 10

Mt 8,29   ἦλθες ὧδε πρὸ καιροῦ   βασανίσαι ἡμᾶς ;
Mc 5,7   ὁρκίζω σε τὸν θεόν,   μή με βασανίσῃς.
Lc 8,28   δέομαί σου,   μή με βασανίσῃς.

         Rushbrooke, Hawkins(IA), Easton.

Mt 8,30   ἀγέλη χοίρων πολλῶν βοσκομένη.
Mc 5,11   ἀγέλη χοίρων μεγάλη βοσκομένη·
Lc 8,32   ἀγέλη χοίρων ἱκανῶν βοσκομένη ἐν τῷ ὄρει·

         Rushbrooke.

Mt 8,31   οἱ δὲ δαίμονες παρεκάλουν αὐτὸν λέγοντες·
Mc 5,12   καὶ   παρεκάλεσαν αὐτὸν λέγοντες·
Lc 8,32   καὶ   παρεκάλεσαν αὐτόν
Lc (8,31)   καὶ   παρεκάλουν αὐτόν

         Rushbrooke, Abbott(VII), Keech.
         Lc 8,31 παρεκαλουν : παρεκαλει TR Ti ; 8,32 παρεκαλεσαν : παρεκαλουν TR.

Mt 8,31   ἀπόστειλον ἡμᾶς εἰς τὴν ἀγέλην τῶν χοίρων.
Mc 5,12   πέμψον   ἡμᾶς εἰς   τοὺς χοίρους, ἵνα εἰς αὐτοὺς εἰσέλθωμεν.
Lc 8,32   ἵνα ἐπιτρέψῃ αὐτοῖς   εἰς ἐκείνους εἰσελθεῖν·

         Rushbrooke, Allen, Schmid(31). 34

Mt 8,32   οἱ ¹δὲ ἐξελθόντες... (v. 31 :) οἱ δὲ ²δαίμονες
Mc 5,13   καὶ ἐξελθόντα   τὰ πνεύματα τὰ ἀκάθαρτα
Lc 8,33   ἐξελθόντα δὲ   τὰ δαιμόνια

         1 : Rushbrooke, Hawkins(VII), Abbott(VI), Easton, Schmid(4), De Solages(a),
             Keech. 1
         2 : Rushbrooke, Schmid(27), Keech. 32

Mt 8,32   εἰς τὴν θάλασσαν,   καὶ ἀπέθανον   ἐν τοῖς ὕδασιν.
Mc 5,13   εἰς τὴν θάλασσαν, ¹ὡς δισχίλιοι, καὶ ²ἐπνίγοντο ἐν τῇ θαλάσσῃ.
Lc 8,33   εἰς τὴν λίμνην   καὶ ἀπεπνίγη.

    1 : Wilke(t), Holtzmann(r), Simons, Rushbrooke, Wright, Wernle, Allen,
        Easton, Schmid(29), Keech.
    2 : 11

Mt 8,33   οἱ ¹δὲ   βόσκοντες   ἔφυγον, καὶ ... ἀπήγγειλαν
Mc 5,14   καὶ   οἱ βόσκοντες ²αὐτοὺς ἔφυγον καὶ ἀπήγγειλαν
Lc 8,34   ἰδόντες δὲ οἱ βόσκοντες τὸ γεγονὸς ἔφυγον καὶ ἀπήγγειλαν

    1 : Rushbrooke, Hawkins(VII), Abbott(VI), Easton, Schmid(4), De Solages(a),
        Keech. 1
    2 : Rushbrooke, Easton, Keech, Boismard(Mt).   (23)
        Mc απηγγειλαν : αν- S.

Mt 8,34   καὶ ἰδοὺ πᾶσα ἡ πόλις ¹ἐξῆλθεν   εἰς ὑπάντησιν τῷ Ἰησοῦ,
Mc 5,14-15 καὶ ἦλθον ἰδεῖν ²τί ἐστιν τὸ γεγονός. (15) καὶ ³ἔρχονται πρὸς τὸν Ἰησοῦν,
Lc 8,35   ἐξῆλθον δὲ ἰδεῖν   τὸ γεγονός,   καὶ ἦλθον πρὸς τὸν Ἰησοῦν,

    1 : Rushbrooke, Veit, Wernle, Abbott(VII), Easton, Schmid(19), Glasson,
        Keech, Brown, Boismard(Mt). 18
    2 : Rushbrooke, Easton.
    3 : Simons, Rushbrooke, Hawkins(VI), Abbott(III), Schmid(5). 10

Mt 8,34   καὶ ἰδόντες (cf. v. 33 : τὰ τῶν δαιμονιζομένων)
Mc 5,15   καὶ ¹θεωροῦσιν τὸν δαιμονιζόμενον καθήμενον ..., ²τὸν ἐσχηκότα τὸν λεγιῶνα,
Lc 8,35   καὶ εὗρον   καθήμενον τὸν ἄνθρωπον ἀφ᾽ οὗ τὰ δαιμόνια ἐξῆλθεν

    1 : Rushbrooke, Schmid(5). 10
    2 : Rushbrooke, Wernle(t), Hawkins(II). 34

Mt 8,34   αὐτὸν παρεκάλεσαν ὅπως   μεταβῇ ἀπὸ τῶν ὁρίων αὐτῶν.
Mc 5,17   καὶ ἤρξαντο παρακαλεῖν αὐτὸν ἀπελθεῖν ἀπὸ τῶν ὁρίων αὐτῶν.
Lc 8,37   καὶ ἠρώτησεν αὐτὸν ...   ἀπελθεῖν ἀπ᾽   αὐτῶν,

    Rushbrooke, Allen, Easton, Schmid(8). 13

Mt (9,1)   καὶ ¹ἐμβὰς   εἰς   πλοῖον ²διεπέρασεν,
Mc 5,18   καὶ ἐμβαίνοντος αὐτοῦ εἰς ³τὸ πλοῖον
Lc 8,37   αὐτὸς δὲ ἐμβὰς   εἰς   πλοῖον ὑπέστρεψεν.

    1 : Simons, Easton, Boismard(Mt). 14
    2 : Boismard(Mt).
    3 : Rushbrooke, Boismard(Mt). 33b

§ 33. Mc 5,21-43; (Mt 9,18-26); Lc 8,40-56

Mt (9,1)   καὶ ἐμβὰς εἰς πλοῖον διεπέρασεν,
Mc 5,21   καὶ ¹διαπεράσαντος τοῦ Ἰησοῦ ἐν τῷ πλοίῳ ²πάλιν εἰς τὸ πέραν
Lc 8,40   ἐν δὲ τῷ ὑποστρέφειν τὸν Ἰησοῦν

    1 : Rushbrooke. **14**
      Mc εν τω πλοιω : — GNT¹ ²(B), [GNT³](D).
    2 : Rushbrooke, Wright, Hawkins(II), Easton. **27 34**

Mt (9,1)   om.
Mc 5,21   καὶ ἦν παρὰ τὴν θάλασσαν.
Lc 8,40   om.

    Simons, Rushbrooke, Wright, Hawkins(III).

Mt 9,18   ¹ἰδοὺ   ²ἄρχων εἷς   ³προσελθών
Mc 5,22   καὶ   ⁴ἔρχεται   εἷς ⁵τῶν ἀρχισυναγώγων,   καί
Lc 8,41   καὶ ἰδοὺ ἦλθεν ἀνήρ..., καὶ οὗτος ἄρχων   τῆς συναγωγῆς

    1 : Weiss, Simons, Rushbrooke, Wright, Veit, Wernle, Abbott(H), Stanton(2),
      Easton, Schmid(33), De Solages(d), Keech, Brown, Boismard(r). **25**
    2 : Weiss, Simons, Rushbrooke, Veit, Wernle, Lagrange, Schmid, De Solages(b),
      Keech, McLoughlin(ML), Boismard(r). **32**
    3 : Rushbrooke, Abbott.
      Mt εις προσελθων : ελθων TR, εισελθων Ti T h, εις ελθων GNT, τις προσελθων S.
    4 : Weiss, Rushbrooke, Veit, Hawkins(VI), Abbott(III), Easton, Schmid(5),
      Keech. **10**
    5 : Rushbrooke.

Mt 9,18   προσελθὼν προσεκύνει αὐτῷ   λέγων ὅτι
Mc 5,22-23   ¹ἰδὼν αὐτὸν ²πίπτει πρὸς τοὺς πόδας αὐτοῦ, (23) ³καὶ ⁴παρακαλεῖ αὐτὸν ⁵πολλὰ
                                               λέγων ὅτι
Lc 8,41   πεσὼν παρὰ τοὺς πόδας Ἰησοῦ   παρεκάλει αὐτὸν ... ὅτι

    1 : Rushbrooke, Easton.
    2 : Hawkins(VI), Schmid(5). **10**
    3 : Rushbrooke, Schmid(7). Cf. v. 22 : **3n**
    4 : Cf. 2.
      Mc παρακαλει : παρεκαλει h W.
    5 : Simons, Rushbrooke, Easton, Schmid(16).

Mt 9,18   ἡ ¹θυγάτηρ μου   ἄρτι ²ἐτελεύτησεν·
Mc 5,23   τὸ θυγάτριόν μου   ³ἐσχάτως ἔχει,
Lc 8,42   θυγάτηρ μονογενὴς ἦν αὐτῷ ... καὶ αὕτη ἀπέθνησκεν.

    1 : Simons, Rushbrooke, Veit, Hawkins(IVa), Abbott(VII), Streeter(d),
      Easton, Schmid(26), De Solages(b), Keech, Boismard(McR). **33a**
    2 : Weiss, Simons, Hawkins(IVa), Schmid(5). **32**
    3 : Wilke(r), Rushbrooke.

Mt 9,18   ἀλλὰ ἐλθὼν ἐπίθες τὴν χεῖρά σου ἐπ᾽ αὐτήν,   καὶ ζήσεται.
Mc 5,23   ¹ἵνα ἐλθὼν ἐπιθῇς τὰς χεῖρας   αὐτῇ, ²ἵνα σωθῇ καὶ ζήσῃ.
Lc (8,41)   εἰσελθεῖν εἰς τὸν οἶκον αὐτοῦ,

    1 : Rushbrooke, Hawkins(IVb), Schmid(23).   **7A 8B**
    2 : Holtzmann, Rushbrooke.

Mt 9,19   καὶ ... ἠκολούθει αὐτῷ
Mc 5,24   ªκαὶ ἀπῆλθεν μετ᾽ αὐτοῦ. ᵇκαὶ   ἠκολούθει αὐτῷ
Lc 8,42   ἐν δὲ τῷ ὑπάγειν αὐτόν

    Hansen. **34**

Mt 9,20   om.
Mc 5,26   καὶ πολλὰ παθοῦσα ὑπὸ πολλῶν ἰατρῶν καὶ δαπανήσασα τὰ παρ᾽ αὐτῆς πάντα,
           καὶ μηδὲν ὠφεληθεῖσα ἀλλὰ μᾶλλον εἰς τὸ χεῖρον ἐλθοῦσα,
Lc 8,43   ἥτις οὐκ ἴσχυσεν ἀπ᾽ οὐδενὸς θεραπευθῆναι,

    Weiss, Rushbrooke, Wright, Easton, Schmid(7,31), Boismard(McR).
    Lc ητις : + ιατροις προσαναλωσασα ολον τον βιον TR Ti T S L GNT(D).

Mt 9,20   om.
Mc 5,27   ἀκούσασα τὰ περὶ τοῦ Ἰησοῦ,
Lc 8,44   om.

    Rushbrooke, Hawkins(III), Easton, Schmid(7,32).

Mt 9,20   ¹προσελθοῦσα   ὄπισθεν ἥψατο ²τοῦ κρασπέδου τοῦ ἱματίου αὐτοῦ·
Mc 5,27   ἐλθοῦσα ³ἐν τῷ ὄχλῳ ὄπισθεν ἥψατο   τοῦ ἱματίου αὐτοῦ·
Lc 8,44   προσελθοῦσα   ὄπισθεν ἥψατο τοῦ κρασπέδου τοῦ ἱματίου αὐτοῦ,

    1 : Wilke, Holtzmann, Weiss, Simons, Veit, Wernle, Abbott, Easton, Schmid
        (19,33), De Solages(c), Keech, Fuchs. **18**
    2 : Holtzmann, Weiss, Simons, Rushbrooke, Wright, Veit, Wernle(t), Haw-
        kins(*), Abbott(I vel H), Burton, Stanton(3b vel 4), Lagrange, Streeter(t),
        Larfeld, Easton, Schmid, Chapman, Da Fonseca, De Solages(f), Keech,
        Brown, McLoughlin(T), Fuchs. **23**
    3 : Wilke(t), Holtzmann, Rushbrooke, Hawkins(III), Easton, Schmid(32),
        Keech, Fuchs.

Mt 9,22   om.
Mc 5,29   καὶ ἔγνω τῷ σώματι ὅτι ἴαται ἀπὸ τῆς μάστιγος.
Lc 8,44   om.

    Rushbrooke, Wright, Boismard(McR).

Mt 9,22   ὁ δὲ Ἰησοῦς στραφεὶς ...   [1]εἶπεν·

Mc 5,30   καὶ [2]εὐθὺς ὁ Ἰησοῦς [3a]ἐπιγνοὺς ἐν ἑαυτῷ τὴν ἐξ αὐτοῦ δύναμιν ἐξελθοῦσαν,
              [b]ἐπιστραφεὶς [4]ἐν τῷ ὄχλῳ ἔλεγεν·

Lc 8,45   καὶ εἶπεν ὁ Ἰησοῦς·

Lc (8,46)   ὁ δὲ Ἰησοῦς εἶπεν· ... ἐγὼ γὰρ ἔγνων δύναμιν ἐξεληλυθυῖαν ἀπ' ἐμοῦ.

       1 : Schmid(6). **11**
       2 : Rushbrooke.
       3 : ἐπιγνούς (cf. Lc), ἐπιστραφείς (cf. Mt). **34**
       4 : Rushbrooke, Wright.

Mt   om.

Mc 5,31   βλέπεις ..., καὶ λέγεις· τίς μου ἥψατο ;

Lc 8,46   ὁ δὲ Ἰησοῦς εἶπεν· ἥψατό μού τις·

       Rushbrooke, Hawkins(IB).

Mt 9,22   καὶ   ἰδὼν αὐτήν

Mc 5,32-33   καὶ περιεβλέπετο ἰδεῖν τὴν τοῦτο ποιήσασαν. (33) ἡ δὲ γυνή

Lc 8,47   ἰδοῦσα δὲ   ἡ γυνή

       Simons, Rushbrooke, Wright, Hawkins(II), Schmid(32).

Mt   om.

Mc 5,33   εἰδυῖα ὃ γέγονεν αὐτῇ,

Lc   om.

       Rushbrooke, Boismard(McR).

Mt 9,22   θάρσει, θύγατερ· ἡ πίστις σου σέσωκέν σε.

Mc 5,34   θυγάτηρ, ἡ πίστις σου σέσωκέν σε·

Lc 8,48   (θύγατερ), ἡ πίστις σου σέσωκέν σε·

       Stephenson.
       Lc θυγατηρ : -τερ T S L.
       Mc θυγατηρ : -τερ T S L.

Mt 9,22   καὶ ἐσώθη ἡ γυνὴ ἀπὸ τῆς ὥρας ἐκείνης.

Mc 5,34   ὕπαγε εἰς εἰρήνην, καὶ ἴσθι ὑγιὴς ἀπὸ τῆς μάστιγός σου.

Lc 8,48   πορεύου εἰς εἰρήνην.

       Holtzmann, Simons, Rushbrooke, Wright, Wernle, Hawkins(II), Schmid(31).

Mt 9,23   καὶ ¹ἐλθὼν ὁ Ἰησοῦς εἰς ²τὴν οἰκίαν τοῦ ἄρχοντος
Mc 5,38-39   καὶ ἔρχονται   εἰς τὸν οἶκον τοῦ ἀρχισυναγώγου, ... (39) καὶ εἰσελθὼν
Lc 8,51   ἐλθὼν δὲ   εἰς τὴν οἰκίαν

> 1 : Weiss(r), Simons, Rushbrooke, Veit, Hawkins(VI), Abbott(III), Easton,
> Schmid(7,30), De Solages(b), Keech, Brown, Boismard(McR).   3 10
> Lc ελθων : εισελθων TR Ti.
> 2 : Weiss(r), Simons, Rushbrooke, Veit, Abbott(VII), Easton, Schmid(28),
> De Solages(b), Keech, Brown, Boismard(McR).   32

Mt 9,23   καὶ ἰδὼν ... καὶ τὸν ὄχλον θορυβούμενον
Mc 5,38   καὶ θεωρεῖ   ¹ᵃθόρυβον, καὶ ᵇκλαίοντας ²καὶ ἀλαλάζοντας ³πολλά,
Lc 8,52   ἔκλαιον δὲ πάντες καὶ ἐκόπτοντο αὐτήν.

> 1 : Boismard(Mc).   34
> 2 : Rushbrooke, Hawkins(II).
> 3 : Easton, Schmid(16).   28

Mt 9,23-24   ¹ὁ Ἰησοῦς... ἔλεγεν·   (24) ἀναχωρεῖτε·
Mc 5,39   ²καὶ εἰσελθὼν ³λέγει ⁴αὐτοῖς·   ⁵τί ᵃθορυβεῖσθε καὶ ᵇκλαίετε ;
Lc 8,52   ὁ δὲ   εἶπεν·   μὴ κλαίετε·

> 1 : 22
> 2 : Cf. v.38.
> 3 : Hawkins(VI), Schmid(5).   10
> 4 : Rushbrooke.   (23)
> 5 : Rushbrooke, Hawkins(V), Easton, Boismard(Mc : cf. v. 38).   34

Mt 9,24   οὐ ¹γὰρ ἀπέθανεν τὸ κοράσιον ἀλλὰ καθεύδει.
Mc 5,39   ²τὸ παιδίον οὐκ   ἀπέθανεν   ἀλλὰ καθεύδει.
Lc 8,52   (οὐ γὰρ) ἀπέθανεν   ἀλλὰ καθεύδει.

> 1 : Rushbrooke, Hawkins(IVc), Abbott(II), Easton, Schmid(3), De Solages(d),
> Keech.   4
> Lc ουκ : ου γαρ Ti H Ru S GNT.
> 2 : Rushbrooke, Keech.

Mt 9,25   ὅτε   δὲ ἐξεβλήθη ὁ ὄχλος εἰσελθών
Mc 5,40   αὐτὸς δὲ ἐκβαλὼν πάντας παραλαμβάνει τὸν πατέρα τοῦ παιδίου καὶ τὴν
             μητέρα καὶ τοὺς μετ' αὐτοῦ, καὶ εἰσπορεύεται ⌜ὅπου ἦν τὸ παιδίον.
Lc 8,54   αὐτὸς δέ

> Rushbrooke, Hawkins(II), Keech, Boismard(⌜ Mc).

Mt 9,25   εἰσελθὼν ἐκράτησεν τῆς χειρὸς ¹αὐτῆς,
Mc 5,41   ²καὶ   κρατήσας τῆς χειρὸς ³τοῦ παιδίου λέγει αὐτῇ·
Lc 8,54   αὐτὸς δὲ κρατήσας τῆς χειρὸς αὐτῆς   ἐφώνησεν λέγων·

> 1 : Rushbrooke, Veit, Abbott(VII), Easton, Schmid(31), De Solages(e), Keech,
> Boismard. Cf. 3.   (23)
> 2 : Rushbrooke, Schmid(4).   2
> 3 : Rushbrooke.

Mt   om.
Mc 5,41   ¹ταλιθὰ κοῦμ, ὅ ἐστιν μεθερμηνευόμενον· τὸ κοράσιον, ²σοὶ λέγω, ἔγειρε.
Lc 8,54   ἡ παῖς,   ἔγειρε.

    1 : Wilke, Simons, Rushbrooke, Hawkins(IIIa), Stanton(2), Easton, Schmid
    (1,31), Keech.
    2 : Rushbrooke, Keech, Boismard(McR).

Mt 9,25   καὶ   ἠγέρθη τὸ κοράσιον.
Mc 5,42   καὶ ¹εὐθὺς ἀνέστη τὸ κοράσιον ²καὶ περιεπάτει· ³ἦν γὰρ ἐτῶν δώδεκα.
Lc 8,55   καὶ   ἀνέστη παραχρῆμα,
Lc (8,42)   ὡς ἐτῶν δώδεκα

    1 : Rushbrooke, Stephenson, Schmid. **26**
    2 : Simons, Rushbrooke, Hawkins(II), Stanton(2), Easton, Boismard(McR).
    3 : Rushbrooke.

Mt   om.
Mc 5,43   καὶ εἶπεν δοθῆναι αὐτῇ φαγεῖν.
Lc   om.

    Rushbrooke.

§ 34. Mc 6,1-6a; Mt 13,53-58; (Lc 4,16-30)

Mt 13,54   καὶ ἐλθὼν εἰς τὴν πατρίδα αὐτοῦ
Mc 6,1   καὶ ¹ἔρχεται εἰς τὴν πατρίδα αὐτοῦ, ²καὶ ἀκολουθοῦσιν αὐτῷ οἱ μαθηταὶ αὐτοῦ.
Lc 4,16   καὶ ἦλθεν εἰς Ναζαρά,

    1 : Rushbrooke, Hawkins(VI), Schmid(5). **10**
    2 : Rushbrooke.

Mt 13,54   ἐδίδασκεν   αὐτοὺς ἐν τῇ συναγωγῇ αὐτῶν,
Mc 6,2   ἤρξατο   διδάσκειν   ἐν τῇ συναγωγῇ·
Lc 4,21   ἤρξατο δὲ λέγειν πρὸς αὐτούς

    Rushbrooke, Abbott, Keech. **23**

Mt 13,54   ὥστε   ἐκπλήσσεσθαι αὐτοὺς ¹καὶ λέγειν·
Mc 6,2   καὶ ²οἱ πολλοὶ ³ἀκούοντες   ἐξεπλήσσοντο   λέγοντες·
Lc 4,22   καὶ πάντες ἐμαρτύρουν αὐτῷ καὶ ἐθαύμαζον ...,   καὶ ἔλεγον·

    1 : Rushbrooke, Veit, Abbott, Keech. **(3) (15)**
    2 : Rushbrooke.
      Mc οι : — TR GNT(A).
    3 : Hansen.

Mt 13,54   καὶ αἱ δυνάμεις ;
Mc 6,2   καὶ αἱ δυνάμεις <u>τοιαῦται διὰ τῶν χειρῶν αὐτοῦ γινόμεναι</u> ;
Lc (4,23) ὅσα ἠκούσαμεν   γενόμενα

Rushbrooke, Hawkins(II), Boismard(McR).
Mc : και δυναμεις ... γινονται TR(+ οτι) T S ; ινα και δυναμεις δ. τ. χ. αυτου γινωνται GNT[1][2](B).

Mt 13,55   οὐχ οὗτός   ἐστιν ὁ [1]τοῦ τέκτονος υἱός ; οὐχ ἡ μήτηρ αὐτοῦ λέγεται Μαριάμ
Mc 6,3   οὐχ οὗτός   ἐστιν ὁ   [2]τέκτων, ὁ υἱὸς τῆς   Μαρίας
Lc 4,22   οὐχὶ   υἱός ἐστιν   <u>Ἰωσὴφ</u> οὗτος ;

1 : Holtzmann(r), Simons, Stanton(r), Keech, Brown.
2 : Wernle(t), Hawkins(IAb), Allen, Vaganay, Keech, Boismard(McR).
Mt [2]ουχ : ουχι TR S.

Mt 13,57   ὁ [1]δὲ Ἰησοῦς [2]εἶπεν αὐτοῖς·
Mc 6,4   καὶ   ἔλεγεν αὐτοῖς ὁ Ἰησοῦς [3]ὅτι
Lc 4,24   εἶπεν δέ·   ἀμὴν λέγω ὑμῖν ὅτι

1 : Rushbrooke, Veit, Abbott(VI?), Keech. **1**
2 : Rushbrooke, Veit, Abbott(V), Keech. **11**
3 : Hansen. **5**

Mt 13,57   ἐν τῇ πατρίδι   καὶ ἐν τῇ οἰκίᾳ αὐτοῦ.
Mc 6,4   ἐν τῇ πατρίδι αὐτοῦ <u>καὶ ἐν τοῖς συγγενεῦσιν αὐτοῦ</u> καὶ ἐν τῇ οἰκίᾳ αὐτοῦ.
Lc 4,24   ἐν τῇ πατρίδι αὐτοῦ.

Rushbrooke, Hawkins(II), Boismard(McR). **34**

Mt 13,58   καὶ οὐκ   ἐποίησεν [1]/ ἐκεῖ   δυνάμεις πολλὰς διὰ τὴν ἀπιστίαν αὐτῶν.
Mc 6,5   καὶ οὐκ [2]ἐδύνατο ἐκεῖ ποιῆσαι   οὐδεμίαν δύναμιν, [3]εἰ μὴ ὀλίγοις ἀρρώστοις
          <u>ἐπιθεὶς τὰς χεῖρας ἐθεράπευσεν.</u>   [4]καὶ ἐθαύμασεν διὰ τὴν ἀπιστίαν αὐτῶν.
Lc (4,23)   ποίησον / καὶ ὧδε ἐν τῇ πατρίδι σου.

1 : **21B**
2 : Rushbrooke, Hawkins(IAa), Allen.
3 : Rushbrooke, Boismard(McR).
4 : Hawkins(IAa), Allen, Vaganay.
Mc εθαυμασεν : -αζεν TR Ti h S GNT.

§ 35. Mc 6,6b-13; (Mt 9,35-10,16); Lc 9,1-6; (10,1-12)

Mt 9,35   καὶ περιῆγεν ὁ Ἰησοῦς τὰς [1]πόλεις πάσας   καὶ τὰς κώμας, διδάσκων
Mc 6,6b   καὶ περιῆγεν   τὰς <u>κώμας</u> [2]κύκλῳ   διδάσκων.
Lc (8,1) καὶ αὐτὸς διώδευεν   κατὰ πόλιν   καὶ   κώμην κηρύσσων
Lc (13,22) καὶ διεπορεύετο   κατὰ <u>πόλεις</u>   καὶ   κώμας διδάσκων

1 : (Lc 8,1) Rushbrooke, Larfeld, Cerfaux.
  (Lc 13,22) Abbott(H).
2 : Rushbrooke.

Mt 9,35 κηρύσσων τὸ εὐαγγέλιον   τῆς βασιλείας
Mc 6,6b om.
Lc (8,1) κηρύσσων καὶ εὐαγγελιζόμενος τὴν βασιλείαν τοῦ θεοῦ,

Stanton(3a), Larfeld, Cerfaux.

Mt 10,1 καὶ [1]προσκαλεσάμενος   τοὺς δώδεκα [2]μαθητὰς αὐτοῦ
Mc 6,7   καὶ προσκαλεῖται   τοὺς δώδεκα,   [3]καὶ ἤρξατο
Lc 9,1   συγκαλεσάμενος δὲ τοὺς δώδεκα (ἀποστόλους)

1 : Simons, Rushbrooke, Wernle, Hawkins(VI), Abbott(III), Stanton(2),
    Streeter(q), Easton(q), Schmid(5), Keech, Fuchs, Boismard(Mt). **3 10**
2 : Simons.
    Lc τους δωδεκα : + αποστολους S ; + μαθητας αυτου TR.
3 : Wernle, Stanton(2).

Mt 10,1.5 [1]ἔδωκεν αὐτοῖς ἐξουσίαν ...   [2]// (5) τούτους τοὺς δώδεκα [3]ἀπέστειλεν
Mc 6,7   [4]ἤρξατο αὐτοὺς ἀποστέλλειν [5]δύο δύο, [6]καὶ ἐδίδου αὐτοῖς ἐξουσίαν
Lc 9,1-2   ἔδωκεν αὐτοῖς δύναμιν καὶ ἐξουσίαν ... // (2) καὶ ἀπέστειλεν αὐτούς

1 : Simons, Rushbrooke, Veit, Wernle, Abbott, Allen, Streeter(q), Easton(q),
    Keech, Turner, Fuchs, Boismard(Mt). **11**
2 : Weiss, Simons, Cerfaux, Fuchs, Boismard(Mt). **35**
3 : Simons, Rushbrooke, Veit, Abbott, Easton, Schmid(8), De Solages(Q), Keech.
4 : Rushbrooke, Easton, Keech. Cf. 3. **13**
5 : Hawkins(IVa), Easton, Schmid(1,29), Keech.
6 : Rushbrooke.

Mt (10,8)   [1]δαιμόνια ἐκβάλλετε·
Mt 10,1 ἐξουσίαν πνευμάτων ἀκαθάρτων ὥστε ἐκβάλλειν αὐτά,
                        [2]καὶ θεραπεύειν πᾶσαν νόσον
Mc 6,7   ἐξουσίαν τῶν πνευμάτων τῶν ἀκαθάρτων,
Lc 9,1   ἐξουσίαν ἐπὶ πάντα τὰ δαιμόνια   καὶ νόσους θεραπεύειν·

1 : Rushbrooke, Abbott, Streeter(q).
2 : Weiss, Simons, Rushbrooke, Veit, Wernle, Hawkins(IB), Abbott(H),
    Burton, Stanton(3a), Streeter(q), Easton(q), Chapman, Keech, Turner,
    McLoughlin(ML), Fuchs, Boismard(Mt).

Mt (10,7) κηρύσσετε λέγοντες ὅτι ἤγγικεν   ἡ βασιλεία τῶν οὐρανῶν.
Mc 6,7   om.
Lc 9,2   κηρύσσειν   τὴν βασιλείαν τοῦ θεοῦ
Lc 10,9 λέγετε αὐτοῖς·   ἤγγικεν ἐφ' ὑμᾶς ἡ βασιλεία τοῦ θεοῦ.

Rushbrooke, Veit, Abbott(H), Stanton(3a), Easton(q), Schmid, Keech,
McLoughlin(DMRI), Boismard(Mt).
+ Lc 10,9 : Streeter(q), Keech.

Mt (10,8)   ἀσθενοῦντας θεραπεύετε,
Mc 6,7   om.
Lc 9,2   καὶ   ἰᾶσθαι (τοὺς ἀσθενοῦντας)
Lc (10,9)   θεραπεύετε τοὺς ἐν αὐτῇ ἀσθενεῖς,

Easton(q), Schmid.
+ Lc 10,9 : Streeter, Keech, Boismard(Mt).

Mt 10,5.9   παραγγείλας αὐτοῖς λέγων·... (9) μὴ   κτήσησθε
Mc 6,8   καὶ παρήγγειλεν αὐτοῖς   ἵνα μηδὲν αἴρωσιν
Lc 9,3   καὶ εἶπεν πρὸς αὐτούς·   μηδὲν αἴρετε

Simons, Rushbrooke, Hawkins(IVb), Schmid(23), Fuchs. **7A**

Mt 10,9-10   μὴ   κτήσησθε ... (10) μὴ πήραν εἰς   ὁδόν... [1]μηδὲ ῥάβδον·
Mc 6,8   ἵνα μηδὲν αἴρωσιν   εἰς   ὁδόν [2]εἰ μὴ   ῥάβδον μόνον,
Lc 9,3   μηδὲν αἴρετε   εἰς τὴν ὁδόν,   μήτε ῥάβδον

1 : Wilke, Weiss(r), Simons, Rushbrooke, Wernle(t), Abbott, Streeter, Lagrange,
Schmid, Da Fonseca, Vaganay, McLoughlin(R), Fuchs.
2 : Rushbrooke.

Mt 10,9   μὴ κτήσησθε   χρυσὸν μηδὲ ἄργυρον μηδὲ χαλκὸν εἰς τὰς ζώνας ὑμῶν,
Mc 6,8   μὴ   ἄρτον, μὴ   πήραν   μὴ   εἰς τὴν ζώνην χαλκόν,
Lc 9,3   μήτε πήραν, μήτε ἄρτον μήτε ἀργύριον

Wilke, Holtzmann, Weiss(r), Simons, Rushbrooke, Abbott(VII), Stanton(3a),
Streeter(q), Easton(q), Schmid, De Solages(Q), Keech, Fuchs.

Mt (10,9-10) μὴ κτήσησθε ... (10) ... [1]μηδὲ ὑποδήματα
Mc 6,9   [2]ἀλλὰ ὑποδεδεμένους σανδάλια,
Lc 9,3   om.
Lc 10,4   μὴ βαστάζετε ...,   μὴ   ὑποδήματα·

1 : Wilke, Weiss, Simons, Rushbrooke, Streeter(q), Schmid, Da Fonseca,
Keech.
2 : Wilke(t), Wernle(t), Hawkins(IVb).

Mt 10,9-10 μὴ κτήσησθε ... (10) ... μηδὲ   δύο χιτῶνας
Mc 6,9   καὶ μὴ ἐνδύσησθε δύο χιτῶνας.
Lc 9,3   μήτε   ἀνὰ δύο χιτῶνας ἔχειν.

Simons, Rushbrooke, Fuchs.
Mc ενδυσησθε : -σασθαι TR H(h -σησθε) Ru GNT.

Mt 10,10   ¹ἄξιος γὰρ ὁ ἐργάτης τῆς τροφῆς αὐτοῦ.
Mc 6,10   ²καὶ ἔλεγεν αὐτοῖς·
Lc 9,4   om.
Lc 10,7   ἄξιος γὰρ ὁ ἐργάτης τοῦ μισθοῦ αὐτοῦ.

      1 : Rushbrooke, Streeter(q), Keech.
      2 : Weiss, Simons, Rushbrooke, Easton, Schmid.

Mt 10,11   εἰς ¹ἣν δ' ἂν πόλιν ἢ κώμην ²// εἰσέλθητε,
Mc 6,10   ³ὅπου ἐὰν εἰσέλθητε εἰς οἰκίαν,
Lc 9,4   καὶ εἰς ἣν ἂν οἰκίαν   // εἰσέλθητε,
Lc 10,10   εἰς ἣν δ' ἂν πόλιν   // εἰσέλθητε

      1 : Wilke, Holtzmann, Simons, Rushbrooke, Veit, Stanton(3a), Schmid, Keech,
      Fuchs.
      Mc εαν : αν Holtzmann.
      2 : Veit, Easton, McLoughlin, Fuchs. **21B**
      3 : Rushbrooke, Fuchs.
      εἰς ἣν δ' ἂν πόλιν (Lc 10,10) : Streeter(q), Keech.

Mt 10,13   καὶ ἐὰν μὲν ᾖ ἡ οἰκία ἀξία, ἐλθάτω ἡ εἰρήνη ὑμῶν ἐπ' αὐτήν·
            ἐὰν δὲ μὴ ᾖ ἀξία, ἡ εἰρήνη ὑμῶν πρὸς ὑμᾶς ἐπιστραφήτω.
Mc 6,10   om.
Lc 9,4   om.
Lc (10,6)   καὶ ἐὰν ἐκεῖ ᾖ υἱὸς εἰρήνης, ἐπαναπαήσεται ἐπ' αὐτὸν ἡ εἰρήνη ὑμῶν·
            εἰ δὲ μή γε,   ἐφ' ὑμᾶς ἀνακάμψει.

      Rushbrooke, Streeter(q).

Mt 10,14   καὶ ὃς ἂν   μὴ δέξηται ὑμᾶς μηδὲ ἀκούσῃ τοὺς λόγους ὑμῶν,
Mc 6,11   καὶ ὃς ἂν ¹τόπος μὴ ²δέξηται ὑμᾶς μηδὲ ἀκούσωσιν   ὑμῶν,
Lc 9,5   καὶ ὅσοι ἂν   μὴ δέχωνται ὑμᾶς,

      1 : Simons, Rushbrooke, Easton, Schmid, Fuchs.
      2 : Sing. (cf. Mt), plur. (cf. Lc).

Mt 10,14   ἐξερχόμενοι ἔξω τῆς οἰκίας ἢ τῆς πόλεως ἐκείνης
Mc 6,11   ἐκπορευόμενοι   ἐκεῖθεν
Lc 9,5   ἐξερχόμενοι ἀπὸ   τῆς πόλεως ἐκείνης
Lc 10,10   ἐξελθόντες εἰς τὰς πλατείας αὐτῆς

      Wilke, Holtzmann, Weiss, Simons, Rushbrooke, Veit, Abbott(H), Stanton(3a),
      Streeter(q), Easton(q), Schmid, Chapman, De Solages(Q), Keech, Fuchs. **20**

Mt 10,14   ἐκτινάξατε τὸν ¹κονιορτὸν   τῶν ποδῶν ὑμῶν.
Mc 6,11   ἐκτινάξατε τὸν χοῦν ²τὸν ὑποκάτω τῶν ποδῶν ὑμῶν
Lc 9,5   τὸν κονιορτὸν ἀπὸ τῶν ποδῶν ὑμῶν ἀποτινάσσετε
Lc 10,11   καὶ τὸν κονιορτὸν ... εἰς τοὺς πόδας   ἀπομασσόμεθα

1 : Wilke, Weiss, Simons, Rushbrooke, Veit, Abbott(H), Stanton(3a), Stree-
ter(q), Easton(q), Schmid, Chapman, De Solages(Q), Keech, Fuchs. **32**
2 : Rushbrooke, Schmid(28).
Mt των ποδων : εκ τ.π. h S [GNT].

Mt 10,15   ἀμὴν λέγω ὑμῖν, ἀνεκτότερον ἔσται γῆ Σοδόμων καὶ Γομόρρων
                                  ἐν ἡμέρᾳ κρίσεως ἢ τῇ πόλει ἐκείνῃ.
Mc 6,11   om.
Lc 10,12   λέγω ὑμῖν, ὅτι Σοδόμοις ἐν τῇ ἡμέρᾳ ἐκείνῃ ἀνεκτότερον ἔσται
                                          ἢ τῇ πόλει ἐκείνῃ.
Rushbrooke, Streeter(q), Keech.

Mt 10,16   ἰδοὺ ἐγὼ ἀποστέλλω ὑμᾶς ὡς πρόβατα ἐν μέσῳ λύκων·
Mc 6,11   om.
Lc (10,3)   ὑπάγετε· ἰδοὺ (ἐγὼ) ἀποστέλλω ὑμᾶς ὡς ἄρνας ἐν μέσῳ λύκων.

Streeter(q), Keech.
Lc : + εγω TR.

Mt (11,1)   καὶ ... μετέβη ἐκεῖθεν τοῦ διδάσκειν καὶ κηρύσσειν ἐν ¹ταῖς πόλεσιν αὐτῶν.
Mc 6,12   καὶ ἐξελθόντες   ἐκήρυξαν ²ἵνα μετανοῶσιν,
Lc 9,6   ἐξερχόμενοι δὲ διήρχοντο κατὰ τὰς κώμας εὐαγγελιζόμενοι

1 : Easton, De Solages(f).
2 : Easton.

Mt   om.
Mc 6,13   καὶ ἤλειφον ἐλαίῳ πολλοὺς ἀρρώστους καὶ ἐθεράπευον.
Lc 9,6   καὶ θεραπεύοντες πανταχοῦ.

Wilke, Holtzmann(r), Rushbrooke, Wright, Stanton(1), Easton.

§ 36. Mc 6,14-16; Mt 14,1-2; Lc 9,7-9

Mt 14,1   ἐν ἐκείνῳ τῷ καιρῷ ἤκουσεν Ἡρώδης ¹/ ὁ ²τετραάρχης
Mc 6,14   ³καὶ ἤκουσεν ὁ βασιλεὺς Ἡρώδης,
Lc 9,7   ἤκουσεν δὲ Ἡρώδης / ὁ τετραάρχης

1 : Simons, Veit, Keech. **21B**
2 : Holtzmann, Weiss(r), Simons, Rushbrooke, Veit, Wernle, Hawkins(*),

Abbott, Allen, Stanton(2), Lagrange, Streeter(d), Easton, Schmid, Da
Fonseca, De Solages(c), Keech, McLoughlin(I), Boismard(r). **32**
3 : Rushbrooke, Schmid(4). **2**

Mt 14,1   ἤκουσεν   ῾Ηρῴδης... ¹τὴν ἀκοὴν ᾿Ιησοῦ,
Mc 6,14   ἤκουσεν ... ῾Ηρῴδης,   ²φανερὸν γὰρ ἐγένετο τὸ ὄνομα αὐτοῦ,
Lc 9,7   ἤκουσεν δὲ ῾Ηρῴδης... τὰ γινόμενα πάντα,

1 : Weiss(r), Simons, Schmid(33). **23**
2 : Weiss(r), Rushbrooke, Schmid(13). **8**

Mt 14,2   om.
Mc 6,14-15 καὶ ἔλεγον ...   (15) ἄλλοι δὲ ἔλεγον ...· ἄλλοι δὲ ἔλεγον
Lc 9,7-8   διὰ τὸ λέγεσθαι ὑπό τινων ..., (8) ὑπό τινων δὲ ..., ἄλλων δέ

Schmid(12).
Mc ελεγον : -γεν TR Ti T h S.

Mt 14,2   ᾿Ιωάννης ὁ βαπτιστής· αὐτὸς ¹ἠγέρθη   ἀπὸ τῶν νεκρῶν,
Mc 6,14   ὅτι ᾿Ιωάννης ²ὁ βαπτίζων   ἐγήγερται ἐκ   νεκρῶν,
Lc 9,7   ὅτι ᾿Ιωάννης   ἠγέρθη   ἐκ   νεκρῶν,

1 : Rushbrooke, Veit, Easton, Schmid(17), Brown, Keech. **11n**
2 : Schmid.

Mt 14,2   καὶ   εἶπεν τοῖς παισὶν αὐτοῦ·
Mc 6,16   ἀκούσας δὲ ὁ ῾Ηρῴδης ἔλεγεν·
Lc 9,9   εἶπεν δὲ [ὁ] ῾Ηρῴδης·

Rushbrooke, Abbott(V), De Solages(a). **11**

Mt (14,2)   οὗτός ἐστιν ᾿Ιωάννης ὁ βαπτιστής· αὐτὸς ἠγέρθη
Mc 6,16   οὗτος ἠγέρθη.
Lc 9,9   τίς δέ ἐστιν οὗτος περὶ οὗ ἀκούω τοιαῦτα ;

Rushbrooke, De Solages(d).

§ 37. Mc 6,17-29; Mt 14,3-12; (Lc 3,19-20)

Mt 14,3   διὰ ῾Ηρῳδιάδα τὴν γυναῖκα (om.)   τοῦ ἀδελφοῦ αὐτοῦ·
Mc 6,17   διὰ ῾Ηρῳδιάδα τὴν γυναῖκα Φιλίππου τοῦ ἀδελφοῦ αὐτοῦ,
Lc 3,19   περὶ ῾Ηρῳδιάδος τῆς γυναικὸς   τοῦ ἀδελφοῦ αὐτοῦ

Wernle.
Mt Φιλιππου : — Ti L,[T].

§ 38. Mc 6,30-44; Mt 14,13-21; Lc 9,10-17

Mt (14,12)	καὶ ἐλθόντες	ἀπήγγειλαν τῷ Ἰησοῦ.
Mc 6,30	καὶ ¹συνάγονται ... πρὸς τὸν Ἰησοῦν, ²καὶ ἀπήγγειλαν αὐτῷ	
Lc 9,10	καὶ ὑποστρέψαντες ...	διηγήσαντο αὐτῷ

1 : Rushbrooke. **10**
2 : Rushbrooke. **3**

Mt	om.
Mc 6,30	¹πάντα ὅσα ἐποίησαν ²καὶ ὅσα ἐδίδαξαν.
Lc 9,10	ὅσα ἐποίησαν.

1 : Rushbrooke.
2 : Wright.

Mt	om.
Mc 6,31	καὶ λέγει αὐτοῖς· δεῦτε ὑμεῖς αὐτοὶ κατ' ἰδίαν εἰς ἔρημον τόπον καὶ ἀναπαύσασθε ὀλίγον. ἦσαν γὰρ οἱ ἐρχόμενοι καὶ οἱ ὑπάγοντες πολλοί, καὶ οὐδὲ φαγεῖν εὐκαίρουν.
Lc	om.

Wilke, Rushbrooke, Wright, Wernle, Hawkins(III), Allen, Stanton(1 vel 2),
Schmid(32), Vaganay, Keech, Boismard(McR).

Mt 14,13	ἀκούσας δὲ ὁ Ἰησοῦς	¹ἀνεχώρησεν ἐκεῖθεν ἐν	πλοίῳ
Mc 6,32	καὶ	²ἀπῆλθον	ἐν ³τῷ πλοίῳ
Lc 9,10	καὶ παραλαβὼν αὐτοὺς	ὑπεχώρησεν	

1 : Weiss, Simons, Rushbrooke, Wernle, Abbott(H), Stanton(1 vel 2), Easton,
Schmid(20,28), Chapman, Da Fonseca, De Solages(c), Keech, Fuchs,
Boismard(Mt). **32**
2 : Rushbrooke, Vaganay (+ εν τω πλοιω : om. in Mt).
3 : Rushbrooke.

Mt 14,13	καὶ ¹ἀκούσαντες ²οἱ	ὄχλοι	ἠκολούθησαν αὐτῷ
Mc 6,33	³καὶ εἶδον αὐτοὺς ὑπάγοντας καὶ ἐπέγνωσαν πολλοί, ... ἀπὸ πασῶν ...		
			συνέδραμον ἐκεῖ καὶ προῆλθον αὐτούς.
Lc 9,11	οἱ δὲ ὄχλοι		γνόντες ἠκολούθησαν αὐτῷ·

1 : Simons, Hawkins(*), Lagrange, Schmid(7), Vaganay, Fuchs, Boismard(Mt). **3**
2 : Weiss, Simons, Rushbrooke, Veit, Wernle, Hawkins(*), Abbott(H), Stanton
(1 vel 2), Lagrange, Streeter(d), Easton, Schmid(12), Chapman, Vaganay,
Da Fonseca, De Solages(e), Keech, Brown, McLoughlin(MLIC?), Fuchs,
Boismard(Mt). **22**
3 : Simons, Rushbrooke, Hawkins(III), Easton, Schmid, Vaganay.

Mt 14,14   καὶ (om.) εἶδεν πολὺν ὄχλον,
Mc 6,34   καὶ ἐξελθὼν εἶδεν πολὺν ὄχλον,
Lc 9,11   καὶ   ἀποδεξάμενος αὐτούς

Vaganay.
Mt ἐξελθών : — sy^s c.

Mt 14,14   καὶ ἐσπλαγχνίσθη ἐπ᾽ αὐτοῖς
Mc 6,34   καὶ ἐσπλαγχνίσθη ἐπ᾽ αὐτοὺς ὅτι ἦσαν ὡς πρόβατα μὴ ἔχοντα ποιμένα,
Lc 9,11   καὶ ἀποδεξάμενος   αὐτούς

Wilke(r), Simons, Wright, Stanton(1 vel 2), Easton, Schmid, Keech.

Mt 14,14   om.
Mc 6,34   καὶ ἤρξατο διδάσκειν αὐτοὺς πολλά.
Lc 9,11   ἐλάλει   αὐτοῖς περὶ τῆς βασιλείας τοῦ θεοῦ,

Rushbrooke, Allen, Vaganay, Boismard(Mt). 13

Mt 14,14   καὶ ἐθεράπευσεν τοὺς ἀρρώστους αὐτῶν.
Mc 6,34   om.
Lc 9,11   καὶ τοὺς χρείαν ἔχοντας θεραπείας ἰᾶτο.

Wilke, Holtzmann, Weiss, Simons, Rushbrooke, Wright, Veit, Wernle, Haw-
kins(*), Abbott(H), Burton, Stanton(1 vel 2), Lagrange, Streeter(d), Easton,
Schmid, Vaganay, Da Fonseca, De Solages(f), Keech, McLoughlin(DMLC),
Fuchs, Boismard(Mt).

Mt 14,15   ὀψίας ¹δὲ   γενομένης
Mc 6,35   καὶ ²ἤδη ὥρας πολλῆς γενομένης
Lc 9,12   ἡ δὲ ἡμέρα ἤρξατο κλίνειν·

1 : Rushbrooke, Hawkins(VII), Abbott(VI), Schmid(4), De Solages(a), Keech. 1
2 : Rushbrooke, Schmid.
Mc γενομενης : γινομενης T h.

Mt 14,15   προσῆλθον   αὐτῷ οἱ μαθηταὶ   λέγοντες·
Mc 6,35   προσελθόντες αὐτῷ οἱ μαθηταὶ ¹αὐτοῦ ²ἔλεγον   ³ὅτι
Lc 9,12   προσελθόντες δὲ   οἱ δώδεκα   εἶπαν αὐτῷ·

1 : Rushbrooke, Easton, Schmid(30).
Mc αυτω : — T, [GNT].
2 : Schmid(6). 11
3 : Schmid(21). 5

Mt 14,15   καὶ ἡ ὥρα ἤδη παρῆλθεν·
Mc 6,35   καὶ   ἤδη ὥρα πολλή·
Lc 9,12   om.

Rushbrooke, Schmid.

Mt 14,15   ἀπόλυσον οὖν [1]τοὺς ὄχλους, ἵνα ἀπελθόντες εἰς [2]τὰς   κώμας
Mc 6,36   ἀπόλυσον   αὐτούς,   ἵνα ἀπελθόντες εἰς τοὺς κύκλῳ ἀγροὺς καὶ κώμας
Lc 9,12   ἀπόλυσον   τὸν ὄχλον, ἵνα πορευθέντες εἰς τὰς κύκλῳ κώμας καὶ ἀγρούς

    1 : Weiss, Rushbrooke, Abbott(I), Schmid(33), De Solages(e), Keech, Fuchs. **23**
    2 : Rushbrooke, Veit, De Solages(b).

Mt 14,15   ἀγοράσωσιν ἑαυτοῖς   βρώματα.
Mc 6,36   ἀγοράσωσιν ἑαυτοῖς   τί φάγωσιν.
Lc 9,12   καταλύσωσιν καὶ εὕρωσιν   ἐπισιτισμόν,
Lc (9,13)   ἀγοράσωμεν εἰς πάντα τὸν λαὸν τοῦτον βρώματα.

    Weiss, Simons, Rushbrooke, Abbott(VII), Streeter(d), Easton, Schmid(27),
    Keech. **14n**
    Lc 9,12 (ἐπισιτισμόν) : Schmid(27).

Mt 14,16   ὁ δὲ Ἰησοῦς   εἶπεν   αὐτοῖς· οὐ [1]χρείαν ἔχουσιν ἀπελθεῖν·
Mc 6,37   ὁ δὲ [2]ἀποκριθεὶς εἶπεν   αὐτοῖς·
Lc 9,13   εἶπεν δὲ πρὸς αὐτούς·
Lc (9,11)   τοὺς χρείαν ἔχοντας... ἰᾶτο.

    1 : Hansen.
    2 : Rushbrooke, Easton, Schmid(33). **16**

Mt 14,17   [1]οἱ δὲ λέγουσιν αὐτῷ·   [2]οὐκ ἔχομεν ὧδε εἰ μὴ πέντε [3]ἄρτους
Mc 6,37   καὶ λέγουσιν αὐτῷ· ... (v. 38 : πόσους ἔχετε ἄρτους ; ... πέντε, ...)
Lc 9,13   οἱ δὲ εἶπαν·   οὐκ εἰσὶν ἡμῖν πλεῖον ἢ ἄρτοι πέντε ... εἰ μήτι

    1 : Rushbrooke, Veit, Hawkins(VII), Abbott(VI), Easton, Schmid(4), De
    Solages(d,a), Keech, Fuchs. **1 22**
    2 : Weiss, Simons, Rushbrooke, Veit, Abbott(H), Easton, De Solages(f),
    Keech(Lc : εἰ μήτι), Fuchs.
    Mc εχετε αρτους : αρτους εχετε TR Ti T(Syn : εχ.α.) S GNT.
    3 : Fuchs (+ πέντε).
    Lc αρτοι πεντε : πεντε αρτοι TR Ti h S.

Mt   om.
Mc 6,37   [1]ἀπελθόντες ἀγοράσωμεν [2]δηναρίων διακοσίων] ἄρτους, [3]καὶ δώσομεν αὐτοῖς
          φαγεῖν ;
Lc 9,13   εἰ μήτι πορευθέντες ἡμεῖς ἀγοράσωμεν

    1 : Simons, Rushbrooke, Wernle, Hawkins(IB), Allen, Easton, Vaganay,
    Keech, Boismard(Mc).
    2 : Wilke(t), Rushbrooke, Wright, Schmid(29).
    3 : Holtzmann.

Mt   om.

Mc 6,38   ὁ δὲ λέγει αὐτοῖς· πόσους ἔχετε ἄρτους ; ὑπάγετε ἴδετε. καὶ γνόντες λέγουσιν· πέντε, καὶ δύο ἰχθύας.

Lc   om.

> Holtzmann, Simons, Wernle, Hawkins(III), Allen, Easton, Schmid, Vaganay, Keech, Fuchs, Boismard(Mc).

Mt 14,18-19   ὁ ¹δὲ εἶπεν...(19) καὶ κελεύσας ²τοὺς ὄχλους   ἀνακλιθῆναι
Mc 6,39   καὶ ἐπέταξεν αὐτοῖς   ἀνακλιθῆναι πάντας
Lc 9,14   εἶπεν δὲ   πρὸς τοὺς μαθητὰς αὐτοῦ· κατακλίνατε αὐτούς

> 1 : Rushbrooke, Fuchs.
> 2 : De Solages(e).

Mt 14,19   ἐπὶ τοῦ   χόρτου,
Mc 6,39   ¹συμπόσια συμπόσια ἐπὶ τῷ ²χλωρῷ χόρτῳ.
Lc 9,14   κλίσιας

> 1 : Wilke, Weiss, Rushbrooke, Hawkins(IVa), Schmid(1), Boismard(Mc).
> 2 : Rushbrooke, Allen, Vaganay.

Mt   om.

Mc 6,40   ¹καὶ ἀνέπεσαν ²πρασιαὶ πρασιαὶ⌐ ³κατὰ ἑκατὸν καὶ⌐ κατὰ πεντήκοντα.

Lc 9,15   καὶ ἐποίησαν οὕτως (v. 14 : κλίσιας ὡσεὶ ἀνὰ πεντήκοντα) καὶ κατέκλιναν ἅπαντας.

> 1 : Wilke, Weiss, Rushbrooke, Allen, Schmid(32), Vaganay, Boismard(Mc).
> 2 : Hawkins(IVa), Easton, Schmid(1).
> 3 : Easton.

Mt 14,19   λαβὼν... εὐλόγησεν,   καὶ   κλάσας
Mc 6,41   ¹καὶ λαβὼν... εὐλόγησεν   καὶ κατέκλασεν ²τοὺς ἄρτους
Lc 9,16   λαβὼν δὲ ... εὐλόγησεν αὐτοὺς καὶ κατέκλασεν,

> 1 : Rushbrooke, Fuchs. 2
> 2 : Rushbrooke, Fuchs(?).

Mt 14,19   ἔδωκεν τοῖς μαθηταῖς τοὺς ἄρτους, οἱ δὲ μαθηταὶ   ¹τοῖς ὄχλοις.
Mc 6,41   καὶ ἐδίδου τοῖς μαθηταῖς   ²ἵνα παρατιθῶσιν αὐτοῖς,
Lc 9,16   καὶ ἐδίδου τοῖς μαθηταῖς   παραθεῖναι τῷ ὄχλῳ.

> 1 : Weiss, Simons, Rushbrooke, Abbott(I), Schmid(33), De Solages(e), Keech, Fuchs. 23
> 2 : Rushbrooke, Schmid(23).
>   Mc μαθηταις : + αυτου TR S [GNT](C).

Mt 14,19   om.
Mc 6,41   καὶ τοὺς δύο ἰχθύας ἐμέρισεν πᾶσιν.
Lc 9,16   om.

         Wilke(t), Simons, Rushbrooke, Wernle, Stanton(1), Lagrange, Easton, Schmid,
         Vaganay, Keech, Fuchs, Boismard.

Mt 14,20   [1]τὸ περισσεῦον τῶν κλασμάτων, δώδεκα κοφίνους πλήρεις.
Mc 6,43   κλάσματα δώδεκα κοφίνων [2]πληρώματα [3]καὶ ἀπὸ τῶν ἰχθύων.
Lc 9,17   τὸ περισσεῦσαν αὐτοῖς κλασμάτων   κόφινοι δώδεκα.

         1 : Weiss, Simons, Rushbrooke, Wright, Veit, Wernle, Abbott(H), Stanton(3b),
             Streeter(d), Easton, Schmid, Chapman, De Solages(e,b), Keech, Brown,
             Fuchs, Boismard(Mt).
         2 : Streeter, Schmid.
         3 : Wilke(t), Weiss, Rushbrooke, Lagrange, Easton, Schmid, Vaganay, Keech.

Mt 14,21   οἱ δὲ ἐσθίοντες ἦσαν   ἄνδρες [1]/[2]ὡσεὶ πεντακισχίλιοι
Mc 6,44   [3]καὶ ἦσαν οἱ φαγόντες τοὺς ἄρτους πεντακισχίλιοι ἄνδρες.
Lc (9,14)   ἦσαν γὰρ   ὡσεὶ ἄνδρες /πεντακισχίλιοι.

         1 : Keech, Fuchs.   21B
         2 : Weiss, Simons, Rushbrooke, Wernle, Abbott(VII), Stanton(2 vel 4), Stree-
             ter(t), Easton, Schmid(33), De Solages(f), Keech, Fuchs.
         3 : Rushbrooke.
             Mc τους αρτους : [GNT](C).

§ 39. Mc 6,45-52; Mt 14,22-33

§ 40. Mc 6,53-56; Mt 14,34-36

§ 41. Mc 7,1-23; Mt 15,1-20

§ 42. Mc 7,24-30; Mt 15,21-28

§ 43. Mc 7,31-37; Mt 15,29-31

Mt 15,30-31   Multi aegroti
Mc 7,32-37   καὶ φέρουσιν αὐτῷ κωφὸν καὶ μογιλάλον, καὶ παρακαλοῦσιν αὐτὸν ἵνα ἐπιθῇ
              αὐτῷ τὴν χεῖρα. (33) καὶ ἀπολαβόμενος αὐτὸν ἀπὸ τοῦ ὄχλου κατ' ἰδίαν ἔβαλεν
              τοὺς δακτύλους αὐτοῦ εἰς τὰ ὦτα αὐτοῦ καὶ πτύσας ἥψατο τῆς γλώσσης αὐτοῦ,
              (34) καὶ ἀναβλέψας εἰς τὸν οὐρανὸν ἐστέναξεν, καὶ λέγει αὐτῷ· ἐφφαθά, ὅ
              ἐστιν διανοίχθητι. (35) καὶ ἠνοίγησαν αὐτοῦ αἱ ἀκοαί, καὶ εὐθὺς ἐλύθη ὁ
              δεσμὸς τῆς γλώσσης αὐτοῦ, καὶ ἐλάλει ὀρθῶς. (36) καὶ διεστείλατο αὐτοῖς ἵνα

μηδενὶ λέγωσιν· ὅσον δὲ αὐτοῖς διεστέλλετο, αὐτοὶ μᾶλλον περισσότερον
ἐκήρυσσον. (37) ὑπερπερισσῶς ἐξεπλήσσοντο λέγοντες· καλῶς πάντα πεποίηκεν,
καὶ τοὺς κωφοὺς ποιεῖ ἀκούειν, καὶ ἀλάλους λαλεῖν.

Lc   om.

Wright, Hawkins(IAa), Schmid, Vaganay, Boismard.

§ 44. Mc 8,1-10; Mt 15,32-39

§ 45. Mc 8,11-13; Mt 16,1-4; (Lc 11,16.29)

Mt 16,1   om.
Mt (12,38)   λέγοντες·
Mc 8,11   ἤρξαντο συζητεῖν αὐτῷ,
Lc 11,16   om.

Rushbrooke, Hawkins(V), Boismard(McR).

Mt 16,1   πειράζοντες ¹/ ἐπηρώτησαν αὐτὸν σημεῖον ²ἐκ τοῦ οὐρανοῦ ἐπιδεῖξαι αὐτοῖς.
Mt (12,38)   λέγοντες· διδάσκαλε, θέλομεν ἀπὸ σοῦ σημεῖον ἰδεῖν.
Mc 8,11   ζητοῦντες παρ' αὐτοῦ σημεῖον ἀπὸ τοῦ οὐρανοῦ, πειράζοντες ³αὐτόν.
Lc 11,16   πειράζοντες / σημεῖον ἐξ οὐρανοῦ ἐζήτουν παρ' αὐτοῦ.

   1 : Simons. **21B**
   2 : Rushbrooke, Abbott(VII), Schmid(20), De Solages(c), Keech. **31b**
   3 : Rushbrooke.

Mt 16,2   ὁ ¹δὲ ἀποκριθεὶς   εἶπεν αὐτοῖς·
Mt (12,39)   ὁ δὲ ἀποκριθεὶς   εἶπεν αὐτοῖς·
Mc 8,12   ²καὶ ἀναστενάξας τῷ πνεύματι αὐτοῦ   ³λέγει·
Lc 11,29   τῶν δὲ ὄχλων ἐπαθροιζομένων   ἤρξατο λέγειν·

   1 : Farmer. **1**
   2 : Rushbrooke, Hawkins(IAa), Allen, Boismard(McR).
   3 : Hansen.

Mt 16,4   γενεὰ   ¹πονηρὰ καὶ μοιχαλὶς   σημεῖον ²/ ἐπιζητεῖ,
Mt (12,39)   γενεὰ   πονηρὰ καὶ μοιχαλὶς   σημεῖον / ἐπιζητεῖ,
Mc 8,12   ³τί ἡ γενεὰ αὕτη   ζητεῖ σημεῖον ; ἀμὴν λέγω ὑμῖν,
Lc 11,29   ἡ γενεὰ αὕτη γενεὰ πονηρά ἐστιν·   σημεῖον / ζητεῖ,

   1 : Rushbrooke, Abbott(H), Stanton(3a), Streeter(q), Chapman, Da Fonseca, Keech.
   2 : Wright. **(21A)**
   3 : Rushbrooke, Allen, Keech. **6**
     Mc τι : οτι Turner

Mt 16,4   ¹καὶ σημεῖον οὐ δοθήσεται αὐτῇ εἰ μὴ τὸ σημεῖον Ἰωνᾶ.
Mt (12,39)   καὶ σημεῖον οὐ δοθήσεται αὐτῇ εἰ μὴ τὸ σημεῖον Ἰωνᾶ τοῦ προφήτου.
Mc 8,12   ²εἰ   δοθήσεται ³τῇ γενεᾷ ταύτῃ σημεῖον.
Lc 11,29   καὶ σημεῖον οὐ δοθήσεται αὐτῇ εἰ μὴ τὸ σημεῖον Ἰωνᾶ.

> 1 : Rushbrooke, Abbott(H), Stanton(3a), Streeter(q), Chapman, Da Fonseca,
> Keech, Boismard(Mc vel McR).
> 2 : Rushbrooke, Hawkins(IVa).
> 3 : Rushbrooke.

Mt 16,4-5   καὶ καταλιπὼν αὐτοὺς   ἀπῆλθεν. καὶ ἐλθόντες ... εἰς τὸ πέραν
Mc 8,13   καὶ ἀφεὶς αὐτοὺς πάλιν ἐμβὰς ἀπῆλθεν   εἰς τὸ πέραν.
Lc 11,29   om.

> Rushbrooke, Keech.

§ 46. Mc 8,14-21; Mt 16,5-12; (Lc 12,1)

Mt 16,5   om.
Mc 8,14   καὶ εἰ μὴ ἕνα ἄρτον οὐκ εἶχον μεθ' ἑαυτῶν ἐν τῷ πλοίῳ.
Lc 12,1   om.

> Rushbrooke, Wright, Hawkins(III).

Mt 16,5-6   καὶ ἐλθόντες οἱ ¹μαθηταὶ ... ἐπελάθοντο ... (6) ὁ δὲ Ἰησοῦς εἶπεν αὐτοῖς·
Mc 8,14-15   καὶ   ἐπελάθοντο ...(15) ²καὶ διεστέλλετο αὐτοῖς ³λέγων·
Lc 12,1   ἤρξατο λέγειν πρὸς τοὺς μαθητὰς αὐτοῦ πρῶτον·

> 1 : Rushbrooke, Abbott(I), Keech.
> 2 : Rushbrooke. 11
> 3 : (15)

Mt 16,6   ὁρᾶτε καὶ ¹προσέχετε ἀπὸ τῆς ζύμης τῶν Φαρισαίων καὶ Σαδδουκαίων.
Mc 8,15   ὁρᾶτε, βλέπετε ἀπὸ τῆς ζύμης τῶν Φαρισαίων καὶ ²τῆς ζύμης Ἡρῴδου.
Lc 12,1   προσέχετε ἑαυτοῖς ἀπὸ τῆς ζύμης, ἥτις ἐστὶν ὑπόκρισις, τῶν Φαρισαίων.

> 1 : Weiss(r), Simons, Rushbrooke, Veit, Hawkins(II,IVa), Abbott(H), Stanton
> (3a), Chapman, De Solages(c), Keech, Fuchs. 32
> 2 : Weiss(r), Simons, Rushbrooke, Boismard(McR).

§ 47. Mc 8,22-26

Mt   om.
Mc 8,22-26   καὶ ἔρχονται εἰς Βηθσαϊδάν. καὶ φέρουσιν αὐτῷ τυφλόν, καὶ παρακαλοῦσιν
αὐτὸν ἵνα αὐτοῦ ἅψηται. (23) καὶ ἐπιλαβόμενος τῆς χειρὸς τοῦ τυφλοῦ ἐξήνεγκεν

αὐτὸν ἔξω τῆς κώμης, καὶ πτύσας εἰς τὰ ὄμματα αὐτοῦ, ἐπιθεὶς τὰς χεῖρας αὐτῷ, ἐπηρώτα αὐτόν· εἴ τι βλέπεις ; (24) καὶ ἀναβλέψας ἔλεγεν· βλέπω τοὺς ἀνθρώπους, ὅτι ὡς δένδρα ὁρῶ περιπατοῦντας. (25) εἶτα πάλιν ἐπέθηκεν τὰς χεῖρας ἐπὶ τοὺς ὀφθαλμοὺς αὐτοῦ, καὶ διέβλεψεν καὶ ἀπεκατέστη, καὶ ἐνέβλεπεν τηλαυγῶς ἅπαντα. (26) καὶ ἀπέστειλεν αὐτὸν εἰς οἶκον αὐτοῦ λέγων· μηδὲ εἰς τὴν κώμην εἰσέλθῃς.

Lc   om.

Wright, Hawkins(IA), Schmid, Vaganay, Boismard.

§ 48. Mc 8,27-30 ; Mt 16,13-20 ; Lc 9,18-21

Mt 16,13   ἐλθὼν δὲ   ὁ Ἰησοῦς   εἰς τὰ μέρη   Καισαρείας
Mc 8,27   καὶ ἐξῆλθεν   ὁ Ἰησοῦς ... εἰς τὰς κώμας Καισαρείας
Lc 9,18   καὶ ἐγένετο ἐν τῷ εἶναι αὐτὸν προσευχόμενον κατὰ μόνας

Rushbrooke, Boismard(McR).   32

Mt 16,13   ἠρώτα   τοὺς μαθητὰς αὐτοῦ
                                                             λέγων·
Mc 8,27   [1a]καὶ οἱ μαθηταὶ αὐτοῦ ... καὶ [2]ἐν τῇ ὁδῷ ἐπηρώτα [1b]τοὺς μαθητὰς αὐτοῦ
                                                             λέγων [3]αὐτοῖς·
Lc 9,18   οἱ μαθηταί,   καὶ   ἐπηρώτησεν αὐτοὺς λέγων·

[1a] : Rushbrooke, Boismard(McR) ; [1a,b] : Hansen.   34
[2] : Rushbrooke, Hawkins(III), Easton, Schmid, Boismard.
[3] : Rushbrooke, Hawkins(II), Easton, Schmid, Glasson, Keech, Boismard. (23)

Mt 16,14   οἱ δὲ   εἶπαν·   οἱ μὲν Ἰωάννην τὸν βαπτιστήν,
Mc 8,28   οἱ δὲ   εἶπαν [1]αὐτῷ [2]λέγοντες [3]ὅτι   Ἰωάννην τὸν βαπτιστήν,
Lc 9,19   οἱ δὲ ἀποκριθέντες εἶπαν·   Ἰωάννην τὸν βαπτιστήν,

[1] : Rushbrooke, Easton, Schmid, Keech.   (23)
[2] : Rushbrooke, Hawkins(V), Schmid, Keech.   (15)
[3] : Rushbrooke, Easton, Schmid(21), Keech.   5
     Mc οτι : — TR, [S][GNT].
     Mc ειπαν : απεκριθησαν TR (— αυτω λεγοντες) S.

Mt 16,14   ἄλλοι [1]δὲ Ἠλίαν, ἕτεροι δὲ   Ἰερεμίαν ἢ ἕνα τῶν προφητῶν.
Mc 8,28   καὶ ἄλλοι Ἠλίαν, ἄλλοι δὲ ὅτι   [2]εἷς τῶν προφητῶν.
Lc 9,19   ἄλλοι δὲ Ἠλίαν, ἄλλοι δὲ ὅτι   προφήτης τις ... ἀνέστη.

[1] : Rushbrooke, Veit, Hawkins(VII), Abbott(VI), Easton, Schmid(4), De
     Solages(a), Keech.   1
[2] : (nom.) Boismard(r).

Mt 16,15   ¹λέγει   ²αὐτοῖς· ὑμεῖς δὲ τίνα με λέγετε εἶναι ;
Mc 8,29   ³καὶ ⁴αὐτὸς ⁵ἐπηρώτα αὐτούς· ὑμεῖς δὲ τίνα με λέγετε εἶναι ;
Lc 9,20   εἶπεν δὲ αὐτοῖς· ὑμεῖς δὲ τίνα με λέγετε εἶναι ;

1 : Simons, Schmid(33), De Solages(a), Keech. **19**
2 : Rushbrooke, Veit, Easton, De Solages(b), Keech.
3 : Simons, Rushbrooke, Schmid(4). **2**
4 : Simons, Rushbrooke, Easton, Schmid, Keech. **(22)**
5 : Cf. 1. **11**

Mt 16,16   ἀποκριθεὶς ¹δὲ Σίμων Πέτρος ²εἶπεν·
Mc 8,29   ἀποκριθεὶς   ³ὁ Πέτρος λέγει ⁴αὐτῷ·
Lc 9,20   Πέτρος δὲ ἀποκριθεὶς   εἶπεν·

1 : Rushbrooke, Veit, Hawkins(IVc), Abbott(II), Easton, Schmid(3), De
    Solages(d). **4**
    Mc : + δε S.
2 : Rushbrooke, Veit, Wernle, Hawkins(VI), Abbott(V), Easton, Schmid(5),
    De Solages(a). **10**
3 : Easton, Schmid, Keech. **33b**
4 : Easton, Keech. **(23)**

Mt 16,16   σὺ εἶ ὁ χριστὸς ὁ υἱὸς τοῦ θεοῦ τοῦ ζῶντος.
Mc 8,29   σὺ εἶ ὁ χριστός.
Lc 9,20   τὸν χριστὸν   τοῦ θεοῦ.

Simons, Rushbrooke, Wright, Veit, Hawkins(*), Abbott(H), Streeter(d),
Larfeld, Easton, Schmid, Da Fonseca, De Solages(f), Keech, Brown, McLoughlin
(ML).

Mt 16,20   τότε   ¹(διεστείλατο) τοῖς μαθηταῖς ἵνα ... ὅτι αὐτός ἐστιν
Mc 8,30   ²καὶ ἐπετίμησεν αὐτοῖς   ἵνα ... ³περὶ αὐτοῦ.
Lc 9,21   ὁ δὲ ἐπιτιμήσας αὐτοῖς παρήγγειλεν   ... τοῦτο,

1 : Veit.
    Mt επετιμησεν : διεστειλατο TR T h S L GNT.
2 : Rushbrooke, Schmid(4). **2**
3 : Rushbrooke.

§ 49. Mc 8,31-33; Mt 16,21-23; Lc 9,22

Mt 16,21   ἀπὸ τότε ἤρξατο Ἰησοῦς Χριστὸς δεικνύειν τοῖς μαθηταῖς αὐτοῦ ὅτι
Mc 8,31   καὶ   ἤρξατο   διδάσκειν αὐτοὺς   ὅτι
Lc 9,22   εἰπὼν   ὅτι

Rushbrooke. **2**

Mt 16,21   καὶ πολλὰ παθεῖν   ἀπὸ τῶν πρεσβυτέρων
Mc 8,31   πολλὰ παθεῖν καὶ ἀποδοκιμασθῆναι ὑπὸ τῶν πρεσβυτέρων
Lc 9,22   πολλὰ παθεῖν καὶ ἀποδοκιμασθῆναι ἀπὸ τῶν πρεσβυτέρων

Weiss(r), Simons, Rushbrooke, Veit, Wernle, Abbott, Easton, Schmid(20), De Solages(c), Keech, Brown. **31c**

Mt 16,21   καὶ   ἀρχιερέων καὶ   γραμματέων ... καὶ [1]τῇ τρίτῃ ἡμέρᾳ [2]ἐγερθῆναι.
Mc 8,31   καὶ [3]τῶν ἀρχιερέων καὶ τῶν γραμματέων ... καὶ μετὰ τρεῖς ἡμέρας ἀναστῆναι·
Lc 9,22   καὶ   ἀρχιερέων καὶ   γραμματέων ... καὶ τῇ τρίτῃ ἡμέρᾳ ἐγερθῆναι.

1 : Wilke, Holtzmann, Weiss(or), Simons, Rushbrooke, Veit, Wernle, Hawkins (IC), Abbott(H), Stanton(3b), Streeter(d), Easton, Schmid(29), Chapman, De Solages(e,b), Keech, Brown, Turner, Boismard(r). **31c**
2 : Wilke, Holtzmann, Rushbrooke, Veit, Abbott(H), Stanton(3b), Easton, Schmid, Chapman, De Solages(c), Keech, Turner, Boismard(r). **32**
    Lc εγερθηναι : αναστηναι h.
3 : Weiss(r), Simons, Rushbrooke, Easton, Schmid, Keech, Turner. **33b**

Mt   om.
Mc 8,32   καὶ παρρησίᾳ τὸν λόγον ἐλάλει.
Lc   om.

Holtzmann, Rushbrooke, Wright, Wernle, Hawkins(IC), Schmid, Boismard (McR).

§ 50. Mc 8,34-9,1; Mt 16,24-28; Lc 9,23-27

Mt 16,24   τότε ὁ Ἰησοῦς εἶπεν   τοῖς μαθηταῖς αὐτοῦ·
Mc 8,34   [1]καὶ [2]προσκαλεσάμενος [3]τὸν ὄχλον [4]σὺν τοῖς μαθηταῖς αὐτοῦ εἶπεν [5]αὐτοῖς·
Lc 9,23   ἔλεγεν δὲ πρὸς πάντας·

1 : Rushbrooke. **2**
2 : Rushbrooke, Easton, Keech.
3 : Schmid(30).
4 : Rushbrooke.
5 : Rushbrooke, Schmid. **23**

Mt 16,24   [1]εἴ τις θέλει ὀπίσω μου [2]ἐλθεῖν,
Mc 8,34   (ὅστις) θέλει ὀπίσω μου (ἀκολουθεῖν),
Lc 9,23   εἴ τις θέλει ὀπίσω μου ἔρχεσθαι,

1 : Veit, Easton, Schmid, Turner.
    Mc ει τις : οστις TR Ti T.
2 : Wernle, Turner.
    Mc ελθειν : ακολουθειν Ti T S ; Lc ερχεσθαι : ελθειν TR.

Mt 16,25   ὃς γὰρ ἐὰν θέλῃ τὴν ψυχὴν ¹/ αὐτοῦ σῶσαι, ... ²ἀπολέσῃ τὴν ψυχὴν αὐτοῦ
Mc 8,35   ὃς γὰρ ἐὰν θέλῃ τὴν ᵃ(ἑαυτοῦ ψυχὴν) σῶσαι, ... ἀπολέσει τὴν ᵇψυχὴν αὐτοῦ
Lc 9,24   ὃς γὰρ ἐὰν θέλῃ τὴν ψυχὴν / αὐτοῦ σῶσαι, ... ἀπολέσῃ τὴν ψυχὴν αὐτοῦ

        1 : Wright. 21B
           Mc ψυχην αυτου : ᵃεαυτου ψυχην H(h ψ. αυτου) s ; ᵇεαυτου ψυχην Ti S(s ψ. αυτου).
        2 : Rushbrooke, De Solages(b), Keech.
           Mc απολεσει : -ση TR W S ; Lc 17,33 απολεσει : -ση TR Ti W S GNT.

Mt 16,25   ἕνεκεν ἐμοῦ,
Mc 8,35   ἕνεκεν ἐμοῦ καὶ τοῦ εὐαγγελίου,
Lc 9,24   ἕνεκεν ἐμοῦ,

        Wilke, Holtzmann, Weiss(r /q), Simons, Rushbrooke, Wright, Wernle, Hawkins,
        Stanton(1), Easton, Schmid, Keech. 34
        ἐμοῦ (Mc : ἕνεκεν τοῦ εὐαγγελίου) : Turner, Boismard(McR).
        Mc εμου και : [H] [GNT¹²](C).

Mt 16,26   τί γὰρ ¹ὠφεληθήσεται ἄνθρωπος, ἐὰν τὸν κόσμον ὅλον κερδήσῃ,
Mc 8,36   τί γὰρ ὠφελεῖ   ἄνθρωπον ²κερδῆσαι τὸν κόσμον ὅλον
Lc 9,25   τί γὰρ ὠφελεῖται   ἄνθρωπος κερδήσας τὸν κόσμον ὅλον

        1 : Wilke, Holtzmann, Weiss(r), Simons, Rushbrooke, Wernle, Abbott(VIII),
           Stanton(2), Easton, Schmid(18), De Solages(bᵇⁱˢ), Keech, Turner. 17
           Lc ωφελειται : -λει h ; Mc ωφελει : -λησει TR h.
        2 : Schmid.
           Mc ανθρωπον : + τον Ti h.

Mt 16,26   τὴν   ¹δὲ ψυχὴν αὐτοῦ ²// ζημιωθῇ ;
Mc 8,36   καὶ ζημιωθῆναι τὴν ψυχὴν αὐτοῦ ;
Lc 9,25   ἑαυτὸν δὲ // ἀπολέσας ἢ ζημιωθείς ;

        1 : Rushbrooke, Hawkins(VII), Abbott(VI), Stanton(2), Schmid(4), De
           Solages(a), Keech. 1
        2 : Wright, Veit. (21A)

Mt   om.
Mc 8,38   ἐν τῇ γενεᾷ ταύτῃ τῇ μοιχαλίδι καὶ ἁμαρτωλῷ,
Lc 9,26   om.

        Holtzmann, Weiss(r), Rushbrooke, Wright, Hawkins(IC), Easton, Schmid,
        Vaganay.

Mt 16,28   ἀμὴν λέγω   ὑμῖν   ὅτι
Mc 9,1   καὶ ἔλεγεν αὐτοῖς· ἀμὴν λέγω   ὑμῖν   ὅτι
Lc 9,27   λέγω δὲ ὑμῖν ἀληθῶς,

        Weiss(r), Simons, Rushbrooke, Wright, Wernle, Easton, Schmid, Keech.

Mt 16,28   εἰσίν τινες τῶν ¹/ ὧδε   ἑστώτων   ... ἐρχόμενον ἐν τῇ βασιλείᾳ αὐτοῦ.
Mc 9,1   εἰσίν τινες ὧδε   τῶν   ἑστηκότων ... ²ἐληλυθυῖαν ἐν δυνάμει.
Lc 9,27   εἰσίν τινες τῶν | αὐτοῦ ἑστηκότων

        1 : Weiss(r), Wright, Veit, Hawkins(IVa) Easton, Schmid, Brown.   **21B**
             Mc : των ωδε TR S.
        2 : Rushbrooke, Keech.

§ 51. Mc 9,2-10; Mt 17,1-9; Lc 9,28-36

Mt 17,1   τὸν Πέτρον καὶ   Ἰάκωβον καὶ   Ἰωάννην τὸν ἀδελφὸν αὐτοῦ,
Mc 9,2   τὸν Πέτρον καὶ τὸν Ἰάκωβον καὶ (τὸν) Ἰωάννην,
Lc 9,28   Πέτρον καὶ   Ἰωάννην καὶ   Ἰάκωβον

        Easton, Schmid, Keech, Boismard(Mt).   **33b**
        Mt Ιακωβον : + τον h.
        Mc Ιωαννην : + τον TR h S GNT.

Mt 17,1   καὶ ἀναφέρει αὐτοὺς εἰς   ὄρος ὑψηλὸν κατ' ἰδίαν.
Mc 9,2   καὶ ἀναφέρει αὐτοὺς εἰς   ὄρος ὑψηλὸν κατ' ἰδίαν μόνους.
Lc 9,28   ἀνέβη   εἰς τὸ ὄρος   προσεύξασθαι.

        Rushbrooke, Wright, Hawkins(II,V), Easton, Schmid.

Mt 17,2   καὶ μετεμορφώθη ... καὶ ἔλαμψεν   τὸ πρόσωπον αὐτοῦ ὡς ὁ ἥλιος,
Mc 9,2   καὶ μετεμορφώθη ...
Lc 9,29   καὶ ἐγένετο ...   τὸ εἶδος τοῦ προσώπου αὐτοῦ ἕτερον

        Weiss, Simons, Rushbrooke, Veit, Wernle, Abbott(H), Burton, Streeter(t),
        Schmid, Chapman, De Solages(g), Keech, McLoughlin(I).   **22**

Mt 17,2   τὰ δὲ ἱμάτια   αὐτοῦ ἐγένετο   λευκὰ ὡς τὸ φῶς.
Mc 9,3   καὶ τὰ ἱμάτια   αὐτοῦ ἐγένετο ¹στίλβοντα λευκὰ ²λίαν,
       ³οἷα γναφεὺς ἐπὶ τῆς γῆς οὐ δύναται οὕτως λευκᾶναι.
Lc 9,29   καὶ ὁ ἱματισμὸς αὐτοῦ   λευκὸς ἐξαστράπτων.

        1 : Rushbrooke, Veit, Schmid(32).   **12**
        2 : Holtzmann(r), Rushbrooke, Schmid(32), Keech.
        3 : Wilke, Holtzmann(r), Weiss, Simons, Rushbrooke, Wright, Wernle, Hawkins
            (II,IVa), Allen, Stanton(2 vel 1), Easton, Schmid(32), Glasson, Keech,
            Boismard(McR).

124   MC 9,4-7

Mt 17,3   καὶ ¹ἰδοὺ   ὤφθη αὐτοῖς   Μωϋσῆς ²/ καὶ Ἠλίας
Mc 9,4   καὶ   ὤφθη αὐτοῖς   Ἠλίας σὺν Μωϋσεῖ,
Lc 9,30   καὶ ἰδοὺ ἄνδρες δύο … οἵτινες ἦσαν Μωϋσῆς / καὶ Ἠλίας,

    1 : Weiss, Simons, Rushbrooke, Veit, Wernle, Abbott(H), Stanton(2), Easton,
        Schmid(33), Chapman, De Solages(d), Keech, Brown. 25
    2 : Weiss, Simons, Wright, Veit, Schmid, Keech, Boismard(McR). 21B

Mt 17,3   ¹Μωϋσῆς καὶ Ἠλίας   συλλαλοῦντες ²μετ᾽ αὐτοῦ.
Mc 9,4   Ἠλίας σὺν Μωϋσεῖ, ³καὶ ἦσαν συλλαλοῦντες τῷ Ἰησοῦ.
Lc 9,30   συνελάλουν αὐτῷ, οἵτινες ἦσαν Μωϋσῆς καὶ Ἠλίας,

    1 : Rushbrooke, Veit, Abbott(VII), Schmid, De Solages(c), Keech.
    2 : Rushbrooke, Veit, Abbott(VII), De Solages(e), Keech. (23)
    3 : Hawkins(IVa). 12

Mt 17,4   ἀποκριθεὶς δὲ ὁ Πέτρος ¹εἶπεν τῷ Ἰησοῦ· κύριε, …· εἰ θέλεις, ποιήσω
                                                        ὧδε τρεῖς σκηνάς,
Mc 9,5   καὶ ἀποκριθεὶς ὁ Πέτρος λέγει τῷ Ἰησοῦ· ²ῥαββί, …, καὶ   ποιήσωμεν
                                                        τρεῖς σκηνάς,
Lc 9,33   εἶπεν ὁ Πέτρος πρὸς τὸν Ἰησοῦν· ἐπιστάτα, …, καὶ   ποιήσωμεν
                                                        σκηνὰς τρεῖς,

    1 : Simons, Rushbrooke, Veit, Wernle, Hawkins(VI), Abbott(V), Easton,
        Schmid(5), De Solages(a), Keech, Boismard(Mt). 10
    2 : Weiss, Rushbrooke, Schmid(1). 30
    Mt τρεις σκηνας : σκηνας τρεις h.

Mt (17,6) καὶ ¹ἐφοβήθησαν σφόδρα.
Mc 9,6   ²ἔκφοβοι γὰρ ἐγένοντο.
Lc (9,34) ἐφοβήθησαν δὲ ἐν τῷ εἰσελθεῖν αὐτοὺς εἰς τὴν νεφέλην.

    1 : Weiss, Simons, Rushbrooke, Wright, Abbott(VII), Stanton(3b), Easton,
        Schmid, De Solages(g), Keech, McLoughlin(PMI), Boismard(Mt).
    2 : Wilke(t), Rushbrooke.

Mt 17,5   ¹ἔτι   αὐτοῦ λαλοῦντος, ἰδοὺ   νεφέλη φωτεινὴ ²ἐπεσκίασεν ³αὐτούς,
Mc 9,7   ⁴καὶ   ἐγένετο νεφέλη   ἐπισκιάζουσα αὐτοῖς,
Lc 9,34   ταῦτα δὲ αὐτοῦ λέγοντος ἐγένετο νεφέλη καὶ   ἐπεσκίαζεν αὐτούς·

    1 : Weiss, Simons, Wright, Veit, Wernle, Hawkins(*), Abbott(H), Stanton
        (3b), Lagrange, Streeter(t), Easton, Schmid(25,33), Da Fonseca, De Solages
        (g), Keech, McLoughlin(DML), Boismard(Mt). (14)
        αὐτοῦ : Rushbrooke.
    2 : Weiss, Simons, Rushbrooke, Easton, Schmid(9), Boismard(Mt). 12
    3 : Weiss, Rushbrooke, Veit, Easton, Schmid, De Solages(b), Keech, Boismard
        (Mt).
    4 : Rushbrooke. 2

Mt 17,5   καὶ ἰδοὺ   φωνὴ ἐκ τῆς νεφέλης λέγουσα·
Mc 9,7   καὶ ἐγένετο φωνὴ ἐκ τῆς νεφέλης·
Lc 9,35   καὶ φωνὴ ἐγένετο ἐκ τῆς νεφέλης λέγουσα·

Weiss, Simons, Rushbrooke, Wright, Veit, Wernle, Abbott(VII), Stanton(3b), Easton, Schmid(33), Chapman, De Solages(d), Keech, Brown, Boismard(Mt).
15

Mt 17,8   ἐπάραντες δὲ τοὺς ὀφθαλμοὺς αὐτῶν
Mc 9,8   καὶ ¹ἐξάπινα ²περιβλεψάμενοι
Lc 9,36   καὶ ἐν τῷ γενέσθαι τὴν φωνήν

1 : Rushbrooke. 26
2 : Rushbrooke, Boismard(McR).

Mt 17,8   οὐδένα εἶδον εἰ μὴ αὐτὸν Ἰησοῦν μόνον.
Mc 9,8   ¹οὐκέτι οὐδένα εἶδον ²(ἀλλὰ) τὸν Ἰησοῦν μόνον ³μεθ᾽ ἑαυτῶν.
Lc 9,36 εὑρέθη			Ἰησοῦς μόνος.

1 : Rushbrooke, Allen, Easton. 34
2 : Rushbrooke, Schmid(15). 9B
   Mc ει μη : αλλα TR Ti T h S GNT.
3 : Wright, Hawkins(II), Easton.

Mt 17,9   μηδενὶ εἴπητε   // τὸ ὅραμα
Mc 9,9   ἵνα μηδενὶ ἃ εἶδον διηγήσωνται,
Lc 9,36   καὶ οὐδενὶ ἀπήγγειλαν ... // οὐδὲν ὧν ἑώρακαν.

Veit. 21A

Mt 17,9   ἐνετείλατο   αὐτοῖς ὁ Ἰησοῦς λέγων· μηδενὶ εἴπητε τὸ ὅραμα
Mc 9,9-10 ᵃδιεστείλατο αὐτοῖς ἵνα   μηδενὶ ἃ εἶδον διηγήσωνται, ...
           (10) ᵇκαὶ τὸν λόγον ἐκράτησαν πρὸς ἑαυτούς
Lc 9,36   καὶ αὐτοὶ ἐσίγησαν καὶ οὐδενὶ ἀπήγγειλαν ... οὐδὲν ὧν ἑώρακαν.

Weiss, Rushbrooke, Hawkins(II,V).

Mt 17,9   om.
Mc 9,10   καὶ τὸν λόγον ἐκράτησαν πρὸς ἑαυτοὺς συζητοῦντες τί ἐστιν τὸ ἐκ νεκρῶν
           ἀναστῆναι.
Lc 9,36   om.

Weiss(r), Rushbrooke, Wright, Allen, Easton.

§ 52. Mc 9,11-13; Mt 17,10-13

§ 53. Mc 9,14-29; Mt 17,14-21; Lc 9,37-43a

Mt 17,14   καὶ ¹ἐλθόντων πρὸς τὸν   ὄχλον
Mc 9,14   καὶ ἐλθόντες ²πρὸς τοὺς μαθητὰς εἶδον   ὄχλον πολύν
Lc 9,37   κατελθόντων αὐτῶν ἀπὸ τοῦ ὄρους συνήντησεν αὐτῷ ὄχλος πολύς.

        1 : Simons, Rushbrooke, Wernle. Cf. Mc 9,9.
        2 : Stanton(2), Easton, Schmid(30), Vaganay.

Mt 17,14   τὸν ὄχλον
Mc 9,14   ὄχλον πολὺν περὶ αὐτοὺς καὶ γραμματεῖς συζητοῦντας πρὸς αὐτούς.
Lc 9,37   ὄχλος πολύς.

        Wilke, Simons, Rushbrooke, Wernle, Hawkins(III), Stanton(1), Easton,
        Schmid(30), Vaganay, Keech, Boismard.

Mt 17,14   om.
Mc 9,15-16 ¹καὶ εὐθὺς πᾶς ὁ ὄχλος ἰδόντες αὐτὸν ²ἐξεθαμβήθησαν⌝, καὶ προστρέχοντες
            ἠσπάζοντο αὐτόν. (16) καὶ ἐπηρώτησεν αὐτούς· τί συζητεῖτε πρὸς αὐτούς;
Lc 9,37   om.

        1 : Wilke, Simons, Rushbrooke, Wright, Wernle, Hawkins(III), Allen, Stanton
            (2), Easton, Schmid(32), Vaganay, Keech, Boismard(McR).
        2 : Hawkins(IC).

Mt 17,14-15 προσῆλθεν   αὐτῷ ¹ἄνθρωπος   γονυπετῶν αὐτὸν (15) καὶ   ²λέγων·
Mc 9,17   καὶ ³ἀπεκρίθη αὐτῷ εἷς ἐκ τοῦ ὄχλου·
Lc 9,38   καὶ ἰδοὺ   ἀνὴρ ἀπὸ τοῦ ὄχλου   ἐβόησεν λέγων·

        1 : Schmid, Keech. 32
        2 : Simons, Rushbrooke, Wright, Veit, Wernle, Abbott(VII), Easton, Schmid
            (33), Vaganay, De Solages(d), Keech. 15
        3 : Rushbrooke. Cf. 2. 16n

Mt 17,15   κύριε,   ¹ἐλέησόν   μου τὸν υἱόν,
Mc 9,17   διδάσκαλε, ²ἤνεγκα   τὸν υἱόν μου ³πρὸς σέ,
Lc 9,38   διδάσκαλε, δέομαί σου ἐπιβλέψαι ἐπὶ τὸν υἱόν μου,

        1 : Vaganay.
        2 : Vaganay.
        3 : Rushbrooke, Easton.

Mt 17,15   ¹ὅτι σεληνιάζεται καὶ κακῶς ἔχει·
Mc 9,17-18   ²ἔχοντα πνεῦμα ἄλαλον· (18) καὶ ³ὅπου ἐὰν αὐτὸν καταλάβῃ,
Lc 9,38-39   ὅτι μονογενής μοί ἐστιν,   (39) καὶ ἰδοὺ πνεῦμα   λαμβάνει αὐτόν,

1 : Rushbrooke, Wernle, Abbott(VII), Vaganay, De Solages(f), Keech.
2 : Simons, Rushbrooke, Easton, Schmid, Vaganay.
3 : Rushbrooke.

Mt 17,15   om.
Mc 9,18   ῥήσσει αὐτόν, καὶ ἀφρίζει καὶ τρίζει τοὺς ὀδόντας καὶ ξηραίνεται·
Lc 9,39   καὶ ἐξαίφνης κράζει καὶ σπαράσσει αὐτὸν μετὰ ἀφροῦ,

Rushbrooke, Stanton(1 vel 2), Easton, Vaganay.

Mt 17,16   καὶ προσήνεγκα αὐτὸν ... καὶ οὐκ ¹ἠδυνήθησαν αὐτὸν θεραπεῦσαι.
Mc 9,18   καὶ ²εἶπα ...   καὶ οὐκ ἴσχυσαν.
Lc 9,40   καὶ ἐδεήθην ...   καὶ οὐκ ἠδυνήθησαν.

1 : Weiss(r), Simons, Rushbrooke, Veit, Wernle, Abbott, Stanton(2), Easton,
    Schmid(28), Chapman, Vaganay, De Solages(c), Keech, Brown, Boismard
    (McR). 32
2 : Rushbrooke, Vaganay.

Mt 17,17   ἀποκριθεὶς ¹/ δὲ ὁ ²·Ἰησοῦς   ³εἶπεν·
Mc 9,19   ὁ δὲ ἀποκριθεὶς   ⁴αὐτοῖς λέγει·
Lc 9,41   ἀποκριθεὶς / δὲ ὁ Ἰησοῦς   εἶπεν·

1 : Simons, Easton, Keech. 21B
    Mt ἀποκριθεις δε : [τοτε] απ. h.
2 : Wilke, Holtzmann, Weiss, Simons, Rushbrooke, Veit, Easton, Schmid,
    Vaganay, De Solages(d), Keech. 22
3 : Wilke, Holtzmann, Weiss, Simons, Rushbrooke, Veit, Hawkins(VI),
    Abbott(V), Easton, Schmid(5), Vaganay, De Solages(a), Keech. 10
4 : Weiss, Simons, Rushbrooke, Schmid, Vaganay, Keech. (23)

Mt 17,17   ὦ γενεὰ ἄπιστος ¹καὶ διεστραμμένη, ἕως ...; φέρετέ μοι αὐτὸν ²ὧδε.
Mc 9,19   ὦ γενεὰ ἄπιστος,   ἕως ...; φέρετε   αὐτὸν πρός με.
Lc 9,41   ὦ γενεὰ ἄπιστος καὶ διεστραμμένη, ἕως ...; προσάγαγε   ὧδε τὸν υἱόν σου.

1 : Wilke, Holtzmann, Weiss, Simons, Rushbrooke, Wright, Veit, Wernle(t),
    Hawkins(*), Abbott(H), Stanton(4 vel 3b), Lagrange, Streeter(t), Easton,
    Schmid, Chapman, Da Fonseca, Vaganay, De Solages(f), Keech, Brown,
    McLoughlin(T), Boismard(t).
2 : Weiss, Simons, Rushbrooke, Wright, Veit, Wernle, Abbott(H), Streeter(t),
    Easton, Schmid, Vaganay, De Solages(e), Keech, Boismard(t). (23)

Mt 17,17   om.
Mc 9,20   καὶ ¹ἤνεγκαν αὐτὸν πρὸς αὐτόν. καὶ ἰδὼν αὐτὸν τὸ πνεῦμα εὐθὺς συνεσπάραξεν
            αὐτόν,²καὶ πεσὼν ἐπὶ τῆς γῆς ἐκυλίετο ἀφρίζων.
Lc 9,42   ἔτι δὲ προσερχομένου αὐτοῦ   ἔρρηξεν αὐτὸν τὸ δαιμόνιον καὶ συνεσπάραξεν·

            1 : Rushbrooke, Vaganay.
            2 : Rushbrooke, Simons, Stanton(1 vel 2), Easton, Schmid, Vaganay, Keech.

Mt 17,17   om.
Mt 9,21   καὶ ἐπηρώτησεν τὸν πατέρα αὐτοῦ· πόσος χρόνος ἐστὶν ὡς τοῦτο γέγονεν αὐτῷ;
            ὁ δὲ εἶπεν· ἐκ παιδιόθεν·
Lc 9,42   om.

            Wilke, Holtzmann, Weiss, Simons, Rushbrooke, Wright, Wernle, Allen,
            Stanton(1 vel 2), Easton, Schmid, Vaganay, Keech, Boismard(McR).

Mt (17,15b) πολλάκις γὰρ πίπτει   εἰς τὸ πῦρ   καὶ πολλάκις εἰς τὸ ὕδωρ.
Mc 9,21-22 καὶ πολλάκις   καὶ εἰς   πῦρ αὐτὸν ἔβαλεν καὶ   εἰς   ὕδατα
            ἵνα ἀπολέσῃ αὐτόν· ἀλλ’ εἴ τι δύνῃ, βοήθησον ἡμῖν σπλαγχνισθεὶς ἐφ’ ἡμᾶς.
Lc 9,42   om.

            Wilke, Holtzmann, Weiss, Simons, Rushbrooke, Wright, Hawkins(IC), Stanton
            (1 vel 2), Easton, Schmid, Vaganay, Keech, Boismard(McR).

Mt 17,17   om. (17,20 : ἐὰν ἔχητε πίστιν ... καὶ οὐδὲν ἀδυνατήσει ὑμῖν.)
Mc 9,23   ὁ δὲ Ἰησοῦς εἶπεν αὐτῷ· τὸ εἰ δύνῃ, πάντα δυνατὰ τῷ πιστεύοντι.
Lc 9,42   om.

            Wilke, Holtzmann, Weiss, Simons, Rushbrooke, Wright, Wernle, Hawkins(IC),
            Stanton(1 vel 2), Easton, Schmid, Vaganay, Keech, Boismard(McR).

Mt 17,17   om.
Mc 9,24   εὐθὺς κράξας ὁ πατὴρ τοῦ παιδίου ἔλεγεν· πιστεύω· βοήθει μου τῇ ἀπιστίᾳ.
Lc 9,42   om.

            Wilke, Holtzmann, Weiss, Simons, Rushbrooke, Wright, Wernle, Hawkins(IC),
            Stanton(1 vel 2), Easton, Schmid, Vaganay, Keech, Boismard(McR).

Mt 17,18   καὶ ἐπετίμησεν αὐτῷ ¹// ²ὁ Ἰησοῦς,
Mc 9,25   ³ἰδὼν δὲ ὁ Ἰησοῦς ὅτι ἐπισυντρέχει ὄχλος, ἐπετίμησεν   τῷ
Lc 9,42   ἐπετίμησεν δὲ   // ὁ Ἰησοῦς τῷ

            1 : Keech.   21B
            2 : Veit.   22
            3 : Simons, Rushbrooke, Wright, Stanton(1 vel 2), Easton, Schmid, Vaganay,
                Keech.

Mt 17,18   om.
Mc 9,25   λέγων αὐτῷ· τὸ ἄλαλον καὶ κωφὸν πνεῦμα, ἐγὼ ἐπιτάσσω σοι, ἔξελθε ἐξ αὐτοῦ
           καὶ μηκέτι εἰσέλθῃς εἰς αὐτόν.
Lc 9,42   om.

           Simons, Rushbrooke, Wright, Stanton(1 vel 2), Easton, Schmid, Vaganay,
           Keech.

Mt 17,18   καὶ   ἐξῆλθεν ἀπ' ¹αὐτοῦ τὸ δαιμόνιον,
Mc 9,26   καὶ ²κράξας καὶ πολλὰ σπαράξας ἐξῆλθεν·
Lc 9,42   καὶ   (ἀφῆκεν   αὐτόν)

           1 : Vaganay.
           Lc ιασατο τον παιδα : αφηκεν αυτον (D e).
           2 : Simons, Rushbrooke, Wernle, Hawkins(III), Stanton(1 vel 2), Easton,
           Schmid, Vaganay, Keech.

Mt 17,18   om.
Mc 9,26   καὶ ἐγένετο ὡσεὶ νεκρός, ὥστε τοὺς πολλοὺς λέγειν ὅτι ἀπέθανεν.
Lc 9,42   om.

           Wilke, Simons, Rushbrooke, Wright, Wernle, Hawkins(III), Stanton(1 vel 2),
           Easton, Schmid, Vaganay, Keech, Boismard(McR).

Mt 17,18   om.
Mc 9,27   ὁ δὲ Ἰησοῦς κρατήσας τῆς χειρὸς αὐτοῦ ἤγειρεν αὐτόν, καὶ ἀνέστη.
Lc 9,42   om.

           Rushbrooke, Wright, Stanton(1 vel 2), Easton, Vaganay, Keech, Boismard
           (McR).

Mt 17,18   ¹καὶ   ²ἐθεραπεύθη ³ὁ παῖς   ἀπὸ τῆς ὥρας ἐκείνης.
Mc 9,27   ὁ δὲ ... ἤγειρεν   αὐτόν, καὶ ἀνέστη.
Lc 9,42   καὶ   ἰάσατο   τὸν παῖδα καὶ ἀπέδωκεν αὐτὸν τῷ πατρὶ αὐτοῦ.

           1 : Rushbrooke, Veit, De Solages(a), McLoughlin(DML). 1
           Lc : v.l. ad Mc 9,26.
           2 : Weiss, Simons, Schmid, Vaganay, Keech, McLoughlin(DML).
           3 : Weiss, Simons, Rushbrooke, Veit, Abbott(I), Schmid(33), Vaganay,
           De Solages(e), Keech, McLoughlin(DML). 23 33a

Mt 17,19   τότε προσελθόντες   οἱ μαθηταὶ τῷ Ἰησοῦ κατ' ἰδίαν
Mc 9,28   καὶ εἰσελθόντος αὐτοῦ εἰς οἶκον οἱ μαθηταὶ αὐτοῦ   κατ' ἰδίαν
Lc 9,43   om.

           Rushbrooke.

Mt 17,20   ὁ δὲ λέγει αὐτοῖς· ...   καὶ οὐδὲν ἀδυνατήσει ὑμῖν.
Mc 9,29   καὶ εἶπεν αὐτοῖς· τοῦτο τὸ γένος ἐν οὐδενὶ δύναται ἐξελθεῖν εἰ μὴ ἐν προσευχῇ.
Lc 9,43   om.

Rushbrooke, Schmid, Vaganay.

§ 54. Mc 9,30-32; Mt 17,22-23; Lc 9,43b-45

Mt 17,22   ¹συστρεφομένων ²δὲ αὐτῶν ἐν τῇ Γαλιλαίᾳ
Mc 9,30   ³κἀκεῖθεν ἐξελθόντες παρεπορεύοντο   διὰ τῆς Γαλιλαίας,
Lc 9,43   πάντων δὲ θαυμαζόντων

    1 : Simons. (14)
    2 : Rushbrooke, Hawkins(VII), Abbott(VI), Schmid(4), Keech. 1
    3 : Rushbrooke.

Mt 17,22   om.
Mc 9,30   καὶ οὐκ ἤθελεν ἵνα τις γνοῖ·
Lc 9,43   om.

Wilke, Rushbrooke, Wright, Allen, Stanton(1), Schmid.

Mt 17,22   ¹εἶπεν αὐτοῖς ὁ Ἰησοῦς·
Mc 9,31   ²ἐδίδασκεν γὰρ τοὺς μαθητὰς αὐτοῦ, καὶ ἔλεγεν αὐτοῖς   ³ὅτι
Lc 9,43   εἶπεν πρὸς τοὺς μαθητὰς αὐτοῦ·

    1 : Simons, Rushbrooke, Veit, Wernle, Abbott(V), Easton, Schmid(6), De
        Solages(a), Keech. 11
    2 : Wilke, Rushbrooke, Easton, Schmid(31).
    3 : Rushbrooke, Easton, Schmid(21). 5
        Mc αυτοις : [H].

Mt 17,22   μέλλει ὁ   υἱὸς τοῦ ἀνθρώπου   παραδίδοσθαι
Mc 9,31   ὁ   υἱὸς τοῦ ἀνθρώπου   παραδίδοται
Lc 9,44   ὁ γὰρ υἱὸς τοῦ ἀνθρώπου μέλλει παραδίδοσθαι

Wilke, Holtzmann, Weiss, Simons, Rushbrooke, Wright, Wernle, Hawkins(IC),
Abbott(H), Stanton(2 vel 3b), Easton, Schmid(17), De Solages(e,b), Keech,
Boismard(Mt). 11n

Mt 17,23   καὶ ἀποκτενοῦσιν αὐτόν, καὶ   τῇ τρίτῃ ἡμέρᾳ ἐγερθήσεται.
Mc 9,31   καὶ ἀποκτενοῦσιν αὐτόν, καὶ ἀποκτανθεὶς μετὰ τρεῖς ἡμέρας ἀναστήσεται.
Lc 9,44   om.

Rushbrooke, Easton, Schmid.

§ 55. Mc 9,33-37; Mt 18,1-5; Lc 9,46-48

Mt(17,24-25) ἐλθόντων ¹δὲ αὐτῶν εἰς Καφαρναούμ ...(25)... καὶ ἐλθόντα εἰς τὴν οἰκίαν
Mt 18,1   ἐν ἐκείνῃ τῇ ὥρᾳ
Mc 9,33   ²καὶ ἦλθον εἰς Καφαρναούμ.   καὶ ἐν τῇ οἰκίᾳ γενομένος
Lc 9,46   εἰσῆλθεν δέ

    1 : Hansen. **1**
    2 : Rushbrooke, Wright, Schmid(32). **2**

Mt 18,1   προσῆλθον οἱ μαθηταὶ τῷ Ἰησοῦ λέγοντες·
Mc 9,33-34   ἐπηρώτα αὐτούς· τί ἐν τῇ ὁδῷ διελογίζεσθε; (34) οἱ δὲ ἐσιώπων· πρὸς ἀλλήλους
                             γὰρ διελέχθησαν ἐν τῇ ὁδῷ
Lc 9,46   εἰσῆλθεν δὲ   διαλογισμὸς   ἐν αὐτοῖς,

    Wilke, Simons, Rushbrooke, Wernle, Hawkins(III), Allen, Easton, Schmid(31),
    Vaganay, Boismard(McR).

Mt 18,1   τίς ἄρα   μείζων ἐστὶν ἐν τῇ βασιλείᾳ τῶν οὐρανῶν ;
Mc 9,34   τίς   μείζων.
Lc 9,46   τὸ τίς ἂν εἴη μείζων αὐτῶν.

    Schmid(33), De Solages(d). **24**

Mt   om.
Mc 9,35   καὶ καθίσας ἐφώνησεν τοὺς δώδεκα καὶ λέγει αὐτοῖς· εἴ τις θέλει πρῶτος
            εἶναι, ἔσται πάντων ἔσχατος καὶ πάντων διάκονος.
Lc   om.

    Wilke(t), Rushbrooke, Wright, Hawkins(III), Stanton(1), Easton, Schmid,
    Glasson.
    Wernle(t) : Mt 18,4 ; Lc 9,48b.
    Vaganay : Mt 23,11 ; Lc 22,26.

Mt 18,4   ὅστις οὖν ταπεινώσει ἑαυτὸν ... ¹// ²οὗτός ἐστιν ὁ μείζων
Mt (23,11)   ³ὁ δὲ   μείζων   ὑμῶν ἔσται ὑμῶν διάκονος. (cf. Mc 10,43 ; Mt 20,26)
Mc 9,35   εἴ τις θέλει ⁴πρῶτος εἶναι, ἔσται ⁵πάντων ἔσχατος καὶ πάντων διάκονος.
Lc 9,48   ὁ γὰρ μικρότερος ἐν πᾶσιν ὑμῖν ὑπάρχων, // οὗτός ἐστιν μέγας.
Lc (22,26)   ἀλλ' ὁ μείζων ἐν ὑμῖν γινέσθω ὡς ὁ νεώτερος, καὶ ὁ ἡγούμενος ὡς ὁ διακονῶν.
            (cf. Mc 10,43)

    1 : Hansen. **21B**
    2 : Simons.
    3 : Rushbrooke, Abbott(H).
    4 . Rushbrooke.
    5 : Rushbrooke, Hawkins(V).

Mt 18,2-3   καὶ ¹προσκαλεσάμενος παιδίον ... (3) καὶ   εἶπεν·
Mc 9,36   καὶ   λαβὼν   παιδίον ...   καὶ ²ἐναγκαλισάμενος αὐτὸ εἶπεν αὐτοῖς·
Lc 9,47-48 ἐπιλαβόμενος   παιδίον ...(48) καὶ   εἶπεν αὐτοῖς·

1 : Schmid, Boismard(r). 32
2 : Wilke, Simons, Rushbrooke, Wright, Wernle, Hawkins(III), Stanton(2),
    Easton, Schmid(32), Vaganay, Keech, Boismard(McR).

Mt 18,5   καὶ ὃς ¹ἐὰν δέξηται ²// ἓν ³παιδίον τοιοῦτο
Mc 9,37   ὃς ἂν ἓν τῶν τοιούτων παιδίων δέξηται ...· καὶ ὃς ἂν ἐμὲ δέχηται,
Lc 9,48   ὃς ἐὰν δέξηται // τοῦτο τὸ παιδίον ...·   καὶ ὃς ἂν ἐμὲ δέξηται,

1 : Veit, Vaganay, Keech.
   Lc εαν : αν H Ru S GNT.
2 : Veit, Easton, Schmid(14), Vaganay, Keech. 21A
3 : Schmid, De Solages(b), Keech.
Add. Mt 18,4 ; Lc 9,48c : Simons, Schmid.

Mt 18,5   om.
Mc 9,37   οὐκ ἐμὲ δέχεται ἀλλὰ τὸν ἀποστείλαντά με.
Lc 9,48   δέχεται   τὸν ἀποστείλαντά με·

Rushbrooke, Keech.

§ 56. Mc 9,38-41; Lc 9,49-50

§ 57. Mc 9,42-48; Mt 18,6-9; (Lc 17,1-2)

Mt 18,7   ἀνάγκη γὰρ   ἐλθεῖν τὰ σκάνδαλα,   πλὴν οὐαὶ τῷ ἀνθρώπῳ δι' οὗ
            τὸ σκάνδαλον ἔρχεται.
Mc 9,42   om.
Lc 17,1   ἀνένδεκτόν ἐστιν τοῦ   τὰ σκάνδαλα μὴ ἐλθεῖν, οὐαὶ δὲ   δι' οὗ
                                  ἔρχεται·

Weiss, Rushbrooke, Veit, Stanton(3a), Easton(q), Chapman, Keech.
Mt : + εστιν T Ru ; Lc ουαι δε : πλην ουαι H Ru GNT.

§ 58. Mc 9,49-50; (Mt 5,13); (Lc 14,34-35)

Mt 5,13   ὑμεῖς ἐστε   τὸ ἅλας τῆς γῆς·
Mc 9,49-50 πᾶς γὰρ πυρὶ ἁλισθήσεται. (50) καλὸν   τὸ ἅλας·
Lc 14,34   καλὸν οὖν τὸ ἅλας·

Holtzmann, Rushbrooke, Wright, Schmid, Keech.

Mt 5,13   ἐὰν δὲ   τὸ ἅλας ¹μωρανθῇ,   ἐν τίνι   ²ἁλισθήσεται ;
Mc 9,50   ἐὰν δὲ   τὸ ἅλας ἄναλον γένηται, ἐν τίνι ³αὐτὸ ἀρτύσετε ;
Lc 14,34   ἐὰν δὲ καὶ τὸ ἅλας μωρανθῇ,   ἐν τίνι   ἀρτυθήσεται ;

1 : Weiss, Rushbrooke, Veit, Abbott(H), Streeter(q), Schmid, Vaganay, Da
Fonseca, De Solages(Q), Keech. 32
2 : Veit (Lc : ἁλισθήσεται), Vaganay. 17
Lc : αλισθησεται (sa bo).
3 : Rushbrooke, Vaganay.

Mt 5,13   εἰς οὐδὲν   ἰσχύει ἔτι εἰ μὴ βληθὲν ἔξω
Mc 9,50   om.
Lc 14,35   οὔτε εἰς γῆν οὔτε εἰς κοπρίαν εὔθετόν ἐστιν· ἔξω βάλλουσιν αὐτό.

Streeter, Schmid, Vaganay, De Solages(Q), Keech.

Mt (5,13) ὑμεῖς ἐστε τὸ ἅλας τῆς γῆς·
Mc 9,50   ἔχετε ἐν ἑαυτοῖς ἅλα καὶ εἰρηνεύετε ἐν ἀλλήλοις.
Lc 14,35   om.

Holtzmann, Rushbrooke, Wright, Stanton(1), Schmid, Vaganay, Keech,
Boismard(McR).

§ 59. Mc 10,1-12; Mt 19,1-12

Mt 19,1   καὶ ¹ἐγένετο ὅτε ἐτέλεσεν ὁ Ἰησοῦς τοὺς λόγους ... καὶ ἦλθεν   εἰς
Mc 10,1   καὶ ἐκεῖθεν ἀναστὰς   ²ἔρχεται   εἰς
Lc (9,51) ἐγένετο δὲ ἐν τῷ συμπληροῦσθαι τὰς ἡμέρας ... τοῦ πορεύεσθαι εἰς

1 : Schmid.
2 : Schmid(5).

Mt 19,1   καὶ ἐγένετο ὅτε ἐτέλεσεν ...   μετῆρεν ἀπὸ τῆς   Γαλιλαίας
Mc 10,1   καὶ   ἐκεῖθεν ἀναστὰς ἔρχεται
Lc (17,11) καὶ ἐγένετο ἐν τῷ πορεύεσθαι ... διὰ μέσον Σαμαρείας καὶ Γαλιλαίας.

Rushbrooke, Veit, Abbott(H), Keech.

Mt 19,9   ὃς ἂν ἀπολύσῃ τὴν γυναῖκα ... καὶ γαμήσῃ ἄλλην, μοιχᾶται.
Mt (5,32) ¹πᾶς ὁ ἀπολύων τὴν γυναῖκα ...   ποιεῖ αὐτὴν ²μοιχευθῆναι,
Mc 10,11   ὃς ἂν ἀπολύσῃ τὴν γυναῖκα ... καὶ γαμήσῃ ἄλλην, μοιχᾶται ³ἐπ' αὐτήν·
Lc (16,18) πᾶς ὁ ἀπολύων τὴν γυναῖκα ... καὶ γαμῶν ἑτέραν μοιχεύει,

1 : Rushbrooke, Abbott(V), Keech.
2 : Rushbrooke, Abbott.
3 : Rushbrooke.

Mt (5,32)   καὶ ὃς ἐὰν ¹ἀπολελυμένην   γαμήσῃ,   μοιχᾶται.
Mt 19,9   om.
Mc 10,12   ²καὶ ἐὰν αὐτὴ ἀπολύσασα τὸν ἄνδρα αὐτῆς γαμήσῃ ἄλλον, μοιχᾶται.
Lc (16,18) καὶ ὁ   ἀπολελυμένην ἀπὸ ἀνδρὸς γαμῶν   μοιχεύει.

1 : Rushbrooke, Abbott, Keech.
2 : Abbott, Stanton(1).
Mt : + και ο απολελυμενην γαμησας μοιχαται TR Ti h S (γαμων).

§ 60. Mc 10,13-16; Mt 19,13-15; Lc 18,15-17

Mt 19,13   τότε ¹προσηνέχθησαν αὐτῷ ... ἐπετίμησαν αὐτοῖς.
Mc 10,13   ²καὶ προσέφερον   αὐτῷ ... ἐπετίμησαν αὐτοῖς.
Lc 18,15   προσέφερον δὲ   αὐτῷ ... ἐπετίμων αὐτοῖς.

1 : Weiss(r) : bis aor. (Mt), bis impf. (Lc). **11n**
2 : Weiss(r), Rushbrooke, Schmid(4). **2**
   αὐτοῖς : Wilke, Weiss(1865), Veit.
   Mc επετιμησαν αυτοις : -μων τοις προσφερουσιν TR Ti T S.

Mt 19,14   ὁ δὲ Ἰησοῦς   εἶπεν·
Mc 10,14   ¹ἰδὼν δὲ ὁ Ἰησοῦς ²ἠγανάκτησεν καὶ εἶπεν ³αὐτοῖς·
Lc 18,16   ὁ δὲ Ἰησοῦς προσεκαλέσατο αὐτὰ λέγων·

1 : Wilke, Weiss(r), Simons, Wernle, Easton, Schmid(33), Keech.
2 : Wilke, Weiss(r), Simons, Rushbrooke, Wernle, Hawkins(IAb), Allen,
    Stanton(2), Easton, Schmid(32), Vaganay, Keech.
3 : Weiss(r). **(23)**
   Mt : + αυτοις T h.

Mt 19,14   ἄφετε τὰ παιδία   καὶ μὴ κωλύετε αὐτὰ ἐλθεῖν πρός με·
Mc 10,14   ἄφετε τὰ παιδία ἔρχεσθαι πρός με,   μὴ κωλύετε αὐτά·
Lc 18,16   ἄφετε τὰ παιδία ἔρχεσθαι πρός με καὶ μὴ κωλύετε αὐτά·

Weiss(r), Simons, Rushbrooke, Wright, Hawkins(IVc), Abbott(II), Easton,
Schmid(3), De Solages(d), Keech. **4**

Mt 19,15   καὶ   ἐπιθεὶς τὰς χεῖρας αὐτοῖς
Mc 10,16   καὶ ἐναγκαλισάμενος αὐτὰ⁷ κατευλόγει τιθεὶς τὰς χεῖρας ἐπ᾽ αὐτά.
Lc 18,17   om.

Wilke(t :⁷), Weiss(r), Rushbrooke, Wright, Hawkins(III,V), Stanton(2),
Easton.

§ 61. Mc 10,17-22; Mt 19,16-22; Lc 18,18-23

Mt 19,(15).16   ἐπορεύθη ἐκεῖθεν.   (16) καὶ ἰδοὺ   εἷς προσελθὼν αὐτῷ
Mc 10,17   ¹καὶ ἐκπορευομένου αὐτοῦ εἰς ὁδὸν προσδραμὼν εἷς ²καὶ γονυπετήσας αὐτόν
Lc 18,18   καὶ...   τις ... ἄρχων

    1 : Weiss(r /q), Simons, Rushbrooke, Hawkins(III), Easton, Schmid(32),
       Keech, Boismard(McR).
    2 : Wilke, Weiss(r /q), Simons, Rushbrooke, Hawkins(III), Stanton(2 vel 1),
       Easton, Schmid(32), Keech, Boismard(McR).

Mt 19,16   αὐτῷ ¹εἶπεν·
Mc 10,17   ²ἐπηρώτα   αὐτόν·
Lc 18,18   καὶ ἐπηρώτησέν τις αὐτὸν ἄρχων λέγων·

    1 : Hansen.
    2 : Schmid(6). **11**

Mt 19,18   οὐ ψευδομαρτυρήσεις,
Mc 10,19   μὴ ψευδομαρτυρήσῃς, μὴ ἀποστερήσῃς,
Lc 18,20   μὴ ψευδομαρτυρήσῃς,

    Holtzmann, Weiss(r /q), Simons, Rushbrooke, Wright, Wernle, Stanton(2),
    Easton, Schmid, Glasson, Keech.

Mt 19,20   ¹λέγει αὐτῷ ὁ νεανίσκος·
Mc 10,20   ὁ δὲ ἔφη   αὐτῷ·   ²διδάσκαλε,
Lc 18,21   ὁ δὲ εἶπεν·

    1 : Schmid, De Solages(a). **11**
    2 : Weiss(r /q), Simons, Rushbrooke, Wernle, Stanton(2), Easton, Schmid,
       Keech. **30**

Mt 19,20   ταῦτα πάντα ἐφύλαξα·
Mc 10,20   ταῦτα πάντα ἐφυλαξάμην ἐκ νεότητός μου.
Lc 18,21   ταῦτα πάντα ἐφύλαξα   ἐκ νεότητος.

    Weiss(r /q), Simons, Rushbrooke, Wernle, Easton, Schmid(27), De Solages(b),
    Keech, Boismard(Mt). **17n**

Mt 19,21   ἔφη αὐτῷ ὁ Ἰησοῦς·
Mc 10,21   ὁ δὲ Ἰησοῦς ἐμβλέψας αὐτῷ ἠγάπησεν αὐτὸν καὶ εἶπεν αὐτῷ·
Lc 18,22   ἀκούσας δὲ ὁ Ἰησοῦς   εἶπεν αὐτῷ·

    Wilke(r), Weiss(r /q), Simons, Rushbrooke, Wernle, Hawkins(III), Allen,
    Stanton(2), Easton, Schmid(32), Keech, Boismard(McR).

Mt 19,(20).21 τί ¹ἔτι   ὑστερῶ ; (21) ... καὶ   δὸς   πτωχοῖς,
Mc 10,21   ἔν σε ὑστερεῖ· ...   καὶ   δὸς ²τοῖς πτωχοῖς,
Lc 18,22   ἔτι ἔν σοι λείπει· ...   καὶ διάδος   πτωχοῖς,

1 : Weiss(r /q), Simons, Wright, Easton, Schmid, De Solages(f), Boismard(Mt).
2 : Schmid, Keech. **33b**
   Mc τοις : — Ti, [H] [Ru] [GNT] ; Mt : + τοις Ti GNT, [H] [Ru].

Mt 19,21   καὶ ἔξεις θησαυρὸν ἐν   οὐρανοῖς,
Mc 10,21   καὶ ἔξεις θησαυρὸν ἐν   οὐρανῷ,
Lc 18,22   καὶ ἔξεις θησαυρὸν ἐν τοῖς οὐρανοῖς,

Weiss(r /q), Simons, Rushbrooke, Abbott(VIII), Easton, Schmid, De Solages
(b), Keech, Boismard(Mt). **33c**

Mt 19,22   ¹ἀκούσας δὲ ὁ νεανίσκος τὸν λόγον [τοῦτον] ἀπῆλθεν λυπούμενος·
Mc 10,22   ὁ δὲ ²στυγνάσας ἐπὶ   τῷ λόγῳ   ἀπῆλθεν λυπούμενος,
Lc 18,23   ὁ δὲ ἀκούσας   ταῦτα περίλυπος ἐγενήθη,

1 : Wilke, Holtzmann, Weiss(r /q), Simons, Rushbrooke, Veit, Wernle, Abbott
   (H), Stanton(2), Easton, Schmid(33), De Solages(e), Keech, Boismard(Mt). **23**
   Mt τον λογον [τουτον] : — Ti T ; τον λογον TR S GNT³(C) ; τ.λ. τουτον W L.
2 : Wilke, Holtzmann, Rushbrooke, Hawkins(III,V), Easton, Schmid, Keech. **32**

Mt 19,22.23   ἔχων κτήματα πολλά. (23) ... πλούσιος
Mc 10,22.23   ἔχων κτήματα πολλά. (23) ... οἱ τὰ χρήματα ἔχοντες
Lc 18,23.24   πλούσιος   σφόδρα. (24) ... οἱ τὰ χρήματα ἔχοντες

Schmid.

§ 62. Mc 10,23-27 ; Mt 19,23-26 ; Lc 18,24-27

Mt 19,23   ὁ ¹δὲ ᾽Ιησοῦς ²εἶπεν τοῖς μαθηταῖς αὐτοῦ·
Mc 10,23   καὶ ³περιβλεψάμενος ὁ ᾽Ιησοῦς λέγει τοῖς μαθηταῖς αὐτοῦ·
Lc 18,24   ἰδὼν δὲ αὐτὸν   ὁ ᾽Ιησοῦς εἶπεν·

1 : Rushbrooke, Hawkins(VII), Abbott(VI), Easton, Schmid(4), De Solages(a),
   Keech, Boismard(Mt). **1**
2 : Simons, Rushbrooke, Veit, Hawkins(VI), Abbott(V), Easton, Schmid(5),
   De Solages(a), Keech, Fuchs, Boismard(Mt). **10**
3 : Wilke, Holtzmann(r), Weiss(r), Rushbrooke, Hawkins(III), Schmid(32),
   Boismard(Mt).

Mt 19,24   πάλιν δὲ λέγω ὑμῖν,

Mc 10,24   οἱ δὲ μαθηταὶ ἐθαμβοῦντο ἐπὶ τοῖς λόγοις αὐτοῦ.⌐ ὁ δὲ Ἰησοῦς πάλιν ἀποκριθεὶς

        λέγει αὐτοῖς· ⌐⌐τέκνα, πῶς δύσκολόν ἐστιν εἰς τὴν βασιλείαν τοῦ θεοῦ εἰσ-

        ελθεῖν·⌐⌐

Lc   om.

      Wilke⌐(ΓΓ: t), Weiss, Simons, Rushbrooke, Wright, Wernle(t), Stanton(1 vel
      2), Easton, Schmid, Glasson, Keech, Brown(W), Fuchs.
      Mc δυσκολον εστιν : + τους πεποιθοτας επι χρημασιν TR Ti hʳ S.

Mt 19,24   πάλιν δὲ λέγω ὑμῖν, εὐκοπώτερόν   ἐστιν

Mc 10,25   εὐκοπώτερόν   ἐστιν

Lc 18,25   εὐκοπώτερον γάρ ἐστιν

      Weiss(r), Hawkins(IVc).   **4**

Mt 19,24   διὰ   ¹τρήματος   ῥαφίδος ²εἰσελθεῖν ἢ πλούσιον εἰς

Mc 10,25   διὰ ³τῆς τρυμαλιᾶς τῆς ῥαφίδος διελθεῖν ἢ πλούσιον εἰς ... εἰσελθεῖν.

Lc 18,25   διὰ   τρήματος   βελόνης εἰσελθεῖν ἢ πλούσιον εἰς ... εἰσελθεῖν.

      1 : Rushbrooke, Abbott(H), Allen, Stanton(2), Streeter(t), Easton, Schmid(27),
         Chapman, Keech, Fuchs, Boismard(Mt).   **32**
      2 : Weiss(r), Rushbrooke, Veit, Abbott(H), Allen, Stanton(3b vel 4), Streeter(t),
         Easton, Schmid(20), Chapman, De Solages(c), Keech, Fuchs, Boismard(Mt).
         31a
         Mt εισελθειν η πλουσιον : διελθειν η πλ. εισελθειν TR h GNT.
         Lc εισελθειν : δι- GNT.
      3 : Simons, Schmid, Keech, Fuchs, Boismard(Mt).   **33b**

Mt 19,25   ¹ἀκούσαντες δὲ οἱ μαθηταὶ   ἐξεπλήσσοντο σφόδρα λέγοντες·

Mc 10,26   οἱ δὲ   περισσῶς ἐξεπλήσσοντο   λέγοντες ²πρὸς ἑαυτούς·

Lc 18,26   εἶπαν δὲ οἱ ἀκούσαντες·

      1 : Weiss(r), Simons, Rushbrooke, Wright, Veit, Wernle, Abbott(H), Stanton
         (2), Schmid(33), De Solages(e), Keech, Fuchs, Boismard.   **22**
      2 : Rushbrooke, Easton, Schmid(24), Fuchs.   **(23)**

Mt 19,26   ἐμβλέψας ¹δὲ   ὁ Ἰησοῦς ²εἶπεν αὐτοῖς·

Mc 10,27   ἐμβλέψας   αὐτοῖς ὁ Ἰησοῦς λέγει·

Lc 18,27   ὁ δὲ   εἶπεν·

      1 : Weiss(r), Rushbrooke, Hawkins(Vc), Abbott(II), Easton, Schmid(3),
         De Solages(d), Fuchs.   **4**
      2 : Weiss(r), Rushbrooke, Veit, Hawkins(VI), Abbott(V), Easton, Schmid(5),
         De Solages(a), Keech, Fuchs.   **10**

Mt 19,26   παρὰ ἀνθρώποις τοῦτο   ἀδύνατόν [1]ἐστιν,   παρὰ δὲ θεῷ πάντα δυνατά.
Mc 10,27   παρὰ ἀνθρώποις   ἀδύνατον,   [2]ἀλλ' οὐ παρὰ   θεῷ·
                           πάντα γὰρ   δυνατὰ   παρὰ τῷ θεῷ.
Lc 18,27   τὰ ἀδύνατα παρὰ ἀνθρώποις δυνατὰ   παρὰ τῷ θεῷ ἐστιν.

1 : Wright, Easton, Schmid(33), De Solages(d), Keech. 24
2 : Weiss(r), Rushbrooke, Hawkins(II), Allen, Easton, Schmid(31), Glasson, Keech, Fuchs. 9B

§ 63. Mc 10,28-31; Mt 19,27-30; Lc 18,28-30

Mt 19,27   [1]τότε ἀποκριθεὶς   ὁ Πέτρος [2]εἶπεν αὐτῷ·
Mc 10,28   [3]ἤρξατο λέγειν ὁ Πέτρος   αὐτῷ·
Lc 18,28   εἶπεν δὲ   ὁ Πέτρος·

1 : Hawkins(IVc), Schmid(3). 4
2 : Weiss(r), Simons, Rushbrooke, Wernle, Abbott(V), Stanton(2), Easton, Schmid(8), De Solages(a), Keech, Fuchs. Cf. 3.
3 : Rushbrooke, Allen, Easton, Keech. 13

Mt 19,27   ἰδοὺ ἡμεῖς ἀφήκαμεν πάντα καὶ ἠκολουθήσαμέν σοι·
Mc 10,28   ἰδοὺ ἡμεῖς ἀφήκαμεν πάντα καὶ ἠκολουθήκαμέν σοι.
Lc 18,28   ἰδοὺ ἡμεῖς ἀφέντες   τὰ ἴδια   ἠκολουθήσαμέν σοι.

Weiss(r), Simons, Rushbrooke, Wernle, Abbott(VII), Easton, Schmid(17), De Solages(b), Keech, Brown, Fuchs, Boismard(Mt). 11n

Mt 19,28   ὁ [1]δὲ Ἰησοῦς [2]/ [3]εἶπεν [4]αὐτοῖς· ἀμὴν λέγω ὑμῖν [5]ὅτι ὑμεῖς
Mc 10,29   ἔφη ὁ   Ἰησοῦς·   ἀμὴν λέγω ὑμῖν,   οὐδείς
Lc 18,29   ὁ δὲ   / εἶπεν αὐτοῖς· ἀμὴν λέγω ὑμῖν ὅτι οὐδείς

1 : Simons, Rushbrooke, Wright, Veit, Hawkins(IVc), Abbott(II), Stanton(2), Easton, Schmid(3), De Solages(d), Keech, Fuchs, Boismard(Mt). 4
2 : Wright. 21B
3 : Simons, Rushbrooke, Veit, Wernle, Abbott, Easton, Schmid, De Solages(a), Keech, Fuchs, Boismard(Mt). 11
4 : Simons, Rushbrooke, Veit, Abbott(I), Easton, Schmid(33), De Solages(d), Keech, Fuchs, Boismard(Mt). 23
5 : Wright, De Solages(d), Keech, Fuchs, Boismard(Mt). (5)
     Lc οτι : — Ti T Ru.

Mt 19,29   ἕνεκεν τοῦ ἐμοῦ ὀνόματος,
Mc 10,29   ἕνεκεν   ἐμοῦ   καὶ ἕνεκεν τοῦ εὐαγγελίου,
Lc 18,29   εἵνεκεν   τῆς βασιλείας τοῦ θεοῦ,

Wilke, Holtzmann, Weiss, Rushbrooke, Hawkins(V), Stanton(1), Easton, Schmid, Keech, Boismard(McR). 34

Mt 19,29   ¹πολλαπλασίονα λήμψεται,
Mc 10,30   ²ἐὰν   μὴ λάβῃ ἑκατονταπλασίονα
Lc 18,30   ὃς οὐχὶ μὴ λάβῃ   πολλαπλασίονα

    1 : Weiss, Simons, Rushbrooke, Veit, Wernle, Hawkins(*), Abbott(H), Stanton
    (2 vel 3b), Streeter(t), Easton, Schmid(29), Chapman, Da Fonseca, Vaganay
    (t), Keech, McLoughlin(IT), Fuchs, Boismard(Mt,t). **32**
    Mt πολλαπλασιονα : εκατοντα- TR S GNT(B) ; Lc : επτα- h.
    2 : Rushbrooke, Hawkins(IVb).

Mt 19,29   om.
Mc 10,30   ¹ªνῦν ᵇἐν τῷ καιρῷ τούτῳ ²οἰκίας καὶ ἀδελφοὺς καὶ ἀδελφὰς καὶ μητέρας καὶ
           τέκνα καὶ ἀγροὺς ³μετὰ διωγμῶν,
Lc 18,30   ἐν τῷ καιρῷ τούτῳ

    1 : Weiss, Rushbrooke, Hawkins(V), Easton, Schmid(31), Boismard(McR).
    2 : Wilke, Weiss, Simons, Rushbrooke, Wright, Wernle, Stanton(2 vel 1),
    Easton, Schmid(31), Keech.
    3 : Boismard(McR).

Mt 19,30   πολλοὶ δὲ ἔσονται πρῶτοι ἔσχατοι   καὶ   ἔσχατοι πρῶτοι.
Mc 10,31   πολλοὶ δὲ ἔσονται πρῶτοι ἔσχατοι   καὶ οἱ ἔσχατοι πρῶτοι.
Lc 18,30   om.
Lc (13,30)   καὶ ἰδοὺ εἰσὶν ἔσχατοι οἳ ἔσονται πρῶτοι, καὶ εἰσὶν πρῶτοι οἳ ἔσονται ἔσχατοι.

    Rushbrooke. **33b**
    Mc : [οι] H S GNT.

§ 64. Mc 10,32-34; Mt 20,17-19; Lc 18,31-34

Mt 20,17   μέλλων δὲ ἀναβαίνειν Ἰησοῦς εἰς Ἱεροσόλυμα
Mc 10,32   ἦσαν δὲ ἐν τῇ ὁδῷ ἀναβαίνοντες   εἰς Ἱεροσόλυμα, καὶ ἦν προάγων αὐτοὺς
           ὁ Ἰησοῦς, καὶ ἐθαμβοῦντο, οἱ δὲ ἀκολουθοῦντες ἐφοβοῦντο.
Lc 18,31   om.
Lc (19,28)   ἐπορεύετο ἔμπροσθεν ἀναβαίνων   εἰς Ἱεροσόλυμα.

    Wilke, Holtzmann, Simons, Rushbrooke, Wright, Wernle, Stanton(2), Easton,
    Schmid(31), Vaganay, Keech.
    Mt μελλων δε αναβαινειν : και αναβαινων ο TR Ti T h S GNT(C).

Mt 20,17   παρέλαβεν   τοὺς δώδεκα κατ᾽ ἰδίαν, καὶ ... ¹εἶπεν ²/ αὐτοῖς·
Mc 10,32-33   ³καὶ παραλαβὼν ⁴πάλιν τοὺς δώδεκα   ⁵ἤρξατο αὐτοῖς λέγειν
         ⁶τὰ μέλλοντα αὐτῷ συμβαίνειν, (33) ⁷ὅτι
Lc 18,31   παραλαβὼν δὲ   τοὺς δώδεκα   εἶπεν / πρὸς αὐτούς·

    1 : Simons, Rushbrooke, Veit, Wernle, Abbott(V), Easton, Schmid(8), De
    Solages(a), Keech, Boismard(McR). Cf. 5.

2 : Veit, Schmid(14), Vaganay. **21A**
3 : Schmid(4). **2**
4 : Wilke, Rushbrooke, Easton, Schmid(11), Keech. **27**
5 : Simons, Rushbrooke, Allen, Schmid, Boismard(McR). Cf. 1. **13**
6 : Wilke, Rushbrooke, Hawkins(II), Easton, Schmid(31), Keech, Boismard (McR). **(23)**
7 : Simons, Rushbrooke, Schmid(21), Keech. **5**

Mt 20,19   εἰς τὸ ἐμπαῖξαι
Mc 10,34   καὶ   ¹ἐμπαίξουσιν ²αὐτῷ καὶ ἐμπτύσουσιν αὐτῷ
Lc 18,32   καὶ   ἐμπαιχθήσεται ... καὶ ἐμπτυσθήσεται,

1 : Stanton(2).
2 : Rushbrooke.

Mt 20,19   καὶ τῇ τρίτῃ ἡμέρᾳ ἐγερθήσεται.
Mc 10,34   καὶ μετὰ τρεῖς ἡμέρας ἀναστήσεται.
Lc 18,33   καὶ τῇ ἡμέρᾳ τῇ τρίτῃ ἀναστήσεται.

Weiss(or), Simons, Rushbrooke, Veit, Wernle, Hawkins(IC), Abbott(H), Stanton(3b), Streeter(d), Easton, Schmid(29), De Solages(b,e), Keech. **31c**

§ 65. Mc 10,35-40; Mt 20,20-23

Mt 20,22   πιεῖν τὸ ποτήριον ὃ ἐγὼ μέλλω πίνειν ;
    20,23   τὸ μὲν ποτήριόν μου πίεσθε,
Mc 10,38   ᵃπιεῖν τὸ ποτήριον ὃ ἐγὼ πίνω, ἢ ᵇτὸ βάπτισμα ὃ ἐγὼ βαπτίζομαι βαπτισθῆναι ;
    10,39   ᵃτὸ ποτήριον ὃ ἐγὼ πίνω πίεσθε, καὶ ᵇτὸ βάπτισμα ἐγὼ ὃ βαπτίζομαι βαπτισθήσεσθε·
Lc   om.
Lc (12,50)   βάπτισμα δὲ ἔχω   βαπτισθῆναι,

Hawkins(V). **34**

§ 66. Mc 10,41-45; Mt 20,24-28; (Lc 22,24-27)

Mt 20,24   καὶ ἀκούσαντες οἱ δέκα   ἠγανάκτησαν
Mc 10,41   καὶ ἀκούσαντες οἱ δέκα ἤρξαντο ἀγανακτεῖν
Lc 22,24   ἐγένετο δὲ καὶ φιλονεικία ἐν αὐτοῖς,

Rushbrooke.

Mt 20,25   ὁ ¹δὲ Ἰησοῦς προσκαλεσάμενος αὐτοὺς   ²εἶπεν·
Mc 10,42   καὶ   προσκαλεσάμενος αὐτοὺς ὁ Ἰησοῦς λέγει αὐτοῖς·
Lc 22,25   ὁ δὲ   εἶπεν αὐτοῖς·

1 : Rushbrooke, Abbott(VI), Schmid(4), Keech. **1**
2 : Rushbrooke, Hawkins(VI), Abbott(V), Schmid(5), Keech. **10**

Mt 20,25   οἴδατε ὅτι οἱ   ἄρχοντες τῶν ἐθνῶν
Mc 10,42   οἴδατε ὅτι οἱ δοκοῦντες ἄρχειν   τῶν ἐθνῶν
Lc 22,25   οἱ   βασιλεῖς τῶν ἐθνῶν

Rushbrooke, Boismard(McR).

§ 67. Mc 10,46-52; Mt 20,29-34; Lc 18,35-43

Mt 20,29   καὶ ἐκπορευομένων αὐτῶν ἀπὸ Ἰεριχώ
Mc 10,46   ¹ᵃκαὶ ²ἔρχονται⌐ εἰς Ἰεριχώ. ᵇκαὶ ἐκπορευομένου αὐτοῦ ἀπὸ Ἰεριχὼ ³καὶ τῶν
            μαθητῶν αὐτοῦ
Lc 18,35   ἐγένετο δὲ ἐν τῷ ἐγγίζειν αὐτὸν εἰς Ἰεριχώ
Lc (19,1)   καὶ εἰσελθὼν διήρχετο τὴν Ἰεριχώ.

    1 : Hawkins(V), Allen.
    2 : Hawkins(VI), Schmid(5).
    3 : Simons, Rushbrooke, Easton, Schmid(30), Vaganay, Keech, Boismard(McR).

Mt 20,30   καὶ ἰδοὺ   δύο τυφλοὶ   καθήμενοι
Mc 10,46   ¹ὁ υἱὸς Τιμαίου Βαρτιμαῖος, τυφλὸς ²προσαίτης, ἐκάθητο
Lc 18,35   τυφλός τις   ἐκάθητο ... ἐπαιτῶν.

    1 : Wilke(t), Holtzmann, Simons, Rushbrooke, Wright, Wernle(t), Hawkins
        (IIIB), Stanton(2), Easton, Schmid(1,32), Vaganay, Keech, Boismard(McR).
    2 :
        Mc προσαιτης, εκαθητο παρα την οδον : εκ. π. τ. οδ. προσαιτων TR GNT¹ ²(C)

Mt (9,27)   παράγοντι ἐκεῖθεν τῷ Ἰησοῦ
Mt 20,30   ἀκούσαντες   ὅτι Ἰησοῦς   ¹παράγει,
Mc 10,47   ²καὶ ἀκούσας   ὅτι Ἰησοῦς ὁ Ναζαρηνός ἐστιν,
Lc 18,36-37 ἀκούσας δὲ ... (37) ... ὅτι Ἰησοῦς ὁ Ναζωραῖος παρέρχεται.

    1 : Wilke, Holtzmann, Weiss(r), Simons, Rushbrooke, Hawkins, Abbott(H),
        Easton, Schmid, Keech. 32
    2 : Rushbrooke. 2

Mt (9,27)   κράζοντες καὶ λέγοντες·
Mt 20,30   ¹ἔκραξαν   ²λέγοντες·
Mc 10,47   ³ἤρξατο κράζειν   καὶ λέγειν·
Lc 18,38   ἐβόησεν   λέγων·

    1 : Easton, Schmid(8). Cf. 3.
    2 : Simons, Easton, Schmid(7), Keech, Boismard(r). 3
    3 : Rushbrooke, Allen, Easton. 13

Mt 20,31   ¹ὁ δὲ ὄχλος   ²// ἐπετίμησεν αὐτοῖς ἵνα σιωπήσωσιν·
Mc 10,48   καὶ ἐπετίμων αὐτῷ ³πολλοὶ   ἵνα σιωπήσῃ·
Lc 18,39   καὶ οἱ προάγοντες // ἐπετίμων αὐτῷ ἵνα σιγήσῃ·

        1 : De Solages(e). Cf. 3. **22**
        2 : Wright, Veit. **21B**
        3 : Rushbrooke, Schmid.

Mt 20,32   ἐφώνησεν αὐτούς
Mc 10,49   εἶπεν· φωνήσατε αὐτόν.
Lc 18,40   ἐκέλευσεν   αὐτὸν ἀχθῆναι πρὸς αὐτόν.

        Rushbrooke.

Mt (9,28)   προσῆλθον αὐτῷ οἱ τυφλοί,
Mt 20,32   om.
Mc 10,49-50 καὶ φωνοῦσιν τὸν τυφλὸν λέγοντες αὐτῷ· θάρσει, ἔγειρε, φωνεῖ σε. (50) ὁ δὲ ἀποβαλὼν τὸ ἱμάτιον αὐτοῦ ἀναπηδήσας ἦλθεν πρὸς τὸν Ἰησοῦν.
Lc 18,40   ἐγγίσαντος δὲ αὐτοῦ

        Wilke, Holtzmann(r), Weiss(r), Simons, Rushbrooke, Wright, Wernle, Hawkins
        (III), Stanton(2), Easton, Schmid(32), Vaganay, Keech, Boismard.

Mt (9,28)   καὶ   λέγει αὐτοῖς ὁ Ἰησοῦς·
Mt 20,32   καὶ   εἶπεν·
Mc 10,51   καὶ ἀποκριθεὶς αὐτῷ ὁ Ἰησοῦς εἶπεν·
Lc 18,40   ἐπηρώτησεν αὐτόν·

        Rushbrooke, Easton, Schmid, Keech. **16 (22)**

Mt (9,28)   λέγουσιν αὐτῷ· ναί, ¹κύριε.
Mt 20,33   λέγουσιν αὐτῷ·   κύριε, ἵνα ἀνοιγῶσιν οἱ ὀφθαλμοὶ ἡμῶν.
Mc 10,51   ὁ δὲ ²τυφλὸς εἶπεν αὐτῷ· ῥαββουνί, ἵνα ἀναβλέψω.
Lc 18,41   ὁ δὲ   εἶπεν·   κύριε, ἵνα ἀναβλέψω.

        1 : Weiss(r /q), Simons, Rushbrooke, Veit, Wernle, Abbott(VII), Stanton(2),
        Easton, Schmid(1), De Solages(c), Keech, Brown, Boismard(r). **30**
        2 : Rushbrooke, Easton, Schmid, Keech. **(22)**

Mt (9,29)   τότε   ἥψατο τῶν ὀφθαλμῶν αὐτῶν λέγων· κατὰ τὴν πίστιν ὑμῶν
Mt 20,34   ὁ Ἰησοῦς ἥψατο τῶν ὀμμάτων αὐτῶν,
Mc 10,52   καὶ ὁ Ἰησοῦς   εἶπεν αὐτῷ· ὕπαγε, ἡ πίστις σου
Lc 18,42   καὶ ὁ Ἰησοῦς   εἶπεν αὐτῷ· ἀνάβλεψον· ἡ πίστις σου

        Schmid.

Mt 20,34   καὶ εὐθέως   ἀνέβλεψαν καὶ ἠκολούθησαν αὐτῷ.
Mc 10,52   καὶ [1]εὐθὺς   ἀνέβλεψεν, καὶ ἠκολούθει   αὐτῷ [2]ἐν τῇ ὁδῷ.
Lc 18,43   καὶ παραχρῆμα ἀνέβλεψεν, καὶ ἠκολούθει   αὐτῷ δοξάζων τὸν θεόν.

1 : Stephenson, Schmid(10). **26**
2 : Rushbrooke, Hawkins(II), Easton, Schmid(31), Keech, Boismard(McR).

§ 68. Mc 11,1-10; Mt 21,1-9; Lc 19,29-38

Mt 21,1   καὶ   ὅτε ἤγγισαν   εἰς Ἱεροσόλυμα
Mc 11,1   καὶ   ὅτε ἐγγίζουσιν εἰς Ἱεροσόλυμα
Lc 19,29   καὶ ἐγένετο ὡς ἤγγισεν   εἰς Βηθφαγή

Weiss(r), Simons, Rushbrooke, Veit, Wernle, Hawkins(VI), Abbott(III), Easton, Schmid(5), Keech, Boismard(Mt). **10**

Mt 21,1   εἰς Ἱεροσόλυμα καὶ ἦλθον εἰς [1]Βηθφαγὴ   εἰς τὸ ὄρος
Mc 11,1   [2]εἰς Ἱεροσόλυμα   εἰς Βηθφαγὴ καὶ Βηθανίαν πρὸς τὸ ὄρος
Lc 19,29   εἰς Βηθφαγὴ καὶ Βηθανίαν πρὸς τὸ ὄρος
Lc (19,28)   εἰς Ἱεροσόλυμα.

1 : (Mc om.) Veit, Wernle(t), Hawkins(*), Streeter(t), Easton.
   Mc εις Βηθφαγη και : και εις T h s.
2 : Weiss(r).

Mt 21,1   τότε Ἰησοῦς [1]ἀπέστειλεν δύο   μαθητάς
Mc 11,1   ἀποστέλλει δύο τῶν μαθητῶν [2]αὐτοῦ
Lc 19,29   ἀπέστειλεν δύο τῶν μαθητῶν

1 : Weiss(r), Simons, Rushbrooke, Veit, Wernle, Hawkins(VI), Abbott(III), Larfeld, Easton, Schmid(5), Chapman, De Solages(b), Keech, Boismard(Mt). **10**
2 : Weiss(r), Simons, Rushbrooke, Easton, Keech. **(23)**

Mt 21,2   [1]λέγων αὐτοῖς· πορεύεσθε..., καὶ εὐθύς
Mc 11,2   καὶ λέγει αὐτοῖς· ὑπάγετε..., καὶ [2a]εὐθὺς [b]εἰσπορευόμενοι [3]εἰς αὐτήν
Lc 19,30   λέγων· ὑπάγετε...,   ἐν ᾗ εἰσπορευόμενοι

1 : Weiss(r), Simons, Rushbrooke, Hawkins(VI), Abbott(IV), Easton, Schmid (5,7), De Solages(b), Keech, Boismard. **3 10**
   Lc λεγων : ειπων Ti T S.
2 : Hawkins(II,V), Easton, Schmid(31). **34**
   Mt ευθυς : ευθεως TR Ti W S GNT.
3 : Rushbrooke, Keech.

Mt 21,2   εὑρήσετε ὄνον δεδεμένην...· ¹λύσαντες   ²ἀγάγετέ μοι.
Mc 11,2   εὑρήσετε πῶλον δεδεμένον...· λύσατε αὐτὸν καὶ φέρετε.
Lc 19,30 εὑρήσετε πῶλον δεδεμένον..., καὶ λύσαντες αὐτὸν   ἀγάγετε.

1 : Weiss(r), Simons, Rushbrooke, Wernle, Abbott(IV), Stanton(2), Streeter(d),
    Larfeld, Easton, Schmid(7), Chapman, Da Fonseca, De Solages(b), Keech,
    Boismard(Mt). **3**
2 : Weiss(r), Simons, Rushbrooke, Veit, Wernle, Abbott, Stanton(2), Streeter(d),
    Larfeld, Easton, Schmid(27), Chapman, Da Fonseca, De Solages(c), Keech,
    Brown, Boismard(Mt). **29**

Mt 21,3   ¹ἐρεῖτε ²ὅτι ὁ κύριος αὐτῶν χρείαν ἔχει·
Mc 11,3   εἴπατε·   ὁ κύριος αὐτοῦ χρείαν ἔχει,
Lc 19,31 οὕτως ἐρεῖτε· ὅτι ὁ κύριος αὐτοῦ χρείαν ἔχει.

1 : Wilke, Holtzmann, Weiss(r), Simons, Rushbrooke, Veit, Wernle, Abbott
    (VII), Stanton(2), Larfeld, Easton, Schmid, Chapman, De Solages(a),
    Keech, Boismard(Mt). **11B**
2 : Weiss(r), Simons, Rushbrooke, Veit, Abbott(VII), Stanton(2), Larfeld,
    Easton, Schmid, Keech, Boismard(Mt). **(5)**

Mt 21,3   εὐθὺς δὲ   ἀποστελεῖ αὐτούς.
Mc 11,3   καὶ εὐθὺς αὐτὸν ἀποστέλλει   πάλιν ὧδε.
Lc 19,31 om.

Simons, Rushbrooke, Hawkins(IAb), Easton, Schmid, Keech.

Mt 21,6   ¹πορευθέντες ²δὲ ³οἱ μαθηταὶ   καὶ ποιήσαντες ⁴καθὼς συνέταξεν ⁵αὐτοῖς
Mc 11,4   καὶ ἀπῆλθον   καὶ εὗρον
Lc 19,32 ἀπελθόντες δὲ οἱ ἀπεσταλμένοι εὗρον   καθὼς εἶπεν   αὐτοῖς.

1 : Weiss(r), Larfeld, Easton, Schmid(7), Boismard(Mt). **3**
2 : Weiss(r), Rushbrooke, Veit, Hawkins(VII), Larfeld, Easton, Schmid(4),
    De Solages(a), Keech, Boismard(Mt). **1**
3 : Weiss(r), Rushbrooke, Veit, De Solages(d). **22**
4 : Veit, Boismard(Mt).
5 : Weiss(r), Rushbrooke, Veit, Abbott(I), De Solages(d), Keech.

Mt 21,6   om.
Mc 11,4   καὶ εὗρον πῶλον δεδεμένον πρὸς θύραν ἔξω ἐπὶ τοῦ ἀμφόδου,
Lc 19,32 εὗρον καθὼς εἶπεν αὐτοῖς.

Wilke, Rushbrooke, Wright, Wernle, Hawkins(II,III), Stanton(2), Easton,
Schmid(32), Keech, Boismard(McR).

Mt 21,6   om.
Mc 11,6   καὶ ἀφῆκαν αὐτούς.
Lc 19,34 om.

Rushbrooke, Hawkins(II), Stanton(2), Easton, Keech, Boismard(McR).

Mt 21,7   ἤγαγον τὴν ὄνον καὶ τὸν πῶλον,

Mc 11,7   καὶ φέρουσιν   τὸν πῶλον πρὸς τὸν Ἰησοῦν,

Lc 19,35   καὶ ἤγαγον   αὐτὸν   πρὸς τὸν Ἰησοῦν,

> Weiss(r), Simons, Rushbrooke, Veit, Wernle, Hawkins(VI), Abbott(III), Stanton(2), Streeter(d), Larfeld, Schmid(5,27), Chapman, Da Fonseca, De Solages(c), Keech, Brown, Boismard(Mt). **10 29**

Mt 21,7   καὶ ἐπέθηκαν [1]ἐπ᾽ αὐτῶν τὰ ἱμάτια,   καὶ ἐπεκάθισεν ἐπάνω αὐτῶν.

Mc 11,7   καὶ [2]ἐπιβάλλουσιν αὐτῷ τὰ ἱμάτια αὐτῶν, καὶ ἐκάθισεν ἐπ᾽ αὐτόν.

Lc 19,35   καὶ ἐπιρίψαντες αὐτῶν τὰ ἱμάτια ἐπὶ τὸν πῶλον ἐπεβίβασαν τὸν Ἰησοῦν.

> 1 : Rushbrooke, Abbott(VII), Larfeld, Easton, Schmid(20), Keech. **31c**
> 2 : Rushbrooke, Hawkins(VI), Schmid(5). **10**

Mt 21,8   ὁ [1]δὲ πλεῖστος ὄχλος ἔστρωσαν [2]// [3]ἑαυτῶν τὰ ἱμάτια   [4]ἐν τῇ ὁδῷ,

Mc 11,8   καὶ πολλοὶ   τὰ ἱμάτια αὐτῶν ἔστρωσαν   εἰς τὴν ὁδόν,

Lc 19,36   πορευομένου δὲ αὐτοῦ ὑπεστρώννυον // τὰ ἱμάτια ἑαυτῶν ἐν τῇ ὁδῷ.

> 1 : Weiss(r), Rushbrooke, Veit, Hawkins(VII), Abbott(VI), Schmid(4), De Solages(a), Keech. **1**
> 2 : Wright, Veit, Boismard(Mt). **21A**
> 3 : Rushbrooke, Veit, Abbott(VII), Easton, Schmid, De Solages(b), Keech, Boismard(Mt).
>   Lc εαυτων : αυτων Ti T S GNT ; αὑτων TR.
> 4 : Weiss(r), Simons, Rushbrooke, Veit, Wernle, Abbott(VII), Larfeld, Easton, Schmid(20), De Solages(c,b), Keech, Boismard(Mt). **31a**

Mt 21,8   ἔστρωσαν ἑαυτῶν τὰ ἱμάτια..., ἄλλοι δὲ ἔκοπτον... καὶ ἐστρώννυον ἐν τῇ ὁδῷ.

Mc 11,8   τὰ ἱμάτια αὐτῶν ἔστρωσαν..., ἄλλοι δὲ στιβάδας, κόψαντες ἐκ τῶν ἀγρῶν.

Lc 19,36   ὑπεστρώννυον τὰ ἱμάτια ἑαυτῶν ἐν τῇ ὁδῷ.

> Weiss(r), Larfeld, Schmid. **(11)**
> Mt εστρωννυον : εστρωσαν T.

Mt 21,9   οἱ [1]δὲ [2]ὄχλοι οἱ προάγοντες αὐτὸν καὶ οἱ ἀκολουθοῦντες

Mc 11,9   καὶ   οἱ προάγοντες   καὶ οἱ ἀκολουθοῦντες

Lc 19,37   ἐγγίζοντος δὲ αὐτοῦ ἤδη ... ἅπαν τὸ πλῆθος τῶν μαθητῶν

> 1 : Weiss(r), Rushbrooke, Hawkins(VII), Abbott(VI), Schmid(4), Keech. **1**
> 2 : **22**

Mt 21,9   ἔκραζον   λέγοντες· ὡσαννά

Mc 11,9   ἔκραζον·   ὡσαννά·

Lc 19,37-38 ἤρξαντο ... αἰνεῖν τὸν θεὸν φωνῇ μεγάλῃ ..., (38) λέγοντες·

> Weiss(r), Simons, Rushbrooke, Wright, Veit, Wernle, Abbott, Larfeld, De Solages(d), Keech, Boismard(Mt). **15**

Mt (21,15)   ἰδόντες δὲ ... τὰ θαυμάσια
Mc 11,9   om.
Lc 19,37   περὶ πασῶν ὧν εἶδον   δυνάμεων,

Boismard(Mt).

Mt 21,9   om.   (cf. v. 9b : τῷ υἱῷ Δαυίδ)
Mc 11,10   εὐλογημένη ἡ ἐρχομένη βασιλεία τοῦ πατρὸς ἡμῶν Δαυίδ·
Lc 19,38   om.   (cf. v. 38a : ὁ βασιλεύς)

Wilke, Holtzmann, Weiss(r), Rushbrooke, Stanton(3b), Schmid, Keech, Boismard(McR).

Mt (21,16)   καὶ   εἶπαν   αὐτῷ·
Mc 11,10   om.
Lc 19,39   καί τινες τῶν Φαρισαίων ἀπὸ τοῦ ὄχλου εἶπαν πρὸς αὐτόν·

McLoughlin(PD).
Mt 21,15-16 ; Lc 19,38-40 : Boismard(Mt).

§ 69. Mc 11,11; Mt 21,10-17

Mt   om.
Mc 11,11   καὶ περιβλεψάμενος πάντα, ὀψὲ ἤδη οὔσης τῆς ὥρας,
Lc (21,37)   τὰς δὲ νύκτας (cf. Mc 11,19)

Wright, Hawkins(III), Stanton(1), Schmid.

Mt 21,17   ἐξῆλθεν ἔξω τῆς πόλεως εἰς Βηθανίαν, καὶ [1]ηὐλίσθη ἐκεῖ.
Mc 11,11   ἐξῆλθεν   εἰς Βηθανίαν   [2]μετὰ τῶν δώδεκα.
Mc (11,19)   ἐξεπορεύετο ἔξω τῆς πόλεως.
Lc (21,37)   ἐξερχόμενος   ηὐλίζετο εἰς τὸ ὄρος

1 : Rushbrooke, Veit, Hawkins(*), Abbott(H), Streeter(d), Larfeld, Da Fonseca, Keech, McLoughlin(PI), Boismard(Mt).
2 : Rushbrooke.
Mc 11,19 εξεπορευοντο : -ενετο TR Ti T h S (s -οντο).

§ 70. Mc 11,12-14; Mt 21,18-19

Mt 21,18-19   Post purgationem templi (12-13).
Mc 11,12-14   Ficulnea maledicta.
Lc 19,44   om.

Weiss(r), Simons, Stanton(1), Schmid, Keech, Sanders. 35

§ 71. Mc 11,15-19; (Mt 21,12-16); Lc 19,45-48

Mt 21,12		καὶ εἰσῆλθεν Ἰησοῦς εἰς τὸ ἱερόν
Mc 11,15	καὶ ἔρχονται εἰς Ἱεροσόλυμα. καὶ εἰσελθὼν	εἰς τὸ ἱερόν
Lc 19,45		καὶ εἰσελθὼν εἰς τὸ ἱερόν

Rushbrooke, Wright, Hawkins(II), Schmid.

Mt   om.
Mc 11,16   καὶ οὐκ ἤφιεν ἵνα τις διενέγκῃ σκεῦος διὰ τοῦ ἱεροῦ,
Lc   om.

Wilke(r), Holtzmann, Weiss(r), Simons, Rushbrooke, Wright, Wernle, Stanton
(2 vel 1), Easton, Schmid, Keech, Boismard(McR).

Mt 21,13	καὶ λέγει αὐτοῖς·
Mc 11,17	καὶ ἐδίδασκεν καὶ ἔλεγεν αὐτοῖς·
Lc 19,46	λέγων αὐτοῖς·

Weiss(r), Schmid(31), Keech. **11**
Mc αυτοις : — Ti H(h +) ; και ελεγεν : λεγων TR.

Mt 21,13	γέγραπται· ... οἶκος προσευχῆς κληθήσεται,
Mc 11,17	[1]οὐ γέγραπται [2]ὅτι ... οἶκος προσευχῆς κληθήσεται [3]πᾶσιν τοῖς ἔθνεσιν ;
Lc 19,46	γέγραπται· καὶ ἔσται ... οἶκος προσευχῆς·

1 : Simons, Rushbrooke, Easton, Schmid, Keech.
2 : Schmid(21), Keech. **5**
3 : Weiss(r), Simons, Rushbrooke, Wright, Wernle(t), Stanton(1), Easton,
    Schmid, Glasson, Keech. **(23)**

Mt 21,13	ὑμεῖς δὲ αὐτὸν [1]/ ποιεῖτε σπήλαιον λῃστῶν.
Mc 11,17	ὑμεῖς δὲ [2]πεποιήκατε αὐτὸν σπήλαιον λῃστῶν.
Lc 19,46	ὑμεῖς δὲ αὐτὸν / ἐποιήσατε σπήλαιον λῃστῶν.

1 : Weiss(r), Simons, Wright, Veit, Easton, Keech. **(21A)**
2 : Weiss(r), Schmid(17). **11n**

Mt (21,15)	ἰδόντες [1]δὲ οἱ ἀρχιερεῖς καὶ οἱ γραμματεῖς τὰ θαυμάσια
Mc 11,18	καὶ [2]ἤκουσαν οἱ ἀρχιερεῖς καὶ οἱ γραμματεῖς,
Lc 19,47	οἱ δὲ ἀρχιερεῖς καὶ οἱ γραμματεῖς ... καὶ οἱ πρῶτοι τοῦ λαοῦ,

1 : Rushbrooke, Veit, Hawkins(VII), Abbott(VI). Schmid(4), Keech. **1**
2 : Rushbrooke, Keech.

148 MC 11,22-28

§ 72. Mc 11,20-25; Mt 21,20-22; (Lc 17,6)

Mt (17,20)   ¹ἐὰν ἔχητε πίστιν ²ὡς κόκκον σινάπεως,   ἐρεῖτε   τῷ ὄρει τούτῳ·
Mt 21,21   ἐὰν ἔχητε πίστιν ...   κἂν   τῷ ὄρει τούτῳ εἴπητε·
Mc 11,22-23   ἔχετε πίστιν θεοῦ. (23) ... ὅτι ὃς ἂν εἴπῃ   τῷ ὄρει τούτῳ·
Lc (17,6)   εἰ ἔχετε πίστιν ὡς κόκκον σινάπεως, ἐλέγετε ἂν τῇ συκαμίνῳ ταύτῃ·

1 : Rushbrooke, Abbott(H).
Mc : + εἰ GNT¹²(B).
2 : Weiss, Rushbrooke, Stanton(3a).

§ 73. Mc 11,27-33; Mt 21,23-27; Lc 20,1-8

Mt 21,23   καὶ ἐλθόντος αὐτοῦ εἰς   τὸ ἱερόν
Mc 11,27   καὶ ἔρχονται πάλιν εἰς Ἱεροσόλυμα. καὶ ἐν τῷ ἱερῷ
Lc   om.

Weiss(r), Simons, Rushbrooke, Wright, Hawkins(II), Schmid, Keech.

Mt 21,23   ἐλθόντος αὐτοῦ εἰς τὸ ἱερὸν   προσῆλθον αὐτῷ ¹διδάσκοντι
Mc 11,27   ἐν τῷ ἱερῷ ²περιπατοῦντος αὐτοῦ   ³ἔρχονται πρὸς αὐτόν
Lc 20,1   διδάσκοντος αὐτοῦ τὸν λαὸν ἐν τῷ ἱερῷ ... ἐπέστησαν

1 : Simons, Wright, Wernle, Hawkins(*), Stanton(2 vel 3b), Streeter(t), Easton
Schmid(33), Da Fonseca, De Solages(d), Keech, McLoughlin(T), Fuchs
Boismard(r).
2 : Simons, Rushbrooke, Easton, Fuchs.
3 : Rushbrooke, Hawkins(VI), Schmid(5).   10

Mt 21,23   καὶ οἱ πρεσβύτεροι ¹τοῦ λαοῦ   ²λέγοντες·
Mc 11,27-28   καὶ οἱ πρεσβύτεροι,   (28) καὶ ³ἔλεγον αὐτῷ·
Lc 20,1-2   διδάσκοντος αὐτοῦ τὸν λαὸν ... σὺν τοῖς πρεσβυτέροις, ...
(2) καὶ εἶπαν λέγοντες πρὸς αὐτόν

1 : Simons, Fuchs.
2 : Rushbrooke, Veit, Wernle, Abbott(IV vel V), Easton, De Solages(b)
Keech.   15
3 : Schmid(6).   11

Mt 21,23   ἐν ποίᾳ ἐξουσίᾳ ταῦτα ποιεῖς ; (cf. v. 23a : διδάσκοντι)
Mc 11,28   ἐν ποίᾳ ἐξουσίᾳ ταῦτα ποιεῖς ;
Lc 20,2   ἐν ποίᾳ ἐξουσίᾳ ταῦτα ποιεῖς, (cf. v. 1 : διδάσκοντος)

Schmid (Mc ταῦτα = purgatio templi).

Mt 21,23   καὶ τίς σοι ἔδωκεν   [1]// τὴν ἐξουσίαν ταύτην ;
Mc 11,28   ἢ τίς σοι (τὴν ἐξουσίαν ταύτην ἔδωκεν)   [2]ἵνα ταῦτα ποιῇς ;
Lc 20,2   ἢ τίς ἐστιν ὁ δούς σοι // τὴν ἐξουσίαν ταύτην ;

    1 : Veit, Schmid(14), Vaganay.   21A
       Mc εδωκεν την εξουσιαν ταυτην : 2-3-4 1 TR Ti T.
    2 : Weiss(r), Simons, Rushbrooke, Wernle, Hawkins(II), Allen, Stanton(2 vel
       3b), Easton, Schmid(31), Keech.   7A

Mt 21,24   ἀποκριθεὶς δὲ ὁ ᾿Ιησοῦς εἶπεν   αὐτοῖς·
Mc 11,29   ὁ δὲ ᾿Ιησοῦς εἶπεν   αὐτοῖς·
Lc 20,3   ἀποκριθεὶς δὲ   εἶπεν πρὸς αὐτούς·

    Weiss(r), Simons, Rushbrooke, Wright, Veit, Wernle, Abbott(H), Stanton(2
    vel 3b), Stieeter(t), Easton, Schmid(33), Chapman, De Solages(d), Keech,
    Brown, Fuchs, Boismard(r).   (16)

Mt 21,24   [1]ἐρωτήσω ὑμᾶς [2]κἀγὼ   λόγον ἕνα, ὃν ἐὰν   [3]εἴπητέ μοι, κἀγὼ ὑμῖν ἐρῶ
Mc 11,29   ἐπερωτήσω ὑμᾶς   ἕνα λόγον,   καὶ ἀποκρίθητέ μοι, καὶ ἐρῶ ὑμῖν
Lc 20,3   ἐρωτήσω ὑμᾶς κἀγὼ   λόγον,   καὶ   εἴπατέ μοι·

    1 : Weiss(r), Simons, Veit, Abbott, Easton, Schmid, De Solages(c), Keech,
       Fuchs.   (18)
    2 : Weiss(r), Rushbrooke, Wright, Veit, Abbott(H), Stanton(2 vel 3b), Streeter
       (d), Easton, Schmid, De Solages(f), Keech, Brown, Fuchs, Boismard(r).   22
    3 : Weiss(r), Simons, Rushbrooke, Abbott(H), Streeter(d), Schmid, De Solages
       (a), Keech, Fuchs, Boismard(r).   16n

Mt 21,25   πόθεν ἦν ; ἐξ οὐρανοῦ   ἢ ἐξ ἀνθρώπων ;
Mc 11,30   ἐξ οὐρανοῦ ἦν ἢ ἐξ ἀνθρώπων ; ἀποκρίθητέ μοι.
Lc 20,4   ἐξ οὐρανοῦ ἦν ἢ ἐξ ἀνθρώπων ;

    Wilke, Weiss(r), Simons, Rushbrooke, Wright, Hawkins(III), Easton, Schmid
    (31), Keech. Cf. v. 29.   34

Mt 21,25   [1]οἱ δὲ διελογίζοντο   ἐν ἑαυτοῖς λέγοντες·   ἐὰν εἴπωμεν·
Mc 11,31   καὶ [2]διελογίζοντο πρὸς ἑαυτοὺς λέγοντες·   ἐὰν εἴπωμεν·
Lc 20,5   οἱ δὲ συνελογίσαντο πρὸς ἑαυτοὺς λέγοντες ὅτι ἐὰν εἴπωμεν·

    1 : Weiss(r), Simons, Rushbrooke, Veit, Wernle, Hawkins(VII), Abbott(VI),
       Stanton(2 vel 3b), Easton, Schmid(4), De Solages(d,a), Keech, Fuchs. 1 22
    2 : Weiss(r).   31c
       Mc διελογιζοντο : ελογ- TR T(Syn) S.

Mt 21,26   [1]ἐὰν δὲ εἴπωμεν· ἐξ ἀνθρώπων,   [2]φοβούμεθα τὸν ὄχλον·
Mc 11,32   ἀλλὰ εἴπωμεν· ἐξ ἀνθρώπων ; — ἐφοβοῦντο τὸν ὄχλον·
Lc 20,6   ἐὰν δὲ εἴπωμεν· ἐξ ἀνθρώπων, ὁ λαὸς ἅπας καταλιθάσει ἡμᾶς·

    1 : Weiss(r), Simons, Rushbrooke, Veit, Wernle, Hawkins(IV), Abbott(H,VII),
       Stanton(2 vel 3b), Easton, Schmid(15), De Solages(c), Keech, Fuchs,
       Boismard(r).   9A
    2 : Hawkins(IVb), Schmid(13), Boismard(r).   8B

Mt 21,26   πάντες γὰρ   ὡς ¹προφήτην ²ἔχουσιν τὸν Ἰωάννην.
Mc 11,32   ἅπαντες γὰρ εἶχον τὸν Ἰωάννην ³ὄντως ὅτι προφήτης ἦν.
Lc 20,6   πεπεισμένος γάρ ἐστιν Ἰωάννην   προφήτην εἶναι.

1 : Easton, De Solages(b), Keech.
2 : Hansen.
3 : Rushbrooke, Schmid.

Mt 21,27   καὶ ἀποκριθέντες τῷ Ἰησοῦ εἶπαν·   ...   ἔφη αὐτοῖς καὶ αὐτός·
Mc 11,33   καὶ ἀποκριθέντες τῷ Ἰησοῦ λέγουσιν·... καὶ ὁ Ἰησοῦς λέγει αὐτοῖς·
Lc 20,7-8   καὶ ἀπεκρίθησαν...   (8) καὶ ὁ Ἰησοῦς εἶπεν αὐτοῖς·

Weiss(r), Simons, Rushbrooke, Hawkins(VI), Schmid(5).   **10**

§ 74. Mc 12,1-12; Mt 21,33-46; Lc 20,9-19

Mt 21,33   ἄλλην ¹παραβολὴν ἀκούσατε.
Mc 12,1   ²καὶ ἤρξατο αὐτοῖς   ἐν παραβολαῖς λαλεῖν.
Lc 20,9   ἤρξατο δὲ πρὸς τὸν λαὸν λέγειν τὴν παραβολὴν ταύτην.

1 : Weiss(r), Simons, Rushbrooke, Wernle, Abbott(VII), Easton, Schmid,
    De Solages(b), Keech. (33c)
2 : Rushbrooke, Schmid(4).   **2**

Mt 21,33   ἄνθρωπος ἦν οἰκοδεσπότης ὅστις ἐφύτευσεν // ἀμπελῶνα,
Mc 12,1   ἀμπελῶνα ἄνθρωπος   ἐφύτευσεν,
Lc 20,9   ἄνθρωπος   ἐφύτευσεν // ἀμπελῶνα,

Weiss, Simons, Wright, Veit, Easton, Schmid, Keech, Brown.   **21A**
Mc : εφυτευσεν ανθρωπος TR.
Lc ανθρωπος : + τις TR GNT(C).

Mt 21,34   ὅτε δὲ ἤγγισεν ὁ καιρὸς τῶν καρπῶν, // ἀπέστειλεν τοὺς δούλους αὐτοῦ πρός
Mc 12,2   καὶ   ἀπέστειλεν πρὸς τοὺς γεωργοὺς τῷ καιρῷ   δοῦλον,
Lc 20,10   καὶ καιρῷ // ἀπέστειλεν πρὸς τοὺς γεωργοὺς   δοῦλον,

Weiss, Wright, Veit, Easton.   **21B**

Mt 21,34   λαβεῖν τοὺς καρποὺς αὐτοῦ.
Mc 12,2   ἵνα παρὰ τῶν γεωργῶν λάβῃ ἀπὸ τῶν καρπῶν τοῦ ἀμπελῶνος·
Lc 20,10   ἵνα   ἀπὸ τοῦ καρποῦ τοῦ ἀμπελῶνος δώσουσιν αὐτῷ·

Weiss, Rushbrooke, Hawkins(II), Easton, Schmid(31).

Mt 21,35   καὶ λαβόντες οἱ γεωργοὶ   τοὺς δούλους αὐτοῦ ὃν μὲν ἔδειραν,
Mc 12,3   καὶ λαβόντες   αὐτὸν ἔδειραν   καὶ ἀπέστειλαν κενόν.
Lc 20,10   οἱ δὲ γεωργοὶ ἐξαπέστειλαν αὐτὸν δείραντες   κενόν.

Simons, Rushbrooke, Wright, Veit, Wernle, Abbott(I), Stanton(3b vel 2), Easton, Schmid(33), De Solages(d), Keech. **22**

Mt 21,36   πάλιν ἀπέστειλεν   ἄλλους   δούλους
Mc 12,4   καὶ πάλιν ἀπέστειλεν πρὸς αὐτοὺς ἄλλον   δοῦλον·
Lc 20,11   καὶ προσέθετο   ἕτερον πέμψαι δοῦλον·

Rushbrooke. **(23)**

Mt 21,36   καὶ ἐποίησαν αὐτοῖς ὡσαύτως.
Mc 12,4-5   κἀκεῖνον [1]ἐκεφαλαίωσαν καὶ ἠτίμασαν. (5) καὶ ἄλλον ἀπέστειλεν·
            [2]κἀκεῖνον ἀπέκτειναν,
Lc 20,11   οἱ δὲ κἀκεῖνον δείραντες   καὶ ἀτιμάσαντες ἐξαπέστειλεν κενόν.

1 : Rushbrooke, Hawkins(IVa), Schmid.
2 : Rushbrooke, Boismard(McR).

Mt 21,37   ὕστερον [1]δὲ   ἀπέστειλεν ... [2]τὸν υἱὸν αὐτοῦ λέγων·
Mc 12,6   [3]ἔτι ἕνα εἶχεν, υἱὸν ἀγαπητόν· ἀπέστειλεν αὐτὸν ἔσχατον ... λέγων [4]ὅτι
Lc 20,13   εἶπεν δὲ ὁ κύριος ...·   πέμψω   τὸν υἱόν μου τὸν ἀγαπητόν·

1 : Rushbrooke, Abbott(II), Schmid(3), Keech. **4**
2 : Veit, De Solages(d). **(33b)**
3 : Simons, Rushbrooke, Wernle.
4 : Rushbrooke. **5**

Mt 21,38   οἱ δὲ γεωργοὶ [1]ἰδόντες τὸν υἱόν
Mc 12,7   [2]ἐκεῖνοι δὲ οἱ γεωργοί
Lc 20,14   ἰδόντες δὲ αὐτὸν οἱ γεωργοί

1 : Weiss, Simons, Rushbrooke, Wright, Wernle, Hawkins, Abbott(H), Stanton (3b), Easton, Schmid(33), Chapman, Glasson, De Solages(d), Keech.
2 : Rushbrooke, Easton, Schmid, Glasson, Keech. **(22n)**

Mt 21,38   εἶπον   [1]/ ἐν ἑαυτοῖς·   οὗτός ἐστιν ὁ κληρονόμος·
Mc 12,7   πρὸς ἑαυτοὺς εἶπαν   [2]ὅτι οὗτός ἐστιν ὁ κληρονόμος·
Lc 20,14   διελογίζοντο / πρὸς ἀλλήλους λέγοντες·   οὗτός ἐστιν ὁ κληρονόμος·

1 : Weiss, Rushbrooke, Wright, Veit. **21A**
2 : Simons, Rushbrooke, Schmid(21). **5**

Mt 21,38   καὶ σχῶμεν   τὴν κληρονομίαν αὐτοῦ·
Mc 12,7   καὶ ἡμῶν ἔσται   ἡ κληρονομία.
Lc 20,14   ἵνα ἡμῶν γένηται ἡ κληρονομία.

Rushbrooke.

Mt 21,39   καὶ λαβόντες αὐτὸν ἐξέβαλον   ἔξω τοῦ ἀμπελῶνος [1] // καὶ ἀπέκτειναν.
Mc 12,8   καὶ λαβόντες ἀπέκτειναν [2]αὐτόν,   καὶ ἐξέβαλον αὐτὸν ἔξω τοῦ ἀμπελῶνος.
Lc 20,15   καὶ   ἐκβαλόντες αὐτὸν ἔξω τοῦ ἀμπελῶνος //   ἀπέκτειναν.

1 : Weiss, Simons, Wright, Veit, Wernle, Hawkins(IC), Stanton(3b), Easton,
Schmid, Vaganay, Keech, Brown. **21B**
2 : Rushbrooke, Keech. **(23)**

Mt 21,40   ὅταν [1]οὖν ἔλθῃ ὁ κύριος..., τί   ποιήσει τοῖς γεωργοῖς [2]ἐκείνοις ;
Mc 12,9   τί   ποιήσει   ὁ κύριος
Lc 20,15   τί οὖν ποιήσει   αὐτοῖς ὁ κύριος

1 : Weiss(r), Simons, Rushbrooke, Wright, Hawkins(IVc), Abbott(II), Easton,
Schmid(3), Keech, Brown. **4**
Mc τι : + ουν TR S GNT.
2 : Simons, Wright, Abbott(I), Easton, Schmid(33). **23**

Mt (21,41)   [1]λέγουσιν αὐτῷ·
Mt 21,42   [2]λέγει αὐτοῖς ὁ Ἰησοῦς·
Mc 12,10   om.
Lc 20,16-17   ἀκούσαντες δὲ εἶπαν· μὴ γένοιτο. (17) ὁ δὲ ἐμβλέψας αὐτοῖς εἶπεν·

1 : Easton.
2 : Simons, Rushbrooke, Wright, Easton, Schmid, De Solages(f).

Mt 21,42   οὐδέποτε   ἀνέγνωτε ἐν ταῖς γραφαῖς·
Mc 12,10   οὐδὲ   τὴν   γραφὴν   ταύτην ἀνέγνωτε·
Lc 20,17   τί οὖν ἐστιν τὸ   γεγραμμένον τοῦτο·

Weiss.

Mt 21,[44]   [καὶ ὁ πεσὼν ἐπὶ τὸν λίθον τοῦτον συνθλασθήσεται· ἐφ' ὃν δ' ἂν πέσῃ, λικμή-
σει αὐτόν.]
Mc 12,11   om.
Lc 20,18   πᾶς ὁ πεσὼν ἐπ' ἐκεῖνον τὸν λίθον συνθλασθήσεται· ἐφ' ὃν δ' ἂν πέσῃ, λικμή-
σει αὐτόν.

Simons, Rushbrooke, Abbott, Stanton(3b vel 4), Streeter(t), Easton(t), Keech.
Mt [21,44] : + TR W, — Ti T L.

Mt 21,45   καὶ <u>ἀκούσαντες οἱ ἀρχιερεῖς</u>
Mc 12,12   om.
Lc (20,16)   <u>ἀκούσαντες</u> δὲ εἶπαν·

     Wernle, Keech.

Mt 21,45-46   καὶ <u>ἀκούσαντες</u> [1]οἱ ἀρχιερεῖς <u>καὶ</u> οἱ Φαρισαῖοι ...
           (46) καὶ ζητοῦντες   αὐτὸν κρατῆσαι
Mc 12,12   καὶ [2]ἐζήτουν   αὐτὸν κρατῆσαι,
Lc 20,19   καὶ ἐζήτησαν   οἱ γραμματεῖς <u>καὶ</u> οἱ ἀρχιερεῖς ἐπιβαλεῖν ἐπ' αὐτὸν τὰς χεῖρας

     1 : Rushbrooke, Veit, Wernle, Abbott(I), Streeter(d), Easton, Schmid(33),
       De Solages(d : + οἱ), Keech. **22**
     2 : **11**

Mt 21,46   om. (cf. 22,22).
Mc 12,12   <u>καὶ ἀφέντες αὐτὸν ἀπῆλθον.</u>
Lc 20,19   om.

     Weiss(r), Rushbrooke, Easton, Schmid, Keech.

§ 75. Mc 12,13-17; Mt 22,15-22; Lc 20,20-26

Mt 22,16   [1]λέγοντας·
Mc 12,14   καὶ [2]ἐλθόντες   λέγουσιν [3]αὐτῷ·
Lc 20,21   καὶ   ἐπηρώτησαν αὐτὸν λέγοντες·

     1 : Rushbrooke, Veit, Hawkins(VI), Easton, Schmid(5), De Solages(b), Bois-
       mard(Mt). **10 15**
       Mt λέγοντας : -ντες TR Ti S GNT.
     2 : Rushbrooke, Wright, Schmid.
     3 : Keech, Boismard(Mt).

Mt 22,16   [1]καὶ ... διδάσκεις, [2]// καὶ οὐ μέλει σοι
Mc 12,14   καὶ οὐ μέλει σοι ..., ἀλλ' ἐπ' ἀληθείας ... διδάσκεις·
Lc 20,21   καὶ   διδάσκεις // καὶ οὐ λαμβάνεις ... ἀλλ' ἐπ' ἀληθείας ... διδάσκεις·

     1 : Rushbrooke.
     2 : Easton, Keech.

Mt 22,17   εἰπὸν οὖν [1]ἡμῖν, ... ἔξεστιν δοῦναι κῆνσον Καίσαρι ἢ οὔ ;
Mc 12,14   ἔξεστιν δοῦναι κῆνσον Καίσαρι ἢ οὔ ; [2]δῶμεν ἢ μὴ δῶμεν ;
Lc 20,22   ἔξεστιν ἡμᾶς Καίσαρι φόρον δοῦναι ἢ οὔ ;

     1 : Weiss(r).
     2 : Wilke, Holtzmann, Weiss(r), Simons, Rushbrooke, Wright, Wernle, Hawkins
       (II,V), Allen, Stanton(2), Easton, Schmid(31), Glasson, Keech, Boismard(Mt).
     34

Mt 22,18 ¹γνοὺς δὲ ὁ Ἰησοῦς   τὴν ²πονηρίαν αὐτῶν εἶπεν·   ..., ³ὑποκριταί ;
Mc 12,15 ὁ δὲ εἰδὼς   αὐτῶν τὴν ὑπόκρισιν   εἶπεν   αὐτοῖς·
Lc 20,23 κατανοήσας δὲ   αὐτῶν τὴν πανουργίαν   εἶπεν πρὸς αὐτούς·
Lc (20,20) ὑποκρινομένους ἑαυτοὺς δικαίους εἶναι,

1 : Weiss(r), Simons, Schmid. 32
    Mc ειδως : ιδων T.
2 : Weiss(r), Simons, Schmid. 32
3 : Weiss(r).

Mt 22,19 ¹ἐπιδείξατέ μοι τὸ νόμισμα τοῦ κήνσου.
Mc 12,15 φέρετέ μοι   δηνάριον   ²ἵνα ἴδω.
Lc 20,24 δείξατέ μοι   δηνάριον·

1 : Holtzmann, Weiss(r), Simons, Rushbrooke, Wernle, Abbott(VII), Stanton
    (2 vel 3b), Easton, Schmid(27), De Solages(c), Keech, Boismard(Mt). 29
2 : Holtzmann, Simons, Rushbrooke, Wernle, Stanton(2), Easton, Schmid(31),
    Keech. 7B

Mt 22,21 λέγουσιν·   Καίσαρος.   τότε   λέγει   ¹αὐτοῖς·
Mc 12,16-17 οἱ δὲ εἶπαν ²αὐτῷ· Καίσαρος. (17) ὁ δὲ ³Ἰησοῦς εἶπεν   αὐτοῖς·
Lc 20,24-25 οἱ δὲ εἶπαν·   Καίσαρος. (25) ὁ δὲ   εἶπεν πρὸς αὐτούς·

1 : (Mc om. αὐτοῖς) Rushbrooke, Abbott(I), Schmid(33).
    Mc αυτοις : — Ti H Ru.
2 : Rushbrooke, Easton, Schmid, Keech. (23)
    Mt : + αυτω TR Ti S GNT.
    Lc οι δε ειπαν : αποκριθεντες δε ειπον TR Ti (-παν) S.
3 : Rushbrooke, Easton, Schmid, Keech. (22)

Mt 22,21 ἀπόδοτε ¹οὖν ²|| τὰ Καίσαρος Καίσαρι καὶ τὰ τοῦ θεοῦ τῷ θεῷ.
Mc 12,17 τὰ Καίσαρος ἀπόδοτε   Καίσαρι καὶ τὰ τοῦ θεοῦ τῷ θεῷ.
Lc 20,25 τοίνυν ἀπόδοτε || τὰ Καίσαρος Καίσαρι καὶ τὰ τοῦ θεοῦ τῷ θεῷ.

1 : Weiss(r), Hawkins(IVc), Stanton(2), Schmid. 4
2 : Weiss(r), Simons, Wright, Veit, Wernle, Easton, Schmid(14), Keech,
    Brown, Boismard(Mt). 21A

Mt 22,22 καὶ ἀκούσαντες ¹ἐθαύμασαν,   καὶ ²ἀφέντες αὐτὸν ἀπῆλθαν.
Mc 12,17 καὶ   ³ἐξεθαύμαζον   ἐπ’   αὐτῷ. (cf. 12,12)
Lc 20,26 καὶ   θαυμάσαντες ἐπὶ τῇ ἀποκρίσει αὐτοῦ ἐσίγησαν.

1 : Weiss(r), Simons, Wernle, Easton, Schmid(19), Keech, Brown, Boismard(Mt).
    Cf. 3.
2 : Weiss(r), Simons.
3 : Simons. 11 (18)

§ 76. Mc 12,18-27; Mt 22,23-33; Lc 20,27-38

Mt 22,23   ἐν ἐκείνῃ τῇ ἡμέρᾳ ¹προσῆλθον αὐτῷ Σαδδουκαῖοι,   ²λέγοντες
Mc 12,18   ³καὶ   ἔρχονται Σαδδουκαῖοι πρὸς αὐτόν,   ⁴οἵτινες λέγουσιν
Lc 20,27   προσελθόντες δέ τινες τῶν Σαδδουκαίων, οἱ ἀντιλέγοντες

1 : Weiss(r), Simons, Rushbrooke, Wernle, Hawkins(VI), Abbott, Allen,
   Easton, Schmid(5,19), Keech, Fuchs, Boismard(Mt). **10 18**
2 : Weiss(r), Simons, Rushbrooke, Wernle, Abbott, Allen, Easton, Schmid,
   De Solages(b), Keech, Boismard(Mt).
   Lc ἀντιλεγοντες : λεγοντες H Ru, [αντι]λεγοντες GNT³(C).
3 : Rushbrooke, Schmid(4). **2**
4 : Rushbrooke.

Mt 22,23-24   καὶ ¹ἐπηρώτησαν αὐτὸν (24) λέγοντες· διδάσκαλε, Μωϋσῆς εἶπεν·
Mc 12,18-19   καὶ ἐπηρώτων αὐτὸν λέγοντες· (19) διδάσκαλε, Μωϋσῆς ἔγραψεν ἡμῖν ²ὅτι
Lc 20,27-28   ἐπηρώτησαν αὐτὸν (28) λέγοντες· διδάσκαλε, Μωϋσῆς ἔγραψεν ἡμῖν,

1 : Weiss(r), Simons, Rushbrooke, Abbott(V), Easton, Schmid(6), De Solages(b),
   Keech, Fuchs, Boismard(McR). **11**
   Lc επηρωτησαν : -ρωτων h W.
2 : Simons, Rushbrooke, Easton, Schmid(21), Keech. **5**

Mt 22,24   ἐάν τις   ἀποθάνῃ   μὴ ¹ἔχων τέκνα,
Mc 12,19   ἐάν τινος ἀδελφὸς ἀποθάνῃ καὶ ²καταλίπῃ γυναῖκα καὶ μὴ ἀφῇ τέκνον,
Lc 20,28   ἐάν τινος ἀδελφὸς ἀποθάνῃ   ἔχων   γυναῖκα, καὶ οὗτος ἄτεκνος ᾖ,

1 : Simons, Rushbrooke, Abbott(IV), Easton, Keech.
2 : Rushbrooke.

Mt 22,25   ἦσαν ¹δὲ παρ᾽ ἡμῖν ἑπτὰ ἀδελφοί· καὶ ὁ πρῶτος ²γήμας ³ἐτελεύτησεν,
Mc 12,20   ἑπτὰ   ἀδελφοὶ ἦσαν· καὶ ὁ πρῶτος ἔλαβεν γυναῖκα, καὶ ἀποθνῄσκων
Lc 20,29   ἑπτὰ οὖν ἀδελφοὶ ἦσαν· καὶ ὁ πρῶτος λαβὼν γυναῖκα   ἀπέθανεν

1 : Weiss(r), Hawkins(IVc), Schmid(3). **4**
2 : Simons, Schmid(7). **3**
3 : (Gaechter). **(3)**

Mt 22,26   ὁμοίως καὶ ὁ δεύτερος
Mc 12,21   καὶ ὁ δεύτερος ¹ἔλαβεν αὐτήν, ²καὶ ἀπέθανεν μὴ καταλιπὼν σπέρμα·
Lc 20,30   καὶ ὁ δεύτερος

Rushbrooke, Wernle, Hawkins(II), Schmid(32), Keech, Boismard(Mt).

Mt 22,27 ὕστερον δὲ πάντων   ἀπέθανεν ἡ γυνή.
Mc 12,22 ἔσχατον πάντων καὶ ἡ γυνὴ ἀπέθανεν.
Lc 20,32 ὕστερον   καὶ ἡ γυνὴ ἀπέθανεν.

Wilke, Holtzmann, Weiss(r), Simons, Rushbrooke, Veit, Wernle, Hawkins, Abbott(VII), Stanton(2), Streeter(t), Easton, Schmid(27), Chapman, De Solages(c), Keech, Fuchs, Boismard(Mt). **32**
Wilke : Mc ἐσχάτη.
Mc εσχατον : -τη TR.

Mt 22,28 ἐν τῇ ἀναστάσει [1]οὖν
Mc 12,23 ἐν τῇ ἀναστάσει,   [2]ὅταν ἀναστῶσιν,
Lc 20,33 ἡ γυνὴ οὖν ἐν τῇ ἀναστάσει

1 : Weiss(r), Simons, Rushbrooke, Hawkins(IVc), Abbott(II), Stanton(2), Schmid(3), De Solages(d), Keech, Brown, Boismard(Mt). **4**
2 : Wilke(t), Hawkins(V), Easton, Schmid(31), Keech, Boismard(Mt). **34**
Mc οταν αναστωσιν : — H(h[r] +) Ru, [GNT](D).

Mt 22,29 ἀποκριθεὶς [1]δὲ ὁ Ἰησοῦς [2]εἶπεν αὐτοῖς·   πλανᾶσθε
Mc 12,24   ἔφη αὐτοῖς ὁ Ἰησοῦς· [3]οὐ διὰ τοῦτο πλανᾶσθε
Lc 20,34   καὶ   εἶπεν αὐτοῖς ὁ Ἰησοῦς·

1 : Hawkins(IVc), Stanton(2), Schmid(3). **4**
2 : Simons, Rushbrooke, Veit, Wernle, Abbott(VII?), Schmid, De Solages(a), Keech. **11**
3 : Weiss(r), Rushbrooke, Keech.

Mt 22,30 ἐν γὰρ τῇ ἀναστάσει
Mc 12,25 ὅταν γὰρ ἐκ νεκρῶν ἀναστῶσιν,
Lc 20,35 καὶ   τῆς ἀναστάσεως τῆς ἐκ νεκρῶν

Rushbrooke, Easton, De Solages(e), Keech, Boismard(Mt).

Mt 22,30 ἀλλ᾽   ὡς ἄγγελοι ἐν τῷ οὐρανῷ // εἰσιν.
Mc 12,25 ἀλλ᾽ εἰσιν ὡς ἄγγελοι ἐν τοῖς οὐρανοῖς.
Lc 20,36   ἰσάγγελοι γάρ   // εἰσιν,

Veit, Boismard(Mt). **21B**

Mt 22,31 περὶ δὲ τῆς ἀναστάσεως [1]// τῶν νεκρῶν
Mc 12,26 [2a]περὶ δὲ τῶν νεκρῶν   [b]ὅτι ἐγείρονται,
Lc 20,37   ὅτι δὲ ἐγείρονται // οἱ νεκροί,

1 : McLoughlin. **21B**
2 : Weiss(r).

Mt 22,32   ἀλλὰ ζώντων.
Mc 12,27   ἀλλὰ ζώντων. ¹(ὑμεῖς οὖν) ²πολὺ πλανᾶσθε.
Lc 20,38   ἀλλὰ ζώντων· πάντες γὰρ αὐτῷ ζῶσιν.

> 1 : Wilke.
>   Mc : + υμεις ουν TR s.
> 2 : Wilke, Holtzmann, Weiss(r), Simons, Rushbrooke, Wright, Wernle, Hawkins(II), Stanton(2 vel 1), Schmid(16), Keech.

§ 77. Mc 12,28-34; Mt 22,34-40; Lc 20,39-40; (10,25-28)

Mt 22,35   καὶ ἐπηρώτησεν εἷς ἐξ αὐτῶν ¹νομικὸς   ²πειράζων αὐτόν·
Mc 12,28   καὶ ³προσελθὼν εἷς τῶν   γραμματέων, ...   ἐπηρώτησεν αὐτόν·
Lc 10,25   καὶ ἰδοὺ   νομικός τις ἀνέστη ἐκπειράζων αὐτὸν λέγων·
Lc 20,39   ἀποκριθέντες δέ τινες τῶν γραμματέων   εἶπαν·

> 1 : Weiss, Simons, Rushbrooke, Abbott(II), Stanton(3a), Streeter(t), Larfeld, Schmid, Chapman, De Solages(Q), Keech, Simpson, Boismard(t). **32**
>   Mt : [νομικος] GNT(C).
> 2 : Weiss, Simons, Rushbrooke, Wernle, Abbott(H), Stanton(3a), Streeter (t vel q), Larfeld, Schmid(33), Chapman, De Solages(Q), Keech, Simpson, Boismard(Mt). **19n**
> 3 : Rushbrooke.

Mt (22,34)   οἱ ¹δὲ Φαρισαῖοι ἀκούσαντες ὅτι   ²ἐφίμωσεν τοὺς Σαδδουκαίους,
Mc 12,28   ἀκούσας ³αὐτῶν συζητούντων, εἰδὼς ὅτι καλῶς ἀπεκρίθη αὐτοῖς,
Lc 20,39-40   ἀποκριθέντες δέ τινες ...· διδάσκαλε,   καλῶς εἶπας.
                (40) οὐκέτι γὰρ ἐτόλμων ἐπερωτᾶν αὐτὸν οὐδέν.

> 1 : **1**
> 2 : Simons.
> 3 : Rushbrooke.

Mt 22,36   ¹διδάσκαλε, ποία   ἐντολὴ μεγάλη ²ἐν τῷ νόμῳ ;
Mc 12,28   ποία ἐστὶν ἐντολὴ ³πρώτη πάντων ;
Lc 10,25-26   διδάσκαλε, ... (26) ...   ἐν τῷ νόμῳ τί γέγραπται ;
Lc 20,39   διδάσκαλε,

> 1 : Weiss, Simons, Rushbrooke, Wernle, Abbott(H), Stanton(3a), Streeter (t vel q), Larfeld, Schmid(33), Chapman, De Solages(Q), Keech, Simpson, Boismard(Mt). **30**
> 2 : Weiss, Simons, Rushbrooke, Abbott(H), Stanton(3a), Larfeld, Schmid, Chapman, Keech, Boismard(Mt).
> 3 : Rushbrooke.

Mt 22,37   ὁ ¹δὲ ἔφη   ²αὐτῷ·
Mc 12,29-30   ἀπεκρίθη ὁ ³'Ιησοῦς ⁴ὅτι... ⁵ἄκουε, 'Ισραήλ, κύριος ὁ θεὸς ἡμῶν κύριος εἷς
                       ἐστιν, (30) καί
Lc 10,26   ὁ δὲ εἶπεν πρὸς αὐτόν·

> 1 : Rushbrooke, Abbott(II), Larfeld, De Solages(Q), Keech, Boismard(Mt). **4**
> 2 : Larfeld, De Solages(Q), Boismard(Mt). **23**
> 3 : Rushbrooke, Keech. **(22)**
> 4 : Rushbrooke, Schmid(21). **5**
> 5 : Rushbrooke, Wright, Schmid, Keech, Simpson.

Mt 22,37   ἐν ὅλῃ τῇ καρδίᾳ σου καὶ ἐν ὅλῃ τῇ ψυχῇ σου
                                       καὶ ἐν ὅλῃ τῇ διανοίᾳ σου.
Mc 12,30   ἐξ ὅλης τῆς καρδίας σου καὶ ἐξ ὅλης τῆς ψυχῆς σου καὶ
                       ἐξ ὅλης τῆς διανοίας σου καὶ ἐξ ὅλης τῆς ἰσχύος σου
Lc 10,27   ἐξ ὅλης τῆς καρδίας σου καὶ ἐν ὅλῃ τῇ ψυχῇ σου καὶ
                       ἐν ὅλῃ τῇ ἰσχύϊ σου καὶ ἐν ὅλῃ τῇ διανοίᾳ σου,

> Weiss, Simons, Rushbrooke, Abbott(VII), Stanton(3a vel 3b), Schmid(20),
> Chapman, De Solages(Q), Keech, Simpson, Boismard(Mt). **31b**

Mt 22,40   ἐν ταύταις ταῖς δυσὶν ἐντολαῖς
Mc 12,31   μείζων τούτων ἄλλη ἐντολὴ οὐκ ἔστιν.
Lc 10,27   om.

> Rushbrooke, Wright.

Mt   om.
Mc 12,32-34   καὶ εἶπεν αὐτῷ ὁ γραμματεύς· καλῶς, διδάσκαλε, ἐπ' ἀληθείας εἶπες ὅτι εἷς
                       ἐστιν καὶ οὐκ ἔστιν ἄλλος πλὴν αὐτοῦ· (33) καὶ τὸ ἀγαπᾶν αὐτὸν ἐξ ὅλης τῆς
                       καρδίας καὶ ἐξ ὅλης τῆς συνέσεως καὶ ἐξ ὅλης τῆς ἰσχύος, καὶ τὸ ἀγαπᾶν τὸν
                       πλησίον ὡς ἑαυτὸν περισσότερόν ἐστιν πάντων τῶν ὁλοκαυτωμάτων καὶ θυσιῶν.
                       (34) καὶ ὁ 'Ιησοῦς, ἰδὼν αὐτὸν ὅτι νουνεχῶς ἀπεκρίθη, εἶπεν αὐτῷ· οὐ μακρὰν
                       εἶ ἀπὸ τῆς βασιλείας τοῦ θεοῦ.
Lc   om.

> Rushbrooke, Wright, Hawkins(IAb), Schmid, Keech, Boismard(McR).

Mt (22,46)   ¹οὐδὲ ἐτόλμησέν τις ... ἐπερωτῆσαι ²|| αὐτὸν οὐκέτι.
Mc 12,34   καὶ οὐδεὶς οὐκέτι ἐτόλμα αὐτὸν ἐπερωτῆσαι.
Lc 20,40   οὐκέτι γὰρ ἐτόλμων ἐπερωτᾶν || αὐτὸν οὐδέν.

> 1 : **1a**
> 2 : Schmid (14). **21A**

§ 78. Mc 12,35-37a; Mt 22,41-46; Lc 20,41-44

Mt 22,41   συνηγμένων ¹δὲ τῶν Φαρισαίων ²ἐπηρώτησεν ³αὐτοὺς ὁ Ἰησοῦς λέγων·
Mc 12,35   καὶ ⁴ἀποκριθεὶς ὁ Ἰησοῦς   ἔλεγεν   ⁵διδάσκων ἐν τῷ ἱερῷ·
Lc 20,41   εἶπεν   δὲ   πρὸς αὐτούς·

    1 : Weiss(r), Rushbrooke, Hawkins(VII), Abbott(VI), Easton, Schmid(4),
       De Solages(a), Keech. **1**
    2 : Schmid(6). **11**
    3 : Weiss(r), Rushbrooke, Veit, Abbott(I), Easton, De Solages(d), Keech. **23**
    4 : Rushbrooke. **16**
    5 : Rushbrooke, Wright, Hawkins(III), Easton, Schmid(32), Keech.

Mt 22,42   τίνος ¹/ υἱός ἐστιν ; λέγουσιν αὐτῷ· τοῦ Δαυίδ.
Mc 12,35   πῶς λέγουσιν ²οἱ γραμματεῖς ὅτι ... υἱὸς Δαυίδ ἐστιν ;
Lc 20,41   πῶς λέγουσιν ...   εἶναι Δαυὶδ / υἱόν ;

    1 : Weiss(r /or). **21B**
    2 : Rushbrooke, Easton.

Mt 22,43   πῶς ¹οὖν Δαυὶδ   ἐν   πνεύματι   ²καλεῖ αὐτὸν κύριον ³λέγων·
Mc 12,36   αὐτὸς   Δαυὶδ εἶπεν ἐν τῷ πνεύματι ⁴τῷ ἁγίῳ·
Lc 20,42   αὐτὸς γὰρ Δαυὶδ λέγει ἐν   βίβλῳ ψαλμῶν·

    1 : Hawkins(IVc), Schmid(3). **4**
       Lc αυτος γαρ : και αυτος TR Ti S (s αυτος γαρ).
    2 : Schmid. **10n**
    3 : Rushbrooke, Abbott.
    4 : Rushbrooke.

Mt 22,44   κάθου   ἐκ δεξιῶν μου
Mc 12,36   (κάθισον) ἐκ δεξιῶν μου
Lc 20,42   κάθου   ἐκ δεξιῶν μου

    Simons.
    Mc καθου : καθισον Ti h W.

Mt 22,45   εἰ ¹οὖν Δαυὶδ ²καλεῖ αὐτὸν κύριον,   ³πῶς υἱὸς αὐτοῦ   ⁴// ἐστιν ;
Mc 12,37   ⁵αὐτὸς   Δαυὶδ λέγει αὐτὸν κύριον, καὶ πόθεν   αὐτοῦ   ἐστιν υἱός ;
Lc 20,44   Δαυὶδ οὖν   αὐτὸν κύριον καλεῖ, καὶ πῶς   αὐτοῦ υἱός // ἐστιν ;

    1 : Weiss(or), Simons, Rushbrooke, Wright, Veit, Hawkins(IVc), Abbott(II),
       Stanton(2), Easton, Schmid(3), De Solages(d), Keech, Boismard(Mt). **4**
    2 : Wilke, Holtzmann, Weiss(or), Simons, Rushbrooke, Veit, Wernle, Hawkins,

Abbott(VII), Stanton(2), Easton, Schmid(28), De Solages(c), Keech, Boismard(Mt). **32**

3 : Weiss(or), Simons, Rushbrooke, Veit, Abbott(VII), Easton, Schmid, De Solages(c), Keech, Brown, Boismard(Mt). **32**

4 : Easton. **21B**

5 : Rushbrooke, Easton, Schmid, Keech.

§ 79. Mc 12,37b-40; Mt 23,1-2.5-7; Lc 20,45-47

Mt 23,1   τότε ὁ Ἰησοῦς   ¹ἐλάλησεν τοῖς ὄχλοις καὶ ²τοῖς μαθηταῖς αὐτοῦ λέγων·

Mc 12,37-38   ³καὶ ὁ πολὺς ὄχλος ἤκουεν αὐτοῦ ἡδέως. (38) καὶ ⁴ἐν τῇ διδαχῇ αὐτοῦ ἔλεγεν·

Lc 20,45   ἀκούοντος δὲ παντὸς τοῦ λαοῦ εἶπεν   τοῖς μαθηταῖς·

1 : Schmid(6). **11**

2 : Simons, Rushbrooke, Wright, Veit, Wernle, Abbott(H), Stanton(3a vel 3b), Schmid, Keech, Boismard(Mt).
    Lc μαθηταις : + αυτου TR S GNT(C) ; προς αυτους Ti.

3 : Simons, Rushbrooke, Wernle, Stanton(2), Schmid. **2**
    Mc : [ο] GNT.

4 : Wilke, Rushbrooke, Stanton(3a vel 3b), Schmid(31).

Mt 23,6   ¹φιλοῦσιν δὲ τήν

Mc 12,38   τῶν ²θελόντων ἐν στολαῖς περιπατεῖν καὶ   ἀσπασμούς

Lc 20,46   τῶν   θελόντων περιπατεῖν ἐν στολαῖς καὶ φιλούντων ἀσπασμούς

1 : Weiss, Simons, Rushbrooke, Veit, Hawkins(IVb), Abbott(H), Stanton(3a vel 3b), Schmid(13), De Solages(c), Keech, Boismard(Mt).

2 : Schmid. **8B**

§ 80. Mc 12,41-44; Lc 21,1-4

§ 81. Mc 13,1-4; Mt 24,1-3; Lc 21,5-7

Mt 24,1   καὶ προσῆλθον οἱ   μαθηταὶ αὐτοῦ ἐπιδεῖξαι αὐτῷ

Mc 13,1   ¹λέγει αὐτῷ ²εἷς τῶν μαθητῶν αὐτοῦ·   ³διδάσκαλε, ἴδε

Lc 21,5   καὶ   τινων λεγόντων περὶ τοῦ ἱεροῦ, ὅτι

1 : Hawkins(VI), Schmid(5). **10**

2 : Rushbrooke, Easton, Schmid(33), Boismard(Mt). **33c**
    Mc εις : + εκ Ti [GNT].

3 : Rushbrooke, Easton, Schmid.
    Oratio recta : Schmid, Boismard(Mt).

Mt 24,1   τὰς οἰκοδομὰς τοῦ ἱεροῦ.
Mc 13,1   ἴδε ¹ποταποὶ ²ᵃλίθοι   καὶ ¹ποταπαὶ ²ᵇοἰκοδομαί.
Lc 21,5   λίθοις καλοῖς καὶ ἀναθήμασιν   κεκόσμηται,

    1 : Rushbrooke.
    2 : Weiss(r). **34**

Mt 24,2   ὁ δὲ ἀποκριθεὶς εἶπεν αὐτοῖς· οὐ ¹βλέπετε ²ταῦτα πάντα ;
Mc 13,2   καὶ ὁ ³ʼΙησοῦς εἶπεν αὐτῷ·   βλέπεις ταύτας ⁴τὰς μεγάλας οἰκοδομάς;
Lc 21,5-6   εἶπεν·   (6) ταῦτα ἃ θεωρεῖτε,

    1 : Keech.
    2 : Rushbrooke, Hawkins(II), Easton, Schmid, De Solages(b), Keech, Boismard
        (Mt).
    3 : Rushbrooke, Schmid. **(22)**
    4 : Rushbrooke, Schmid, Keech. **(23)**

Mt 24,2   ¹ἀμὴν λέγω ὑμῖν,   οὐ μὴ ἀφεθῇ ὧδε ... ὃς οὐ   ²καταλυθήσεται.
Mc 13,2   οὐ μὴ ἀφεθῇ   ... ὃς οὐ ³μὴ καταλυθῇ.
Lc 21,6   ἐλεύσονται ἡμέραι ἐν αἷς οὐκ   ἀφεθήσεται ... ὃς οὐ   καταλυθήσεται.

    1 : Weiss(r).
    2 : Wilke, Holtzmann, Weiss(r), Simons, Rushbrooke, Wernle, Abbott(VII?),
        Easton, Schmid(17), De Solages(b), Keech, Brown, Boismard(Mt). **11n**
    3 : Wilke, Holtzmann, Weiss(r), Schmid(28), Keech, Boismard(Mt).

Mt 24,3   καθημένου ¹δὲ αὐτοῦ ἐπὶ τοῦ ὄρους τῶν ἐλαιῶν
Mc 13,3   καὶ καθημένου αὐτοῦ εἰς τὸ ὄρος τῶν ἐλαιῶν ²κατέναντι τοῦ ἱεροῦ,
Lc 21,7   ἐπηρώτησαν δὲ αὐτόν

    1 : Weiss(r), Rushbrooke, Hawkins(VII), Abbott(VI), Schmid(4), De Solages(a),
        Keech.
    2 : Weiss(r), Rushbrooke, Wright, Easton, Boismard(McR).

Mt 24,3   προσῆλθον   αὐτῷ οἱ μαθηταὶ κατʼ ἰδίαν ¹λέγοντες·
Mc 13,3   ²ἐπηρώτα   αὐτὸν   κατʼ ἰδίαν   ³Πέτρος καὶ Ἰάκωβος
           καὶ Ἰωάννης καὶ Ἀνδρέας·
Lc 21,7   ἐπηρώτησαν δὲ αὐτὸν   λέγοντες·

    1 : Rushbrooke, Wright, Abbott(II?), Easton, Schmid(33), De Solages(d),
        Keech, Boismard(Mt). **15**
    2 : Weiss(r). **11**
    3 : Wilke, Simons, Rushbrooke, Wright, Wernle, Hawkins(III), Easton,
        Schmid(32), Keech, Boismard(McR).

Mt 24,3   τί τὸ σημεῖον τῆς σῆς παρουσίας καὶ συντελείας τοῦ αἰῶνος ;
Mc 13,4   τί τὸ σημεῖον ὅταν μέλλῃ ¹ᵃταῦτα ᵇσυντελεῖσθαι ²πάντα ;
Lc 21,7   τί τὸ σημεῖον ὅταν μέλλῃ ταῦτα γίνεσθαι ;

    1 : Weiss(r).
    2 : Rushbrooke, Easton.

§ 82. Mc 13,5-8; Mt 24,4-8; Lc 21,8-11

Mt 24,4   καὶ ἀποκριθεὶς ὁ Ἰησοῦς [1]εἶπεν   αὐτοῖς·
Mc 13,5   ὁ δὲ   Ἰησοῦς [2]ἤρξατο λέγειν αὐτοῖς·
Lc 21,8   ὁ δὲ   εἶπεν·

> 1 : Simons, Rushbrooke, Wernle, Abbott(V), Allen, Schmid(8), De Solages(a),
> Keech. Cf. 2.
> 2 : Simons, Rushbrooke, Easton. **13**

Mt 24,5   πολλοὶ [1]γὰρ ἐλεύσονται ἐπὶ τῷ ὀνόματί μου λέγοντες·   ἐγώ εἰμι ὁ χριστός,
Mc 13,6   πολλοὶ   ἐλεύσονται ἐπὶ τῷ ὀνόματί μου λέγοντες [2]ὅτι ἐγώ εἰμι,
Lc 21,8   πολλοὶ γὰρ ἐλεύσονται ἐπὶ τῷ ὀνόματί μου λέγοντες·   ἐγώ εἰμι,

> 1 : Rushbrooke, Wright, Veit, Wernle, Hawkins(IVc), Abbott(II), Easton,
> Schmid(3), De Solages(d), Keech, Brown. **4**
> 2 : Rushbrooke, Easton, Schmid(21), Keech. **5**

Mt 24,6   δεῖ γὰρ   γενέσθαι,
Mc 13,7   δεῖ   γενέσθαι,
Lc 21,9   δεῖ γὰρ ταῦτα γενέσθαι πρῶτον,

> Rushbrooke, Wright, Veit, Wernle, Hawkins(IVc), Abbott(II), Schmid(3),
> De Solages(d), Keech, Brown. **4**
> Mc : + γαρ TR [S].

Mt 24,7   [1]καὶ ἔσονται λιμοὶ καὶ σεισμοὶ κατὰ τόπους·
Mc 13,8   [2a]ἔσονται   σεισμοὶ κατὰ τόπους,   [b]ἔσονται λιμοί·
Lc 21,11   σεισμοί τε μεγάλοι καὶ   κατὰ τόπους λοιμοὶ καὶ λιμοὶ ἔσονται,

> 1 : Rushbrooke, Abbott(II), Schmid, De Solages(d), Keech. **4**
> Lc λοιμοι και λιμοι : λιμοι και λοιμοι TR T h S GNT.
> Mt λιμοι : + και λοιμοι TR W.
> 2 : Rushbrooke, Hawkins(IVc), Schmid. **34**

§ 83. Mc 13,9-13; Mt 24,9-14; (10,17-22); Lc 21,12-19

Mt (10,17) προσέχετε δὲ ἀπὸ τῶν ἀνθρώπων·
Mt 24,9   τότε
Mc 13,9   βλέπετε δὲ ὑμεῖς ἑαυτούς·
Lc 21,12   πρὸ δὲ τούτων πάντων

> Rushbrooke.

Mt (10,17)   παραδώσουσιν ¹γὰρ ὑμᾶς εἰς συνέδρια, καὶ ἐν ²ταῖς συναγωγαῖς αὐτῶν
Mc 13,9   παραδώσουσιν   ὑμᾶς εἰς συνέδρια καὶ εἰς   συναγωγάς
Lc 21,12   παραδιδόντες   εἰς τὰς συναγωγὰς καὶ φυλακάς,
Lc (12,11) εἰσφέρουσιν   ὑμᾶς   εἰς τὰς συναγωγάς

        1 : 4
        2 : Rushbrooke, De Solages(d).   33b
        Lc ταs : — TR Ti S.

Mt (10,17-18) μαστιγώσουσιν ὑμᾶς· (18) καὶ ἐπὶ ¹ἡγεμόνας δὲ καὶ βασιλεῖς ἀχθήσεσθε
Mc 13,9   ²δαρήσεσθε   καὶ ἐπὶ ἡγεμόνων καὶ βασιλέων σταθήσεσθε
Lc 21,12   ἀπαγομένους   ἐπὶ βασιλεῖς   καὶ ἡγεμόνας
Lc (12,11)   καὶ τὰς ἀρχὰς   καὶ τὰς ἐξουσίας,

        1 : Rushbrooke, Abbott(VIII?), Schmid(20), De Solages(b,c), Keech, Fuchs.
        29 31c
        2 : Rushbrooke.

Mt (10,18)   εἰς μαρτύριον αὐτοῖς   καὶ   τοῖς ἔθνεσιν.
Mt (24,14)   καὶ   κηρυχθήσεται...
        εἰς μαρτύριον   πᾶσιν τοῖς ἔθνεσιν, καὶ τότε ἥξει τὸ τέλος.
Mc 13,9-10 εἰς μαρτύριον αὐτοῖς. (10) καὶ εἰς πάντα τὰ ἔθνη πρῶτον δεῖ κηρυχθῆναι
Lc 21,13   ἀποβήσεται ὑμῖν εἰς μαρτύριον.

        Rushbrooke, Fuchs ; v. 10 : 8A

Mt (10,19)   ὅταν ¹δὲ   παραδῶσιν ὑμᾶς,
Mc 13,11   καὶ ὅταν ²ἄγωσιν   ὑμᾶς παραδιδόντες,
Lc (12,11) ὅταν δὲ εἰσφέρωσιν ὑμᾶς

        1 : Rushbrooke, Veit, De Solages(Q), Fuchs.   1
        2 : Rushbrooke, Fuchs.   (29)   34

Mt (10,19)   μὴ   μεριμνήσητε πῶς ἢ τί λαλήσητε·
Mc 13,11   μὴ προμεριμνᾶτε   τί λαλήσητε,
Lc 21,14   μὴ προμελετᾶν   ἀπολογηθῆναι·
Lc (12,11) μὴ   μεριμνήσητε πῶς ἢ τί ἀπολογήσηθε ἢ τί εἴπητε·

        Weiss, Simons, Rushbrooke, Wright, Veit, Hawkins(IVa), De Solages(Q),
        Fuchs, Boismard(q).   18
        Lc πως η τι : πως [η τι] H GNT¹²(C).

Mt (10,19)   δοθήσεται ¹γὰρ   ὑμῖν ἐν ἐκείνῃ τῇ ὥρᾳ τί   λαλήσητε·
Mc 13,11   ²ἀλλ᾽ ὃ ἐὰν δοθῇ   ὑμῖν ἐν ἐκείνῃ τῇ ὥρᾳ, τοῦτο λαλεῖτε·
Lc 21,15   ἐγὼ γὰρ δώσω   ὑμῖν   στόμα καὶ σοφίαν,
Lc (12,12) τὸ γὰρ ἅγιον πνεῦμα διδάξει ὑμᾶς ἐν αὐτῇ τῇ ὥρᾳ ἃ δεῖ εἰπεῖν.

        1 : Weiss, Rushbrooke, Abbott(VIII), De Solages(e), Keech.   9B
        2 : Rushbrooke. Cf. 1.

Mt (10,21) παραδώσει   δὲ ἀδελφὸς ἀδελφὸν εἰς θάνατον καὶ πατὴρ τέκνον,
Mc 13,12   καὶ παραδώσει   ‾ ἀδελφὸς ἀδελφὸν εἰς θάνατον καὶ πατὴρ τέκνον,
Lc 21,16   παραδοθήσεσθε δὲ καὶ ὑπὸ γονέων καὶ ἀδελφῶν

Rushbrooke, Veit, Abbott(VI), Schmid(4), De Solages(a), Keech. **1**

Mt (10,21) καὶ θανατώσουσιν αὐτούς.
Mt 24,9   καὶ ἀποκτενοῦσιν ὑμᾶς,
Mc 13,12   καὶ θανατώσουσιν αὐτούς·
Lc 21,16   καὶ θανατώσουσιν ἐξ ὑμῶν,

§ 84. Mc 13,14-20; Mt 24,15-22; Lc 21,20-24; (17,31)

Mt 24,16-17 τότε οἱ ἐν τῇ Ἰουδαίᾳ..., (17) ὁ   ἐπὶ τοῦ δώματος
Mc 13,14-15 τότε οἱ ἐν τῇ Ἰουδαίᾳ..., (15) ὁ (δὲ) ἐπὶ τοῦ δώματος
Lc 21,21   τότε οἱ ἐν τῇ Ἰουδαίᾳ..., καὶ οἱ ‾ ἐν ταῖς χώραις
Lc (17,31)   ἐν ἐκείνῃ τῇ ἡμέρᾳ   ὃς ἔσται ἐπὶ τοῦ δώματος

Mc : δε TR Ti T h S.

Mt 24,17   μὴ καταβάτω   ἆραι [1]τὰ ἐκ τῆς οἰκίας αὐτοῦ,
Mc 13,15   [a]μὴ καταβάτω [2b]μηδὲ εἰσελθάτω τι ἆραι ‾ ἐκ τῆς οἰκίας αὐτοῦ,
Lc 21,21   μὴ   εἰσερχέσθωσαν   εἰς αὐτήν,
Lc (17,31) ἐν τῇ οἰκίᾳ, μὴ καταβάτω   ἆραι αὐτά,

1 : Farmer. **33c**
   Mc τι αραι : αραι τι TR T GNT.
2 : Weiss, Rushbrooke. **34**

Mt 24,18   καὶ ὁ ἐν τῷ ἀγρῷ   μὴ ἐπιστρεψάτω   ὀπίσω
Mc 13,16   καὶ ὁ εἰς τὸν ἀγρὸν   μὴ ἐπιστρεψάτω εἰς τὰ ὀπίσω
Lc 21,21   καὶ οἱ ἐν ταῖς χώραις μὴ εἰσερχέσθωσαν εἰς αὐτήν,
Lc (17,31) καὶ ὁ ἐν   ἀγρῷ ὁμοίως μὴ ἐπιστρεψάτω εἰς τὰ ὀπίσω.

Rushbrooke, Hawkins(IV), Abbott(VII), Schmid(20), De Solages(c,b), Keech.
Lc 21,21 : Veit. **31c**

Mt 24,21   [1]ἔσται γὰρ τότε   θλῖψις [2]μεγάλη,
Mc 13,19   ἔσονται γὰρ [3]αἱ ἡμέραι ἐκεῖναι θλῖψις,
Lc 21,23   ἔσται γὰρ   ἀνάγκη μεγάλη

1 : Simons, Rushbrooke, Veit, Hawkins(IVa), Streeter(d), Schmid, De Solages
   (b), Keech, McLoughlin(RI).
2 : Simons, Wright, Veit, Wernle, Hawkins(IVa), Abbott(VII), Burton,
   Streeter(d), Schmid(33), De Solages(e), McLoughlin(RI).
3 : Rushbrooke.

§ 85. Mc 13,21-23; Mt 24,23-28; (Lc 17,23)

Mt (24,26) ἰδοὺ ἐν τῇ ἐρήμῳ ἐστίν,   μὴ ¹ἐξέλθητε· ἰδοὺ ..., μὴ   πιστεύσητε.
Mt 24,23   ²ἰδοὺ ὧδε ὁ χριστός, ἤ· ὧδε,   μὴ   πιστεύσητε·
Mc 13,21   ἴδε ὧδε ὁ χριστός,   ἴδε ἐκεῖ,   μὴ   ³πιστεύετε·
Lc (17,23) ἰδοὺ ἐκεῖ,   (ἤ·) ἰδοὺ ὧδε· μὴ ἀπέλθητε   μηδὲ διώξητε.

1 : Rushbrooke, Abbott(H?).
2 : Rushbrooke, Abbott(VII). **4**
   Lc : η TR (ωδε η ι. εκει) H (h om) Ru, [S] [GNT](D).
   Mc : ιδου ... η ιδου TR ; και ι. εκει W.
3 : Mc πιστευετε : -ευσητε TR ; Mt 24,23 : πιστευετε W.

§ 86. Mc 13,24-27; Mt 24,29-31; Lc 21,25-28

Mt 24,29   εὐθέως δὲ   μετὰ τὴν θλῖψιν τῶν ἡμέρων ἐκείνων
Mc 13,24   ἀλλὰ ἐν ἐκείναις ταῖς ἡμέραις μετὰ τὴν θλῖψιν   ἐκείνην
Lc 21,25   καί

Rushbrooke. **9**

Mt 24,29   πεσοῦνται...,   καὶ αἱ δυνάμεις   ¹τῶν οὐρανῶν σαλευθήσονται.
Mc 13,25   ἔσονται... ²πίπτοντες, καὶ αἱ δυνάμεις αἱ ἐν τοῖς οὐρανοῖς σαλευθήσονται.
Lc 21,25-26 ἔσονται...   (26) ... αἱ γὰρ δυνάμεις   τῶν οὐρανῶν σαλευθήσονται.

1 : Simons, Rushbrooke, Veit, Wernle, Abbott(VIII), Schmid(28), De Solages
   (b), Keech.
2 : Rushbrooke. **12 33b**

Mt 24,30   ¹καὶ τότε κόψονται πᾶσαι αἱ φυλαὶ τῆς γῆς ... μετὰ δυνάμεως καὶ δόξης ²/ πολλῆς·
Mc 13,26   μετὰ δυνάμεως πολλῆς καὶ δόξης.
Lc 21,26-27 ἀποψυχόντων ἀνθρώπων ἀπὸ φόβου καὶ προσδοκίας τῶν ἐπερχομένων τῇ
             οἰκουμένῃ·   (27) ... μετὰ δυνάμεως καὶ δόξης / πολλῆς.

1 : Simons.
2 : Weiss, Simons, Wright, Veit, Wernle, Keech. **21B**

§ 87. Mc 13,28-32; Mt 24,32-36; Lc 21,29-33

Mt 24,34   ἕως ἂν   πάντα ταῦτα γένηται.
Mc 13,30   μέχρις οὗ ταῦτα πάντα γένηται.
Lc 21,32   ἕως ἂν   πάντα γένηται.

Weiss, Simons, Rushbrooke, Veit, Wernle, Abbott(VII), Stanton(2), Easton,
Schmid(27), De Solages(c), Keech, Brown.
Mt Lc αν : [H].

Mt 24,35   οἱ δὲ λόγοι μου οὐ μὴ παρέλθωσιν.
Mc 13,31   οἱ δὲ λόγοι μου οὐ ‾‾‾ παρελεύσονται.
Lc 21,33   οἱ δὲ λόγοι μου οὐ μὴ παρελεύσονται.

   Weiss, Rushbrooke, Abbott(VII), Stanton(2), Schmid(28), Keech, Brown.
   Mc ου : ου μη TR Ti T h S.

§ 88. Mc 13,33-37; (Mt 25,13-15); Lc (19,12-13); 21,36

Mt 25,13   γρηγορεῖτε ¹οὖν, ὅτι οὐκ οἴδατε τὴν ἡμέραν οὐδὲ τὴν ὥραν.
Mc 13,33   ²βλέπετε, ἀγρυπνεῖτε·   οὐκ οἴδατε γὰρ πότε ὁ καιρός ἐστιν.
Lc 21,36   ἀγρυπνεῖτε δὲ   ἐν παντὶ καιρῷ

   1 : Schmid(3).
      Lc δε : ουν TR s.
   2 : Rushbrooke.

Mt 25,14   ὥσπερ γὰρ ἄνθρωπος   ἀποδημῶν
Mc 13,34   ὡς   ἄνθρωπος   ἀπόδημος ἀφεὶς τὴν οἰκίαν αὐτοῦ
Lc 19,12   ἄνθρωπός τις εὐγενὴς ἐπορεύθη εἰς χώραν μακράν

   Rushbrooke.

Mt 25,14   ¹ἐκάλεσεν τοὺς ἰδίους δούλους καὶ παρέδωκεν αὐτοῖς   τὰ ὑπάρχοντα αὐτοῦ,
Mc 13,34   καὶ   δοὺς τοῖς δούλοις αὐτοῦ ²τὴν ἐξουσίαν
Lc 19,13   καλέσας δὲ δέκα δούλους ἑαυτοῦ ἔδωκεν αὐτοῖς   δέκα μνᾶς,

   1 : Hansen.
   2 : Rushbrooke.

Mt 25,15   ἑκάστῳ κατὰ τὴν ἰδίαν δύναμιν,
Mc 13,34   ἑκάστῳ τὸ ἔργον αὐτοῦ,   καὶ τῷ θυρωρῷ ἐνετείλατο ἵνα γρηγορῇ.
Lc 19,13   om.

   Rushbrooke, Boismard(McR).

Mt (25,14-30) Parabola talentorum.
Mc 13,34   om.
Lc (19,12-27) Parabola mnarum.

   Sanders.

Mt (24,42) γρηγορεῖτε οὖν,   ¹ὅτι οὐκ οἴδατε ποίᾳ ἡμέρᾳ ὁ κύριος
Mc 13,35   γρηγορεῖτε οὖν·   οὐκ οἴδατε ²γὰρ πότε   ὁ κύριος
Lc (12,40) καὶ ὑμεῖς γίνεσθε ἕτοιμοι, ὅτι ᾗ ὥρᾳ οὐ δοκεῖτε   ὁ υἱὸς τοῦ ἀνθρώπου

   1 : Rushbrooke, Abbott(VIII), Keech.
   2 : Rushbrooke.

Mt (24,44)   ¹καὶ ὑμεῖς γίνεσθε ἕτοιμοι, ²ὅτι⌉ ᾗ οὐ δοκεῖτε ὥρᾳ ὁ υἱὸς τοῦ ἀνθρώπου
Mt (24,42)   γρηγορεῖτε οὖν,   ὅτι οὐκ οἴδατε ... ὁ κύριος ὑμῶν
Mc 13,35   γρηγορεῖτε οὖν·   οὐκ οἴδατε ³γὰρ ... ὁ κύριος τῆς οἰκίας
Lc (12,40)   καὶ ἡμεῖς γίνεσθε ἕτοιμοι, ὅτι ᾗ ὥρᾳ οὐ δοκεῖτε ὁ υἱὸς τοῦ ἀνθρώπου

1 : Rushbrooke.
2 : Rushbrooke, Abbott(VII), Keech.
3 : Rushbrooke.

Mt (24,44)   ᾗ ... ὥρᾳ ὁ υἱὸς τοῦ ἀνθρώπου ἔρχεται.
Mt 24,42   ποίᾳ ἡμέρᾳ ὁ κύριος ὑμῶν   ἔρχεται.
Mc 13,35   πότε   ὁ κύριος τῆς οἰκίας ἔρχεται, ἢ ὀψὲ ἢ μεσονύκτιον ἢ ἀλεκτοροφω-
              νίας ἢ πρωΐ·
Lc (12,40)   ᾗ ὥρᾳ ... ὁ υἱὸς τοῦ ἀνθρώπου ἔρχεται.

Rushbrooke, Boismard(McR).

Mt   om.
Mc 13,36-37   μὴ ἐλθὼν ἐξαίφνης εὕρῃ ὑμᾶς καθεύδοντας. (37) ὃ δὲ ὑμῖν λέγω, πᾶσιν λέγω,
              γρηγορεῖτε.
Lc   om.

Rushbrooke, Boismard(McR).

§ 89. Mc 14,1-2; Mt 26,1-5; Lc 22,1-2

Mt 26,2   οἴδατε ὅτι μετὰ δύο ἡμέρας τὸ πάσχα   γίνεται,
Mc 14,1   ¹ἦν δὲ   ²ᵃτὸ πάσχα καὶ ᵇτὰ ἄζυμα μέτα δύο ἡμέρας.
Lc 22,1   ἤγγιζεν δὲ   ἡ ἑορτὴ   τῶν ἀζύμων ἡ λεγομένη πάσχα.

1 : Rushbrooke.
2 : Schmid. 34

Mt 26,4   ἵνα   τὸν Ἰησοῦν   δόλῳ κρατήσωσιν
Mc 14,1   ᵃπῶς   αὐτὸν ᵇἐν δόλῳ κρατήσαντες
Lc 22,2   τὸ πῶς   ἀνέλωσιν   αὐτόν·

Rushbrooke, Schmid(27).

§ 90. Mc 14,3-9; Mt 26,6-13; (Lc 7,36-50)

Mt 26,6-7   τοῦ ¹δὲ Ἰησοῦ γενομένου ἐν Βηθανίᾳ ἐν   οἰκίᾳ..., (7) προσῆλθεν αὐτῷ
Mc 14,3   καὶ ²ὄντος αὐτοῦ   ἐν Βηθανίᾳ ἐν τῇ οἰκίᾳ... κατακειμένου αὐτοῦ ἦλθεν
Lc 7,36   ἠρώτα δέ τις ...· καὶ εἰσελθὼν εἰς τὸν οἶκον τοῦ Φαρισαίου κατεκλίθη.

1 : Rushbrooke.
2 : Rushbrooke, Hawkins(IV), Schmid(7).

Mt 26,7   ἔχουσα   ἀλάβαστρον μύρου   βαρυτίμου
Mc 14,3   ἔχουσα   ἀλάβαστρον μύρου νάρδου πιστικῆς πολυτελοῦς·
Lc 7,37   κομίσασα ἀλάβαστρον μύρου

Rushbrooke, Wright, Hawkins(III).
Mt βαρυτιμου : πολυτιμου T.

Mt 26,7   ¹καὶ   κατέχεεν ἐπὶ   τῆς κεφαλῆς αὐτοῦ ἀνακειμένου.
Mc 14,3   ²συντρίψασα τὴν ἀλάβαστρον κατέχεεν αὐτοῦ τῆς κεφαλῆς.
Lc 7,38   καὶ   ἤλειφεν τῷ μύρῳ.

1 : Rushbrooke. **4**
2 : Rushbrooke, Wright.

Mt 26,8   ¹ἰδόντες δὲ οἱ μαθηταὶ ἠγανάκτησαν   λέγοντες·
Mc 14,4   ²ἦσαν δέ   τινες   ἀγανακτοῦντες πρὸς ἑαυτούς·
Lc 7,39   ἰδὼν   δὲ ὁ Φαρισαῖος ... εἶπεν   ἐν ἑαυτῷ λέγων·

1 : Rushbrooke, Schmid(33). **15**
2 : Rushbrooke. **12**

Mt 26,10   γνοὺς δὲ   ὁ Ἰησοῦς εἶπεν   ¹αὐτοῖς·
Mc 14,5-6 ²καὶ ἐνεβριμῶντο αὐτῇ.   (6) ὁ δὲ Ἰησοῦς εἶπεν·
Lc 7,40   καὶ ἀποκριθεὶς ὁ Ἰησοῦς εἶπεν πρὸς αὐτόν·

1 : Rushbrooke. **23**
2 : Rushbrooke, Wright.

Mt 26,12   om.
Mc 14,8   ὃ ἔσχεν ἐποίησεν·
Lc 7,46   om.

Rushbrooke.

Mt 26,12   βαλοῦσα ¹γὰρ ²αὕτη τὸ ³μύρον τοῦτο ἐπὶ τοῦ σώματός μου πρὸς τὸ ἐνταφιάσαι
           με ἐποίησεν.
Mc 14,8   προέλαβεν   μυρίσαι   τὸ σῶμά   μου εἰς τὸν ἐνταφιασμόν.
Lc 7,46   αὕτη δὲ   μύρῳ ἤλειψεν   τοὺς πόδας   μου.

1 : Hawkins(IV), Schmid(3). **4**
2 : Hansen.
3 : Hansen.

§ 91. Mc 14,10-11 ; Mt 26,14-16 ; Lc 22,3-6

Mt 26,14   τότε πορευθεὶς ... ¹ὁ λεγόμενος Ἰούδας   ²'Ἰσκαριώτης,
Mc 14,10   ³καὶ   Ἰούδας   Ἰσκαριώθ,
Lc 22,3   εἰσῆλθεν δὲ σατανᾶς εἰς   Ἰούδαν τὸν καλούμενον Ἰσκαριώτην,

    1 : Weiss(r), Simons, Wright, Schmid, De Solages(d), Keech. **15n**
      Mc Ιουδας Ισκαριωθ : ο I. ο I. TR, [ο] I. ο I. S.
    2 : Simons, Rushbrooke, Wernle, Abbott(VII), Schmid(1), Keech, Brown,
      Léon-Dufour(4).
    3 : Schmid(4). **2**

Mt 26,15   κἀγὼ   ὑμῖν   ¹/ παραδώσω ²/ αὐτόν ;
Mc 14,10   ³ἵνα   αὐτὸν παραδοῖ αὐτοῖς.
Lc 22,4   τὸ πῶς αὐτοῖς / παραδῶ   / αὐτόν·

    1 : Wright, Veit, Easton, Schmid(14). **21A**
      Mc αυτοις : [GNT].
    2 : Wright, Veit, Easton, Schmid(14), Keech. **21A**
      Mc : παραδοι αυτον αυτοις TR S.
    3 : Rushbrooke, Boismard(McR). **7B**

Mt 26,15   οἱ δὲ   ἔστησαν   αὐτῷ τριάκοντα ἀργύρια.
Mc 14,11   οἱ δὲ ἀκούσαντες ἐχάρησαν καὶ ἐπηγγείλαντο αὐτῷ   ἀργύριον δοῦναι.
Lc 22,5   καὶ   ἐχάρησαν, καὶ συνέθεντο αὐτῷ   ἀργύριον δοῦναι.

    Rushbrooke, Hawkins(II), Schmid(33).

Mt 26,16   καὶ ἀπὸ τότε ἐζήτει   ¹εὐκαιρίαν ἵνα αὐτὸν παραδῷ.
Mc 14,11   καὶ   ἐζήτει ²πῶς αὐτὸν εὐκαίρως   παραδοῖ.
Lc 22,6   καὶ   ἐζήτει   εὐκαιρίαν τοῦ   παραδοῦναι αὐτόν

    1 : Wilke, Holtzmann, Weiss(or), Simons, Rushbrooke, Wernle, Abbott(VIII?),
      Stanton(2), Easton, Schmid(27), Chapman, De Solages(b), Keech, Léon-
      Dufour(4), Boismard(McR). **32**
    2 : Rushbrooke, Boismard(McR).

§ 92. Mc 14,12-16 ; Mt 26,17-19 ; Lc 22,7-13

Mt 26,17   τῇ   δὲ πρώτῃ   τῶν ἀζύμων
Mc 14,12   καὶ τῇ   πρώτῃ ἡμέρᾳ τῶν ἀζύμων, ὅτε τὸ πάσχα ἔθυον,
Lc 22,7   ἦλθεν δὲ ἡ ἡμέρα τῶν ἀζύμων, ᾗ ἔδει θύεσθαι τὸ πάσχα·

    Rushbrooke, Hawkins(VII), Abbott(VI), Schmid(4), De Solages(a), Keech. **1**

Mt 26,17   προσῆλθον οἱ μαθηταὶ τῷ Ἰησοῦ λέγοντες· ποῦ θέλεις   ἑτοιμάσωμεν
Mc 14,12   ¹λέγουσιν αὐτῷ οἱ μαθηταὶ αὐτοῦ·   ποῦ θέλεις ²ἀπελθόντες ἑτοιμάσωμεν
Lc 22,9   οἱ δὲ εἶπαν αὐτῷ·   ποῦ θέλεις   ἑτοιμάσωμεν ;

        1 : Hawkins(VI), Schmid(5).   10
        2 : Rushbrooke, Keech.

Mt 26,18   om.
Mc 14,13   καὶ ἀποστέλλει δύο τῶν μαθητῶν αὐτοῦ
Lc (22,8)   καὶ ἀπέστειλεν Πέτρον καὶ Ἰωάννην

        Rushbrooke, Keech.

Mt 26,18   ¹ὁ δὲ ²εἶπεν·   ὑπάγετε   εἰς τὴν πόλιν
Mc 14,13   καὶ λέγει αὐτοῖς· ὑπάγετε   εἰς τὴν πόλιν,
Lc 22,10   ὁ δὲ εἶπεν αὐτοῖς· ἰδοὺ εἰσελθόντων ὑμῶν εἰς τὴν πόλιν

        1 : Rushbrooke, Veit, Abbott(VI), Easton, Schmid(4), De Solages(d,a), Keech.
            1   22
        2 : Rushbrooke, Veit, Wernle, Hawkins(VI), Abbott(V), Easton, Schmid(5),
            De Solages(a), Keech, Léon-Dufour(4).   10

Mt 26,18   καὶ   εἴπατε αὐτῷ·
Mc 14,14   καὶ ¹ὅπου ἐὰν εἰσέλθῃ   εἴπατε τῷ οἰκοδεσπότῃ   ²ὅτι
Lc 22,10-11   εἰς ἣν εἰσπορεύεται· (11) καὶ ἐρεῖτε τῷ οἰκοδεσπότῃ τῆς οἰκίας·

        1 : Rushbrooke.
        2 : Rushbrooke, Schmid(21), Keech.   5

Mt 26,18   πρὸς σὲ   ποιῶ τὸ πάσχα
Mc 14,14   ποῦ ἐστιν τὸ κατάλυμά μου, ὅπου   τὸ πάσχα ... φάγω ;
Lc 22,11   ποῦ ἐστιν τὸ κατάλυμα   ὅπου   τὸ πάσχα ... φάγω ;

        Rushbrooke, Hawkins(IAb).

Mt 26,19   καὶ ἐποίησαν οἱ μαθηταί
Mc 14,16   καὶ ἐξῆλθον οἱ μαθηταὶ καὶ ἦλθον εἰς τὴν πόλιν
Lc 22,13   ἀπελθόντες δέ

        Rushbrooke, Hawkins(II), Schmid.

§ 93. Mc 14,17-21; Mt 26,20-25; Lc 22,14.(21-23)

Mt 26,20   ¹ἀνέκειτο μετὰ τῶν δώδεκα [μαθητῶν].
Mc 14,17-18 ²ἔρχεται μετὰ ³τῶν δώδεκα. (18) καὶ ἀνακειμένων αὐτῶν
Lc 22,14   ἀνέπεσεν, καὶ οἱ ἀπόστολοι σὺν αὐτῷ.

        1 : Simons, Rushbrooke, Hawkins, Easton, Schmid(5). Cf. 2.
        2 : Rushbrooke. **10**
        3 : Mt [μαθητων] : — TR Ti GNT(C).

Mt 26,22   ¹καὶ   λυπούμενοι σφόδρα ἤρξαντο λέγειν αὐτῷ εἷς ἕκαστος·
Mc 14,19   ἤρξαντο λυπεῖσθαι   ²καὶ   λέγειν αὐτῷ εἷς ³κατὰ εἷς·
Lc (22,23)   καὶ αὐτοὶ ἤρξαντο   συζητεῖν πρὸς ἑαυτούς

        1 : Rushbrooke, Veit, Hawkins(IVc), Abbott(II), Schmid(3), De Solages(d),
            Keech. **4**
        2 : Rushbrooke.
        3 : Rushbrooke, Hawkins(IVa).

Mt 26,22   μήτι ἐγώ εἰμι, κύριε ;
Mc 14,19   μήτι ἐγώ ;
Lc (22,23)   τὸ τίς ἄρα εἴη ἐξ αὐτῶν ὁ τοῦτο μέλλων πράσσειν.

        De Solages(d). **24**

Mt 26,23   ὁ ἐμβάψας   μετ᾽ ἐμοῦ ¹τὴν χεῖρα ἐν τῷ τρυβλίῳ,
                      οὗτός ²με παραδώσει.
Mc 14,20   ³εἷς (ἐκ) τῶν δώδεκα ὁ ἐμβαπτόμενος μετ᾽ ἐμοῦ   εἰς τὸ [ἐν] τρύβλιον.
Lc 22,21   πλὴν ἰδοὺ ἡ χεὶρ τοῦ παραδιδόντος με μετ᾽ ἐμοῦ   ἐπὶ τῆς τραπέζης.

        1 : Weiss(r), Simons, Schmid, De Solages(f), Keech, Brown, Léon-Dufour(5),
            Boismard(McR). **23**
        2 : McLoughlin.
        3 : Wilke(t), Holtzmann, Rushbrooke, Hawkins(II), Boismard(McR).
            Mc : + εκ TR Ti, [S] [GNT].

§ 94. Mc 14,22-25; Mt 26,26-29; Lc 22,15-20

Mt 26,26   εὐλογήσας   ἔκλασεν καὶ δοὺς   τοῖς μαθηταῖς   εἶπεν·
Mc 14,22   εὐλογήσας   ἔκλασεν καὶ ἔδωκεν αὐτοῖς   καὶ εἶπεν·
Lc 22,19   εὐχαριστήσας ἔκλασεν καὶ ἔδωκεν αὐτοῖς   λέγων·

        Rushbrooke, Schmid(7). **3**

Mt 26,27   ἔδωκεν αὐτοῖς   ¹λέγων· πίετε ἐξ αὐτοῦ πάντες·

Mc 14,23-24 ἔδωκεν αὐτοῖς,   καὶ ἔπιον ἐξ αὐτοῦ πάντες. (24) ²καὶ εἶπεν αὐτοῖς·

Lc 22,20   μετὰ τὸ δειπνῆσαι, λέγων·

        1 : Veit, Schmid(7), De Solages(b), Keech, Léon-Dufour(4).   **3 15**

        2 : Rushbrooke. **(23)**

Mt 26,28   τοῦτο γάρ ἐστιν τὸ αἷμά μου τῆς (καινῆς) διαθήκης

Mc 14,24   τοῦτό   ἐστιν τὸ αἷμά μου τῆς   διαθήκης

Lc 22,20   τοῦτο   τὸ ποτήριον ἡ καινὴ διαθήκη ἐν τῷ αἷματι

        De Solages(f).

        Mt : καινης TR S.

Mt 26,28   τὸ περὶ πολλῶν // ἐκχυννόμενον

Mc 14,24   τὸ ἐκχυννόμενον ὑπὲρ πολλῶν.

Lc 22,20   τὸ ὑπὲρ ὑμῶν // ἐκχυννόμενον.

        Veit. **21B**

Mt 26,29   λέγω ¹δὲ   ὑμῖν,   οὐ μὴ πίω ²// ³ἀπ' ἄρτι

Mc 14,25   ⁴ἀμὴν λέγω ὑμῖν ⁵ὅτι ⁶οὐκέτι οὐ μὴ πίω

Lc (22,18)   λέγω γὰρ ὑμῖν,   οὐ μὴ πίω   // ἀπὸ τοῦ νῦν

Lc (22,16)   λέγω γὰρ ὑμῖν ὅτι οὐκέτι οὐ μὴ φάγω

        1 : Schmid(3). **1a**

        2 : Veit. **21B**

        3 : Simons, Rushbrooke, Abbott(H), Schmid, De Solages(c), Keech, Léon-
            Dufour(3). **32**

        4 : Rushbrooke, Schmid, Keech.

        5 : Rushbrooke, Schmid(21), Keech. **5**

           Lc 22,18 : + οτι TR T [GNT].

        6 : Rushbrooke, Schmid.

           Lc 22,16 ουκετι : — H Ru S GNT.

§ 95. Mc 14,26-31; Mt 26,30-35; Lc 22,31-34

Mt 26,33-34 ἀποκριθεὶς δὲ ὁ Πέτρος ¹εἶπεν αὐτῷ· ... (34)   ἔφη αὐτῷ ὁ Ἰησοῦς·

Mc 14,29-30   ὁ δὲ Πέτρος ἔφη αὐτῷ· ... (30) ²καὶ ³λέγει αὐτῷ ὁ Ἰησοῦς·

Lc 22,33-34   ὁ δὲ   εἶπεν αὐτῷ· ... (34) ὁ δὲ εἶπεν·

        1 : Rushbrooke, Abbott, Keech, Léon-Dufour(4). **11**

        2 : Rushbrooke, Schmid(4). **2**

        3 : Rushbrooke, Hawkins(VI), Schmid(5). **10**

Mt 26,34   ὅτι   ἐν ταύτῃ τῇ νυκτὶ πρὶν   ἀλέκτορα φωνῆσαι
Mc 14,30   ὅτι ¹σὺ   ²ᵃσήμερον ᵇταύτῃ τῇ νυκτὶ πρὶν ³ἢ δὶς ἀλέκτορα φωνῆσαι
Lc 22,34   οὐ φωνήσει σήμερον   ἀλέκτωρ   ἕως

1 : Weiss(or), Simons, Rushbrooke, Schmid. (22)
2 : Hawkins(V), Schmid(31). 34
3 : Wilke(t), Holtzmann, Weiss(or), Simons, Rushbrooke, Wright, Wernle(t),
    Stanton(1), Lagrange, Schmid(29), Keech, Brown, Léon-Dufour(1).

Mt 26,34   τρὶς ἀπαρνήσῃ // με.
Mc 14,30   τρίς με ἀπαρνήσῃ.
Lc 22,34   τρίς (ἀπαρνήσῃ // μὴ εἰδέναι με).

Veit, Schmid(14), Vaganay. 21A
Lc με απαρνηση μη ειδεναι : 2 3 4 1 TR Ti T, 2 1 4 Ru, 1 2 4 H S GNT.

Mt 26,35   ¹λέγει αὐτῷ ὁ Πέτρος·
Mc 14,31   ὁ δὲ ²ἐκπερισσῶς ἐλάλει·
Lc (22,33) ὁ δὲ   εἶπεν αὐτῷ·

1 : De Solages(a,d), Boismard(McR). 32
2 : Rushbrooke, Hawkins(IVa).

§ 96. Mc 14,32-42 ; Mt 26,36-46 ; Lc 22,39-46

Mt 26,36   τότε ¹ἔρχεται μετ' αὐτῶν ὁ Ἰησοῦς εἰς χωρίον..., καὶ λέγει
Mc 14,32   ²καὶ ἔρχονται   εἰς χωρίον..., καὶ λέγει
Lc 22,40   γενόμενος δὲ   ἐπὶ τοῦ τόπου   εἶπεν

1 : Schmid(30). (33c)
2 : Rushbrooke, Schmid(4). 2

Mt 26,39   καὶ προελθὼν μικρὸν   ἔπεσεν ἐπὶ πρόσωπον αὐτοῦ
Mc 14,35   καὶ προελθὼν μικρὸν   ἔπιπτεν ἐπὶ τῆς γῆς,
Lc 22,41   καὶ αὐτὸς ἀπεσπάσθη ἀπ' αὐτῶν ὡσεὶ λίθου βολήν, καὶ θεὶς τὰ γόνατα

Rushbrooke. 11

Mt 26,39   προσευχόμενος   καὶ ¹λέγων·
Mc 14,35-36 ²καὶ προσηύχετο ³ἵνα εἰ δυνατόν ἐστιν παρέλθῃ ἀπ' αὐτοῦ ἡ ὥρα, (36) καὶ ἔλεγεν·
Lc 22,41-42   προσηύχετο   (42)   λέγων·

1 : Weiss(r), Simons, Rushbrooke, Veit, Wernle, Abbott(IV), Schmid(7),
    De Solages(b), Keech. 11 15
2 : Schmid(7). 3
3 : Allen, Schmid(23), Keech. 7A

Mt 26,39 ^{1}πάτερ μου, ^{2}εἰ   δυνατόν ἐστιν,
Mc 14,36 ^{3}ἀββὰ ὁ πατήρ, ^{4}πάντα δυνατά σοι·
Lc 22,42   πάτερ,   εἰ   βούλει

1 : Rushbrooke, Veit, Stanton(3b), Schmid, De Solages(b), Keech, Léon-Dufour(4). **32**
    Mt πατερ μου : — μου Ti T.
2 : Veit, De Solages(e), Keech, Boismard(Mt).
3 : Weiss(r), Simons, Rushbrooke, Wright, Wernle, Hawkins(IIIa), Stanton (3b), Schmid(1), Keech. Cf. 1.
4 : Rushbrooke (cf. v. 35). **24**

Mt (26,42)   ἐὰν μὴ αὐτὸ πίω, ^{1}γενηθήτω τὸ θέλημά σου.
Mt 26,39 ^{2}πλὴν οὐχ ὡς ἐγὼ θέλω   ἀλλ' ὡς σύ.
Mc 14,36   ἀλλ' οὐ ^{3}τί ἐγὼ θέλω   ἀλλὰ τί σύ.
Lc 22,42   πλὴν μὴ   τὸ θέλημά μου ἀλλὰ τὸ σὸν γινέσθω.

1 : Weiss(or), Simons, Léon-Dufour(4), McLoughlin(PDRIQ), Boismard(Mt).
2 : Weiss(or), Simons, Rushbrooke, Veit, Wernle, Abbott(VII), Stanton(3b), Schmid(15), De Solages(c), Keech, Léon-Dufour(4), Boismard(Mt). **9A**
3 : Rushbrooke, Hawkins(IVa).

Mt 26,40   καὶ ἔρχεται πρὸς τοὺς μαθητὰς καὶ εὑρίσκει αὐτοὺς καθεύδοντας,
Mc 14,37   καὶ ἔρχεται   καὶ εὑρίσκει αὐτοὺς καθεύδοντας,
Lc 22,45   ἐλθὼν πρὸς τοὺς μαθητὰς   εὗρεν κοιμωμένους αὐτούς

Weiss(r), Simons, Rushbrooke, Veit, Wernle, Abbott(I), Stanton(2), Schmid(33), De Solages(d), Keech, Léon-Dufour(4). **23**

Mt 26,40   οὕτως   οὐκ ^{1}ἰσχύσατε μίαν ὥραν γρηγορῆσαι μετ' ἐμοῦ ;
Mc 14,37 ^{2}Σίμων, ^{3a}καθεύδεις ; ^{b}οὐκ ἴσχυσας μίαν ὥραν γρηγορῆσαι ;
Lc 22,46   τί   καθεύδετε ;

1 : Rushbrooke.
2 : Rushbrooke.
3 : Schmid(31). **33c 34**

Mt 26,41   ἵνα μὴ εἰσέλθητε εἰς πειρασμόν·
Mc 14,38   ἵνα μὴ   ἔλθητε εἰς πειρασμόν·
Lc 22,46   ἵνα μὴ εἰσέλθητε εἰς πειρασμόν.

Rushbrooke, Veit, Abbott(VII), Schmid, De Solages(c), Keech, Brown, Léon-Dufour(4). **18**

Mt 26,43   ἦσαν γὰρ αὐτῶν οἱ ὀφθαλμοὶ   [1]βεβαρημένοι.

Mc 14,40   ἦσαν γὰρ αὐτῶν οἱ ὀφθαλμοὶ καταβαρυνόμενοι, [2]καὶ οὐκ ᾔδεισαν τί ἀποκριθῶσιν αὐτῷ.

Lc 22,46   om.

Lc (9,32) ἦσαν   βεβαρημένοι ὕπνῳ·

1 : Hansen.
2 : Rushbrooke, Léon-Dufour(1).

§ 97. Mc 14,43-52; Mt 26,47-56; Lc 22,47-53

Mt 26,47   καὶ   ἔτι αὐτοῦ λαλοῦντος, [1]ἰδοὺ   Ἰούδας... [2]// [3]ἦλθεν,

Mc 14,43   καὶ [4]εὐθὺς ἔτι αὐτοῦ λαλοῦντος [5]παραγίνεται   [ὁ] Ἰούδας

Lc 22,47   ἔτι αὐτοῦ λαλοῦντος ἰδοὺ ὄχλος, καὶ ὁ λεγόμενος Ἰούδας ... //
προήρχετο αὐτούς,

1 : Weiss(r), Simons, Rushbrooke, Wright, Veit, Wernle, Abbott(H), Stanton(2),
    Easton, Schmid(33), De Solages(d), Keech, Léon-Dufour(4), Boismard(Mt).
    25
2 : Veit.   **21B**
3 : Schmid(5), De Solages(c), Boismard(Mt).
4 : Weiss(r), Simons, Rushbrooke, Wright, Hawkins(II,V), Stephenson,
    Schmid(10), Keech, Boismard(Mt).   **26**
5 : Rushbrooke, Hawkins(VI), Abbott(III), Schmid(5).   **10**

Mt 26,49   καὶ   εὐθέως προσελθὼν [1]τῷ Ἰησοῦ εἶπεν·

Mc 14,45   καὶ [2]ἐλθὼν εὐθὺς προσελθὼν αὐτῷ   [3]λέγει·

Lc 22,47   καὶ   ἤγγισεν   τῷ Ἰησοῦ

1 : Veit, Easton, De Solages(e), Keech, Léon-Dufour(4), Boismard(Mt).   **23**
2 : Rushbrooke, Hawkins(II,IVa), Boismard(Mt).
3 : Rushbrooke, Schmid(5).

Mt 26,50   ὁ δὲ Ἰησοῦς   εἶπεν αὐτῷ· ἑταῖρε, ἐφ᾽ ὃ πάρει.

Mc 14,45   om.

Lc 22,48   Ἰησοῦς δὲ εἶπεν αὐτῷ· Ἰούδα, φιλήματι τὸν υἱὸν τοῦ ἀνθρώπου παραδίδως ;

Simons, Rushbrooke, Veit, Wernle, Hawkins(*), Abbott(H), Stanton(3b),
Streeter(d), Easton, Schmid, Da Fonseca, De Solages(f), Keech, Léon-Dufour
(2), McLoughlin(D), Sanders, Boismard(Mt).

Mt 26,51   [1]καὶ [2]ἰδοὺ   εἷς   τῶν μετὰ Ἰησοῦ   ἐκτείνας τὴν χεῖρα

Mc 14,47   εἷς δέ τις τῶν [3]παρεστηκότων

Lc 22,49   [2]ἰδόντες δὲ   οἱ περὶ αὐτὸν   τὸ ἐσόμενον εἶπαν·

Lc 22,50   καὶ ἐπάταξεν εἷς   τις ἐξ αὐτῶν

1 : Rushbrooke, Veit, Easton, De Solages(a).   **1**
2 : Simons.
3 : Rushbrooke, Schmid.

Mt 26,51   ἀπέσπασεν τὴν μάχαιραν αὐτοῦ, καὶ πατάξας τὸν δοῦλον τοῦ ἀρχιερέως
Mc 14,47   σπασάμενος τὴν μάχαιραν   ἔπαισεν τὸν δοῦλον τοῦ ἀρχιερέως
Lc 22,49-50 εἰ πατάξομεν ἐν μαχαίρῃ ; (50) καὶ ἐπάταξεν ... τοῦ ἀρχιερέως τὸν δοῦλον

Weiss(or), Simons, Rushbrooke, Wernle, Abbott(H), Allen, Streeter(d), Easton,
Schmid(28), Chapman, De Solages(c), Keech, Léon-Dufour(4), Boismard(Mt).
32

Mt 26,51   ἀφεῖλεν αὐτοῦ τὸ ¹ὠτίον.
Mc 14,47   καὶ ἀφεῖλεν αὐτοῦ τὸ ²ὠτάριον.
Lc 22,50   καὶ ἀφεῖλεν   τὸ οὖς αὐτοῦ τὸ δεξιόν.
Lc (22,51) καὶ ἁψάμενος   τοῦ ὠτίου   ἰάσατο αὐτόν.

1 : Weiss(or), Simons, Rushbrooke, Wernle, Schmid. 33a
2 : Weiss(or), Schmid(26).
Mc : ωτιον TR s.

Mt 26,52   τότε λέγει αὐτῷ ὁ Ἰησοῦς· ἀπόστρεψον τὴν μάχαιράν σου
Mc 14,47   om.
Lc 22,51   ἀποκριθεὶς δὲ ὁ Ἰησοῦς εἶπεν· ἐᾶτε ἕως τούτου·

Simons, Rushbrooke, Léon-Dufour(2).

Mt 26,52   οἱ λαβόντες μάχαιραν ἐν μαχαίρῃ ἀπολοῦνται.
Mc 14,47   om.
Lc (22,49) κύριε, εἰ πατάξομεν ἐν μαχαίρῃ ;

Rushbrooke, Léon-Dufour(5), Boismard(Mt).

Mt (26,52) τότε   λέγει αὐτῷ ὁ Ἰησοῦς·
Mt 26,55   ¹ἐν ἐκείνῃ τῇ ὥρᾳ εἶπεν ²/ ὁ Ἰησοῦς τοῖς ὄχλοις·... ἐκαθεζόμην διδάσκων,
Mc 14,48-49 ³καὶ ⁴ἀποκριθεὶς ὁ Ἰησοῦς εἶπεν ⁵αὐτοῖς· ... (49) ... ⁶ἤμην πρὸς ὑμᾶς ... διδά-
                                                                              σκων
Lc 22,52-53   εἶπεν δὲ / Ἰησοῦς πρὸς τοὺς παραγενομένους ἐπ᾽ αὐτόν...·
            (53) ... ὄντος μου μεθ᾽ ὑμῶν...· ἀλλ᾽ αὕτη ἐστὶν ὑμῶν ἡ ὥρα

1 : Simons.
2 : Veit. 21B
3 : Rushbrooke, Schmid(4). 2
4 : Rushbrooke, Schmid, Glasson. 16
5 : Rushbrooke, Schmid. 23
6 : Rushbrooke. 12

Mt   om.
Mc 14,51-52 καὶ νεανίσκος τις συνηκολούθει αὐτῷ περιβεβλημένος σινδόνα ἐπὶ γυμνοῦ, καὶ
            κρατοῦσιν αὐτόν. (52) ὁ δὲ καταλιπὼν τὴν σινδόνα γυμνὸς ἔφυγεν.
Lc   om.

Wilke(t), Simons, Rushbrooke, Wright, Wernle, Allen, Stanton(2), Schmid,
Vaganay, Léon-Dufour(1).

§ 98. Mc 14,53-54; Mt 26,57-58; Lc 22,54-55

Mt 26,57 οἱ ¹δὲ ²κρατήσαντες τὸν Ἰησοῦν ³/ ἀπήγαγον
Mc 14,53 καὶ   ἀπήγαγον τὸν Ἰησοῦν
Lc 22,54 συλλαβόντες δὲ   αὐτὸν   / ἤγαγον καὶ εἰσήγαγον

> 1 : Simons, Rushbrooke, Hawkins(VII), Abbott(VI), Easton, Schmid(4), De Solages(a), Keech, Schneider(V). 1
> 2 : Weiss(r), Simons, Wright, Schmid, Schneider(V).
> 3 : Veit. 21B

Mt 26,57 ὅπου οἱ γραμματεῖς καὶ οἱ πρεσβύτεροι ¹συνήχθησαν.
Mc 14,53 καὶ ²συνέρχονται ³πάντες οἱ ἀρχιερεῖς καὶ οἱ πρεσβύτεροι καὶ γραμματεῖς.
Lc (22,66) καὶ ... συνήχθη τὸ πρεσβυτέριον τοῦ λαοῦ, ἀρχιερεῖς τε καὶ γραμματεῖς,

> 1 : Simons, Veit, Wernle, Léon-Dufour(4), Schneider(I). 17
> 2 : Rushbrooke, Schmid(5). Cf. 1. 10
> 3 : Rushbrooke.

Mt 26,58 ὁ ¹δὲ Πέτρος ²ἠκολούθει αὐτῷ ³// ἀπὸ μακρόθεν
Mc 14,54 καὶ ὁ Πέτρος ⁴ἀπὸ μακρόθεν ἠκολούθησεν αὐτῷ
Lc 22,54 ὁ δὲ Πέτρος ἠκολούθει   //   μακρόθεν.

> 1 : Weiss(r), Rushbrooke, Veit, Hawkins(VII), Abbott(VI), Easton, Schmid(4), De Solages(a), Keech, Brown, Schneider(V), Fuchs. 1
> 2 : Weiss(r), Rushbrooke, Veit, Abbott(H), Easton, Schmid, De Solages(b), Keech, Brown, Léon-Dufour(4), Schneider(V vel VI), Fuchs. (11)
> 3 : Wright, Veit, Easton, Schmid, Fuchs. 21B
> 4 : (Mt om. ἀπό) Schmid(27).
> Mt απο : — T S, [H] [Ru] [N].

Mt 26,58   ἕως   ¹τῆς αὐλῆς τοῦ ἀρχιερέως, καὶ εἰσελθὼν ἔσω
Mc 14,54   ἕως ²ἔσω εἰς τὴν αὐλὴν τοῦ ἀρχιερέως,
Lc 22,55 περιαψάντων δὲ πῦρ ἐν μέσῳ τῆς αὐλῆς

> 1 : Rushbrooke, Veit, Abbott(H), Easton, Schmid, De Solages(b), Keech, Léon-Dufour(4), Schneider(V).
> 2 : Rushbrooke, Allen, Schneider(V).

Mt 26,58 καὶ   ¹ἐκάθητο   μετὰ τῶν ὑπηρετῶν
Mc 14,54 καὶ ἦν ²ᵃσυγκαθήμενος   ᵇμετὰ τῶν ὑπηρετῶν
Lc 22,55 καὶ   συγκαθισάντων ἐκάθητο ὁ Πέτρος μέσος αὐτῶν.

> 1 : Weiss(r), Rushbrooke, Veit, Abbott(H), Schmid(9,19), De Solages(b), Keech, Léon-Dufour(4), Schneider(V), Boismard(McR). (11) 12 (18)
> 2 : Weiss(r). Cf. 1. 34

Mt 26,58   ἰδεῖν τὸ τέλος.
Mc 14,54   καὶ θερμαινόμενος πρὸς τὸ φῶς.
Lc 22,55   om.
Lc (22,56)   καθήμενον   πρὸς τὸ φῶς

Rushbrooke, Hawkins(III), Boismard(McR).

§ 99. Mc 14,55-65; Mt 26,59-68; Lc 22,67-71. (63-65)

Mt 26,63   καὶ ὁ ἀρχιερεὺς   εἶπεν   αὐτῷ· ἐξορκίζω σε
Mc 14,61   ¹πάλιν ὁ ἀρχιερεὺς ἐπηρώτα αὐτὸν καὶ   ²λέγει   αὐτῷ·
Lc 22,66-67 ἀπήγαγον αὐτὸν εἰς τὸ συνέδριον αὐτῶν, (67) λέγοντες·

1 : Rushbrooke. **19**
2 : Hawkins(VI), Schmid(5), Schneider(V). **10**

Mt 26,63   ἵνα ¹ἡμῖν εἴπῃς ²εἰ σὺ   εἶ ὁ χριστὸς   ὁ υἱὸς τοῦ ³θεοῦ.
Mc 14,61   σὺ   εἶ ὁ χριστὸς   ὁ υἱὸς τοῦ εὐλογητοῦ;
Lc 22,67   εἰ σὺ   εἶ ὁ χριστός, εἰπὸν ἡμῖν.
Lc (22,70)   σὺ οὖν εἶ   ὁ υἱὸς τοῦ θεοῦ ;

1 : Weiss(or /r), Simons, Rushbrooke, Abbott, Easton, De Solages(g), Keech,
    Léon-Dufour(3), McLoughlin(I), Schneider(I).
2 : Simons, Rushbrooke, Veit, Abbott, Easton, Schmid, De Solages(g), Keech,
    Léon-Dufour(3), Schneider(I).
3 : Weiss(r), Simons, Rushbrooke, Abbott(H), Stanton(1 vel 2), Streeter(d),
    Schmid, De Solages(c), Keech, Léon-Dufour(3), Schneider(V), Boismard(Mt).
    32

Mt 26,64   λέγει   ¹αὐτῷ ὁ Ἰησοῦς· ²σὺ εἶπας·
Mc 14,62   ὁ δὲ Ἰησοῦς εἶπεν·   ³ἐγώ εἰμι,
Lc 22,67   εἶπεν δὲ   αὐτοῖς·   ἐὰν ὑμῖν εἴπω,
Lc (22,70)   ὁ δὲ πρὸς αὐτοὺς ἔφη·   ὑμεῖς λέγετε ὅτι ἐγώ εἰμι.

1 : De Solages(d), Schneider(I vel V). **23**
2 : Weiss(or /r), Simons, Hawkins(*), Streeter(t vel d), Easton, De Solages(g),
    Keech, Brown, Léon-Dufour(3), McLoughlin(PDMT), Schneider(I).
3 : Schneider(I).

Mt 26,64   ¹πλὴν λέγω ὑμῖν, ²ἀπ᾽ ἄρτι   ὄψεσθε τὸν υἱὸν τοῦ ἀνθρώπου
Mc 14,62   ³καὶ   ὄψεσθε τὸν υἱὸν τοῦ ἀνθρώπου
Lc 22,69   ἀπὸ τοῦ νῦν δὲ ἔσται ὁ υἱὸς τοῦ ἀνθρώπου

1 : Schneider(I vel V).
2 : Holtzmann, Weiss(or), Simons, Rushbrooke, Wernle, Hawkins(*), Abbott(H),
    Burton, Stanton(1), Streeter(d), Easton, Schmid, De Solages(g), Keech,
    Léon-Dufour(3), McLoughlin(DML), Schneider(I vel V).
3 : Rushbrooke.

Mt 26,64   τὸν υἱὸν τοῦ ἀνθρώπου καθήμενον || ἐκ δεξιῶν τῆς δυνάμεως
Mc 14,62   τὸν υἱὸν τοῦ ἀνθρώπου ἐκ δεξιῶν καθήμενον   τῆς δυνάμεως
Lc 22,69   ὁ   υἱὸς τοῦ ἀνθρώπου καθήμενος || ἐκ δεξιῶν τῆς δυνάμεως τοῦ θεοῦ.

     Weiss(r /or), Simons, Schmid, Keech, Léon-Dufour(4), McLoughlin, Schneider
     (V). **21B**

Mt 26,65   τότε ὁ ἀρχιερεὺς διέρρηξεν τὰ   ἱμάτια   αὐτοῦ λέγων·
Mc 14,63   ὁ δὲ ἀρχιερεὺς   διαρήξας τοὺς χιτῶνας αὐτοῦ λέγει·
Lc 22,71   οἱ δὲ   εἶπαν·

     Hawkins(VI), Schmid(5). **10**

Mt 26,65-66   [1]ἴδε νῦν   ἠκούσατε... (66)... ; οἱ   δὲ ἀποκριθέντες [2]εἶπαν·
Mc 14,64   ἠκούσατε... ;   οἱ   δὲ πάντες κατέκριναν
Lc 22,71   αὐτοὶ γὰρ ἠκούσαμεν
Lc (22,70)   εἶπαν δὲ πάντες·

     1 : **4**
     2 : Schneider(V).

Mt 26,67   τότε ἐνέπτυσαν εἰς   τὸ πρόσωπον αὐτοῦ
Mc 14,65   καὶ ἤρξαντό τινες ἐμπτύειν αὐτῷ   καὶ περικαλύπτειν   αὐτοῦ τὸ πρόσωπον
Lc (22,63-64) καὶ ... ἐνέπαιζον αὐτῷ δέροντες, (64) καὶ περικαλύψαντες αὐτόν

     Rushbrooke, Schmid(8), Schneider(V). **13**

Mt 26,67-68   καὶ ἐκολάφισαν αὐτόν, οἱ δὲ ἐρράπισαν (68) [1]λέγοντες·
Mc 14,65   καὶ κολαφίζειν   αὐτὸν   [2]καὶ   λέγειν   [3]αὐτῷ·
Lc (22,64)   ἐπηρώτων   λέγοντες·

     1 : Simons, Rushbrooke, Veit, Wernle, Abbott(IV), Schmid(7), De Solages(b),
       Keech, Léon-Dufour(2), Schneider(V). **3** **15**
     2 : Rushbrooke.
     3 : Rushbrooke, Keech. **(23)**

Mt 26,68   προφήτευσον ἡμῖν, χριστέ, τίς ἐστιν ὁ παίσας σε ;
Mc 14,65   προφήτευσον,
Lc (22,64)   προφήτευσον,   τίς ἐστιν ὁ παίσας σε ;

     Holtzmann, Weiss(or), Simons, Rushbrooke, Wright, Veit, Wernle, Hawkins(*),
     Abbott(H), Burton, Stanton(4 vel 3b), Lagrange, Streeter(t), Larfeld, Easton,
     Schmid, Chapman, Da Fonseca, De Solages(g), Keech, Brown, Léon-Dufour(2),
     McLoughlin(T), Schneider(II,III, I vel IV).

Mt (26,67)   οἱ δὲ   ἐρράπισαν
Mt 26,68   om.
Mc 14,65   καὶ οἱ ὑπηρέται ῥαπίσμασιν αὐτὸν ἔλαβον.
Lc (22,65)   καὶ ἕτερα πολλὰ βλασφημοῦντες ἔλεγον εἰς αὐτόν.

     Rushbrooke.

§ 100. Mc 14,66-72; Mt 26,69-75; (Lc 22,56-62)

Mt 26,69   ὁ ¹δὲ   Πέτρος   ²ἐκάθητο ἔξω ἐν τῇ αὐλῇ·
Mc 14,66   καὶ ³ὄντος τοῦ Πέτρου   κάτω ἐν τῇ αὐλῇ
Lc 22,56   ἰδοῦσα δὲ   αὐτὸν παιδίσκη τις καθήμενον πρὸς τὸ φῶς

1 : De Solages(a).
2 : Rushbrooke, Abbott(H), Easton, De Solages(e), Keech, Léon-Dufour(3) Schneider(V).
3 : Rushbrooke. **14**

Mt 26,69   καὶ   προσῆλθεν αὐτῷ μία   ¹παιδίσκη
Mc 14,66   ²ἔρχεται   μία τῶν παιδισκῶν ³τοῦ ἀρχιερέως,
Lc 22,56   ἰδοῦσα δὲ   αὐτὸν   παιδίσκη τις

1 : Rushbrooke, Easton, De Solages(b), Keech, Léon-Dufour(4), Schneider(V)
2 : Schmid(5), Schneider(V).
3 : Hawkins(II), Keech. **(22n)**

Mt 26,69   λέγουσα
Mc 14,67   καὶ ἰδοῦσα τὸν Πέτρον ¹θερμαινόμενον   ἐμβλέψασα αὐτῷ ²λέγει·
Lc 22,56   ἰδοῦσα δὲ αὐτὸν ... καθήμενον πρὸς τὸ φῶς καὶ ἀτενίσασα αὐτῷ εἶπεν·

1 : Rushbrooke.
2 : Hawkins(VI), Schmid(5), Schneider(V). **10**

Mt 26,70   ¹οὐκ οἶδα   τί λέγεις.
Mc 14,68   οὔτε οἶδα ²οὔτε ἐπίσταμαι ³σὺ τί λέγεις.
Lc 22,57   οὐκ οἶδα   αὐτόν, γύναι.

1 : Rushbrooke, Abbott(H), Easton, De Solages(b), Keech, Léon-Dufour(4) Schneider(V).
2 : Holtzmann, Rushbrooke, Hawkins(V), Schmid, Keech, Boismard(McR). **3**
3 : Rushbrooke, Schmid, Keech.

Mt 26,71   ἐξελθόντα δὲ   εἰς τὸν πυλῶνα
Mc 14,68   καὶ ἐξῆλθεν ¹ἔξω εἰς τὸ προαύλιον ²(καὶ ἀλέκτωρ ἐφώνησεν)
Lc 22,57   om.

1 : Rushbrooke, Schneider(V vel VI).
2 : Wilke, Holtzmann, Weiss(r), Rushbrooke, Wernle(t), Brown, Schneider(VI)
Mc : + και αλεκτωρ εφωνησεν TR Ti T hʳ S [GNT](D).

Mt 26,71   εἶδεν αὐτὸν ¹ἄλλη καὶ   λέγει τοῖς ἐκεῖ·
Mc 14,69   ἡ παιδίσκη ἰδοῦσα αὐτὸν   ²ἤρξατο ³πάλιν λέγειν τοῖς παρεστῶσιν ⁴ὅτι
Lc 22,58   ἕτερος ἰδὼν αὐτὸν   ἔφη·

1 : Schmid, Léon-Dufour(3), Schneider(V vel VI).
2 : Rushbrooke, Allen, Schmid(8), Schneider(V).   13
   Mc ηρξατο λεγειν : ειπεν h W.
3 : Rushbrooke, Schmid(11).   27
4 : Rushbrooke, Schmid(21), Keech.   5

Mt 26,71   οὗτος ¹ἦν ²μετὰ 'Ιησοῦ τοῦ Ναζωραίου.
Mc 14,69   οὗτος   ἐξ   αὐτῶν ἐστιν.
Lc 22,58   καὶ σὺ   ἐξ   αὐτῶν εἶ.
Lc (22,59) ἐπ' ἀληθείας καὶ οὗτος   μετ' αὐτοῦ ἦν,

1 : De Solages(b), Léon-Dufour(5,2).   (11)
2 : Rushbrooke, Abbott(H), Keech, Léon-Dufour(5,2), Schneider(V).   31b

Mt 26,72   καὶ πάλιν ἠρνήσατο μετὰ ὅρκου ὅτι ¹οὐκ οἶδα τὸν ²ἄνθρωπον.
Mc 14,70   ὁ δὲ πάλιν ἠρνεῖτο.
Lc 22,58   ὁ δὲ Πέτρος ἔφη·   ἄνθρωπε, οὐκ εἰμί.

1 : Simons, Rushbrooke, Wright, Veit, Abbott(H), Keech, Schneider(V).
2 : Simons, Wright, Veit, Abbott(H), Keech, Schneider(V).

Mt (26,71)   εἶδεν αὐτὸν ¹ἄλλη   καὶ λέγει τοῖς ἐκεῖ·
Mt 26,73   μετὰ μικρὸν δὲ προσελθόντες οἱ   ἑστῶτες εἶπον τῷ Πέτρῳ·
Mc 14,70   καὶ μετὰ μικρὸν ²πάλιν   οἱ παρεστῶτες ³ἔλεγον τῷ Πέτρῳ·
Lc 22,59   καὶ διαστάσης ὡσεὶ ὥρας μιᾶς ἄλλος τις διϊσχυρίζετο λέγων·

1 : Schneider(V vel VI).
2 : Rushbrooke, Schmid(11).   27
3 : 11

Mt 26,73   ἀληθῶς καὶ σὺ   ἐξ   αὐτῶν εἶ,
Mc 14,70   ἀληθῶς   ἐξ   αὐτῶν εἶ·
Lc 22,59 ἐπ' ἀληθείας καὶ οὗτος μετ' αὐτοῦ ἦν,
Lc (22,58)   καὶ σὺ   ἐξ   αὐτῶν εἶ.

Rushbrooke, Wright, Abbott(H), Streeter(t), De Solages(f), Keech, Léon-
Dufour(5,2), Schneider(V), Boismard.   22
   Lc καὶ οὗτος : Weiss(r), Easton.

Mt 26,74   οὐκ οἶδα τὸν ἄνθρωπον.
Mc 14,71   οὐκ οἶδα τὸν ἄνθρωπον τοῦτον ὃν λέγετε.
Lc 22,60 ἄνθρωπε, οὐκ οἶδα   ὃ λέγεις.

Rushbrooke.

Mt 26,74   καὶ εὐθὺς   ἀλέκτωρ ἐφώνησεν.
Mc 14,72   καὶ εὐθὺς   ἐκ δευτέρου ἀλέκτωρ ἐφώνησεν.
Lc 22,60   καὶ παραχρῆμα ἔτι λαλοῦντος αὐτοῦ   ἐφώνησεν ἀλέκτωρ.

Wilke, Holtzmann, Weiss(r), Simons, Rushbrooke, Wright, Wernle(t), Lagrange, Schmid(29), Keech, Brown, Léon-Dufour(1), Schneider(V).
Mc εκ δευτερου : — hʳ.
Mc ευθυς : — TR Ti S ; Mt : ευθεως TR Ti T S GNT.

Mt 26,75   καὶ ἐμνήσθη ὁ Πέτρος ¹τοῦ ῥήματος Ἰησοῦ   ²|| εἰρηκότος   ὅτι
Mc 14,72   καὶ ἀνεμνήσθη ὁ Πέτρος τὸ ῥῆμα   ὡς εἶπεν αὐτῷ ὁ Ἰησοῦς   ὅτι
Lc 22,61   καὶ ὑπεμνήσθη ὁ Πέτρος τοῦ λόγου   τοῦ κυρίου, || ὡς εἶπεν αὐτῷ ὅτι

1 : Weiss(r), Rushbrooke, Veit, Abbott(VII?), Streeter(t), Easton, Schmid(27), De Solages(b), Keech, Brown, Schneider(V). 32
Lc τοῦ ῥήματος : Rushbrooke.
Lc λογου : ρηματος H Ru GNT.
2 : Wright. 21B

Mt 26,75   πρὶν ἀλέκτορα   φωνῆσαι   τρὶς   ἀπαρνήσῃ ¹/ με·
Mc 14,72   πρὶν ἀλέκτορα ²δὶς φωνῆσαι   τρίς με ἀπαρνήσῃ·
Lc 22,61   πρὶν ἀλέκτορα   φωνῆσαι σήμερον   ἀπαρνήσῃ / με τρίς.

1 : Easton, Keech, Schneider(V). 21A
2 : Wilke(t), Holtzmann, Weiss(or), Rushbrooke, Wright, Wernle(t), Stanton(1), Lagrange, Schmid(29), Keech, Brown, Léon-Dufour(1), Schneider(V).

Mt 26,75   καὶ ¹ἐξελθὼν ἔξω⌝ ἔκλαυσεν πικρῶς.
Mc 14,72   καὶ ²ἐπιβαλὼν   ἔκλαιεν.
Lc 22,62   καὶ ἐξελθὼν ἔξω ἔκλαυσεν πικρῶς.

1 : Wilke(⌐), Holtzmann(⌐), Weiss(or), Simons, Rushbrooke, Veit, Wernle, Hawkins(*), Abbott(H), Burton, Allen, Stanton(4), Lagrange, Streeter(t), Larfeld, Easton(t), Schmid, Da Fonseca, De Solages(c,d,c,f), Keech, Léon-Dufour(2), McLoughlin(IT), Schneider(II), Boismard(t). 11
Lc vs. : [H].
2 : Simons, Rushbrooke, Hawkins(IVa), Allen. 32

§ 101. Mc 15,1; Mt 27,1-2; Lc 23,1

Mt 27,1   πρωΐας δὲ ¹γενομένης συμβούλιον ἔλαβον   ²πάντες οἱ ἀρχιερεῖς
Mc 15,1   καὶ ³εὐθὺς πρωΐ   συμβούλιον ἑτοιμάσαντες   οἱ ἀρχιερεῖς
Lc 23,1   καὶ   ἀναστὰν ἅπαν   τὸ πλῆθος αὐτῶν
Lc (22,66)   καὶ ὡς ἐγένετο ἡμέρα,

1 : De Solages(d).
2 : Simons, Rushbrooke, Abbott, Schmid, Keech, Léon-Dufour(5).
3 : Rushbrooke, Stephenson, Schmid(10). 26

Mt 27,1   οἱ ἀρχιερεῖς καὶ οἱ πρεσβύτεροι ¹τοῦ λαοῦ
Mc 15,1   οἱ ἀρχιερεῖς ²μετὰ τῶν πρεσβυτέρων καὶ γραμματέων καὶ ὅλον τὸ συνέδριον,
Lc 23,1   ἅπαν τὸ πλῆθος αὐτῶν
Lc (22,66)   τὸ πρεσβυτέριον τοῦ λαοῦ, ἀρχιερεῖς τε καὶ γραμματεῖς, ... εἰς τὸ συνέδριον
              αὐτῶν,

              1 : Easton, De Solages(f), Keech, Léon-Dufour(4), Schneider(V).   22n
              2 : Rushbrooke.

Mt 27,2   ¹καὶ δήσαντες ²αὐτὸν   ³ἀπήγαγον καὶ παρέδωκαν Πιλάτῳ ⁴τῷ ἡγεμόνι.
Mc 15,1   δήσαντες τὸν Ἰησοῦν ἀπήνεγκαν καὶ παρέδωκαν Πιλάτῳ.
Lc 23,1   καὶ ἀναστὰν ...   ἤγαγον αὐτὸν ἐπὶ τὸν Πιλᾶτον.

              1 : De Solages(d).   4
              2 : Rushbrooke, Veit, Abbott(VII), De Solages(e), Keech.   (23)
              3 : Simons, Rushbrooke, Veit, Wernle, Abbott(VII), Streeter(d), Schmid(27),
                  De Solages(c), Keech(cf. Lc 22,66), Brown, Léon-Dufour(4).   29
              4 : Rushbrooke.   (33b)

Mt 27,3-10   Mors Judae.
Mc 15,1   om.
Lc   Mors Judae (Act 1,15-20).

              Schmid.

§ 102. Mc 15,2-5; Mt 27,11-14; Lc 23,2-5

Mt 27,11   καὶ   ἐπηρώτησεν αὐτὸν ὁ ἡγεμὼν λέγων·
Mc 15,2   καὶ   ἐπηρώτησεν αὐτὸν ὁ Πιλᾶτος·
Lc 23,3   ὁ δὲ Πιλᾶτος ἠρώτησεν αὐτὸν   λέγων.

              Weiss(r), Simons, Rushbrooke, Wright, Veit, Wernle, Abbott(II), Schmid(33),
              De Solages(d), Keech, Léon-Dufour(4), Boismard(Mt).   15
              Mc επηρωτησεν : επηρωτα GNT.

Mt 27,11   ὁ δὲ Ἰησοῦς   ἔφη·
Mc 15,2   ὁ δὲ   ἀποκριθεὶς αὐτῷ λέγει·
Lc 23,3   ὁ δὲ   ἀποκριθεὶς αὐτῷ ἔφη·

              Weiss(r), Simons, Rushbrooke, Veit, Wernle, Hawkins(VI), Abbott(V), Easton,
              Schmid(5), De Solages(a), Keech, Léon-Dufour(4), Boismard(Mt).   10   (11)

Mt 27,12 καὶ ἐν τῷ κατηγορεῖσθαι αὐτὸν ὑπὸ τῶν ἀρχιερέων [1]καὶ πρεσβυτέρων
Mc 15,3 καὶ κατηγόρουν αὐτοῦ οἱ ἀρχιερεῖς [2]πολλά.
Lc (23,10) οἱ ἀρχιερεῖς καὶ οἱ γραμματεῖς εὐτόνως κατηγοροῦντες αὐτοῦ.

1 : Hansen.
2 : Rushbrooke, Schmid(16). 28

Mt 27,13 τότε λέγει αὐτῷ ὁ Πιλᾶτος·
Mc 15,4 ὁ δὲ Πιλᾶτος πάλιν ἐπηρώτα αὐτὸν λέγων·
Lc (23,9) ἐπηρώτα δὲ αὐτὸν ἐν λόγοις ἱκανοῖς·

Rushbrooke. 27
Mc λεγων : — T, [H] [N].
Mc επηρωτα : -τησεν TR W s.

Mt (27,12) οὐδὲν [1]ἀπεκρίνατο.
Mt 27,14 καὶ οὐκ ἀπεκρίθη [2]αὐτῷ πρὸς οὐδὲ ἕν ῥῆμα,
Mc 15,5 [3]ὁ δὲ Ἰησοῦς [4]οὐκέτι οὐδὲν ἀπεκρίθη,
Lc (23,9) αὐτὸς δὲ οὐδὲν ἀπεκρίνατο αὐτῷ.

1 : Farmer.
2 : Rushbrooke, Abbott(I), Keech, Léon-Dufour(4). 23
3 : Rushbrooke. (22)
4 : Hansen. 34

§ 103. Mc 15,6-15; Mt 27,15-26; Lc 23,13-25

Mt 27,16 εἶχον δὲ τότε δέσμιον ἐπίσημον λεγόμενον Βαραββᾶν.
Mc 15,7 ἦν δὲ ὁ λεγόμενος Βαραββᾶς μετὰ τῶν στασιαστῶν δεδεμένος,
οἵτινες ἐν τῇ στάσει φόνον πεποιήκεισαν.
Lc (23,19) ὅστις ἦν διὰ στάσιν τινὰ ... καὶ φόνον βληθεὶς ἐν τῇ φυλακῇ.

Rushbrooke, Stanton(1 vel 2).

Mt 27,17 συνηγμένων οὖν αὐτῶν
Mc 15,8 καὶ ἀναβὰς ὁ ὄχλος ἤρξατο αἰτεῖσθαι καθὼς ἐποίει αὐτοῖς.
Lc 23,13 om.

Rushbrooke, Hawkins(III).

Mt 27,17 [1]συνηγμένων οὖν αὐτῶν εἶπεν αὐτοῖς ὁ Πιλᾶτος·
Mc 15,9 ὁ δὲ Πιλᾶτος [2]ἀπεκρίθη αὐτοῖς λέγων·
Lc 23,13-14 Πιλᾶτος δὲ συγκαλεσάμενος τοὺς ἀρχιερεῖς ... (14) εἶπεν πρὸς αὐτούς·

1 : Rushbrooke, Abbott(VIII?), Keech, Léon-Dufour(3). 16n
2 : Rushbrooke.

Mt 27,20   ἵνα   αἰτήσωνται   ¹// τὸν Βαραββᾶν, τὸν ²δὲ Ἰησοῦν ἀπολέσωσιν.
Mc 15,11   ἵνα ³μᾶλλον τὸν Βαραββᾶν   ἀπολύσῃ αὐτοῖς.
Lc 23,18   αἶρε τοῦτον, ἀπόλυσον δὲ ἡμῖν // τὸν Βαραββᾶν·

    1 : 21A
    2 : Rushbrooke, Abbott, De Solages(f), Keech.
    3 : Rushbrooke.

Mt 27,21-22   εἶπεν   αὐτοῖς· τίνα ¹θέλετε ἀπὸ τῶν δύο ἀπολύσω ὑμῖν ; …
              (22) λέγει αὐτοῖς ὁ Πιλᾶτος· τί οὖν ποιήσω
Mc 15,12   ²ἔλεγεν   αὐτοῖς·   τί οὖν ποιήσω
Lc 23,20   προσεφώνησεν αὐτοῖς,   θέλων   ἀπολῦσαι τὸν Ἰησοῦν.

    1 : Rushbrooke, Veit, Abbott(H), Easton, Keech, Léon-Dufour(5).
       Mc ουν : + θελετε TR Ti T [GNT](D).
    2 : 11

Mt 27,21   οἱ δὲ εἶπαν·   τὸν Βαραββᾶν.
Mc 15,12   om.
Lc (23,18) λέγοντες· αἶρε τοῦτον, ἀπόλυσον δὲ ἡμῖν τὸν Βαραββᾶν·

    Simons, Schmid.

Mt 27,22   τί οὖν ποιήσω   ¹Ἰησοῦν τὸν λεγόμενον χριστόν ;
Mc 15,12   τί οὖν ποιήσω   ²ὃν λέγετε τὸν βασιλέα τῶν Ἰουδαίων ;
Lc 23,20   θέλων ἀπολῦσαι τὸν Ἰησοῦν.

    1 : Easton, Schmid, De Solages(e).   23
    2 : Rushbrooke.

Mt 27,22   ¹λέγουσιν πάντες· σταυρωθήτω.
Mc 15,13   οἱ δὲ ²πάλιν ἔκραξαν·   σταύρωσον   αὐτόν.
Lc 23,21   οἱ δὲ   ἐπεφώνουν λέγοντες·   σταύρου σταύρου αὐτόν.

    1 : Rushbrooke, Abbott(II), Easton, Schmid, De Solages(d), Keech, Léon-
       Dufour(4).   32
    2 : Rushbrooke, Schmid(11).   27

Mt 27,23   ὁ δὲ   ἔφη·   τί γὰρ κακὸν ¹/ ἐποίησεν ;
Mc 15,14   ὁ δὲ ²Πιλᾶτος ³ἔλεγεν   αὐτοῖς· τί γὰρ ἐποίησεν κακόν ;
Lc 23,22   ὁ δὲ τρίτον εἶπεν πρὸς αὐτούς· τί γὰρ κακὸν / ἐποίησεν οὗτος ;

    1 : Wright, Veit, Easton, Keech, Brown, Léon-Dufour(4).   (21A)
    2 : Rushbrooke, Schmid(6).   (22)
    3 : Rushbrooke, Schmid.

Mt 27,23   οἱ δὲ περισσῶς [1]ἔκραζον λέγοντες·   [2]σταυρωθήτω.
Mc 15,14   οἱ δὲ περισσῶς ἔκραξαν·   σταύρωσον αὐτόν.
Lc 23,23   οἱ δὲ ἐπέκειντο φωναῖς μεγάλαις αἰτούμενοι αὐτὸν σταυρωθῆναι,

            1 : (11)
            2 : Simons, Rushbrooke, Wernle, Abbott, Easton, Schmid(18), Keech.   17

Mt 27,24   ὁ Πιλᾶτος ... λέγων· ἀθῷός εἰμι ἀπὸ τοῦ αἵματος τούτου·
Mc 15,14   om.
Lc (23,22)   οὐδὲν αἴτιον θανάτου εὗρον ἐν αὐτῷ·

            Léon-Dufour(3).

Mt 27,26   τότε   ἀπέλυσεν αὐτοῖς
Mc 15,15   ὁ δὲ Πιλᾶτος βουλόμενος τῷ ὄχλῳ τὸ ἱκανὸν ποιῆσαι   ἀπέλυσεν αὐτοῖς
Lc 23,24-25 καὶ Πιλᾶτος ἐπέκρινεν γενέσθαι τὸ αἴτημα αὐτῶν· (25) ἀπέλυσεν δέ

            Rushbrooke, Hawkins(IVa), Glasson, Brown(W), Boismard(McR).

Mt 27,26   τὸν [1]δὲ Ἰησοῦν   φραγελλώσας [2]// παρέδωκεν ἵνα σταυρωθῇ.
Mc 15,15   καὶ παρέδωκεν τὸν Ἰησοῦν φραγελλώσας   ἵνα σταυρωθῇ.
Lc 23,25   τὸν δὲ Ἰησοῦν   // παρέδωκεν τῷ θελήματι αὐτῶν.

            1 : Rushbrooke, Veit, Hawkins(VII), Abbott(VI), Schmid(4), De Solages(a),
                Keech, Boismard(Mt).   1
            2 : Veit, Easton, Keech, Léon-Dufour(4), Boismard(Mt).   (21A)

§ 104. Mc 15,16-20 ; Mt 27,27-31 ; Lc 23,26a

Mt 27,28   καὶ ἐκδύσαντες   αὐτὸν χλαμύδα κοκκίνην περιέθηκαν   αὐτῷ,
Mc 15,17   καὶ ἐνδιδύσκουσιν αὐτὸν πορφύραν   καὶ περιτιθέασιν αὐτῷ... στέφανον·
Lc (23,11) περιβαλὼν   ἐσθῆτα λαμπράν

            Hawkins(VI), Schmid(5).   10

Mt 27,29   ἐνέπαιξαν   αὐτῷ   λέγοντες· χαῖρε, βασιλεῦ
Mc 15,18   ἤρξαντο ἀσπάζεσθαι αὐτόν·   χαῖρε, βασιλεῦ
Lc (23,36-37) ἐνέπαιξαν δὲ αὐτῷ ... (37) καὶ λέγοντες· εἰ σὺ εἶ ὁ βασιλεύς

            Boismard(Mt).

Mt 27,31   καὶ ἀπήγαγον αὐτὸν εἰς τὸ σταυρῶσαι.
Mc 15,20   καὶ ἐξάγουσιν αὐτὸν ἵνα   σταυρώσωσιν αὐτόν.
Lc 23,26   καὶ ὡς ἀπήγαγον αὐτόν,

            Weiss(r), Simons, Rushbrooke, Veit, Wernle, Hawkins(VI), Abbott(III),
            Schmid(5,20), De Solages(c), Keech, Léon-Dufour(2), Boismard(Mt).   10   31b
            Lc απηγαγον : απηγον h.

§ 105. Mc 15,21; Mt 27,32; Lc 23,26

Mt 27,32   ἐξερχόμενοι δὲ εὗρον ἄνθρωπον ...· τοῦτον ἠγγάρευσαν
Mc 15,21   καὶ ἀγγαρεύουσιν   παράγοντά τινα
Lc 23,26   ἐπιλαβόμενοι   Σίμωνά τινα Κυρηναῖον ... ἐπέθηκαν

Hawkins(VI), Schmid(5).   **10**

Mt 27,32   ἄνθρωπον   Κυρηναῖον, ὀνόματι Σίμωνα·
Mc 15,21   ¹παράγοντά τινα Σίμωνα Κυρηναῖον   ἐρχόμενον ἀπ᾽ ἀγροῦ,
           ²τὸν πατέρα Ἀλεξάνδρου καὶ Ῥούφου,
Lc 23,26   Σίμωνά τινα Κυρηναῖον   ἐρχόμενον ἀπ᾽ ἀγροῦ

1 : Rushbrooke, Hawkins(V), Easton.
2 : Wilke(t), Holtzmann, Simons, Rushbrooke, Wright, Wernle(t), Hawkins
(IIIb), Allen, Stanton(2), Easton, Schmid(32), Vaganay, Keech, Léon-
Dufour(1), Boismard(McR).

§ 106. Mc 15,22-32; Mt 27,33-44; Lc 23,33-43

Mt 27,33   καὶ   ¹ἐλθόντες   εἰς   τόπον   ²λεγόμενον   Γολγοθά,
Mc 15,22   καὶ   ³φέρουσιν αὐτὸν ἐπὶ τὸν Γολγοθὰν τόπον,
Lc 23,33   καὶ ὅτε   ἦλθον   ἐπὶ τὸν   τόπον τὸν καλούμενον Κρανίον,

1 : Rushbrooke, Abbott(H), Easton, Schmid(27), De Solages(c), Keech.   **29**
2 : Simons, Schmid, Keech, Boismard(Mt).   **15n**
3 : Rushbrooke, Hawkins(VI), Abbott(III), Schmid(5). Cf. 1.   **10**

Mt 27,33   ὅ ἐστιν   κρανίου τόπος λεγόμενος,
Mc 15,22   ὅ ἐστιν μεθερμηνευόμενος κρανίου τόπος.
Lc 23,33   τὸν   καλούμενον   Κρανίον,

Rushbrooke, Schmid.

Mt (27,36)   καὶ καθήμενοι ἐτήρουν   αὐτὸν ¹ἐκεῖ.
Mt 27,35   σταυρώσαντες δὲ αὐτόν
Mc 15,24   ²καὶ   ³σταυροῦσιν   αὐτόν,
Lc 23,33   καὶ ὅτε..., ἐκεῖ ἐσταύρωσαν   αὐτόν

1 : Rushbrooke, Abbott(H), Keech, Léon-Dufour(5).
2 : Rushbrooke, Schmid(4).
3 : Hawkins(VI), Easton, Schmid(5), Keech, Brown.   **10**
   Mc σταυρουσιν : σταυρωσαντες TR s.

Mt 27,35 σταυρώσαντες ... διεμερίσαντο τὰ ἱμάτια αὐτοῦ βάλλοντες κλῆρον,
Mc 15,24 ¹καὶ ²διαμερίζονται τὰ ἱμάτια αὐτοῦ, βάλλοντες κλῆρον ³ἐπ' αὐτὰ τίς τί ἄρῃ.
Lc 23,34 διαμεριζόμενοι δὲ τὰ ἱμάτια αὐτοῦ ἔβαλον κλήρους.

1 : Rushbrooke, Schmid(7). **2 3**
2 : Hawkins(VI), Schmid(5). **10**
3 : Weiss(r), Simons, Rushbrooke, Wright, Hawkins(II), Stanton(1 vel 2), Schmid(31), Glasson, Keech. **34**

Mt 27,36 καὶ καθήμενοι ¹ἐτήρουν αὐτὸν ἐκεῖ.
Mc 15,25 ²ἦν δὲ ὥρα τρίτη καὶ ἐσταύρωσαν αὐτόν.
Lc 23,35 καὶ εἱστήκει ὁ λαὸς θεωρῶν.

1 : Glasson, Brown.
Mc εσταυρωσαν : εφυλασσον h^r.
2 : Wilke(t), Weiss(r), Simons, Rushbrooke, Wright, Hawkins(IC,II), Stanton (1), Easton, Schmid(29), Vaganay, Keech, Léon-Dufour(1).
Mc 15,25 τρίτη : Boismard(t).

Mt 27,37 καὶ ἐπέθηκαν ¹ἐπάνω τῆς κεφαλῆς αὐτοῦ τὴν αἰτίαν αὐτοῦ γεγραμμένην·
Mc 15,26 καὶ ²ἦν ἡ ³ᵃἐπιγραφὴ τῆς αἰτίας αὐτοῦ ᵇἐπιγεγραμμένη·
Lc (23,38) ἦν δὲ καὶ ἐπιγραφὴ ἐπ' αὐτῷ·

1 : Rushbrooke, Abbott(H), Easton, Keech, Léon-Dufour(3).
2 : **12**
3 : Rushbrooke, Hawkins(V). **34**

Mt 27,37 οὗτός ἐστιν Ἰησοῦς ὁ βασιλεὺς τῶν Ἰουδαίων.
Mc 15,26 ὁ βασιλεὺς τῶν Ἰουδαίων.
Lc (23,38) ὁ βασιλεὺς τῶν Ἰουδαίων οὗτος.

Simons, Rushbrooke, Veit, Abbott(I vel VII), Stanton(3b vel 2), Easton, Schmid(33), De Solages(f), Keech, Léon-Dufour(2), Boismard(Mt). **22**

Mt 27,38 τότε σταυροῦνται / σὺν αὐτῷ δύο λῃσταί,
Mc 15,27 καὶ σὺν αὐτῷ σταυροῦσιν δύο λῃστάς,
Lc (23,33) ἐκεῖ ἐσταύρωσαν / αὐτὸν καὶ τοὺς κακούργους,

Veit. **21B**

Mt 27,40 σῶσον σεαυτόν, ¹εἰ υἱὸς ²εἶ ³τοῦ θεοῦ,
Mc 15,30 σῶσον σεαυτόν
Lc (23,35) σωσάτω ἑαυτόν, εἰ οὗτός ἐστιν ὁ χριστὸς τοῦ θεοῦ ὁ ἐκλεκτός.
Lc (23,37) εἰ σὺ εἶ ὁ βασιλεὺς τῶν Ἰουδαίων, σῶσον σεαυτόν.

1 : Simons, Rushbrooke, Veit, Hawkins(*), Abbott(H), Stanton(3b), Streeter (d), Larfeld, Easton, Schmid, De Solages(f), Keech, Léon-Dufour(2), McLoughlin(PDM).

2 : Simons, Schmid, De Solages(f), McLoughlin(PDM).
3 : Simons, Rushbrooke, Veit, Hawkins(*), Abbott(H), Stanton(3b), Streeter(d).
Larfeld, Schmid, De Solages(f), Keech, Léon-Dufour(5), McLoughlin(PDM).

Mt 27,41   οἱ ἀρχιερεῖς ἐμπαίζοντες   μετὰ τῶν γραμματέων καί
Mc 15,31   οἱ ἀρχιερεῖς ἐμπαίζοντες πρὸς ἀλλήλους μετὰ τῶν γραμματέων
Lc 23,35   ἐξεμυκτήριζον δὲ καὶ οἱ ἄρχοντες

            Rushbrooke, Keech.   (23)

Mt 27,42   ἑαυτὸν οὐ δύναται σῶσαι·   βασιλεὺς Ἰσραήλ ἐστιν,
Mc 15,31-32 ἑαυτὸν οὐ δύναται σῶσαι·   (32) ὁ χριστὸς ὁ βασιλεὺς Ἰσραήλ
Lc 23,35   σωσάτω ἑαυτόν,   εἰ οὗτός ἐστιν ὁ χριστὸς τοῦ θεοῦ ὁ ἐκλεκτός.

            Wright.

Mt 27,42   καὶ πιστεύσομεν ἐπ᾽ αὐτόν.
Mc 15,32   ἵνα ἴδωμεν καὶ πιστεύσωμεν.
Lc 23,35   om.

            Rushbrooke.

Mt 27,44   τὸ [1]δ᾽ αὐτὸ καὶ οἱ [2]λῃσταὶ οἱ   συσταυρωθέντες σὺν αὐτῷ
Mc 15,32   καὶ   οἱ   συνεσταυρωμένοι σὺν αὐτῷ
Lc 23,39   εἷς δὲ   τῶν κρεμασθέντων κακούργων

            1 : Rushbrooke, Abbott(VI), De Solages(a), Keech.   1
            2 : 22

§ 107. Mc 15,33-41; Mt 27,45-56; Lc 23,44-49

Mt 27,45   ἀπὸ δὲ   ἕκτης ὥρας   σκότος ἐγένετο
Mc 15,33   καὶ γενομένης   ὥρας ἕκτης   σκότος ἐγένετο
Lc 23,44   καὶ ἦν ἤδη ὡσεὶ ὥρα ἕκτη καὶ σκότος ἐγένετο

            Rushbrooke.   14

Mt 27,50   ὁ δὲ Ἰησοῦς πάλιν [1]κράξας [2]φωνῇ μεγάλῃ
Mc 15,37   ὁ δὲ Ἰησοῦς   ἀφεὶς   φωνὴν μεγάλην
Lc 23,46   καὶ   φωνήσας φωνῇ μεγάλῃ ὁ Ἰησοῦς εἶπεν·

            1 : Fuchs.   32
            2 : Simons, Rushbrooke, Veit, Abbott(H), Easton, Schmid, De Solages(b),
                Keech, Léon-Dufour(4), Fuchs. Cf. 1.

Mt 27,50　　　　　　　　　ἀφῆκεν τὸ πνεῦμα.
Mc 15,37　　　　　　　　　ἐξέπνευσεν.
Lc 23,46　　πάτερ, εἰς χεῖράς σου παρατίθεμαι τὸ πνεῦμά μου.

Simons, Fuchs.

Mt 27,54　　　　ὁ δὲ [1]ἑκατόνταρχος
Mc 15,39　　ἰδὼν δὲ ὁ　κεντυρίων　[2]παρεστηκὼς ἐξ ἐναντίας αὐτοῦ
Lc 23,47　　ἰδὼν δὲ ὁ　ἑκατοντάρχης

1 : Wilke, Holtzmann, Weiss(r), Simons, Rushbrooke, Veit, Wernle, Hawkins
(IVa), Abbott(VII), Stanton(2), Streeter(d), Easton, Schmid(2), De Solages
(c), Keech, Léon-Dufour(2), Boismard(McR). **32**
2 : Rushbrooke, Keech.
Mt εκατονταρχος : -ης T.

Mt 27,54　　ἰδόντες　τὸν σεισμὸν καὶ [1]τὰ γινόμενα [2]ἐφοβήθησαν σφόδρα, [3]λέγοντες·
Mc 15,39　　ἰδὼν ... [4]ὅτι οὕτως ἐξέπνευσεν,　　　　　　　　εἶπεν·
Lc 23,47　　ἰδὼν ...　　　　　　　τὸ γενόμενον ἐδόξαζεν τὸν θεὸν λέγων·

1 : Simons, Rushbrooke, Hawkins(*), Abbott(H), Streeter(t?), Easton, Schmid,
Da Fonseca, De Solages(e), Keech, Léon-Dufour(2), McLoughlin(D,I),
Boismard(r).
2 : Schmid.
3 : Simons, Rushbrooke, Wernle, Abbott(VII), Easton, Keech, Léon-Dufour(2).
4 : Wilke(+ κράξας), Easton, Boismard(r).　　　　　　　　　**15**
Mc εξεπνευσεν : κραξας εξ. TR GNT[1](B).

Mt 27,56　　ἐν αἷς ἦν　Μαρία ἡ Μαγδαληνή, καὶ Μαρία ἡ τοῦ Ἰακώβου
　　　　　καὶ Ἰωσὴφ　μήτηρ, καὶ ἡ μήτηρ τῶν υἱῶν Ζεβεδαίου.
Mc 15,40　　ἐν αἷς καὶ Μαρία ἡ Μαγδαληνὴ καὶ Μαρία ἡ　　Ἰακώβου τοῦ μικροῦ
　　　　　καὶ Ἰωσῆτος μήτηρ ⌜καὶ Σαλώμη,
Lc 23,49　　om. (cf. 24,10).

Holtzmann(⌜), Rushbrooke(cf. Mc 16,1).

Mt (27,55)　αἵτινες [1]ἠκολούθησαν τῷ Ἰησοῦ [2]// [3]ἀπὸ τῆς Γαλιλαίας
Mc 15,41　　αἳ ὅτε ἦν ἐν τῇ Γαλιλαίᾳ [4]ἠκολούθουν αὐτῷ
Lc 23,49　　αἱ (συνακολουθήσασαι) αὐτῷ　　// ἀπὸ τῆς Γαλιλαίας,

1 : Boismard(Mt).
Lc συνακολουθουσαι : -θησασαι TR Ti.
2 : Keech, Boismard(Mt).　**21B**
3 : Simons, Rushbrooke, Veit, Abbott(H), Easton, Schmid, De Solages(e,b),
Keech, Léon-Dufour(2), Fuchs.　**31c**
4 : Rushbrooke.　**11**

Mt (27,55)　　　　πολλαί
Mc 15,41　　καὶ ἄλλαι πολλαὶ αἱ συναναβᾶσαι αὐτῷ εἰς Ἱεροσόλυμα.
Lc (23,49a)　　　　πάντες

Wilke, Rushbrooke, Wright.

§ 108. Mc 15,42-47; Mt 27,57-61; Lc 23,50-56

Mt 27,57   ὀψίας δὲ   γενομένης
Mc 15,42   [1a]καὶ ἤδη ὀψίας γενομένης, [b]ἐπεὶ ἦν παρασκευή, [2]ὅ ἐστιν προσάββατον,
Lc (23,54)   καὶ ἡμέρα ἦν παρασκευῆς, καὶ σάββατον ἐπέφωσκεν.

    1ab : Hawkins(V), Schmid(31). **34**
    1b : Wilke(t), Rushbrooke, Wright.
    2 : Boismard(McR).

Mt 27,57   om., cf. v. 62 : τῇ δὲ ἐπαύριον, ἥτις ἐστὶν μετὰ τὴν παρασκευήν,
Mc 15,42   ἐπεὶ ἦν παρασκευή, ὅ ἐστιν προσάββατον,
Lc 23,50   om., cf. v. 54 : καὶ ἡμέρα ἦν παρασκευῆς, καὶ σάββατον ἐπέφωσκεν.

    Weiss(r), Simons, Boismard(Mt).

Mt 27,57   [1]ἄνθρωπος πλούσιος   ἀπὸ ʽΑριμαθαίας, [2]τοὔνομα ᾽Ιωσήφ,
Mc 15,43   ᾽Ιωσὴφ ὁ ἀπὸ ʽΑριμαθαίας,   [3]εὐσχήμων βουλευτής,
Lc 23,50-51   ἀνὴρ ὀνόματι ᾽Ιωσὴφ   βουλευτὴς ὑπάρχων,
    ἀνὴρ ἀγαθὸς καὶ δίκαιος, (51) ... ἀπὸ ʽΑριμαθαίας

    1 : Weiss(r), Easton, Keech.
        Mc o : — H (h : o) Ru, [GNT].
    2 : Rushbrooke, Abbott, Stanton(2), Cladder, Streeter(d), Easton, Schmid,
        De Solages(d), Keech, Léon-Dufour(4), Boismard(Mt). **15n**
    3 : Rushbrooke, Schmid, Boismard(McR).

Mt 27,57   ὃς καὶ αὐτὸς   ἐμαθητεύθη   τῷ ᾽Ιησοῦ·
Mc 15,43   ὃς καὶ αὐτὸς ἦν προσδεχόμενος τὴν βασιλείαν τοῦ θεοῦ,
Lc 23,51   ὃς   προσεδέχετο   τὴν βασιλείαν τοῦ θεοῦ,

    Rushbrooke, Boismard(McR). **12**

Mt 27,58   [1]οὗτος   [2]προσελθὼν   [3]τῷ Πιλάτῳ   ἠτήσατο τὸ σῶμα τοῦ ᾽Ιησοῦ.
Mc 15,43   [4]τολμήσας   εἰσῆλθεν πρὸς   τὸν Πιλᾶτον [5]καὶ ἠτήσατο τὸ σῶμα τοῦ ᾽Ιησοῦ.
Lc 23,52   οὗτος   προσελθὼν   τῷ Πιλάτῳ   ἠτήσατο τὸ σῶμα τοῦ ᾽Ιησοῦ,

    1 : Weiss(r), Simons, Rushbrooke, Veit, Wernle, Abbott(H), Stanton(2),
        Cladder, Streeter(t), Easton, Schmid(33), De Solages(d), Keech, Léon-
        Dufour(4), Boismard. **22**
    2 : Weiss(r), Simons, Rushbrooke, Veit, Wernle, Abbott(IV), Stanton(2),
        Cladder, Streeter(t), Easton, Schmid(20), De Solages(b), Keech, Léon-
        Dufour(4), Boismard. **3 18 31a**
    3 : Weiss(r), Rushbrooke, Abbott(VII), Easton, De Solages(b), Keech. **31a**
    4 : Holtzmann, Rushbrooke, Wernle, Schmid(7), Keech, Boismard(McR).
    5 : Simons, Rushbrooke, Keech. Cf. 2.

Mt 27,58   τότε ὁ Πιλᾶτος ἐκέλευσεν ἀποδοθῆναι.
Mc 15,44-45 ὁ δὲ Πιλᾶτος ¹ἐθαύμασεν εἰ ἤδη τέθνηκεν, καὶ προσκαλεσάμενος τὸν κεντυ-
            ρίωνα ἐπηρώτησεν αὐτὸν εἰ πάλαι ἀπέθανεν· (45) καὶ γνοὺς ἀπὸ τοῦ κεντυρίω-
            νος ἐδωρήσατο ²τὸ πτῶμα τῷ Ἰωσήφ.
Lc   om.

1 : Wilke, Simons, Rushbrooke, Wright, Wernle, Hawkins(IAa), Allen, Stanton
(2), Schmid, Vaganay, Keech, Léon-Dufour(1), Boismard(McR).
2 : Hawkins(IC), Vaganay.

Mt 27,59   καὶ   λαβὼν τὸ σῶμα ...¹ἐνετύλιξεν ²/³αὐτὸ [ἐν] σινδόνι καθαρᾷ,
Mc 15,46   καὶ⁴ἀγοράσας σινδόνα καθελὼν αὐτὸν   ἐνείλησεν   ⁵τῇ σινδόνι
Lc 23,53   καὶ   καθελὼν   ἐνετύλιξεν / αὐτὸ   σινδόνι,

1 : Holtzmann, Weiss(r /or), Simons, Rushbrooke, Veit, Wernle, Hawkins(*),
Abbott(H), Allen, Stanton(2 vel 3b), Streeter(t), Easton, Schmid(28),
Chapman, Da Fonseca, De Solages(c), Keech, Léon-Dufour(2), McLoughlin
(I), Boismard(Mt). 32
2 : Keech. 21A
3 : Holtzmann, Weiss(r /or), Rushbrooke, Veit, Hawkins(*), Abbott, Streeter
(d), Easton, Schmid, Keech.
4 : Wilke, Rushbrooke, Stanton(2 vel 3b), Schmid, Boismard(McR).
5 : Rushbrooke, Schmid, Keech.
Mt [ἐν] : — TR T S GNT.

Mt 27,60   καὶ ¹ἔθηκεν ²αὐτὸ ἐν τῷ ³καινῷ αὐτοῦ μνημείῳ ὃ   ἐλατόμησεν
Mc 15,46   καὶ κατέθηκεν αὐτὸν ἐν   μνήματι ὃ⁴ἦν λελατομημένον
Lc 23,53   καὶ ἔθηκεν (αὐτὸ) ἐν   μνήματι   λαξευτῷ,
                          οὗ οὐκ ἦν οὐδεὶς οὔπω κείμενος.

1 : Weiss(or), Simons, Veit, Streeter(d vel t?), Schmid(19), Keech, Boismard
(Mt). (18)
Mc κατεθηκεν : εθηκεν H Ru GNT.
2 : Easton, Schmid, De Solages(b).
Lc αυτον : αυτο TR.
3 : Weiss(or), Simons, Wernle, Easton, Schmid, Léon-Dufour(3).
4 : 11n   12

Mt 27,61   ἦν ... καθήμεναι ἀπέναντι ¹τοῦ τάφου.
Mc 15,47   ἐθεώρουν   ποῦ ²τέθειται.
Lc 23,55   ἐθεάσαντο   τὸ μνημεῖον καὶ ὡς ἐτέθη τὸ σῶμα αὐτοῦ,

1 : De Solages(e).
2 : 11n

§ 109. Mc 16,1-8; Mt 28,1-20; Lc 24,1-53

Mt 28,1   ὀψὲ δὲ   σαββάτων,   τῇ ... εἰς μίαν   σαββάτων,
Mc 16,1-2   καὶ διαγενομένου τοῦ σαββάτου ... (2) καὶ ... τῇ   μιᾷ τῶν σαββάτων
Lc 24,1   τῇ δὲ   μιᾷ τῶν σαββάτων

     Rushbrooke, Hawkins(VII), Abbott(VI), Schmid(4), De Solages(a), Keech.   **1**

Mt 28,1   Μαριὰμ ἡ Μαγδαληνὴ καὶ   ἡ ἄλλη Μαρία
Mc 16,1   [ἡ] Μαρία   ἡ Μαγδαληνὴ καὶ   Μαρία ἡ [τοῦ] Ἰακώβου ⌐καὶ Σαλώμη
Lc 24,1   om.
Lc (24,10)   ἡ Μαγδαληνὴ Μαρία καὶ Ἰωάννα καὶ Μαρία ἡ   Ἰακώβου·

     Holtzmann(⌐), Rushbrooke, Wright(⌐), Hawkins(IIIb).
     Mc [η] : — TR Ti T S L GNT.
     Mc [του] : — T L GNT.

Mt 28,1   ἦλθεν ... θεωρῆσαι τὸν τάφον.
Mc 16,1   ἠγόρασαν ἀρώματα ἵνα ἐλθοῦσαι ἀλείψωσιν αὐτόν.
Lc 24,1   ἦλθον   φέρουσαι ἃ ἡτοίμασαν ἀρώματα.

     Rushbrooke, Boismard(McR).

Mt 28,1   τῇ [1]ἐπιφωσκούσῃ εἰς μίαν   σαββάτων,
Mc 16,2   καὶ λίαν πρωΐ τῇ   μιᾷ τῶν σαββάτων..., [2]ἀνατείλαντος τοῦ ἡλίου.
Lc 24,1   τῇ   δὲ μιᾷ τῶν σαββάτων   ὄρθρου βαθέως
Lc (23,54)   καὶ σάββατον ἐπέφωσκεν.

     1 : Simons, Hawkins(*), Streeter(t vel d), Schmid, Da Fonseca, Keech, Léon-
       Dufour(5), McLoughlin(P), Boismard(Mt).
     2 : Simons, Rushbrooke, Wright, Hawkins(V), Schmid, Boismard(McR).

Mt 28,1   ἦλθεν Μαριὰμ ἡ Μαγδαληνή
Mc 16,2   ἔρχονται ἐπὶ τὸ μνῆμα,
Lc 24,1   ἐπὶ τὸ μνῆμα ἦλθον φέρουσαι ἃ ἡτοίμασαν ἀρώματα.

     Rushbrooke, Hawkins(VI), Abbott(VII), Easton, Schmid(5), Keech.   **10**
     Lc ηλθον : -αν H Ru.

Mt 28,2   om.
Mc 16,3   καὶ ἔλεγον πρὸς ἑαυτάς· τίς ἀποκυλίσει ἡμῖν τὸν λίθον ἐκ τῆς θύρας τοῦ μνη-
       μείου ;
Lc 24,2   om.

     Rushbrooke, Wright, Wernle, Schmid, Keech, Léon-Dufour(1), Boismard(McR).
     Cf. Mc 16,4.

Mt 28,2   καὶ προσελθὼν   ¹ἀπεκύλισεν ²τὸν λίθον
Mc 16,4   καὶ ³ἀναβλέψασαι θεωροῦσιν ⁴ὅτι   ἀνακεκύλισται ὁ λίθος·
           ⁵ἦν γὰρ μέγας σφόδρα.
Lc 24,2   εὗρον δὲ   τὸν λίθον ἀποκεκυλισμένον ἀπὸ τοῦ μνημείου,

           1 : Easton, Keech. **31b**
           2 : Veit, Easton, De Solages(b).
           3 : Rushbrooke.
           4 : Easton.
           5 : Wright, Boismard(McR). **8A**

Mt 28,2   ¹καὶ ἰδοὺ σεισμὸς ἐγένετο μέγας· ἄγγελος γὰρ... καὶ ἐκάθητο ἐπάνω αὐτοῦ.
Mc 16,5   εἶδον   νεανίσκον   καθήμενον ²ἐν τοῖς δεξιοῖς
Lc 24,4   καὶ ἰδοὺ   ἄνδρες δύο ἐπέστησαν αὐταῖς

           1 : Simons, Schmid. **25**
           2 : Rushbrooke, Wright, Boismard(McR).

Mt 28,3   ἦν δὲ ἡ εἰδέα αὐτοῦ ὡς ¹ἀστραπή,
Mc 16,5   ²περιβεβλημένον στολὴν λευκήν,
Lc 24,4   ἐν ἐσθῆτι   ἀστραπτούσῃ·

           1 : Weiss(r), Simons, Rushbrooke, Hawkins(*), Abbott(H), Streeter(t?),
               Easton, Schmid, Da Fonseca, De Solages(f), Keech, Léon-Dufour(5),
               McLoughlin(DIC).
           2 : Rushbrooke, Boismard(McR). **32**

Mt 28,4   ἀπὸ ¹δὲ τοῦ ²φόβου αὐτοῦ ἐσείσθησαν οἱ τηροῦντες καὶ ἐγενήθησαν ὡς νεκροί.
Mc 16,5   καὶ ³ἐξεθαμβήθησαν.
Lc 24,5   ἐμφόβων δὲ γενομένων αὐτῶν   καὶ κλινουσῶν τὰ πρόσωπα εἰς τὴν γῆν,

           1 : De Solages(a).
           2 : Easton, De Solages(c). Cf. 3. **32**
           3 : Rushbrooke, Easton, Schmid, Keech, Boismard(McR). Cf. 2.

Mt 28,5   ἀποκριθεὶς δὲ ὁ ἄγγελος εἶπεν ταῖς γυναιξίν·
Mc 16,6   ὁ   δὲ   λέγει αὐταῖς·
Lc 24,5   εἶπαν πρὸς αὐτάς·

           Rushbrooke, Hawkins(VI), Abbott(V), Easton, Schmid(5), Keech. **10**

Mt 28,5   μὴ ¹φοβεῖσθε ὑμεῖς·   ²οἶδα γὰρ ὅτι Ἰησοῦν ... ζητεῖτε·
Mc 16,6   μὴ ἐκθαμβεῖσθε·   Ἰησοῦν   ζητεῖτε
Lc 24,5   ἐμφόβων δὲ γενομένων αὐτῶν ... εἶπαν πρὸς αὐτάς· τί ζητεῖτε

           1 : Rushbrooke, Abbott(VII), Schmid, Boismard(McR). **32**
           2 : Weiss(Mc : asyndeton). **4**

Mt 28,5   ὅτι Ἰησοῦν   τὸν ἐσταυρωμένον ζητεῖτε·
Mc 16,6   Ἰησοῦν ζητεῖτε τὸν Ναζαρηνὸν τὸν ἐσταυρωμένον·
Lc 24,5   τί   ζητεῖτε   τὸν ζῶντα μετὰ τῶν νεκρῶν;

    Rushbrooke, Schmid(32), Boismard(McR).

Mt 28,6   οὐκ ἔστιν ὧδε· [1]//   ἠγέρθη [2]γὰρ   [3]καθὼς εἶπεν·
Mc 16,6   ἠγέρθη,   οὐκ ἔστιν ὧδε·
Lc 24,6   οὐκ ἔστιν ὧδε, // ἀλλὰ ἠγέρθη. μνήσθητε ὡς ἐλάλησεν ὑμῖν

    1 : Holtzmann, Weiss(r), Simons, Veit, Wernle, Easton, Schmid, Keech,
        McLoughlin. 21B
    2 : Weiss(r), Hawkins(IV), Schmid(3). 4
        Lc : ⟦ουκ εστιν ωδε αλλα ηγερθη⟧ H N, [GNT¹].
    3 : Keech. Cf. Mc 16,7c : 8A

Mt 28,7   εἴπατε τοῖς μαθηταῖς αὐτοῦ   ὅτι ἠγέρθη   ἀπὸ [1]τῶν νεκρῶν,
Mc 16,7   εἴπατε τοῖς μαθηταῖς αὐτοῦ [2]καὶ τῷ Πέτρῳ ὅτι
Lc 24,(5-)6   τὸν ζῶντα μετὰ τῶν νεκρῶν;
    (6) ... μνήσθητε ὡς ἐλάλησεν ὑμῖν

    1 : Rushbrooke, Abbott, Keech, Léon-Dufour(5).
    2 : Wilke(t), Rushbrooke, Wright, Boismard(McR).

Mt 28,8   καὶ ἀπελθοῦσαι ταχὺ ἀπὸ τοῦ μνημείου μετὰ φόβου καὶ χαρᾶς μεγάλης
Mc 16,8   καὶ ἐξελθοῦσαι ἔφυγον ἀπὸ τοῦ μνημείου, ⌐εἶχεν γὰρ αὐτὰς τρόμος καὶ ἔκστα-
          σις· καὶ οὐδενὶ οὐδὲν εἶπαν· ἐφοβοῦντο γάρ.
Lc 24,9   ὑποστρέψασαι   ἀπὸ τοῦ μνημείου

    Wilke(t : ⌐), Rushbrooke, Schmid, Boismard(McR). 8A

Mt 28,8   ἔδραμον ἀπαγγεῖλαι   τοῖς μαθηταῖς αὐτοῦ.
Mc 16,8   καὶ οὐδενὶ οὐδὲν εἶπαν·
Lc 24,9   ἀπήγγειλαν ταῦτα πάντα τοῖς ἕνδεκα καὶ πᾶσιν τοῖς λοιποῖς.

    Weiss(r), Simons, Rushbrooke, Veit, Hawkins(*), Wernle, Abbott(H), Streeter
    (d), Easton, Schmid, Da Fonseca, De Solages(f), Keech, Léon-Dufour(2),
    McLoughlin(RI), Boismard(McR). 32
    (Lc ἕνδεκα, cf. Mt 28,16 : Pesch).

Mt 28,19 μαθητεύσατε πάντα τὰ ἔθνη, βαπτίζοντες αὐτοὺς εἰς τὸ ὄνομα τοῦ πατρὸς καὶ
          τοῦ υἱοῦ καὶ τοῦ ἁγίου πνεύματος,
Mc 16,8   om.
Lc 24,47 καὶ κηρυχθῆναι ἐπὶ τῷ ὀνόματι αὐτοῦ μετάνοιαν εἰς ἄφεσιν ἁμαρτιῶν εἰς πάντα
          τὰ ἔθνη,

    Simons, Larfeld.

A CLASSIFICATION OF STYLISTIC AGREEMENTS
with Comparative Material from the Triple Tradition

INTRODUCTION

The phenomena of literary style cover a great deal of the coincidences between Matthew and Luke against Mark. In the following lists the main categories are presented with comparative material from the Triple Tradition. The titles indicate the principal direction of the changes but instances of the inverse are also included [161].

CONJUNCTIONS AND SENTENCE STRUCTURE

1. καί in Mark and δέ in Matthew and Luke (p. 203) ;
   δέ in Matthew only (p. 204), in Luke only (p. 205) ;
2. καί in Mark : δέ in Luke and τότε, ἐν ἐκείνῳ(-η)... or asyndeton in Matthew (p. 205) ;
   Other instances of (a) τότε and (b) asyndeton in Matthew (p. 206) ;

---

161. The bibliographical notes refer to former attempts of classification of the minor agreements by Hawkins (see n. 64, cf. n. 62), Abbott (see n. 40, cf. n. 38), Turner (see n. 87), Schmid (see n. 108, cf. n. 103) and De Solages (see n. 113, cf. n. 111). The number added to the name (in parentheses) indicates the author's own division. For Turner no. 1 refers to *JTS* 25 (1924), nos. 2-6 to 26 (1925), no. 7(1) to 27 (1926), nos. 7(2)-8 to 28 (1927) and nos. 9-10 to 29 (1928). — Some special studies which present valuable descriptions of the evidence are also referred to by the name of the author : J. H. SCHOLTEN, *Das älteste Evangelium*, Elberfeld, 1869 ; *Das Paulinische Evangelium*, Elberfeld, 1881 ; M. KRENKEL, *Josephus und Lukas. Der schriftstellerische Einfluss des jüdischen Geschichtschreibers auf den christlichen nachgewiesen*, Leipzig, 1894 ; Wernle's *Die synoptische Frage* (see n. 28) ; Allen's commentary on Matthew (see n. 89), Cadbury's work on the style of Luke (see n. 108), Larfeld's *Evangelien* (see n. 108) and the more recent contributions of H. Schürmann. Schürmann I, II, III, refers to the three volumes of his *Quellenkritische Untersuchung des lukanischen Abendmahlsberichtes Lk 22,7-38* : I. *Der Abendmahlsbericht Lk 22,(7-14.)15-18* ; II. *Der Einsetzungsbericht Lk 22,19-20* ; III. *Der Abschiedsrede Lk 22,21-38* (Neutest. Abh., 19/5 ; 20/4-5), Munster, 1953, 1955, 1957. We should mention also, besides the commonly used tools (concordance, lexicon and grammar), the commentaries of Lagrange (see n. 84 and 86) and Taylor (see n. 86), Sanders's *Tendencies* (see n. 134) ; M. ZERWICK, *Untersuchungen zum Markus-Stil. Ein Beitrag zur stilistischen Durcharbeitung des Neuen Testaments*, Rome, 1937 ; J. C. DOUDNA, *The Greek of the Gospel of Mark* (JBL Monograph Series, 12), Philadelphia, 1961 ; G. D. KILPATRICK, ' Notes on Marcan Usage ', *The Bible Translator* 7 (1956) 2-9.51-56.146 ; F. NEIRYNCK, *Duality in Mark* (see n. 57).

3. Finite verb with καί in Mark and participle in Matthew and Luke
(p. 207) ;
Participle in Matthew only (p. 208), in Luke only (p. 209) ;
Genitive absolute in Matthew or Luke (p. 210) ;
4. Asyndeton in Mark and conjunction in Matthew and Luke (p. 211);
Conjunction in Matthew only (p. 212), in Luke only (p. 213);
Other instances of asyndeton in Mark (p. 213) ;
5. ὅτι recitative in Mark and not in Matthew and Luke (p. 213) ;
ὅτι recitative not in Matthew (p. 215), not in Luke (p. 215) ;
Other instances of ὅτι recitative in Mark (p. 215) ;
6. ὅτι interrogative in Mark and not in Matthew and Luke (p. 216);
7. ἵνα in Mark and not in Matthew and Luke (p. 217) ;
8. Parenthesis and anacoluthon in Mark (p. 220) ;
9. ἀλλά in Mark (p. 221).

USE OF VERBS

10. The historic present in Mark and not in Matthew and Luke (p. 223) ;
The historic present in Mark (p. 224), in Matthew (p. 228), in
Luke (p. 229) ;
11. The imperfect in Mark and not in Matthew and Luke (p. 229) ;
The imperfect in Mark (p. 230), in Matthew (p. 236), in Luke
(p. 237) ;
Additional note : other changes of tense (p. 239) ;
12. The periphrastic construction (ἦν with participle) in Mark and not
in Matthew and Luke (p. 240) ;
13. ἤρξατο with infinitive in Mark and not in Matthew and Luke (p. 242) ;
14. Genitive absolute in Mark and not in Matthew and Luke (p. 244) ;
15. λέγων /λέγοντες in Matthew and Luke and not in Mark (p. 246) ;
16. ἀποκριθείς in Mark and not in Matthew and Luke (p. 249) ;
Additional note : ἀποκρίνομαι and λέγω (p. 250) ;
17. Active or middle voice in Mark and passive in Matthew and Luke
(p. 251) ;
18. Simple verb in Mark and compound verb in Matthew and Luke
(p. 252) ;
19. ἐπερωτάω /ἐρωτάω in Mark and λέγω in Matthew and Luke (p. 255) ;
20. πορεύομαι and ἔρχομαι (and compounds) (p. 256).

WORD ORDER, VOCABULARY AND MISCELLANEOUS

21A. Word order : object-verb in Mark and verb-object in Matthew and
Luke (p. 257) ;
21B. Other instances of change in word order (indicated in the cumulative list) (p. 259) ;

22. Matthew and Luke defining the subject (p. 261) ;
23. Matthew and Luke defining the object (p. 267) ;
24. Verb supplied in Matthew and Luke (p. 272) ;
25. καὶ ἰδού (in narrative) in Matthew and Luke and not in Mark (p. 273) ;
26. εὐθύς in Mark and not in Matthew and Luke (p. 274) ;
27. πάλιν in Mark and not in Matthew and Luke (p. 276) ;
28. πολλά adverbial in Mark and not in Matthew and Luke (p. 278) ;
29. φέρω in Mark (in the sense of " lead " or " bring ") (p. 279) ;
30. Titles used in addressing Jesus (p. 280) ;
31. Prepositions changed in Matthew and Luke :
    (a) εἰς in Mark and ἐν in Matthew and Luke (p. 281) ;
    (b) ἐκ in Mark and ἀπό in Matthew and Luke (p. 282) ;
    (c) other prepositions (p. 283) ;
32. Changes in vocabulary (p. 284) ;
33. Miscellaneous :
    (a) diminutive in Mark and not in Matthew and Luke (p. 285) ;
    (b) the article in Mark and not in Matthew and Luke (p. 286);
    (c) singular in Mark and plural in Matthew and Luke (p. 286) ;
34. Duplicate expressions in Mark and simple phrases in Matthew and Luke (p. 287) ;
35. Agreements in order (p. 287).

1. καί IN MARK AND δέ IN MATTHEW AND LUKE [162]

Mk	Mt	Lk	Mk	Mt	Lk
1,7	(3,7)	3,15	8,36	16,26	9,25
1,16	4,18	(5,1)	9,30	17,22	9,43
2,24	12,2	6,2	9,33	(17,24)	9,46
3,4	12,11	6,9	10,23	19,23	18,24
3,6	12,14	6,11	10,42	20,25	(22,25)
3,13	(5,1)	6,12	11,4	21,6	19,32
3,22	12,24(9,34)	11,15	11,8	21,8	19,36
3,23	12,25	11,17	11,9	21,9	19,37
3,32	[12,47]	8,20	11,18	(21,15)	19,47
3,33	12,48	8,21	11,31	21,25	20,5
4,11	13,11	8,10	12,28	22,34	20,39
4,16	13,20	8,13	12,35	22,41	20,41
4,18	13,22	8,14	13,3	24,3	21,7
4,20	13,23	8,15	13,11	(10,19)	(12,11)
4,35	8,18	8,22	13,12	(10,21)	21,16
4,38	8,24	8,23	14,12	26,17	22,7
4,41	8,27	8,25	14,13	26,18	22,10
5,13	8,32	8,33	14,53	26,57	22,54
5,14	8,33	8,34	14,54	26,58	22,54
6,4	13,57	(4,24)	14,66	26,69	22,56
6,35	14,15	9,12	15,15	27,26	23,25
6,37	14,17	9,13	15,32	27,44	23,39
8,12	16,2	(11,29)	16,1	28,1	24,1
8,28	16,14	9,19	16,5	28,4	24,5

(1) The inverse : δέ in Mark and καί in Matthew and Luke

2,6	9,3	5,21	Compare		
9,27	17,18	9,42	3,10 γάρ	12,15	6,18
14,47	26,51	22,50			

---

162. The instances are marked in our list as positive agreements (underlining in Matthew and Luke). See Hawkins(VII), Abbott(VI), Schmid(4), De Solages(a). Abbott's list is the most complete (36 cases). The 26 instances signaled by Hawkins (p. 150) are in that list (with the exception of Mk 4,35) and also Schmid's 7 additional cases (p. 37, n. 4). De Solages (total : 34) gives some new examples but omits others (e.g., Mk 9,30 ; 11,9.18). — Comp. Larfeld, pp. 14-20 (pp. 18-19 : the inverse) ; Cadbury, pp. 142-145 (p. 143 : list of Luke's substitutions of δέ for καί) ; Schürmann I, pp. 76-77 (see also II, p. 3 and 44) ; Sanders, pp. 233-237 (" The use of καί in one Gospel but not in another " ; only 24 instances of καί : δέ/δέ are signaled).

1a. *Other instances of* καί *in Mark and* δέ *in Matthew*

*καί in Luke

Mk	Mt		Mk	Mt
1,6	(3,4)		9,5*	17,4
1,9b(*)	3,16		9,8*	17,8
1,18	4,20		9,42	18,6
1,20*	4,22		9,43	18,8
2,17*	9,12		10,11	19,11 (cf. 9)
2,23b*	12,1		10,48*	20,31
2,25*	12,3		10,52a*	20,34
3,7*	12,15		11,3b	21,3
4,5*	13,5		11,12	21,18
4,6	13,6		11,22	21,21
4,7*	13,7		12,2*	21,34
4,8a*	13,8a		12,28*	22,34
4,17*	13,21		12,34b	22,46b οὐδέ (Lk 20,40 γάρ)
4,32*	13,32		13,2	24,2 (Lk gen. abs., see No. **3c**)
5,12*	8,31		13,3	24,3
5,30*	9,22		13,19b	24,21 οὐδ'
6,21	14,6		14,3	26,6 (cf. Lk 7,36)
6,32*	14,13		14,17*	26,20
6,44	14,21 (Lk 9,14 γάρ)		14,22*	26,26
6,47a	14,23		14,25	26,29 (Lk 22,18 γάρ)
6,47b	14,24		14,57	26,59
6,48a	14,25		14,68*	26,70
6,51b	14,33		14,69*	26,71
7,17	15,15		14,70b*	26,73
7,18	15,16		15,1*	27,1
7,27	15,26		15,21*	27,32
8,15	16,6		15,29	27,39
8,16	16,7		15,33*	27,45
8,17	16,8		15,34	27,46
8,18	16,9 οὐδέ		15,35	27,47
8,27*	16,13		15,42*	27,57
9,3*	17,2			

The inverse δέ in Mark and καί in Matthew
*δέ in Luke

Mk	Mt		Mk	Mt
4,34	13,34		15,5	27,14
7,24	15,21		15,23	27,34
9,25*	17,18		15,24	27,35
13,5*	24,4		15,36	27,48
14,70a*	26,72			

1b. *Other instances of* καί *in Mark and* δέ *in Luke* (See also No. **2.**)

*καί in Matthew

Mk	Lk		Mk	Lk
1,29*	4,38		5,32	8,46
1,34a*	4,40b		5,38a*	8,51
1,34b*	4,41		5,38b*	8,52a
1,35	4,42		5,39	8,52b
1,38	4,43		5,41	8,54 (Mt participle)
2,8*	5,22		5,43	8,56
2,19*	5,34		6,7*	9,1
3,1*	6,6		6,12	9,6
3,2*	6,7		6,33*	9,11
3,3	6,8		6,39*	9,14
3,5b	6,10b		9,2*	9,28
3,26*	(11,18)		9,14*	9,37
4,1* (cf. No. 2)	8,4		9,20	9,42
4,10*	8,9		10,46*	18,35
4,38b*	8,24a		10,49*	18,40a
4,40*	8,25		10,51*	18,40b
5,2(*)	8,27		12,3*	20,10
5,6(*)	8,28		12,22	20,31 (Mt diff.)
5,9a	8,30a		12,41	21,1
5,9b	8,30b		12,42	21,2
5,14b	8,35		14,16*	22,13
5,16	8,36		14,62	22,69 (Mt πλήν...)
5,18* (Mt 9,1a)	8,37		15,2*	23,3
5,19	8,38b		15,26*	(23,38)
5,21* (Mt 9,1b)	8,40		15,38*	(23,45)
5,24*	8,42		16,4	24,2
5,31	8,45		16,5a	24,3

The inverse : δέ in Mark and καί in Luke
*δέ in Matthew

Mk	Lk		Mk	Lk
10,31*	(13,30)		14,55*	(22,66)
14,11*	22,5		15,37*	23,46

2. καί IN MARK : δέ IN LUKE AND τότε, ἐν ἐκείνῳ(-η)... OR ASYNDETON IN MATTHEW [163]

Mk	Mt		Lk	
1,9	3,13	τότε (cf. Mk ἐν ἐκείναις ταῖς ἡμέραις)	3,21	
		comp. 3,1 ἐν δὲ ταῖς ἡμέραις ἐκείναις	3,1	ἐν ἔτει δέ

---

163. In our list Mark's καί is underlined (negative agreement). Comp. Larfeld (espec. pp. 19-20), Schmid and Sanders (cf. n. 162).

Mk	Mt		Lk
1,12	4,1	τότε	4,1
2,18	9,14	τότε	5,33
2,23	12,1	ἐν ἐκείνῳ τῷ καιρῷ	6,1
4,1	13,1	ἐν τῇ ἡμέρᾳ ἐκείνῃ	8,4
4,39	8,26	τότε	8,24
5,41	9,25	participle (cf. No. 3a)	8,54
6,14	14,1	ἐν ἐκείνῳ τῷ καιρῷ (cf. 11,25)	9,7
6,41	14,19	asyndeton	9,16
8,29	16,15	asyndeton	9,20
8,30	16,20	τότε	9,21
8,34	16,24	τότε	9,23
9,7	17,5	asyndeton (cf. No. (14) : gen. abs.)	9,34
9,33	18,1	ἐν ἐκείνῃ τῇ ὥρᾳ	9,46
10,13	19,13	τότε	18,15
10,32	20,17	participle (cf. No. 3a)	18,31
10,47	20,30	asyndeton	18,36
12,1	21,33	asyndeton (ἄλλην παραβολὴν ἀκούσατε)	20,9
12,18	22,23	ἐν ἐκείνῃ τῇ ἡμέρᾳ	20,27
12,37	23,1	τότε	20,45
14,10	26,14	τότε	22,3
14,30	26,34	asyndeton	22,34
14,32	26,36	τότε	22,40
14,48	26,52	τότε (cf. v. 55 ἐν ἐκείνῃ τῇ ὥρᾳ)	22,52
15,24	27,35	participle (cf. No. 3)	23,33

Note

Mk	Mt		Lk	
1,5	3,5	τότε	3,7	οὖν (cf. Mt 3,7 δέ)
8,31	16,21	ἀπὸ τότε	9,22	participle
4,30	13,31	ἄλλην παραβολήν	13,18	οὖν

2a. *Other instances of καί in Mark and*

(a) τότε in Matthew

*καί in Luke

Mk	Mt		Mk	Mt
1,5	3,5		14,27	26,31
3,5a*	12,13		14,34	26,38
7,1	15,1		14,41	26,45
7,29	15,28		14,50	26,56
9,28	17,19		14,65*	26,67
10,35	20,20		15,27	27,38
14,1b*	26,3		15,45	27,58

Note 1. δέ in Mark and τότε in Matthew
*δέ in Luke

Mk	Mt		Mk	Mt
12,17*	22,21		15,4	27,13
14,46	26,50		15,15	27,26 (Lk καί)
14,63*	26,65		15,16	27,27
14,71*	26,74			

Note 2. καὶ τότε (in sayings)
Mk 2,20 (Mt) ; 3,27 (Mt) ; 13,14 (ὅταν... τότε, Mt).21 (Mt τότε).26 (Mt).27 (Mt καί).

Note 3. ἐν ἐκείναις ταῖς ἡμέραις in Mark

Mk	Mt	Lk
1,9 post καὶ ἐγένετο	3,13 τότε (see No. 2)	3,21 ἐν τῷ
8,1	15,32 δέ (see No. 4a)	
13,24 post ἀλλά	24,29 εὐθέως δέ (see No. 26)	

(b) asyndeton in Matthew

diff. Mk 4,33 ; 10,10 ; 11,33*b* ; 14,39 (see No. 4a).

3. Finite Verb with καί in Mark and Participle in Matthew and Luke [164]

Mk		Mt		Lk	
1,41	καὶ λέγει	8,3	λέγων	5,13	λέγων
2,12	ἠγέρθη καί	9,7	ἐγερθείς	5,25	ἀναστάς
4,38	καὶ λέγουσιν	8,25	λέγοντες	8,24	λέγοντες
4,41	καὶ ἔλεγον	8,27	λέγοντες	8,25	λέγοντες
5,38	ἔρχονται... καί	9,23	ἐλθών	8,51	ἐλθών
6,7	προσκαλεῖται... καί	10,1	προσκαλεσάμενος	9,1	συγκαλεσάμενος
6,30	συνάγονται... καί	14,12	ἐλθόντες	9,10	ὑποστρέψαντες
6,33	εἶδον... καὶ ἐπέγνωσαν... καί	14,13	ἀκούσαντες	9,11	γνόντες
10,47	καὶ λέγειν	20,30	λέγοντες	18,38	λέγων
11,2	καὶ λέγει	21,2	λέγων	19,30	λέγων
11,2b	λύσατε... καί	21,2	λύσαντες	19,30	λύσαντες
11,4	ἀπῆλθον καί	21,6	πορευθέντες	19,32	ἀπελθόντες
12,20b	ἔλαβεν... καί	22,25	γήμας	20,29	λαβών
14,22	ἔδωκεν... καὶ εἶπεν	26,26	δούς... εἶπεν	22,19	ἔδωκεν... λέγων
14,24	καὶ εἶπεν	26,27	λέγων	22,20	λέγων

---

164. The agreements are underlined in Matthew and Luke ; with the exception of 6,30 ; 14,22 ; 15,24 (marked as negative agreements). See Abbott(IV) : 10 cases ; Schmid(7), pp. 39-40 : 17 cases. Comp. Wernle, pp. 21-23 ; Larfeld, pp. 19-20 (p. 20 : the inverse) ; Cadbury, pp. 134-135 (Lk) ; Schürmann II, p. 60 ; Sanders, pp. 237-240. — Cf. *infra*, n. 178.

Mk		Mt		Lk	
14,35	ἔπιπτεν...	26,39	ἔπεσεν...	22,41	θεὶς...
	καὶ προσηύχετο		προσευχόμενος		προσηύχετο
14,65	ἤρξαντο... καὶ λέγειν	26,68	λέγοντες	22,64	λέγοντες
15,24	σταυροῦσιν... καὶ	27,35	σταυρώσαντες...	23,33-34	ἐσταύρωσαν...
	διαμερίζονται		διαμερίσαντο		διαμεριζόμενοι
15,43	εἰσῆλθεν... καὶ	27,58	προσελθών	23,52	προσελθών

(3) *The inverse*

12,20c	(cf. 20b) ἀποθνήσκων	22,25	ἐτελεύτησεν, καί	20,29	ἀπέθανεν + adj.
6,2	λέγοντες	13,54	καὶ λέγειν	4,22	καὶ ἔλεγον

Note: Mk 5,22, see No. **3a** and **3b**.

3a. *Other instances of finite verb with* καί *in Mark and participle in Matthew*

* Paratactic καί in Luke

Mk		Mt	
1,44	καὶ λέγει	(9,30)	λέγων
2,18	καὶ λέγουσιν	9,14	λέγοντες
4,2	καὶ ἔλεγεν	13,3	λέγων
4,4	ἦλθεν... καί	13,4	ἐλθόντα
5,15	θεωροῦσιν... καί	8,34	ἰδόντες
5,22	ἔρχεται... καί	9,18	προσελθών
5,38	θεωρεῖ... καί	9,23	ἰδών
5,40-41	εἰσπορεύεται... καί	9,25	εἰσελθών
6,1-2*	ἔρχεται... καί	13,54	ἐλθών (cf. Lk 4,16 ἦλθεν... καί)
6,(7-)8*	(ἤρξατο...) καὶ παρήγγειλεν	10,5	παραγγείλας λέγων
6,17	ἐκράτησεν... καί	14,3	κρατήσας
6,29	ἦλθαν καί	14,12	προσελθόντες
6,34*	εἶδεν... καί (= Mt 14,14)	(9,36)	ἰδών
6,41*	κατέκλασεν... καί	14,19	κλάσας
6,49(-50)	ἔδοξαν... καί	14,26	λέγοντες
6,50	καὶ λέγει	14,27	λέγων
7,5	καὶ ἐπερωτῶσιν	15,1	λέγοντες
7,26	καὶ ἠρώτα	15,25	λέγουσα
8,11	ἐξῆλθον... καί	16,11	προσελθόντες
8,27	ἐξῆλθεν... καί	16,13	ἐλθών
9,4	καὶ ἦσαν συλλαλοῦντες	17,3	συλλαλοῦντες (Lk relative clause)
11,(4-)7*	ἀπῆλθον... καί	21,6	πορευθέντες
11,28*	καὶ ἔλεγον	21,23	λέγοντες (Lk 20,2 καὶ εἶπαν λέγοντες)
12,12*	ἐζήτουν... καί	21,46	ζητοῦντες
12,14*	καὶ λέγουσιν	22,16	λέγοντας (Lk 20,28 καὶ ἐπηρώτησαν... λέγοντες)
12,19	καὶ μὴ ἀφῇ	22,24	μὴ ἔχων (cf. Lk)
14,19	(ἤρξαντο) λυπεῖσθαι καί	26,22	λυπούμενοι
14,33	παραλαμβάνει... καί	26,37	παραλαβών

Mk		Mt	
14,66-67	καὶ... λέγει	26,69	λέγουσα
15,16	ἀπήγαγον... καί	27,27	παραλαβόντες
15,22	φέρουσιν... καί	27,33	ἐλθόντες (Lk relative clause)
15,41	καὶ διηκόνουν	27,55	διακονοῦσαι

The inverse : finite verb with καί in Matthew and participle in Mark
* Participle in Luke

Mk		Mt	
6,22	ὀρχησαμένης	14,6	ὠρχήσατο... καί
9,12	ἐλθών	17,11	ἔρχεται καί
11,15*	εἰσελθών	21,12	εἰσῆλθεν... καί
12,28	προσελθών	22,(34-)35	συνήχθησαν... καί (cf. Lk 10,25)
14,69*	ἰδοῦσα	26,71	εἶδεν... καί
15,1	ἑτοιμάσαντες (See No. 4.)	27,(1-)2	ἔλαβον... καί
15,30	καταβάς	27,40	καὶ κατάβηθι
15,36	λέγων	27,49	οἱ δὲ λοιποὶ εἶπαν

More complex instances

| Mk 1,9-10 | ἐβαπτίσθη... καὶ ἀναβαίνων... εἶδεν |
| Mt 3,16 | βαπτισθείς... ἀνέβη... καὶ ἰδού |

| Mk 8,9-10 | ἀπέλυσεν... καὶ ἐμβὰς... ἦλθεν |
| Mt 15,39 | ἀπολύσας ἐνέβη καὶ ἦλθεν |

| Mk 10,32 | ἦσαν ἀναβαίνοντες... καὶ παραλαβὼν... ἤρξατο λέγειν |
| Mt 20,17 | μέλλων ἀναβαίνειν παρέλαβεν... καὶ εἶπεν |

| Mk 14,47 | σπασάμενος... ἔπαισεν... καὶ ἀφεῖλεν |
| Mt 26,51 | ἀπέσπασεν... καὶ πατάξας ἀφεῖλεν |

| Mk 15,17 | ἐνδιδύσκουσιν... καὶ περιτιθέασιν πλέξαντες |
| Mt 27,28-29 | ἐκδύσαντες περιέθηκαν... καὶ πλέξαντες ἐπέθηκαν |

3b. Other instances of finite verb with καί in Mark and participle in Luke

* Paratactic καί in Matthew

Mk		Lk	
1,35	ἐξῆλθεν καί	4,42	ἐξελθών
2,11*	ἆρον... καί	5,24	ἄρας
3,11	καὶ ἔκραζον	4,41	κραυγάζοντα
4,5*	ἐξανέτειλεν... καί	8,6	φυέν
4,7*	ἀνέβησαν... καί	8,7	συμφυεῖσαι
4,20*	ἀκούουσιν... καί	8,15	ἀκούσαντες
5,20	καὶ ἤρξατο κηρύσσειν	8,39	κηρύσσων
5,22-23*	πίπτει... καί	8,41	πεσών
5,33	προσέπεσεν... καί	8,47	προσπεσοῦσα
8,31	καὶ ἤρξατο διδάσκειν	9,21	εἰπών (cf. Mt 16,2 ἀπὸ τότε)
9,2*	παραλαμβάνει... καί	9,28	παραλαβών
10,14	καὶ εἶπεν	18,16	λέγων
10,28*	ἀφήκαμεν... καί	18,26	ἀφέντες

Mk		Lk	
10,34*	μαστιγώσουσιν... καί	18,33	μαστιγώσαντες
11,7*	ἐπιβάλλουσιν... καί	19,35	ἐπιρίψαντες
11,17*	καὶ ἔλεγεν	19,46	λέγων
12,3	ἔδειραν καί	20,10	δείραντες
12,4	καὶ ἠτίμασαν	20,11	ἀτιμάσαντες
12,8*	καὶ ἐξέβαλον	20,15	ἐκβαλόντες
12,18*	ἔρχονται... καί	20,27	προσελθόντες
12,19	καὶ καταλίπῃ	20,28	ἔχων (cf. Mt)
14,13	καὶ λέγει	22,8	εἰπών
14,16	ἐξῆλθον... (καὶ ἦλθον...) καί	22,13	ἀπελθόντες
14,36*	καὶ ἔλεγεν	22,42	λέγων (Mt καὶ λέγων, see No. 15.)
14,37*	ἔρχεται καί	22,45	ἐλθών
14,61	καὶ λέγει	22,67	λέγοντες
14,65	ἤρξαντο περικαλύπτειν... καί	22,64	περικαλύψαντες

The inverse : finite verb with καί in Luke and participle in Mark

9,7   (ἐγένετο...) ἐπισκιάζουσα (see No. 12)   9,34 καὶ ἐπεσκίαζεν (Mt 17,5 ἰδού... ἐπεσκίασεν)

More complex instances

Mk 12,28 προσελθών... ἐπηρώτησεν
Lk 10,25 ἀνέστη... λέγων

Mk 14,35 προελθών... ἔπιπτεν... καὶ προσηύχετο
Lk 22,41 ἀπεσπάσθη καὶ θείς...   προσηύχετο

3c. *Finite verb with καί in Mark and genitive absolute in Matthew or Luke* [165]

Matthew

Mk		Mt	
6,51	ἀνέβη... καί	14,32	ἀναβαινόντων αὐτῶν
9,33	ἦλθον... καί	17,24	ἐλθόντων δὲ αὐτῶν
11,11	εἰσῆλθεν... καί	21,10	εἰσελθόντος αὐτοῦ
15,(8-)9	ἤρξατο... δέ	27,17	συνηγμένων οὖν αὐτῶν

The inverse

Mk		Mt	
14,66	ὄντος τοῦ Πέτρου	26,69	ἐκάθητο... καί

Luke
* Paratactic καί in Matthew

Mk		Lk	
1,(9-)10	ἐβαπτίσθη... καί	3,21	Ἰησοῦ βαπτισθέντος καὶ προσευχομένου (Mt 3,17 βαπτισθείς)

165. Schmid(25), pp. 25-26 ; comp. Cadbury, pp. 133-134 ; Larfeld, pp. 223-225 ; Schürmann I, p. 94 ; cf. L. HARTMAN, *Testimonium Linguae* (Coniectanea Neotestamentica, 19), Lund, 1963, pp. 5-56 : *Participial Constructions in the Synoptic Gospels.* Cf. *infra*, n. 177.

Mk		Lk	
4,(1-)2*	συνάγεται... καί	8,4	συνιόντος δὲ ὄχλου πολλοῦ
9,20	ἤνεγκαν... καί	9,42	ἔτι δὲ προσερχομένου αὐτοῦ
10,(50-)51	ἦλθεν... καί	18,40	ἐγγίσαντος δὲ αὐτοῦ
11,(4-)5	λύουσιν... καί	19,33	λυόντων δὲ αὐτῶν
12,(37-)38	ἤκουεν... καί	20,45	ἀκούοντος δὲ παντὸς τοῦ λαοῦ
13,(1-)2	λέγει... καί	21,5	τινων λεγόντων
			(Mt 24,2 ὁ δέ)
14,13*	ὑπάγετε... καί	22,10	εἰσελθόντων ὑμῶν
14,49*	ἤμην... καί	22,53	ὄντος μου
cf.16,(5-)6	ἐξεθαμβήθησαν. ὁ δέ	24,5	ἐμφόβων δὲ γενομένων αὐτῶν

The inverse

Mk		Lk	
15,33	γενομένης ὥρας ἕκτης	23,44	ἦν... καί
cf. 6,35	ὥρας πολλῆς γενομένης	9,12	ἤρξατο κλίνειν·... δέ (Mt 14,15 = Mk).

4. Asyndeton in Mark and Conjunction in Matthew and Luke [166]

† Narrative material

Mk	Mt	Lk
1,8a	3,11 μέν	3,16 μέν
2,21	9,16 δέ	5,36 ἔλεγεν δὲ... ὅτι
4,24b	(7,2b) καί (2a γάρ)	6,38 γάρ
5,39	9,24 γάρ	8,52 γάρ v.l.
8,29† (ἀποκριθεὶς λέγει)	16,16 δέ	9,20 δέ
10,14	19,14 καί	18,16 καί
10,25	19,24 πάλιν δὲ λέγω ὑμῖν	18,25 γάρ
10,27† (ἐμβλέψας λέγει)	19,26 δέ	18,27 δέ
10,28†	19,27 τότε	19,28 δέ
10,29† (ἔφη)	19,28 δέ	18,29 δέ
12,6	21,37 δέ	20,13 δέ
12,9	21,40 οὖν	20,15 οὖν
12,17	22,21 οὖν	20,25 τοίνυν
12,20	22,25 δέ	20,29 οὖν
12,23	22,28 οὖν	20,33 οὖν
12,24† (ἔφη)	22,29 δέ	20,34 καί
12,29† (ἀπέκριθη)	22,37 δέ	(10,26) δέ
12,36	22,43 οὖν	20,42 γάρ
12,37	22,45 οὖν	20,44 οὖν
13,6	24,5 γάρ	21,8 γάρ

---

166. Schmid(3), pp. 36-37 : 11 cases ; cf. Turner(7,3), pp. 15-19 ; comp. Abbott(II) ; Hawkins (IVc) ; Cadbury, pp. 147-148 ; Schürmann III, pp. 9-10 ; Sanders, pp. 240-242.

Mk		Mt		Lk	
13,7		24,6	γάρ	21,9	γάρ
13,8		24,7	καί καί	21,11	τε καί καί
13,9		(10,17)	γάρ	21,12	participle
13,21		24,23	ἤ	(17,23)	ἤ v.l.
14,3†	(κατέχεεν)	26,7	καί	(7,38)	καί
14,8		26,12	γάρ	(7,46)	δέ
14,19†	(ἤρξατο... λέγειν)	26,22	καί	(22,23)	καί
14,64		26,65	ἴδε νῦν	22,71	γάρ
15,1†	(δήσαντες)	27,2	καί	23,1	καί
16,6a		28,5	οἶδα γὰρ ὅτι	24,5	τί
16,6c		28,6	γάρ	24,6	ἀλλά

(4) The inverse

1,8a	δέ (cf. 1,8a)	3,11		3,16	

4a. *Asyndeton in Mark and conjunction in Matthew*

* Asyndeton in Luke

Mk	Mt			Mk	Mt	
2,9*	9,5	γάρ		13,8c	24,8	δέ
2,17*	9,13b	γάρ (add. v. 13a)		13,34	(25,14)	γάρ
3,35	12,50	γάρ		14,6	26,10	γάρ
6,36*	14,15	οὖν		14,23*†	26,27	καί (ante εὐχαρ.)
8,1†	15,32	δέ				(cf. Lk 22,17 ptc.)
8,6†	15,36	καί (ante εὐχαρ.)		14,25	26,29	δέ
8,15	16,6	καί		14,41c (ἰδού)	26,45	καί
12,22*	22,27	δέ		14,61† (πάλιν)	26,63	καί

The inverse : asyndeton in Matthew

* Luke identical with Mark

See No. **2** : καί in Mark and δέ in Luke

diff. Mk 4,30† ; 6,41† ; 8,29a†(λέγει) ; (9,7†) ; 10,47† ; 14,30†(ἔφη).

Other instances

Mk		Mt	
2,25	οὐδέποτε	12,3	οὐκ (Lk 6,3 οὐδέ)
4,11*	δέ	13,13	διὰ τοῦτο
4,33†	καί	13,34	ταῦτα πάντα
10,4†	δέ	19,7	λέγουσιν
10,5†	δέ	19,8	λέγει
10,10†	καί	19,10	λέγουσιν
10,20*†	δέ	19,20	λέγει
10,21*†	δέ	19,21	ἔφη (v.l. λέγει)
10,37†	δέ	20,21	λέγει

Mk		Mt	
10,39a†	δέ	20,22b	λέγουσιν
10,39b†	δέ	20,23a	λέγει
10,43*	δέ	20,26	οὐχ οὕτως
10,51*†	δέ	20,33	λέγουσιν
11,33*†	καί	21,27	ἔφη
12,4*	καί	21,36	(πάλιν) ἀπέστειλεν
12,16*†	δέ	22,21	λέγουσιν
14,9	δέ	26,13	ἀμήν
14,31a†	δέ	26,35a	λέγει
14,31b†	δέ	26,35b	ὁμοίως
14,39†	καί	26,42	πάλιν
14,62*†	δέ	26,64	λέγει
15,13*†	δέ	27,22b	λέγει

4b. Asyndeton in Mark and conjunction in Luke

* Asyndeton in Matthew

Mk	Lk			Mk	Lk	
1,27	4,36	ὅτι		11,2	19,30	καί
1,44*	5,14	ptc.		12,4	20,11	δέ
2,11*	5,24	καί		12,5	20,12	δέ
4,24a	8,18	οὖν		12,27a*	20,38	δέ
9,38† (ἔφη)	9,49	δέ		13,4*	21,7	οὖν
9,50	14,34	οὖν		14,67† (ἐμβλέψασα)	(22,56)	καί

The inverse: asyndeton in Luke

* Matthew identical with Mark

Mk		Lk	
3,27	ἀλλ'	11,21	ὅταν (Mt 12,29 ἢ πῶς)
4,9†	καί	8,8	ταῦτα λέγων
13,10*	καί	21,13	ἀποβήσεται
13,13b*	δέ	21,19	ἐν τῇ ὑπομονῇ
13,17*	δέ	21,23	οὐαί
14,43*†	καί εὐθὺς ἔτι...	22,47	ἔτι αὐτοῦ λαλοῦντος

4c. Other instances of asyndeton in Mark

4,28 ; 8,19 ; 9,24 ; 12,27b ; 13,33 ; 14,8a.41a.41b (Mt ἰδού).

5. Ὅτι RECITATIVE IN MARK AND NOT IN MATTHEW AND LUKE [167]

* ἀμὴν λέγω ὑμῖν ὅτι

Mk	Mt	Lk
1,40	8,2	5,12
2,17	9,12	5,31

---

167. Schmid(21), p. 53 ; cf. Turner(7,2), pp. 9-15 : 45 instances in Mark and 12 agreements Matthew/Luke " in simply dropping the ὅτι of Mark ". Mk 12,6 should be added ; see also 6,4 ;

Mk	Mt	Lk
3,22bis	12,24	11,15
6,4	13,57	(4,24* !)
6,35	14,15	9,12
8,28	16,14	9,19
9,31	17,22	9,43
10,33	20,17	18,31
11,17 γέγραπται	21,13	19,46
12,6	21,37	20,13
12,7	21,38	20,14
12,19 ἔγραψεν	22,24	20,28
12,29	22,37	(10,26)
13,6	24,5	21,8
14,14	26,18	22,11
14,25*	26,29	22,18 (cf. v. 16 ὅτι)
14,69	26,71	22,58

(5) *The inverse: ὅτι recitative in Matthew and Luke and not in Mark*

10,29 ἀμὴν λέγω ὑμῖν	19,28*	18,29*
11,3	21,3	19,31

12,29 and 14,25 (in our list). In 1,15.37.40 ; 2,12.17 ; 3,11 ; 5,23.28.35 ; 6,18.23.35 ; 10,33 ; 13,6 ; 14,14.27.58a.b.71.72 ; 16,7 ὅτι is followed by a first or second person (necessarily in *oratio recta*), but in other instances ὅτι could introduce indirect discourse (e.g., 3,21.22 ; 6,14-15 ; 8,28.31). In 7,6a the text is doubtful (see also 6,23), but not in 1,15 (contra Schmid : — λέγων). Compare the first edition of Hawkins's *Horae Synopticae*, pp. 28 and 41 (omitted in the second edition) : ὅτι recitative is characteristic of Mark : 34 instances (Mt 14 ; Lk 28 ; without ἀμὴν λέγω ὑμῖν ὅτι) ; if only the more certain cases are included : 24 (Mt 8 ; Lk 13). Cf. Cadbury, pp. 139-141 ; Larfeld, p. 262 (Mk 26, comp. Bruder : 27 ; Mt 10 ; Lk 13 ; Acts 13) ; Schürmann I, pp. 75 (n. 311) and 98. B. WEISS, *Das Marcusevangelium* (see n. 21), p. 53 : " so oft Marcus auch dasselbe gebraucht, so lässt sich doch beobachten, dass er dasselbe nur da anwendet, wo er auf den Wortlaut eines Ausspruchs kein Gewicht legen will, sondern ihn nur ungefähr seinem Inhalt nach anführt ". The use of ὅτι recitative indicates that Mark gives his own free formulation of the saying : 1,15 (p. 53) ; 1,37 (p. 69) ; 1,40 (p. 72) ; 2,7! (p. 81) ; 2,12 (p. 85) ; 2,16! (p. 88) ; 3,11 (p. 115) ; 3,21 (p. 124) ; 3,22a.b (p. 120) ; 4,21 (p. 154) ; 5,23 (p. 184, n. 1) ; 5,28 (p. 187) ; 5,35 (p. 192) ; 6,4 (p. 201) ; 6,18 (p. 216) ; 6,35 (p. 229) ; 7,20 (p. 253) ; 8,4 (p. 266) ; 8,28 (p. 283) ; 9,11! (p. 300) ; 9,26 (p. 310) ; 9,28! (p. 311) ; 10,33 (p. 350) ; 11,17 (p. 372) ; 12,67 (p. 386) ; 12,19 (p. 395) ; 12,29 (p. 401) ; 13,6 (p. 413) ; 14,14 (p. 445) ; 14,27 (p. 454) ; 14,58a (p. 472) ; 14,69 (p. 480) ; 14,71.72 (p. 482) ; 16,7 (p. 511, n.1). Comp. V. Taylor, p. 166 : " Sometimes, instead of indirect speech, which Mark avoids, the construction is used for what is said repeatedly (cf. ii.12, iii.11, v. 28) or summarily (cf. iii.12, vii.20, xiii.6), but this cannot be inferred from the construction itself ; the context must decide. " J. SUNDWALL, *Om bruket av ὅτι recitativum i Markusevangeliet*, in *Eranos* 31 (1933) 73-84 ; and *Die Zusammensetzung des Markusevangeliums* (Acta Academiae Aboensis. Humaniora IX, 2), Åbo, 1934 : ὅτι recitative as introduction of the first utterance in an unitary composition or of a free-floating logion in the pre-Markan tradition. For criticism of this form-critical theory, see Zerwick, pp. 39-48. (He notes : " ὅτι rec. steht bei Mk im ganzen nahezu 50 mal ", p. 39.)

5a. ὅτι recitative in Mark and not in Matthew (without parallel in Luke)

Mk		Mt	
1,15		4,17	
3,28*		12,31	(διὰ τοῦτο λέγω ὑμῖν)
5,28		9,21	
6,18		14,4	
7,6b	γέγραπται	15,7	(λέγων)
8,4		15,33	
11,23*		21,21	
14,27	γέγραπται	26,31	
14,58a		26,61a	
14,58b		26,61b	

The inverse : ὅτι recitative in Matthew and not in Mark

Mk		Mt	
4,11		13,11	(causal ?)
6,49	indirect	14,26	(λέγοντες) ὅτι
8,16	indirect (interrogative ?)	16,7	(λέγοντες) ὅτι
10,5		19,8	(causal ?)
10,11		19,9	(λέγω δὲ ὑμῖν) ὅτι (cf. v. 11)
10,23	πῶς	19,23	
14,70		26,72	add.
15,35	ἴδε	27,47	

5b. ὅτι recitative in Mark (and Matthew) and not in Luke

Mk	Mt	Lk	
9,1*	16,28	9,27	(λέγω δὲ ὑμῖν ἀληθῶς)
14,30*	26,34	22,34	(λέγω σοι)
14,71	26,74	22,60	

The inverse : ὅτι recitative in Luke and not in Mark

Mk	Lk
1,38	4,43
11,31	20,5

5c. Other instances of ὅτι recitative in Mark

Mk		Mt		Lk	
1,37				4,42	diff.
2,12		9,8	diff.	5,26	ὅτι
3,11				(4,41)	ὅτι
3,21	(indirect ?)				
4,21				8,16	diff.
5,23		9,18	ὅτι (v.l.)	8,42	(causal ὅτι)
5,35				8,49	ὅτι
6,14.15bis	(indirect ?)			9,7.8bis	ὅτι

Mk		Mt		Lk	
6,23		14,7	diff.		
7,6a	(Turner)	15,3	diff. (cf. Mk 15,9)		
7,20		15,18	diff.		
8,28b		16,14	diff.	9,19	ὅτι
8,31	(indirect ?)	16,21	ὅτι	9,22	ὅτι
9,41b*		10,42*			
12,32	(indirect ?)				
12,35	(indirect ?)	22,42	diff.	20,41	diff.
12,43*				21,3	(ἀληθῶς...) ὅτι
13,30*		24,34*		21,32*	
14,18*		26,21*		22,21	(πλήν)
14,72		26,75	ὅτι	22,61	ὅτι
16,7		28,7	ὅτι	24,6	diff.

6. ῞Οτι Interrogative in Mark and not in Matthew and Luke [168]

Mk	Mt	Lk
2,16 ὅτι	9,11 διὰ τί	5,30 διὰ τί

Note

(a) ὅτι in Mark and not in Matthew (without parallel in Luke)

9,11 ὅτι	17,10 τί οὖν
9,28 ὅτι	17,19 διὰ τί (v. 20 διά)

(b) διὰ τί (cf. diff. Mk 2,16 Mt Lk ; 9,28 Mt)

2,18	9,14	5,33 diff.
7,5	15,2 (and 3)	
11,31	21,25	20,5

Mt 13,10 (diff. Mk 4,10) : διὰ τί (v. 11 ὅτι ; v. 13 διὰ τοῦτο)
Lk 19,23.24 ; 24,38 ; Acts 5,3

---

168. Schmid(22), p. 53 ; cf. Turner(7,1), pp. 58-62. On 2,16 ; 9,11.28 see Grimm's Lexicon, s.v. ὅστις, 4 (contra Winer § 53,4) ; Hawkins, *Horae Synopticae*, p. 35 (characteristic of Mk) ; Blass-Debrunner, § 300,2 ; see, however, Bauer, *s.v.* ὅστις, 4 : the use is doubtful, " since all the passages where this use might occur are textcritically uncertain ". But the reading ὅτι is beyond doubt in 9,11 (τι ουν W Θ lat sys·p sa bo, cf. Mt) and 9,28 (δια τι D 33 al, cf. Mt) ; also in 2,16 ὅτι (B pc bopt) is not so uncertain : δια τι (ℵ D W latt sa bopt) is an harmonization and τι (Θ syp) may be a correction, as well as τι οτι (C ℜ A λ φ pl ; cf. Textus Receptus, von Soden, Vogels and De Wette, Meyer etc.). In the three instances ὅτι is understood as recitative (introducing a statement) by B. Weiss, G. Wohlenberg (cf. Blass), RV and ASVmg, and in 2,16 (but not in 9,11.28) by P. Schanz, W. Bauer, W. Grundmann, R. Pesch and NEB. In 2,7 ὅτι (B Θ), printed as recitative by Weiss, is understood as interrogative by Westcott-Hort(h) and Turner, Taylor, Cranfield. In 14,60 h has again the interrogative (B W Ψ) ; on the double question, cf. *Duality in Mark*, p. 57, n. 195 (contra Weiss, Tischendorf, Nestle-Aland). In 8,12 ὅτι in only poorly attested (cf. Turner : C and Origen).

(c) ὅτι as variant reading for τί

2,7 (ὅτι) οὗτος	9,3 οὗτος (statement)	5,31 τίς ἐστιν οὗτος ὅς
8,12 (ὅτι)	16,4 om. (statement, cf. 12,39)	11,29 om. (statement)
14,60 (ὅτι) (indirect ?)	26,62 τί	

Cf. Acts 9,6

(d) ὅτι in indirect interrogative

8,16 ὅτι... ἔχουσιν	16,7 λέγοντες ὅτι... ἐλάβομεν
8,17 ὅτι... ἔχετε	16,8 ὅτι... ἔχετε

7. ἵνα IN MARK AND NOT IN MATTHEW AND LUKE [169]

7A. ἵνα Non-Purposive

Substitution by the *oratio recta* (†) or the infinitive (*)

5,23 παρακάλει... ἵνα ἐλθὼν ἐπιθῇς	Mt 9,18† ἀλλὰ ἐλθὼν ἐπίθες
	Lk 8,41* παρεκάλει... εἰσελθεῖν
6,8 παρήγγειλεν... ἵνα μηδὲν αἴρωσιν	Mt 10,5.9† παραγγείλας... μὴ κτήσησθε
	Lk 9,3† εἶπεν... μηδὲν αἴρετε

Omission of the ἵνα clause

Mk

11,28 ἔδωκεν ἐξουσίαν... ἵνα ταῦτα ποιῇς	Mt 21,23 ἔδωκεν... ἐξουσίαν
	Lk 20,2 δοὺς... ἐξουσίαν
14,35 προσηύχετο ἵνα... παρέλθῃ... ἡ ὥρα	Mt 26,39† προσευχόμενος... παρελθάτω
	Lk 22,41 προσηύχετο (+ oratio recta)

(v. 36 *oratio recta*)

Other instances of ἵνα in Mark

Infinitive : in Matthew diff. Mk 14,12 ; in Luke diff. Mk 5,12.18.43 ; 8,30 ; 14,38 ; 15,21.
Oratio recta : in Matthew diff. Mk 6,25 ; 7,26 ; 9,9 ; in Luke diff. Mk 15,11.

Mk

3,9 εἶπεν...	ἵνα... προσκαρτερῇ		
3,12 ἐπετίμα...	ἵνα μὴ ποιήσωσιν	Mt 12,16	ἐπετίμησεν... ἵνα μὴ ποιήσωσιν
		Lk 4,41	ἐπιτιμῶν οὐκ εἴα... λαλεῖν (= Mk 1,34)

---

169. Schmid(23), pp. 53-54 ; cf. Turner(10,4), pp. 356-359 : 31 instances in Mark (Schmid's correction : the infinitive in Luke *five* times, cf. par. Mk 5,23 ; but see Turner : the *oratio recta* in Mt *five* times, cf. par. Mk 9,9 ; Lk omits par. Mk 14,12, and not 15,11 ; see also Cadbury, pp. 137-138 ; Schürmann III, p. 48 (additions : Mk 5,10.12 ; 14,38) ; comp. P. Lampe, 'Die markinische Deutung des Gleichnisses vom Sämann Markus 4,10-12', ZNW 65 (1974) 140-150, espec. pp. 142-143 (" Exkurs zu ἵνα bei Markus ") : 28 instances of " explicatives ἵνα mit finalen Sinn " (including 3,12 and 13,18, but without 5,12 ; 14,12 ; 15,11.15.20.21 ; in 4,12 ; 9,12 and 11,16 ἵνα is " rein explikativ "). — For the omission of purpose clauses in Luke : cf. Cadbury, p. 90 ; Schürmann I, pp. 41 and 91.

Mk

5,10	παρεκάλει...	ἵνα μὴ... ἀποστείλῃ	Lk 8,31	παρεκάλουν... ἵνα μὴ ἐπιτάξῃ... ἀπελθεῖν
5,12	παρεκάλεσαν...	πέμψον...	Mt 8,31	παρεκάλουν... ἀπόστειλον
		ἵνα... εἰσέλθωμεν	Lk 8,32*	παρεκάλεσαν... ἵνα ἐπιτρέψῃ... εἰσελθεῖν
5,18	παρεκάλει...	ἵνα... ᾖ	Lk 8,38*	ἐδεῖτο... εἶναι
5,43	διεστείλατο...	ἵνα μηδεὶς γνοῖ	Lk 8,56*	παρήγγειλεν... μηδενὶ εἰπεῖν
6,12	ἐκήρυξαν	ἵνα μετανοῶσιν	Lk 9,6	εὐαγγελιζόμενοι
6,25	θέλω	ἵνα... δῷς	Mt 14,8†	δός μοι
6,56	παρεκάλουν...	ἵνα... ἅψωνται	Mt 14,36	παρεκάλουν... ἵνα... ἅψωνται
7,26	ἠρώτα...	ἵνα... ἐκβάλῃ	Mt 15,25†	βοήθει μοι
7,32	παρακαλοῦσιν...	ἵνα ἐπιθῇ		
7,36	διεστείλατο...	ἵνα... λέγωσιν		
8,22	παρακαλοῦσιν...	ἵνα... ἅψηται		
8,30	ἐπετίμησεν...	ἵνα... λέγωσιν	Mt 16,20	διεστείλατο... ἵνα... εἴπωσιν
			Lk 9,21*	ἐπιτιμήσας... παρήγγειλεν... λέγειν
9,9	διεστείλατο...	ἵνα μηδενὶ... διηγήσωνται	Mt 17,9†	λέγων μηδενὶ εἴπητε
			Lk 9,36	οὐδενὶ ἀπήγγειλαν
9,12	γέγραπται...	ἵνα... παθῇ	Mt (17,12)	μέλλει πάσχειν (diff.)
9,18	εἶπα...	ἵνα... ἐκβάλωσιν	Lk 9,40	ἐδεήθην... ἵνα ἐκβάλωσιν
9,30	οὐκ ἤθελεν	ἵνα... γνοῖ		
10,35	θέλομεν	ἵνα... ποιήσῃς	Mt 20,20	diff.
10,37	δός...	ἵνα... καθίσωμεν	Mt 20,21	εἰπὲ ἵνα καθίσωσιν
10,48	ἐπετίμων...	ἵνα σιωπήσῃ	Mt 20,31	ἐπετίμησεν... ἵνα σιωπήσωσιν
			Lk 18,39	ἐπετίμων... ἵνα σιγήσῃ
10,51	(θέλεις ποιήσω)...	ἵνα ἀναβλέψω	Mt 20,33	(θέλετε ποιήσω)... ἵνα ἀνοιγῶσιν
			Lk 18,41	(θέλεις ποιήσω)... ἵνα ἀναβλέψω
11,16	οὐκ ἤφιεν	ἵνα... διενέγκῃ		
12,19	ἔγραψεν...	ἵνα λάβῃ	Mt 22,24	εἶπεν... ἐπιγαμβρεύσει
			Lk 20,28	ἔγραψεν... ἵνα λάβῃ
13,18	προσεύχεσθε...	ἵνα μὴ γένηται	Mt 24,20	προσεύχεσθε... ἵνα μὴ γένηται
13,34	ἐνετείλατο	ἵνα γρηγορῇ		
14,12	ποῦ θέλεις...	ἑτοιμάσωμεν ἵνα φάγῃς	Mt 26,17*	ποῦ θέλεις ἑτοιμάσωμεν... φαγεῖν
			Lk 22,9	ποῦ θέλεις ἑτοιμάσωμεν
			Lk (22,8)	ἑτοιμάσατε... ἵνα φάγωμεν
14,38	προσεύχεσθε,	ἵνα μὴ ἔλθητε	Mt 26,41	προσεύχεσθε, ἵνα μὴ εἰσέλθητε
			Lk 22,46	προσεύχεσθε, ἵνα μὴ εἰσέλθητε
			Lk (22,40)*	προσεύχεσθε μὴ εἰσελθεῖν
15,11	ἀνέσεισαν...	ἵνα... ἀπολύσῃ	Mt 27,20	ἔπεισαν... ἵνα ἀπολέσωσιν
			Lk 23,18†	ἀνέκραγον... ἀπόλυσον
15,15	παρέδωκεν...	ἵνα σταυρωθῇ	Mt 27,26	παρέδωκεν ἵνα σταυρωθῇ
			Lk 23,25	παρέδωκεν τῷ θελήματι αὐτῶν
15,20	ἐξάγουσιν...	ἵνα σταυρώσωσιν	Mt 27,31	ἀπήγαγον... εἰς τὸ σταυρῶσαι
15,21	ἀγγαρεύουσιν...	ἵνα ἄρῃ	Mt 27,32	ἠγγάρευσαν ἵνα ἄρῃ
			Lk 23,26*	ἐπέθηκαν... φέρειν

The inverse (with ὅπως)

5,17*	παρακαλεῖν... ἀπελθεῖν		Mt 8,44	παρεκάλεσαν... ὅπως μεταβῇ
			Lk 8,37	ἠρώτησεν... ἀπελθεῖν

7B. ἵνα *Purposive*

12,15 φέρετε... <u>ἵνα ἴδω</u>

14,10 ἀπῆλθεν... <u>ἵνα... παραδοῖ</u>

Mt 22,19 ἐπιδείξατε
Lk 20,24 δείξατε
Mt 26,15† εἶπεν· ... παραδώσω
Lk 22,4 ἀπελθὼν συνελάλησεν...
τὸ πῶς... παραδοῖ

cf. 14,11 ζήτει πῶς... εὐκαίρως παραδοῖ

Mt 26,16 ἐζήτει εὐκαιρίαν ἵνα... παραδοῖ
Lk 22,6 ἐζήτει εὐκαιρίαν τοῦ παραδοῦναι

Other instances of ἵνα in Mark

1,38	ἄγωμεν... ἵνα... κηρύξω	Lk 4,43	εὐαγγελίσασθαί με δεῖ
3,10	ἐπιπίπτειν... ἵνα... ἅψωνται	Lk 6,19*	ἐζήτουν ἅπτεσθαι
4,12	(γίνεται) ἵνα... βλέπωσιν	Mt 13,13	λαλῶ, ὅτι... βλέπουσιν
		Lk 8,10	δέδοται... ἵνα... βλέπωσιν
4,21a	μήτι ἔρχεται... ἵνα... τεθῇ	Lk 8,16a	οὐδεὶς... τίθησιν
4,21b	οὐχ ἵνα... τεθῇ	Lk 8,16b	ἀλλ'... τίθησιν
4,22a	οὐ... ἐὰν μὴ ἵνα φανερωθῇ	Lk 8,17a	οὐ... ὃ οὐ
4,22b	οὐδὲ... ἀλλ' ἵνα ἔλθῃ	Lk 8,17b	οὐδὲ... ὃ οὐ
6,41	ἐδίδου... ἵνα παρατιθῶσιν	Mt 14,19	ἔδωκεν... οἱ δέ
		Lk 9,16*	ἐδίδου... παραθεῖναι
7,9	ἀθετεῖτε... ἵνα... τηρήσητε	Mt 15,3	παραβαίνετε... διά
10,17	τί ποιήσω ἵνα... κληρονομήσω	Mt 19,16	τί... ποιήσω... ἵνα σχῶ
		Lk 18,18	τί ποιήσας... κληρονομήσω
12,2	ἀπέστειλεν... ἵνα... λάβῃ	Mt 21,34*	ἀπέστειλεν... λαβεῖν
		Lk 20,10	ἀπέστειλεν... ἵνα... δώσουσιν
12,13	ἀποστέλλουσιν... ἵνα ἀγρεύσωσιν	Mt 22,15	συμβούλιον ἔλαβον ὅπως
		Lk 20,20	ἀπέστειλαν... ἵνα ἐπιλάβωνται
15,32	καταβάτω... ἵνα ἴδωμεν	Mt 27,42	καταβάτω... καὶ πιστεύσομεν
	καὶ πιστεύσωμεν	Lk 23,35.37	om.

Compare the omission of the infinitive: Lk 22,52, diff. Mk 14,48 ἐξήλθατε... (συλλαβεῖν με).

The inverse
ἵνα in Matthew and not in Mark

Mk 9,42 καλόν ἐστιν... μᾶλλον εἰ περίκειται
Mk 14,1 ἐζήτουν... πῶς... ἀποκτείνωσιν
Mk 14,2 μήποτε ἔσται θόρυβος

Mt 18,6 συμφέρει... ἵνα κρεμασθῇ
Mt 26,4 συνεβουλεύσαντο ἵνα... κρατήσωσιν
Mt 26,5 ἵνα μὴ θόρυβος γένηται

Compare: Mk 14,55 εἰς τὸ θανατῶσαι

Mt 26,59 ὅπως... θανατώσωσιν

ἵνα in Luke and not in Mark

Mk 12,7 ἀποκτείνωμεν... καὶ... ἔσται

Mt 21,38 ἀποκτείνωμεν... καὶ σχῶμεν
Lk 20,14 ἀποκτείνωμεν... ἵνα... γένηται

Mk 4,15   Lk 8,12   add.
Mk 4,21   Lk 8,16   add. (but ἀλλ' = οὐχ ἵνα in Mk!)

8. Parenthesis and Anacoluthon in Mark

8A. *Parenthesis* [170]

* A delayed parenthesis

Mk	Mt	Lk
1,2-3 καθὼς γέγραπται...	3,1-2 *ante* v. 3	3,2b-3 *ante* v. 3
2,15b ἦσαν γὰρ... αὐτῷ (N. Turner : ἦσαν... πολλοί)	9,10 om.	5,29 om.
2,22c* ἀλλὰ... καινούς (Turner : εἰ δὲ μὴ... ἀσκοί)	9,17 + βάλλουσιν	5,38 + βλητέον
2,26b οὓς... ἱερεῖς	12,4 om. (ἔφαγον) ἔδωκεν	6,4 post ἔδωκεν
6,14b-15 φανερὸν γὰρ... προφητῶν	14,1 τὴν ἀκοὴν Ἰησοῦ,	9,7 τὰ γινόμενα πάντα, καὶ διηπόρει διὰ...
12,12* ἔγνωσαν γὰρ... εἶπεν (Turner-Schmid : καὶ ἐφοβήθησαν τὸν ὄχλον)	21,45 ante ἐφοβήθησαν	20,19 om. καὶ ἄφεντες
13,10	24,14 post Mk 13,11-13	21,13 om.
16,4b* ἦν γὰρ μέγας σφόδρα (Turner : καὶ ἀναβλέψασαι... λίθος)	28,2 om. (27,60 μέγαν)	24,2 om.
16,7c* καθὼς εἶπεν ὑμῖν (Turner : ἐκεῖ αὐτὸν ὄψεσθε)	28,7 ἰδοὺ εἶπον ὑμῖν 6b καθὼς εἶπεν	24,6 ὡς ἐλάλησεν ὑμῖν
16,8 ἐφοβοῦντο γάρ (post καὶ... εἶπαν)	28,8 om.	24,9 om.

Other instances of parenthesis in Mark

2,10b λέγει τῷ παραλυτικῷ (Mt 9,6 ; Lk 5,24) ; 7,2 τοῦτ' ἔστιν ἀνίπτοις ; 7,3-4 ; 7,19b καθαρίζων πάντα τὰ βρώματα (om. Mt 15,18) ; 7,26a ἡ δὲ γύνη... τῷ γένει (om. Mt 15,25, cf. 22 Χαναναία) ; 8,15 (Mt 16,6) ; 13,14 ὁ ἀναγινώσκων νοείτω (Mt 24,15 ; om. Lk 21,20).

---

170. Schmid(13a), pp. 43-45 ; cf. Turner(4), pp. 145-156 ; comp. Lagrange, *Marc*, pp. LXXXI-LXXXII ; Taylor, p. 50 ; M. Zerwick, pp. 130-138 ; N. Turner, *Grammatical Insights into the New Testament*, Edinburgh, 1965, pp. 28.64-67.77-79 (delayed parentheses : also in Mk 5,42b, cf. v. 41b ; 6,15 ὡς εἷς τῶν προφητῶν, cf. v. 14 end ; and 14,2c).

8B. *Anacoluthon* [171]

Mk		Mt	Lk
3,16	καὶ ἐποίησεν τοὺς δώδεκα καὶ ἐπέθηκεν ὄνομα τῷ Σίμωνι Πέτρον· (see also v. 17)	10,2	6,14
4,31-32	ὡς κόκκῳ... ὃς ὅταν σπαρῇ..., μικρότερον ὂν πάντων..., καὶ ὅταν σπαρῇ,	13,31-32	13,19
5,23	λέγων ὅτι... ἐσχάτως ἔχει, ἵνα ἐλθὼν ἐπιθῇς	9,18	8,42
11,32	ἀλλὰ εἴπωμεν..., — ἐφοβοῦντο τὸν ὄχλον	21,26 φοβούμεθα	20,6 ἡμᾶς
12,38-39	τῶν θελόντων... περιπατεῖν καὶ ἀσπασμοὺς...	23,6 om. add. φιλοῦσιν	20,46 add. φιλούντων

Other instances of anacoluthon in Mark

12,19 ἔγραψεν ἡμῖν ὅτι ἐάν τινος... ἵνα λάβῃ (Lk 20,28 ; Mt 22,24 diff. ; cf. No. **7**)
12,40 (τῶν θελόντων)... οἱ κατέσθοντες (cf. Lk 20,47 relative)
13,14 ἑστηκότα (Mt 24,15 ἑστός ; Lk diff.)
14,49 ἀλλ' ἵνα (cf. No. **9**).

9. ἀλλά IN MARK [172]

9A. *ἀλλά at the Beginning of a Sentence*

Matthew/Luke agreements : diff. Mk 11,32 ; 14,36 ; (negative) 3,27 ; 13,24.

Mk		Mt		Lk	
3,27	ἀλλ' οὐ δύναται	12,29	ἢ πῶς δύναται	11,21	ὅταν
9,13	ἀλλὰ λέγω	17,12	λέγω δέ		
9,22	ἀλλ' εἴ τι δύνῃ				
11,32	ἀλλὰ εἴπωμεν (cf. v. 31 ἐὰν εἴπωμεν)	21,26	ἐὰν δὲ εἴπωμεν	20,6	ἐὰν δὲ εἴπωμεν
13,7	ἀλλ' οὔπω	24,6	ἀλλ' οὔπω	21,9	ἀλλ' οὐκ εὐθέως
13,20	ἀλλὰ διά (εἰ μὴ ἐκολόβωσεν... ἀλλά... ἐκολόβωσεν)	24,22	διὰ δέ		
13,24	ἀλλὰ ἐν ἐκείναις ταῖς ἡμέραις	24,29	εὐθέως δέ	21,25	καί

---

171. Schmid(13b), pp. 45-46 ; comp. Hawkins(IVb), pp. 135-137 ; Cadbury, pp. 148-149 ; Taylor, p. 50.
172. Schmid(15), p. 47 ; cf. Turner(9,2), pp. 279-280 ; comp. Schürmann III, pp. 84 and 121, πλήν p. 6 ; N. Turner, *Syntax*, pp. 329-330 ; *Duality in Mark*, pp. 35, n. 83, 58-63, 89-94.

Mk	Mt	Lk
14,28 ἀλλὰ μετά	26,32 μετὰ δέ	
14,36 ἀλλ' οὐ... ἀλλά	26,39 πλὴν οὐχ... ἀλλά	22,42 πλὴν μή... ἀλλά
14,49 ἀλλ' ἵνα	26,56 τοῦτο δὲ ὅλον γέγονεν ἵνα	22,53 ἀλλ' αὕτη ἐστίν
(οὐκ ἐκρατήσατέ με· ἀλλ')		
16,7 ἀλλὰ ὑπάγετε	28,7 καὶ ταχὺ πορευθεῖσαι	24,6
(6) ἠγέρθη,	(6) οὐκ ἔστιν ὧδε·	(6) οὐκ ἔστιν ὧδε,
οὐκ ἔστιν ὧδε...	ἠγέρθη γάρ...	ἀλλὰ ἠγέρθη
(7) ἀλλά... ἐκεῖ	(7) καὶ... ἐκεῖ	

Note : ἀλλά in Matthew or Luke
Lk 6,27 (diff. Mt 5,44 δέ) ; 11,42 (Mt 23,23 asyndeton) ; 22,36 ἀλλὰ νῦν (+ impf.)
Lk 7,25.26, par. Mt 11,8.9 (with preceding question : answer implied).
Lk 16,21 ; 24,21.22 : ἀλλὰ (γε) καί

Additional note : πλήν (cf. diff. Mk 14,36)
Other instances in Luke (and Matthew) : Lk 6,24 πλὴν οὐαί ; 6,35 πλὴν ἀγαπᾶτε (cf. v. 27 : ἀλλὰ
ὑμῖν λέγω... ἀγαπᾶτε) ; 10,11 ; 10,14 (Mt 11,22,24) ; 10,20 ; 12,31 (Mt 6,33 δέ) ; 13,33 ; 17,1 v.l. πλὴν
οὐαί (Mt 18,7) ; 18,8 ; 19,27 ; 22,21 (Mk 14,18 ἀμὴν λέγω ὑμῖν) ; 22,22 πλὴν οὐαί (Mk 14,21 οὐαὶ δέ) ;
23,28.

9B. ἀλλά with Preceding Negative

* In narrative

Mk	Mt	Lk	
3,26 οὐ δύναται	12,26 πῶς οὖν	11,18 πῶς	
ἀλλὰ τέλος ἔχει			
3,29 οὐκ ἔχει ἄφεσιν...	12,32 οὐκ ἀφεθήσεται	12,10 οὐκ ἀφεθήσεται	
ἀλλὰ ἔνοχός ἐστιν			
9,8* οὐδένα...	17,8 οὐδένα...	9,36	
εἰ μὴ (v.l. ἀλλά)...	εἰ μή...		
μόνον	μόνον	μόνος	
10,27 (followed by οὐ)			
ἀδύνατον,	19,26 ἀδύνατον...	18,27 τὰ ἀδύνατα	
ἀλλ' οὐ παρὰ θεῷ			
πάντα γάρ...	παρὰ δέ...	δυνατά...	
13,11 μή...	10,19 μή...	21,14 μή...	12,11 μή...
ἀλλ' ὃ ἐὰν δοθῇ	δοθήσεται γάρ...	(15) ἐγὼ γὰρ δώσω	
οὐ γάρ ἐστε ὑμεῖς	(20) οἱ γὰρ ὑμεῖς		
ἀλλὰ τὸ πνεῦμα	ἀλλὰ τὸ πνεῦμα	(12) τὸ γάρ... πνεῦμα	

Comp. Mk 13,20 ; 14,49 ; 16,7 (ἀλλά at the beginning of a sentence).

Additional Notes

(a) ἀλλά in Mark and not in Matthew or Luke
† ἀλλά in the parallel text of Matthew or Luke

Not in Matthew : Mk 6,9 (cf. Mt 10,10 $\mu\eta\delta\acute{\epsilon}$) ; 7,5 (cf. Mt 15,2 inversion of $o\vec{v}\ \gamma\acute{a}\rho$) ; 7,19 (cf. Mt 15,17 om. negative phrase) ; 7,25 (cf. Mt 15,22 om. negative phrase) ; 12,14† (cf. Mt 21,16 inversion $\kappa a\acute{\iota}$) ; 14,29 (cf. Mt 26,33 asyndeton).

Not in Luke : Mk 1,45* (cf. Lk 5,16 om. negative phrase) ; 4,17† (cf. Lk 8,13 $o\acute{\iota}$) ; 4,22 (cf. Lk 8,17 $\acute{o}\ o\vec{v}\ \mu\acute{\eta}$ instead of $\dot{a}\lambda\lambda$' $\acute{\iota}\nu a = \dot{\epsilon}\dot{a}\nu\ \mu\grave{\eta}\ \acute{\iota}\nu a$) ; 5,19* (cf. Lk 8,38 positive and participle) ; 5,26* (cf. Lk 8,43 om. negative phrase) ; 9,37 (cf. Lk 9,48 om. negative phrase) ; 10,45† (cf. Lk 22,27 diff. $\delta\acute{\epsilon}$) ; 12,25† (cf. Lk 20,36 $\gamma\acute{a}\rho$).

(b) $o\vec{v}$... $\dot{a}\lambda\lambda\acute{a}$ in Mark and in both Matthew and Luke : Mk 1,44 ; 2,17a.b.22 ; 5,39 ; 10,13 ; 12,27 ; 14,36b.

In Mark and Matthew only : (diff. Lk) Mk 4,17 ; 10,45 ; 12,25 ; (without parallel in Lk) Mk 7,15 ; 8,33 ; 9,6 ; 10,40 ; 11,23 (diff.).

In Mark and Luke only : (diff. Mt) Mk 12,14.

— Other instances of $o\vec{v}$... $\dot{a}\lambda\lambda\acute{a}$ in Matthew :

Parallel Lk : Mt 5,15 (cf. Lk 11,33, diff. Mk 4,21) ; 7,8 (cf. Lk 7,[6-]7) ; 10,34 (cf. Lk 12,51 $o\dot{v}\chi\acute{\iota}$, $\dot{a}\lambda\lambda\acute{a}$).

Peculiar : Mt 4,4 (Lk om. positive phrase) ; 5,17.39 ; 6,13.18 ; 7,21 (diff. Lk) ; 16,12* (add. Mk) ; 16,17 ; 17,12* (diff. Mk 9,13, but see v. 13a) ; 18,22 (diff. Lk) ; 18,30 ; 19,11.

— Other instances of $o\vec{v}$... $\dot{a}\lambda\lambda\acute{a}$ in Luke :

Diff. Mk : Lk 8,16 (cf. Mk 4,21 $o\dot{v}\chi\ \acute{\iota}\nu a$; comp. 11,33 and Mt 5,15) ; 8,27 (cf. Mk 5,3) ; 24,6 (cf. first list of $\dot{a}\lambda\lambda\acute{a}$).

Diff. Mt : Lk 12,7 (v. 6 $o\dot{v}\kappa$, cf. Mt 10,30 $\delta\acute{\epsilon}$).

$o\dot{v}\chi\acute{\iota}$, $\dot{a}\lambda\lambda\acute{a}$: Lk 1,60 ; 12,51 (= M) ; 13,3.5 ; 16,30 ; $\dot{a}\lambda\lambda$' $o\dot{v}\chi\acute{\iota}$: Lk 17,8.

Comp. Lk 14,10 (v. 8a $\mu\acute{\eta}$) ; 14,13 (v. 12 $\mu\acute{\eta}$) ; 23,15 (v. 14 $o\dot{v}\delta\acute{\epsilon}\nu$).

10. HISTORIC PRESENT IN MARK AND NOT IN MATTHEW AND LUKE [173]

† Historic present in the parallel text of Matthew or Luke

Matthew/Luke agreements against Mark

(1) aorist : diff. Mk 2,5.8.15.17.25 ; 3,4.13.32[Mt].34 ; 4,35.37(Mt $\imath\delta o\acute{v}$).38 ; 5,15a (Mt $\imath\delta o\acute{v}$) ; 8,29 ; 9,5.19 ; 10,23.27.42 ; 11,1bis.7.27.33 ; 14,13.53 ; 15,20.21 ; 16,2.16.

(2) participle : diff. Mk 1,41 ; 4,38 ; 5,38 ; 6,7.30 ; 11,2 ; 12,14.

(3) imperfect ($\acute{\epsilon}\phi\eta$) : diff. Mk 15,2.

(4) ($\kappa a\acute{\iota}$) $\imath\delta o\acute{v}$: diff. Mk 1,40 (Mt part.) ; 2,3 ; 5,22 ; 14,43.

---

173. The agreements are signaled here by underlining in Mark only (negative) or by underlining both in Mark and Matthew/Luke (positive). (In the cumulative list only the coincident text of Matthew and Luke is underlined for cases of *complete* verbal agreement.) — The list of the historic presents in the Synoptic Gospels can be found in Hawkins's *Horae Synopticae*, pp. 144-149 (one omission on p. 149 : Mt 25,26) ; see also p. 34 : $\acute{\epsilon}\rho\chi\epsilon\tau a\iota$, $\acute{\epsilon}\rho\chi o\nu\tau a\iota$ in Mark. Comp. Cadbury, pp. 158-159 ; Larfeld, pp. 13-14 ; Schmid(5), p. 38 ; Zerwick, pp. 49-57. Zerwick concludes : " die Begriffe des Kommens, Bringens, Führens, sich Versammelns erscheinen bei Mk am Anfang der Perikope präsentisch markiert, wenn mit ihnen für den Schriftsteller das Neue beginnt " (p. 57 ; comp. our Table B) ; on $\lambda\acute{\epsilon}\gamma\epsilon\iota$ see p. 64, and p. 65 ; " Die beiden Tempora ($\epsilon\imath\pi\epsilon\nu$ and $\lambda\acute{\epsilon}\gamma\epsilon\iota$) müssen für das Sprachempfinden des Mk sich äusserst nähestehen "). See also Schürmann I, p. 83, 88 ($\lambda\acute{\epsilon}\gamma\epsilon\iota$) and 106, n. 487 ($\acute{\epsilon}\rho\chi\epsilon\tau a\iota$). On Lk 24,12 see F. NEIRYNCK, 'The Uncorrected Historic Present in Lk xxiv.12 ', *ETL* 48 (1972) 548-553.

Negative agreements (differences in tense or mood)

(1) aorist in Mt and (a) participle in Lk : diff. Mk 4,1 (gen. abs.) ; 11,7 ; 12,18 ; 13,1
    (gen. abs.) ; 14,61 ; 15,17 (Mt part.) ; 15,24b ; (b) imperfect in Lk : diff. Mk 1,12 ;
    14,43 (cf. ἰδού).
(2) aorist in Lk and (a) participle in Mt : diff. Mk 1,21 ; 2,18 ; 4,36 ; 5,7.15b.22a
    (cf. ἰδού) ; 6,1 ; 14,21.63.67 ; 15,22.24a ; (b) imperfect in Mt : diff. Mk 5,39 ; 11,33
    (ἔφη) ; 14,17.30 (ἔφη) ; (c) ἰδού in Mt : diff. Mk 3,31.
(3) imperfect in Mt : diff. Mk 3,31.

Other instances of

(1) aorist, (a) in Mt : diff. Mk 3,33 ; 6,48 ; 7,18.28.32bis ; 8,1.12.17.33 ; 10,1bis.11.35 ; 11,22 ;
    14,45.66 ; 15,16 ; (b) in Lk : diff. Mk 1,30.38.44† ; 2,4.10†.14† ; 3,3.5†.13 ; 5,36 ; 6,37† ;
    9,2b† ; 12,13a† ; 14,32b†.37b.c†.
(2) participle, (a) in Mt : diff. Mk 1,40 (+ ἰδού) ; 5,38.40 ; 6,50 ; 7,5 ; 8,6 ; 11,21 ; 14,33 ; (b) in Lk :
    diff. Mk 5,19.41 ; 9,2a† ; 11,4 (gen. abs.) ; 14,32a†.37a†.
(3) imperfect in Lk : diff. Mk 5,23.
(4) (καὶ) ἰδού in Mt : diff. Mk 4,37 ; 5,15a (cf. 1).

Historic Present in Mark

A. λέγει /λέγουσιν and other verbs of saying

* Also referred to in Table B (when used at a new beginning in the narrative)

Mk		Mt		Lk	
1,30	λέγουσιν			4,38	ἠρώτησαν
1,37	λέγουσιν				
1,38	λέγει			4,43	εἶπεν
1,41	λέγει	8,3	λέγων	5,13	λέγων
1,44	λέγει	8,4†	λέγει	5,14	παρήγγειλεν
2,5	λέγει	9,2	εἶπεν	5,20	εἶπεν
2,8	λέγει	9,4	εἶπεν	5,22	εἶπεν
2,10	λέγει	9,6†	λέγει	5,24	εἶπεν
2,14	λέγει	9,9†	λέγει	5,27	εἶπεν
2,17	λέγει	9,12	εἶπεν	5,31	εἶπεν
*2,18	λέγουσιν	9,14	λέγοντες	5,33	εἶπαν
2,25	λέγει	12,3	εἶπεν	6,3	εἶπεν
3,3	λέγει			6,8	εἶπεν
3,4	λέγει	12,11	εἶπεν	6,9	εἶπεν
3,5	λέγει	12,13†	λέγει	6,10	εἶπεν
3,32	λέγουσιν	[12,47]	εἶπεν	8,20	ἀπηγγέλη
3,33	λέγει	12,48	εἶπεν	(cf. Mk 3,34)	
3,34	λέγει	14,49	εἶπεν	8,21	εἶπεν
4,13	λέγει				
*4,35	λέγει	8,18	ἐκέλευσεν	8,22	εἶπεν
*4,38	λέγουσιν	8,25	λέγοντες	8,24	λέγοντες
5,7	λέγει	8,29	λέγοντες	8,28	εἶπεν
5,9	λέγει			8,30	εἶπεν
5,19	λέγει			8,38	λέγων

Mk		Mt		Lk	
*5,36	λέγει			8,50	ἀπεκρίθη
*5,39	λέγει	9,23	ἔλεγεν	8,52	εἶπεν
*5,41	λέγει			8,54	ἐφώνησεν λέγων
*6,31	λέγει				
6,37	λέγουσιν	14,17†	λέγουσιν	9,13	εἶπαν
6,38	λέγει				
6,38	λέγουσιν				
6,50	λέγει	14,27	λέγων		
*7,5	ἐπερωτῶσιν	15,1	λέγοντες		
7,18	λέγει	15,16	εἶπεν		
7,28	λέγει	15,27	εἶπεν		
7,34	λέγει				
*8,1	λέγει	15,32	εἶπεν		
8,6	παραγγέλλει	15,35	παραγγείλας		
8,12	λέγει	16,2	εἶπεν		
8,17	λέγει	16,8	εἶπεν		
8,19	λέγουσιν				
8,20	λέγουσιν				
8,29	λέγει	16,16	εἶπεν	9,20	εἶπεν
8,33	λέγει	16,23	εἶπεν		
9,5	λέγει	17,4	εἶπεν	9,33	εἶπεν
9,19	λέγει	17,17	εἶπεν	9,41	εἶπεν
9,35	λέγει				
10,11	λέγει	(19,11)	εἶπεν		
10,23	λέγει	19,23	εἶπεν	18,24	εἶπεν
10,24	λέγει				
10,27	λέγει	19,26	εἶπεν	18,27	εἶπεν
10,42	λέγει	20,25	εἶπεν	(22,25)	εἶπεν
10,49	φωνοῦσιν				
*11,2	λέγει	21,2	λέγων	19,30	λέγων
11,21	λέγει	21,20	λέγοντες		
11,22	λέγει	21,21	εἶπεν		
11,33	λέγουσιν	21,27	εἶπαν	20,7	ἀπεκρίθησαν
11,33	λέγει	21,27	ἔφη	20,8	εἶπεν
*12,14	λέγουσιν	22,16	λέγοντας	20,21	ἐπηρώτησαν λέγοντες
12,16	λέγει	22,20†	λέγει		
*13,1	λέγει	24,1	προσῆλθον... ἐπιδεῖξαι	21,5	λεγόντων
*14,12	λέγουσιν	26,17	προσῆλθον... λέγοντες	22,9	εἶπαν
*14,13	λέγει	26,18	εἶπεν	22,10	εἶπεν
*14,27	λέγει	26,31†	λέγει		
14,30	λέγει	26,34	ἔφη	22,34	εἶπεν
*14,32	λέγει	26,36†	λέγει	22,40	εἶπεν
14,34	λέγει	26,38†	λέγει		
*14,37	λέγει	26,40†	λέγει	22,46	εἶπεν
*14,41	λέγει	26,45†	λέγει		
14,45	λέγει	26,49	εἶπεν		
14,61	λέγει	26,63	εἶπεν	22,67	λέγοντες
14,63	λέγει	26,65	λέγων	22,71	εἶπαν
*14,67	λέγει	26,69	λέγουσα	22,56	εἶπεν
15,2	λέγει	27,11	ἔφη	23,3	ἔφη
16,6	λέγει	28,5	εἶπεν	24,5	εἶπαν

B. Other instances of historic present

* The asterisk indicates the historic present at a new beginning in the narrative ; the chapter reference is not repeated for a second or third historic present used continuously.

( ) Verbs of saying already mentioned in Table A.

Mk		Mt		Lk	
*1,12	ἐκβάλλει	4,1	ἀνήχθη	4,1	ἤγετο
*1,21	εἰσπορεύονται	4,13	ἐλθών	4,31	κατῆλθεν
*1,40	ἔρχεται	8,2	(καὶ) ἰδοὺ... προσελθών	5,12	(καὶ) ἰδού
*2,3	ἔρχονται	9,2	(καὶ) ἰδού	5,18	(καὶ) ἰδού
2,4	χαλῶσι			5,19	καθῆκαν
*2,15	γίνεται	9,10	ἐγένετο	5,29	ἐποίησεν
*2,18	ἔρχονται	9,14†	προσέρχονται		
	(λέγουσιν)		λέγοντες	5,33	εἶπαν
*3,13	ἀναβαίνει	(5,1)	ἀνέβη	6,12	ἐγένετο... ἐξελθεῖν
	προσκαλεῖται		(cf. 10,1, par. Mk 6,7)	13	προσεφώνησεν
*3,20	ἔρχεται				
	συνέρχεται				
*3,31	ἔρχονται	12,46	(gen. abs.) ἰδού	8,19	παρεγένετο
*4,1	συνάγεται	13,2	συνήχθησαν	8,4	συνιόντος
*4,35	(λέγει)	8,18	ἐκέλευσεν	8,22	εἶπεν
36	παραλαμβάνουσιν	8,23	ἐμβάντι	8,22	ἐνέβη
4,37	γίνεται	8,24	καὶ ἰδοὺ... ἐγένετο	8,23	κατέβη
4,38	ἐγείρουσιν	8,25	ἤγειραν	8,24	διήγειραν
	(λέγουσιν)		λέγοντες		λέγοντες
*5,15	ἔρχονται	3,34	καὶ ἰδοὺ... ἐξῆλθεν	8,35	ἦλθον
	θεωροῦσιν		ἰδόντες		εὗρον
*5,22	ἔρχεται	9,18	(gen. abs.) ἰδοὺ... προσελθών	8,41	καὶ ἰδοὺ ἦλθεν
	πίπτει		προσεκύνει		πεσών
23	παρακαλεῖ				παρεκάλει
*5,35	(gen. abs.) ἔρχονται			8,49†	(gen. abs.) ἔρχεται
36	(λέγει)			50	ἀπεκρίθη
5,38	ἔρχονται	9,23	ἐλθών	8,51	ἐλθών
	θεωρεῖ		ἰδών		
39	(λέγει)		ἔλεγεν	52	εἶπεν
5,40	παραλαμβάνει				
	εἰσπορεύεται	9,25	εἰσελθών	(cf. 8,51	εἰσελθεῖν)
41	(λέγει)			54	ἐφώνησεν λέγων
*6,1	ἔρχεται		ἐλθών	(4,16)	ἦλθεν
	ἀκολουθοῦσιν				
*6,7	προσκαλεῖται	10,1	προσκαλεσάμενος	9,1	συγκαλεσάμενος
*6,30	συνάγονται	14,12	ἐλθόντες	9,10	ὑποστρέψαντες
31	(λέγει)				
6,48	ἔρχεται	14,25	ἦλθεν		
*7,1	συνάγονται	15,1†	προσέρχονται		
5	(ἐπερωτῶσιν)		λέγοντες		
*7,32	φέρουσιν	15,30	προσῆλθον		
	παρακαλοῦσιν		ἔρριψαν		
*8,1	(λέγει)	15,32	εἶπεν		
*8,22	ἔρχονται				
	φέρουσιν				
	παρακαλοῦσιν				

Mk		Mt		Lk	
*9,2	παραλαμβάνει	17,1†	παραλαμβάνει	9,28	παραλαβών
	ἀναφέρει	†	ἀναφέρει		ἀνέβη
*10,1	ἔρχεται	19,1	ἦλθεν	(cf. 9,51 ; 17,11 πορεύεσθαι)	
	συμπορεύονται	2	ἠκολούθησαν		
*10,35	προσπορεύονται	20,20	προσῆλθεν		
*10,46	ἔρχονται	20,29		18,35	ἐγένετο... ἐν τῷ
					ἐγγίζειν
*11,1	(ὅτε) ἐγγίζουσιν	21,1	(ὅτε) ἤγγισαν	19,29	(ὡς) ἤγγισεν
	ἀποστέλλει		ἀπέστειλεν		ἀπέστειλεν
2	(λέγει)		λέγων		λέγων
11,4	λύουσιν			19,33	λυόντων
11,7	φέρουσιν	21,7	ἤγαγον	19,35	ἤγαγον
	ἐπιβάλλουσιν		ἐπέθηκαν		ἐπιρίψαντες
*11,15	ἔρχονται				
*11,27	ἔρχονται				
	ἔρχονται	21,23	προσῆλθον	20,1	ἐπέστησαν
*12,13	ἀποστέλλουσιν	22,16†	ἀποστέλλουσιν	20,20	ἀπέστειλαν
14	(λέγουσιν)		λέγοντας	21	ἐπηρώτησαν... λέγοντες
*12,18	ἔρχονται	22,23	προσῆλθον	20,27	προσελθόντες
*13,1	(λέγει)	24,1	προσῆλθον... ἐπιδεῖξαι	21,5	λεγόντων
*14,12	(λέγουσιν)	26,17	προσῆλθον... λέγοντες	22,9	εἶπαν
13	ἀποστέλλει			(8)	ἀπέστειλεν
	(λέγει)	18	εἶπεν	10	εἶπεν
*14,17	ἔρχεται (cf. 18a)	26,20	(ἀνέκειτο)	22,14	(ἀνέπεσεν)
*14,27	(λέγει)	26,31†	λέγει		
*14,32	ἔρχονται	26,36†	ἔρχεται	22,40	γενόμενος
					(39 ἐπορεύθη)
	(λέγει)	†	λέγει		εἶπεν
33	παραλαμβάνει	37	παραλαβών		
14,37	ἔρχεται	26,40†	ἔρχεται	22,45	ἐλθών
	εὑρίσκει	†	εὑρίσκει		εὗρεν
	(λέγει)	†	λέγει	46	εἶπεν
14,41	ἔρχεται	26,45†	ἔρχεται		
	(λέγει)	†	λέγει		
*14,43	παραγίνεται	26,47	ἰδού... ἦλθεν	22,47	ἰδού... προήρχετο
14,51	κρατοῦσιν				
*14,53	συνέρχονται	26,57	συνήχθησαν	(22,66)	συνήχθη
*14,66	ἔρχεται	26,69	προσῆλθεν		
67	(λέγει)		λέγουσα	22,56	εἶπεν
*15,16	συγκαλοῦσιν	27,27	συνήγαγον		
17	ἐνδιδύσκουσιν	28	ἐκδύσαντες... περιέθηκαν	(23,11)	περιβαλών
	περιτιθέασιν		ἐπέθηκαν		
*15,20b	ἐξάγουσιν	27,31	ἀπήγαγον	23,26	(ὡς) ἀπήγαγον
21	ἀγγαρεύουσιν	32	ἠγγάρευσαν		ἐπιλαβόμενοι...
					ἐπέθηκαν
22	φέρουσιν	33	ἐλθόντες	33	(ὅτε) ἦλθον
15,24	σταυροῦσιν	27,35	σταυρώσαντες	23,33	ἐσταύρωσαν
	διαμερίζονται		διεμερίσαντο	34	διαμεριζόμενοι
15,27	σταυροῦσιν	27,38†	σταυροῦνται	(23,32)	ἤγοντο... ἀναιρεθῆναι
*16,2	ἔρχονται	28,1	ἦλθεν	24,1	ἦλθον
16,4	θεωροῦσιν			24,2	εὗρον (cf. 12 βλέπει!)

Note

12,36 (Δαυὶδ) εἶπεν	22,43 καλεῖ	20,42 λέγει
(ἐν τῷ πνεύματι τῷ ἁγίῳ)	(ἐν πνεύματι)	(ἐν βίβλῳ ψαλμῶν)
cf. 12,37 λέγει	22,45 καλεῖ	20,44 καλεῖ

Historic Present in Matthew

P indicates parable material.

A. λέγει /λέγουσιν

Par. Mk 1,44 ; 2,10,14 ; 3,5 ; 6,37 ; 12,16 ; 14,27.32.34.37.41 (pp. 224-225).
Diff. Mk :

Mk		Mt		Lk	
1,17	εἶπεν	4,19	λέγει	5,10	εἶπεν
4,40	εἶπεν	8,26	λέγει	8,25	εἶπεν
6,25	ᾐτήσατο λέγουσα	14,8	φησίν		
8,4	ἀπεκρίθησαν	15,33	λέγουσιν		
8,5	ἠρώτα	15,34	λέγει		
8,29	ἐπηρώτα	16,15	λέγει	9,20	εἶπεν
9,29	εἶπεν	17,20	λέγει	[17,6]	εἶπεν
10,4	εἶπαν	19,7	λέγουσιν		
10,5	εἶπεν	19,8	λέγει		
10,10	ἐπηρώτων	(19,10)	λέγουσιν		
10,20	ἔφη	19,20	λέγει	18,21	εἶπεν
10,37	εἶπαν	20,21	λέγει		
10,39	εἶπαν	20,22	λέγουσιν		
10,39	εἶπεν	20,23	λέγει		
10,51a	εἶπεν	(9,28)	λέγει (20,32 εἶπεν)	18,40	ἐπηρώτησεν
10,51b	εἶπεν	20,33	λέγουσιν	18,41	εἶπεν
11,14	εἶπεν	21,19	λέγει		
11,17	ἔλεγεν	21,13	λέγει	19,46	λέγων
12,16	εἶπαν	22,21	λέγουσιν	20,24	εἶπαν
12,17	εἶπεν	22,21	λέγει	20,25	εἶπεν
14,31	ἐλάλει	26,35	λέγει		
14,48	εἶπεν	26,52	λέγει (55 εἶπεν)	22,51	εἶπεν (52 εἶπεν)
14,62	εἶπεν	26,64	λέγει	26,67	εἶπεν (70 ἔφη)
14,69	ἤρξατο... λέγειν	26,71	λέγει	22,57	ἔφη
15,4	ἐπηρώτα	27,13	λέγει	(23,4	εἶπεν)
15,12	ἔλεγεν	27,22	λέγει (21 εἶπεν)	(23,20	προσεφώνησεν)
15,13	ἔκραξαν	27,22	λέγουσιν	23,21	ἐπεφώνουν λέγοντες

Diff. Lk (εἶπεν) : λέγει in Mt 4,6.10 ; 8,7 (— Lk).20.22 ; 9,37 (Lk ἔλεγεν) ; 22,8(P).
Peculiar to Mt : λέγει /λέγουσιν in 13,28(P).29 φησίν (P).51 ; 14,31 ; 15,12 ; 17,25 ; 18,22 (add. Lk). 32(P) ; 19,18 (add. Mk) ; 20,6(P).7 bis(P).8(P) ; 21,16.31bis.41.42 (add. Mk ; cf. Lk εἶπεν) ; 22,12(P).42 (add. Mk).43 (add. Mk) ; 26,25 (add. Mk) ; 28,10.

B. Other instances

Par. Mk 2,18 ; 7,1 ; 9,2 bis ; 12,13 ; 14,32(+ λέγει).37 bis(+ λέγει).41(+ λέγει) ; 15,27 (pp. 226-228).

Diff. Mk:

Mk	Mt	Lk
1,4 ἐγένετο	(3,1) παραγίνεται	(3,3) ἦλθεν
1,9 ἐγένετο... ἦλθεν	3,13 παραγίνεται	3,21 diff.

Diff. Lk in Mt 4,5 παραλαμβάνει (ἤγαγεν).8 παραλαμβάνει (ἀναγαγών).8 δείκνυσιν (ἔδειξεν).11 ἀφίησιν (ἀπέστη) ; 25,19 ἔρχεται (P ἐν τῷ ἐπανελθεῖν).19 συναίρει (P εἶπεν φωνηθῆναι). Variant reading : 4,5 ἵστησιν TR Ti S GNT (ἔστησεν).
Peculiar to Mt : 2,13 φαίνεται.19 φαίνεται ; 3,15 ἀφίησιν ; 13,44 ὑπάγει, πωλεῖ, ἀγοράζει (P) ; 25,11 ἔρχονται (P).

Historic Present in Luke

A. Verbs of saying :

Diff. Mt in Lk 19,22 λέγει (P ἀποκριθείς... εἶπεν).
Peculiar to Lk : 7,40 φησίν ; 11,37 ἐρωτᾷ ; 11,45 λέγει ; 13,8 λέγει (P) ; 16,7 λέγει (P).29 λέγει (P) ; 24,36 λέγει.
Acts (*φησίν) : 8,36* ; 10,31* ; 12,8 λέγει ; 19,35* ; 21,37 λέγει. 22,2* ; 23,18* ; 25,5*.22*.24* ; 26,24*.

B. Other instances

Par. Mk 5,35 (p. 226).
Peculiar to Lk : 24,12 βλέπει (comp. Mk 16,4 θεωροῦσιν) ; 16,23 ὁρᾷ (P).
Acts : 10,11 θεωρεῖ.27 εὑρίσκει.

11. IMPERFECT IN MARK AND NOT IN MATTHEW AND LUKE [174]

† Imperfect in the parallel text of Matthew or Luke

Matthew /Luke agreements against Mark

(1) aorist : diff. Mk 1,32 ; 2,24 ; 3,22.23 ; 4,2 (Mt + λέγων).11 ; 5,13.(30) ; 6,4.7.16 ; 9,31b ; 10,17.29 ; 12,18.24.35 (Mt + λέγων).38 (Mt + λέγων) ; 14,29.72 ; 15,12.
(2) participle : diff. Mk 4,41 ; 11,28 (Lk + εἶπαν) ; 13,3 (Lk + ἐπηρώτησαν) ; 14,36.

Negative agreements (differences in tense or mood)

(1) aorist in Mt and (a) participle in Lk : diff. Mk 12,17 ; 14,35.70b (Lk + impf.) ; 15,41 ; (b) ἦν + participle in Lk : diff. Mk 11,17a ; (c) ἤρξατο in Lk : diff. Mk 8,15.
(2) aorist in Lk and (a) participle in Mt : diff. Mk 6,35 ; 12,12 ; (b) present in Mt : diff. Mk 8,29 ; 10,20.
(3) participle in Lk and present in Mt : diff. Mk 11,17b.

---

174. Schmid(6), pp. 38-39 ; comp. Hawkins, p. 51 : (excluding the verb substantive) Mt 94 Mk 228 Lk 259 Acts 329 Jn 163 ; Cadbury, pp. 160-162 : " Imperfect and Aorist " (for cases of the inverse see the note on variant readings, p. 161) ; Schürmann I, p. 80. — For the change of the perfect and other tenses (No. **11n**), see Schmid(17), p. 48.

Other instances of

(1) aorist, (a) in Mt : diff. Mk (1,32) ; 3,2†.6†.12 ; 4,10†.30(+ ptc.).33 ; 6,(5).20.41†.56 ; 7,(9). 14.17.27 ; 8,15 ; 9,11.12.13.28.32† ; 10,(1).13†.48†bis.52† ; 11,(17) ; 12,34 ; 14,31.55.(57).70† ; 15,23 ; (b) in Lk : diff. Mk 1,7 ; 4,8† ; 5,9.30 ; 8,27† ; 9,38 ; 11,5.28 (cf. ptc.). 31† ; 12,41 ; 15,14†.47 ;

(2) participle, (a) in Mt : diff. Mk (1,30) ; 4,2 (+ aor.).30† (+ aor.) ; 6,19 ; 10,2 ; 12,35 (+ aor.).38 (+ aor.) ; 14,35 ; 15,19bis.41 ; (b) in Lk : diff. Mk (1,30) ; 2,16 (+ impf.) ; 3,11.12 ; 6,12 (+ impf.) ; 11,9†.17.37 (gen.abs.) ; 15,31 (+ impf.)

(3) ἦν + participle in Lk : diff. Mk 1,21.30.(35).45 ; 2,2.15 ; 11,17a. See No. 12.

Imperfect in Mark

ἦν + participle is not included ; see No. 12.

Mk		Mt		Lk	
1,5	ἐξεπορεύετο	3,5†	ἐξεπορεύετο		(cf. 3,7)
	ἐβαπτίζοντο	3,6†	ἐβαπτίζοντο		(cf. 3,7)
1,7	ἐκήρυσσεν			3,16	ἀπεκρίνατο
1,13b	ἦν				
	διηκόνουν	4,11†	διηκόνουν		
1,16	ἦσαν	4,18†	ἦσαν		
1,21	ἐδίδασκεν	(5,2†)	ἐδίδασκεν	4,31	ἦν διδάσκων
					(cf. Mk 1,22)
1,22	ἐξεπλήσσοντο	8,28†	ἐξεπλήσσοντο	4,32†	ἐξεπλήσσοντο
1,23	ἦν			4,33†	ἦν
1,30	κατέκειτο	8,14	βεβλημένην	4,38	ἦν συνεχομένη
1,31	διηκόνει	8,15†	διηκόνει	4,39†	διηκόνει
1,32	ἔφερον	8,16	προσήνεγκαν	4,40	ἤγαγον
1,34	ἤφιεν			4,41†	εἴα
1,35	προσηύχετο			4,42	(cf. 5,16 ἦν...
					προσευχόμενος)
1,45	ἦν			5,16	ἦν ὑποχωρῶν
	ἤρχοντο			5,15†	συνήρχοντο
2,2	ἐλάλει			5,17	ἦν διδάσκων
2,4	ἦν			5,19	
	κατέκειτο			5,19	
2,13	ἤρχετο				
	ἐδίδασκεν				
2,15	συνανέκειντο	9,10†	συνανέκειντο	5,29	ἦσαν κατακείμενοι
	ἦσαν				
	ἠκολούθουν				
2,16	ἔλεγον	9,11†	ἔλεγον	5,30†	ἐγόγγυζον... λέγοντες
2,24	ἔλεγον	12,2	εἶπαν	6,2	εἶπαν
2,27	ἔλεγεν			6,5†	ἔλεγεν
3,1	ἦν	12,10	καὶ ἰδού	6,6†	ἦν
3,2	παρετήρουν	12,10	ἐπηρώτησαν	6,7†	παρετηροῦντο
3,4	ἐσιώπων				(cf. 6,11)
3,6	ἐδίδουν	12,14	ἔλαβον	6,11†	διελάλουν
3,11	ἐθεώρουν				
	προσέπιπτον				
	ἔκραζον			(4,41)	κραυγάζοντα

Mk		Mt		Lk	
3,12	ἐπετίμα	12,16	ἐπετίμησεν	(4,41)	ἐπιτιμῶν
3,21	ἔλεγον				
3,22	ἔλεγον	12,24	εἶπον	(11,15)	εἶπαν
3,23	ἔλεγεν	12,25	εἶπεν	(11,17)	εἶπεν
3,30	ἔλεγον				
3,32	ἐκάθητο				(cf. 8,19)
4,1	ἦσαν	13,2	εἰστήκει		
4,2	ἐδίδασκεν	13,3	ἐλάλησεν...	8,4	εἶπεν
	ἔλεγεν		λέγων		
4,5	εἶχεν	13,5†	εἶχεν		
4,8	ἐδίδου	13,8†	ἐδίδου	8,8	ἐποίησεν
	ἔφερεν				
4,9	ἔλεγεν			8,8†	λέγων... ἐφώνει
4,10	ἠρώτων	13,10	εἶπαν	8,9†	ἐπηρώτων
4,11	ἔλεγεν	13,11	εἶπεν	8,10	εἶπεν
4,21	ἔλεγεν			8,16	
4,24	ἔλεγεν			8,18	
4,26	ἔλεγεν		(cf. 13,24)		
4,30	ἔλεγεν	13,31	παρέθηκεν λέγων	13,18†	ἔλεγεν
4,33	ἐλάλει	13,34	ἐλάλησεν		
	ἠδύνατο				
4,34	ἐλάλει	13,34†	ἐλάλει		
	ἐπέλυεν				
4,36	ἦν				
	ἦν				
4,37	ἐπέβαλλεν	8,24		8,23†	diff.
	(ὥστε γεμίζεσθαι)		(ὥστε καλύπτεσθαι)		συνεπληροῦντο
4,41	ἔλεγον	8,27	λέγοντες	8,25	λέγοντες
5,3	εἶχεν			8,27†	diff. ἔμενεν
	ἐδύνατο				
5,4	ἴσχυεν				
5,8	ἔλεγεν			8,29†	παρήγγελλεν
5,9	ἐπηρώτα			8,30	ἐπηρώτησεν
5,10	παρεκάλει			8,31†	παρεκάλουν
5,13	ἐπνίγοντο	9,32	ἀπέθανον	8,33	ἀπεπνίγη
5,18	παρεκάλει			8,38†	ἐδεῖτο
5,20	ἐθαύμαζον				
5,21	ἦν				
5,24	ἠκολούθει	9,19†	ἠκολούθει	8,42	diff. ἐν τῷ
	συνέθλιβον			8,42†	συνέπνιγον
5,28	ἔλεγεν	9,21†	ἔλεγεν		
5,30	ἔλεγεν	9,22	εἶπεν (cf. Mk 5,34)	8,45	εἶπεν
	ἔλεγον			8,45	εἶπεν
5,32	περιεβλέπετο				
5,40	κατεγέλων	9,24†	κατεγέλων	8,53†	κατεγέλων
5,42	περιεπάτει				
	ἦν				(cf. 8,42)
6,2	ἐξεπλήσσετο	13,54	ὥστε ἐκπλήσσεσθαι	(4,22†)	ἐμαρτύρουν, ἐθαύμαζον
6,3	ἐσκανδαλίζοντο	13,57†	ἐσκανδαλίζοντο		
6,4	ἔλεγεν	13,57	εἶπεν	(4,24)	εἶπεν
6,5	ἐδύνατο	13,58	(ἐποίησεν)		

Mk		Mt		Lk	
6,6	περιῆγεν	9,35†	περιῆγεν		
6,7	ἐδίδου	10,1	ἔδωκεν	9,1	ἔδωκεν
6,10	ἔλεγεν				
6,13	ἐξέβαλλον				
	ἤλειφον				
	ἐθεράπευον			9,6†	διήρχοντο...
					θεραπεύοντες
6,14	ἔλεγον			9,7	διὰ τὸ λέγεσθαι
6,15	ἔλεγον			9,8	
	ἔλεγον			9,8	
6,16	ἔλεγεν	14,2	εἶπεν	9,9	εἶπεν
6,18	ἔλεγεν	14,4†	ἔλεγεν		
6,19	ἐνεῖχεν				
	ἤθελεν	14,5	θέλων		
	ἠδύνατο				
6,20	ἐφοβεῖτο	14,5	ἐφοβήθη		
	συνετήρει				
	ἠπόρει			cf. 9,7†	διηπόρει
	ἤκουεν				
6,31	ἦσαν				
	εὐκαίρουν				
6,34	ἦσαν	(cf. 9,36)			
6,35	ἔλεγον	14,15	λέγοντες	9,12	εἶπαν
6,41	ἐδίδου	14,19	ἔδωκεν	9,16†	ἐδίδου
6,43	ἦσαν	14,21†	ἦσαν	9,14†	ἦσαν
6,47	ἦν	14,24†	ἀπεῖχεν		
6,48	ἦν	14,24†	ἦν		
	ἤθελεν				
6,56	εἰσεπορεύετο				
	ἐτίθεσαν				
	παρεκάλουν	14,36†	παρεκάλουν		
	ἐσῴζοντο	14,36	διεσώθησαν		
7,9	ἔλεγεν	15,3	εἶπεν (cf. Mk 7,3)		
7,14	ἔλεγεν	15,10	εἶπεν		
7,17	ἐπηρώτων	15,15	εἶπεν		
7,20	ἔλεγεν				
7,24	ἤθελεν				
7,25	εἶχεν	15,22	δαιμονίζεται (dir.)		
7,26	ἦν	15,22			
	ἠρώτα	15,22	ἔκραζεν λέγουσα		
7,27	ἔλεγεν	15,26	εἶπεν		
7,35	ἐλάλει				
7,36	διεστέλλετο				
	ἐκήρυσσεν				
7,37	ἐξεπλήσσοντο	15,31	ὥστε... θαυμάσαι		
8,5	ἠρώτα	15,34	λέγει		
8,6	ἐδίδου	15,36†	ἐδίδου		
8,7	εἶχον	15,36			
8,9	ἦσαν	15,38†	ἦσαν		
8,14	εἶχον				
8,15	διεστέλλετο... λέγων	16,6	εἶπεν	(12,1)	ἤρξατο λέγειν

Mk		Mt		Lk	
8,16	διελογίζοντο	16,7†	διελογίζοντο		
8,21	ἔλεγεν				
8,23	ἐπηρώτα				
8,24	ἔλεγεν				
8,25	ἐνέβλεπεν				
8,27	ἐπηρώτα	16,13†	ἠρώτα	9,18	ἐπηρώτησεν
8,29	ἐπηρώτα	16,15	λέγει	9,20	εἶπεν
8,32	ἐλάλει				
9,1	ἔλεγεν				
9,11	ἐπηρώτων	17,10	ἐπηρώτησεν		
9,12	ἔφη	17,11	εἶπεν		
9,13	ἤθελον	17,12	ἠθέλησαν		
9,15	ἠσπάζοντο				
9,20	ἐκυλίετο				
9,24	ἔλεγεν				
9,27	ἤγειρεν				
9,28	ἐπηρώτων	17,19	εἶπεν		
9,30	παρεπορεύοντο	17,22	gen. abs.		
	ἤθελεν				
9,31	ἐδίδασκεν				
	ἔλεγεν	17,22	εἶπεν	9,43	εἶπεν
9,32	ἠγνόουν			9,45†	ἠγνόουν
	ἐφοβοῦντο	17,23	λυπήθησαν	9,45†	ἐφοβοῦντο
9,33	ἐπηρώτα				
	ἐσιώπων				
9,38	ἔφη			9,49	εἶπεν
	ἐκωλύομεν			9,49†	ἐκωλύομεν
	ἠκολούθει			9,49	ἀκολουθεῖ
10,1	ἐδίδασκεν	19,2	(ἐθεράπευσεν)		
10,2	ἐπηρώτων	19,3	λέγοντες		
10,10	ἐπηρώτων	(19,10)	λέγουσιν		
10,13	προσέφερον	19,13	προσηνέχθησαν	18,15†	προσέφερον
10,16	κατευλόγει				
10,17	ἐπηρώτα	19,16	εἶπεν	18,18	ἐπηρώτησεν
10,20	ἔφη	19,20	λέγει	18,21	εἶπεν
10,24	ἐθαμβοῦντο				
10,26	ἐξεπλήσσοντο	19,25†	ἐξεπλήσσοντο		
10,29	ἔφη	19,28	εἶπεν	18,29	εἶπεν
10,32	ἐθαμβοῦντο				
	ἐφοβοῦντο				
10,46	ἐκάθητο	20,30	καὶ ἰδού... καθήμενοι	18,35†	ἐκάθητο
10,48	ἐπετίμων	20,31	ἐπετίμησεν	18,39†	ἐπετίμων
10,48	ἔκραζεν	20,31	ἔκραξαν λέγοντες	18,39†	ἔκραζεν
10,52	ἠκολούθει	20,34	ἠκολούθησαν	18,43†	ἠκολούθει
11,5	ἔλεγον			19,33	εἶπαν
11,9	ἔκραζον	21,9†	ἔκραζον	19,37	ἤρξαντο... χαίροντες αἰνεῖν... (38) λέγοντες
11,13	ἦν				
11,14	ἤκουον				
11,16	ἤφιεν				

Mk		Mt			Lk	
11,17	ἐδίδασκεν	(21,14)	(ἐθεράπευσεν)		(19,47)	ἦν διδάσκων (cf. 21,37)
	ἔλεγεν	21,13	λέγει		19,46	λέγων
11,18	ἐζήτουν				19,47†	ἐζήτουν (cf. v. 48)
	ἐφοβοῦντο					
	ἐξεπλήσσετο				19,48†	ἐξεκρέματο
11,19	ἐξεπορεύοντο				cf. 21,37	ἐξερχόμενος ηὐλίζετο
11,28	ἔλεγον	21,23	λέγοντες		20,2	εἶπαν λέγοντες
11,31	διελογίζοντο	21,25†	διελογίζοντο		20,5	συνελογίσαντο
11,32	ἐφοβοῦντο	21,26	φοβούμεθα (dir.)		20,6	diff. καταλιθάσει (dir.)
	εἶχον	21,26	ἔχουσιν		20,6	πεπεισμένος... ἐστιν
	ἦν				20,6	εἶναι
12,6	εἶχεν					
12,12	ἐζήτουν	21,45	ζητοῦντες		20,19	ἐζήτησαν
12,17	ἐξεθαύμαζον	22,22	ἐθαύμασαν		20,26	θαυμάσαντες
12,18	ἐπηρώτων	22,23	ἐπηρώτησαν		20,27	ἐπηρώτησαν
12,20	ἦσαν	22,25†	ἦσαν		20,29†	ἦσαν
12,24	ἔφη	22,29	ἀποκριθεὶς εἶπεν		20,34	εἶπεν
12,34	ἐτόλμα	22,46	ἐτόλμησεν		(20,40†)	ἐτόλμων
12,35	ἔλεγεν	22,41	ἐπηρώτησεν λέγων		20,41	εἶπεν
12,37	ἤκουεν				20,45	ἀκούοντος (gen. abs.)
12,38	ἔλεγεν	23,1	ἐλάλησεν λέγων		20,45	εἶπεν
12,41	ἐθεώρει				21,1	εἶδεν
	ἔβαλλον				21,1	diff. βάλλοντες
12,44	εἶχεν				21,4†	εἶχεν
13,3	ἐπηρώτα	24,3	προσῆλθον λέγοντες		21,7	ἐπηρώτησαν... λέγοντες
14,1	ἦν	26,2	γίνεται (dir.)		22,1†	ἤγγιζεν
	ἐζήτουν	26,3-4			22,2†	ἐζήτουν
14,2	ἔλεγον	26,5†	ἔλεγον		22,2†	diff. ἐφοβοῦντο
14,3	κατέχεεν	26,7†	κατέχεεν			
14,5	ἠδύνατο	26,9†	ἐδύνατο			
	ἐνεβριμῶντο					
14,11	ἐζήτει	26,16†	ἐζήτει		22,6†	ἐζήτει
14,12	ἔθυον				22,7†	diff. ἔδει θύεσθαι
14,29	ἔφη	26,33	εἶπεν		22,33	εἶπεν
14,31	ἐλάλει	26,35	λέγει			
	ἔλεγον	26,35	εἶπαν			
14,35	ἔπιπτεν	26,39	ἔπεσεν		22,41	θεὶς τὰ γόνατα
	προσηύχετο	26,39	προσευχόμενος		22,41†	προσηύχετο
14,36	ἔλεγεν	26,39	λέγων		22,42	λέγων
14,51	συνηκολούθει					
14,55	ἐζήτουν	26,59†	ἐζήτουν			
	ηὕρισκον	26,60	εὗρον			
14,56	ἐψευδομαρτύρουν	26,60	diff. (gen. abs.)			
	ἦσαν					
14,57	ἐψευδομαρτύρουν λέγοντες	26,61	εἶπαν			
14,59	ἦν					
14,61	ἐσιώπα	26,63†	ἐσιώπα			
	ἐπηρώτα					
14,67	ἦσθα	26,69†	ἦσθα		22,56†	ἦν
14,70	ἠρνεῖτο	26,72	ἠρνήσατο		22,58b†	ἔφη
	ἔλεγον	26,73	εἶπον		22,59	διϊσχυρίζετο λέγων

Mk		Mt		Lk	
14,72	ἔκλαιεν	26,75	ἔκλαυσεν	22,62	ἔκλαυσεν
15,3	κατηγόρουν	27,12	ἐν τῷ κατηγορεῖσθαι	(23,2)	ἤρξαντο κατηγορεῖν
				(23,10)	εἱστήκεισαν
					κατηγοροῦντες
15,4	ἐπηρώτα	27,13	λέγει		
15,6	ἀπέλυεν	27,15	εἰώθει ἀπολύειν		
	παρῃτοῦντο	27,15†	ἤθελον	(23,25)	ᾐτοῦντο
15,8	ἐποίει				
15,10	ἐγίνωσκεν	27,18	ᾔδει		
15,12	ἔλεγεν	27,21	εἶπεν	23,20	προσεφώνησεν
15,14	ἔλεγεν	27,23	ἔφη	23,22	εἶπεν
15,19	ἔτυπτον	27,30†	ἔτυπτον		
	ἐνέπτυον	27,30	ἐμπτύσαντες		
	προσεκύνουν	27,29	γονυπετήσαντες		
15,23	ἐδίδουν	27,34	ἔδωκαν		
15,25	ἦν				
15,29	ἐβλασφήμουν	27,39†	ἐβλασφήμουν		
15,31	ἔλεγον	27,41†	ἔλεγον	23,35†	ἐξεμυκτήριζον λέγοντες
15,32	ὠνείδιζον	27,44†	ὠνείδιζον	23,39†	ἐβλασφήμει
15,35	ἔλεγον	27,47†	ἔλεγον		
15,36	ἐπότιζεν	27,48†	ἐπότιζεν		
15,39	ἦν	27,54†	ἦν	23,47†	ἦν
15,41	ἦν	27,55		23,49	
	ἠκολούθουν	27,55	ἠκολούθησαν	23,49	συνακολουθοῦσαι
	διηκόνουν	27,55	διακονοῦσαι	(8,3†)	διηκόνουν
15,42	ἦν			(23,54†)	ἦν
15,47	ἐθεώρουν	27,61†	ἦν..., καθήμεναι	23,55	ἐθεάσαντο
16,3	ἔλεγον				
16,4	ἦν				
16,8	εἶχεν				
	ἐφοβοῦντο	28,8	diff. (μετὰ φόβου)		

Note : εἰώθει 10,1 ; ᾔδει(-σαν) 1,34 (= Lk) ; 9,6 ; 14,40.

(11) *The inverse : Imperfect in Matthew and Luke and not in Mark*

Mk		Mt		Lk	
2,14	ἠκολούθησεν	9,9	(ἠκολούθει)	5,28	ἠκολούθει
11,8	ἔστρωσαν	21,8	ἐστρώννυον	19,36	ἐπεστρώννυον
14,54	ἠκολούθησεν	26,58	ἠκολούθει	22,54	ἠκολούθει
14,69	ἐστίν	26,71	ἦν	(22,59)	ἦν
15,14	ἔκραξαν	27,23	ἔκραζον (λέγοντες)	23,23	ἐπέκειντο
					(αἰτούμενοι)

Compare No. **12** and No. **10** :

Mk		Mt		Lk	
14,54	ἦν συγκαθήμενος	26,58	ἐκάθητο	22,55	ἐκάθητο
15,2	λέγει	27,11	ἔφη	23,3	ἔφη

Imperfect in Matthew

* Participial construction in Mark

Par. Mk 1,5bis.13.16.21.22.31 ; 2,15.16 ; 4,5.8.34 ; 5,24.28.40 ; 6,3.6.18.43.47.48.56 ; 7,26 ; 8,6.9.16.27 ; 10,26 ; 11,9.31 ; 14,2.3.5.11.55.61.67 ; 15,6.14.19.29.31.32.35.36.39.47 (pp. 230-235).

Matthew /Luke agreements against Mark : diff. Mk (2,14) ; 11,8 ; 14,54a.b* ; 15,2.14 (p. 235).

Other instances diff. Mk :

Mk		Mt	
1,6*	ἦν ἐνδεδυμένος καὶ ἔσθων	3,4	εἶχεν (τὸ ἔνδυμα αὐτοῦ) (ἡ δὲ τροφή) ἦν
1,39*	ἦλθεν (v.l. ἦν) κηρύσσων	4,23	περιῆγεν (cf. 9,35 = Mk 6,6)
1,40*	γονυπετῶν	8,2	προσεκύνει
2,3*	ἔρχονται φέροντες (πρός)	9,2	προσέφερον
4,1	ἤρξατο διδάσκειν	13,1	ἐκάθητο
4,31	ὅταν σπαρῇ	13,31	ἔσπειρεν
4,38*	ἦν καθεύδων	8,24	ἐκάθευδεν
5,12	παρεκάλεσαν	8,31	παρεκάλουν
5,22	πίπτει (πρός)	9,18	προσεκύνει
5,39	λέγει	9,23	ἔλεγεν
6,2	ἤρξατο διδάσκειν	13,54	ἐδίδασκεν
6,20*	εἰδώς	14,5	εἶχον
6,47		14,23	ἦν
7,25		15,23	ἠρώτα (add.)
7,25	προσέπεσεν	15,25	προσεκύνει
7,31		15,29	ἐκάθητο (add.)
10,19		19,18	ἔφη (add.)
10,21	εἶπεν	19,21	ἔφη
11,11		21,11	ἔλεγον (add.)
11,33	λέγει	21,27	ἔφη
12,12		21,46	εἶχον
12,27		22,33	ἐξεπλήσσοντο (add.)
12,29	ἀπεκρίθη	22,37	ἔφη
12,37		22,46	ἐδύνατο (add.)
13,1*	ἐκπορευομένου (gen. abs.)	24,1	ἐπορεύετο
14,(17-)18*	(ἔρχεται) ἀνακειμένων (gen. abs.)	26,20	ἀνέκειτο
14,21		26,24	ἦν
14,30	λέγει	26,34	ἔφη (cf. Mk v. 29)
14,58*	λέγοντος	26,61	ἔφη
14,66*	ὄντος (gen. abs.)	26,69	ἐκάθητο
14,69	ἐστιν	26,71	ἦν (cf. Mk v. 67)
15,7*	ἦν δεδεμένος	27,16	εἶχον
15,24		27,36	ἐτήρουν (add.)
15,40*	ἦσαν θεωροῦσαι	27,55	ἦσαν ἐκεῖ (θεωροῦσαι)
16,5*	καθήμενον	28,2	ἐκάθητο
16,5*	περιβεβλημένον	28,3	ἦν (τὸ ἔνδυμα αὐτοῦ)
16,7	ἔθηκαν	28,6	ἔκειτο

Diff. Lk in Mt 4,7 ἔφη (εἶπεν) ; 7,27 ἦν (ἐγένετο) ; 8,8 ἔφη (λέγων) ; 9,34 ἔλεγον ; 12,23 ἔλεγον (cf. Mk 3,21.22).40 ἦν (ἐγένετο) ; 22,3 ἤθελον (P). 8 ἦσαν (P) ; 23,23 ἔδει. 30 ἤμεθα bis ; 25,21 ἔφη (P εἶπεν). 23 ἔφη (P εἶπεν). 27 ἔδει (P).

Peculiar to Mt in 1,18 ; 2,4.9.15 ; 3,14.28.46 ; 17,26 ; 18,26(P).28(P) bis.29(P).30(P).33(P) ; 20,11(P) ; 21,28(P) ; 25,2(P).5(P).35(P).36(P).42(P) ; 27,65.

Note : εἰώθει 27,15 (Mk impf.) ; ᾔδει 27,18 (Mk impf.) ; comp. 24,43 ; 25,26 (= Lk). For εἱστήκει, see No. 12.

Imperfect in Luke

* ἤρξατο with infinitive in Mark
** Periphrastic construction
† ὥστε with infinitive

Par. Mk 1,22.23.31.34.45 ; 2,16.27 ; 3,1.2.6 ; 4,9.10.30.37 ; 5,3.8.10.18.24.40 ; 6,2.12.(20).41.43 ; 9,32bis.38 ; 10,13.46.48bis.52 ; 11,18bis.(19) ; 12,20.34.44 ; 14,1bis.2.11.12.35.67.70bis ; 15,6.39.42 (pp. 230-235).
Matthew/Luke agreements : diff. Mk 2,14 ; 11,8 ; 14,54a.b** ; 15,2.14 (p. 235).
Other instances diff. Mk :

Mk		Lk	
1,27†	ὥστε συζητεῖν	4,36	συνελάλουν
1,28	ἐξῆλθεν	4,37	ἐξεπορεύετο
1,32		4,40	εἶχον
1,34	ἐθεράπευσεν	4,40	ἐθεράπευεν (v.l. -σεν)
1,34	ἐξέβαλεν	4,41	ἐξήρχετο
1,36	κατεδίωξεν (cf. 37 ζητοῦσιν)	4,42a	ἐπεζήτουν
1,37	λέγουσιν	4,42b	κατεῖχον
1,45	ἐξελθών (cf. 28 ἐξῆλθεν)	5,15	διήρχετο
2,2		5,17	ἦν (add.)
2,4	μὴ δυνάμενοι	5,18	ἐζήτουν
2,12†	ὥστε... δοξάζειν	5,26	ἐδόξαζον
2,21		5,36	ἔλεγεν (add.)
2,23	τίλλοντες	6,1	ἔτιλλον
			ἤσθιον (add.)
3,1		6,6	ἦν (add.)
3,10	ἐθεράπευσεν	6,18	ἐθεραπεύοντο
3,10†	ὥστε... ἐπιπίπτειν	6,19	ἐζήτουν
			ἐξήρχετο (add.)
			ἰᾶτο (add.)
3,31	ἀπέστειλαν	8,19	ἠδύναντο
4,37†	ὥστε γεμίζεσθαι	8,23	ἐκινδύνευον (add.)
5,22		8,41	ὑπῆρχεν (add.)
5,38	κλαίοντας	8,52	ἔκλαιον
	ἀλαλάζοντας		ἐκόπτοντο
6,2	(ἐξεπλήσσοντο) λέγοντες	(4,22)	(ἐμαρτύρουν, ἐθαύμαζον) ἔλεγον
6,34*	ἤρξατο διδάσκειν	9,11	ἐλάλει
			ἰᾶτο (add.)
8,11*	(ἤρξαντο συζητεῖν) ζητοῦντες	(11,16)	ἐζήτουν
8,34	εἶπεν	9,23	ἔλεγεν
9,4**	ἦσαν συλλαλοῦντες	9,30	συνελάλουν
			ἦσαν
		9,31	ἔλεγον (add.)
			ἤμελλεν (add.)
9,7**	ἐγένετο ἐπισκιάζουσα	9,34	ἐπεσκίαζεν
9,27		9,43a	ἐξεπλήσσοντο (add.)
			ἐποίει (add.)
10,13	ἐπετίμησαν	18,15	ἐπετίμων
10,22**	ἦν ἔχων	18,23	ἦν (+ adjective)
10,32**	ἦν προάγων	(19,28)	ἐπορεύετο (ἔμπροσθεν)
10,34		18,34	ἐγίνωσκεν (add.), cf. Mk 9,32
10,47		18,36	ἐπυνθάνετο

Mk		Lk	
12,7	εἶπαν	20,14	διελογίζοντο
13,8		21,10	ἔλεγεν (add.)
14,36		[22,44]	προσηύχετο (add.)
14,43	παραγίνεται	22,47	προήρχετο
14,62	εἶπεν	22,70	ἔφη (67 εἶπεν)
14,65*	ἤρξαντο ἐμπτύειν	22,63	ἐνέπαιζον
	... λέγειν	64	ἐπηρώτων λέγοντες
		65	ἔλεγον (add.)
14,69*	ἤρξατο λέγειν	22,58	ἔφη (cf. v. 58b)
14,70	εἶ	22,59	ἦν (cf. Mk 14,67)
15,13	ἔκραξαν	23,21	ἐπεφώνουν λέγοντες
15,14		23,23	κατίσχυον (add.)
15,15	βουλόμενος	23,24	ἐπέκρινεν
15,22		23,32	ἤγοντο (add.)
15,24		[23,34]	ἔλεγεν (add.)
15,33	γενομένης	23,44	ἦν
15,39		23,47	ἐδόξαζεν (add.)
		48	ὑπέστρεφον (add.)
15,42		(23,54)	ἐπέφωσκεν (add.)
15,43**	ἦν προσδεχόμενος	23,51	προσεδέχετο

Diff. Mt in Lk 3,7 ἔλεγεν (εἶπεν) ; 4,1 ἤγετο (ἀνήχθη ; cf. Mk 1,12 ἐκβάλλει) ; 6,20 ἔλεγεν (λέγων).48 ἐβάθυνεν add. ; 7,2 ἤμελλεν (τελευτᾶν).4 παρεκάλουν add.6 ἐπορεύετο (cf. Mk 5,24 ἀπῆλθεν) ; 10,1 ἔλεγεν (λέγει) ; 11,14 ἦν add. ; 12,54 ἔλεγεν (16,2 εἶπεν) ; 14,16 ἐποίει (ἐποίησεν) ; 17,27 ἤσθιον, ἔπινον, ἐγάμουν, ἐγαμίζοντο (ἦσαν τρώγοντες...).28 ἤσθιον, ἔπινον, ἠγόραζον, ἐπώλουν, ἐφύτευον, ᾠκοδόμουν add. ; 19,14 ἐμίσουν add. (P).20 εἶχον (25,25 ἔκρυψα P).

Peculiar to Lk in 1,6.7ter.29.58bis.59.62.64.65.66.80ter ; 2,3.7bis.8.15.19.25bis.38bis.39ter.41.44. 51.52 ; 3,10.11.14.18.23bis ; 4,15.25.27.29.30 ; 5,2.3bis.6.10 ; 7,11,12ter.16.36.37.38ter.39bis.41. 44.45 ; 8,1.3 ; 10,1.18.30(P).31(P).39bis.40bis ; 13,1.4.6a.b(P).13.14.15.17bis.22 ; 14,2.7.12.25 ; 15,2.16bis(P).17(P).24bis(P).25(P).26(P).28bis(P).32(P) ; 16,1a.b(P).c(P).5(P).14bis.19bis(P).21(P) ; 18,1.2(P).3bis(P).4(P).11(P).13bis(P) ; 19,1.2.3.4.7 ; 21,38bis ; 23,5.8.9.12.27ter.40.42 ; 24,10.11. 14.15.16.21.26.28.30.32bis.35.37.51.

Note : ᾔδει(-σαν) 4,41 (= Mk) ; 6,8 (diff. Mk) : 12,39 ; 19,22 (= Mt) ; 2,49. For εἱστήκει, see No. 12.

Additional note : ἔφη

Matthew Luke agreements

Mk		Mt		Lk	
10,20	ἔφη	19,20	λέγει	18,21	εἶπεν
10,29	ἔφη	19,28	εἶπεν	18,29	εἶπεν
12,24	ἔφη	22,29	ἀποκριθεὶς εἶπεν	20,34	εἶπεν

The inverse

15,2	ἀποκριθεὶς λέγει	27,11	ἔφη	23,3	ἀποκριθεὶς ἔφη

Other instances of ἔφη in Mark (ἀποκριθεὶς εἶπεν in Matthew or Luke)

9,12	Mt 17,11	
14,29	26,33	
9,38	Lk 9,49	

Compare : λέγω in Mark († and Mt or Lk) and ἔφη in Matthew or Luke

Mk		Mt	
10,21 †		19,21	(cf. v. 20 and λέγει-ἔφη in v. 18)
11,33 †		21,27	
14,30 †		26,34	(cf. v. 33 par. Mk 14,29)
14,58		26,61	
15,14 †		27,23	
cf. 6,25	ἠτήσατο λέγουσα	14,8	φησίν
12,29	ἀπεκρίθη	22,37	ἔφη

Mk	Lk	
14,69 †	22,58a	(cf. also 58b, par. Mk 14,70 ἠρνεῖτο)
14,62 †	22,70	(but see v. 67 εἶπεν)

11n. *Additional Note : Other Changes of Tense*

A. Perfect in Mark and not in Matthew and Luke

Mk		Mt		Lk	
3,1	ἐξηραμμένην	12,10	ξηράν	6,6	ξηρά
6,14	ἐγήγερται	14,2	ἠγέρθη	9,7	ἠγέρθη
	(Kilpatrick : ἀνέστη)				
10,28	ἠκολουθήκαμεν	19,27	ἠκολουθήσαμεν	18,28	ἠκολουθήσαμεν
11,17	πεποιήκατε	21,13	ποιεῖτε	19,46	ἐποίησατε
15,46	ἦν λελατομημένον	27,60	ἐλατόμησεν	23,53	λαξευτῷ
15,47	τέθειται	27,62	τοῦ τάφου	23,55	ἐτέθη

B. Other changes

1,8	ἐβάπτισα	3,11	βαπτίζω	3,16	βαπτίζω
9,31	παραδίδοται	17,22	μέλλει παραδίδοσθαι	9,44	μέλλει παραδίδοσθαι
11,3	εἴπατε	21,3	ἐρεῖτε	19,31	ἐρεῖτε
13,2	καταλυθῇ	24,2	καταλυθήσεται	21,6	καταλυθήσεται

Comp. 10,13 impf., aor.   19,13 aor. (bis)   18,15 impf. (bis)

Other instances of perfect in Mark

1,6	ἦν ἐνδεδυμένος	Mt	3,4	εἶχεν τὸ ἔνδυμα αὐτοῦ
9,1	ἐληλυθυῖαν		16,28	ἐρχόμενον
9,13	ἐλήλυθεν		17,12	ἦλθεν
11,21	ἐξήρανται		21,20	ἐξηράνθη
14,44	δεδώκει		26,48	ἔδωκεν
15,10	παραδεδώκεισαν		27,18	παρέδωκαν
5,15	(τὸν δαιμονιζόμενον)	Lk	8,35	ἀφ' οὗ τὰ δαιμόνια ἐξῆλθεν
	τὸν ἐσχηκότα τὸν λεγιῶνα			
5,19	πεποίηκεν		8,39	ἐποίησεν
11,2 v.l.	κεκάθικεν		19,30	ἐκάθισεν
12,43 v.l.	βέβληκεν		21,3	ἔβαλεν

12. PERIPHRASTIC CONSTRUCTION (ἦν WITH PARTICIPLE) IN MARK AND NOT IN MATTHEW AND LUKE [175]

* Perfect participle
† Periphrastic construction in the parallel text of Matthew or Luke

Matthew/Luke agreement against Mark : diff. Mk 14,54.

Other (negative) agreements : diff. Mk 1,13 ; 2,6 ; 4,38 ; 9,4 ; 14,4.49 ; 15,26.43.46, as indicated in the following list.

Note the imperfect in Mt : diff. Mk 1,6.39 ; 4,38 ; (15,40) ; in Lk : diff. Mk 9,4.(7) ; 10,32 ; 15,43.

ἦν with Participle in Mark

1,6*	ἦν ἐνδεδυμένος καὶ ἔσθων	3,4	εἶχεν (τὸ ἔνδυμα αὐτοῦ) (ἡ δὲ τροφὴ) ἦν (αὐτοῦ)			
1,13	ἦν (ἐν τῇ ἐρήμῳ...)	4,1		4,1	(ἤγετο ἐν τῇ ἐρήμῳ)	
	πειραζόμενος		πειρασθῆναι		πειραζόμενος	
1,22	ἦν διδάσκων	7,29†	ἦν διδάσκων	(4,31†)	ἦν διδάσκων	
1,33*	ἦν ἐπισυνηγμένη					
1,39	(v.l. ἦν) ἦλθεν κηρύσσων	4,23	περιῆγεν	4,44†	ἦν κηρύσσων	
2,6	ἦσαν καθήμενοι			(5,17†)	ἦσαν καθήμενοι	
	καὶ διαλογιζόμενοι	9,3	εἶπαν	5,21	ἤρξαντο διαλογί-ζεσθαι λέγοντες	
2,18	ἦσαν νηστεύοντες					
4,38	ἦν (ἐν τῇ πρύμνῃ...) καθεύδων	8,24	ἐκάθευδεν	(8,23)	ἀφύπνωσεν	
5,5	(ἐν τοῖς μνήμασιν...) ἦν κράζων καὶ κατακόπτων					
5,11	ἦν (ἐκεῖ πρὸς τῷ ὄρει) βοσκομένη	8,30†	ἦν (μακρὰν ἀπ' αὐτῶν) βοσκομένη	8,32†	ἦν (ἐκεῖ) βοσκομένη (ἐν τῷ ὄρει) v.l. βοσκομένων	

---

175. Schmid(9), pp. 40-41 ; cf. Turner(8,1), pp. 349-351. Comp. Krenkel, pp. 324-326.335 ; Moulton-Geden, *Concordance, s.v.* ἤμην (1) and ἔσομαι (1) : he includes Lk 3,23 and 4,33 ; Mt 8,30 but not 27,61 ; Winer, § 45,5 : ἦν is not the mere auxiliary in Mk 5,5.11 ; 10,32 ; 14,4 ; and the participle is adjectival in 10,22 ; Larfeld, pp. 220-223 : " εἶναι c. part. praes. " : 13 cases in Mk (he includes 7,15 and 19,25, but 1,13.39 ; 4,38 ; 5,5.11 ; 10,32a ; 14,49 ; 15,40 are excluded), 4 in Mt, 30 in Lk, 24 in Acts (but Lk 3,23 ἦν... ἐτῶν ; 12,35 ἔστωσαν ; 17,7.35 are included) ; Hawkins, p. 51 : Mk 16, Mt 4, Lk 28, Acts 24 (with any participles : 22,6,45,36). Comp. Wernle, p. 147 (Mt) ; Allen, p. XXII ; Cadbury, pp. 161-162 (Lk) ; Lagrange, *Luc*, pp. CV-CVI ; Howard, pp. 451-452 (p. 452 : list of 16 instances ; 1,6.22.39 are not mentioned) ; Taylor, p. 45 ; Blass-Debrunner, § 353,1 ; Zerwick, p. 117 ; G. BJÖRCK, *HN ΔΙΔΑΣΚΩΝ. Die periphrastischen Konstruktionen im Griechischen*, Uppsala, 1940 ; Kilpatrick, pp. 8-9 (he includes 2,4 ; 3,1! ; 5,40) ; Doudna, p. 109 ; L. HARTMAN, *Testimonium Linguae* (see n. 165), pp. 12-13.23-27.

6,52*	ἦν πεπωρωμένη				
9,4	ἦσαν συλλαλοῦντες	17,3	συλλαλοῦντες	9,30	συνελάλουν
10,22	ἦν ἔχων (κτήματα)	19,22†	ἦν ἔχων (κτήματα)	18,23	ἦν πλούσιος
10,32	ἦσαν (ἐν τῇ ὁδῷ) ἀναβαίνοντες	20,17	μέλλων ἀναβαίνειν (v.l. ἀναβαίνων)		
10,32	ἦν προάγων			(19,28)	ἐπορεύετο ἔμπροσθεν ἀναβαίνων
14,4	ἦσαν ἀγανακτοῦντες	26,8	ἠγανάκτησαν λέγοντες	(7,39)	εἶπεν... λέγων
14,40	ἦσαν καταβαρυνόμενοι	26,43*†	ἦσαν βεβαρημένοι	(cf. 9,32*†)	ἦσαν βεβαρημένοι
14,49	ἤμην (πρὸς ὑμᾶς ἐν τῷ ἱερῷ) διδάσκων	26,55	(ἐν τῷ ἱερῷ) ἐκαθεζόμην διδάσκων	22,53	ὄντος μου μεθ' ὑμῶν ἐν τῷ ἱερῷ
14,54	ἦν συγκαθήμενος καὶ θερμαινόμενος	26,58	ἐκάθητο	22,55	ἐκάθητο
15,7*	ἦν δεδεμένος	27,16	εἶχον δέσμιον	(cf. 23,19)	ἦν βληθείς
15,26*	ἦν (ἡ ἐπιγραφή) ἐπιγεγραμμένη	27,37	ἐπέθηκαν... γεγραμμένην	(23,28)	ἦν (ἐπιγραφή)
15,40	ἦσαν (... ἀπὸ μακρόθεν) θεωροῦσαι	27,55†	ἦσαν (ἐκεῖ) θεωροῦσαι	23,49	εἱστήκεισαν ὁρῶσαι
15,43	ἦν προσδεχόμενος	27,57	ἐμαθητεύθη	23,51	προσεδέχετο
15,46*	ἦν λελατομημένον	27,60	ἐλατόμησεν	23,53	λαξευτῷ

Variant readings (Kilpatrick)

2,4   ἦν κατακείμενος (D)   Lk 5,19 diff. (cf. 25 ἐφ' ὃ κατέκειτο)
      (instead of κατέκειτο)
5,40 ἦν (add. :) ἀνακείμενον (TR S)
      (v.l. κατακείμενον)

Other Instances of εἶναι with Participle

Mk		Mt		Lk	
7,15	ἐστιν... εἰσπορευόμενον	15,11	τὸ εἰσερχόμενον		
13,13	ἔσεσθε μισούμενοι	24,9†	ἔσεσθε μισούμενοι	21,17†	ἔσεσθε μισούμενοι
		(10,22†)	ἔσεσθε μισούμενοι		
13,25	ἔσονται πίπτοντες	24,29	πεσοῦνται	21,25	ἔσονται σημεῖα

Note : ἐγένετο with participle

1,4	ἐγένετο (ἐν τῇ ἐρήμῳ) κηρύσσων v.l. ἐγένετο βαπτίζων καὶ κηρύσσων	3,1	παραγίνεται κηρύσσων (ἐν τῇ ἐρήμῳ)	3,3	ἦλθεν (εἰς...) κηρύσσων
9,3	ἐγένετο στίλβοντα (λευκά)	17,2	ἐγένετο λευκά	9,29	ἐγένετο λευκὸς ἐξαστράπτων
9,7	ἐγένετο ἐπισκιάζουσα	17,5	ἐπεσκίασεν	9,34	ἐγένετο καὶ ἐπεσκίαζεν

ἦν with Participle in Matthew

Par. Mk 1,22 ; 5,11 ; 10,22 ; 14,40* ; 15,40.

Diff. Mk		Mt	
2,26	ἔξεστιν	12,4	ἐξὸν ἦν (cf. 3,15 πρέπον ἐστίν)
6,34	ἦσαν (ὡς)	9,36*	ἦσαν ἐσκυλμένοι καὶ ἐριμμένοι (ὡσεί)

Other instances in Mt :

24,38 ἦσαν τρώγοντες καὶ πίνοντες, γαμοῦντες καὶ γαμίζοντες (Lk 17,27 ἤσθιον, ἔπινον, ἐγάμουν, ἐγαμί-
      ζοντο)
5,25 ἴσθι εὐνοῶν (cf. Lk 12,57-58)
16,19* ἔσται δεδεμένον, ἔσται λελυμένον ; 18,18* ἔσται δεδεμένα, ἔσται λελυμένα

ἦν with Participle in Luke

Par. Mk 1,22.39 ; 2,6 ; 5,11 ; 14,40* ; 15,40.

Diff. Mk		Lk	
1,16	παράγων (παρά...)	(5,1)	ἦν ἑστὼς (παρά...)
1,30	κατέκειτο πυρέσσουσα	4,38	ἦν συνεχομένη (πυρετῷ)
1,45	(ἐπ' ἐρήμοις τόποις) ἦν	5,16	ἦν ὑποχωρῶν (ἐν ταῖς ἐρήμοις) καὶ προσευχόμενος
2,2a	συνήχθησαν	5,17c*	ἦσαν ἐληλυθότες
2,2b	ἐλάλει	5,17a	ἦν διδάσκων
2,15	συνανέκειντο	5,29	ἦσαν κατακείμενοι
3,13		6,12	ἦν διανυκτερεύων (add.)
5,21		8,40	ἦσαν προσδοκῶντες (add.)
11,17	ἐδίδασκεν	19,47	ἦν διδάσκων (ἐν τῷ ἱερῷ) cf. 21,37 ἦν (ἐν τῷ ἱερῷ) διδάσκων
15,46	(cf. Mt 27,60 καίνῳ)	23,53	ἦν κείμενος
1,17	ποιήσω... γενέσθαι ἁλεεῖς	5,10	ἔσῃ ζωγρῶν
14,62	ὄψεσθε καθήμενον	22,69	ἔσται καθήμενος
8,27	(cf. 6,46 ἀπῆλθεν προσεύξασθαι)	9,18	ἐν τῷ εἶναι αὐτὸν προσευχόμενον (add.)

Other instances in Luke : 1,10.21.22 ; 2,33.51 ; 4,20 ; 9,53 ; 11,14 (diff. Mt 12,22) ; 13,10.11 ;
14,1 (cf. Mk 3,2) ; 15,1 ; 23,8 ; 24,13.32.

— 1,20 (ἔσῃ) ; 11,1 (ἐν τῷ εἶναι) ; 12,52 (ἔσονται, diff. Mt 10,35) ; 19,17 (ἴσθι) ; 21,24 (ἔσται).

— ἦν with perfect participle : 1,7 ; 2,26 (pluperf.) ; 4,16 (pluperf.) ; 4,17 ; 5,17 (pluperf.) ; 5,18 ;
8,2 (pluperf.) ; 9,32.45 ; 15,24 (pluperf.) ; 18,34 ; 23,51 (pluperf.) ; 23,55 (pluperf.).

Note : εἰστήκει(-σαν) with ptc. in Lk 23,10.35.49 (cf. Mk 15,40) ; Mt 12,46 (diff. Mk) ; comp. 13,2.

13. ἤρξατο WITH INFINITIVE IN MARK AND NOT IN MATTHEW AND LUKE [176]

† ἤρξατο with infinitive in the parallel text of Matthew or Luke

Matthew/Luke agreements against Mark

(1) aorist : diff. Mk 5,17 ; 6,7 ; 10,28.32.47 ; 13,5.
(2) participle : diff. Mk (10,47, cf. aorist) ; 14,65b.

---

176. Schmid(8), p. 40 ; cf. Turner(8,2), pp. 352-353, and J. W. Hunkin, '" Pleonastic " ἄρχομαι
in the New Testament ', JTS 25 (1924) 390-402. Comp. Wernle, p. 147 ; Allen, pp. XXI-XXII ;
Cadbury, pp. 162-163 ; Lagrange, Matthieu, pp. XCI-CXII ; Larfeld, p. 234 ; Howard, pp. 455-456
(list) ; Taylor, pp. 48 and 63-64 ; Schürmann III, p. 8, n. 28.

(3) aorist in Mt and imperfect in Lk : diff. Mk 6,34 ; 14,65a.
(4) present in Mt and imperfect (ἔφη) in Lk : diff. Mk 14,69.

Other instances of

(1) aorist, in Mt only : diff. Mk 6,55 ; 8,11(†) ; 10,41 ; 11,15† ; in Lk only : diff. Mk 14,71†.
(2) participle, in Mt only : diff. Mk 15,18(+ aor.) ; in Lk only : diff. Mk 5,20 ; 8,31† ; 14,33†.
(3) imperfect, in Mt only : diff. Mk 4,1 ; 6,2† ; in Lk only : diff. Mk 1,45 ; 2,23†.

ἤρξατο with Infinitive in Mark

Mk		Mt		Lk	
1,45	ἤρξατο κηρύσσειν καὶ διαφημίζειν			5,15	διήρχετο
2,23	ἤρξαντο ὁδὸν ποιεῖν (τίλλοντες)	12,1†	ἤρξαντο τίλλειν καὶ ἐσθίειν	6,1	ἔτιλλον καὶ ἤσθιον
4,1	ἤρξατο διδάσκειν	13,1	ἐκάθητο		
5,17	ἤρξαντο παρακαλεῖν	8,34	παρεκάλεσαν	8,37	ἠρώτησεν
5,20	ἤρξατο κηρύσσειν			8,39	κηρύσσων (cf. No. 3b)
6,2	ἤρξατο διδάσκειν	13,54	ἐδίδασκεν	(4,21†)	ἤρξατο λέγειν
6,7	ἤρξατο ἀποστέλλειν	(10,5)	ἀπέστειλεν	9,2	ἀπέστειλεν
6,34	ἤρξατο διδάσκειν	14,14	(ἐθεράπευσεν)	9,11	ἐλάλει (καὶ ἰᾶτο)
6,55	ἤρξαντο περιφέρειν	14,35	προσήνεγκαν		
8,11	ἤρξαντο συζητεῖν	16,1	ἐπηρώτησαν	(11,29†)	ἤρξαντο λέγειν
8,31	ἤρξατο διδάσκειν	16,21†	ἤρξατο δεικνύειν	9,22	εἰπών (cf. No. 3b)
8,32	ἤρξατο ἐπιτιμᾶν	16,22†	ἤρξατο ἐπιτιμᾶν		
10,28	ἤρξατο λέγειν	19,27	εἶπεν	18,28	εἶπεν
10,32	ἤρξατο λέγειν	20,17	εἶπεν	18,31	εἶπεν
10,41	ἤρξαντο ἀγανακτεῖν	20,24	ἠγανάκτησαν	(22,24)	ἐγένετο φιλονεικία
10,47	ἤρξατο κράζειν καὶ λέγειν	20,30	ἔκραξαν λέγοντες	18,38	ἐβόησεν λέγων
11,15	ἤρξατο ἐκβάλλειν	21,12	ἐξέβαλεν	19,45†	ἤρξατο ἐκβάλλειν
12,1	ἤρξατο λαλεῖν	21,33	(ἀκούσατε)	20,9†	ἤρξατο λέγειν
13,5	ἤρξατο λέγειν	24,4	εἶπεν	21,8	εἶπεν
14,19	ἤρξαντο λυπεῖσθαι καὶ λέγειν	26,22†	λυπούμενοι ἤρξαντο λέγειν	(22,23†)	ἤρξαντο συζητεῖν
14,33	ἤρξατο ἐκθαμβεῖσθαι καὶ ἀδημονεῖν	26,37†	ἤρξατο λυπεῖσθαι καὶ ἀδημονεῖν	(22,44)	γενόμενος ἐν ἀγωνίᾳ
14,65	ἤρξαντο ἐμπτύειν καὶ περικαλύπτειν καὶ κολαφίζειν καὶ λέγειν	26,67	ἐνέπτυσαν καὶ ἐκολάφισαν (ἐρράπισαν) (68) λέγοντες	22,63 64	ἐνέπαιζον καὶ περικαλύψαντες ἐπηρώτων λέγοντες
14,69	ἤρξατο λέγειν	26,71	λέγει	22,57	ἔφη
14,71	ἤρξατο ἀναθεματίζειν καὶ ὀμνύναι	26,74†	ἤρξατο καταθεματίζειν καὶ ὀμνύειν	22,60	εἶπεν
15,8	ἤρξατο αἰτεῖσθαι				
15,18	ἤρξαντο ἀσπάζεσθαι	27,29	(ἐνέπαιξαν) λέγοντες		

ἤρξατο *with Infinitive in Matthew*

Par. Mk 2,23 ; 8,31.32 ; 14,19.33.71.

Other instances :

Mt

4,17 ἤρξατο κηρύσσειν καὶ λέγειν   Mk 1,14 κηρύσσων καὶ λέγων
     (ἀπὸ τότε cf. 16,21)
11,7 ἤρξατο λέγειν   Lk 7,24 ἤρξατο λέγειν
11,20 ἤρξατο ὀνειδίζειν

ἄρχομαι in other tenses (in sayings) :

14,30 ἀρξάμενος ; 18,24 ἀρξαμένου ; 24,49 ἄρξηται (= Lk 12,45)

ἤρξατο *with Infinitive in Luke*

Par. Mk 11,15 ; 12,1 ; 14,19 ; see also 6,2 ; 8,11 ; par. Mt : Lk 7,24.

Other instances :

Mk	Lk
2,6 ἦσαν... διαλογιζόμενοι	5,21 ἤρξαντο διαλογίζεσθαι λέγοντες
6,35 ὥρας πολλῆς γενομένης	9,12 ἤρξατο κλίνειν
11,9	19,37 ἤρξαντο αἰνεῖν (add.)
15,3 κατηγόρουν	23,2 ἤρξαντο κατηγορεῖν

Lk 14,18 ἤρξαντο παραιτεῖσθαι (diff. Mt 22,5)
Lk 7,15.38.49 ; 11,53 ; 12,1 ; 14,30 ; 15,14.24.

ἄρχομαι in other tenses (in sayings) :

3,8 ἄρξησθε (δόξητε) ; 12,45 (= Mt) ; 13,25 ἄρξησθε ; 13,26 ἄρξεσθε ; 14,9 ἄρξῃ ; 14,29 ἄρξωνται ; 21,28 ἀρχομένων ; 23,30 ἄρξονται.

Acts 1,1 ; 2,4 ; 18,26 ; 24,2 ; 27,35. Comp. Jn 13,5.

14. GENITIVE ABSOLUTE IN MARK AND NOT IN MATTHEW OR LUKE [177]

* The participle of the verb γίνομαι or (*) εἰμί.
† Genitive absolute in the parallel text of Matthew and Luke

Conjunctive participle (ἐμβάς) : diff. Mk 5,18.
Negative agreements : diff. Mk 5,21 ; 14,66 ; 15,33.

Mk		Mt	Lk	
1,32*	ὀψίας δὲ γενομένης	8,16†	4,40	om. (40a †)
4,17*	εἶτα γενομένης θλίψεως ἢ διωγμοῦ	13,21†	8,13	diff.

177. See n. 165. Comp. Larfeld, pp. 224-225.

Mk		Mt		Lk	
4,35*	... ὀψίας γενομένης	8,18	om.	8,22	om.
5,2	καὶ ἐξελθόντος αὐτοῦ	8,28	om. (28a †)	8,27	ptc.
5,18	καὶ ἐμβαίνοντος αὐτοῦ	9,1	ptc.	8,37	ptc.
5,21	καὶ διαπεράσαντος τοῦ Ἰησοῦ	9,1	diff.	8,40	diff.
5,35	ἔτι αὐτοῦ λαλοῦντος	(cf. 9,18†)		8,49†	
6,2*	καὶ γενομένου σαββάτου	13,54	om.	(4,16)	diff.
6,21*	καὶ γενομένης ἡμέρας εὐκαίρου	14,6a	dat.		
6,22	καὶ εἰσελθούσης τῆς θυγατρὸς...	14,6b	om.		
	καὶ ὀρχησαμένης		diff.		
6,35*	καὶ ἤδη ὥρας πολλῆς γενομένης	14,15†		9,12	diff.
6,47*	καὶ ὀψίας γενομένης	14,23†			
6,54	καὶ ἐξελθόντων αὐτῶν	14,53	om.		
8,1(*)	... πολλοῦ ὄχλου ὄντος	15,32	om.		
	καὶ μὴ ἐχόντων τί φάγωσιν				
9,9	καὶ καταβαινόντων αὐτῶν	17,9†		(9,37†)	
9,28	καὶ εἰσελθόντος αὐτοῦ	17,19	om.		
10,17	καὶ ἐκπορευομένου αὐτοῦ	(19,15)	diff.	18,18	om.
10,46	καὶ ἐκπορευομένου αὐτοῦ	20,29†		18,35	om.
11,11(*)	... ὀψὲ ἤδη οὔσης τῆς ὥρας	21,17	om.		
11,12	... ἐξελθόντων αὐτῶν	21,18	diff.		
11,27	καὶ... περιπατοῦντος αὐτοῦ	21,36b	om. (23a †)	20,1†	
13,1	καὶ ἐκπορευομένου αὐτοῦ	24,1	ptc.	21,5	om.
13,3	καὶ καθημένου αὐτοῦ	24,3†		21,7	om.
14,3a(*)	καὶ ὄντος αὐτοῦ	26,6†			
14,3b	κατακειμένου αὐτοῦ	(26,7)	ptc.		
14,17	καὶ ὀψίας γενομένης	26,20†		22,14	diff.
14,18	καὶ ἀνακειμένων αὐτῶν	(26,20)	diff.	(22,14)	diff.
	καὶ ἐσθιόντων	26,21†			
14,22	καὶ ἐσθιόντων αὐτῶν	26,26†		22,19	om.
14,43	καὶ εὐθὺς ἔτι αὐτοῦ λαλοῦντος	26,47†		22,47†	
14,66(*)	καὶ ὄντος τοῦ Πέτρου	26,69	diff.	22,56	ptc.
15,33*	καὶ γενομένης ὥρας ἕκτης	27,45	diff.	23,44	diff.
15,42*	καὶ ἤδη ὀψίας γενομένης	27,57†		(23,54)	diff.
16,1*	καὶ διαγενομένου τοῦ σαββάτου	28,1	diff.	(23,56b)	diff.
16,2	... ἀνατείλαντος τοῦ ἡλίου	28,1	om.	24,1	om.

(14) The inverse : diff. Mk 9,7(add.).30.

(1) Genitive absolute in Matthew and not in Mark
Instead of a finite verb with καί : diff. Mk 6,51 ; 9,33 ; 11,11 ; 15,9 (see No. **3c**).
Other instances diff. Mk :

Mk	Mt		Mk	Mt	
(1,21)	5,1	add.	5,21	9,18	add. (cf. Mk 5,35)
2,15	9,10		9,14	17,14	
3,31	12,46	add.	12,35	22,41	add.
4,6	13,6		14,56	26,60	
4,15	13,19	(cf. note)	15,1	27,1	
5,1	8,28	(cf. Mk 5,2)			

(2) Genitive absolute in Luke and not in Mark
Instead of a finite verb with καί : diff. Mk 1,10 ; 4,2 ; 9,20 ; 10,51 ; 11,5 ; 12,38 ; 13,2 ; 14,13.49 ; 16,6 (see No. **3c**).

Other instances diff. Mk :

Mk	Lk			Mk	Lk	
1,13	4,2	add.		13,25	21,26	add.
1,32b	4,40	(cf. Mk 1,32a)		13,27	21,28	add.
1,35	4,42			14,54	22,55	
4,38	(8,23)	add.		14,70	22,59	
5,31	8,45	add.		14,72	22,60	
11,8	19,36			15,33	23,45	add. (cf. No. 3c 23,44)
11,9	19,37	add.				

14n. Note : Relative Clause in Mark and Participle in Matthew and Luke

Mk	Mt	Lk
4,9 ὃς ἔχει ὦτα	13,9 ὁ ἔχων ὦτα	8,8 ὁ ἔχων ὦτα
4,15 ὅταν ἀκούσωσιν	13,19 πάντος ἀκούοντος	8,12 οἱ ἀκούσαντες
4,20 οἵτινες ἀκούουσιν... καί	13,23 ὁ ἀκούων... καί	8,15 οἵτινες...ἀκούσαντες
4,23 εἴ τις ἔχει ὦτα	(11,15) ὁ ἔχων ὦτα	(14,35) ὁ ἔχων ὦτα

Compare the use of the substantive :

2,8 ὅτι... διαλογίζονται	9,4 τὰς ἐνθυμήσεις αὐτῶν	5,22 τοὺς διαλογισμοὺς αὐτῶν
3,14 ἵνα ἀποστέλλῃ αὐτούς	(10,2) τῶν... ἀποστόλων	6,13 οὓς καὶ ἀποστόλους ὠνόμασεν
6,36 τί φάγωσιν	14,15 βρώματα	9,12 ἐπισιτισμόν (9,13) βρώματα

15. λέγων /λέγοντες IN MATTHEW AND LUKE AND NOT IN MARK [178]

Instead of a finite verb with καί : diff. Mk 1,41 (Lk *v.l.* εἰπών) ; 4,38.41 ; 10,47 ; 11,2 (*v.l.* εἰπών) ; 14,24.65 ; the inverse : diff. Mk 6,2. See No. **3**.
Other instances

Mk	Mt	Lk
9,7 (ἐγένετο) φωνή	17,5 (καὶ ἰδού) φωνὴ λέγουσα	9,35 φωνὴ (ἐγένετο) λέγουσα
9,17 ἀπεκρίθη	17,15 (προσῆλθεν) λέγων	9,38 ἐβόησεν λέγων
11,9 ἔκραζον	21,9 ἔκραζον λέγοντες	19,38 ἤρξαντο αἰνεῖν... λέγοντες
11,28 ἔλεγον	(21,15) κράζοντας καὶ λέγοντας	20,2 εἶπαν λέγοντες
	21,23 λέγοντες	

---

178. Schmid(33d), pp. 77-78 ; cf. Turner(10,5), pp. 359-361 ; comp. Cadbury, p. 170 ; Schürmann I, p. 85. See also n. 164.

Mk	Mt	Lk
12,14 (ἐλθόντες) λέγουσιν	22,16 (ἀποστέλλουσιν) λέγοντας	20,21 (ἐπηρώτησαν) λέγοντες
13,3 ἐπηρώτα	24,3 (προσῆλθον) λέγοντες	21,7 ἐπηρώτησαν λέγοντες
14,4 ἦσαν ἀγανακτοῦντες	26,8 ἠγανάκτησαν λέγοντες	(7,39) εἶπεν λέγων
15,2 ἐπηρώτησεν	27,11 ἐπηρώτησεν λέγων	23,3 ἐπηρώτησεν λέγων
15,39 εἶπεν	27,54 (ἐφοβήθησαν) λέγοντες	23,47 (ἐδόξαζεν τὸν θεὸν) λέγων

(15) The inverse

8,28 εἶπαν λέγοντες	16,14 εἶπαν	9,19 ἀποκριθέντες εἶπαν
14,36 (προσηύχετο... καὶ) ἔλεγεν	26,39 (προσευχόμενος καὶ) λέγων	22,(42-)43 (προσηύχετο) λέγων

λέγων /λέγοντες *in Matthew only*

Instead of a finite verb with καί :

diff. Mk 1,44 ; 2,18 ; 4,2 ; 6,8.49.50 ; 7,5 (Mk ἐπερωτῶσιν) ; 7,26 (Mk ἠρώτα) ; 11,28 (cf. *infra* Lk) ; 12,14 ; 14,67. See No. **3a**.

Other instances diff. Mk :

Mk	Mt
1,11 φωνὴ [ἐγένετο]	3,17 καὶ ἰδοὺ φωνὴ... λέγουσα
3,2 παρετήρουν	12,10 ἐπηρώτησαν λέγοντες (dir.) cf. Lk 14,3 λέγων
4,26 ἔλεγεν	13,24 παρέθηκεν λέγων
4,31 ἔλεγεν	13,31 παρέθηκεν λέγων
5,7 κράξας λέγει (1,24-25 ἀνέκραξεν λέγων)	8,29 ἔκραξαν λέγοντες
6,35 προσελθόντες ἔλεγον	14,15 προσῆλθον λέγοντες
6,52 ἐξίσταντο	14,33 προσεκύνησαν λέγοντες
7,6 (ἐπροφήτευσεν) ὡς γέγραπται	15,7 ἐπροφήτευσεν λέγων
8,16 διελογίζοντο	16,7 διελογίζοντο λέγοντες
8,32 ἤρξατο ἐπιτιμᾶν	16,22 ἤρξατο ἐπιτιμᾶν λέγων
9,9 διεστείλατο	17,9 ἐνετείλατο λέγων
9,34 διελέχθησαν	18,1 προσῆλθον λέγοντες
10,2 προσελθόντες ἐπηρώτων πειράζοντες	19,3 προσῆλθον πειράζοντες καὶ λέγοντες
10,48 ἔκραζεν	20,31 ἔκραξαν λέγοντες
	(9,27) ἠκολούθησαν κράζοντες καὶ λέγοντες
10,52 εἶπεν (Mt 20,34 ἥψατο)	(9,29) ἥψατο λέγων
11,21 ἀναμνησθεὶς λέγει	21,20 ἐθαύμασαν λέγοντες
12,1 ἤρξατο λαλεῖν	(22,1) εἶπεν λέγων

Mk		Mt	
12,18	οἵτινες λέγουσιν	22,23	προσῆλθον λέγοντες (cf. Lk 20,27)
12,35	ἔλεγεν διδάσκων	22,42	ἐπηρώτησεν λέγων
12,36	εἶπεν	22,43	καλεῖ λέγων
12,38	ἔλεγεν	23,2	ἐλάλησεν λέγων
14,12	λέγουσιν	26,17	προσῆλθον λέγοντες
14,63	διαρρήξας	26,65	διέρρηξεν λέγων
15,14	ἔκραξαν	27,23	ἔκραζον λέγοντες
15,18	ἤρξαντο ἀσπάζεσθαι	27,29	ἐνέπαιξαν λέγοντες
15,34	ἐβόησεν	27,46	ἀνεβόησεν λέγων

The inverse

Mk		Mt	
1,15	κηρύσσων [καὶ λέγων]	4,17	ἤρξατο κηρύσσειν καὶ λέγειν (but see 3,2)
8,15	διεστέλλετο λέγων	16,6	εἶπεν (Lk 12,1 ἤρξατο λέγειν)
10,35	λέγοντες	20,20	αἰτοῦσα (with accusative)
14,57	ἐψευδομαρτύρουν λέγοντες	26,61	προσελθόντες εἶπαν
14,58	αὐτοῦ λέγοντος	26,61	ἔφη
14,60	ἐπηρώτησεν λέγων	26,62	εἶπεν
15,4	ἐπηρώτα (λέγων v.l.)	27,13	λέγει
15,9	ἀπεκρίθη λέγων	27,17	εἶπεν
15,36	(ἐπότιζεν) λέγων	27,49	(οἱ δὲ λοιποὶ) εἶπαν

λέγων /λέγοντες in Luke only

Instead of a finite verb with καί :

diff. Mk 8,31 (εἰπών) ; 10,14 ; 11,17 ; 14,13 (εἰπών) ; 14,22.61. See No. **3b** ; for 14,22 see No. **3**.

Other instances diff. Mk :

Mk		Lk	
1,25	ἐπετίμησεν [λέγων]	4,35	ἐπετίμησεν λέγων
2,6	ἦσαν διαλογιζόμενοι	5,21	ἤρξαντο διαλογίζεσθαι λέγοντες
2,16	ἔλεγον	5,30	ἐγόγγυζον λέγοντες
		(15,2)	διεγόγγυζον λέγοντες
3,4	λέγει (εἶπεν Mt 12,11 ; Lk 6,9)	(14,5)	εἶπεν λέγων
4,9	ἔλεγεν	8,8	ταῦτα λέγων εἶπεν
5,9	ἐπηρώτα	8,30 v.l.	ἐπηρώτησεν (λέγων)
5,19	ἀλλὰ λέγει	8,38	ἀπέλυσεν λέγων
9,7	(add. Mt 17,5 ἔτι αὐτοῦ λαλοῦντος)	9,34	ταῦτα δὲ αὐτοῦ λέγοντος, cf. No. **(14)**
10,17	ἐπηρώτα	18,18	ἐπηρώτησεν λέγων
11,28	ἔλεγον	20,2	εἶπαν λέγοντες
12,7	εἶπαν	20,14	διελογίζοντο λέγοντες
12,14	λέγουσιν	20,21	ἐπηρώτησαν λέγοντες
12,18	οἵτινες λέγουσιν	20,27	οἱ ἀντιλέγοντες (v.l. λέγοντες)
12,28	προσελθὼν ἐπηρώτησεν	(10,25)	ἀνέστη λέγων
13,1	λέγει	21,5	τινων λεγόντων
14,14	εἴπατε	22,11 v.l.	ἐρεῖτε (λέγοντες)
14,70	ἔλεγον	22,59	διϊσχυρίζετο λέγων
15,3	κατηγόρουν	(23,2)	ἤρξαντο κατηγορεῖν λέγοντες (dir.)
15,11	ἀνέσεισαν	23,18	ἀνέκραγον λέγοντες

Mk		Lk	
15,13	ἔκραξαν	23,21	λέγοντες
15,31	ἔλεγον	23,35	λέγοντες
16,7	εἶπεν	24,6	ἐλάλησεν λέγων

The inverse : λέγων in Mark (and Matthew) and not in Luke

Mk		Mt	Lk	
1,24	ἀνέκραξεν λέγων	(cf. 8,29)	4,33	ἀνέκραξεν (φωνῇ μεγάλῃ)
5,12	παρεκάλεσαν λέγοντες	8,31	8,32	παρεκάλεσαν (indirect)
5,23	παρακαλεῖ λέγων	9,18	8,41	παρεκάλει (indirect)
10,26	ἐξεπλήσσοντο λέγοντες	19,25	18,26	εἶπαν
12,6	λέγων	21,37	20,13	εἶπεν (var.)
12,26	εἶπεν λέγων	22,31	20,37	λέγει

Other instances of λέγων in Mark : 1,7.25(v.l.).27.40; 2,12; 3,11; 5,35; 9,14; 11,31; 12,18; 13,5; 14,44.68 ; 15,29.

15n. Note : λεγόμενος in Matthew

2,14	Λευίν	9,9	Μαθθαῖον λεγόμενον	5,27	ὀνόματι Λευίν
3,16	ἐπέθηκεν ὄνομα	10,2	ὁ λεγόμενος	6,14	ὃν... ὠνόμασεν
14,10	Ἰούδας Ἰσκαριώθ	26,14	ὁ λεγόμενος Ἰ.Ἰ.	22,3	Ἰ. τὸν καλούμενον Ἰ.
15,22	τὸν Γολγοθὰν τόπον	27,33	τόπον λεγόμενον Γολγοθά	23,33	τὸν τόπον τὸν καλούμενον Κρανίον

Compare

15,43	Ἰωσήφ	27,57	τοὔνομα Ἰωσήφ	23,50	ὀνόματι Ἰωσήφ

16. ἀποκριθείς IN MARK AND NOT IN MATTHEW AND LUKE [179]

* ἀποκριθεὶς εἶπεν

Mk		Mt		Lk	
6,37*	ἀποκριθεὶς εἶπεν	14,16	εἶπεν	9,13	εἶπεν
10,51*	ἀποκριθεὶς εἶπεν	20,32	εἶπεν	18,40	ἐπηρώτησεν
12,35	ἀποκριθεὶς ἔλεγεν	22,41	ἐπηρώτησεν	20,41	εἶπεν
14,48*	ἀποκριθεὶς εἶπεν	26,55	εἶπεν (52 λέγει)	22,52	εἶπεν

(16) The inverse

11,29	εἶπεν	21,24*	ἀποκριθεὶς εἶπεν	20,3*	ἀποκριθεὶς εἶπεν

ἀποκριθείς in Mark and not in Matthew

10,24	ἀποκριθεὶς λέγει	19,24			
11,14	ἀποκριθεὶς εἶπεν	21,19	λέγει		
15,2	ἀποκριθεὶς λέγει	27,11	ἔφη	23,3	ἀποκριθεὶς ἔφη

---

179. Schmid(33e), p. 78 ; comp. Cadbury, pp. 170-171.

The inverse

Mk		Mt		Mk		Mt
4,11	εἶπεν	13,11*		10,38	εἶπεν	20,22*
7,6	εἶπεν	15,3*		13,2	εἶπεν	24,2*
7,17	ἐπηρώτησεν	15,15*		13,5	ἤρξατο λέγειν	24,4*
7,27	ἔλεγεν	15,26*		14,20	εἶπεν	26,23*
8,12	λέγει	16,2*		14,29	ἔφη	26,33*
9,12	ἔφη	17,11*		14,64	κατέκριναν	26,66* (plur.)
10,28	ἤρξατο λέγειν	19,27*		16,6	λέγει	28,5*

ἀποκριθείς in Mark and not in Luke

Mk		Mt		Lk	
9,5	ἀποκριθεὶς λέγει	17,4*		9,33	εἶπεν
11,33	ἀποκριθέντες λέγουσιν	21,27* (plur.)		20,7	ἀπεκρίθησαν (!)
15,12	ἀποκριθεὶς ἔλεγεν	27,11*		23,20	προσεφώνησεν

The inverse

Mk		Lk		Mk		Lk	
2,8	λέγει	5,22*		9,38	ἔφη	9,49*	
2,17	λέγει	5,31*		12,29	ἀπεκρίθη	(10,27)*	
2,25	λέγει	6,3*		12,34	ἀπεκρίθη	(20,39)*	
3,2	λέγει	(14,3)* (6,9 εἶπεν)		15,2	λέγει	23,3 ἀποκριθεὶς ἔφη	
8,28	εἶπαν λέγοντες	9,19* (plur.)				(cf. Mt 27,11 ἔφη)	

Note : ἀποκριθεὶς λέγει in Mark and ἀποκριθεὶς εἶπεν in Matthew /Luke

Mk	Mt	Lk		Mk	Mt	Lk
3,33	12,48	8,21		9,19	17,17	9,41
8,29	16,16	9,20		11,22	21,22	
9,5	17,4	9,41		11,33 (plur.)	21,27	(20,7 ἀπεκρίθησαν)

Comp. Mk 10,3 ἀποκριθεὶς εἶπεν Mt 19,4*
    15,12 ἀποκριθεὶς ἔλεγεν   27,21*

16n. Additional Note : ἀποκρίνομαι and λέγω

Matthew /Luke agreements

Mk		Mt		Lk	
9,17	ἀπεκρίθη	17,15	λέγων	9,38	ἐβόησεν λέγων
11,29	ἀποκρίθητε	21,24	εἴπητε	20,3	εἴπατε (but see 22,68)
	(cf. 11,30 ἀποκρίθητε)				
15,9	ἀπεκρίθη... λέγων	27,17	εἶπεν	23,14	εἶπεν

ἀποκρίνομαι in Mark and λέγω in Matthew or Luke

7,28 (+ καὶ λέγει)	Mt	15,27 (cf. v. 23)
8,4		15,33
9,6	Lk	9,33
12,28 (Mt ἐφίμωσεν)		20,39 (cf. Mk 12,32)
12,29 (Mt ἔφη)		(10,26)

The inverse

Mk 5,36   Lk 8,50

Other instances of ἀποκρίνομαι in Mark : 12,34 (cf. Lk 10,28) ; 14,40 (cf. 9,6) ; 14,60 (Mt).61 om. Mt) ; 15,4 (cf. Mt 27,12) ; 15,5 (Mt).

17. Active or Middle Voice in Mark and Passive in Matthew and Luke [180]

† Active in Matthew or Luke
* Impersonal plural in Mark (see No. 22)

Mk		Mt		Lk	
1,12	ἐκβάλλει	4,1	ἀνήχθη	4,1	ἤγετο
8,36	ὠφελεῖ	16,26	ὠφεληθήσεται	9,25	ὠφελεῖται
9,50	ἀρτύσετε	(5,13)	ἁλισθήσεται	(14,34)	ἀρτυθήσεται
4,53	συνέρχονται	26,57	συνήχθησαν	(22,66)	συνήχθη
5,14	σταύρωσον	27,23	σταυρωθήτω	23,23	σταυρωθῆναι

Active or middle voice in Mark and passive in Matthew

Mk		Mt	
1,31	ἤγειρεν	8,15	ἠγέρθη (Lk 4,39 ἀναστᾶσα)
5,40	ἐκβαλών	9,25	ἐξεβλήθη
6,28a	ἤνεγκεν	14,11a	ἠνέχθη
6,28b	ἔδωκεν	14,11b	ἐδόθη
7,19	ἐκπορεύεται	15,17	ἐκβάλλεται
9,43	ἀπελθεῖν	18,8	βληθῆναι
10,13	προσέφερον	19,13	προσηνέχθησαν (Lk 18,15†)
13,20	ἐκολόβωσεν	24,22	ἐκολοβώθησαν
13,20	ἐκολόβωσεν	24,22	κολοβωθήσονται
5,27	σταυροῦσιν	27,38	σταυροῦνται (Lk 23,33†)

Comp. diff. Lk in Mt 5,13 βληθέν (βάλλουσιν).
The inverse

5,46	ἦν λελατομημένον	27,60	ἐλατόμησεν (Lk 23,53 λαξευτῷ)

Active in Mark and passive in Luke

Mk		Mt	Lk	
3,31*	ἀπέστειλαν καλοῦντες	[12,47†]	8,20	ἀπηγγέλη
4,19	συμπνίγουσιν	13,22†	8,14	συμπνίγονται
6,14*	ἔλεγον		9,7	λέγεσθαι ὑπό
6,43*	ἦραν	14,20†	9,17	ἤρθη
9,8	εἶδον	17,8†	9,36	εὑρέθη
10,33b	παραδώσουσιν	20,19†	18,32	παραδοθήσεται (cf. Mk 10,33a)
10,34	ἐμπαίξουσιν	20,19†	18,32	ἐμπαιχθήσεται
10,34	ἐμπτύσουσιν		18,32	ἐμπτυσθήσεται
13,5	τις πλανήσῃ	24,4†	21,8a	πλανηθῆτε

---

180. Schmid(18), pp. 48-49 ; comp. Cadbury, pp. 164-165 ; Schürmann I, p. 79.

Mk	Mt	Lk
13,6 πλανήσουσιν	24,5†	21,8b πορευθῆτε ὀπίσω
13,12 παραδώσει	24,21†	21,16 παραδοθήσεσθε
14,12* ἔθυον		22,7 θύεσθαι

Comp. diff. Mt in Lk 11,51 ἐκζητηθήσεται (ἥξει) ; 12,3 ἀκουσθήσεται, κηρυχθήσεται (εἴπατε, κηρύξατε) 12,9 ἀπαρνηθήσεται (ἀρνήσομαι) ; 12,53 διαμερισθήσονται (ἦλθον διχάσαι).

17n. Note : Middle in Mark and Active in Matthew and Luke

10,20 ἐφυλαξάμην (v.l. -ξα) 19,20 ἐφύλαξα   18,21 ἐφύλαξα

The inverse : Middle in Luke and active in Mark (and Matthew)

3,2 παρετήρουν (v.l. -ουντο)	12,10 ἐπηρώτησαν	6,7 παρετηροῦντο
		(14,1) ἦσαν παρατηρούμενοι
10,49 στάς	20,32 στάς	18,40 σταθείς

Comp. Lk 17,27 ἐγαμίζοντο, diff. Mt 24,38 γαμίζοντες.

18. Simple Verb in Mark and Compound Verb in Matthew and Luke [181]

Matthew/Luke agreements

Mk	Mt		Lk	
5,14 ἦλθον (15 ἔρχονται)	8,34	ἐξῆλθεν	8,35	ἐξῆλθον
5,27 ἐλθοῦσα	9,20	προσελθοῦσα	8,44	προσελθοῦσα
12,18 ἔρχονται πρός	22,23	προσῆλθον	20,27	προσελθόντες
14,38 ἔλθητε	26,41	εἰσέλθητε	22,46	εἰσέλθητε
				(cf. 40 εἰσελθεῖν)
15,43 εἰσῆλθεν πρός	27,58	προσελθών	23,52	προσελθών
4,38	8,25	προσελθόντες	8,24	προσελθόντες

(18) The inverse

3,1 εἰσῆλθεν	12,9	ἦλθεν	(14,1)	ἐλθεῖν
11,29 ἐπερωτήσω	21,24	ἐρωτήσω	20,3	ἐρωτήσω
12,17 ἐξεθαύμαζον ἐπ'	22,22	ἐθαύμασαν	20,26	θαυμάσαντες ἐπί
13,11 προμεριμνᾶτε	(10,19)	μεριμνήσητε	(12,11)	μεριμνήσητε
14,54 ἦν συγκαθήμενος	26,58	ἐκάθητο	22,55	ἐκάθητο (55 συγ-
				καθισάντων,
				56 καθήμενον)
15,46 κατέθηκεν (47 τέ-	27,60	ἔθηκεν	23,53	ἔθηκεν
θειται ; 16,6 ἔθηκαν)				

---

181. Schmid(19), pp. 49-50 ; comp. Krenkel, pp. 41-42.320 ; Allen, pp. XXVI-XXVII ; Cadbury, pp. 166-168 ; Schürmann I, p. 30 ; III, p. 70.

Simple verb in Mark and compound verb in Matthew

* προσέρχομαι
† προσφέρω

Mk		Mt		Lk	
1,32	ἔφερον πρός	8,16†	προσήνεγκαν	4,40	ἤγαγον πρός
		(4,24†)	προσήνεγκαν		
1,40	ἔρχεται πρός	8,2*	προσελθών		
2,3	ἔρχονται φέροντες πρός	9,2†	προσέφερον	5,18	φέροντες
	(4 προσενέγκαι)				εἰσενεγκεῖν
2,18	ἔρχονται	9,14*	προσέρχονται		
5,22	ἔρχεται	9,18*	προσελθών	8,41	ἦλθεν
6,29	ἦλθαν	14,12*	προσελθόντες		
7,32	φέρουσιν	15,30*	προσῆλθον ἔχοντες		
8,12	ζητεῖ (11 ζητοῦντες)	16,4	ἐπιζητεῖ		
		12,39	ἐπιζητεῖ	11,29	ζητεῖ (16 ἐζήτουν)
9,17	ἤνεγκα πρός	17,16†	προσήνεγκα		
11,27	ἔρχονται πρός	21,23*	προσῆλθον	20,1	ἐπέστησαν
12,16	ἤνεγκαν	22,19†	προσήνεγκαν		
14,3	ἦλθεν	26,7	προσῆλθεν		
14,66	ἔρχεται	26,69*	προσῆλθεν		
15,34	ἐβόησεν	27,46	ἀνεβόησεν		

The inverse

† Compound verb in Luke

1,16	ἀμφιβάλλοντας	4,18	βάλλοντας ἀμφίβληστρον		
1,23	ἀνέκραξεν (cf. 5,29)				
2,1	εἰσελθὼν εἰς	9,1	ἦλθεν εἰς		
3,1	εἰσῆλθεν εἰς	12,9	ἦλθεν εἰς	6,6†	
3,27	διαρπάσαι	12,29	ἁρπάσαι	11,22	διαδίδωσιν
4,7	συνέπνιξαν	13,7 v.l. ἔπνιξαν		8,7	ἀπέπνιξαν
4,39	διεγερθείς	8,26	ἐγερθείς	8,24†	
5,7	κράξας, but see 1,23	8,29	ἔκραξαν	8,28	ἀνακράξας
5,30	ἐπιστραφείς	9,22	στραφείς		
6,26	περίλυπος γενόμενος	14,9	συνανακειμένους		
6,49	ἀνέκραξαν	14,26	ἔκραξαν		
8,27	ἐξῆλθεν	16,13	ἐλθών		
8,27	ἐπηρώτα	16,13	ἠρώτα	9,18†	
8,33	ἐπιστραφείς	16,23	στραφείς		
10,17	ἐκπορευομένου	19,15	ἐπορεύθη		
11,2	ὑπάγετε εἰς	21,2	πορεύεσθε εἰς	19,30†	ὑπάγετε εἰς
	εἰσπορευόμενοι εἰς				ἐν ᾗ εἰσπορευόμενοι
12,19	ἐξαναστήσῃ	22,24	ἀναστήσει	20,28†	
13,1	ἐκπορευομένου (ἐκ)	24,1	ἐπορεύετο (ἀπό)		
14,31	συναποθανεῖν	26,35	ἀποθανεῖν	(22,33)	εἰς θάνατον πορεύεσθαι
14,70	παρεστῶτες	26,73	ἑστῶτες	22,59	ἄλλος
14,72	ἀνεμνήσθη	26,75	ἐμνήσθη	22,61	ὑπεμνήσθη
15,26	ἐπιγεγραμμένη	27,37	γεγραμμένη	(22,38)	
15,35	παρεστηκότων	27,47	ἑστηκότων		

Simple verb in Mark and compound verb in Luke

† Simple verb in Matthew

Mk		Mt		Lk	
1,29	ἦλθον εἰς	8,14†		4,38	εἰσῆλθεν
1,37	ζητοῦσιν			4,42	ἐπεζήτουν
1,45	ἤρχοντο			5,15	συνήρχοντο
3,24	μερισθῇ	12,25†		11,17	διαμερισθεῖσα
3,26	ἐμερίσθη	12,26†		11,18	διεμερίσθη
4,5	ἔπεσεν	13,5†		8,6	κατέπεσεν
4,10	ἠρώτων	13,10	εἶπαν	8,9	ἐπηρώτων
4,24	μετρηθήσεται	(7,2†)		(6,38) v.l.	ἀντιμετρηθήσεται
4,38	ἐγείρουσιν	8,25†		8,24	διήγειραν
5,7	κράξας	8,29†		8,28	ἀνακράξας
5,13	ἐπνίγοντο	8,32	ἀπέθανον	8,33	ἀπεπνίγη
5,23	ἐλθών	9,18†		8,41	εἰσελθεῖν
6,20	ἠπόρει			(9,7)	διηπόρει
9,20	ἤνεγκαν πρός			9,42	προσερχομένου
9,36	λαβών	18,2	προσκαλεσάμενος	9,47	ἐπιλαβόμενος
10,21	δός	19,21†		18,22	διάδος
10,30	λάβῃ			18,30 v.l.	ἀπολάβῃ
11,8	ἔστρωσαν	21,8†		19,36	ὑπεστρώννυον
12,3	ἀπέστειλαν			20,10	ἐξαπέστειλαν
12,18	λέγουσιν	22,23†		20,27	ἀντιλέγοντες
15,36	δραμών	27,49†		(23,36)	προσερχόμενοι
15,41	ἠκολούθουν	27,55†		23,49	συνακολουθοῦσαι
				(23,55)	συνεληλυθυῖαι

The inverse

† Compound verb in Matthew

Mk		Mt		Lk	
4,19	εἰσπορευόμεναι			8,14	πορευόμενοι
5,36	παρακούσας			8,50	ἀκούσας
6,33	ἐπέγνωσαν	9,11	γνόντες	14,13	ἀκούσαντες
8,34	ἀπαρνησάσθω	16,24		9,23	ἀρνησάσθω
9,18	καταλάβῃ			9,39	λαμβάνει
9,32	ἐπερωτῆσαι	17,22		9,45	ἐρωτῆσαι
10,42	κατακυριεύουσιν	20,25†		22,25	κυριεύουσιν
10,42	κατεξουσιάζουσιν	20,25†		22,25	ἐξουσιάζοντες
14,53	ἀπήγαγον	26,57†		22,54	ἤγαγον (καὶ εἰσήγαγον)
15,1	ἀπήνεγκαν	27,2	ἀπήγαγον	23,1	ἤγαγον
15,2	ἐπηρώτησεν	27,11†		23,3	ἠρώτησεν

Note : Simple verb in Matthew and compound verb in Luke

Mt		Lk	
10,26	κεκαλυμμένον	12,2	συγκεκαλυμμένον
10,33	ἀρνήσομαι	12,9	ἀπαρνηθήσεται
11,25	ἔκρυψας	10,21	ἀπέκρυψας
15,14	πεσοῦνται	6,39	ἐμπεσοῦνται
23,34	διώξετε	11,49	ἐκδιώξουσιν
24,28	συναχθήσεται	17,37	ἐπισυναχθήσεται

Diff. Mk 12,28 : Mt 22,35 πειράζων, Lk 10,25 ἐκπειράζων
Lk 6,38 ; 11,17.18 : see par. Mk.

The inverse

Mt		Lk	
4,1	ἀνήχθη (cf. Mk 1,12)	4,1	ἤγετο
11,27	ἐπιγινώσκει (bis)	10,22	γινώσκει (bis)
(12,11)	ἐμπέσῃ	14,5	πεσεῖται
16,4	ἐπιζητεῖ	11,29	ζητεῖ (cf. Mk 8,12)

19. ἐπερωτάω /ἐρωτάω IN MARK AND λέγω IN MATTHEW AND LUKE

Matthew /Luke agreements

Mk		Mt		Lk	
8,29	ἐπηρώτα	16,15	λέγει	9,20	εἶπεν
14,61	ἐπηρώτα (καὶ λέγει)	26,63	εἶπεν	22,67	λέγοντες

ἐπερωτάω in Mark († and Luke) and λέγω in Matthew

Mk	Mt		Mk	Mt
7,5	15,1		10,17†	19,16
7,17	15,15		13,3†	24,3
9,28	17,19		14,60 (+ λέγων)	26,62
10,10	(19,10)		15,4	27,13
10,2	19,3			

ἐρωτάω in Mark and λέγω in Matthew

4,10	13,10	(Lk 8,9 ἐπερωτάω)
7,26	15,25	
8,5	15,34	

The inverse : λέγω in Mark and (ἐπ)ερωτάω in Matthew or Luke
† λέγω in the parallel text of Mt or Lk

10,18†	Mt 19,17 ἐρωτᾷς (cf. Mk 10,17 ἐπηρώτα)

1,30	Lk 4,38	
(5,17† παρακαλεῖν)	8,37	
10,51†	18,40 (ἐπ-)	
11,3†	19,31	
12,14†	20,21 (ἐπ- λέγοντες)	
14,65 †	22,64 (ἐπ- λέγοντες)	

19n. Note

3,2	παρετήρουν (εἰ)	12,10	ἐπηρώτησεν (εἰ ἔξεστιν)	6,7	παρετηροῦντο (εἰ)
4	λέγει	11	εἶπεν	9	εἶπεν
	(ἔξεστιν)	12	(... ὥστε ἔξεστιν)		ἐπερωτῶ ὑμᾶς εἰ
					(ἔξεστιν)

12,28 ἐπηρώτησεν	22,35 ἐπηρώτησεν πειράζων	(10,25) ἐκπειράζων λέγων (!)
10,2 ἐπηρώτων πειράζοντες	19,3 πειράζοντες καὶ λέγοντες (!)	
cf. 8,11 ζητοῦντες πειράζοντες	16,1 πειράζοντες ἐπηρώτησεν (!)	(11,16) πειράζοντες ἐζήτουν

See also No. **(18)**, Simple and compound verb :

ἐπερωτάω Mk 11,29 and ἐρωτάω Mt 21,24 ; Lk 20,3

Compare Mk 8,27† (Mt 16,13) ; 9,32 (Lk 9,45) ; 15,2† (Lk 23,3).
The inverse : Mk 4,10 (Lk 8,9).
Other instances of ἐπερωτάω in Mark : 5,9 (Lk) ; 8,23 ; 9,11 (Mt).16.21.33 ; 12,18 (Mt, Lk).34
(Mt, Lk) ; 15,44.

20. πορεύομαι AND ἔρχομαι (AND COMPOUNDS)

Matthew /Luke agreements

Mk		Mt		Lk	
1,21	εἰσπορεύονται	(4,13)	ἐλθών	4,31	κατῆλθεν
5,40	εἰσπορεύονται	9,25	εἰσελθών	(8,51)	εἰσελθεῖν
6,10	ἐκπορευόμενοι	10,14	ἐξερχόμενοι	9,5	ἐξερχόμενοι

(a) ἔρχομαι in Matthew only

7,25	εἰσπορευόμενον	15,11	εἰσερχόμενον		
7,21	ἐκπορεύονται	15,19	ἐξέρχονται		
10,35	προσπορεύονται	20,20	προσῆλθεν		
13,1	ἐκπορευομένου	24,1	ἐξελθὼν ἐπορεύετο		

The inverse

11,4	ἀπῆλθον	21,6	πορευθέντες	19,32	ἀπελθόντες
14,10	ἀπῆλθεν	26,14	πορευθείς	22,4	ἀπελθών

(b) ἔρχομαι in Luke only

11,19	ἐξεπορεύοντο (cf. 11)		(21,37)	ἐξερχόμενος

The inverse

1,28	ἐξῆλθεν	(4,24)	ἀπῆλθεν	4,37	ἐξεπορεύετο
1,35	ἀπῆλθεν			4,42	ἐπορεύθη
6,36	ἀπελθόντες	14,15†		9,12	πορευθέντες
6,37	ἀπελθόντες	(14,16)	ἀπελθεῖν	9,13	πορευθέντες
10,23	εἰσελεύσονται	19,23	εἰσελεύσεται	18,24	εἰσπορεύονται
14,12	ἀπελθόντες	26,17		(22,8)	πορευθέντες
14,14	εἰσελθῇ			22,10	εἰσπορεύεται
14,26	ἐξῆλθεν	26,30†		22,39	ἐξελθὼν ἐπορεύθη

Note : ὑπάγω in Mark and πορεύομαι in Matthew or Luke

Mk		Mt		Lk	
11,2	ὑπάγετε	21,2	πορεύεσθε	19,30†	
16,7	ὑπάγετε	28,7	πορευθεῖσαι (cf. 10,11)		
2,11	ὕπαγε	9,6†		5,24	πορεύου
5,34	ὕπαγε			8,48	πορεύου
14,21	ὑπάγει	26,24†		(22,22)	πορεύεται
1,44	ὕπαγε	8,4†		5,14	ἀπελθών
5,24	ἀπῆλθεν	9,19	ἠκολούθει (cf. Mk)	8,42	ὑπάγειν
14,13	ὑπάγετε	26,18†		22,10	εἰσελθόντων

21A. WORD ORDER : OBJECT-VERB IN MARK AND VERB-OBJECT IN MATTHEW AND LUKE [182]

Mk		Mt	Lk
1,34	δαιμόνια / ἐξέβαλεν	8,16	4,41 (subject)
1,41	αὐτοῦ / ἥψατο	8,3	5,13
3,12	αὐτὸν / φανερὸν ποιήσωσιν	12,16	(4,41)
3,27b	τὸν ἰσχυρὸν / δήσῃ	12,29b	11,22a
3,33	αὐτοῖς / λέγει	12,48	8,21
9,9	ἃ εἶδον / διηγήσωνται	17,9	9,36
9,37	ἓν τῶν τοιούτων παιδίων / δέξηται	18,5	9,48
10,32	αὐτοῖς / λέγειν	20,17	18,31
11,8	τὰ ἱμάτια αὐτῶν / ἔστρωσαν	21,8	19,36
11,28 v.l.	τὴν ἐξουσίαν ταύτην / ἔδωκεν	21,23	20,2
12,1	ἀμπελῶνα / ἐφύτευσεν	21,33	20,9
12,7	πρὸς ἑαυτοὺς / εἶπαν	21,38	20,14
12,17	τὰ Καίσαρος / ἀπόδοτε	22,21	20,25
12,34	αὐτὸν / ἐπερωτῆσαι	(22,46)	(20,40)
14,10	αὐτὸν / παραδοῖ / αὐτοῖς	26,15	22,4 (interchanged)
14,30	με / ἀπαρνήσῃ	26,34	22,34 v.l.
14,72	με / ἀπαρνήσῃ	26,75	22,61
15,11	τὸν Βαραββᾶν / ἀπολύσῃ	27,20	23,18
15,46	(καθελὼν) αὐτὸν / ἐνείλησεν	27,59	23,53

(21A) The inverse

Mk		Mt	Lk
1,8	βαπτίσει / ὑμᾶς	3,11	3,16
8,12	ζητεῖ / σημεῖον	16,4	(11,29)
8,36	ζημιωθῆναι / τὴν ψυχὴν αὐτοῦ	16,26	9,25
11,17	πεποιήκατε / αὐτόν	21,13	19,46
15,14	(τί) ἐποίησεν / κακόν	27,23	23,22
15,15	παρέδωκεν / τὸν Ἰησοῦν	27,26	23,25

---

182. Schmid(14), pp. 46-47 ; cf. Turner(10,3), pp. 352-356. Comp. Cadbury, pp. 152-154 ; Zerwick, pp. 108-117 : " Zur Schluss-Stellung des Verbums " (' Le phénomène de Turner ') ; Schürmann I, p. 81 (nouns), p. 40 (pronouns). On Luke's transpositions, see Appendix, pp. 311-321 (n. 76 and 117).

Object-verb in Mark (and Luke) and verb-object in Matthew

Mk	Mt	Lk
2,21 ἐπίβλημα / ἐπιράπτει	9,16	5,36
5,7 με / βασανίσῃς	8,29	8,28
6,50 αὐτὸν / εἶδον	14,26 (part.)	
6,55 τοὺς κακῶς ἔχοντας / περιφέρειν	14,35	
6,56 τοῦ κρασπέδου τοῦ ἱματίου αὐτοῦ / ἅψωνται	14,36	
8,27 με / εἶναι	16,13 (τὸν υἱὸν τ.ἀ.)	9,18
10,2 γυναῖκα / ἀπολῦσαι	19,3	
10,13 αὐτῶν / ἅψηται (v.l. ἅψηται αὐτῶν)	19,13	18,15
10,51 σοι / ποιήσω	20,32	18,41
11,3c αὐτὸν / ἀποστέλλει	21,3	
11,14 καρπὸν / φάγοι	21,19 (pass.)	
14,6 αὐτῇ / κόπους παρέχετε	26,1	
14,14 τὸ πάσχα / φάγω	26,18	22,7 (cf. 15 τ)

πάσχα φαγεῖν)

The inverse

4,41 (but v.l.: Ti T Ru S)	8,27 αὐτῷ / ὑπακούουσιν	8,25 (=Mk)

Object-verb in Mark (and Matthew) and verb-object in Luke

Mk	Mt	Lk
1,44 σεαυτὸν / δεῖξον	8,4	5,14
3,6 αὐτὸν / ἀπολέσωσιν	12,14	6,11
3,10 αὐτοῦ / ἅψωνται		6,19
4,30 αὐτὴν / παραβολῇ θῶμεν	13,31	(13,18)
5,30 μου / ἥψατο		8,45
5,31 μου / ἥψατο		8,46
6,7 αὐτοὺς / ἀποστέλλει	10,5	9,2
9,18a αὐτὸν / καταλάβῃ		9,39
9,18b αὐτὸ / ἐκβάλωσιν	9,16	9,40
9,19 πρὸς ὑμᾶς / ἔσομαι	9,17	9,41
9,32 αὐτὸν / ἐπερωτῆσαι		9,45
11,28 σοι / ἔδωκεν		20,2
12,12a αὐτὸν / κρατῆσαι	21,46	20,19a
12,12b τὴν παραβολὴν / εἶπεν		20,19b
12,13 αὐτὸν / ἀγρεύσωσιν	22,15	20,20
14,1 αὐτὸν / ἀποκτείνωσιν	26,4	22,2
14,11 αὐτὸν / παραδοῖ	26,16	22,6
14,12 τὸ πάσχα / ἔθυον		22,7
14,25 αὐτὸ / πίνω	26,29	22,16 (φάγω αὐτό)
14,63 χρείαν / ἔχομεν	26,56	22,71
15,1 (δήσαντες) τὸν Ἰησοῦν / ἀπήνεγκαν	27,2	23,1
15,31b ἑαυτὸν / σῶσαι	27,42	23,35 (σωσάτω)

The inverse

Mk	Mt	Lk	
2,7		5,21	ἁμαρτίας / ἀφεῖναι
4,17	13,21	8,13	ῥίζαν / οὐκ ἔχουσιν
4,41		8,25	τοῖς ἀνέμοις / ἐπιτάσσει (καὶ τῷ ὕδατι)
4,41 v.l. cf. Mt			
6,11	10,14	9,5	τὸν κονιορτόν... / ἀποτινάσσετε

Mk	Mt	Lk	
8,38		9,26	τοῦτον / ἐπαισχυνθήσεται
9,7	17,5	9,35	αὐτοῦ / ἀκούετε
12,4	21,36	20,11	ἕτερον / πέμψαι (δοῦλον)
12,6	21,37	20,13	τοῦτον / ἐντραπήσονται
12,14	22,17	20,22	Καίσαρι / δοῦναι
12,37	22,45	20,44	αὐτὸν κύριον / καλεῖ
comp. 12,37b		(19,48)	αὐτοῦ / ἀκούων
14,44	26,48	(22,48)	τὸν υἱὸν τοῦ ἀνθρώπου / παραδίδως
(2,3)		5,18	αὐτὸν / εἰσενεγκεῖν (add.)
(14,62)		22,70	πρὸς αὐτοὺς / ἔφη (add.)

21B. OTHER INSTANCES OF CHANGES IN WORD ORDER (INDICATED IN THE CUMULATIVE LIST)

Mk 1,10	6,10	12,26
1,12	6,14	12,35
1,13	6,44	12,37
1,31	8,11	13,26
1,40	8,35	14,24
2,10	9,1	14,25
2,22	9,4	14,43
2,24	9,19	14,48
2,28	9,25 (cf. No. 22)	14,53
3,1	9,35	14,54
3,17-18	10,29	14,62
4,11	10,48	14,72a
4,20a	12,2	15,27
4,20b	12,8	15,41
4,32	12,25	16,6

See also No. **35** (agreement in order) and No. **8A** (parenthesis).

Other instances in Luke

Mk	Lk	Mk	Lk
1,8	3,16	1,45	5,16
1,10	3,22	2,5	5,20
1,11bis	3,22	2,6	5,21
1,21	4,31	2,9	5,23
1,22	4,32	2,10	5,24
1,23	4,33	2,12	5,25
1,27	4,36	2,15	5,29
1,32	4,40	2,16	5,30
1,34	4,40	2,18	5,33
1,34	4,41	2,19	5,34
1,40	5,12	2,23	6,1
1,42	5,13	2,25	6,3

Mk	Lk	Mk	Lk
3,1bis	6,6	9,5quinq.	9,33
3,3	6,8	9,7bis	9,35
3,7bis	6,6	9,17	9,38
3,8	6,17	9,19bis	9,41
3,10	6,18	9,20	9,42
3,16	(6,14)	9,38	9,49
3,31	(8,20)	9,39	9,50
3,35	(8,21)	9,42	17,2
4,1	8,4	10,13	18,15
4,6	8,6	10,17	18,18
4,8	8,8	10,18	18,19
4,15	8,12	10,19	18,20
4,16	8,13	10,21	18,22
4,21ter	8,16	10,22	18,32
4,22	8,17	10,27	18,27
5,6-7	8,28	10,31bis	(13,30)
5,8	8,29	10,34bis	18,33
5,9	8,30	10,43bis	(22,26)
5,10	8,31	10,46	18,35
5,11	8,32	10,47	18,35
5,15	8,35	11,2	19,30
5,18	8,38	11,5	19,33
5,19	8,39	11,18	19,48
5,20	9,39	12,1	20,9
5,21	8,40	12,3	20,10
5,22	8,41	12,25	20,35
5,25	8,43	12,27	20,38
5,35	8,49	12,28	(10,25)
5,37bis	8,51	12,30	(10,27)
5,42	8,55	12,38	20,46
6,3	(4,22)	12,41	21,1
6,8	9,3	12,42	21,2 *v.l.*
6,10	9,4	12,43	21,3 *v.l.*
6,11	9,5	12,44	21,4
6,16	9,9	13,8	21,11
6,32	9,10	13,9	21,12
6,33	9,11	13,28	21,30
6,36	9,12	14,1	22,1
6,37	9,13	14,14	22,11
6,38	9,13	14,17	22,14
6,40	9,14-15	14,24	22,20
6,42	9,17	14,21bis	22,22
6,43	9,17	14,30	22,34
6,44	(9,14)	14,36	22,42
8,27	9,18	14,37	22,45
8,29	9,20	14,47bis	22,50
8,38	9,26	14,63	22,71
9,1bis	9,27	14,72bis	(22,60)
9,2	9,28	15,2	23,3
9,3	9,29	15,12	23,20
9,4	9,30	15,14	23,23

Mk	Lk		Mk	Lk
15,21	23,26		15,40	23,49
15,37	23,46		16,2bis	24,1
15,39	23,47		16,4	24,2

22. MATTHEW AND LUKE DEFINING THE SUBJECT [183]

* Impersonal plural in Mk (cf. note, p. 266)

Mk		Mt		Lk	
1,9b	(cf. 9a)	3,16	ὁ Ἰησοῦς	3,21	Ἰησοῦ
1,12	αὐτόν (obj.)	4,1	ὁ Ἰησοῦς	4,1	Ἰησοῦς
1,44		8,4	ὁ Ἰησοῦς	5,14	αὐτός
2,18b*		9,14	οἱ μαθηταὶ Ἰωάννου	5,33	οἱ (δέ)
2,25		12,3	ὁ (δέ)	6,3	ὁ Ἰησοῦς
3,4		12,11	ὁ (δέ)	6,9	ὁ Ἰησοῦς
3,33		12,48	ὁ (δέ)	8,21	ὁ (δέ)
4,4	(inf.)	13,4	αὐτόν	8,5	αὐτόν
4,11		13,11	ὁ (δέ)	8,10	ὁ (δέ)
4,35		8,18	ὁ Ἰησοῦς	8,22	αὐτός
5,39		9,23	ὁ Ἰησοῦς	8,52	ὁ (δέ)
6,33*	(33a πολλοί)	14,13	οἱ ὄχλοι	9,11	οἱ (δέ) ὄχλοι
6,37		14,17	οἱ (δέ)	9,13	οἱ (δέ)
9,2		17,2	(ἔλαμψεν) τὸ πρόσωπον αὐτοῦ	9,29	(τὸ εἶδος) τοῦ προσώπου αὐτοῦ
9,19	ὁ (δέ)	17,17	ὁ Ἰησοῦς	9,41	ὁ Ἰησοῦς
9,25b	(cf. No. **21B**)	17,18	ὁ Ἰησοῦς	9,42	ὁ Ἰησοῦς
9,29		17,20	ὁ (δέ)	(cf. 17,6)	ὁ κύριος
10,26	οἱ (δέ)	19,25	(ἀκούσαντες) οἱ μαθηταί	18,26	οἱ ἀκούσαντες
10,48	πολλοί	20,31	ὁ (δὲ) ὄχλος	18,39	οἱ προάγοντες
11,4		21,6	οἱ μαθηταί	19,32	οἱ ἀπεσταλμένοι
11,9		21,9	οἱ ὄχλοι	19,37	ἅπαν τὸ πλῆθος
11,29		21,24	κἀγώ	20,3	κἀγώ
11,31		21,25	οἱ (δέ)	20,5	οἱ (δέ)
12,3		21,35	οἱ γεωργοί	20,10	οἱ (δὲ) γεωργοί
12,12		21,45	οἱ ἀρχιερεῖς καὶ οἱ Φαρισαῖοι	20,19	οἱ γραμματεῖς καὶ οἱ ἀρχιερεῖς
14,13		26,18	ὁ (δέ)	22,10	ὁ (δέ)
14,70		26,73	καὶ σύ	22,59	καὶ οὗτος (v. 58: καὶ σύ)

---

183. Schmid(33a), p. 76, n. 3 ; comp. Wernle, pp. 19-20 ; Cadbury, p. 150 ; Schürmann I, p. 83 ; III, p. 22 ; Sanders, pp. 152-157. For the impersonal plural in Mark, see Schmid(12), p. 43 ; cf. Turner(1), pp. 378-386 ; comp. Cadbury, p. 165 ; Schürmann I, p. 79.

Mk	Mt	Lk
15,26	27,37 οὗτος	23,38 οὗτος
15,43	27,58 οὗτος	23,52 οὗτος

Compare also :

2,16	(ἐσθίει)	9,11	(ἐσθίει) ὁ διδάσκαλος ὑμῶν	5,30	(ἐσθίετε)
2,24	(ποιοῦσιν)	12,2	οἱ μαθηταί σου (ποιοῦσιν)	6,2	(ποιεῖτε)

Note

15,1	τῶν πρεσβυτέρων	27,1	+ τοῦ λαοῦ	(22,66)	+ τοῦ λαοῦ

(22) The inverse

Mk		Mt		Lk	
8,29	αὐτός	16,15		9,20	
10,51	ὁ Ἰησοῦς	20,32		18,40	
10,51	ὁ (δὲ) τυφλός	20,33		18,41	ὁ (δέ)
12,17	ὁ (δὲ) Ἰησοῦς	22,21		20,25	ὁ (δέ)
12,29	ὁ Ἰησοῦς	22,37	ὁ (δέ)	(10,26)	ὁ (δέ)
13,2	ὁ Ἰησοῦς	24,2	ὁ (δέ) (cf. v. 1)	21,5	
14,30	σύ	26,34		22,34	
15,5	ὁ Ἰησοῦς	27,14	(cf. v. 11)	(23,9)	
15,14	ὁ (δὲ) Πιλᾶτος	27,23	ὁ (δέ)	23,22	ὁ (δέ)

Note

3,31	(ἡ μήτηρ) αὐτοῦ	12,46		8,19
12,7	ἐκεῖνοι (οἱ γεωργοί)	21,38		20,14
14,66	τοῦ ἀρχιερέως	26,69		22,56

22a. Matthew defining the subject

Mk		Mt	
1,6		1,4	+ αὐτός
1,18		4,20	οἱ (δέ)
1,20		4,22	οἱ (δέ)
1,22*		(7,28)	οἱ ὄχλοι
1,29		(8,14)	ὁ Ἰησοῦς
2,14		9,9	ὁ Ἰησοῦς
2,23		12,1	ὁ Ἰησοῦς
3,22		12,24	οὗτος
3,31*	(ἀπέστειλαν)	[12,47]	τις
4,1		13,1	ὁ Ἰησοῦς
4,33		13,34	ὁ Ἰησοῦς
4,41		8,27	οἱ (δὲ) ἄνθρωποι
5,12		8,31	οἱ (δὲ) δαίμονες

Mk		Mt	
5,15*	(cf. 14b)	8,34	πᾶσα ἡ πόλις
5,24		9,19	ὁ Ἰησοῦς
5,38	(and 39)	9,23	ὁ Ἰησοῦς
6,6		9,35	ὁ Ἰησοῦς
6,31		14,13	ὁ Ἰησοῦς
6,37	ὁ (δέ)	14,16	ὁ (δὲ) Ἰησοῦς
6,49	οἱ (δέ)	14,26	οἱ (δέ) μαθηταί
6,50	ὁ (δέ)	14,27	ὁ Ἰησοῦς
6,55*		14,35	οἱ ἄνδρες τοῦ τόπου ἐκείνου
7,18		15,16	ὁ (δέ)
7,24		15,21	ὁ Ἰησοῦς
7,27		15,26	ὁ (δέ)
7,29		15,28	ὁ Ἰησοῦς
7,31		15,29	ὁ Ἰησοῦς
7,32*		15,30	ὄχλοι πολλοί
8,1		15,32	ὁ (δὲ) Ἰησοῦς
8,5		15,34	ὁ Ἰησοῦς
8,6		15,36	οἱ μαθηταί
8,8		15,37	πάντες
8,9		15,38	οἱ (δὲ) ἐσθίοντες
8,12		16,2	ὁ (δέ)
8,14		16,5	οἱ μαθηταί
8,15		16,6	ὁ (δὲ) Ἰησοῦς
8,16		16,7	οἱ (δέ)
8,17		16,8	ὁ Ἰησοῦς
8,31		16,21	Ἰησοῦς Χριστός
8,34		16,24	ὁ Ἰησοῦς
9,9		17,9	ὁ Ἰησοῦς
9,11		17,10	οἱ μαθηταί
9,31		17,22	ὁ Ἰησοῦς
9,34		18,1	οἱ μαθηταί
10,1		19,1	ὁ Ἰησοῦς
10,2* v.l.	om. Φαρισαῖοι	19,3	Φαρισαῖοι
10,5		(19,7)	ὁ Μωϋσῆς
10,6		19,4	ὁ κτίσας
10,11		(19,11)	ὁ (δέ)
10,20	ὁ (δέ)	19,20	ὁ νεανίσκος
10,22	ὁ (δέ)	19,22	ὁ νεανίσκος
10,27		19,26	τοῦτο
11,1		21,1	Ἰησοῦς
11,15		21,12	Ἰησοῦς
12,13		22,15	οἱ Φαρισαῖοι
12,15	ὁ (δέ)	22,18	ὁ Ἰησοῦς
12,38		23,1	ὁ Ἰησοῦς
13,1		24,1	ὁ Ἰησοῦς (cf. v. 2)
13,18		24,20	ἡ φυγὴ ὑμῶν
14,3	αὐτοῦ (gen. abs.)	26,6	τοῦ (δὲ) Ἰησοῦ
14,8		26,12	αὕτη
14,9	τὸ εὐαγγέλιον	26,13	+ τοῦτο
14,16		26,19	ὁ Ἰησοῦς
14,22		26,26	ὁ Ἰησοῦς

Mk		Mt	
14,31	ὁ (δέ)	26,35	ὁ Πέτρος
14,31	πάντες	26,35	+ οἱ μαθηταί
14,32		26,36	ὁ Ἰησοῦς
14,50		26,56	οἱ μαθηταί
14,53		26,57	οἱ (δέ) κρατήσαντες τὸν Ἰησοῦν
14,61	ὁ (δέ)	26,63	ὁ (δὲ) Ἰησοῦς
15,2	ὁ (δέ)	27,11	ὁ (δὲ) Ἰησοῦς
15,6		27,15	ὁ ἡγεμών
15,13	οἱ (δέ)	27,22	πάντες
15,35		27,47	οὗτος
15,36	τις	27,48-49	εἶς ἐξ αὐτῶν... οἱ (δέ) λοιποί
15,45	(cf. v. 44)	27,58	ὁ Πιλᾶτος
15,46		27,59	ὁ Ἰωσήφ
16,6	ὁ (δέ)	28,5	ὁ ἄγγελος

Cf. Lk 9,60 and Mt 8,22 : ὁ Ἰησοῦς

The inverse

Mk		Mt	
1,14	ὁ Ἰησοῦς	4,12	(cf. v. 17)
1,17	ὁ Ἰησοῦς	4,19	
2,17	ὁ Ἰησοῦς	9,12	
2,22	οὐδεὶς (βάλλει)	9,17	(οὐδὲ βάλλουσιν)
2,25	αὐτός	12,3	
3,5	ἡ χεὶρ αὐτοῦ	12,13	(ὡς ἡ ἄλλη)
5,13	τὰ πνεύματα τ.ἀ.	8,32	οἱ (δέ), cf. v. 31
6,2	οἱ πολλοὶ ἀκούσαντες	13,54	αὐτούς
6,27	ὁ βασιλεύς	14,10	
6,28	τὸ κοράσιον	14,11	
6,45	αὐτός	14,22	
7,14	πάντες	15,10	
8,31	τὸν υἱὸν τοῦ ἀνθρώπου (inf.)	16,21	αὐτόν
10,2	ἀνδρί (+ inf.)	19,3	
10,4	οἱ (δέ)	(19,7)	
10,5	ὁ (δὲ) Ἰησοῦς	(19,8)	
10,18	ὁ (δὲ) Ἰησοῦς	19,17	ὁ (δέ)
10,37	οἱ (δέ)	20,21	
10,39	οἱ (δέ)	20,22	
10,39	ὁ (δὲ) Ἰησοῦς	20,23	
11,33	ὁ Ἰησοῦς	21,27	καὶ αὐτός
12,16	οἱ (δέ)	22,21	
12,19	τινος ἀδελφός	22,24	τις
13,2	ὁ Ἰησοῦς	24,2	ὁ (δέ), cf. v. 1
13,19	αἱ ἡμέραι ἐκεῖναι	24,21	
14,5	τοῦτο τὸ μύρον	26,9	τοῦτο
14,18	ὁ Ἰησοῦς	26,21	
14,68	σύ	26,70	
14,70	ὁ (δέ)	26,72	
15,10	οἱ ἀρχιερεῖς (v.l. om. ; cf. 8 ὁ ὄχλος)	27,18	
15,39	οὗτος ὁ ἄνθρωπος	27,54	οὗτος

22b. Luke defining the subject

Mk		Lk	
1,27	τοῦτο	4,36	ὁ λόγος οὗτος
1,32*		4,40	ἅπαντες ὅσοι εἶχον ἀ.ν.π.
1,34		4,40	ὁ (δέ)
1,38		4,43	ὁ (δέ)
1,45*		5,15	ὄχλοι πολλοί
2,3*		5,18	ἄνδρες
3,2*	(cf. v. 6) (cf. Mt 12,9 αὐτῶν)	6,7	οἱ γραμματεῖς καὶ οἱ Φαρισαῖοι
3,5b		6,10	ὁ (δέ)
3,23	(cf. Mt 12,25)	(11,17)	αὐτὸς (δέ)
4,17	(cf. v. 16)	8,13	οὗτοι
4,39		8,24	ὁ (δέ)
5,9		8,30	ὁ Ἰησοῦς
5,9		8,30	ὁ (δέ)
5,17		8,37	ἅπαν τὸ πλῆθος τῆς περιχώρου τ.Γ.
5,35*		8,49	τις
5,41		8,54	αὐτὸς (δέ)
5,42		8,56	οἱ γονεῖς αὐτῆς
5,43		8,56	ὁ (δέ)
8,30		9,21	ὁ (δέ)
8,35		9,24	οὗτος
10,48	ὁ δέ	18,39	αὐτὸς (δέ)
11,9		19,38	ὁ βασιλεύς
12,4		20,11	οἱ (δέ)
12,5		20,12	οἱ (δέ)
12,14	(inf.)	20,22	ἡμᾶς
12,23		20,33	ἡ γυνή
13,7	(inf.)	21,9	ταῦτα
13,29		21,31	ἡ βασιλεία τοῦ θεοῦ
14,19		22,23	αὐτοί
14,35		22,41	αὐτός
15,14		23,22	οὗτος
15,47		23,55	τὸ σῶμα αὐτοῦ

Compare also

13,12	παραδώσει	21,16	παραδοθήσεσθε

Diff. Mt : Lk 6,22 ; 7,33.34 ; 11,33 (cf. 8,16) ; 11,17 (cf. *supra*).

The inverse

Mk		Lk	
1,31	ὁ πυρετός	4,39	(cf. 33a)
1,34	τὰ δαιμόνια (inf.)	4,41	αὐτά
2,5	ὁ Ἰησοῦς	5,20	
3,6	οἱ Φαρισαῖοι μ.τ.ʽΗ.	6,11	αὐτοὶ (δέ), cf. v. 7.
3,7	ὁ Ἰησοῦς	6,17	
5,9	ὄνομά μοι	8,30	
5,39	τὸ παιδίον	8,52	

Mk		Lk	
5,42	τὸ κοράσιον	8,55	
6,4	ὁ Ἰησοῦς	(4,24)	
6,37	ὁ (δέ)	9,13	
8,27	ὁ Ἰησοῦς	9,18	αὐτόν (inf.)
9,2	ὁ Ἰησοῦς	9,28	
10,27	ὁ Ἰησοῦς	18,27	ὁ (δέ)
10,29	ὁ Ἰησοῦς	18,29	ὁ (δέ)
10,42	ὁ Ἰησοῦς	(22,25)	ὁ (δέ)
11,29	ὁ Ἰησοῦς	20,3	
12,15	ὁ δέ	20,23	
12,35	ὁ Ἰησοῦς	20,41	
12,35	οἱ γραμματεῖς	20,41	
13,2	ὁ Ἰησοῦς	21,5	
13,3	Πέτρος κ. Ἰ.κ. Ἰ.κ. Ἀ.	21,7	
13,5	ὁ (δὲ) Ἰησοῦς	21,8	ὁ (δέ)
14,11	οἱ (δέ)	22,5	
14,12	οἱ μαθηταὶ αὐτοῦ	22,9	οἱ (δέ), cf. v. 8.
14,14	μου	22,11	
14,16	οἱ μαθηταί	22,13	
14,21	ὁ υἱὸς τοῦ ἀνθρώπου	22,22	
14,29	ὁ (δὲ) Πέτρος	22,33	ὁ (δέ)
14,30	ὁ Ἰησοῦς	22,34	ὁ (δέ)
14,62	ὁ (δὲ) Ἰησοῦς	22,67	cf. v. 70 ὁ (δέ)
14,63	ὁ (δὲ) ἀρχιερεύς	22,71	οἱ (δέ)
15,43	ὃς καὶ αὐτός	23,51	ὅς

Diff. Mt 8,11

22n. Note : Impersonal Plural in Mark

Matthew /Luke agreements

Mk	Mt	Lk	
2,18 (cf. p. 261)	9,17	5,33	
3,2	12,10 (cf. 9 αὐτῶν)	6,7	
3,32	[12,47]	8,20	(passive)
6,33 (cf. p. 261)	14,13	9,11	

Subject inserted
Matthew : diff. Mk 1,22 (Lk 4,32) ; 5,15 (Lk 8,30) ; 6,55 ; 7,32 ; 10,2 v.l.
Luke : diff. Mk 1,32 (Mt 8,16).45 ; 2,3 (Mt 9,2) ; 5,35.
The inverse in Matthew : diff. Mk 2,22 (Lk 5,37) ; 15,10 v.l.
  Passive substituted (see No. 17)
Matthew : diff. Mk 10,13 (Lk 18,15).
Luke : diff. Mk 3,31 cf. *supra* ; 6,14.43 (Mt 14,20) ; 14,12.
  Other instances of impersonal plural
Mk 1,30 (Lk 4,38) ; 8,22 ; 10,49 ; 13,9.11 (Mt 24,9 ; Lk 12,12 ; Mt 10,17.19 ; Lk 12,11 ; but see Mt 10,17a ἀπὸ τῶν ἀνθρώπων !).
  Turner adds Mk 3,21.30 ; 14,2 (Mt 26,5) ; 15,10 v.l. (doubtful).

23. MATTHEW AND LUKE DEFINING THE OBJECT, DIRECT OR INDIRECT [184]

* The asterisk indicates a verb of saying

Mk		Mt		Lk	
1,10	τὸ πνεῦμα	3,16	πνεῦμα θεοῦ	3,22	τὸ πνεῦμα τὸ ἅγιον (subj.)
3,5	τὴν χεῖρα	12,13	+ σου (ante)	6,10	+ σου (post)
4,14	τὸν λόγον	13,19	+ τῆς βασιλείας	8,11	+ τοῦ θεοῦ
5,27	τοῦ ἱματίου αὐτοῦ	9,20	+ τοῦ κρασπέδου	8,44	+ τοῦ κρασπέδου
6,2*		13,54	(διδάσκειν) αὐτούς	(4,21)	(λέγειν) πρὸς αὐτούς
6,14		14,1	τὴν ἀκοὴν Ἰησοῦ	9,7	τὰ γινόμενα πάντα
6,36	αὐτούς	14,15	τοὺς ὄχλους	9,12	τὸν ὄχλον
6,41	αὐτοῖς	14,19	τοῖς ὄχλοις	9,16	τῷ ὄχλῳ
8,34*	αὐτοῖς	16,24	τοῖς μαθηταῖς αὐτοῦ	9,23	πρὸς πάντας
9,27	αὐτόν	17,18	ὁ παῖς (subj.)	9,42	τὸν παῖδα
10,22	τῷ λόγῳ	19,22	τὸν λόγον [τοῦτον]	18,23	ταῦτα
10,29*		19,28	αὐτοῖς	18,29	αὐτοῖς
12,9		21,40	τοῖς γεωργοῖς ἐκείνοις	20,15	αὐτοῖς
12,29*		22,37	αὐτῷ	10,26	πρὸς αὐτόν
12,35*		22,41	αὐτούς	20,41	πρὸς αὐτούς
14,10*		26,10	αὐτοῖς	(7,40)	πρὸς αὐτόν
14,20		26,23	τὴν χεῖρα	22,21	ἡ χείρ (subj.)
14,37	(ἔρχεται)	26,40	πρὸς τοὺς μαθητάς	22,45	πρὸς τοὺς μαθητάς
14,45	αὐτῷ	26,49	τῷ Ἰησοῦ	22,47	τῷ Ἰησοῦ
14,48*	αὐτοῖς	26,55	τοῖς ὄχλοις	22,52	πρὸς τοὺς παραγενομένους ἐπ᾽ αὐτὸν ἀρχιερεῖς καὶ στρατηγοὺς τοῦ ἱεροῦ καὶ πρεσβυτέρους
14,62*		26,64	αὐτῷ	22,67	αὐτοῖς (v. 70 πρὸς αὐτούς)
15,5*		27,14	αὐτῷ	(23,9)	αὐτῷ

Compare

3,13	οὓς ἤθελεν αὐτός	(5,1)	οἱ μαθηταὶ αὐτοῦ (subj.)	6,13	τοὺς μαθητὰς αὐτοῦ
3,18	Ἀνδρέαν	(10,2)	+ ὁ ἀδελφὸς αὐτοῦ	6,14	+ τὸν ἀδελφὸν αὐτοῦ

---

184. Schmid(33a), p. 76, n. 3 ; also p. 77, n. 1 ; comp. Larfeld, p. 238 ; Schürmann I, pp. 91 and 101 ; Sanders, pp. 155-159 : (2) direct objects ; (3) indirect objects and equivalent πρός phrases ; also pp. 165-168 : (6) genitive nouns, (7) genitive pronouns.

(23) The inverse

Mk		Mt		Lk	
1,40*	αὐτῷ	8,2	(ante λέγων)	5,12	
1,41*	αὐτῷ	8,3		5,13	
1,44	μηδέν (double negative)	8,4		5,14	
2,9*	τῷ παραλυτικῷ	9,5		5,23	
3,2	αὐτόν	12,10		6,7	
4,11*	αὐτοῖς	13,11		8,10	
4,15	τὸν λόγον ἐσπαρμένον	13,19	τὸ ἐσπαρμένον	8,12	τὸν λόγον
4,38	αὐτῷ	8,25	(part.)	8,24	(part.)
5,14	αὐτούς	8,33		8,34	
5,39*	αὐτοῖς	9,23		8,52	
5,41	(τῆς χειρὸς) τοῦ παιδίου	9,25	αὐτῆς	8,54	αὐτῆς
8,27*	αὐτοῖς	16,13		9,18	
8,28*	αὐτῷ	16,14		9,19	
8,29	αὐτῷ	16,16		9,20	
9,4*	τῷ Ἰησοῦ	17,3	μετ' αὐτοῦ	9,30	αὐτῷ
9,17*	αὐτῷ	17,15	(cf. v. 14)	9,38	
9,19	αὐτοῖς	17,17		9,41	
10,14*	αὐτοῖς	19,14		18,16	
10,26*	πρὸς ἑαυτούς	19,25		18,26	
10,32	τὰ μέλλοντα αὐτῷ συμβαίνειν	20,17		18,31	
11,1	(μαθητῶν) αὐτοῦ	21,1	(μαθητάς)	19,29	(μαθητῶν)
11,17	πᾶσιν τοῖς ἔθνεσιν	21,13		19,46	
12,8	αὐτόν	21,39		20,15	
12,16*	αὐτῷ	22,21		20,24	
13,2	ταύτας τὰς μεγάλας οἰκοδομάς	24,2	ταῦτα πάντα	21,6	ταῦτα ἅ
14,24*	αὐτοῖς	26,27		22,20	
14,65*	αὐτῷ	26,68		22,64	
15,1	τὸν Ἰησοῦν	27,2	αὐτόν (cf. 1)	23,1	αὐτόν
15,31*	πρὸς ἀλλήλους	27,41		23,35	

Compare

1,40	(ἔρχεται) πρὸς αὐτόν	8,2	(προσελθών)	5,12	
9,19	(φέρετε)... πρός με	17,17	(φέρετέ) μοι... ὧδε	9,41	(προσάγαγε) ὧδε
12,4	(ἀπέστειλεν) πρὸς αὐτούς	21,36		20,11	

Matthew defining the object

Mk		Mt	
1,44	ἅ	8,4	τὸ δῶρον ὅ
2,18	ταῦτα	9,4	πονηρά

Mk		Mt	
4,30*		13,31	αὐτοῖς
4,33*	αὐτοῖς	13,34	τοῖς ὄχλοις
5,14		8,33	πάντα καὶ τὰ τῶν δαιμονιζομένων
6,2		13,54	αὐτούς
6,27	αὐτόν	14,10	Ἰωάννην
6,30*	αὐτῷ	14,12	τῷ Ἰησοῦ
6,45		14,22	αὐτόν
6,46	αὐτοῖς	14,23	τοὺς ὄχλους
7,1	πρὸς αὐτόν	15,1	τῷ Ἰησοῦ
8,9	αὐτοῖς	15,38	τοὺς ὄχλους
8,12*		16,2	αὐτοῖς
8,30*	αὐτοῖς	16,20	τοῖς μαθηταῖς
8,31*	αὐτούς	16,21	τοῖς μαθηταῖς
9,8	τὸν Ἰησοῦν	17,8	αὐτὸν Ἰησοῦν
9,28(*)	αὐτόν	17,19	τῷ Ἰησοῦ
10,2		19,3	αὐτῷ
10,4*		19,7	αὐτῷ
10,40		20,23	τοῦτο
11,2*		21,2	μοι
11,6*		21,6	αὐτοῖς
11,9		21,9	αὐτόν
11,31*		21,25	ἡμῖν
12,1		21,33	αὐτῷ (ἐν αὐτῷ)
12,9	ἄλλοις	21,41	+ γεωργοῖς (cf. v. 41a)
12,16		22,19	αὐτῷ
12,16		22,19	δηνάριον
12,23	τίνος αὐτῶν	22,28	τίνος τῶν ἑπτά
14,6	αὐτῇ	26,10	τῇ γυναικί
14,12*	αὐτῷ	26,17	τῷ Ἰησοῦ
14,22	αὐτοῖς	26,26	τοῖς μαθηταῖς
14,27	πάντες	26,31	+ ὑμεῖς
14,31*		26,35	αὐτῷ
14,46	αὐτῷ	26,50	ἐπὶ τὸν Ἰησοῦν
14,69	ἐξ αὐτῶν	26,71	μετὰ Ἰησοῦ τοῦ Ναζωραίου
15,6	αὐτοῖς	27,15	τῷ ὄχλῳ
15,12		27,22	Ἰησοῦν (cf. Lk 23,20)
15,16	αὐτόν	27,27	τὸν Ἰησοῦν
15,32		27,42	ἐπ' αὐτόν
15,41	αὐτῷ	27,55	τῷ Ἰησοῦ

Compare

| 14,41 | (ἔρχεται) | 26,45 | (ἔρχεται) πρὸς τοὺς μαθητάς |
| 14,66 | (ἔρχεται) | 26,69 | (προσῆλθεν) αὐτῷ |

The inverse

Mk		Mt	
1,14	τὸ εὐαγγέλιον τοῦ θεοῦ	4,17	(cf. v. 23)
2,8*	αὐτοῖς	9,4	

Mk		Mt	
2,16	ὅτι ἐσθίει... τελωνῶν	9,11	
2,17*	αὐτοῖς	9,12	
4,35*	αὐτοῖς	8,18	
4,41*	πρὸς ἀλλήλους	8,27	
5,15	τὸν δαιμονιζόμενον... λεγιῶνα	8,34	
5,34*	αὐτῇ	9,22	(ἰδὼν αὐτήν ante)
6,18*	τῷ Ἡρῷδῃ	14,4	αὐτῷ
6,18	τὴν γυναῖκα τοῦ ἀδελφοῦ σου	14,4	αὐτήν
5,34*	αὐτῇ	9,22	
6,28b	αὐτήν	14,11b	
6,28c	αὐτήν	14,11c	
6,39	αὐτοῖς	14,19	
6,41	τοὺς ἄρτους	14,19	
6,44	τοὺς ἄρτους	14,21	
6,56	αὐτοῦ	14,36	
7,14	μου	15,10	
7,18*	αὐτοῖς	15,16	
7,27*	αὐτῇ	15,28	
7,28*	αὐτῷ	15,27	
8,1*	αὐτοῖς	15,32	
8,17*	αὐτοῖς	16,8	
9,12*	αὐτοῖς	17,11	
9,36*	αὐτοῖς	18,3	
10,2(*)	αὐτόν	19,2	
10,3*	αὐτοῖς	19,4	
10,34	αὐτῷ	20,19	
10,34	αὐτόν	20,19	
10,36	με ποιήσω ὑμῖν (cf. v. 35)	20,21	
10,38*	αὐτοῖς	20,22	
10,42*	αὐτοῖς	20,25	
10,51*	αὐτῷ	20,32	
11,2	αὐτόν	21,2	
11,7	πρὸς τὸν Ἰησοῦν	21,7	
11,21*	αὐτῷ	21,20	
11,28*	αὐτῷ	21,23	
12,9	τοὺς γεωργούς	21,41	αὐτούς (cf. v. 41b)
12,14*	αὐτῷ	22,16	
12,15*	αὐτοῖς	22,18	
12,19	ἡμῖν	22,24	
13,23	πάντα	24,25	
14,4	πρὸς ἑαυτούς	26,8	
14,13*	αὐτοῖς	26,18	
14,14	τῷ οἰκοδεσπότῃ	26,18	αὐτῷ
14,20*	αὐτοῖς	26,23	
14,58	ἄλλον	26,61	
14,60(*)	τὸν Ἰησοῦν	26,62	αὐτῷ
14,71	τοῦτον	26,74	
15,2*	αὐτῷ	27,11	
15,14*	αὐτοῖς	27,23	
15,20	αὐτόν	27,31	
16,7*	τοῖς μαθηταῖς αὐτοῦ καὶ τῷ Πέτρῳ	28,7	om. καὶ τῷ Πέτρῳ

Luke defining the object

Mk		Lk	
1,27*	(v.l. πρὸς ἑαυτούς)	4,36	πρὸς ἀλλήλους
1,38		4,43	τὴν βασιλείαν τοῦ θεοῦ
2,4		5,19	αὐτόν (cf. αὐτῷ in Mk)
2,5		5,20	σοι
3,6	αὐτόν	6,11	τῷ ᾿Ιησοῦ
4,3		8,5	τὸν σπόρον αὐτοῦ
6,39	αὐτοῖς	9,14	πρὸς τοὺς μαθητὰς αὐτοῦ
9,19	αὐτόν	9,41	τὸν υἱόν σου
9,39*		9,50	πρὸς αὐτόν
12,1	αὐτοῖς	20,9	πρὸς τὸν λαόν
12,9	τοὺς γεωργούς	20,16	+ τούτους
12,44	πάντες	21,4	+ οὗτοι
14,14*		22,11	σοι
15,40		23,49	ταῦτα

The inverse

Mk		Lk	
1,40	αὐτῷ	5,13	
2,3	πρὸς αὐτόν	5,18	
2,5*	τῷ παραλυτικῷ	5,20	
2,8	ταῦτα	5,22	
2,24*	αὐτῷ	6,2	
3,2	αὐτόν	6,7	(cf. Mt 12,10)
3,5*	τῷ ἀνθρώπῳ	6,10	αὐτῷ
4,2*	αὐτοῖς	8,4	
4,16	τὸν λόγον... αὐτόν	8,13	... τὸν λόγον
4,18	τὸν λόγον	8,14	
5,9*	αὐτῷ	8,30	
5,19*	αὐτῷ	8,38	(αὐτόν ante λέγων)
5,19*	αὐτοῖς	8,39	
5,36	τὸν λόγον λαλούμενον	8,50	
5,36	τῷ ἀρχισυναγώγῳ	8,50	αὐτῷ
5,41*	αὐτῇ	8,54	
6,37*	αὐτῷ	9,13	
6,41	τοὺς ἄρτους	9,16	αὐτούς (cf. εὐλόγησεν)
8,27	τοὺς μαθητὰς αὐτοῦ	9,18	αὐτούς
8,31*	αὐτούς	9,22	
9,38*	αὐτῷ	9,49	
9,39	αὐτόν	9,50	
10,20*	αὐτῷ	18,21	
10,23*	τοῖς μαθηταῖς αὐτοῦ	18,24	
10,27*	αὐτοῖς	18,27	
10,28*	αὐτῷ	18,28	
10,51*	αὐτῷ	18,41	
11,2*	αὐτοῖς	19,30	
11,6*	αὐτοῖς	19,34	
11,27	πρὸς αὐτόν	20,1	
11,33*	τῷ ᾿Ιησοῦ	20,7	

Mk		Lk	
12,18	(ἔρχονται) πρὸς αὐτόν	20,27	(προσελθόντες)
12,32*	αὐτῷ	20,39	
12,43*	αὐτοῖς	21,3	
13,2*	αὐτῷ	21,5	
13,5*	αὐτοῖς	21,8	
14,15	ἡμῖν	22,18	(cf. v. 8)
14,30*	αὐτῷ	22,34	
14,54	αὐτῷ	22,54	
14,61*	αὐτῷ	22,67	(+ 70)
14,67	τὸν Πέτρον	22,56	αὐτόν
14,71	τὸν ἄνθρωπον τοῦτον ὅν	22,60	ὅ
12,6	πρὸς αὐτούς	20,13	

24. Verb Supplied in Matthew and Luke [185]

Mk		Mt		Lk	
2,22a	ὁ οἶνος ἀπόλλυται καὶ οἱ ἀσκοί	9,17	ὁ οἶνος ἐκχεῖται καὶ οἱ ἀσκοὶ ἀπόλλυνται	5,37	αὐτὸς ἐκχυθήσεται καὶ οἱ ἀσκοὶ ἀπολοῦνται
2,22b	ἀλλὰ...	9,17	+ βάλλουσιν	5,38	+ βλητέον
2,23	τίλλοντες	12,1	τίλλειν στάχυας καὶ ἐσθίειν	6,1	ἔτιλλον καὶ ἤσθιον
	τοὺς στάχυας				τοὺς στάχυας
2,24	ὃ οὐκ ἔξεστιν	12,2	+ ποιεῖν	6,2	(+ ποιεῖν)
4,11	τὸ μυστήριον	13,11	γνῶναι τὰ μυστήρια	8,10	γνῶναι τὰ μυστήρια
9,34	τίς μείζων	18,1	+ ἐστίν	9,46	+ εἴη
10,27	ἀδύνατον	19,26	+ ἐστίν	18,27	+ ἐστίν
14,19	μήτι ἐγώ ;	26,22	+ εἰμί	(22,23)	τίς... εἴη
14,36	δυνατά σοι	26,39	εἰ δυνατόν ἐστιν	22,42	εἰ βούλει
(cf. 35	+ ἐστίν)	(26,42)	εἰ οὐ δύναται		

(24) The inverse

2,26	τοῖς σὺν αὐτῷ οὖσιν	12,4	τοῖς μετ᾽ αὐτοῦ	6,4	τοῖς μετ᾽ αὐτοῦ
cf. 25	οἱ μετ᾽ αὐτοῦ	12,3	οἱ μετ᾽ αὐτοῦ	6,3	οἱ μετ᾽ αὐτοῦ ὄντες

Verb supplied in Matthew

6,47	μόνος	Mt 14,23	+ ἦν
14,21	καλόν	26,24	+ ἦν
14,29	ἐγώ	26,33	+ σκανδαλισθήσομαι
15,32	ὁ βασιλεὺς Ἰσραήλ	27,42	+ ἐστίν
15,40	ἐν αἷς	27,56	+ ἦν

---

185. Schmid(33b), p. 77.

Verb supplied in Luke

5,9	ὄνομά σοι	Lk 8,30 + ἐστίν
6,15	προφήτης	9,8 + ἀνέστη
12,16	ἡ εἰκών (Mt 22,20)	20,24 ἔχει εἰκόνα

The inverse

1,27	τί ἐστιν τοῦτο ;	4,36 τίς ὁ λόγος οὗτος
	διδαχὴ καινὴ κατ᾽ ἐξουσίαν	ὅτι ἐν ἐξουσίᾳ

25. καὶ ἰδού (IN NARRATIVE) IN MATTHEW AND LUKE AND NOT IN MARK [186]

Mk	Mt		Lk	
1,40	8,2	καὶ ἰδού... προσελθών	5,12	καὶ ἰδοὺ ἀνήρ
2,3	9,2	καὶ ἰδοὺ προσέφερον	5,18	καὶ ἰδοὺ ἄνδρες φέροντες
3,1	12,10	καὶ ἰδοὺ ἄνθρωπος	(14,2)	καὶ ἰδοὺ ἄνθρωπός τις
5,22	9,18	(gen. abs.) ἰδού... προσελθών	8,41	καὶ ἰδοὺ ἦλθεν ἀνήρ
9,4	17,3	καὶ ἰδοὺ ὤφθη	9,30	καὶ ἰδοὺ ἄνδρες δύο
14,43	26,47	(gen. abs.) ἰδού	22,47	(gen. abs.) ἰδοὺ ὄχλος
16,5	28,2	καὶ ἰδοὺ σεισμὸς... ἄγγελος γάρ	24,4	καὶ ἰδοὺ ἄνδρες δύο

See Nos. **10** and **11**.

καὶ ἰδού in Matthew

Mk		Mt	
1,10	εἶδεν σχιζομένους	3,16	καὶ ἰδοὺ ἠνεῴχθησαν
1,11	καὶ φωνὴ (ἐγένετο)	3,17	καὶ ἰδοὺ φωνή
1,13	καὶ ἄγγελοι	4,11	καὶ ἰδοὺ ἄγγελοι προσῆλθον
2,6	ἦσαν δέ τινες... καθήμενοι	9,3	καὶ ἰδού τινες
2,15	καὶ (post γίνεται with infinitive)	9,10	(gen. abs.) καὶ ἰδοὺ πολλοί (v.l. καί om.)
3,31	καὶ ἔρχονται ἡ μήτηρ	12,46	(gen. abs.) ἰδοὺ ἡ μήτηρ
4,37	καὶ γίνεται	8,24	καὶ ἰδοὺ σεισμὸς μέγας ἐγένετο
5,6-7	καὶ ἰδών... ἔδραμεν... καὶ κράξας	8,29	καὶ ἰδοὺ ἔκραξαν
5,13	καὶ ὥρμησεν	8,32	καὶ ἰδοὺ ὥρμησεν
5,15	καὶ ἔρχονται	8,34	καὶ ἰδοὺ πᾶσα ἡ πόλις
5,25	καὶ γυνή	9,20	καὶ ἰδοὺ γυνή
7,25	ἀλλ᾽ εὐθύς... γυνή	15,22	καὶ ἰδοὺ γυνή
9,7a	καὶ ἐγένετο	17,5a	(gen. abs.) ἰδοὺ νεφέλη
9,7b	καὶ ἐγένετο	17,5b	καὶ ἰδοὺ φωνή
10,17	προσδραμὼν εἷς	19,16	καὶ ἰδοὺ εἷς προσελθών
10,46	ὁ υἱός... ἐκάθητο	20,30	καὶ ἰδοὺ δύο τυφλοὶ καθήμενοι
14,47	εἷς δέ τις	26,51	καὶ ἰδοὺ εἷς
15,38	καὶ τὸ καταπέτασμα	27,51	καὶ ἰδού... καὶ ἡ γῆ ἐσείσθη

---

186. Schmid(33f), p. 78 ; cf. Turner(7,4iii), pp. 21-22 ; comp. Schürmann I, p. 93.

καὶ ἰδού in Luke

Mk		Lk	
9,17	καὶ ἀπεκρίθη αὐτῷ εἷς	9,38	καὶ ἰδοὺ ἀνήρ
9,18	καὶ ὅπου	9,39	καὶ ἰδοὺ πνεῦμα λαμβάνει
12,28	καὶ προσελθὼν εἷς	(10,25)	καὶ ἰδοὺ νομικός τις
15,42-43	καὶ... ἐλθών	23,50	καὶ ἰδοὺ ἀνήρ

Note : ἰδού in sayings in Mk 1,2 ; 3,32 ; 4,3 ; 10,28 ; 10,33 ; 14,41.42 (with parallel in Mt) ; ἴδε in Mk 2,24 ; 3,34 ; 13,21bis (ἰδού in Mt) ; 11,21 ; 13,1 ; 15,4.35 (diff. Mt) ; 16,6 (ἴδετε in Mt).

26. εὐθύς IN MARK AND NOT IN MATTHEW AND LUKE [187]

Matthew/Luke agreements (†) : εὐθέως diff. Mk 1,42 ; εὐθέως/παραχρῆμα diff. Mk 10,52 ; 14,72 v.l. Mt ; omission diff. Mk 1,12.28,29 ; 2,8.12 (Lk παραχρῆμα) ; 3,6 ; 4,15 ; 5,42 ; 14,43 ; 15,1. Comp. ἐξάπινα om. diff. Mk 9,8.

Mk	Mt		Lk	
1,10	3,16	εὐθύς	3,21	om. phrase
1,12†	4,1	om.	4,1	om.
1,18	4,20	εὐθέως		
1,20	4,22	εὐθέως (ante ἀφέντες)	(5,11)	om.
1,21			4,31	om. phrase
1,23			4,33	om.
1,28†	(4,24)	om.	4,37	om.
1,29†	8,14	om.	4,38	om.
1,30	8,14	om. phrase	4,38	om. cf. v. 39 παραχρῆμα
1,42†	8,3	εὐθέως	5,13	εὐθέως
1,43	8,3		5,13	
2,8†	9,4	om.	5,22	om.
2,12†	9,7	om.	5,25	παραχρῆμα (ante ἀναστάς)
3,6†	12,14	om.	6,11	om.
4,5	13,5	εὐθέως	8,6	
4,15†	13,19	om.	8,12	om. (εἶτα)
4,16	13,20	εὐθύς	8,13	om.

---

187. Schmid(10), pp. 41-42 ; cf. Larfeld, p. 14 (list) and 218 (" Differenzierungstrieb " in Mt and Lk). Contra T. Stephenson (see n. 68) and J. WEISS, 'ΕΥΘΥΣ bei Markus ', *ZNW* 11 (1910) 124-133 (proto-Mark). Comp. F. EAKIN, 'Mark's " Straightway " ', *Expositor*, 8th ser., vol. 25 (1923) 185-205 ; H. PERNOT, *Études sur la langue des évangiles*, Paris, 1927, pp. 181-188 ; P. VAN-NUTELLI, ' La voce ΕΥΘΥΣ (εὐθέως) negli evangeli e negli scrittori greci ', *Synoptica* 1 (1936) CXIV-CXXVI ; G. RUDBERG, 'ΕΥΘΥΣ', in *Coniectanea Neotestamentica* 9 (1954) pp. 42-46 ; D. TABACHO-VITZ, *Die Septuagint und das Neue Testament*, Lund, 1956, pp. 29-35 ; Kilpatrick, pp. 3-4 (normally at the beginning of the clause : a connecting particle) ; N. TURNER, *Syntax*, p. 229 ; D. DAUBE, *The Sudden in the Scriptures*, Leiden, 1964, pp. 38-72 ; L. RYDBECK, *Fachprosa, vermeintliche Volkssprache und Neues Testament*, Uppsala, 1967, pp. 167-176. — See *Duality in Mark*, p. 33, n. 78 : repetition of εὐθύς and " Wortresponsion " (cf. J. SUNDWALL, *Zusammensetzung*, see n. 167) ; p. 48, n. 152 and pp. 94-96 : double temporal statement.

Mk		Mt		Lk	
4,17		13,21	εὐθύς	8,13	om.
4,29					
5,2†	(v.l. om.)	8,28	om.	8,27	om.
5,29				8,44	παραχρῆμα
5,30		9,22		8,45	om.
5,42a†		9,25	om.	8,55	παραχρῆμα
5,42b	(v.l. om.)	9,25	om. phrase	8,56	om.
6,25		14,8			
6,27		14,10	om.		
6,45		14,22	εὐθέως		
6,50		14,27	εὐθύς (v.l. εὐθέως)		
6,54		14,35	om.		
7,25		15,22	om.		
7,35	(v.l. om.)				
8,10		15,39	om.		
9,15					
9,20		17,17		9,42	om. (gen. abs. ἔτι)
9,24					
10,52†		20,34	εὐθέως	18,43	παραχρῆμα
11,2		21,2	εὐθύς (v.l. εὐθέως)	19,30	om.
11,3		21,3	εὐθύς	19,31	om. phrase
14,43†		26,47	om.	22,47	om.
14,45		26,49	εὐθέως	22,47	om.
14,72(†)		26,74	εὐθύς (v.l. εὐθέως)	22,60	παραχρῆμα (+ ἔτι λαλοῦντος αὐτοῦ)
15,1†		27,1	om.	22,66	om. (ὡς)
9,8	ἐξάπινα	17,8	om.	9,36	ἐν τῷ γενέσθαι τὴν φωνήν

Note on variant readings

Mk 5,2 ; Mt diff. Mk 11,2 ; 14,72 : see the list.

5,42b εὐθύς : — TR, [GNT³](D).
7,35 εὐθὺς (ἐλύθη) : — Ti H ; εὐθέως (ἠνοίγησαν) TR [S] [GNT](C).

Additional instances (K = Kilpatrick)

Mk		Mt		Lk	
1,31 εὐθέως TR Ti ; εὐθύς S K		8,15 om.		4,39a om. (cf. 39b παραχρῆμα)	
2,2 εὐθέως TR Ti S ; εὐθύς K				5,17	
5,13 εὐθέως TR Ti S ; εὐθύς K		8,32 om.		8,32 om.	
5,36 εὐθέως TR ; εὐθύς S K				8,50 om.	
9,8 εὐθύς (instead of ἐξάπινα) K					

TR εὐθέως, but εὐθύς 1,12.28 ; om. 1,23 ; 7,25 (S) ; 14,72 (Ti S).

εὐθύς, εὐθέως, παραχρῆμα in Matthew

εὐθύς :   par. Mk : Mt 3,16 ; 13,20.21 ; 14,27 ; 21,2 (v.l. εὐθέως). 3 ; 26,74 (v.l. εὐθέως).
           Note : εὐθέως TR S in 14,27 ; 21,3.

εὐθέως :   par. Mk εὐθύς :   Mt 4,20.22 ; 8,3 ; 13,5 ; 14,22 v.l. ; 20,34 ; 26,49.
             other instances : Mt 14,31 (M, cf. 14,29 = Mk 6,50)
                             24,29 (diff. Mk 13,24 ἀλλὰ ἐν ἐκείναις ἡμέραις)
                             25,15 (diff. Lk 19,13ff.)
                             27,48 (add. Mk 15,36)
παραχρῆμα : Mt 21,19 (add. Mk 11,14, cf. v. 15)
             21,20 πῶς παραχρῆμα (Mk 11,21 ἴδε).

εὐθύς, εὐθέως, παραχρῆμα in Luke

εὐθύς :   Lk 6,49 (add. Mt 7,27)
             Acts 10,16.
εὐθέως :   par. Mk εὐθύς :   Lk 5,13.
             other instances : Lk 12,36 ; 12,54 ; 14,5 (diff. Mt 12,11) ; 17,7 ; 21,9 οὐκ εὐθέως (Mk 13,9
             οὔπω).
             Acts 9,18.20.34 ; 12,10 ; 16,10 ; 17,10.14 ; 21,30 ; 22,39.
παραχρῆμα : par. Mk εὐθύς :   Lk 4,39 ; 5,25 ; 8,44.55 ; 18,43 ; 22,60.
             other instances : Lk 1,64 ; 8,47 (cf. v. 44, par. εὐθύς Mk 5,29) ; 13,13 ; 19,11.
             Acts 3,7 ; 5,10 ; 12,23 ; 13,11 ; 16,26.33.

27. πάλιν IN MARK AND NOT IN MATTHEW AND LUKE [188]

† Parallel use in Matthew or Luke
* In the opening sentence of a section or sub-section

Matthew /Luke agreements : omission diff. Mk 3,1 ; 5,21 ; 10,32 ; 14,69.70b ; 15,(4).13.

Mk		Mt		Lk	
2,1*	cf. 1,21	9,1b	om.	5,17	om. phrase
2,13*	cf. 1,16	9,9		5,27	
3,1*	cf. 1,21.39	12,9	om.	6,6	(ἐν ἑτέρῳ σαββάτῳ)
3,20*	cf. 3,7-9				
4,1*	cf. 2,13 (3 7-9)	13,1	om.	8,1.4	om. phrase
5,21*	cf. 4,35 (εἰς τὸ πέραν)	9,1a	om.	8,40	(ἐν τῷ ὑποστρέφειν)
	cf. 4,1 (πάλιν συνήχθη ?)				

---

188. Schmid(11), p. 42 ; cf. Turner(9,2), pp. 283-287 ; comp. Cadbury, p. 199 ; Larfeld, pp. 218-
219. Turner, p. 287 : " The original sense of ' back' seems clear in certain connexions, e.g. 5,21 ;
11,3, and possible in 7,31 ; 10,10 ; 10,32 ; 11,27 " ; Bauer does not include 10,10.32 (Turner : " back
in the house ", " back in the company with him ") but still adds 2,1 and 14,39. There is much
discussion about the meaning of πάλιν in Mark : whether merely connective or really iterative ;
cf. Bultmann : " in der Regel (zu verstehen) : ... einfach als Anreihungsformel für das aramäische
תּוּב : 2,1.13 ; 3,1 ; 4,1 ; 11,27 " (p. 364) ; Lagrange, Marc, p. XCVIII : " πάλιν a toujours dans Mc.
le sens itératif " ; comp. Howard, p. 446 ; Kilpatrick, pp. 4-5 : the close proximity with the verb
suggests that we should treat it as a true adverb ; exceptions are 5,21 (πάλιν συνήχθη) ; 8,1 ; 10,10 ;
11,3 ; 12,5 v.l. ; 14,61 ; N. Turner, Syntax, p. 329 ; Black³, pp. 112-113 (Mk 15,13 " thereupon ",
comp. Bauer, s.v. πάλιν, 5). — The possible cross-references are indicated in the list (e.g., 2,1 cf.
1,21).

Mk		Mt		Lk
7,14(*)	comp. 3,23	15,10	om.	
7,31*	cf. 7,24	15,29	om.	
8,1*	cf. 6,34-36	15,32		
8,13(*)	cf. 8,10	16,4	om.	
8,25	cf. 8,23			
10,1a*	cf. passim	19,2a	om.	
10,1b*	+ ὡς εἰώθει	19,2b	om.	
10,10(*)	cf. (4,10) ; 7,17 ; 9,28	19,10	om.	
10,24	cf. v. 23	19,24†	πάλιν (δὲ λέγω ὑμῖν) (oratio recta)	
10,32*		20,17	om.	18,31 om.
11,3	(" back ")	21,3	om.	19,32 om. phrase
11,27*	cf. 11,15	21,23	om.	20,1 om. phrase
12,4	cf. 12,2	21,36†	πάλιν	20,11 om. (προσέθετο)
14,39	cf. 14,35	26,42†	πάλιν ἐκ δευτέρου	
14,40	cf. 14,37	26,43†	πάλιν	
14,61	cf. 14,60	26,63	om.	22,67 om. phrase
14,69	cf. 14,67	26,71	(ἄλλη)	22,58 (ἕτερος)
14,70a	cf. 14,68	26,72†	πάλιν	22,58 om.
14,70b	cf. 14,67.69	26,73	om.	22,59 (ἄλλος)
15,4	cf. 15,2 (comp. 14,61)	27,13	om.	cf. (23,9)
15,12	cf. 15,9	27,21	om.	23,20† πάλιν
15,13	cf. 15,11	27,22	om.	23,21 om.

Variant reading (TR, Kilpatrick)

| 12,5 | cf. 12,2.4 | | | 20,12 om. (προσέθετο) |

πάλιν in Matthew

Par. Mk : Mt 19,24 ; 21,36 ; 26,42.43.72.
Add. Mk : Mt 26,44 (cf. v. 39.42)   Mk 14,41 (comp. v. 39)
              27,50 (cf. v. 46)   15,37
Diff. Lk : Mt 4,7 (cf. v. 6)   Lk 4,12 (om.)
              4,8 (cf. v. 5)   4,5 (om.)
              22,1 (cf. 21,33 and 28)   14,16 (diff.)
              22,4 (cf. v. 9)   24,21 (diff.)
              (comp. 21,36 par. Mk)

Peculiar to Mt : 5,33 (cf. v. 21.27.[31[) ; 13,45 (cf. v. 44) ; 13,47 (cf. v. 44 and 45) ; 18,49 (cf. v. 18) ; 20,5 (cf. v. 3).

πάλιν in Luke

Par. Mk : Lk 23,20.
Diff. Mt : Lk 6,43b (cf. v. 43a)   Mt 7,18 (om.)
              13,20 (cf. v. 18)   13,33 (ἄλλην)
Acts 10,15 (πάλιν ἐκ δευτέρου, cf. v. 13) ; 11,10 (cf. v. 5) ; 17,32 ; 18,21 ; 27,28b (cf. v. 28a).

28. πολλά Adverbial in Mark and not in Matthew and Luke [189]

* See note.

Matthew/Luke agreements against Mark : diff. Mk 3,12 ; 5,38 ; 15,3.

Mk		Mt		Lk	
1,45*	κηρύσσειν πολλά			5,15	(μᾶλλον)
3,12*	πολλὰ ἐπετίμα	12,16	ἐπετίμησεν	(4,41)	ἐπιτιμῶν
4,2(*)	ἐδίδασκεν πολλά	13,3	ἐλάλησεν πολλά	8,4	diff.
5,10*	παρεκάλει πολλά			8,31	παρεκάλουν
5,23*	παρεκάλει πολλά			8,41	παρεκάλει εἰσελθεῖν
5,26	πολλὰ παθοῦσα		(cf. 27,19 πολλὰ ἔπαθον)	8,43	diff.
5,38*	κλαίοντας καὶ ἀλα-λάζοντας πολλά	9,23	diff. (ὄχλον)	8,52	diff. (πάντες)
5,43*	διεστείλατο πολλά			8,56	παρήγγειλεν
6,20*	πολλὰ ἠπόρει (ἀκούσας πολλά Kilpatrick)			(9,7)	διηπόρει
6,34(*)	διδάσκειν πολλά			9,11	ἐλάλει περί
8,31	πολλὰ παθεῖν	16,21	πολλὰ παθεῖν	9,22	πολλὰ παθεῖν
9,12	πολλὰ παθῇ	17,12	πάσχειν	(cf. 17,25)	πολλὰ παθεῖν
9,26*	πολλὰ σπαράξας (v.l. κράξας πολλά Kilpatrick)				
15,3*	κατηγόρουν πολλά	27,12	κατηγορεῖσθαι	(23,2)	κατηγορεῖν

Variant reading (Taylor, Kilpatrick)

6,23	ὤμοσεν (πολλά)	14,7	μεθ' ὅρκου ὡμολόγησεν		
12,27	πολὺ πλανᾶσθε	22,32	om. phrase	20,38	om. phrase

Cf. Lk 7,47 ἠγάπησεν πολύ

The inverse

2,18	νηστεύουσιν	9,15	v.l. + πολλά	5,33	+ πυκνά

---

189. Schmid(16), p. 48 ; cf. Cadbury, pp. 199-200 ; comp. Hawkins, p. 35, who notes the nine instances marked by an asterisk and regards all other instances as accusatives. See Howard, p. 446 ; Bauer, s.v. πολύς I 2bβ. In addition, 6,34 is referred to in Moulton-Geden's *Concordance* ; (cf. Moffatt, Lagrange and Taylor, p. 190 ; Blass-Debrunner, § 155,1) ; also 4,2 may be interpreted adverbially (cf. B. Weiss, G. Wohlenberg, and Zerwick, p. 123, who adds 8,31 ; on this last passage see G. Strecker, in *ZTK* 64 (1967) p. 27) ; Kilpatrick, pp. 7-8 : πολλά regularly following the verb and πολλὰ παθεῖν a stereotyped phrase.

29. φέρω IN MARK (IN THE SENSE OF " LEAD " OR " BRING ") [190]

* ἄγω (or compound form)
† προσφέρω (see No. **18**)

Mk	Mt	Lk
11,2 φέρετε	21,2* ἀγάγετε	19,30* ἀγάγετε
11,7 φέρουσιν (πρός)	21,7* ἤγαγον	19,35* ἤγαγον (πρός)
12,15 φέρετε (ἵνα ἴδω)	22,19 ἐπιδείξατε	20,24 δείξατε
15,1 ἀπήνεγκαν	27,2* ἀπήγαγον	23,1* ἤγαγον (ἐπί)
		cf. 14† προσηνέγκατε
15,22 φέρουσιν	27,33 ἐλθόντες	23,33 ἦλθον
		cf. 32* ἤγοντο (σὺν αὐτῷ)
cf. 13,9 σταθήσεσθε	10,18* ἀχθήσεσθε	21,12* ἀπαγομένους
(ἐπί + gen.)	(ἐπί + acc.)	(ἐπί + acc.)
See No. **31c**.		

Other instances

1,32 ἔφερον	8,16† προσήνεγκαν	4,40* ἤγαγον
	(4,24†) προσήνεγκαν	
2,3 φέροντες	9,2† προσέφερον	5,18 φέροντες (ἐπὶ κλίνης)
		' carrying (on a bed) ',
		cf. 23,26 ; 24,1
6,27 ἐνέγκαι (cf. 28)		
6,28 ἤνεγκεν	14,11 ἠνέχθη	
7,32 φέρουσιν	15,30 προσῆλθον ἔχοντες	
8,22 φέρουσιν (τυφλόν)		(cf. 18,40* ἀχθῆναι πρός)
9,17 ἤνεγκα	(17,16†) προσήνεγκα	
9,19 φέρετε	17,17 φέρετε	9,41* προσάγαγε
9,20 ἤνεγκαν		9,42 προσερχομένου
12,16 ἤνεγκαν (cf. 15)	22,19† προσήνεγκαν	

(29) The inverse

13,11 ἄγωσιν (παραδιδόντες)	10,19 παραδῶσιν	12,11 εἰσφέρωσιν

---

190. Schmid(27), p. 56 ; cf. Turner(2), pp. 12-14 ; comp. B. H. STREETER, *The Four Gospels* (see n. 96), pp. 298-299 ; W. R. FARMER, *The Synoptic Problem* (see n. 125), pp. 128-130 ; J. A. FITZMYER, ' The Use of *Agein* and *Pherein* in the Synoptic Gospels ', in E. H. BARTH-R. E. COCROFT (ed.), *Festschrift to Honor F. Wilbur Gingrich*, Leiden, 1972, pp. 147-160. He observes that the synonymous use of φέρειν and ἄγειν cannot be limited to Hellenistic times. His list of instances " purports to be exhaustive " (p. 155), but the compound forms in Lk 12,11 (φέρω) and 21,12 (ἄγω) are not mentioned. He objects against Turner's conclusion (p. 150, n. 1), without good reason since the sense of φέροντες in Lk 5,18 differs from Mk 's " bringing to him ", as it is rightly observed by Turner (p. 13). Still, " such issues as the minor agreements of Matthew and Luke against Mark have to be assessed in detail, with such side issues as the use of *agein* and *pherein* treated adequately " (p. 160).

30. TITLES USED IN ADDRESSING JESUS [191]

* κύριε
† ἐπιστάτα

Matthew/Luke agreements (positive) diff. Mk 1,40 ; 10,51 ; 12,28 ; (negative) 4,38 ; 9,5.

Mk		Mt		Lk	
9,5	ῥαββί	17,4*	κύριε	9,33†	ἐπιστάτα
10,51	ῥαββουνί	20,33*	κύριε	18,41*	κύριε
		(9,28)			
11,21	ῥαββί	21,20			
14,45	ῥαββί	26,49	ῥαββί	22,47	
		cf. 26,25			
4,38	διδάσκαλε	8,25*	κύριε	8,24†	ἐπιστάτα ἐπιστάτα
9,17	διδάσκαλε	17,15*	κύριε	9,38	διδάσκαλε
9,38	διδάσκαλε			9,49†	ἐπιστάτα
10,17	διδάσκαλε	19,16	διδάσκαλε	18,18	διδάσκαλε
10,20	διδάσκαλε (cf. 17)	19,20		18,21	
10,35	διδάσκαλε	20,20	diff.		
12,14	διδάσκαλε	22,16	διδάσκαλε	20,21	διδάσκαλε
12,19	διδάσκαλε	22,24	διδάσκαλε	20,28	διδάσκαλε
12,28		22,36	διδάσκαλε	(10,25)	διδάσκαλε
				cf. 20,39	
12,32	διδάσκαλε			(20,39)	διδάσκαλε
13,1	διδάσκαλε	24,1	diff.	21,5	diff.
				cf. 7	διδάσκαλε
1,24	Ἰησοῦ Ναζαρηνέ			4,34	Ἰησοῦ Ναζαρηνέ
5,7	Ἰησοῦ υἱὲ τοῦ θεοῦ	8,29	υἱὲ τοῦ θεοῦ	8,28	Ἰησοῦ υἱὲ τοῦ θεοῦ
	τοῦ ὑψίστου				τοῦ ὑψίστου
10,47	υἱὲ Δαυίδ Ἰησοῦ	20,30*	κύριε,... υἱὸς Δαυίδ	18,38	Ἰησοῦ υἱὲ Δαυίδ
		(9,27)	υἱὸς Δαυίδ		
10,48	υἱὲ Δαυίδ	20,31*	κύριε,... υἱὸς Δαυίδ	18,39	υἱὲ Δαυίδ
7,28*	κύριε	15,27*	κύριε		
		cf. 22*	add. κύριε υἱὸς Δαυίδ		
7,26	(indir.)	15,25*	dir. κύριε		
1,40		8,2*	κύριε	5,12*	κύριε
5,31				8,45†	ἐπιστάτα
8,32		16,22*	add. κύριε		
14,19		26,22*	κύριε	22,23	indir.
		cf. 25	add. ῥαββί		
14,29.(31)		26,33		22,33*	κύριε
14,47		26,51		22,48*	add. κύριε

---

191. Schmid(1), p. 35, n. 1 ; (33,g), pp. 78-79 ; cf. Turner(10,1), pp. 347-349 ; comp. Schürmann III, pp. 28-29.

31. PREPOSITIONS CHANGED IN MATTHEW AND LUKE [192]

31a. εἰς in Mark and ἐν in Matthew and Luke

Matthew/Luke agreements

Mk	Mt	Lk
11,8 εἰς (τὴν ὁδόν)	21,8 ἐν (τῇ ὁδῷ)	19,36 ἐν (τῇ ὁδῷ)
13,16 εἰς (τὸν ἀγρόν)	24,18 ἐν (τῷ ἀγρῷ)	(17,31) ἐν (τῷ ἀγρῷ)

The inverse

4,36 (ὡς ἦν) ἐν (τῷ πλοίῳ)	8,23 ἐμβάντι εἰς (τὸ πλοῖον)	8,22 ἐνέβη εἰς (πλοῖον)

ἐν in Matthew only

1,39 κηρύσσων εἰς... εἰς	4,23 περιῆγεν ἐν διδάσκων ἐν	4,44 κηρύσσων εἰς
9,42 βέβληται εἰς	18,6 καταποντισθῇ ἐν	
13,10 εἰς... κηρυχθῆναι	24,14 κηρυχθήσεται ἐν	
14,9 κηρυχθῇ εἰς	26,13 κηρυχθῇ ἐν	
14,20 ἐμβαπτόμενος εἰς	26,23 ἐμβάψας ἐν	
Cf. 1,9 ἐβαπτίσθη εἰς	(3,13) παραγίνεται ἐπί	
5,14 ἀπήγγειλαν εἰς	8,33 ἀπελθόντες εἰς	

Mk 13,9   παραδώσουσιν
              εἰς συνέδρια καὶ εἰς συναγωγὰς δαρήσεσθε
Mt (10,17) παραδώσουσιν εἰς συνέδρια
              καὶ ἐν ταῖς συναγωγαῖς μαστιγώσουσιν
Lk 21,12   παραδιδόντες εἰς τὰς συναγωγὰς καὶ φυλακάς

The inverse : ἐν in Mark and εἰς in Matthew

1,16 Mt 4,18	
9,41 10,42	
14,6 26,10	

Compare

1,8 πνεύματι	3,11 ἐν πνεύματι	3,16 ἐν πνεύματι
15,43 εἰσῆλθεν πρός + acc.	27,58 προσελθών + dat.	23,52 προσελθών + dat.
cf. 2,4 προσενέγκαι		5,19 εἰσενέγκωσιν
10,25 διελθεῖν	19,24 εἰσελθεῖν	18,25 εἰσελθεῖν

---

192. Schmid(20), pp. 50-52 ; cf. Turner(3), pp. 14-20 (εἰς, ἐν) ; and (9,2), pp. 281-282 (ἐκ, ἀπό) ;
comp. Allen, p. XXVII ; Cadbury, pp. 202-205 ; Schürmann I, p. 102.

31b. *ἐκ in Mark and ἀπό in Matthew and Luke*

Matthew/Luke agreements

Mk	Mt	Lk
2,12 ἐξῆλθεν	9,7 ἀπῆλθεν (εἰς τὸν οἶκον)	5,25 ἀπῆλθεν (εἰς τὸν οἶκον)
15,20 ἐξάγουσιν	27,31 ἀπήγαγον	23,26 ἀπήγαγον

The inverse

8,11 ἀπό	16,1 ἐκ	(11,16) ἐξ

Compare

1,28 ἐξῆλθεν	(4,24) ἀπῆλθεν	
1,34 ἐξέβαλεν	8,16 ἐξέβαλεν	4,41 ἐξήρχετο ἀπό
6,11 ἐκτινάξατε	10,14 ἐκτινάξατε	9,5 ἀποτινάσσετε (+ ἀπό)
14,16 ἐξῆλθεν καὶ ἦλθον	22,13 ἀπελθόντες	
16,8 ἐξελθοῦσαι	28,8 ἀπελθοῦσαι	24,9 ὑποστρέψασαι
Cf. 9,43 ἀπόκοψον	18,8 ἔκκοψον (5,29 βάλε ἀπό)	
9,45 ἔκβαλε	18,9 ἔξελε καὶ βάλε ἀπό (= 5,29)	

Note

12,30 ἐξ (quater)	22,37 ἐν (ter)	(10,27) ἐν (quater)
14,69 ἐξ αὐτῶν (67 μετά)	26,71 μέτα Ἰησοῦ	22,58 ἐξ αὐτῶν
cf. 14,70 ἐξ αὐτῶν	26,73 ἐξ αὐτῶν	22,59 μετ' αὐτοῦ
15,46 ἐκ πέτρας	27,60 ἐν τῇ πέτρᾳ	

ἐκ in Mark and ἀπό in Matthew or Luke

1,10 ἀναβαίνων ἐκ	3,16 ἀνέβη ἀπό	
1,25 ἔξελθε ἐξ		4,35 ἔξελθε ἀπ'
1,26 ἐξῆλθεν ἐξ		4,35 ἐξῆλθεν ἀπ'
1,29 ἐκ ἐξελθόντες		4,38 ἀναστὰς ἀπό
5,8 ἔξελθε ἐκ		8,29 ἐξελθεῖν ἀπό
5,30 ἐξ ἐξελθοῦσαν		8,46 ἐξεληλυθυῖαν ἀπ'
6,14 ἐγήγερται ἐκ	16,2 ἠγέρθη ἀπό	(9,7) ἠγέρθη ἐκ
9,9a καταβαινόντων ἐκ (v.l. ἀπό)	(17,9) καταβαινόντων ἐκ	9,37 κατελθόντων ἀπό
9,17 εἰς ἐκ τοῦ ὄχλου		9,38 ἀνὴρ ἀπὸ τοῦ ὄχλου
9,25 ἔξελθε ἐξ (cf. 26)	17,18 ἐξῆλθεν ἀπ'	
11,8 κόψαντες ἐκ	21,8 ἔκοπτον ἀπό	
13,1 ἐκπορευομένου ἐκ	24,1 ἐξελθὼν ἀπό	
13,25 ἐκ πίπτοντες	24,29 πεσοῦνται ἀπό	
14,25 πίω ἐκ	(26,29) πίω ἐκ	22,18 πίω ἀπό
16,4 ἀνακεκύλισται	28,2 ἀπεκύλισεν	24,2 ἀποκεκυλισμένον ἀπό
cf. 3 ἀποκυλίσει ἐκ		

Comp. Mk 14,13 ἀπαντήσει Lk 22,10 συναντήσει

31c. *Other Prepositions*

Mk	Mt	Lk
2,26 σὺν αὐτῷ (cf. 25)	12,4 μετ' αὐτοῦ	6,4 μετ' αὐτοῦ

The inverse : Mk 5,18   Lk 8,38
                 5,37   8,51
                 14,17   22,14
                 14,67   22,56 (but see μετά in 22,56 par. Mk ἐξ)

Mk	Mt	Lk
4,7 συνέπνιξαν	13,7 ἀπέπνιξαν	8,7 ἀπέπνιξαν
11,31 διελογίζοντο πρός	21,25 διελογίζοντο ἐν	20,5 συνελογίσαντο πρός
12,7 πρὸς ἑαυτοὺς εἶπαν	21,38 εἶπον ἐν ἑαυτοῖς	20,14 διελογίζοντο πρὸς ἀλλήλους

Comp. Mk 14,19 λέγειν   Lk 22,23 συζητεῖν
           1,27 συζητεῖν   4,36 συνελάλουν

Mk	Mt	Lk
8,31 ὑπό	16,21 ἀπό	9,22 ἀπό
15,41 ἐν	(27,55) ἀπό	23,49 ἀπό
1,10 εἰς	3,16 ἐπί	3,22 ἐπί

Compare

1,38 εἰς		4,43 ἐπί + acc.
4,7 εἰς	13,7 ἐπί	8,7 ἐν μέσῳ
4,8 εἰς	13,8 ἐπί	8,8 εἰς
cf. 4,18 εἰς	13,22 εἰς	8,14 εἰς
4,20 ἐπί	13,23 ἐπί	8,15 ἐν

Comp. Mt 18,12 ἐπί + acc., Lk 15,14 ἐν + dat.

Mk	Mt	Lk
11,7 ἐπιβάλλουσιν αὐτῷ	21,7 ἐπέθηκαν ἐπ' αὐτῶν	19,35 ἐπιρίψαντες ἐπὶ τόν
13,9 ἐπί + gen.	10,17 ἐπί + acc.	21,12 ἐπί + acc.

Comp. Mt 19,28 ἐπί + acc., Lk 22,30 ἐπί + gen.

Mk	Mt	Lk
4,31 ἐπὶ τῆς γῆς	13,31 ἐν τῷ ἀγρῷ	13,19 εἰς κῆπον
cf. 13,2 ἐπὶ λίθον	24,2 ἐπὶ λίθον	21,6 ἐπὶ λίθῳ
4,21 ἐπί + acc.	5,15 ἐπί + acc.	11,33 ἐπί + acc.
8,31 μετὰ τρεῖς ἡμέρας	16,21 τῇ τρίτῃ ἡμέρᾳ	9,22 τῇ τρίτῃ ἡμέρᾳ
10,34 μετὰ τρεῖς ἡμέρας	20,19 τῇ τρίτῃ ἡμέρᾳ	18,33 τῇ ἡμέρᾳ τῇ τρίτῃ

32. CHANGES IN VOCABULARY [193]

The mere negative agreements are underlined in the text of Mark.

Mk	Mt	Lk
1,10 σχιζομένους	ἠνεῴχθησαν	ἀνεῳχθῆναι
1,13 σατανᾶ	διαβόλου	διαβόλου
1,14 ἦλθεν	ἀνεχώρησεν	ὑπέστρεψεν
1,20 ἀπῆλθον ὀπίσω	ἠκολούθησαν	ἠκολούθησαν
1,39 ἦλθεν (v.l. ἦν)	περιῆγεν	ἦν
1,40 γονυπετῶν	προσεκύνει	πεσὼν ἐπὶ πρόσωπον
2,6 διαλογιζόμενοι	εἶπαν	λέγοντες
2,11 κράβατον	κλίνην	κλινίδιον
2,12 ἐξίστασθαι	ἐφοβήθησαν	ἔκστασις ἔλαβεν... ἐπλήσθησαν φόβου
2,21 ἐπιράπτει	ἐπιβάλλει	ἐπιβάλλει
2,23 παραπορεύεσθαι	ἐπορεύθη	διαπορεύεσθαι
3,7 πλῆθος	ὄχλοι	ὄχλος
3,10 μάστιγας	νόσοις	νόσων
4,1 (ὄχλος) πλεῖστος	(ὄχλοι) πολλοί	(ὄχλου) πολλοῦ
4,15 σατανᾶς	πονηρός	διάβολος
4,32 ἀναβαίνει	αὐξηθῇ	ηὔξησεν
4,41 ἐφοβήθησαν	ἐθαύμασαν	φοβηθέντες... ἐθαύμασαν
5,2 ἐν πνεύματι ἀκαθάρτῳ	δαιμονιζόμενοι	ἔχων δαιμόνια
5,13 (τὰ) πνεύματα τὰ ἀκάθαρτα	(οἱ) δαίμονες	(τὰ) δαιμόνια
5,22 (εἷς τῶν) ἀρχισυναγώγων	ἄρχων	ἄρχων τῆς συναγωγῆς
5,23 ἐσχάτως ἔχει	ἐτελεύτησεν	ἀπέθνῃσκεν
5,38 τὸν οἶκον	τὴν οἰκίαν	τὴν οἰκίαν
6,11 χοῦν	κονιορτόν	κονιορτόν
6,14 βασιλεύς	τετραάρχης	τετραάρχης
6,32 ἀπῆλθον	ἀνεχώρησεν	ὑπεχώρησεν
8,15 βλέπετε	προσέχετε	προσέχετε
8,27 ἐξῆλθεν (εἰς)	ἐλθὼν (εἰς)	ἐγένετο ἐν τῷ εἶναι
8,31 ἀναστῆναι	ἐγερθῆναι	ἐγερθῆναι
9,17 εἷς	ἄνθρωπος	ἀνήρ
9,18 ἴσχυσαν	ἠδυνήθησαν	ἠδυνήθησαν
9,36 λαβών	προσκαλεσάμενος	ἐπιλαβόμενος
9,50 ἄναλον γένηται	μωρανθῇ	μωρανθῇ
10,22 στυγνάσας ἐπί	ἀκούσας	ἀκούσας
10,25 τρυμαλιᾶς	τρήματος	τρήματος
10,30 ἑκατονταπλασίονα	πολλαπλασίονα	πολλαπλασίονα
10,47 ἐστίν	παράγει	παρέρχεται
12,15 εἰδώς	γνούς	κατανοήσας
12,15 ὑπόκρισιν	πονηρίαν	πανουργίαν
12,22 ἔσχατον	ὕστερον	ὕστερον
12,28 (εἷς) τῶν γραμματέων	(εἷς ἐξ αὐτῶν) νομικός	νομικός (τις)

193. For lists of synonyms see already Scholten, *Das älteste Evangelium*, pp. 92-95 (Mk-Mt) and Krenkel, pp. 41-47 (Mk-Lk).

Mk	Mt	Lk
12,37 λέγει	καλεῖ	καλεῖ
12,37 πόθεν	πῶς	πῶς
14,11 (πῶς) εὐκαίρως	εὐκαιρίαν	εὐκαιρίαν
14,25 οὐκέτι	ἀπ' ἄρτι	ἀπὸ τοῦ νῦν
14,31 ἐλάλει	λέγει	εἶπεν
14,36 (ἀββὰ) ὁ πατήρ	πάτερ μου	πάτερ
14,47 ἔπαισεν	πατάξας	ἐπάταξεν
14,61 εὐλογητοῦ	θεοῦ	θεοῦ
14,72 ἀνεμνήσθη + acc.	ἐμνήσθη + gen.	ὑπεμνήσθη + gen.
14,72 ἐπιβαλών	ἐξελθών	ἐξελθών
15,13 ἔκραξαν	λέγουσιν	ἐπεφώνουν λέγοντες
15,37 ἀφεὶς (φωνήν)	κράξας (φωνῇ)	φωνήσας (φωνῇ)
15,39 κεντυρίων	ἑκατόνταρχος	ἑκατοντάρχης
15,46 ἐνείλησεν	ἐνετύλιξεν	ἐνετύλιξεν
16,5 λευκήν	ὡς ἀστραπή	ἀστραπτούσῃ
16,5 ἐξεθαμβήθησαν	φόβου	ἐμφόβων
6 ἐκθαμβεῖσθε	φοβεῖσθε	
16,8 εἶπαν	ἀπαγγεῖλαι	ἀπήγγειλαν

33. MISCELLANEOUS

33a. *Diminutive in Mark and not in Matthew and Luke* [194]

Mk	Mt	Lk
5,23 θυγάτριον	θυγάτηρ	θυγάτηρ
9,27 αὐτοῦ (cf. 24 τοῦ παιδίου)	ὁ παῖς	τὸν παῖδα
14,47 ὠτάριον	ὠτίον	οὖς, ὠτίου
5,23, cf. 35 ἡ θυγάτηρ		θυγάτηρ
39 τὸ παιδίον	τὸ κοράσιον	
40 τοῦ παιδίου		(51) τῆς παιδός
41 τοῦ παιδίου	αὐτῆς	αὐτῆς
τὸ κοράσιον		ἡ παῖς
42 τὸ κοράσιον	τὸ κοράσιον	(αὐτῆς)
7,25 τὸ θυγάτριον		
26 τῆς θυγατρός	ἡ θυγάτηρ	
29 τῆς θυγατρός		
30 τὸ παιδίον	ἡ θυγάτηρ	
10,13 παιδία	παιδία	τὰ βρέφη
8,7 ἰχθύδια	15,34 ἰχθύδια	
αὐτά	36 τοὺς ἰχθύας	

---

194. Schmid(26), p. 55 ; cf. Turner(10,2), pp. 349-352 ; Larfeld, pp. 199-202.

33b. *The Article in Mark and not in Matthew and Luke*

Mk

1,2	ἐν τῷ Ἠσαΐᾳ
5,18	εἰς τὸ πλοῖον
8,29	ὁ Πέτρος
8,31	τῶν ἀρχιερέων καὶ τῶν γραμματέων
9,2	τὸν Ἰάκωβον
	(τὸν) Ἰωάννην
10,21	τοῖς πτωχοῖς
10,25	τῆς τρυμαλιᾶς
	τῆς ῥαφίδος
10,31	οἱ ἔσχατοι
13,25	αἱ δυναμεῖς αἱ ἐν τοῖς οὐρανοῖς

The inverse

3,1	εἰς συναγωγήν	+ τήν	+ τήν
4,3	σπεῖραι	+ τοῦ	+ τοῦ
12,6	υἱὸν ἀγαπητόν	τὸν υἱὸν αὐτοῦ	τὸν υἱὸν μου
13,9	εἰς συναγωγάς	ἐν ταῖς συναγωγαῖς	εἰς τὰς συναγωγάς
15,1	Πιλάτῳ	Π. τῷ ἡγεμόνι	ἐπὶ τὸν Πιλᾶτον

33c. *Singular in Mark and Plural in Matthew and Luke*

Mk		Mt	Lk
4,11	τὸ μυστήριον	τὰ μυστήρια	τὰ μυστήρια
4,41	ὁ ἄνεμος	οἱ ἄνεμοι	τοῖς ἀνέμοις
10,21	οὐρανῷ	οὐρανοῖς	τοῖς οὐρανοῖς
13,1	εἷς τῶν μαθητῶν	οἱ μαθηταὶ αὐτοῦ	τινῶν
13,15	τι	τά	αὐτά
14,37	καθεύδεις... ἴσχυσας	ἰσχύσατε	καθεύδετε

The inverse :

4,18	οἱ... σπειρόμενοι	ὁ... σπαρείς	τὸ... πεσόν
4,20	οἱ... σπαρέντες	ὁ... σπαρείς	τό
12,1	ἐν παραβολαῖς	παραβολήν	τὴν παραβολήν

Compare

1,29	ἦλθον	ἐλθών (cf. No. **22a**)	εἰσῆλθεν
14,32	ἔρχονται	ἔρχεται (cf. No. **22a**)	γενόμενος

34. DUPLICATE EXPRESSIONS IN MARK AND SIMPLE PHRASES IN MATTHEW AND LUKE [195]

The following instances are signaled in the list; sometimes the two phrases are marked by [a] [b].

Mk		
1,4	5,21	13,1
1,12-13	5,24	13,8
1,32a	5,30	13,11
1,32b	5,38	13,15
1,42	5,39	14,1
2,25	6,4	14,30
3,7-8bis	8,27	14,37
3,13	8,35	14,54
3,22	9,8	14,68
4,8	10,29	15,5
4,15	10,38	15,24
4,40	11,2	15,26
5,2-3	11,30	15,42
5,12	12,14	
5,15	12,23	

35. THE AGREEMENTS IN ORDER

Changes in word order are classified in No. 21. In this category the transpositions of sentences and pericopes are listed. We refer the reader to the Appendix for further discussion. The numbers added in parentheses are those of the table on pp. 292-293 (Sanders). Instances signaled by Morgenthaler (p. 308) and Boismard (n. 118) are marked by M and B.

Mk	Mt	Lk	No.		
1,2-3.(4)	3,(1-2).3	3,(3).4	3	M,B	
1,2b	(11,10b)	(7,27b)	2		(Q)
1,7.(8a)	3,(11a).11b	3,(16a).16b	4	M	(Q)
3,13-19	(10,2-4)	(6,13-16)	9		
3,19	add. 5-7	add. 6,20-49			(Q)
(post 3,7-8)	(post 4,24-25)	(post 6,17-19)		B	
4,23	(11,15 ; 13,43)	(14,35)	11		
4,24c	(7,2b)	(6,38b)	1	M	(Q)
4,24d	(6,33b)	(12,31b)	7		(Q)
6,7b.(c)	10,(1b).5a	9,(1b).2a		B	
9,50a	(5,13b)	(14,34)	8	M	(Q)
11,12-14.(15-19)	21,(12-16).18-19	19,(45-48)	5		
12,34c	(22,46)	(20,40)	12		
14,21	add. 26,25	add. 22,23	21		
14,45	add. 26,50	add. 22,48	22		

---

195. Schmid(31) ; cf. Hawkins(V) ; comp. Krenkel, pp. 41-47 ; *Duality in Mark*.

Note

For obvious reasons Sanders's Nos. 10 (par. Mt), 13-16 (om. Lk) and 23-24 (different material) are omitted here. Nos. 17-20 and 25-29 (expansion of a Marcan passage) refer to some *major agreements* which are usually assigned to the influence of Q :

Mk	Mt	Lk	No.
1,7-8	3,11-12(+7-10)	3,16-17(+7-9)	17,25
1,12-13	4,1-11	4,1-13	26
3,22-30	12,22-32	11,14-23 ; 12,10	19,27
4,30-32	13,31-32(+33)	13,18-19(+20-21)	18
6,7-11	10,1-16	10,1-12	28
9,42	18,6-7(+15-20.21-22)	17,1-2(+3-4)	20
13,21-23	24,23-28	17,21-37	29

APPENDIX
THE ARGUMENT FROM ORDER

Eph. Theol. Lov. 49 (1973) 784-815

THE ARGUMENT FROM ORDER
AND ST. LUKE'S TRANSPOSITIONS [1]

" One of the principal arguments for the two-document hypothesis has always been the phenomenon of order. As has been previously observed, this argument does not logically prove what it is thought to prove ". The quotation is taken from E. P. Sanders who, in a previous observa-

---

1. This paper was prepared for the SNTS Seminar on the Synoptic Problem (Southampton, August 1973), in view of a discussion of E. P. Sanders's article : *The Argument from the Order and the Relationship between Matthew and Luke*, in *NTS* 15 (1968-69) 249-261. — Ed Parish Sanders (McMaster University, Hamilton, Ont.) is the author of a doctoral dissertation on *The Tendencies of the Synoptic Tradition*, prepared at Union Theological Seminary during the years 1964-66, under the supervision of W. D. Davies, and published in 1969 (SNTS Monograph Series 9 ; Cambridge, 1969, XIV-328 pp.). Although a positive definition of the author's synoptic hypothesis can hardly be given, his work has clear connections with the views of W. R. Farmer, who introduced him to the study of the synoptic problem. He agrees with him in a rather radical critique of the two-source theory. Butler's challenge of the argument from order and the importance of the Matthew-Luke agreements are common assumptions. It was the work of Farmer that drew his attention to the question of the criteria required for distinguishing the relative antiquity of the texts. His conclusion, however, moved him away from all ' simple ' solutions, from Marcan priority and also from the Griesbach hypothesis defended by Farmer. He believes that the study of the synoptic gospels " would profit from a period of withholding judgements on the Synoptic problem " (*Tendencies*, p. 279 ; this idea of an ' interim period ' was also suggested by Farmer in 1966). Nevertheless, his article on *The Argument from Order* ends with the suggestion that " we must ( ) become more open to the possibility that there was more contact between Matthew and Luke than their independent employment of the same two sources. The simplest explanation is that one knew the other ; evidence not discussed here makes it likely that Luke used Matthew " (p. 261). In more recent contributions he becomes extremely hesitant, but still maintains his opposition to " any rigid and simple solution of the Synoptic problem " and pleads for a theory which takes into account multiple and overlapping sources. Cf. *Priorités et dépendances dans la tradition synoptique*, in *RSR* 60 (1972) 519-540, p. 539 ; *The Overlaps of Mark and Q and the Synoptic Problem*, in *NTS* 19 (1972-73) 453-465, p. 464 : " While there are doubtless direct literary relationships among the Synoptic Gospels, these relationships were probably complicated by the Evangelists' knowledge of overlapping traditions. ( ) A theory which takes into account multiple sources would also account for the fact that sometimes Matthew or Luke, rather than Mark, is the middle term. "

tion, is referring to Butler and Farmer [2]. In fact, Butler's chapter on *The Lachmann Fallacy* (1951) has become a *locus classicus* in recent synoptic studies. Sanders's personal contribution, however, is a much more radical critique of the argument. He maintains that the usual description of the phenomenon of order is inadequate : " the facts of order as they are usually stated are misleading ". This goes far beyond the positions of Butler (and Farmer) [3].

1. The Agreements Matthew-Luke against Mark

The argument from order discussed by Sanders is the one which depends upon the absence of agreement between Matthew and Luke against Mark. As a first observation he remarks that the usual statement is true " only if one limits one's view to complete pericopes as they are set forth in Tischendorf's synopsis " [4]. In his NTS article (January 1969), he adds a second preliminary remark : the statement that both Matthew and Luke generally support Mark's order is a great over-simplification. It is true only in a most general sense, but to speak more specifically, of the total 101 pericopes of Mark (following Huck's arrangement), only 58 are supported in order by both Matthew and Luke (28 of the 61 pericopes in Mk I-X and 30 of the 40 pericopes in Mk XI-XVI) [5]. Then he presents four groups of exceptions to the traditional claim about order. We give them here in the following list. The continuous numbering is ours ; the asterisk in the margin indicates that, in the author's view, the agreements cannot be attributed to the influence of Q [6].

(a) Matthew and Luke agree against Mark's order :

1.	Mk IV, 24c	: Mt VII, 2b	// Lk VI, 38b	(Q)
2.	Mk I, 2b	: Mt XI, 10b	// Lk VII, 27b	(Q)
* 3.	Mk I, 4	: Mt III, 1	// Lk III, 3	
4.	Mk I, 7b	: Mt III, 11b	// Lk III, 16c	(Q)
* 5.	Mk XI, 15-19	: Mt XXI, 10-17	// Lk XIX, 45-46	
* 6.	Mk XIII, 34	: Mt XXV, 14	// Lk XIX, 12-13	
7.	Mk IV, 24d	: Mt VI, 33b	// Lk XII, 31b	(Q)

---

2. *Tendencies*, p. 277 ; comp. p. 7.

3. Comp. N. B. Stonehouse, *Origins of the Synoptic Gospels*, Grand Rapids, 1963, p. 63 : " But it is important to add that apparently no one challenges the accuracy of the observations concerning order as such. B. C. Butler, for example, admits their accuracy ; it is the inference relating to the dependence of Matthew upon Mark to which he objects ".

4. *Tendencies*, p. 277, n. 2 ; *The Argument from Order*, p. 253, n. 2.

5. *The Argument from Order*, pp. 254-255. In fact the synopsis has 103 pericopes.

6. In nos. 1, 2, 4, 7 and 8 a more precise biblical reference is used (*e.g.* no. 1 : IV, 24c instead of 24b).

(b) Passages differently placed by each of the three evangelists :

```
   8. Mk IX, 50a    : Mt V, 13b ;          Lk XIV, 34        (Q)
*  9. Mk III, 13-19 : Mt X, 2-4 ;          Lk VI, 13-16
*10. Mk VI, 1-6a    : Mt XIII, 53-58 ;     Lk IV, 16-30
*11. Mk IV, 23      : Mt XI, 15 ; XIII, 43 ; Lk XIV, 35
*12. Mk XII, 34c    : Mt XXII, 46 ;        Lk XX, 40
```

(c) Either Matthew or Luke has a different order from that of Mark while the other omits :

```
*13. Mk XI, 25      : Mt VI, 14b ;         Lk om.
*14. Mk I, 4-6      : Mt III, 4-6 ;        Lk om.
*15. Mk IX, 41      : Mt X, 42 ;           Lk om.
*16. Mk VI, 34b     : Mt IX, 36b ;         Lk om.
```

(d) Matthew and Luke agree in placing the same common (Q) material at the same place relative to the Marcan outline :

```
   (verbatim agreement)
  17. Mk I, 1-6     // Mt III, 1-6         Lk III, 1-6
                            7-10                    7-9       (Q)
*18. Mk IV, 30-32   // Mt XIII, 31-32      Lk XIII, 18-19
                            33                      20-21
  19. Mk III, 23-30 // Mt XII, 25-37       Lk XI, 17-23
                        38-42.43-45              24-26.29-32 (Q)
*20. Mk IX, 42-48   // Mt XVIII, 6-9       Lk XVII, 1-2
                       15-20.21-22               3.4
   (approximately the same)
  21. Mk XIV, 21    : Mt XXVI, 25          Lk XXII, 23
  22. Mk XIV, 45    : Mt XXVI, 50          Lk XXII, 48
   (different material)
  23. Mk I, 39      : Mt V-VII             Lk V, 1-11
  24. Mk IV, 26-29  : Mt XIII, 24-30       Lk VIII, 19-21
   (expansions of a Marcan passage)
  25. Mk I, 7-8     : Mt III, 11-12        Lk III, 15-18     (Q)
  26. Mk I, 12-13   : Mt IV, 1-11          Lk IV, 1-13       (Q)
  27. Mk III, 20-30 : Mt XII, 22-37        Lk XI, 14-23      (Q)
  28. Mk VI, 7-13   : Mt X, 1-16           Lk X, 1-12        (Q)
  29. Mk XIII, 21-23 : Mt XXIV, 23-28      Lk XVII, 21-37    (Q)
```

His conclusion : " The assurance with which it is usually said that Matthew and Luke were independent of each other rests on the assertion that they *never* agree together in such a way that it cannot be explained by reference to their independent use of Mark and Q. When we note the number of instances where they do, the assurance we have felt in the traditional hypothesis must be correspondingly weakened " [7].

In fact, a number of Marcan passages are presented as ' inexplicably unsupported ' : nos. 3, 5, (6), 9, 10, 11, 12, 13, 14, 15, 16, (18), (20). Mt XXV, 14 = Lk XIX, 12-13 ; Mt XIII, 33 = Lk XIII, 20-21 and Mt XVIII, 15.21-22 = Lk XVII, 3-4 are commonly assigned to the Q material [8] and therefore nos. 6, 18 and 20 should be placed in the category of the Q texts and the overlaps between Mark and Q. Sanders also mentions passages in which Matthew and Luke break the Marcan order at the same point with different material (nos. 23 and 24). The statement is not quite adequate. No. 23 : the Miraculous Draught of Fishes is placed after Mk I, 39 (= Lk IV, 44), but the Sermon on the Mount is inserted in the Marcan outline at Mk I, 21 (Mt IV, 18-22 / VII, 28-29 = Mk I, 16-20 / 22) [9]. No. 24 : the Parable of the Tares is the Matthean parallel of Mark's Parable of the Seed Growing Secretly, both followed by the Parable of the Mustard Seed and the Conclusion of the Parable Teaching (Mk IV, 30-32.33-34 = Mt XIII, 31-32.34). Luke omits Mk IV, 26-34 and Christ's Real Brethren is appended to the preceding verses of IV, 21-25 (omitted in Matthew). Perhaps Lk VIII, 19-21 has connections with the omitted section of Mk IV, 26-34, but the ending verse on Jesus' own disciples (v. 34b) is a much better ' parallel ' than IV, 26-29. Finally, nos. 21 and 22 should not be in a list of agreements in order. If they are taken as such, other ' minor agreements ' should also be cited (e.g. Mt XXI, 43 (44) // Lk XX, 18 : the words of Jesus added after the Scripture text of Mk XII, 10-11). But these additions or omissions (' add-omissions ') are generally not treated in the category of agreements of order.

The third category gives a list of passages " in which either Matthew or Luke has a different order from that of Mark, while the other omits ". These instances are understood as exceptions to the general assertion : where Matthew or Luke disagrees with Mark's relative order, the other supports it. " The claim is that one *always supports Mark's order* except where both omit " [10]. Sanders refers to Woods's third statement and Streeter's use of it as a proof for the priority of Mark. I wonder, however, if he understands the assertion on the alternating support *in sensu auctoris*. Streeter's expression is clear enough : " there is no case where Matthew

7. *Ib.*, p. 261.
8. Cf. S. SCHULZ, *Q - Die Spruchquelle der Evangelisten*, Zurich, 1972, pp. 288-298, 307-309 and 320-322.
9. Cf. F. NEIRYNCK, *La rédaction matthéenne et la structure du premier évangile*, in I. DE LA POTTERIE (ed.), *De Jésus aux Évangiles* (Bibl. Eph. Theol. Lov. 25), Gembloux-Paris, 1967, pp. 41-73 ; = *Eph. Theol. Lov.* 43 (1967), same pagination ; espec. p. 66, n. 102.
10. *The Argument from Order*, pp. 251-252.

and Luke agree together against Mark in a point of arrangement ",
" they practically never agree together against Mark "[11]. The argument
is that of the absence of agreement, and " wherever Matthew (or Luke)
departs from Mark's order " is apparently understood of a different
placement, not of an omission of the material. The curious mention of
Mk III, 31-35 as the only exception ("which occurs in a different
context in each gospel ")[12] at least does not contradicts this interpretation. The formulation of Burkitt is not ambiguous : " Matthew and
Luke never agree against Mark in *transposing* a narrative "[13]. Sanders
is perfectly conscious that he is innovating with the extension given to
Woods's statement on the order[14]. He is right that the text of Woods
lends itself to that understanding[15], but however influential Woods's
essay may have been, the argument from order was not commonly
proposed with the corollary formulated now by Sanders.

In spite of the general title given to the third category (" either Matthew
or Luke ") it is always Luke who omits and Matthew who rearranges the
Marcan passage. The order of Mk I, (5).6 is inverted in Mt III, 4.(5-6),
but both parts are omitted by Luke ; Mk IX, 41 is omitted together
with the subsequent section (IX, 42-50 — X, 1-12) and Mk XI, 25 is
also part of a much larger omission (XI, 11-14.20-25) (nos. 13, 14, 15).
Because in the three instances the Lucan omissions by no means coincide with the Matthean transpositions, it is hard to see how this evidence
has anything to do with the possibility of Luke's use of Matthew (Sanders's final conclusion). In the fourth case the difference of order is rather
dubious, while Mt IX, 36a is a doublet of Mt XIV, 14a, par. Mk VI, 34a
(no. 16). The author observes that no. 5 (now in the first category)
should ' perhaps ' be placed in this third category. Luke omits Mk XI,
11-14, but he does not depart from Mark's order for the Cleansing of the
Temple (Lk XIX, 45-48 = Mk XI, 15-18). In fact, he could have mentioned more instances of a Marcan passage which is omitted in Luke and

11. B. H. STREETER, *The Four Gospels*, London, 1924, p. 161 and 162.

12. *Ib.*, p. 161. Comp. *The Synoptic Problem*, in *Peake's Commentary on the Bible*,
London, 1920, pp. 672-680, espec. p. 673.

13. F. C. BURKITT, *The Gospel Tradition and its Transmission*, Cambridge, 1906,
p. 36.

14. Cf. *The Argument from Order*, p. 251 : " It is not usually recognized that
this last is a corollary to Woods's point three, but it is ".

15. At least in the passage on p. 63 : " When we say that the order of St. Mark
is maintained either by St. Matthew or St. Luke, we mean the relative order,
without taking into account the insertions by either of what is not in St. Mark at
all, or the omissions from St. Mark by both ". Cf. F. H. WOODS, *The Origin and
Mutual Relation of the Synoptic Gospels*, in *Studia Biblica et Ecclesiastica*. Vol. II,
Oxford, 1890, pp. 59-104. With regard to the instances of Sanders's third category :
for Mk IX, 41 and XI, 25, omitted in Lk, the author notes the ' omission ' in Mt
and the ' quasi-parallel ' in Mt X, 42 and VI, 14 (pp. 65 and 101-102).

differently placed in Matthew (Mt XV, 3-6.7-9, par. Mk VII, 9-13.6-8 ; Mt XIX, 4-6.7-8, par. Mk X, 6-9.3-5) [16].

Let us now examine briefly the instances listed in the first and second category (passages differently placed by Matthew-Luke and Mark or by each of them).

No. 3 : Both evangelists inverted the Marcan order of Mk I, 2-3.4 and placed the presentation of the Baptist before the quotation from Isaiah. They agree against Mark indeed, but it is a rearrangement within the pericope and I can hardly see in it any indication against their independent use of Mark [17].

No. 5 : We have noted that Mk XI, 15-19 should not be listed here, because of the Lucan omission.

No. 9 : Mark has the Call of the Twelve after the Healing of the Multitude, while Matthew (X, 2-4) and Luke (VI, 12-16) put it before the Healing in different places. Matthew has the summary in the Marcan order (XII, 15-16 = Mk III, 7-12), but he anticipates the Call and combines it with the Mission (Mk VI, 6b-11) in Mt X. In Luke there is only an inversion within the same section of Mk III, 7-12.13-19 [18].

No. 10 : The text of Mt XIII, 53-58 is in Marcan order.

Mk	Mt	
III, 31-35	XII, 46-50	
IV, 1-34	XIII, 1-35.(36-52)	
IV, 35-V, 20		VIII, 18-34
V, 21-43		IX, 18-26
VI, 1-6a	XIII, 53-58	
VI, 6b-11.(12-13)		IX, 35a ; X, 1.9-14
VI, 14-16	XIV, 1-2	
VI, 17-29	XIV, 3-12	
etc.	etc.	

---

16. The transpositions in Mt XV, XIX and XXI are the only three of some importance in the second half of Matthew (XIV-XXVIII). In each of them it is within the pericope that some verses are replaced and, more exactly, anticipated. Cf. *La rédaction matthéenne*, pp. 59-60 ; comp. J. SCHMID, *Markus und der aramäische Matthäus*, in *Synoptische Studien. Fs. A. Wikenhauser*, Munich, 1953, pp. 148-183, espec. 168-183.

17. Cf. F. NEIRYNCK, *Une nouvelle théorie synoptique (à propos de Mc., I, 2-6 et par.). Notes critiques*, in *Eph. Theol. Lov.* 44 (1968) 141-153, espec. p. 148 : " (L'ordonnance matthéenne) est plus logique, parce que ' tout est dit sur Jean avant que l'on ne parle des foules qui viennent à lui '. Cette logique a fait avancer la description du vêtement et de la nourriture de Jean (*Mt.*, III, 4) ".

18. On the anticipation of Mk III, 7b-8 in Mt IV, 25 and of Mk III, 11-12 in Lk IV, 41, see F. NEIRYNCK, *Urmarcus redivivus ? Examen critique de l'hypothèse des insertions matthéennes dans Marc* (see p. 46, n. 151), espec. p. 141.

No. 11 : The saying " he who has ears ... " (Mk IV, 23) is omitted in the parallel text but Mt has omitted the whole passage of Mk IV, 21-25. Since both have the same saying in parallel with Mk IV, 9 (Mt XIII, 9 = Lk VIII, 8), the use of it in Mt XI, 15 and XIII, 43 and Lk XIV, 35 may be due to redactional repetition, without any significance for the problem of order [19].

No. 12 : Matthew who made an intimate connection between the pericopes of the Great Commandment and the Question about David's Son (cf. v. 41a) has transferred Mk XII, 34c to the end (XXII, 46), but Luke has simply omitted the Great Commandment pericope here (cf. the doublet in X, 25-28) and preserved Mk XII, 32a and 34c in the parallel place, now after the Question of the Sadducees (XX, 39-40).

It appears from this brief survey that the author's attempt to contribute to an adequate description of the phenomenon of order is not satisfactory in all aspects. He has made an effort at clarification by distinguishing four categories of differences from Mark, but still more distinctions are desirable. The author is perhaps too much inclined to count the instances and not to weigh them. Differences in order are listed indiscriminately : transferences to a distant context and inversions within the same section, transpositions of a full pericope and replacements of a single sentence. The author does not have a high esteem for the argument from order dealing only with full pericopes. He opposes his strictly literary approach to a biographical one which is concerned with the sequence of events in the life of Jesus. This also is an over-simplification. The relative place of individual phrases is one thing, but no less important is the phenomenon of the order of pericopes (*Perikopenfolge, ordo narrationum*). The fact that former discussions were motivated by interest in the ' precise chronology of the history of Jesus ' should not prevent us from studying the relative order of the gospel sections as a literary phenomenon.

2. THE ABSENCE OF AGREEMENT AND ITS SIGNIFICANCE

For too long the discussion of the argument from order has been characterized by abstract reasoning [20]. This is still the case in the post-Butlerian time. W. R. Farmer, for instance, continues to argue on the basis of the absence of agreement. " The problem of Marcan order can

---

19. Compare the judgement on the scribal gloss in Mk VII, 16 : " derived perhaps from 4.9 or 4.23 " ; cf. B. M. METZGER, *A Textual Commentary on the Greek New Testament*, London-New York, 1971, p. 95.

20. One has the impression that Sanders in counting the exceptions is still arguing in the line of the argument he attacks. To the ' absence of agreement ' he opposes the new assertion on the number of agreements, " too large to attribute to chance " (*The Argument from Order*, p. 261, n. 3).

be posed this way : It is as if Matthew and Luke each knew what the other was doing, and that each had agreed to support Mark whenever the other departed from Mark. Such concerted action is excluded by the adherents of Marcan priority in their insistence that Matthew and Luke were completely independent of one another. ( ) This fact of alternating support (the order in Mark, when unsupported by both Matthew and Luke, is almost always supported either by one or the other) suggests some kind of conscious intention for which the Marcan hypothesis offers no ready explanation on either the terms of Lachmann or Streeter ". On the Griesbach hypothesis the phenomenon is readily explicable : " Where his sources departed from one another in order, so that there was no longer a common order to follow, he (Mark) tended to follow the order of one or the other of his sources, rather than depart from both " [21]. Thus the argument from order is brought back to the Griesbach hypothesis where it originated [22]. The absence of agreement is presumed to be a significant literary fact, explainable only by deliberate intention of a writer.

The significance of the phenomenon, however, may become questionable with a more concrete approach. The basic statement remains the common order Mark-Matthew and Mark-Luke. In Luke the alterations

---

21. W. R. FARMER, *The Synoptic Problem*, New York-London, 1964, pp. 212-214. For the Augustinian hypothesis the " unresolved difficulty " is in the " rather erratic redactional procedure " it would suppose for Luke (pp. 214-215).

22. Cf. J. J. GRIESBACH, *Commentatio qua Marci Evangelium totum e Matthaei et Lucae commentariis decerptum esse monstratur*, Jena, 1789-90 ; in P. GABLER (ed.), *Griesbachii Opuscula Academica*, vol. 8, Jena, 1825, pp. 358-425, espec. p. 370 : "(Marcus) ordinem a Matthaeo observatum ita retinuit, ut, sicubi ab eo recederet, Lucae vestigiis insisteret et hunc ordinemque narrationis eius κατα ποδα sequeretur". This is, as far as I know, the earliest description of ' the fact of alternating support ' or ' absence of agreement against Mark '. The combination hypothesis was based upon " die Erscheinung, dass das erste und dritte Evangelium *abwechslungsweise* sowohl hinsichtlich der Anordnung, als in Hinsicht auf den Text in dem zweiten Evangelium sich wiederfinden " (cf. F. J. SCHWARZ, *Neue Untersuchungen über das Verwandschaft-Verhältniss der synoptischen Evangelien mit besonderer Berücksichtigung der Hypothese vom schöpferischen Urevangelisten*, Tübingen, 1844, p. 310). Comp. H. U. MEIJBOOM, *Geschiedenis en kritiek der Marcushypothese*, Amsterdam, 1866, pp. 157-187, espec. p. 162 ("dit feit is ten allen tijde het punt geweest, waarop de volgelingen van Griesbach met nadruk hebben gewezen") and p. 182 ("Maar was het opmerkelijk, zonderling zelfs, dat de beide bewerkers ten naastenbij nooit tegelijk iets invoegden of uitlieten, maar veeleer den schijn op zich laadden, als waren zij in nauwkeurig overleg getreden : datzelfde is weer eveneens bij de verplaatsingen het geval"). The ' concerted action ' and ' conscious intention ' (cf. Farmer) is a traditional motif in the objection against the Marcan hypothesis : " ihre Selbständigkeit, resp. ihre gegenseitige Abweichung von Marcus, um mit ihm und durch ihn ja nicht in gegenseitige Gemeinschaft unter einander zu treten, müsste eine auf Verabredung beruhende seyn " (SCHWARZ, *op. cit.*, p. 308).

of the Marcan order are limited in number and the transpositions in
Matthew are confined to Mt IV, 23-XI, 1. Emphasis on the alternating
support seems to imply that agreements and disagreements with the
relative order of Mark are treated as comparable quantities. In fact, the
disagreement against Mark is the exception and the absence of concur-
rence between Matthew and Luke is less surprising than the somewhat
misleading formulation ' whenever the other departs ' may suggest.

In this question we have to go back to the original statement of
Lachmann [23]. We all know about a Lachmann Fallacy which was not
Lachmann's fallacy, but there is also the Lachmann argument which
was not Lachmann's. Kümmel presents the contribution of Lachmann
as follows : " er führte den Nachweis, dass die Übereinstimmung der
drei Synoptiker in der *Reihenfolge* der Erzählungen nur so weit geht,
als Matthäus und Lukas mit der Reihenfolge des Markus übereinstimmen ; wo sie von dieser Reihenfolge abweichen, weichen sie auch von
einander ab " [24]. Whoever checks this description with the text of
Lachmann will notice that a precision was added which first appeared
some years later in the formulation given by Weisse. The much quoted
passage to which Kümmel also refers is not so explicit : " Sed narrationum evangelicarum ordinis non tanta est quanta plerisque videtur
diversitas ; maxima sane si aut hos scriptores eadem conplexione omnes
aut Lucan cum Matthaeo conposueris, exigua si Marcum cum utroque
seorsum " [25]. It is true that in discussing the differences Matthew-Mark
Lachmann maintains that no good reason can be found by which we
could suppose that Mark altered the order of Matthew : " praesertim
cum Lucas quoque hic paene in omnibus cum Marco consentiat " [26].
This last sentence looks like a corollary ; it is not the point of his
argumentation [27].

---

23. K. LACHMANN, *De ordine narrationum in evangeliis synopticis*, in *Theologische
Studien und Kritiken* 8 (1835) 570-590. For an English translation, cf. N. H. PAL-
MER, *Lachmann's Argument*, in *NTS* 13 (1966-67) 368-378.

24. W. G. KÜMMEL, *Das Neue Testament. Geschichte der Erforschung seiner
Probleme*, Munich, 1958, p. 180.

25. K. LACHMANN, *De ordine narrationum*, p. 574.

26. *Ib.*, p. 577.

27. This is well stated by H. Palmer. He indicates the concern of Lachmann
as follows : " The transpositions in the gospels were not to be explained by chance
and mechanical means, but by finding reasons which could have influenced one or
another evangelist in altering the order that he found " (cf. *Lachmann's Argument*,
p. 377). The author comes back to the question in his *The Logic of Gospel Criticism*,
Edinburgh, 1968, espec. pp. 132-135. — The reader should notice that the passage
on ' majority-voting ' is the author's own reflection : " Lachmann's carefully
restricted conclusion, that Mark's *order* is most nearly original, could also be shown
(on Lachmann's assumptions) by majority-voting ; for, if all three derived
independently from one Grundschrift (G-M, K, L), the agreement of two against

The attention to the absence of agreement Matthew-Luke against
Mark was an essential ingredient of the Griesbach hypothesis from the
very beginning. It appears in the Marcan hypothesis with C. H. Weisse
in 1838 [28] and from that time it became a common feature of the two
theories. In fact, Butler was not the first critic to note that Marcan
priority is not the only solution to the usual statement on the relative
order of the gospels. Nineteenth-century authors had already proposed
Mark as the middle-term in the two alternatives : either as the source
or as the combination of both gospels [29]. In the article that has been
marked as " the earliest evidence of an error that B. C. Butler sixty-

---

the third could be held to reconstitute that original. Now in questions of order,
Mark always votes in the majority (i.e. the others never agree against him). So in
most passages (i.e. except where all three differ) Mark's order must be attributed to
G. This argument, however, requires the assumption that the gospels are ' Brothers-
All ' in a three-branched family " (p. 133). — With regard to the author's
assertion that Lachmann " first tried arguing from the phenomenon of order "
(*Lachmann's Argument*, p. 377), see our note on Griesbach (n. 22).

28. Cf. *Die evangelische Geschichte*, Leipzig, 1838, vol. I, pp. 72-73 : " Auch in
denjenigen Partien, welche alle drei Synoptiker gemeinschaftlich haben, ist die
Einstimmung der beiden andern immer eine durch Marcus vermittelte : das heisst,
die beiden andern stimmen in diesen Partien, sowohl was die Anordnung im Ganzen,
als was die Wortfügung im Einzelnen betrifft, immer nur in so weit unter sich
zusammen, als sie auch mit Marcus zusammenstimmen, so oft sie aber von Marcus
abweichen, weichen sie (einige unbedeutende Weglassungen ausgenommen, wo
das Zusammentreffen als zufällig angesehen werden kann) jederzeit auch gegen-
seitig von einander ab ". It appears clearly from the context of this quotation
that Weisse extends here, to the phenomenon of order, a statement which had
already been made with regard to the formal similarities. Comp. H. MARSH, *A
Dissertation on the Origin and Composition of the First Three Gospels*, in his translation of J. D. MICHAELIS, *Introduction to the New Testament*, London, [2]1802
(the dissertation was finished in 1798 and first published in 1801), pp. 382-383 :
" St. Matthew's Greek text never agrees in $\aleph$ (= *triple tradition*) with that of
St. Luke, except where both agree with that of St. Mark, because the translator
had no recourse to St. Luke, where St. Mark had matter in common with St. Matthew. Consequently, throughout all $\aleph$ the Greek translation of St. Matthew's
Gospel could harmonize with St. Luke's Gospel through no other means than
through the medium of St. Mark's Gospel ".

29. Cf. F. J. SCHWARZ, *Neue Untersuchungen* (see n. 22), p. 307 : " Schon der
Augenschein lehrt, dass Markus mehr ist, als das chronologische Mittelglied zwischen
Matthäus und Lukas ; nicht er, der Schriftsteller und die Zeit der Abfassung,
sondern der Text ist es, der in der Mitte liegt, an dessen Stamm, wie ersichtlich
ist, entweder Matthäus und Lukas sich abwechselnd angehängt haben, oder der
stückweise aus ihnen, bald aus diesem, bald aus jenem entstanden ist. Er ist also
das Bindeglied, und zwar bestimmter entweder die Quell- oder Schlusseinheit
seiner Mitreferenten. So viel darf also auch jetzt als ausgemacht angesehen werden,
dass Markus entweder der Urevangelist ist, oder dass er seine beiden Vorgänger
benützt hat. Diese Alternative ist gestellt, und wir haben uns nun für die eine
oder die andere Seite derselben zu entscheiden ".

five years later was to term the Lachmann fallacy " [30] the two alternatives were still envisaged. It was on other grounds than that of absence of agreement Matthew-Luke that Woods abandoned the Griesbach hypothesis [31]. After the dismissal of that alternative the argument from order easily developed into the fallacious proof of Marcan priority. It should be observed, however, that the logical inference from the absence of agreement in order between Matthew and Luke was never the whole argument from order. Sanders distinguishes two arguments : the one which is based upon the absence of agreement and another one which is the argument of Lachmann [32]. Kümmel tries not to separate the two approaches when he maintains that there is no fallacy " falls sich die Abweichung der Mt. und Lk. von Mk. in der Reihenfolge verständlich machen lässt, die Abweichung des Mk. von Mt. und Lk. aber nicht " [33]. For others this is a different argument, for " it is not the failure of Matthew and Luke to agree as such that would prove the point " [34]. It was, however, the background behind the argument from order and it forms the real excuse for those authors who committed the so execrated logical error. It should be clear for us that an ' argument ' from the failure of Matthew and Luke to agree in order is only the first step, a sort of preliminary : an adequate discussion on the relative order of the gospels should take place in the larger context of a redaction-critical examination of each gospel.

---

30. W. R. FARMER, *The Synoptic Problem*, p. 66.

31. F. H. WOODS, *The Origin*, pp. 66-67.

32. E. P. SANDERS, *The Argument from Order*, p. 249, n. 2 (with reference to Palmer's article).

33. W. G. KÜMMEL, *Einleitung in das Neue Testament* (Feine and Behm's 12th ed.), Heidelberg, 1963, p. 28. Farmer observes that Kümmel's demonstration does not provide decisive evidence for Marcan priority, since Luke's changes of Mark's sequence are no less understandable on the hypothesis that Luke changed the sequence of Matthew. Cf. W. R. FARMER, *The Two-Document Hypothesis as a Methodological Criterion in Synoptic Research*, in *Anglican Theological Review* 48 (1966) 380-396, espec. p. 389, n. 23. A similar objection can easily be raised against the Griesbach hypothesis : Mark where he is said to leave the order of Matthew for that of Luke could be held responsible himself for the change of the Matthean order and Luke could depend upon him for the alteration. This inconclusiveness was precisely Butler's statement on the argument from order. It means for us that the phenomenon cannot be taken in isolation from the general comparative study of the gospels. That was also the view of Butler who for other reasons definitely rejected the priority of Luke.

34. Cf. D. WENHAM, *The Synoptic Problem Revisited : Some New Suggestions about the Composition of Mark 4 : 1-34*, in *Tyndale Bulletin* 23 (1972) 3-38, espec. p. 8, n. 12.

The merely logical argument came to its end with Butler's book [35].

---

35. Cf. G. M. STYLER, *The Priority of Mark*, in C. F. D. MOULE, *The Birth of the New Testament*, London, 1962, pp. 223-232 (Excursus IV), p. 225 : " Now it is obvious that the priority of Mk will satisfactorily *explain* these phenomena. But its advocates have made a serious mistake in arguing (or assuming) that no *other* hypothesis will explain them. Butler is correct in claiming that they are guilty of a fallacy in reasoning " (comp. p. 224 : " it came as a shock "). — On Butler's triple-comparison argument, see the studies of Palmer already mentioned (n. 27). " The precise application of [Quentin's] technique of triple comparison to the Synoptic problem is probably due to Butler himself " (*Lachmann's Argument*, p. 377). Due perhaps to a lack of historical information the author does not mention here the name of J. Chapman. Cf. *Matthew, Mark and Luke. A Study in the Order and Interrelation of the Synoptic Gospels*. Edited by J. M. R. BARTON, London, 1937. Evidence for ' the precise application of this technique ' can already be found in Chapman's biographical notice (pp. 1-8 ; written in 1926, cf. p. 8). His ' conversion ' dates from 1915 : " All this egotistical account of my Synoptic opinions is given to show how rooted I was in my self-sufficiency. My sudden conversion, by a regular knock-down blow, took place during the war... " (p. 3). For the conversion motif compare also Butler (*Originality*, p. 70, n. 2) and Farmer (*Synoptic Problem*, p. VIII) ; it is less exceptional in this literature than Palmer seems to suggest (p. 136 : " in this profession, conversions in middle life are rather rare "). If there is any probability for Palmer's supposition about the influence of Quentin upon Butler, I guess that there is a middle term in the linear pedigree : Chapman who was busy at the Vulgate together with Quentin, from 1918 to 1922 at Rome. Chapman's work was published posthumously and B. C. Butler was one of the collaborators of the editor (cf. p. VII). Surprisingly enough, the name of Chapman is not mentioned in Butler's chapter on the Lachmann fallacy (pp. 62-71 ; see also pp. 2-6 ; only for the essay on Aramaisms, p. 147, he refers to ' Chapman's *Matthew, Mark and Luke* ', as to a well known book. — H. G. JAMESON, *The Origin of the Synoptic Gospels*, Oxford, 1922, is frequently cited by Farmer for his critique of the argument from order ; cf. *Synoptic Problem*, pp. 113-114 ; 127, n. 9 ; 152-153 ; 287-293 (Appendix B : with extracts). Comp. p. 196 : " (Chapman) pointed out the logical fallacy of the conventional argument from order as did Jameson in 1922 ". There is, however, an important divergence between the two authors, both defenders of the Augustinian hypothesis. Chapman accepts the *significance* of the absence of agreement in order between Matthew-Luke ; comp. p. 114 : " Mt. and Lk. virtually never agree against Mk. I call attention to this well-known fact, because it is significant " (see also p. 4). For Jameson, on the contrary, " these are really quite *insignificant* facts " (p. 10). The passage on the relative order deserves to be quoted here : " This state of things, again, is the natural result of the two familiar facts, (1) that Matthew and Mark, after the dislocations of order in the early chapters, agree throughout the rest of their course, and (2) that Luke, when he is following Mark, scarcely ever deserts his order at all except towards the close. It is evidently very unlikely, under these conditions, that variations in order in (1) and (2) should coincide. ( ) Here the only thing with which we are really concerned is the relative order of Matthew and Mark, and any light which it may throw on the question as to the priority of one or the other. But it is evident that, while the *nature* of the dislocations of order found in the early chapters might give some hint as to which was the earlier of the two, the mere fact of their *existence* (which is all that we are concerned with here) leaves the question quite open " (pp. 10-11).

The inconclusiveness of the proof for Marcan priority has been widely recognized. But after correction of the logical error the argument in its revised form now works as a criterion for distinguishing ' orthodox ' and ' unorthodox' solutions of the Synoptic problem (*i.e.* with or without Mark as the middle-term) [36]. It was one of the results of Butler's inter-

---

36. The oral tradition hypothesis and the fragment theory (multiple sources) are excluded and the possible solutions are reduced to :

(*A*) in the Urgospel hypothesis : *ordo Marci*

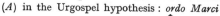

(*B*) in the hypothesis of interdependence :

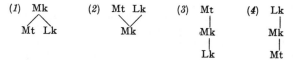

For Chapman the conflation (*2*) is one of the possibilities. For Butler " the absurd theory " (p. 171) is " a surrender of critical principles " (p. 5) : " the so-called ' solution ' does not explain why A and C ever agree together at all " (pp. 2-3, end of note 1). In the Griesbachian theory the objection is answered with the supposed dependence of Luke upon Matthew (which is Butler's solution for the Q passages) :

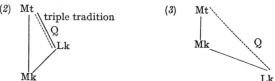

The diagram regards the triple tradition and the hypotheses about the double tradition Mt-Lk (*e.g.* Q source or Lucan dependence upon Mt) are not concerned :

In the hypothesis of interdependence (*B*) the insertion of intermediary stages does not modify the diagram. For instance :

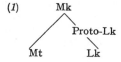

There is no modification of the fundamental diagram in the following variations :

vention that the absence of agreements in order between Matthew and Luke against Mark is explicitly acknowledged by adherents of the Augustinian and the Griesbachian hypothesis as well as by Marcan priorists [37]. Only occasionally one or another instance is noted as a possible exception [38],

---

In some sense the hypothesis of the primitive gospel (*A*) forms a variation on *B1* :

(1')   Proto-Mk

Mt Mk Lk

The middle term is an *Urmarcus, i. e.* a gospel with the Marcan sequence. Thus, for instance, in the solution of L. Vaganay : the common gospel source (*Mg = Matthieu grec*) has the order of Mark.

37. On the argument in a statistical dress see particularly the publications of B. de Solages. Cf. *Critique des évangiles et méthode historique. L'exégèse des synoptiques selon R. Bultmann*, Toulouse, 1972, p. 14 : " J'ai démontré que, dans les passages de triple tradition, Lc et Mt ne sont jamais d'accord contre Mc quant à l'ordre des péricopes. Cette seule constatation suffit à éliminer tout autre schème généalogique des Évangiles synoptiques, que les cinq schèmes mentionnés (*Synopse*, p. 1068). Il s'agit là d'une certitude mathématique. Toute exégèse qui ne veut pas en tenir compte mérite d'être qualifiée d'exégèse pré-pythagoricienne ". Comp. *La composition des évangiles de Luc et de Matthieu et leurs sources*, Leiden, 1973, pp. 11-31 : " La solution du problème synoptique par l'ordre des péricopes ", espec. p. 19 : "On remarquera que, dans ces cinq schèmes, Luc et Matthieu n'ont de rapport qu'à travers Mc (qui est toujours sur les parcours qui les joint). C'est le zéro (pas de rapports directs propres à Luc et à Matthieu) qui impose à tous ces schèmes, cette configuration ". And in a note : " C'est ce zéro qui élimine aussi les schèmes plus compliqués que certains tiennent à envisager. En effet, ce zéro étant incompatible avec une liaison propre à Lc et Mt, il l'est *a fortiori* avec deux ou plusieurs liaisons ". By the same author : *Synopse grecque des évangiles. Méthode nouvelle pour résoudre le problème synoptique*, Leiden, 1959, pp. 1087-1118 : « Solution du problème synoptique », espec. pp. 1108-1109. The diagrams *B1, B3* and *B4* (not *B2*) are among the possible *schèmes* of de Solages. He comes to five solutions by adding the diagrams with the hypothetical source Y (= 3' or 3'') and Z (= 4' or 4'') ; comp. *Synopse*, p. 1066 and 1068 : U and Y. See, however, our note 36 ! — A. M. HONORÉ, *A Statistical Study of the Synoptic Problem*, in *Novum Testamentum* 10 (1968) 95-147, espec. p. 107 : " there are no instances in which Matthew and Luke have the same sequence (= two sections in the same sequence) but not Mark. This is in itself strong evidence that the double-link hypothesis is correct. On the triple-link hypothesis the triple agreements and sequences are accounted for by Luke's use of both Matthew and Mark. But, when the sequences of Matthew and Mark diverge, Luke, if he follows either, always follows Mark. If therefore seems unlikely that Luke used Matthew and probable that the double-link is correct ".

38. Comp. J. C. HAWKINS, *Horae Synopticae*, Oxford, [2]1909, p. 114 : " The different placing of a quotation in Mk I, 2 and in Mt XI, 10, Lk XI, 27 can hardly be called an exception ". In his handwritten notes, he refers also to " Mk III, 31-35 as the one exception to rule ". Cf. F. NEIRYNCK (ed.), *Hawkins's Additional Notes to his ' Horae Synopticae '*, in *Eph. Theol. Lov.* 46 (1970) 78-111, p. 94 (= *Analecta Lovaniensia Biblica et Orientalia*. Ser. V, fasc. 2, Leiden, 1970). This may have to do with Streeter's unexplained mistake : Mk III, 31-35 // Mt XII, 46-50,

unable to modify the general statement [39]. The absence of agreement Matthew-Luke continued to be quoted as unambiguous evidence against Luke's use of Matthew, and authors who accepted Luke's dependence upon Matthew or a common dependence upon a non-Marcan source expressly noticed that their conclusion was based on other grounds [40]. Sanders has a divergent opinion : " The number of agreements in order between Luke and Matthew is too large to attribute to chance " [41]. But Sanders does not say how large would be the number of agreements to attribute to chance [42]. Farmer could be right when he maintains that chance should produce a number of coincidences [43] and,

---

comp. Lk VIII, 19-21 (see our n. 12 ; comp. also Sanders's observation in *Argument from Order*, p. 256). — Authors who refer to exceptions do not seem to make a distinction between dislocated texts placed at the same place or at a different place in Matthew and Luke. Chapman notes an exception for " one single verse, Mk. 3 : 10 " (p. 114 ; see on p. 111 : Mt IV, 24 ; XII, 15b // Mk III, 10.11 // Lk VI, 17b-19). The editor, J. M. T. Barton, adds a further instance : Mk IX, 50, comp. Mt V, 13 and Lk XIV, 34 (p. 14, n. 1). The diagram of Barr points out Mk III, 13-19, comp. Mt X, 1-4 and Lk VI, 12-16 ; cf. A. BARR, *A Diagram of the Synoptic Relationships*, Edinburgh, 1938. For De Solages, the following are differently placed in the three gospels : Mk III, 7b-8, comp. Mt IV, 24-25 and Lk VI, 17b-18 ; Mk IX, 50, comp. Mt V, 13 and Lk XIV, 34 ; cf. *Composition*, p. 18. See also L. VAGANAY, *Le problème synoptique* (Bibliothèque de Théologie. Série III. Théologie Biblique. Vol. I), Tournai, 1954, p. 59 : " Il existe, il est vrai, des très rares accords de Mt.-Lc. contre Mc. dans l'ordonnance particulière des péricopes. Un seul exemple. L'expulsion des vendeurs du temple est placée chez Mc. (*11*, 11-18) le lendemain de l'entrée à Jérusalem. Au contraire, chez Mt. (*21*, 12) et, autant qu'on peut le conjecturer, chez Lc. (*19*, 45-46), la scène semble avoir lieu le jour même " (cf. too on p. 282).

39. A typical example of the ' bagatellization ' : " On the Griesbach hypothesis it simply entails the recognition that Mark did not slavishly adhere to the order common to Matthew and Luke " (about Mk XI, 11-18 : the instance quoted also by Vaganay, see n. 38) ; cf. W. R. FARMER, *The Synoptic Problem*, p. 212.

40. Cf. L. VAGANAY, *Le problème synoptique*, p. 282 : " Péricopes à une place différente chez Mt.-Lc. et chez Mc. — On n'en peut citer qu'un petit nombre et avec une certaine réserve. ( ) Quoi qu'il en soit, ce n'est pas sur cette ressemblance entre Mt. et Lc. que l'on peut établir entre eux un rapport de dépendance ". See also A. M. FARRER, *On Dispensing with Q*, in *Studies in the Gospels. Essays in Memory of R. H. Lightfoot* (ed. D. E. NINEHAM), Oxford, 1955, pp. 55-86, p. 65 : " Anyone who holds that St. Luke knew St. Matthew is bound to say that he threw over St. Matthew's order (where it diverged) in favour of St. Mark's. He made a Marcan, not a Matthean, skeleton for his book ".

41. *The Argument from Order*, p. 261, n. 3.

42. Sanders's expression is characteristic of his proclivity for statistics. In *Tendencies* he employs the same approach : see our remarks on his treatment of the duplicate expressions, in *Duality in Mark. Contributions to the Study of the Markan Redaction* (Bibl. Eph. Theol. Lov. 31), Louvain, 1972, pp. 40-44.

43. He indicates as ' a serious problem ' for the Marcan hypothesis : " why do not their desertions of Mark coincide more frequently ? " (cf. *supra*, n. 21). His question concerns not only alterations of order but also common omissions. —

as R. Morgenthaler observed about such ' statistical ' evaluation, it is
a question of proportion [44]. But more important is this author's statement: " Alles hängt auch hier von der Erklärbarkeit der Umstellungen
ab " [45].

3. THE POSITION OF R. MORGENTHALER

Morgenthaler's partial endorsement of Sanders's new argument from
order deserves our further attention [46]. In *Statistische Synopse* the article

---

On the omissions of whole pericopes in Matthew and Luke, see the reaction of
S. McLoughlin : " By our count Mark has 100 pericopes, of which Matthew omits
four and Luke twenty-five. How many would one expect Matthew and Luke to
coincide in omitting *together* ? The calculation, given in the next paragraph, is
elementary. Luke copies 75/100 of the Marcan pericopes, i. e. three-quarters of
them. Since (on Two Source assumptions) he is acting independently of Matthew,
we may suppose he will treat in the same way the four pericopes Matthew has
selected for omission : he will copy three-quarters of these four, i. e. three. Thus of
the four Matthew omits three will be copied by Luke, and one omitted. So we
expect to find *one* pericope out of the Marcan 100 not copied by either Matthew
or Luke. In fact, consulting the synopsis, we find not one but three pericopes not
copied by either Matthew or Luke. Thus Matthew and Luke coincide in diverging
from Mark *more* than expected, and not less as suggested by Farmer. The new
discrepancy, however, is readily explained by the rigidity of the above arithmetic :
we assumed it was just as likely that Luke would copy a pericope whether Matthew
had copied it or not. But, in fact, if Matthew omits something it is unattractive
to him for some reason, and what is unattractive to one Christian author has by
that very fact an *increased* chance of being unattractive to another. Refining the
argument in this way, therefore, we may improve on the expected number of *one*
common omission suggested by the above calculation, and say we expect more
than one, but not too many : say, between one and four. This, of course, fits the
data perfectly ". Cf. *A Reply* (to H. MEYNELL, *A Note on the Synoptic Problem*),
The Downside Review 90 (1972) 201-206, pp. 201-202. — Comp. R. MORGENTHALER,
Statistische Synopse, Zurich-Stuttgart, 1971, pp. 282-283. On the theoretical (statistical) level he espouses Farmer's opinion. In the supposition that there are three
texts of 100 pericopes and that two of them disagree in order against the third
in 25 instances : " Hätten sie einander wirklich nicht gekannt, dann wäre es ganz
von selber bei 25 Abweichungen von der Mk-Ordnung zu einigen Überschneidungen
der Verschiebungen gekommen ! " (p. 283). His description of the concrete situation,
however, entirely differs from Farmer's statement in *The Synoptic Problem*, p. 213 :
" Since both *frequently* desert Mark, either by departing from his order or by omitting his material... " ; comp. with *Statistische Synopse*, p. 283 : " In Wirklichkeit
stellt sich nun heraus, dass Mt und Lk *fast nie* von der Mk-Folge abweichen ".

    44. *Ib.*, p. 303.

    45. *Ib.* — According to Morgenthaler the valid argument from order is not
statistical but it should be based upon the redactional explanation of the divergences between the gospels. For the order of pericopes he refers to Lachmann
(pp. 283-284) and for the order of sentences he considers three phenomena in
Matthew : the (redactional) doublets, the compositions of sayings and the interpolations (*Perikopenintarsien*), as demonstrating Marcan priority (vis-à-vis Matthew).

    46. *Ib.*, pp. 303-305.

of Sanders is quoted favorably, but with reservations in regard to the broad acceptation of 'agreement' (including texts differently placed in Matthew and Luke or omitted by one of them) and to the appropriateness of the examples. Morgenthaler clearly distinguishes between sentences and pericopes and more particularly Sanders's instances of dislocated pericopes are found unconvincing [47]. For him the agreements in order between Matthew and Luke against Mark are only 'minor agreements' and they cannot challenge the existence of Q [48]. In that connection he discusses Sanders's no. 18 : the Parable of the Mustard Seed (Mk IV, 30-32) followed by the Parable of the Leaven in Mt XIII, 31-32.33 and Lk XIII, 18-19.20-21. According to Sanders we cannot assign the Mustard Seed to Q : the argument from context (the Mustard Seed together with the Leaven in Q) is irrelevant and the Matthew-Luke agreements (the most striking is 'tree' against Mark's 'shrubs') are unsufficient evidence. Thus the sequence of the two parables is counted as an agreement in order against Mark which cannot be attributed to Q [49]. Morgenthaler rightly observes that this is hardly reconcilable with Luke's use of Matthew (Sanders's own conclusion). If Luke was acquainted with Matthew and had read the Mustard Seed in Mt XIII, 31-32, strictly parallel with Mk IV, 30-32, the question remains why Luke omitted the parable, together with the Leaven, in Lk VIII and transferred them to Lk XIII [50].

---

47. Ib., p. 303 : " Die Belege, die Sanders vorbringt, sind freilich wenig überzeugend " ; compare note 183 (p. 311) on the examples of replaced sentences : " eine Belegserie von sehr unterschiedlichem Wert ".

48. Ib., p. 305. — For Morgenthaler Mark and Q are the main sources used by Matthew and Luke (Two Sources) but he admits that Luke had occasionally some subsidiary contact with Matthew as with a third source (Dreiquellentheorie, cf. p. 301 ; compare Simons and Larfeld). The evidence for this direct relationship Matthew-Luke is provided by " die kleineren Übereinstimmungen in Wort-, Satz- und Abschnittfolgen ". The second and third category concern the agreements in order ; they are associated with the phenomena which are commonly understood as 'minor agreements' (first category). As far as the triple tradition is concerned, his position can be compared with Farrer's treatment of the minor agreements : " Now this is just what one would expect, on the supposition that St. Luke had read St. Matthew, but decided to work direct upon the more ancient narrative of St. Mark for himself. He does his own work of adaptation, but small Matthean echoes keep appearing, because St. Luke is after all acquainted with St. Matthew " (On Dispensing with Q, p. 61). Comp. Statistische Synopse, p. 312, n. 196.

49. The Argument from Order, pp. 257, 260 (note 3), 261.

50. Statistische Synopse, p. 304. In a predominantly 'Matthean' wording : ὁμοία ἐστίν, ὃν λαβὼν ἄνθρωπος, om. ἐπὶ τῆς γῆς (bis), ηὔξησεν, δένδρον, ἐν τοῖς κλάδοις αὐτοῦ (after κατεσκήνωσεν). — Sanders mentions only 'the most striking agreement' (tree) and cites, as an objection against the conflation of Mark and Q in Matthew, the analogy of Mk III, 8 : 'beyond the Jordan' (Mt) and 'Tyre and Sidon' (Lk) (p. 260, n. 3 ; comp. Tendencies, p. 271 : " The arguments for

Morgenthaler's *Synopse* is a valuable tool of study, especially for the careful description of the sequences of words, sentences and pericopes. He presents two exhaustive lists of dislocations in Matthew and in Luke. Only four instances of displaced Marcan texts are in both lists [51] :

Mk I, 4   : Mt III, 1.2a // Lk III, 2b.3
Mk I, 7b   : Mt III, 11b // Lk III, 16c
Mk IV, 24c : Mt VII, 2b // Lk VI, 38b
Mk IX, 50a : Mt V, 13b ;   Lk XIV, 34

In the parallels of the saying about Salt (Mk IX, 50a), differently placed in the two gospels, the influence of Q is apparent (compare Sanders's no. 8) [52]. He reckons evidently with Q influence for the inverted order of the sentence of Mk I, 7b (Sanders's no. 4), and, more objectionably, for Mk I, 4 (no. 3) [53]. On this point Sanders may be right [54], but the common inversion in Matthew and Luke is no less understandable without Q influence [55].

For the saying about Measuring of Mk IV, 24c (no. 1) Morgenthaler joins Sanders in protesting " that they are improperly assigned to Q, apparently on the basis of context alone " [56]. He considers Mt VII, 2b as an insertion of Marcan material in the saying composition. It is strictly identical in wording with Mk IV, 24c and even the Marcan sequence can be detected in the Matthean transpositions : Mt V, 15 ; VII, 2b ; XIII, 12 (comp. Mk IV, 21b ; IV, 24c ; IV, 25) [57]. In Luke the sentence is omitted in VIII, 16-18, par. Mk IV, 21-25, and placed in

---

conflation in one Gospel are not appreciably stronger than they are in another Gospel"). However, in the Lucan parallel the omission of ' beyond the Jordan ' has to do with the meaning of ' Judea ' (including ' beyond the Jordan ') and in Mt the omission of ' Tyre and Sidon ' is understandable after the mention of Syria in IV, 24a (compare also the sequence ' Jerusalem-Judea-beyond the Jordan ' in III, 5, diff. Mk).

51. *Statistische Synopse*, pp. 188-189.

52. *Ib.*, p. 169 : μωρανθῇ. In addition : the passive form ἁλισθήσεται /ἀρτυθήσεται (Mk : ἀρτύσετε), together with the second part of the logion (Mt V, 13b ; Lk XIV, 35 : ἔξω βάλλειν).

53. *Ib.*, p. 189.

54. *The Argument from Order*, p. 261, n. 1. He follows Hawkins and Harnack (against Streeter).

55. See n. 17. — Morgenthaler refers to Mt III, 1.2a = Mk I, 4. In fact, λέγων (= 2a, cf. p. 33 and 129) is part of the doublet III, 2 = IV, 17 (cf. Mk I, 14b !).

56. *The Argument from Order*, p. 260, n. 1. Nevertheless, Sanders left the passage in the list of " sayings usually assigned to Q ".

57. *Statistische Synopse*, pp. 169 (on Mk IV, 24c), 172-173 (Mk IV, 21-25), 192 (Mt VII, 1-5), 197, 202, 219 (Marcan insertions). Only on p. 299 the author shows some hesitation : Q ?

VI, 37b, in parallel with Mt VII, 2b. Because of the identical vocabulary [58] the logion must have its origin in one written source. The common omission (in parallel with Mk IV, 24c) and the common insertion (at the same place in the sermon) demand an explanation and here Luke's use of Matthew is one of the possibilities [59]. Morgenthaler also notes Vaganay's treatment of Mk IV, 24c. In fact, the examples quoted by Morgenthaler are the nos. 1 and 2 of Sanders's list but correspond exactly to the instances emphasized by Vaganay : Mk IV, 24c and Mk I, 2b (comp. Mt XI, 10b // Lk VII, 27b) [60]. According to Vaganay Matthew and Luke preserved the logia in their original context (common gospel source) from where they are removed by Mark. Morgenthaler agrees that there is only one form of the saying but he inverts the order : the original form is Mark's, Matthew replaced the saying and was, most probably, followed by Luke. More examples of such inverted re-employment of Vaganay's arguments can be seen where he treats the *Perikopenfolge* : the coincidences in Birth Stories and Resurrection Narratives and the agreement with regard to the Sermon on the Mount are understood as evidence not for a common source but for Luke's use of Matthew [61].

There is something curious about Morgenthaler's exposition. About agreements in sentences he writes: "Ähnliche Beispiele (*as Mk IV, 24c*) gibt es eine ganze Anzahl ", but he dismisses the instances of Sanders's article [62]. Concerning agreements in sections he mentions Mt I-II, XXVIII and V-VII (par. Lk) and then refers to Larfeld for " wertvolle weitere Hinweise auf Übereinstimmungen Mt-Lk gegen Mk in Perikopenfolgen ... " [63]. This last author, however, does not provide complementary examples except the common sections of Mt VIII, 5-13 ; VIII, 19-22 ; XI, 2-6 (par. Lk) [64]. Since the prologue and the epilogue of the gospels are too speculative a basis for establishing either a common gospel

---

58. Comp. S. SCHULZ, *Q - Die Spruchquelle der Evangelisten* (see n. 8), pp. 146-147 : " Das dem Verbum angefügte ἀντί geht auf Lk zurück, der Komposita liebt. Lk wird auch hellenisierend ἐν vor dem Dativ weggelassen haben ".

59. *Statistische Synopse*, p. 303.

60. Cf. L. VAGANAY, *Existe-t-il chez Marc quelques traces du Sermon sur la Montagne ?*, NTS I (1954-55) 192-200. The article concentrates upon the saying as a trace of the Sermon in Mk. On Mk I, 2b, see p. 192 ; cf. *Le problème synoptique*, pp. 353-355.

61. Comp. p. 311, n. 187 : " Lange vor Vaganay hat zB Larfeld dieses Argument verwendet (S 74f) ". For the question of Luke's use of Matthew Morgenthaler is heavily indebted to W. Larfeld's *Die neutestamentlichen Evangelien nach ihrer Eigenart und Abhängigkeit*, Gütersloh, 1925.

62. *Statistische Synopse*, p. 303. Comp. n. 47.

63. *Ib.*, p. 312, n. 195.

64. W. LARFELD, *Die neutestamentlichen Evangelien*, pp. 85-86. Comp. also p. 84 (Mt XXVI, 50 par. Lk : Sanders's no. 22) and pp. 43 and 58 (the inversion of Mk I, 1-6 : Sanders's no. 3).

source or Luke's acquaintance with Matthew, the point at issue in a discussion with Morgenthaler is the Sermon on the Mount (compare Sanders's no. 23). He follows Vaganay in the description of the Matthew-Luke agreement : the localisation on the mountain (comp. Mk III, 13), the presence of the multitude, the thematically identical conclusion and the sequence of the Sermon and the Capernaum pericope. Then he simply declares his preference for the solution of Larfeld and Argyle [65]. No other reason is given than Farrer's argument for omissions in Luke : " St. Luke was not interested in the detail of the anti-Pharisaic controversy " [66]. This is most certainly not a valid reason against Vaganay who similarly explains the omission from the common source : " Il (*Luke*) a écourté d'une façon notable le corps du discours, en supprimant le plan, les oppositions entre la Loi ancienne et la Loi nouvelle, la supériorité de la justice chrétienne sur la justice pharisaïque, thèmes qui devaient moins intéresser ses lecteurs venus de la gentilité " [67]. For Morgenthaler who considers Lk VI, 20-VII, 10 as almost exclusively Q material there should be no need for such an explanation : the Lucan ' omissions ' could be Matthean ' additions '. About Mt VII, 1-2 // Lk VI, 37-38 the author agrees with Vaganay about the Lucan expansion of the text in Lk VI, 37c-38a [68], but he departs from him (and from the common opinion) [69] when he takes away the saying about Measuring from the Q form of Mt VII, 1. True, the vocabulary of Mt VII, 2b is identical with Mk IV, 24c but because of the proverbial character of this short saying it is not a sufficient evidence for the Marcan origin [70].

The instances in Sanders's list where Matthew transposes a Marcan passage while Luke omits it are not accepted by Morgenthaler as agreements in order. The transposition and the omission constitute, however, a negative minor agreement which Morgenthaler employs as such as evidence for Luke's dependence upon Matthew. He refers explicitly to Mt XIV, 14 / Lk IX, 11b, diff. Mk VI, 34b (cf. no. 16). Luke would have omitted the quotation from Mk VI, 34b because, besides Mark, he used also the parallel text of Mt XIV, 14 [71]. In the line of the author's

---

65. *Statistische Synopse*, pp. 304-305 ; cf. p. 312, n. 192.

66. *Ib.*, p. 305 ; cf. p. 312, n. 193.

67. *Le problème synoptique*, p. 255.

68. *Statistische Synopse*, p. 192.

69. There is some hesitation in the reconstruction of the common source : Mt VII, 1-2 is mostly considered as more archaic than Lk VI, 37-38 ; but among others H. Schürmann is in favour of the longer version of Luke. Nevertheless, at least Mt VII, 1.2b (par. Lk VI, 37a.38b) is commonly assigned to Q, to the common gospel source or to the two variant sayings (for authors like H. Th. Wrege who are opposed to a common source).

70. Comp. Sanders's remark : " The sayings ( ) are too short to admit much variation in any case " (p. 260, n. 1).

own reasoning, however, a double objection can be raised. If Luke's indebtedness to his sources is the explanation for the omission, how can we explain that he omitted εἶδεν ... ἐσπλαγχνίσθη, attested here by both Mark and Matthew and used elsewhere by Luke in VII, 13 ; X, 33 and XV, 20 ? According to the author πρόβατα μὴ ἔχοντα ποιμένα in Mt IX, 36 forms an excellent introduction to the saying of IX, 37-38 and in the hypothesis of Mark's dependence upon Matthew the omission would be unexplainable ; but if Luke had read Matthew, is then the omission from the side of Luke, who cites the saying in X, 2, not more unexplainable than it would be for Mark who does not have any parallel ?

The titles given by Morgenthaler to his treatment of the question were very promising for the topic of Sanders's study : " Indizien für eine Bekanntschaft Mt→ Lk : Die kleineren Übereinstimmungen Mt→ Lk in den Satzfolgen, — in den Perikopenfolgen ". In fact, he formulates a thesis but no valuable instances of agreements in order are put forward. Surely, minor agreements Matthew-Luke require an explanation and Luke's use of Matthew is a possible (although unnecessary [72]) solution ; agreements in order, however, do not constitute a valid argument.

4. THE TRANSPOSITIONS IN LUKE

The concentration of dislocations in the first part of the Gospel is the principal problem of order in Matthew [73]. The very existence of such transpositions in Luke is questioned by R. Morgenthaler : " Wir haben also zu schliessen, dass Lk praktisch kein einziges Mal die Perikopenfolgen des Mk verändert " ; " so fehlen bei Lk überhaupt Perikopenumstellungen " [74].

In the recent literature the history of Morgenthaler's assertion starts with J. Jeremias's argument about Lk XXII, 15-18 [75] : Deviation in order must be regarded as an indication that Luke is not following Mark. Luke dislikes transpositions : whenever he follows Mark, he keeps to

---

71. *Statistische Synopse*, p. 285.

72. Comp. F. NEIRYNCK, *Minor Agreements Matthew-Luke in the Transfiguration Story*, in *Orientierung an Jesus. Zur Theologie der Synoptiker. Fs. J. Schmid* (ed. P. HOFFMANN, N. BROX, W. PESCH), Freiburg i. Br., 1973, pp. 253-266.

73. For Matthew I refer to previous studies dealing with the composition of Mt IV, 23 - XI, 1. Cf. F. NEIRYNCK, *La rédaction matthéenne et la structure du premier évangile* (see n. 9) ; *The Gospel of Matthew and Literary Criticism. A Critical Analysis of A. Gaboury's Hypothesis*, in M. DIDIER (ed.), *L'Évangile selon Matthieu. Rédaction et théologie* (Bibl. Eph. Theol. Lov., 29), Gembloux, 1972, pp. 37-69.

74. *Statistische Synopse*, pp. 232 and 283.

75. J. JEREMIAS, *Die Abendmahlsworte Jesu*, Göttingen, ²1949, pp. 56 and 87 ; E. T. by A. Ehrhardt : *The Eucharistic Words of Jesus*, Oxford, 1955, pp. 69 and 116.

Mark's order of the sections most faithfully, and thus we find only two insignificant deviations, Lk VI, 17-19 ; VIII, 19-21, until we come to the Passion narrative. The expression used in this paraphrase : ' order of the sections ' is Jeremias's own translation for *Reihenfolge der Perikopen*. The somewhat inaccurate first English translation, " arrangement of the material ", gave rise to misunderstanding and to the well-known reaction of H. F. D. Sparks in NTS (May 1957) [76]. In the meantime Jeremias's argument had been repeated by H. Schürmann [77], who added an important precision : in Lk VI, 17-19 and VIII, 19-21 there is not *Umstellung* but *Nachtrag* of the Marcan passage. Luke followed Mk I, 21-III, 6 in IV, 31-VI, 11, then he left Mark for the ' interpolation ' of VI, 12-VIII, 3 and came back to Mark in Lk VIII, 4 (= Mk IV, 1). Thus Luke omitted Mk III, 7-35, but two passages of this section (III, 7-11*a* and III, 31-35) were re-introduced where he found a suitable place : in VI, 17-19, as an introduction to the Sermon on the Plain, and in VIII, 19-21, after the Parable section (" nachgetragen, nicht aber eigentlich umgestellt ") [78]. The same scheme of *Nachtrag* (or postposition) applies for Lk XXII, 21-23 and 33-34 (comp. Mk XIV, 18*b*-21 and 29-31), where Mk XIV, 18*b*-31 has been omitted for the non-Marcan section of Lk XXII, 15-38 [79]. Jeremias sanctioned this explanation in his reply to Sparks, at least for Lk VI, 17-19 and VIII, 19-21 : " Er (*Luke*) hat an keiner Stelle eine Perikopenumstellung vorgenommen, nur zweimal

---

76. H. F. D. SPARKS, *St Luke's Transpositions*, in *NTS* 3 (1956-57) 219-223. The author reproduces a list of Lucan transpositions, including instances from the Passion narrative : words, phrases, or subject-matter transposed (*a*) within a sentence, (*b*) within a section, (*c*) from one section to another, (*d*) transpositions of sections, or the subject-matter of sections. He concludes : Luke's dislike of transpositions is unsupported by the evidence which tends in opposite direction.

77. H. SCHÜRMANN, *Der Paschamahlbericht Lk 22, (7-14.)15-18* (Neutest. Abh. 19,5), Münster, 1953, p. 2, n. 9 (with reference to Jeremias) ; *Die Dubletten im Lukasevangelium*, in *ZKTh* 75 (1953) 338-345, p. 339, n. 9; = *Traditionsgeschichtliche Untersuchungen zu den synoptischen Evangelien*, Düsseldorf, 1968, pp. 272-278, p. 273, n. 9 ; comp. also *Die Dublettenvermeidungen im Lukasevangelium*, in *ZKTh* 76 (1954) 83-93; = *Traditionsgeschichtliche Untersuchungen*, pp. 279-289, espec. p. 280.

78. *Ib.* : Lk IV, 41, par. Mk I, 34, is not a true transposition but merely a reminiscence of Mk III, 11*b*-12 or another similar exorcism story ; this should explain its omission in Lk VI, 19.

79. For a full discussion see *Jesu Abschiedsrede Lk 22, 21-38* (Neutest. Abh. 20, 5), Münster, 1957, pp. 3-35. — The author signals another instance of *Nachtrag* in Lk XIX, 45-48 = Mk XI, 15-19, after the non-Marcan insertion of Lk XIX, 39-44 and the omission of Mk XI, 11-25. He gives a similar treatment of the Marcan materials in Lk III, 1-6.19-20.21-22, in the non-Marcan section of Lk III, 1-IV, 30. Cf. *Die Dubletten*, pp. 273-274 (n. 8, 9, 10, 11 and 14) ; *Die Dublettenvermeidungen*, p. 280 (n. 5, 6, 9, 11, 12, 13) ; *Jesu Abschiedsrede*, p. 35.

je eine kurze Markus-Perikope an späterer Stelle nachgeholt " [80]. Transpositions of pericopes only appear in the Passion narrative : Lk XXII, 15-18.21-23.24-27.33-34.56-62.63-65.66-71 ; XXIII, 26-49 : *passim* ; they are unmistakable evidence for Luke's use of a non-Marcan source in Lk XXII, 14ff. [81]. The view of Jeremias (and Rehkopf) that there is an undeniable contrast between Luke's Passion narrative and the pre-Passion chapters, was contested from different viewpoints, by Sparks who presents the list of the transpositions in Lk III-XXI and by Morgenthaler who observes that the transposed passages in the Passion narrative are not really pericopes [82].

With regard to the Passion the position of Jeremias is also different from that of Schürmann. The latter considers Lk XXII, 21-23 and 33-34 as Marcan insertions in the non-Marcan source. His conclusion is based on content analysis but has its *confirmatur* in the analogy of other examples of *Nachtrag* [83]. Jeremias does not consider the phenomenon of *Nachtrag* in the Passion narrative and simply refers to transpositions as evidence for the non-Marcan character. F. Rehkopf explicitly notes the deviation from the Marcan order as one of the indications against Schürmann's exegesis of Lk XXII, 21-23 and 33-34 [84]. The Proto-Luke hypothesis of Jeremias and Rehkopf is clearly more radical than the theory of Streeter and Taylor. Both British scholars accepted an impor-

---

80. J. JEREMIAS, *Perikopen-Umstellungen bei Lukas ?*, in *NTS* 4 (1957-58) 115-119 ; = *Abba*, Göttingen, 1966, pp. 93-97, espec. 95-96. Jeremias's approval is noted by Schürmann in his commentary, *Das Lukasevangelium*, t. 1, Freiburg i. Br., 1969, p. 323, n. 30 (about Lk VI, 17-19) ; see also p. 471, on Lk VIII, 19-21 (" nicht ' umgestellt ' — wie das landläufige Urteil lautet ").

81. Comp. also the third edition of *Die Abendmahlsworte Jesu*, Göttingen, 1960, pp. 91-93 (E. T. by N. Perrin : London, 1966). — See p. 93, n. 3, for another inference from Luke's dislike of transpositions : the proto-Lucan setting (i. e. before Luke was acquainted with Mark) of Lk IV, 16-30 (cf. Mk VI, 1-6a) ; V, 1-11 (cf. Mk I, 16-20) ; VII, 36-50 (cf. Mk XIV, 3-9) ; X, 25-28 (cf. Mk XII, 28-34) ; XIII, 6-9 (cf. Mk XI, 12-14). Luke's dislike of transpositions becomes an argument for the Proto-Luke hypothesis. Comp. F. REHKOPF, *Die lukanische Sonderquelle* (Wiss. Unters. N. T. 5), Tübingen, 1959, p. 89 : " Die Art der Verarbeitung des MkSt (Blöcke, Einhaltung der Reihenfolge) macht wahrscheinlich, dass jedenfalls Sondergut und Redenquelle bereits zusammengestellt waren, ehe Lukas diese Zusammenstellung durch MkSt bereicherte ". See also pp. 1-2 and 88 (cf. n. 5, on Lk VI, 17-19 ; VIII, 19-21) ; on Lk XXII, 21-23 : pp. 7-30 (espec. 29-30, comp. 3-4).

82. *Statistische Synopse*, p. 283. The author seems to make a distinction between Lk VI, 17-19 ; VIII, 19-21 (" als Perikopennachtragungen gewertet ") and XXII, 21-23 and 33-34 (" wegen besonderer Verhältnisse ausgeklammert ").

83. Cf. *Jesu Abschiedsrede*, p. 35.

84. Cf. *Die lukanische Sonderquelle*, pp. 29 and 88 (for XXII, 21-23) and p. 84, n. 1, g (for XXII, 33-34).

tant number of Marcan ' insertions ' in the Lucan Passion narrative [85]. Taylor compared them with Hawkins's list of the twelve inversions of order and he concluded that in five instances the difference of order is due to preference for another source and that the remaining seven insertions " are found in a different sequence because they are inserted by Luke " [86]. Thus for those ' Marcan insertions ' in inverted order (Lk XX, 19a, 22.34.54b-61 ; XXIII, 38.44-45.54) his solution is not that of Jeremias but rather a solution of the Schürmann-type. It sounds like Schürmann's description of *Nachtrag* when Taylor concludes : " We are left with the impression that, coming to the Markan story with his special source in mind, the evangelist has noted features which he desires to incorporate in his Gospel and has introduced these borrowings (...) at such points as the special source permitted " [87]. The words omitted in this quotation are : " in their original Markan order ". Taylor observed that if a list be made of all Marcan elements in the Passion narrative, they would occur in Luke in the same relative order in which they stand in Mark [88]. The Marcan elements are ' insertions ' in an existing document,

---

85. For a survey of the Marcan insertions in the Passion narrative compare F. NEIRYNCK, *La matière marcienne dans l'Évangile de Luc*, in *L'Évangile de Luc. Mémorial L. Cerfaux* (Bibl. Eph. Theol. Lov. 32), Gembloux, 1973, pp. 157-201, espec. 196-197. For Rehkopf only Lk XXII, 20b.52b-53a ; XXIII, 26b are Marcan material. Possible Marcan influences are not excluded by Jeremias in *Neutestamentliche Theologie. I. Die Verkündigung Jesu*, Gütersloh, 1971, p. 48 : " Lediglich bei dem letzten *(non-Marcan block)*, der Passionsgeschichte (22,14-24,53), kann man an einigen Stellen fragen, ob gemein-urchristliche Tradition vorliegt oder Markuseinfluss ". But the argument from order is still the same : " Mit der Feststellung, dass Lukas in der Akoluthie unentwegt Markus folgt, ist auch das Urteil über die Passionsgeschichte Lk 22,14-24,53 gefällt. Sie weicht so stark in der Reihefolge der Perikopen von Markus ab, dass sie dem neuen Stoff zugerechnet werden muss. "

86. V. TAYLOR, *The Passion Narrative of St Luke* (SNTS Mon. Ser. 19), Cambridge, 1972, p. 123. Comp. *Behind the Third Gospel*, Oxford, 1926, p. 72.

87. *The Passion Narrative*, p. 124.

88. Taylor gives the following table :

Lk XXII, 1-13	Mk XIV, 1-2.10-16
22	21
34	30
46b	38
50b	47b
52b-53a	48b-49
54b-61	54.66-72
XXIII, 3	XV, 2
25	15
26	21
34b	24b
38	26
44-45	33.38

LUKE'S TRANSPOSITIONS   315

but Luke's relation to Mark's order in XXII-XXIV is not so radically
different from what happened in III-XXI : " wherever and however he
uses Mark he observes its order " [89]. Schürmann's exegesis of Lk XXII,
21-23 and 33-34 is also supported by G. Schneider. His analysis of XXII,
54-71 leads to the conclusion that Peter's denial (XXII, 56-62) is a Marcan
insertion in the non-Marcan source, and only in the pericope of the mocking
(XXII, 63-65) is the inverted order that of the special source [90].

It appears from this survey that three types of solution are proposed
for the ' transpositions ' in Luke : (1) a non-Marcan section transmitted
by Luke in the original sequence of the special source ; (2) an extract
from Mark displaced under the influence of the non-Marcan source
and inserted by Luke in a different non-Marcan (or Marcan) context ;
(3) an editorial inversion of the Marcan order, a genuine transposition
to another place in the Marcan sequence. Jeremias and Schürmann agree
in arguing that all transpositions of pericopes are deviations of type
(1) or (2), explainable only by the influence of a non-Marcan source.

Let us examine Lk VI, 17-19 and VIII, 19-21. Schürmann considers
both passages as *Nachtrag* from the omitted section, Mk III, 7-35. In
the more common interpretation the omission is limited to Mk III,
20-30 and the two preceding pericopes, Mk III, 7-12.13-19, are presented
in inverted order in Lk VI, 12-16.17-19. For Schürmann, however, the
non-Marcan source already begins with Lk VI, 12-16 (and not in VI,
20, i.e. after Mk III, 19) and Lk VI, 17-19, although it depends on Mk
III, 7-8.10, contains in v. 17 the following traces of the Q source : ὄχλος
πολύς, the descent from the mountain (the presentation of the sermon as
" Predigt am Berge ") and probably the Semitic form of Ἰερουσαλήμ [91].

However, this last evidence is extremely weak and Schürmann immediately adds that it is a mere suspicion, a possibility that cannot be
proven : " Luk schreibt in Lk — anders in Apg — immer die semitische

49	40
50-54	42-47
XXIV, 10a	XVI, 1

" The passages, xxii. 47, 69, 71, and xxiv. 1-3, which may reflect the influence
of Mark linguistically, stand in a different order because of their non-Markan con-
tents " (p. 124).

89. *Ib.*, p. 125.

90. G. SCHNEIDER, *Verleugnung, Verspottung und Verhör Jesu nach Lukas 22,
54-71* (StANT 22), Munich, 1969, pp. 144-151. The author, who reckons *Periko-
penakoluthie* as source-critical criterion, makes a clear distinction between pericopes
and sentences : " Akoluthieabweichungen von einem lk Vers und weniger können
in lk Quellenfragen keinen Ausschlag geben " (p. 151).

91. *Lukasevangelium*, p. 323 ; comp. *Die Warnung des Lukas vor der Falschlehre
in der " Predigt am Berge " Lk 6, 20-49*, in *Traditionsgeschichtliche Untersuchungen*,
pp. 291-293.

Form (auch 5, 17; 18, 31; 21, 20.24 diff Mk und 4, 9 diff Mt), wenn er es nicht vergisst (wie 2, 22 ; 13, 22 v. l. ; 19, 28 ; 23, 7), weil er hier ' sacred prose' schreiben will " [92]. It is also less convincing that, already in a pre-Lucan form, Lk VI, 17 should have referred to the scene at Sinai. The descent from the mountain after the transfiguration in Mk IX, 9.14 (par. Lk IX, 37) is a more probable model for Luke. In Mk III, 7 Jesus is accompanied by his disciples and in III, 13 he calls the twelve. Is that not enough to suggest the distinction between the disciples and the group of the twelve ? In parallel with Mk III, 13-14 Jesus calls his disciples to him and from among them he chooses twelve (Lk VI, 13). Then, Jesus comes down with them (the twelve ' apostles ') and stands on level ground where also are ὄχλος πολὺς τῶν μαθητῶν αὐτοῦ and πλῆθος πολὺ τοῦ λαοῦ (VI, 17). This is a striking parallel with Mk IX, 9.14 : Jesus comes down with Peter, John and James, and they rejoin the other disciples and see that they are surrounded by a ὄχλος πολύς. Is it really necessary to have recourse to the Q source with ὄχλος πολύς designating the audience of the sermon (cf. Lk VII, 1 = Mt VII, 28) ? There is the double expression πολὺ πλῆθος and πλῆθος πολύ in Mk III, 7-8 and " the combination of similarity and variation " (Cadbury) is a well known feature of Lucan style. Schürmann compares it with τὸ πλῆθος τῶν μαθητῶν in XIX, 37 and although he aptly notes the distinction between the disciples (the inner circle) and the crowd, he emphasizes the ' Massiertheit' of the disciples in Lk VI, 17 [93]. It should not be overlooked, however, that the only other employment of ὄχλος πολύς + genitive in Lk designates the guests at the dinner of Levi (V, 29, par. Mk II, 15 : πολλοί). Finally, once we admit with Schürmann that Mt IV, 25 depends on Mk III, 7-8, it is hardly provable that recourse to Q is still needed for the explanation of the term ὄχλοι in Mt IV, 25 ; V, 1 and VII, 28 [94].

The hypothesis of a non-Marcan source for Lk VI, 12-16 is mainly based upon the agreements Matthew-Luke against Mark: vv. 12-13a, comp. Mt V, 1 ; vv. 13b-16, comp. Mt X, 2-4 [95]. However, the motif of the mountain and the approach of the disciples in Mt V, 1 are borrowed from Mk III, 13 :

ἰδὼν δὲ τοὺς ὄχλους	(cf. IV, 25 ; comp. VIII, 18a)
ἀνέβη εἰς τὸ ὄρος	καὶ ἀναβαίνει εἰς τὸ ὄρος (Mk)
καὶ καθίσαντος αὐτοῦ	(comp. XV, 29b)
προσῆλθαν αὐτῷ οἱ μαθηταὶ αὐτοῦ	καὶ ἀπῆλθον πρὸς αὐτόν (Mk)

92. *Lukasevangelium*, p. 323, n. 37 ; comp. *Die Sprache des Christus*, in *Traditionsgeschichtliche Untersuchungen*, pp. 85-86.

93. *Lukasevangelium*, pp. 320-321.

94. Cf. F. NEIRYNCK, *The Gospel of Matthew and Literary Criticism* (see n. 73), pp. 65-67. On Lk IV, 42 and Mt IV, 25, see p. 61, n. 39.

95. *Lukasevangelium*, pp. 318-319.

How can we appeal to Mt V, 1, against Mk III, 13, for εἰς τὸ ὄρος in Luke [96] ? For προσεφώνησεν (comp. Mk III, 13 : προσκαλεῖται) Schürmann refers to Mt V, 1 and X, 1a : καὶ προσκαλεσάμενος τοὺς δώδεκα μαθητὰς αὐτοῦ [97]. Still, this last sentence has its basis in Mk VI, 7 : καὶ προσκαλεῖται τοὺς δώδεκα. The author seems to explain more particularly Luke's τοὺς μαθητὰς αὐτοῦ (diff. Mk) by Mt V, 1 and X, 1. But the composition of Lk VI, 12-13a follows immediately after VI, 11 = Mk III, 6, that means that it is parallel to Mk III, 7a : καὶ ὁ Ἰησοῦς μετὰ τῶν μαθητῶν αὐτοῦ ἀνεχώρησεν. For the remaining elements in Lk VI, 12-13 which have no parallel in Mk III, 13, there is no need to emphasize here their Lucan character [98]. Only the term ἀποστόλους can cause difficulty in view of Mt X, 2a :

δώδεκα, οὓς καὶ	τῶν δὲ δώδεκα
ἀποστόλους	ἀποστόλων
ὠνόμασεν	τὰ ὀνόματά ἐστιν ταῦτα.

In addition to this agreement there are some resemblances in the list of the apostles (VI, 14-16, cf. Mt X, 2b-4). Yet, it should be accepted that some contact of Luke and Matthew with a traditional list which is independent from Mk III, 16-19, does not necessarily imply that such a list was part of an account like Lk VI, 12ff. (cf. Acts I, 13). But even here the indications are not convincing. Καὶ Ἀνδρέαν τὸν ἀδελφὸν αὐτοῦ, cited after Peter, has its model in Mk I, 16. The mere mention of James and John is but a partial agreement with Matthew, who omits as well the imposition of the name of Boanerges but who retains " son of Zebedee " and " his brother ". The enumeration two by two, which is clear in Matthew, has only slight correspondence in Luke, at the beginning

---

96. Ib., p. 318, n. 52 : " Vgl. V. 12 εἰς τὸ ὄρος = Mt 5, 1 (freilich auch Mk 3, 13 ; aber Matth schiebt die Rede bei Mk 1, 21 ein, nicht hinter Mk 3, 13-19) ". However, the insertion of the sermon in Mk I, 21/22 does not dispense one from the search of the sources of the introduction in Mt IV, 23-25 ; V, 1. The author himself refers to Mk I, 28.32.34a.39 ; III, 7-8 (p. 323). In addition : Mk VI, 6b (for IV, 23a) ; Mk I, 14-15 (for IV, 23b : rather than " Q vgl. Lk IV, 43 ") ; cf. The Gospel of Matthew, p. 61, n. 39) and Mk III, 13 (for Mt V, 1). If one admits that the sermon is inserted at Mk I, 21, it becomes difficult to conclude to a traditional introduction : V, 1 (ἐδίδασκεν = Mk I, 21) ; VII, 27b-28 (= Mk I, 22). Finally, only καθίσαντος αὐτοῦ (v. 1) and ἀνοίξας τὸ στόμα αὐτοῦ (v. 2) do not have their origin in Mk : Matthean solemnization ?

97. Ib., p. 318, n. 53.

98. On the construction ἐγένετο (comp. Lk XI, 1), cf. F. NEIRYNCK, La matière marcienne dans l'évangile de Luc (see n. 85), pp. 157-201, espec. pp. 184-193. On Jesus' prayer on the mountain, see Mk VI, 46 (and Lk IX, 18.28 ; cf. ib., p. 171, n. 66) ; ὅτε ἐγένετο : II, 42 ; XXII, 14 (ἡ ὥρα) ; Acts XXI, 5.35 ; XXVII, 39 (ἡμέρα) ; ἐγένετο ἡμέρα : XXII, 66 ; Acts XXVII, 39 (!). On ἐκλεξάμενος (cf. Acts I, 2), οὓς καί, ὠνόμασεν, cf. H. SCHÜRMANN, Lukasevangelium, p. 318, n. 55.

(Peter and Andrew, cf. Mk I, 16) and perhaps at the end. The last pair, Judas son of James and Judas Iscariot, might explain an inversion of order, since *Judas Jacobi*, cited after Simon, replaces Thaddaeus of Mk/Mt (before Simon). Simon's surname, the Zealot, may be a translation of κανavaῖoς which cannot be attributed to Luke [99], but the use of a traditional name does not imply a traditional account, nor even a traditional list of the twelve. The agreement with Acts I, 13, " Simon the Zealot and Judas son of James ", is not very helpful, since Luke can copy Luke ; on the other hand, it should be noted that the list of Acts gives the name of Andrew in the order of Mk. Finally, the title ἀπόστoλoι in Luke and Matthew : in Lk VI, 13 the redactional character is recommended by the very Lucan context of vv. 12-13 in parallel with Mk III, 13-14 (ἵνα ἀπoστέλλῃ αὐτoὺς...) and by the general use of the term ἀπόστoλoς in Luke and Acts (for ὠνόμασεν, cf. v. 14, diff. Mk). The Matthean expression, ' the twelve apostles ' (X, 2 : unique in Mt) can be understood in the light of Mk VI, 7 : " the twelve, to send them out two by two " (cf. Mt X, 1a.5a) and Mk VI, 30 : the return of the ' apostles ' [100]. In these conditions, it becomes difficult to see valuable reasons for assigning Lk VI, 12-13 to a non-Marcan source. " Irgendeine szenische Bemerkung wird man für die Redequelle vor 6, 20 ansetzen müssen " [101] : this is a supposition which is hardly verifiable in the analysis of the text of Lk VI, 12ff. It is more prudent to see the beginning of the non-Marcan source in Lk VI, 20, after Mk III, 19, and to treat VI, 12-16.17-19 as a Lucan transposition. In this case, ' anticipation ' is perhaps a more appropriate definition. The opening pericope in the section of Lk V, 1-VI, 11 (= Mk I, 40-III, 6) was the call of Peter (V, 1-11), due to the transposition of the motifs of Mk I, 16-20. The new section in Lk VI, 12ff. opens now with the choice of the twelve disciples, slightly anticipated from Mk III, (7-12).13-19.

The second passage is Lk VIII, 19-21. The commentary of H. Schürmann has some excellent observations on the significance of the pericope [102]. Although the text greatly differs from Mk III, 31-35, there are no traces of a non-Marcan tradition [103]. The Marcan parallel is placed before the Parables (IV, 1-34), but in Luke the pericope is postponed

99. *Lukasevangelium*, p. 318.

100. Comp. J. DUPONT, *Le nom d'apôtres a-t-il été donné aux douze par Jésus*, Bruges-Louvain, 1956, p. 26: " il ne peut évidemment pas être question de faire remonter cet emploi d'ἀπόστoλoι à une tradition ancienne. Il a été mis là par l'évangéliste, pour des raisons littéraires qui sautent aux yeux " ; on Lk VI, 13, see pp. 38-46.

101. *Lukasevangelium*, p. 318.

102. *Ib.*, pp. 470-471. See especially notes 197 and 198 (versus Conzelmann's interpretation).

103. He notes that the same opinion is held by T. Schramm (p. 471, n. 203).

until after the Parable section (VIII, 4-18). Schürmann considers it as a *Nachtrag* : Luke came back to Mark in VIII, 4 (= Mk IV, 1) and he inserted the passage on the True Relatives (from the omitted section, Mk III, 7-35) as soon as he found a suitable place (after the unit of the Parables). This exegesis presupposes that Lk VIII, 1-3 is part of the non-Marcan source : v. 1 is the end of the Q section (VI, 12-16.20-49 ; VII, 1-10.18-35 ; VIII, 1) and vv. 2-3 pertain to the pre-Lucan account which has been combined with Q (VII, 11-17.36-50 ; VIII, 2-3) [104].

It seems to me that Schürmann correctly understands the redactional intention of Luke in VIII, 1. He writes explicitly : " Mk 3, 14 hatte Luk gelesen (aber par Lk 6, 13 nicht übernommen), dass die Zwölf ausgewählt waren, ἵνα ὦσιν μετ᾽ αὐτοῦ. Als solche schildert Luk sie nunmehr " [105]. Nevertheless he maintains that Lk VIII, 1 is attested by Mt XI, 1 and IX, 35 and that the notice of Lk VIII, 1 should be assigned to Q [106]. For Mt IX, 35 he seems to neglect the identity of the verse with Mt IV, 23. He reckons with three Q influences for κηρύσσων τὸ εὐαγγέλιον τῆς βασιλείας : Lk IV, 43 ; VIII, 1 and X, 9b [107], but Mk I, 14b-15 is a much more probable source of Mt IV, 23b = IX, 35b [108]. In fact, only the expression τὰς πόλεις πάσας καὶ τὰς κώμας is different from IV, 23 and the influence of Mk VI, 6b, already perceptible in IV, 23a, provides a satisfactory explanation (τὰς κώμας κύκλῳ in between περιῆγεν and διδάσκων) [109]. The other parallel in Mt XI, 1 is no more convincing. Καὶ ἐγένετο ὅτε ἐτέλεσεν ὁ Ἰησοῦς is the stereotyped redactional formula (VII, 28 ; XI, 1 ; XIII, 53 ; XIX, 1 ; XXVI, 1) ; διατάσσων τοῖς δώδεκα μαθηταῖς αὐτοῦ refers to the content of the discourse and repeats the

---

104. *Lukasevangelium*, pp. 447-449. Luke is held responsible for the combination of the two sources (versus the Proto-Luke hypothesis).

105. *Ib.*, p. 445. On p. 447, however, he has the following comment : " Wenn aber abschliessend die Zwölf genannt werden, die zu Beginn der Q-Abfolge Lk 6, 12-16 ausgewählt wurden, darf man für V 1 zumindest eine gewisse Grundlage in der Redequelle vermuten ".

106. *Ib.*, p. 447. See also the quotation in n. 105.

107. *Ib.*, pp. 323, 448 and note 38.

108. Cf. *supra*, n. 96. — For Mt IV, 23c (θεραπεύων) he refers to Mk I, 34a and for the same expression in Mt IX, 35c to Lk VIII, 1, or more exactly to τεθεραπευμέναι in v. 2 (!).

109. Comp. Mt X, 11 : πόλιν ἢ κώμην (cf. Lk X, 10 : πόλιν). In his article on the Mission discourse H. Schürmann considers it as the repetition of IX, 35, which is a combination of Mk VI, 6b (τὰς κώμας) and Lk X, 1 Q (πᾶσαν πόλιν). Cf. *Traditionsgeschichtliche Untersuchungen*, p. 140, n. 12. In *Lukasevangelium* he became more sceptical about the influence of Lk X, 1 : " aber 10, 1 färbt sonst auf Mt 9, 35 nicht ab " (p. 448, n. 37). However, there is no convincing evidence for the influence of Lk VIII, 1. It is more acceptable that Matthew has completed the expression of Mk VI, 6b in view of the Mission discourse (cf. X, 11). It is noteworthy that κύκλῳ of Mk III, 34 ; VI, 6 and VI, 36 (τοὺς κύκλῳ ἀγροὺς καὶ κώμας) never has a correspondent in Matthew.

initial designation of the disciples (X, 1) ; μετέβη ἐκεῖθεν is Matthean redaction [110] ; and διδάσκειν καὶ κηρύσσειν ἐν ταῖς πόλεσιν αὐτῶν echoes the summary of IX, 35 [111]. On the other hand, the question of a Q source for Lk VIII, 1 is highly speculative because of the exceptional density of Lucan characteristics in the verse [112].

Lk VIII, 2-3 appears as Luke's own composition on the basis of Mk XV, 40-41. Schürmann's objection is that nothing is said in Mark about Joanna and Susanna, nor about the healing and the cure of evil spirits [113]. However, the theme of the ministering women in Lk VIII, 3b is so close to Mk XV, 41 and so significantly omitted in Lk XXIII, 49.55, that the literary relationship can hardly be denied. In XXIV, 10 Luke inserts the name of Joanna and, moreover, in VIII, 3 the name of Susanna is added, but in a reference to " many other women " some variation in the names is permissible and does not necessarily suggest a different account. In Lk VIII, 2, as well as in Mk XV, 40-41.47 ; XVI, 1 (and par.), Mary of Magdala plays the first role. Αἳ ἦσαν τεθεραπευμέναι ἀπὸ πνευμάτων πονηρῶν καὶ ἀσθενειῶν is characteristically Lucan wording and reminds us of Lk VI, 18, in the subsequent context of the Lucan parallel of Mk III, 14 to which Luke refers in VIII, 2c (καὶ οἱ δώδεκα σὺν αὐτῷ, cf. καὶ ἐποίησεν δώδεκα ἵνα ὦσιν μετ' αὐτοῦ).

This somewhat lengthy discussion may suggest that Lk VIII, 1-3 is a redactional composition, the motifs for which were provided by the Gospel of Mark. In this hypothesis it cannot be maintained that it is only in Lk VIII, 4 that Luke comes back to the Marcan source. Lk VIII, 1-3, the Lucan overture of the section VIII, 1-21, deserves our attention in an examination of the relative order of Mark and Luke. Schleiermacher's suggestion on the inclusion of vv. 1-3 and 19-21 is still noteworthy [114]. One of its implications is that Luke has associated Mk III, 31-35 and IV, 1-25(34) more intimately than they were in the Marcan sequence [115]. In some sense, Lk VIII, 1-3 can be regarded as a Lucan

---

110. Comp. μεταβὰς ἐκεῖθεν in XII, 9 ; XV, 29 (diff. Mk) ; μετάβα ἔνθεν in XVII, 20 (diff. Lk, comp. Mk XI, 23) ; μεταβῇ ἀπό in VIII, 34 (diff. Mk).

111. Schürmann also argues from the relative order : Lk VIII, 1 after VII, 18-35 and Mt XI, 1 before XI, 2-19, the Baptist section ; Mt IX, 35 at the same place as Lk VIII, 1 in the original Q order (Mt's insertion of VIII-IX and transposition of the Baptist section). However, the content analysis does not provide a sufficient basis for the argument, especially in this most hypothetical question of narrative Q elements !

112. Cf. J. DELOBEL, L'onction par la pécheresse. La composition littéraire de Lc., VII, 36-50, in Eph. Theol. Lov. 42 (1966) 415-475, espec. pp. 445-449 (on Lk VIII, 1-3). See also F. NEIRYNCK, La matière marcienne, pp. 184-193 (on καὶ ἐγένετο).

113. Lukasevangelium, p. 448.

114. Cf. J. DELOBEL, L'onction par la pécheresse, pp. 448-449.

115. See also p. 787 (no. 24).

correspondence of Mk III, 31-35 and prepares for the parallel in VIII, 19-21. Here again we have a transposition within the Marcan material and it may be a misleading qualification to call it *Nachtrag* [116].

The examination of Lk VI, 12-16.17-19 and VIII, 4-18.19-21 has shown that we cannot eliminate all transpositions from the Marcan material in Luke. In both instances Luke may have inverted the Marcan order for redactional reasons, and not under the influence of non-Marcan sources. The observation is important in view of the (Proto-Lucan) theory that Luke never changes the sequence of the sections when he copies Mark. This was one of the reasons why Lk IV, 16-30 (cf. Mk VI, 1-6a) ; Lk V, 1-11 (cf. Mk I, 16-20) ; Lk VIII, 36-50 (cf. Mk XIV, 3-9) ; Lk X, 25-28 (cf. Mk X, 28-34) were assigned to Luke's peculiar source L (and to Proto-Luke) or to special pre-Lucan sources (Schürmann's hypothesis for IV, 16-30 and VII, 36-50). More especially in the study of the Passion narrative Luke's dislike of the transposition of sections, not of sentences, was employed as a principle of exegesis. It seems to me that it may have withdrawn attention from the potentialities of the Lucan redaction, and in any case it is only in this direction that the argument of analogy with reference to Lk VI and VIII can be used [117].

CONCLUSION

Luke's divergences from the Marcan order in so far as they supposedly agree with Matthew are attributed by Sanders (and Morgenthaler) to Luke's use of the Gospel of Matthew. Jeremias's and Schürmann's

---

116. Another example of *Nachtrag* outside the Passion narrative according to Schürmann (cf. n. 79) : Luke has omitted Mk XI, 11-25 for the insertion of the non-Marcan passage in XIX, 45-48 from the omitted Marcan section (cf. Mk XI, 15-19). In fact, there is no dislocation in this case : Mk XI, 12-14.20-25 are omitted but Lk XIX, 45-48 (= Mk XI, 15-19) is in the Marcan order. And can we say that Luke omitted Mk XI, 11-25 as one whole ? Mk XI, 11 is not without correspondence in Luke (v. 41 : καὶ ὡς ἤγγισεν, ἰδὼν τὴν πόλιν, cf. καὶ εἰσῆλθεν εἰς Ἱεροσόλυμα ... καὶ περιβλεψάμενος πάντα) and for the various elements of the omission there can be more than one reason : " Dass Lukas Mk 11, 12-14, 20-21 in Rückblick auf Lk 13, 6-9 S fortgelassen habe ist möglich (*note* : Wahrscheinlicher hat Lukas hier aber auch einen unverständlichen Zug von Jesus fernhalten wollen) ; wahrscheinlich ist die Auslassung von Mk 11, 22-24 in Rückblick auf Lk 17, 5-6 par Mt erfolgt " (*Traditionsgeschichtliche Untersuchungen*, p. 283). — On the hypothesis of the variant tradition which replaces Mk I, 1-20 in Lk III, 1-IV, 30 (and the Marcan influences in IV, 1-6.19-20.21-22 as *Nachträge*), cf. J. DELOBEL, *La rédaction de Lc., IV, 14-16a et le " Bericht vom Anfang "*, in F. NEIRYNCK (ed.), *L'évangile de Luc* (see n. 85), pp. 203-223.

117. This examination of Lk VI and VIII serves as a prolegomenon to the study of the transpositions in the Passion narrative. Cf. *La matière marcienne*, pp. 198-199.

denial of transpositions in the Marcan material of Luke is ultimately based on a similar assumption : the dislocations of Marcan sections suggest indebtedness to sources. In both approaches the phenomenon of order is studied with an undue limitation of the creative activity of the evangelist. Thus the argument from order shows us again how interrelated redactional and source-critical study should be [118].

118. Additional Note :

Note 33.

Compare the new edition of Kümmel's *Einleitung* (1973), p. 31, and n. 34. — See also p. 37, n. 50, on Sanders's examples of Mt /Lk agreements in placing the same Q passage at the same place relative to the Marcan outline (" keine der Beispiele ist beweiskräftig "), and p. 102, on the so-called *Nachträge* in Luke (" unbegründetermassen ").

Note 38.

J. C. Hawkins : In his list of transpositions of verbs and sentences he gives one example of Mt /Lk agreement against Mark : diff. Mk I,7-8 (p. 80).
L. Vaganay : Comp. Lagrange, *Luc,* p. LXIX : only one agreement, diff. Mk XI,11-17, " mais cela est plutôt un raccourci, qu'une inversion dans l'ordre des faits "; in the order of phrases : diff. Mk I,2-3.4 and XII,8.
B. de Solages : In a book review of *La composition, RB* 80 (1973) 588-593, M. E. Boismard indicates three cases of agreement in order against Mark : (*1*) the Sermon on the Mount at the same place in Matthew and Luke (after the Triple Tradition pericope of Mk III,7b-8 ; Mt IV,24-25 ; Lk VI,17b-18) ; (*2*) the inversion of the quotation and the presentation of John the Baptist par. Mk I,1-4, and (*3*) the inversion of " mission " and " gift of authority " par. Mk VI,7 (p. 591). He conclu-des :" On pourrait probablement apporter d'autres exemples semblables. Les trois que je viens de mentionner suffisent à prouver qu'il existe effectivement quelques accords *Mt /Lc* contre *Mc* touchant l'ordre des péricopes " (p. 592). However, the two instances from the Triple Tradition concern transpositions within the pericope. For par. Mk I,1-4 he refuses B. de Solages's solution (combination of Mk and Q) : " A ma connaissance, aucun partisan de la théorie des Deux Sources ne l'a admis " (p. 591). But see Streeter (cf. *The Four Gospels,* pp. 291 and 305 ; *Oxford Studies,* p. 186), Taylor and others ; more recently also H. Schürmann, *Das Lukasevangelium,* p. 161. For criticism, cf. *supra,* n. 17 (and 18).

TABLE OF GOSPEL SECTIONS

(Cumulative List, pp. 55-195)

The second column of Matthew and Luke contains the passages which are not in the order of Mark (within parentheses in the cumulative list). The asterisk marks sections with a parallel in Matthew or Luke only.

§	Mk	Mt	Mt	Lk	Lk	page
1.	1,1-6	3,1-6	11,10	3,1-6	7,27	55
2.	1,7-8	3,7-12		3,7-17		56
3.	1,9-11	3,13-17		3,21-22		58
4.	1,12-13	4,1-11		4,1-13		59
5.	1,14-15	4,12-17		4,14-15	4,16	60
6.	1,16-20	4,18-22			5,1-11	61
7.	1,21-22	7,28-29		4,31-32		61
8.	1,23-28		4,24a	4,33-37		62
9.	1,29-31	8,14-15		4,38-39		62
10.	1,32-34	8,16-17		4,40-41		63
11.	1,35-38			4,42-43		64
12.	1,39		4,23	4,44	4,15.43	64
13.	1,40-45		8,1-4 ; 9,30-31	5,12-16		64
14.	2,1-12	9,1-8		5,17-26		67
15.	2,13-17	9,9-13		5,27-32		70
16.	2,18-22	9,14-17		5,33-39		72
17.	2,23-28	12,1-8		6,1-5		74
18a.	3,1-6	12,9-14		6,6-11		76
18b.	3,1-6	12,9-14			14,1-6	78
19.	3,7-12	12,15-16	4,24b-25	6,17-19	4,41	79
20.	3,13-19		10,1-4 ; 5,1		6,12-16	80
21.	3,20-21					82
22.	3,22-30	12,22-32	9,32-34		11,14-23 ; 12,10	82
23.	3,31-35	12,46-50			8,19-21	85
24.	4,1-9	13,1-9		8,4-8		87
25.	4,10-12	13,10-15		8,9-10		89
26.	4,13-20	13,18-23		8,11-15		90
27.	4,21-25			8,16-18		92
	21		5,15	16	11,33	92
	22		10,26	17	12,2	93
	23		11,15		14,35	93
	24c		7,2b		6,38b	93
	24d		6,33b		12,31b	93
28.	4,26-29					94

§	Mk	Mt	Mt	Lk	Lk	page
29.	4,30-32	13,31-32			13,18-19	94
30.*	4,33-34	13,34-35				95
31.	4,35-41		8,18-27 ; 13,36	8,22-25		95
32.	5,1-20		8,28-34	8,26-39		97
33.	5,21-43		9,1.18-26	8,40-56		101
34.	6,1-6a	13,53-58			4,16-30	105
35.	6,6b-13		9,35-10,16	9,1-6	10,1-12 ; 8,1 ; 13,22	106
36.	6,14-16	14,1-2		9,7-9		110
37.	6,17-29	14,3-12			3,19-20	111
38.	6,30-44	14,13-21	14,12	9,10-17		112
39.*	6,45-52	14,22-23				116
40.*	6,53-56	14,34-36				116
41.*	7,1-23	15,1-20				116
42.*	7,24-30	15,21-28				116
43.	7,31-37	15,29-31				116
44.*	8,1-10	15,32-39				117
45.	8,11-13	16,1-4	12,38-39		11,16.29	117
46.	8,14-21	16,5-12			12,1	118
47.	8,22-26					118
48.	8,27-30	16,13-20		9,18-21		119
49.	8,31-33	16,21-23		9,22		120
50.	8,34-9,1	16,24-28		9,23-27		121
51.	9,2-10	17,1-9		9,28-36		123
52.*	9,11-13	17,10-13				126
53.	9,14-29	17,14-21		9,37-43a		126
54.	9,30-32	17,22-23		9,43b-45		130
55.	9,33-37	18,1-5	17,24-25 ; 23,11	9,46-48	22,26	131
56.*	9,38-41			9,49-50		132
57.	9,42-48	18,6-9			17,1-2	132
58.	9,49-50		5,13		14,34-35	132
59.	10,1-12	19,1-12	5,32		9,51 ; 17,11 ; 16,18	133
60.	10,13-16	19,13-15		18,15-17		134
61.	10,17-22	19,16-22	19,15.23	18,18-23		135
62.	10,23-27	19,23-26		18,24-27		136
63.	10,28-31	19,27-30		18,28-30		138
64.	10,32-34	20,17-19		18,31-34		139
65.	10,35-40	20,20-23			12,50	140
66.	10,41-45	20,24-28			22,24-27	140
67.	10,46-52	20,29-34	9,27-30	18,35-43	19,1	141
68.	11,1-10	21,1-9	21,15-16	19,29-38	19,28	143
69.	11,11.19	21,10-17			21,37	146
70.	11,12-14	21,18-19				146
71.	11,15-19		21,12-16	19,45-48		147
72.	11,20-25	21,20-22	17,20		17,6	148
73.	11,27-33	21,23-27		20,1-8		148
74.	12,1-12	21,33-46		20,9-19		150
75.	12,13-17	22,15-22		20,20-26		153
76.	12,18-27	22,23-33		20,27-38		155
77.	12,28-34	22,34-40		20,39-40	10,25-28	157
78.	12,35-37a	22,41-46		20,41-44		159
79.	12,37b-40	23,1-2.5-7		20,45-47		160

§	Mk	Mt	Mt	Lk	Lk	page
80.*	12,41-44			21,1-4		160
81.	13,1-4	24,1-3		21,5-7		160
82.	13,5-8	24,4-8		21,8-11		162
83.	13,9-13	24,9-14	10,17-22	21,12-19	12,11-12	162
84.	13,14-20	24,15-22		21,20-24	17,31	164
85.	13,21-23	24,23-28			17,23	165
86.	13,24-27	24,29-31		21,25-28		165
87.	13,28-32	24,32-36		21,29-33		165
88.	13,33-37		25,13-15 ; 24,42.44	21,36	19,12-13 ; 12,40	166
89.	14,1-2	26,1-5		22,1-2		167
90.	14,3-9	26,6-13			7,36-50	167
91.	14,10-11	26,14-16		22,3-6		169
92.	14,12-16	26,17-19		22,7-13		169
93.	14,17-21	26,20-25		22,14	22,21-23	171
94.	14,22-25	26,26-29		22,15-20		171
95.	14,26-31	26,30-35		22,31-34		172
96.	14,32-42	26,36-46		22,39-46	9,32	173
97.	14,43-52	26,47-56		22,47-53		175
98.	14,53-54	26,57-58		22,54-55	22,56.66	177
99.	14,55-65	26,59-68		22,67-71	22,63-65	178
100.	14,66-72	26,69-75			22,56-62	180
101.	15,1	27,1-2		23,1	22,66	182
102.	15,2-5	27,11-14		23,2-5	23,9-10	183
103.	15,6-15	27,15-26		23,13-25		184
104.	15,16-20	27,27-31		23,26a		186
105.	15,21	27,32		23,26		187
106.	15,22-32	27,33-44		23,33-43		187
107.	15,33-41	27,45-56		23,44-49		189
108.	15,42-47	27,57-61		23,50-56		191
109.	16,1-8	28,1-20		24,1-53		193

DISLOCATED TEXTS

INDEX OF AUTHORS

Heavy type signals the pages in which the author's theory on the minor agreements is exposed.

Full bibliographical references are indicated by the numbers of the footnotes or (for pp. 52-53) by an asterisk added to the number of the page.

BY THE SAME AUTHOR

Duality in Mark. Contributions to the Study of the Markan Redaction. (BETL, 31.) Leuven University Press, 1972. In-8, 214 p. Out of print. New edition in preparation.

Reprinted from *Ephemerides Theologicae Lovanienses* 47 (1971) 144-198 : *Mark in Greek* ; 394-463 : *Duality in Mark* ; 48 (1972) 150-209 : *Duplicate Expressions in the Gospel of Mark.*

*

La rédaction matthéenne et la structure du premier Évangile, pp. 41-73, in :

I. DE LA POTTERIE (ed.), *De Jésus aux Évangiles. Tradition et rédaction dans les Évangiles synoptiques.* Donum Natalicium J. Coppens, II. (BETL, 25.) Gembloux, Duculot & Paris, Lethielleux, 1967. In-8, 272 p. FB 500.

The Gospel of Matthew and Literary Criticism. A Critical Analysis of A. Gaboury's Hypothesis, pp. 37-69, in :

M. DIDIER (ed.), *L'Évangile selon Matthieu. Rédaction et théologie.* (BETL, 29.) Gembloux, Duculot, 1972. In-8, 428 p. FB 750.

La matière marcienne dans l'Évangile de Luc, pp. 157-201, in :

F. NEIRYNCK (ed.), *L'Évangile de Luc. Problèmes littéraires et théologiques.* Mémorial Lucien Cerfaux. (BETL, 32.) Gembloux, Duculot, 1973. In-8, 386 p. FB 650.

Urmarcus redivivus ? Examen critique de l'hypothèse des insertions matthéennes dans Marc, pp. 103-145, in :

M. SABBE (ed.), *L'Évangile selon Marc. Tradition et rédaction.* (BETL, 34.) Gembloux, Duculot & Leuven University Press, 1974. In-8, 594 p. FB 1100.

Jesus and the Sabbath. Some Observations on Mk II, 27, pp. 227-270, in :

J. DUPONT (ed.), *Jésus aux origines de la christologie.* (BETL, 40.) Gembloux, Duculot & Leuven University Press, 1975. In-8, 376 p. FB 950.

*

Hawkins's Additional Notes to his « Horae Synopticae » (Analecta Lovaniensia Biblica et Orientalia, Ser. V, Fasc. 2.) In-8, 37 p. FB 100.

Reprinted from *Ephemerides Theologicae Lovanienses* 46 (1970) 78-111.

Éditions J. DUCULOT B-5800 GEMBLOUX (Belgium)

94

Imprimerie J. Duculot - Gembloux *(Printed in Belgium)*